murder
mayhem
and
mystery

other books by alan hynd

Passport to Treason

Betrayal from the East

The Giant Killers

alan hynd

murder mayhem and mystery

an album of american crime

new york
a. s. barnes and company

Library of Congress Catalog Card Number: 58-6001

Printed in the United States of America
American Book–Stratford Press, Inc., New York

To the Memory of
Joseph and Lizzie Dobbs
and
Archie and Mary Hynd
and to
Evvy, Diane and Noel

Acknowledgments

No book of this kind can possibly be the work of one person. I wish, therefore, to express my deep appreciation to Ralph Daigh, Vice President and Editorial Director of Fawcett Publications; to Douglas S. Kennedy, Editor; Charles N. Barnard, Managing Editor, and Don McKinney, Assistant Managing Editor, all of TRUE, for their encouragement, their patience and their kind and vital assistance during the creative process that made this work possible. I also feel a deep obligation to Don Schiffer of A. S. Barnes & Company, for his meticulous editing of this collection of my work. Nor can I fail to thank Helen Lamoureux, of Fairfield, Connecticut, for her invaluable editorial assistance during the years when the pieces in this book were in preparation. And a deep bow to my lovely wife, Evvy Hynd—just because.

ALAN HYND

All stories in this volume originally appeared in
TRUE—The Man's Magazine

Contents

Acknowledgments   7

Introduction by Doug Kennedy   11

Why the Lindbergh Case Was Never Solved   13

The Case of the Curious Cubs   47

The Man They Couldn't Kill   59

The Stiffs in the Old Folks' Home   69

New York's Easter Murders   81

The Worm That Turned   91

The Case of the Resurrected Girl   101

Oregon's Riddle of the Bodies That Weren't There   111

Who Killed Sir Harry Oakes?   123

The Pied Piper of Boston   153

How Oscar Reaped the Farmers   187

Twenty-three Murders   199

The Pink Ducks   211

The Coronary Con Men   221

The Yellow Kid   233

Prophet Joshua and His Holy Rollers   265

The Riddle of the Ragged Stranger   275

The Wife Who Got Boiled   283

The "Burned-Up" Old Maid   293

The Case of the Extra Husband   303

The Built-in Lover   315

Mr. Coffey Buys—and Buries—A Bride   325

The Lady in the Bath Tub   333

The Snatch That Made the G-Men   343

Chicago's Constant Widow   355

Long Island's Messy Murder   363

Gaston Bullock Means: Con Cum Laude   375

The Redheaded Mouthpiece of Broadway   407

Philadelphia's Murdering Faith Healer   441

Brooklyn's Two Million $ Torch   451

Coster-Musica: Man Who Doped the Drug Houses   463

The Scrambled Sleepers   491

The Captain's Lethal Paradise   501

Introduction

Alan Hynd, whom we at TRUE regard as the top writer in the fact-crime field, has, in the past twelve years, contributed more than one hundred pieces to our magazine. There has been something outstanding about every one of them—either the case itself or the Hynd telling of the story, for when it comes to taking an oblique view of a situation or extracting humor from crime Hynd is in a class with such masters of the past as Edmund Pearson and William Roughead.

One of the most prolific of the top writers in the magazine field today, Hynd has also contributed his studies in murder, mayhem, and mystery to such other magazines as *The Reader's Digest, The American Mercury* and *The Saturday Evening Post.*

Alan Hynd was born in Trenton, New Jersey, of Scottish ancestry, and studied at Columbia University. He is a fastidious character and patronizes the same New York tailor as the Duke of Windsor. A curiosity among the literary set, he neither drinks nor smokes. He is married to the former Evvy Dobbs and they have a daughter Diane, and a son Noel, and live in Westport, Connecticut.

Doug Kennedy
Editor, TRUE

Why the Lindbergh Case Was Never Solved

*Was the Lindbergh kidnaping—the crime of the century—ever really solved?
That is a question that has been puzzling professional and amateur
criminologists for more than a quarter of a century now. Here, at
long last, the searching light of truth is focused on the dark
recesses of the mystery, with results that will startle you.*

When, sometime between nine and ten o'clock on the night of Tuesday, March 1, 1932, twenty-month-old Charles Augustus Lindbergh, Jr., was kidnaped from the home of his parents near Hopewell, New Jersey, the curtain was rung up on considerably more than what has been called the crime of the century—a crime which, in the opinion of some qualified students of the subject, remains today, more than twenty-five years later, only partially solved, if indeed it has been really cleared up to any extent at all. For a variety of reasons, the principal ones being the prominence, gullibility and stubbornness of the victim's father, and the esteem in which he was then held, the Lindbergh kidnaping served to assemble under one tent the most notable congress of clowns, villains, screwballs, exhibitionists and other entertaining characters ever to perform in any arena except that of the Ringling Brothers. As Jimmy Durante would say, everybody wanted to get into the act.

During the seventy-two days that elapsed between the kidnaping and the discovery of a corpse—a corpse which, according to the Lindbergh baby's doctor, may not have been that of the Lindbergh child at all—the good people of the U. S. A. went on a monumental emotional binge. The missing child, being the son of the man known as the Lone Eagle, was continually referred to, even in the austere columns of the New York *Times,* as the little eaglet. He had been, on the authority of Miss Adela Rogers St. John, writing for a newspaper syndicate, stolen from his warm nest. In Tin Pan Alley, derbied, cigar-smoking tunesmiths, sweating at battered uprights, attempted to monetize the mass emotion by hammering out such competition for Rodgers and Hart as this:

His father flew over the ocean,
Is this how we show our devotion?
Who put the snatch on the Lindbergh
    kid?
Did *you?* Did *you?* Did *you?*

Actually, the crime itself was a simple kidnaping, essentially the same as hundreds of others. It followed the classic pattern—the stealing of a child and negotiations for ransom. The unusual factor that complicated this affair and allowed it to assume the status of a major mystery was the awe with which the investigators themselves viewed Lindbergh and their willingness to acquiesce to Lindbergh's insistence on being the chief detective in charge of the hunt.

If it hadn't been for Lindbergh, the New York cops would probably have wrapped up the case after two ransom letters showed up from mailboxes in one particular section of Brooklyn. Police Commissioner Ed Mulrooney, a realistic cop, was visited by the bright thought that whoever had mailed the two ransom letters might just drop a third from the same locality.

Mulrooney wanted to stick a two-man twenty-four-hour cover on every one of the scores of mailboxes in the section. Every time anybody mailed a letter at any of the boxes, a dick was to retrieve it by means of a special device that would hold it just inside the slot. If any letter was addressed either to Lindbergh or to an eccentric old man named John F. Condon, who had by that time become the intermediary in the case, the person who had just mailed the letter could be tailed before he got out of sight.

Lindbergh vetoed Mulrooney on the ground that shadowing the letter writer might jeopardize the life of his son. Mulrooney argued that the letter writer need never know he was under surveillance, and that by shadowing him, or his associates, it was entirely possible that the child could be recovered by a police *coup.*

Lindbergh still said no. He added that if Mulrooney went ahead anyway, he, Lindbergh, would use his influence to see that Mulrooney was broken. Lindbergh, at that time, might really have been able to make such a threat stick. At any rate, Mulrooney laid off. Next day a third ransom note was dropped in one of the very boxes that the cops would have been watching.

The Lindbergh case is the only snatch on record wherein the same victim was grabbed by both a gang and a lone wolf, simultaneously, with neither party aware of the existence of the other. A few months after the kidnaping, the state cops hustled a man into court and convicted him of obstructing justice by withholding information from them that prevented the apprehension of a gang of six specified Lindbergh kidnapers. Three years later, the same state cops, working with the same basic evidence, went into the same courtroom with another man and convicted him of having been the sole perpetrator of the crime. Some advanced thinkers are of the opinion that one of those two men—either the justice obstructor or the lone wolf—had no rightful place in the act. But that, as Wilson Mizner put it, was part of the charm of the Lindbergh case.

The Lindbergh home—a custom-built two-story dwelling of whitewashed fieldstone in the French manor tradition—was situated in precisely the kind of spot Lindbergh would have been expected to choose for privacy. It was smack in the center of five hundred acres of woodland, meadows and pastureland in the Sourland Hills of Hunterdon County, New Jersey, a beautiful, remote section a few miles from Hopewell. Lindbergh's nearest neighbors, farmers, were a good half-mile away.

The Lindberghs had occupied the house less than a year. In the winter time—and this was winter—they occupied it only on weekends, spending most of their time at the home of Mrs. Lindbergh's mother, Mrs. Dwight W. Morrow, in Englewood, an hour's drive distant.

Usually, after week-ending in the Sourlands, the Lindberghs returned to Englewood on Monday afternoon. During the last week end of February, however, little Charles—a curly-haired blond child weighing thirty pounds—developed a cold, and Mrs. Lindbergh decided not to return to Englewood on February 29. She had been taking care of the child herself, but now that she had decided to remain at Hopewell she telephoned the Morrow home, on the morning of Tuesday, March 1, and requested the child's Scottish nurse—Betty Gow, twenty-eight, dark, and attractive—to come to the Sourlands that afternoon.

On the night of March 1, then, there were six persons in the Lindbergh home: Colonel and Mrs. Lindbergh, Betty Gow, the baby, and a middle-aged English couple who had served the Lindberghs for more than a year—Ollie Whately, a butler, and his wife, Elsie, a cook. There was also a male English terrier.

At nine o'clock Mrs. Lindbergh looked in the nursery and found her son asleep. A few minutes later, Lindbergh, doing some desk work in the library on the first floor, heard a noise outside. He ascribed the sound to a loose second-floor shutter—on a window of the nursery—banging in the wind. At ten minutes to ten o'clock, Betty Gow went up to the baby's nursery, which was immediately above the library where the father was still working, to see if the child was properly covered.

When the nurse discovered that the baby was missing from his crib, her immediate supposition was that either the father or the mother must have removed him. Lindbergh himself was a great one for practical jokes that often scared the hell out of people. A few months before, he had taken the baby from the crib, hidden him in a closet and thrown the household into an uproar for twenty minutes. It quickly developed, however, that what was afoot this time was no joke.

It was Lindbergh who discovered an envelope on the sill just inside one of the windows in the child's nursery. The window was not locked, but it was closed, so there was no chance of the note blowing away. Everybody in the household was in the nursery by this time. Lindbergh pointed to the envelope and said, "Don't anybody touch it." Then to Whately, the butler, he said, "Call the police and tell them the baby has been taken." The colonel grabbed a loaded rifle and rushed outside.

The first official to reach the scene was Harry Wolf, the chief of police of Hopewell, in whose jurisdiction the crime had been committed. Chief Wolf, a cop typical of the backwoods, was so stunned at what had happened, and so overwhelmed at finding himself actually in the presence of Colonel Lindbergh, that the blood that nourished his brain had scarcely resumed circulation when the first contingent of state police arrived and took over. That, so far as the public prints were concerned, was about the last ever heard of Chief Wolf. The chief became a victim of a sort of official caste system. He still retains the distinction, however, of being the forgotten man of the Lindbergh kidnaping case—probably the only living adult who really had a right to get into the act and couldn't.

Lindbergh's chief assistant in the investigation that was about to get under way was the superintendent of the state cops—Colonel H. Norman Schwarzkopf, a handsome young man with a crew haircut and a waxed blond mustache, who, between graduating from West Point and embracing crime detection, had served a hitch as a floorwalker in Bamberger's department store in Newark.

It was after midnight before a fingerprint man arrived and opened the envelope on the window sill. For more than two hours, Lindbergh had forbidden anybody, even himself, to touch the envelope. A handwritten letter demanded fifty grand for the safe return of the child and warned Lindbergh against notifying the police. But it was already too late to follow that instruction. The news had leaked; and the whole world now knew about the crime by radio. The spelling, the clumsy sentence structure, the apparent thought processes, and the penmanship itself in the ransom letter indicated that its author was of German origin and not too highly educated. The man said Lindbergh would hear from him again shortly.

A homemade three-section ladder, of good construction, was found disassembled near the house. Marks in the earth just outside Lindbergh's library indicated that the ladder had been placed against the side of the house to afford entrance to the nursery. One rung of the ladder, near the top, was broken. It was surmised that this had given way under the weight of the kidnaper, and that the resultant noise was that which had been heard by Lindbergh. Since the noise had been heard a few minutes after nine o'clock, the hour of the crime was tentatively pegged.

Near the ladder was a chisel. Presumably the chisel had been used to pry open the nursery window.

The top rung of the ladder fell some thirty inches short of reaching the bottom of the nursery window. It would have been quite a trick for one man, carrying a child who weighed thirty pounds, to negotiate in the dark the gap between the nursery to the ladder, not to mention closing the window as well.

In the morning, the investigation was abruptly elevated from a police to a sort of diplomatic-military level. Lindbergh conferred with two friends—Colonel William Joseph (Wild Bill) Donovan, then getting ready to run for Governor of New York State, and Colonel Henry Breckinridge, a Manhattan lawyer who traveled only in upper social and military echelons.

The three colonels, together with Colonel Schwarzkopf, came up with a staggering joint thought. They decided to summon to the Sourlands a dark, sharply dressed little Broadway character known as Mickey Rosner. Rosner claimed, among other things, acquaintanceship with certain underworld figures. This, the top-level thinkers had decided, was just what the case called for, although there was nothing in the ransom letter, or anywhere else, to indicate that the underworld was involved in the job. If anything, a crime involving Lindbergh was precisely the type of thing that the underworld would have wanted no part of.

The little town of Hopewell, which had been suffering a depression, found itself in a boom the morning after the kidnaping. It had become, in the space of a few hours, the news capital of the world. Between editions, metropolitan reporters became acquainted with a marvelous snake-bite antidote distilled within sight of the Lindbergh home and known as applejack or Jersey lightning. The scribes were thus led to embrace the hope that the Lindbergh probe would be long and pleasant.

The Lindbergh home itself was a shambles. Miles of telephone wires were being strung into the place and switchboards installed to handle the calls coming in from all over the world. Headquarters of the state cops had been moved there from near-by Trenton, and caterers were imported from New York. Henry Morton Robinson, in his book *Science Versus Crime,* said it good:

To summon up a ghastly remembrance of police tipstavery, bend your glance backward to the opening chapter of the Lindbergh case. Do you remember—could anyone ever forget—the foaming and senseless cataract of gorgeously uniformed state troopers that descended on the Lindbergh home in motorcycles, roared up and down the road trampling every available clue into the March mud, systematically covering with impenetrable layers of stupidity every fingerprint, footprint, dust trace on the estate?

What serious investigators were left with were the ladder, the chisel, and the ransom letter. There were no prints on the letter. There were, a silver-nitrate treatment revealed, some five hundred prints on the ladder, most of them from the thumbs of state cops.

Curiously, there was not a single fingerprint found in the nursery—on the crib, on the walls, on the window woodwork, on other articles of furniture, or anywhere else. "I'm damned," said one cop, "if I don't think somebody washed everything in that nursery before the print men got there."

Out of the absence of prints in the nursery arose the never-to-die theory of a job carried out with inside help. The Morrow and Lindbergh servants naturally came in for a thorough going-over. Little things came out about the pasts of some of them, though nothing that could be proved to have a connection with the kidnaping. Whately, the English butler who had come to this country two years before, turned out not to be a man of long domestic service, as he had told the Lindberghs when they hired him and his wife through a New York employment agency. He had been, in turn, a jeweler, a munitions worker, and a mechanic.

Betty Gow, the child's nurse, had a Swedish boy friend who, it turned out, was in this country illegally. Violet Sharpe, an English maid in the Morrow home, said she had been at the movies the night of the snatch. When asked to give the plot of the picture she had seen, she couldn't. Then she explained that she had been out with a man other than her regular boy friend.

The dog in the Lindbergh house had not barked at any time the night of March 1. Emphasis was placed on this fact in support of the inside-job theory. The dog was in a downstairs room, on the other side of the house from the spot where the ladder was placed. It couldn't have heard footsteps in the mud from where it was. Moreover, this particular dog was such a friendly little animal that, if anything, he would probably have been only too glad to show an intruder around the place.

It did seem strange, though, that a kidnaper should have chosen, for entry into the house, a time of night when there were lights on all over the place, and when people were up and moving around within. The inside-job theorists pointed to two more supporting facts: The shutter of the window under which the ladder had been placed was the only shutter on the whole house that was broken and could not be locked from within. Nobody could recall how it had got broken. Colonel Lindbergh wasn't expected to be home between the hours of nine and ten the night of the crime. He had been in New York that day and had planned to attend a social affair in midtown Manhattan that night, which would not have allowed him to reach the Sourlands until midnight or later. He canceled his plans at the last minute because he didn't think he would enjoy looking at the faces of some of the people at the social affair.

Mickey Rosner, the Broadway character agented into the act by the four colonels, was, it just happened, a little short of ready scratch. Lindbergh supplied him with twenty-five hundred dollars for expenses. Rosner thereupon extracted a promise from Lindbergh that he would not be followed by state cops or anybody else, wherever he went. "We gotta think of the little eaglet, you know, Colonel," he explained.

Two of Rosner's acquaintances turned out to be a couple of New York speakeasy proprietors named Salvatore Spitale and Irving Bitz—two-watt big-shots. The Lindberghs, on Rosner's say-so, publicly appointed Spitale and Bitz as the official intermediaries to deal with the kidnapers. Police Commissioner Mulrooney rushed to his physician and said, "Doc, you better give me a going-over. Something tells me my blood pressure's up."

What had happened was that Salvy and Irv, as the boys were called, had been sold to Rosner by the New York *Daily News,* the world's greatest tabloid, which thus hoped to get a pipeline into the Sourlands. The speakeasy that Salvy and Irv ran was on East Forty-first Street, right behind the News building, and derived its principal support from the alcoholic capacities of some of the most heroic drinkers in newspaper history.

There were two interlocking circles— one red and one blue—as an identification signature on the first ransom letter. The circles were punctured by three holes, evenly spaced. The presumption was that only the kidnaper would be in a postion to duplicate the circles and the spacing of the three holes.

When the first of a long series of follow-up ransom letters arrived for Lindbergh through the mails, Rosner, who by now was living in the Lindbergh home, grabbed it and rushed to New York. His mission apparently was to show the letter to underworld authorities on penmanship. But somewhere in its travels the letter lay prostrate under a camera lens, for copies of it were soon being peddled by various enterprising characters. Some sharpers were even selling pictures of a *fake* note.

Frequent references in the press to such characters as Mickey Rosner and the speakeasy proprietors catapulted many a jailbird out of the doldrums. Cell bars throughout the land rattled and shook as the altruists behind them screamed for a chance to get out and get into the act. Al Capone, jugged in Chicago on an income-tax rap, said he could, because of his connections, get the baby back if permitted his freedom under guard.

Arthur Brisbane, the celebrated doubledome of the Hearst newspaper empire, took time off from brooding over whether a man could lick a gorilla to interview Capone. Brisbane wrote a column implying it might be a good thing to spring Scarface, make him a dick and put him on the case. Lindbergh was terrifically impressed. He telephoned to Ogden Mills, who didn't have a military title, but who was Secretary of the Treasury, and asked about springing Al. Mills was the man to see because it was the Treasury Department that had removed Capone from circulation, like a bad bill. Some of the best T-men in the business spent a week looking into the Capone thing before deciding that all Al wanted was out.

More ransom letters kept pouring in. The author began to comment bitterly on the character of the men who were surrounding Lindbergh. A gentleman named Murray Garsson, who was to run a shoestring into a few million dollars in the Second World War, was, in 1932, looking around for a shoestring. He latched on as an investigator in the Bureau of Immigration and, using that as a sort of Indian club, juggled his way into the act. He used to sit around the Lindbergh house, glaring at Colonel Schwarzkopf and demanding, "Give us some action! Give us more than fortune-tellers!"

What Garsson meant was that the whole investigative staff, from Lindbergh down, was paying what some observers thought an inordinate amount of attention to people who claimed to be in direct contact with unseen cosmic forces. Anybody with a crystal ball and a deck of cards could get into the act. Part of the bill for $1,181,000, which New Jersey and federal taxpayers were eventually presented with for the Lindbergh case was run up by the purchase of gasoline with which to drive clairvoyants around the countryside.

Two gangsters spent three days with a fat Italian woman who claimed to be something of a human divining rod. They drove her all around the Sourlands while she was in various states of consciousness. She was supposed to lead them to the baby. At the end of the third day, one of the gangsters happened to mention that the window with the broken shutter faced north. "Nort!" screamed the clairvoyant. "Why you no tell me eet is nort? No use huntin' for keed. Keed *dead*."

In the Bronx—two hours by car from the Sourlands—there lived an old gentleman named Condon—Dr. John F. Condon. He was mustached, apple-cheeked and garrulous, a big man of seventy-two. He was a schoolteacher. He was still working—as principal of a Bronx public school and as a lecturer at Fordham University—and he hadn't missed a session in forty years.

Condon, a forty-eight-star patriot, was a sort of male Lucy Monroe. Every Fourth of July he hit the outdoor festival circuit and, sweating in a dark winter suit, sang *The Star-Spangled Banner*. For years he had written poems, essays and letters on current topics for the Bronx *Home News*, a poor man's New York *Times*. He never signed himself Taxpayer or Constant Reader. He was (actually) P. A. Triot (for patriotic stuff), L. O. Nester (Lone Star), L. O. Nehand, and (you could look it up) J. U. Stice. With a mind like that, it was a simple thing for him to become Jafsie, the world-renowned intermediary in the Lindbergh case. He just took his initials —J. F. C.—said them fast, and out came Jafsie.

Condon's entrance into the act was really quite uncomplicated. It was only after he started to perform that the plot thickened. He got in simply by having the *Home News* put a piece in the paper saying that he was offering his services as intermediary, and, out of his own pocket, offering a reward of one thousand dollars for the Lindbergh baby's safe return. Since the Lindberghs had already offered a $50,000 reward, and the state of New Jersey $25,000, Condon's offer had the effect of raising the total rewards from $75,000 to $76,000.

While Condon was waiting for the kidnapers to reply to the *Home News* story a moon-faced big man in his early fifties sat around a house down in Chevy Chase, a Washington suburb, drinking bourbon, listening to radio flashes about the hunt for the little eaglet, and wondering how the hell he could put the thing on a paying basis. The Lindbergh snatch was made to order for Gaston Bullock Means, of the South Carolina Meanses. All of his adult life, Means had successfully played angles in and around

Washington, as an investigator for the Department of Justice, as a money collector for the Ohio Gang during the Harding regime, and as a free-lance swindler.

The phone rang. Who was on the other end of the wire but Evalyn Walsh McLean, the spectacular Washington society woman. Mrs. McLean told Means to come to her home on Massachusetts Avenue that night.

Mrs. McLean was a little chain smoker who was usually dressed either in something by Hattie Carnegie or in an old woolen bathrobe, depending on who was around. She wore so much jewelry that she clanked when she walked. She was always thinking up dramatic cliches. She envisioned herself—she who had done everything—appearing out of the nowhere, with the baby clutched in her arms, like something from the last reel of an old D. W. Griffith movie. In sending for Means, Mrs. McLean was subscribing to the same theory as the four colonels up in Hopewell—that it would take a crook to catch a crook. She knew that Means had underworld connections.

When Means arrived, humble, eager and curious, Mrs. McLean asked him if he knew anything about the Lindbergh kidnaping. Means coughed and said that it just happened that he did. Some underworld acquaintances had just requested him to act as intermediary in the case.

Mrs. McLean asked for proof that Means was in touch with the kidnapers. Means said that the state police had given out for publication the story that the baby had been wearing a certain brand of sleeping suit. "Those suits have little flaps in the back," said Means. "The suit the Lindbergh baby was wearing did not have a flap in the back."

The level of the investigation was raised, if anything, by Mrs. McLean's next move. She telephoned to Emory S. Land of the United States Navy, a relative of Lindbergh's, later head of the Maritime Commission. Land needed to be only a captain to be on equal rank with the Hopewell colonels. He outranked them, however. He was a rear admiral.

When Admiral Land went to New Jersey and charted his way through the stormy sea of state cops, newspapermen and gangsters auditioning for intermediary roles, and told Lindbergh what Means said about the sleeping suit, Lindbergh said, "He's absolutely right. We purposely gave out an erroneous description of the suit so that we could eliminate false tips."

Means advised Mrs. McLean that a representative of the kidnap gang had okayed her as an intermediary. "The trouble is," he added, "that the gang has jumped the ransom price to a hundred thousand dollars and I'll have to have the cash in advance, all ready to give them." Means had it right. The ransom writer—the man who was signing his letters with the red-and-blue circle and the three holes—had just begun to talk about doubling the original demand on the ground that the heat of the hunt warranted it. Mrs. McLean got a go-ahead from Lindbergh.

Evalyn McLean didn't have one hundred thousand dollars in ready cash. She raised the money by hocking a block of business property in downtown Washington. Two messengers arrived with two big boxes containing one hundred thousand dollars in fives, tens and twenties. It took three people two and a half hours to count the money.

Evalyn McLean was a woman of intermittent piety. Means told her that the kidnap gang would insist upon handing the baby over to a Catholic priest. Thus entered the picture the Reverend Francis J. Hurney.

At a little gathering in Mrs. McLean's house the night the money arrived—a gathering attended by Mrs. McLean, Means, Father Hurney and Admiral Land—Means suggested a little prayer by the priest to insure the success of the coming negotiations. Means himself seemed to be undergoing a regeneration right before the eyes of the onlookers —a sort of miracle of the bills. His round face was wet with tears and suffused with beatification as he walked out into Massachusetts Avenue, lugging the hundred thousand with him.

Next morning he added an authentic touch. He put the bite on Mrs. McLean for four thousand dollars expenses. Presently Mrs. McLean, Father Hurney, Admiral Land and a McLean butler and maid holed into a deserted house owned by Mrs. McLean in the wilds of Maryland. Mrs. McLean had seldom gone near the property—a summer hideaway. In years gone by, a gentleman and a lady who lived in the place had participated in a disagreement of some kind and the gentleman had finally slammed the lady fatally over the head. Ever since, the house had been reputed to be haunted. Haunted or not, the place was, Means said, ideal for the safe transfer of the baby. In the middle of the night, the maid woke up screaming . . . of which more later.

Meantime, up in the Bronx, Dr. Condon's offer in the *Home News* to act as intermediary drew a bite. He received through the mails a letter bearing the now-familiar red-and-blue symbol, and the three holes. The letter said that he would be okay as an intermediary.

Condon took the letter to Lindbergh. Lindbergh decided that it was genuine,

since the symbol and the holes, which had not yet even been mentioned to the newspapers, matched exactly with the markings on the previous letters. Lindbergh was not aware that every confidence man, penman, swindler and forger east of the Rockies was in possession of the photograph of the ransom letter that had somehow found its way out of Mickey Rosner's hands long enough to get photographed; and that an extortion plot, separate and distinct from the kidnaping, could conceivably be under way.

Condon was like a breath of fresh air —well, *some* kind of air—in the Lindbergh household. If Mickey Rosner and Salvy and Irv, the speakeasy boys, were out of Damon Runyon, the old Doc was straight from the pages of Sinclair Lewis in his Babbitt phase. He began to drop corn and cliches all over the place and was a walking powerhouse generating good cheer. The first thing he did was to inform Mrs. Lindbergh that he had once won a twenty dollar prize by submitting to a *Home News* New Year's resolution contest the following: "That I shall, to the best of my ability, and at all times, help anyone in distress."

The ransom writer favored the Hearst press. He instructed Condon to acknowledge receipt of the letter by a three-word reply in the agony columns of the New York *American*. Condon inserted this ad:

Money is ready. Jafsie.

The money, of course, wasn't ready at all. Lindbergh, like Mrs. McLean and Mickey Rosner, was a little pressed for ready cash. His credit was good, though, especially at the private banking house of J. P. Morgan, where his father-in-law, forgetful little Dwight Morrow, had been a partner.

Jafsie was out gadding about somewhere when he got a phone call at his home a few hours after the ad appeared. His wife took the call. A man, speaking with a German accent, said he would call back later. Police Commissioner Mulrooney would probably have given five years of his life to know about the promised call, which of course was a secret between the Condon and Lindbergh households. Mulrooney could have traced it and probably put a tail on the man who made it. For it was made, all right, just as the kidnaper promised. Jafsie was told to lie low and wait for further instructions. During the conversation, Jafsie heard the caller in verbal asides to someone else.

The instructions came by way of a taxi driver. Jafsie wound up late at night at Woodlawn Cemetery in the Bronx. There, inside a gate, a man was waving a handkerchief. "I see you!" yelled Jafsie, breaking into a run. "Not so fast!" yelled the kidnaper. The loud conversation woke up a cemetery guard. Jafsie and the kidnaper became brothers under the skin while taking it on the lam together. They wound up on a bench in Van Cortlandt Park.

The night was bitter cold. The kidnaper, whose face Jafsie couldn't see, was shivering. "Why," said Jafsie, "your coat is too thin. Here, take mine." The kidnaper refused, but thanked Jafsie. He was the same man who had phoned.

The talk drifted from the weather to other things. The kidnaper said his name was John and that he was a Scandinavian sailor. There were six members of the kidnap gang—four men and two women. The Lindbergh baby was on a boat somewhere.

Jafsie asked John just where he had left the note in the nursery. "In crib," said John. Jafsie passed over the discrep-

ancy. Lindbergh had found the note on the window sill.

Jafsie had taken two large safety pins from the crib blankets. "What," he asked, "are these?"

"Safety pins," said John.

"But where are they from, John?"

"The crib," said John.

The safety pins settled it for Jafsie. This had to be the man who had been in the nursery.

John grew mercenary. He mentioned money. Jafsie said the Lindberghs were raising the ransom. John was co-operative. He voluntarily offered additional proof that he represented the gang who had the child. He would deliver the sleeping suit the baby had been wearing when kidnaped. The suit did not, said John, have a flap in the back, as the newspapers had said. Now Jafsie was really sold on John.

When Commissioner Mulrooney, who was getting second-hand news of what a criminal was doing in his own bailiwick, learned that a Lindbergh intermediary had spent more than an hour sitting on a park bench with the kidnaper, he thought he was going to have a cerebral hemorrhage. For the third time since the kidnaping, a demander of ransom could easily have been tailed had Lindbergh not been running the show.

While Jafsie and Means were performing, the *Three Virginians* joined the act. The Three Virginians, all from Norfolk, were Commodore John Hughes Curtis, a social leader and boat builder; Dean H. Dobson Peacock, an Episcopal clergyman; and Rear Admiral G. H. Burrage, who had commanded the Navy vessel that returned Lindbergh and his New York-to-Paris plane to the United States after the Lone Eagle's epochal flight.

The rear admiral, the commodore and the dean spent a week trying to get Lindbergh on the phone. All they got was Mickey Rosner, who was now identifying himself as Lindbergh's private secretary. Rosner didn't seem to like the tendency that the investigation had of deserting the underworld for military and naval circles. Once, when Admiral Burrage phoned, Rosner said, "Oh, another admiral, huh?"

Lindbergh happened to be elbowing his way through a mob of state cops in his own living room when he overheard Rosner insulting Burrage. "Is there," Lindbergh asked Rosner, "an *admiral* on the wire?" Rosner nodded glumly and Lindbergh grabbed the phone.

The Three Virginians were in. It was Commodore Curtis who was the talented one of the trio. Curtis—a large, pleasant man in his middle forties—had, he said, been leaving a Norfolk club one night when a desperate-looking character calling himself Sam materialized out of the shadows. Commodore Curtis, a socially correct man, wouldn't have dreamed of carrying on a conversation with a person who hadn't been properly introduced except that this man said he was one of a gang of six who had the Lindbergh kid and that Commodore Curtis had been elected to act as intermediary.

Although not a word of Jafsie's dealings with the man in the cemetery had leaked to the papers, the kidnaper that the Three Virginians were promoting seemed to know about Jafsie. "Sam told me," the commodore informed Lindbergh, "that you are negotiating with another member of the same gang up here. Sam says the man up here wants fifty thousand, maybe as much as a hundred thousand. Sam is willing to deliver the baby to me for twenty-five thousand." The gang, then, seemed to be quarreling among themselves.

Lindbergh said Sam would have to supply proof that his gang had the baby. The accurate description of the sleeping suit was not the only information about the child that had been withheld. Little Charles had a slight but definite deformity of two toes of his right foot; should anyone professing to know the baby's whereabouts divulge that information, Lindbergh would know they were authentic.

Lindbergh told the Virginians to go ahead with negotiations, but cautiously. Commodore Curtis said that Sam wanted twenty-five thousand dollars deposited to the account of the Virginians in a Norfolk bank, to be paid over to him immediately upon delivery of the baby. Lindbergh wouldn't hold still for that. He wanted proof first that Sam's gang really had his son.

Jafsie exploded when Lindbergh told him about the Virginians. "They're frauds!" roared the old man. "Frauds! All three of them—including that dean."

Cemetery John sent Jafsie a sleeping suit through the mails. Lindbergh went to Jafsie's home in the Bronx, examined the suit, and pronounced it the one his son had worn the night of the abduction. This in itself was pretty good going. The suit was a standard garment, bought in a store, and it bore no laundry marks, since the child's nurse did his laundry, or any other identification marks. It was the same as thousands of others.

Jafsie didn't hear from the ransom writer for a few days. He stuck an ad in the Bronx *Home News,* which he had told Cemetery John to cover in the future, reading:

> Money is ready. No cops. No secret service. I come alone, like last time.
>   Jafsie

There were more letters, and more ads, in the *Home News* and the *American*. Jafsie was so busy composing ads and letters to the *Home News,* signed P. A. Triot and J. U. Stice, commenting on the crime, and reading the stuff over the phone to Lindbergh before letting it fly, that he hardly had time for his school work. He was getting increasingly garrulous in his ads. Newspaper editors had spotted the ads, as who wouldn't, and were trying to run them down. "I wish I knew," said Police Commissioner Mulrooney, expressing a widely held feeling about Jafsie, "who that guy is."

Jafsie began to feel frustrated. Nobody had identified him. No newspaper reporters were hanging around his house. He began to travel the streets in a fanfare of secrecy. He dressed as a woman, rolling his pants legs up and covering his mustache with a drawn-up collar. Still nobody recognized him.

He rented a vacant store and conducted a bazaar to raise funds for a prison chapel on Hart's Island. He presided at a booth where violins were being peddled. He played scratchy numbers for prospective purchasers, the while commenting on the Lindbergh case, and asking people if they had any idea who Jafsie was. Nobody had any idea, worse luck.

Mickey Rosner's performers—Salvy and Irv—had by this time been thrown out of the act. Lindbergh had finally learned that the *Daily News* was more than passingly interested in them. Lindbergh hated all newspapers, and especially tabloids.

Finally, on Friday, April Fool's Day—exactly a month after the snatch—Jafsie got a note telling him to be ready with the money. The ransom sum had now been stabilized at seventy thousand dollars. Fifty thousand of it was packed in a wooden box, made of five different kinds of wood for possible later identification. The remaining twenty thousand dollars was done up in brown paper bundles. The dough had been made up at the House of Morgan, and the serial numbers of the bills carefully recorded. Additionally, twenty thousand dollars of the money was in gold notes—bills bearing gold seals, which would make them just that much more easily recognizable.

Meanwhile, in the haunted house in Maryland, where the McLean group had awaited word from Gaston Means, events were taking place which, while they had nothing to do with the Lindbergh kidnaping, were to interest researchers in the field of psychic phenomena. The maid who woke up screaming in the middle of the night did so because the sheets were yanked off her bed and various inanimate articles began to fly about the room—all this despite the fact that there was nobody else in the room and that it was tightly locked from the inside.

Next night exactly the same thing happened when the butler occupied the room alone. The third night Mrs. McLean herself took up the vigil. The clothes were inexplicably yanked off her bed and she was almost struck by books that took flight from between their ends. When Means finally put in an appearance, with word that the child was being held on a boat near Norfolk, Virginia, and suggested that everybody adjourn to Mrs. McLean's mid-South home, in Aiken, South Carolina, the lady and her entourage were only too happy to move on.

In Aiken, everybody sat on a keg of dynamite. Means put in frequent appearances, offering various explanations for the delay in returning the child. One day a businesslike character called at the Aiken house. Means introduced him simply as the Fox—one of the kidnap gang. The Fox inspected the house, apparently to make certain that there were no dictographs around. He wore gloves, but he took the added precaution of wiping with a handkerchief every door knob he touched. He finally satisfied himself that nobody or nothing was going to overhear what he said. Then he departed without saying anything. Means explained later that that was a peculiarity of the Fox's; the man never spoke when he was pleased with things. That meant, then, that the baby's delivery was imminent.

Something, however, went wrong. Mr. Means blamed it on the fact that the Three Virginians had broken into print. He suggested that everybody shift to El Paso. The baby, it seemed, had now been taken to Juarez, Mexico, just across the international bridge from El Paso. So everybody went to Texas.

One of the Three Virginians—Dean Peacock—had many of the qualities of Jafsie Condon, although he was some thirty years younger. The dean, a big pixie-featured man, seemed to be getting his picture in the papers all the time. The dean leaked a little at the mouth, too, especially for someone who was supposed to be hastening hither and yon on secret errands having to do with the return of the baby.

One day the dean, in New York to pose for some special newspaper pictures, ran afoul of a gang of small-time racketeers who were putting the snatch on a paying basis in the Cumberland Hotel, at Broadway and Fifty-fourth Street. The boys convinced him that the baby was being held by a gang in upper New York State, dressed as a girl and with his hair dyed red. On the strength of their story, the dean took the racketeers right into the Lindbergh home, where they had a long talk with the colonel. They wound up in the act when Lindbergh gave them his blessing to form the nucleus of a fourth group to deal with the kidnapers.

Commodore Curtis was reporting to Lindbergh hourly. Sam, the original contact, took Curtis to Newark. There, in front of a railroad station, he introduced him to four men who called themselves John, Olaf, Eric and Nils. Norsemen all. The five men drove Curtis to Cape May, New Jersey. There they took him to a cabin where he was introduced to John's wife, Hilda. The baby was safe on a boat, Hilda said, in charge of a nurse.

The Cape May gang said that the child had been kidnaped with the aid of inside connivance on the part of a female domestic in the Morrow household. They offered as proof of their claim a detailed diagram of the interior of the Lindbergh home—a plan that had not been published. They said that their inside informant had told them that the Lindberghs would be in the Sourlands on a Tuesday, for the first time, on the night of March 1, further divulging that the Lindberghs and their staff were creatures of habit and that at nine o'clock at night they would be settled in various parts of the house, making it possible for an intruder to walk from the nursery, down a flight of stairs and out a certain door, without fear of detection. This, the gang told Curtis, had been done, although entrance to the nursery had been effected by way of the ladder.

The exit through the house, instead of by means of the ladder, made sense to Lindbergh. What Lindbergh didn't get was how Cemetery John, who was dealing with Jafsie, came into the picture.

"I think," said Curtis, "that the John of my gang and the man dealing with Dr. Condon are one and the same."

"We are on the point," said Lindbergh, "of paying Cemetery John seventy thousand dollars."

"Good God!" said Curtis. "Don't do it!"

On the night of Saturday, April 2, a taxi driver, who had been hailed by a stranger on a Bronx street, arrived at Jafsie's home with a letter from the ransom author. Jafsie was told to proceed immediately to a desolate Bronx location and look under a stone in front of a flower shop.

Lindbergh, as it happened, had arrived at Jafsie's home not long previously. It was Lindbergh who drove the old boy to the stone. A note beneath the stone told Jafsie to walk to St. Raymond's Cemetery, near by. Jafsie there met Cemetery John for the second time. It was pitch-black, but Jafsie claims to have got a good look at the man this time. It was such a good look that he described him eight different ways in the months and years to come.

Cemetery John and Jafsie resumed the pleasant relationship that had begun in the other cemetery. Where, John asked, was the money? Jafsie had left the money in the car, with Lindbergh. "I wanted to make sure you were here and everything was all right," Jafsie explained. "But Colonel Lindbergh could raise only fifty thousand. There is a depression on, you know."

"Yes," said John, "I know. Fifty thousand will be all right."

Jafsie went back to the car, pleased as Punch that he had gypped John out of twenty thousand. He returned to the cemetery with the fifty, turned it over to John, and got a note in return. He shook hands with John, who melted into the shadows.

The note said the child was on a boat called the Nelly off Martha's Vineyard, Massachusetts. Lindbergh flew over the Martha's Vineyard vicinity for two days before he realized that the man in the cemetery had hoaxed Condon.

Commodore Curtis, still keeping up his contact with the Cape May group, told Lindbergh that they had now divulged the whereabouts of the boat the child was on. Lindbergh went off on a second wild-goose chase to the vicinity of Norfolk.

In El Paso, the McLean-Means expedition began to disintegrate. Mrs. McLean returned to Washington. Means returned to Chevy Chase. The lady called the gentleman and demanded her money back. Means didn't have it. He and his co-conspirator—a one-time lawyer named Norman Whittaker, who had played the role of the Fox—went off to prison for their hoax.

In the Lindbergh home, Commodore Curtis, unable to lead the police to the six people he had been in contact with —was turned over to Captain John J. Lamb, second in command of the state cops. Lamb, who had a face like an angry tomato, didn't like anybody who had any information about the case that the state cops didn't have. He took Curtis down to the cellar and beat the hell out of him.

After he recovered from his beating, Commodore Curtis signed a confession that Sam and the five other members of the kidnap gang were merely characters in a fiction story he had dreamed up. His purpose in becoming an author had been to sell his story to the New York *Herald-Tribune* and use the proceeds to pay off hot-breathed creditors. Somewhere along the way, however, the confession was forgotten. The commodore was taken into court and charged with obstructing justice. Specifically, he was supposed to have dealt with six persons who had stolen the Lindbergh baby and, by not letting the state police in on what he was doing, prevented the apprehension of the kidnapers. The commodore was fined one thousand dollars and sentenced to a year in jail, though the jail sentence was suspended.

The Lindbergh kidnaping case was largely responsible for divesting the annual Pulitzer prizes, for distinctive work in journalism, literature, the theater and allied fields, of the prestige that had long been associated with them. On the afternoon of May 12—seventy-two days after the snatch—a young man named Francis Jamieson, who covered the State House in Trenton for the Associated Press, wandered into the office of Governor A. Harry Moore just after Moore had been notified that the body of the Lindbergh baby had been found in a patch of thicket just off a secondary highway about four miles from the Lindbergh home. Jamieson ran along almost one hundred fifty feet of marble corridors to a point where he could put this intelligence on the AP wire. For that he got the Pulitzer prize in journalism for the year 1932, and things in Pulitzer circles have never been the same since.

What had happened was that a colored truck driver named William Allen had parked his truck on the highway and gone into the thicket to see a man about a horse. Allen never did get to see the man about the horse, for he saw a small, unclothed corpse first. By his discovery, the colored truckman automatically got into the act. He considered abandoning his amateur standing when he was offered three hundred dollars a week to appear

at Coney Island, there to tell the peasants how it felt to discover the body of the little eaglet. The state cops told him that if he turned pro, he'd be sorry. He went back to his steering wheel.

The body that had been found was taken to a morgue in Trenton, about twelve miles away. There Lindbergh and Betty Gow, the child's nurse, identified it as little Charles. Lindbergh and the nurse were in the morgue exactly one hundred eighty seconds. The remains were quickly cremated without being subjected to pathological or toxicological tests.

How the identification could have been made so quickly and positively was a major mystery all by itself. The body was black with decomposition. The left leg was missing from the knee down, and the right foot was missing. The decomposition around the vital organs was in such an advanced state that it was out of the question to determine by visual inspection even the sex of the child, and the county physician so stated in his report.

The baby's doctor—Dr. Philip Van Ingen of New York—who had examined little Charles only a couple of weeks before the kidnaping, took a long professional look at the body. "If someone were to come in here and offer me ten million dollars," he said to the coroner, "I simply wouldn't be able to identify these remains."

Somebody photographed the corpse. The picture was bootlegged at five dollars a copy.

Among those who saw a picture of the corpse was Ellis Parker, the Old Fox of Burlington County. Parker, as a county detective, had, in thirty-odd years, sent more than a hundred murderers to the gallows, the chair or prison. While he himself was a murderer of the King's

English and a man of little education, he was a deductive and inductive thinker of such attainments that he frequently lectured to psychology classes at the University of Pennsylvania and Columbia University.

As Parker studied the picture, he concluded that Lindbergh and Betty Gow had been victims of a psychological trick. They couldn't possibly have recognized the child, he decided, but they had made an identification because they had gone into the morgue *expecting* to see the remains of little Charles.

Parker had been sitting out the Lindbergh investigation. His pride was deeply hurt that Governor Moore had not invited him, the most famous detective in the history of Jersey justice, to enter the case. The two were political enemies.

But the Old Fox had pipelines. Somebody drove down to Mt. Holly and, over a seidel at the Elks Club, told Parker that it was a very odd thing that the corpse had not been found before. The search of the kidnaping terrain had been thorough and systematic. The very spot where the decomposed body was found had been gone over by searchers not once but two or three times. The body hadn't been buried; it had just been lying there when the truckman came upon it. How it had gone undiscovered did not lend itself to easy explanation.

Parker had picked up considerable medical and scientific knowledge in his time. The thought hit him that the body had decomposed to a remarkable extent, considering the cold weather that had prevailed between the time of the snatch and the discovery of the corpse.

Parker consulted weather records. The average mean temperature for the entire month of March was 37 degrees; the mean average for April only 49 degrees,

and the average for the twelve days in May, 55 degrees. The sun never struck the spot where the corpse was found. It all added up, in the opinion of medical men whom Parker consulted, to the fact that a body couldn't possibly have decomposed, under the circumstances, to the extent of the corpse in the photograph.

The Lindbergh baby was known to have been twenty-nine inches tall. The skeleton measured four and a half inches *longer* than that. Even allowing for the fact that dead tissue does not hold the bones so compactly as live tissue, four and a half inches was an impressive difference.

Parker became convinced that the body had not been that of the Lindbergh child—and he has plenty of informed companionship in that belief to this day. The Old Fox's deduction was that big bootlegging interests had dug up a corpse somewhere—probably from a grave—and planted it so that the whisky and beer traffic between New York and Pennsylvania, which had been seriously impeded by snooping cops searching vehicles for the baby, could return to normal.

The county physician, Dr. Charles Mitchell, stated, on the death certificate, that the corpse had the toe peculiarities the Lindbergh child was known to have had. This was an extraordinary observation, considering that Dr. Mitchell himself testified a few weeks later, in Washington, at the trial of Gaston Means for the McLean swindle, that both feet were missing. He did not, however, correct the death certificate. Thus not only was the Lindbergh case officially recognized as both a gang and a lone-wolf job, but the corpse in the case was officially represented both as having queerly formed toes and no feet.

Nobody, up to this point in the case, had even thought of a lone-wolf job, let alone mentioned such a thing. And now —now that a body that the state called that of the Lindbergh baby—had been found, the lone-wolf theory seemed all the more untenable. If Cemetery John had been the only person in the world who had thought up and executed the crime—which is the theory that a man eventually went to the chair for—and if that body they found really was the corpse of the baby, it is hard to conceive of Cemetery John showing up in St. Raymond's Cemetery, even to collect fifty grand. For when Cemetery John met Jafsie that night, how could he be certain, since he wasn't supposed to have any accomplices, and since that was supposed to be the Lindbergh baby lying in the brush over in Jersey, that the cops hadn't already found the corpse and were keeping the find secret so that they could nail him when he showed up?

In June, three months after the snatch, the state cops were still warmly embracing the gang theory. Violet Sharpe—the maid in the Morrow home who had given contradictory accounts of her activities the night of the crime—committed suicide when faced with continued police questioning. Colonel Schwarzkopf, speaking for the state cops, issued the statement that the maid had been under suspicion for a long time, as a member of the kidnap gang, and that her suicide marked a great forward step toward eventual solution of the case.

Miss Sharpe was an English subject. The British consul general in New York heard rumors that she had been cuffed around. Under such circumstances a neurotic person, as the Sharpe girl was, might well have committed suicide rather than face the police again. The consul general's probe came to nothing. Miss Sharpe returned to England in a box.

A federal kidnaping law—the so-called Lindbergh law—was passed. That opened the door for J. Edgar Hoover to get into the act. The competition among the man hunters was fierce. Hoover and Schwarzkopf got along like Cain and Abel. The New York cops, getting a whiff of twenty-five thousand dollars reward money that the State of New Jersey had laid on the line for the apprehension of the murderers, trusted one another like Hatfields and McCoys as they searched the Bronx for Cemetery John and kept eyes peeled for ransom money.

One school of thought developed that the crime would be broken through the ransom money, particularly the gold-seal bills. The Treasury Department had plastered the country with lists containing the ransom serial numbers, but, as time passed, bank tellers, gas-station attendants, cashiers in restaurants and theaters, and others in possession of the list, paid less and less attention to it. The result was that a trickle of ransom bills began to show up here and there throughout the country, apparently long after they had been laid down. The first ten-spot, a gold certificate, turned up in New Castle, Pennsylvania, in June—sixty days after the cemetery deal.

The year after the kidnaping, the country went off the gold standard. Everybody with gold-seal certificates had to turn them in at banks in exchange for non-gold currency. The deadline was May 1—fourteen months after the snatch. There was such a last-minute rush at the banks by people exchanging money that tellers didn't have a chance to look at serial numbers. Nobody noticed a man who walked into the Federal Reserve Bank in New York City and exchanged $2,990 of the ransom money—two hundred ninety-seven ten-spots and one twenty. A deposit slip, which all holders of gold certificates were required to fill out, bore the name J. J. Faulkner and the address 537 West 149th Street, New York City. The handwriting on the slip, while not in sufficient quantity to base a comparison on, did bear at least an interesting resemblance to that on the ransom notes.

Treasury dicks found that there was no J. J. Faulkner at the address in question, which was an apartment house. On the off-chance that Faulkner, whoever he was, had not just picked 537 West 149th Street out of a hat, the sleuths talked to everybody in the house. Nobody knew anybody named Faulkner. It happened that one letter carrier had been delivering mail to the apartment house for eighteen years. He recalled no Faulkner in all that time. These dicks were really persistent. They examined city directories and telephone books. They peeled off the years, one by one. Finally, when they got to 1913, they found, listed in the city directory, a Miss Jane Faulkner, whose address was exactly the same as that of J. J. Faulkner on the deposit slip.

Jane Faulkner's trail was picked up through marriage-license records in the Bronx. She had, in 1921, married a man named Gerhardt. Gerhardt, according to the marriage-license dope, had been born in Germany. The handwriting on the license records was his. It looked similar to that on both the ransom notes and the deposit slip.

Gerhardt's trail was picked up in city directories. Eventually, the man himself was located. Both he and his wife, the former Jane Faulkner, denied any knowledge of the Lindbergh case, or the gold-certificate deposit.

Gerhardt had a grown son and daughter by a previous marriage. The daughter, a trained nurse, was married to a German landscape gardener. The son, who worked in a flower shop, had, for three years just prior to the kidnaping, lived on Decatur Avenue, in the Bronx, only a block from Jafsie.

Gerhardt and his wife and his son and daughter and son-in-law couldn't prove they had been engaged in innocent pursuits the night of the snatch. The dicks, on the other hand, couldn't prove any of them had been guiltily occupied. Samples of the quintet's handwriting, when compared with the ransom notes and the deposit slip, produced nothing but bad feelings among experts who disagreed.

Old Jafsie, called back into the act for a return engagement, looked at the three male members of the suspected quintet, rolled his eyes, huffed and puffed and said he wanted to hear them talking in the dark. When he did, he said that the son-in-law—the landscape gardener—sounded very much like Cemetery John. Then he said he couldn't be sure. Then he said the man didn't sound like Cemetery John at all. The landscape gardener began to get very unnerved by the whole business. One day he committed suicide. The Faulkner incident was closed. At least, so it was presumed.

The so-called crime of the century had, by the summer of 1933, dropped through a hole into space so far as the newspapers were concerned. But Jafsie, having become addicted to the violet glow of the spotlight, took to obscurity like Napoleon took to Elba. He emerged from retirement to sit in a store window in the Bronx with a disassembled replica of the kidnap ladder. He popped into police stations, jails and prisons up and down the Atlantic seaboard announcing, "I am Jafsie. Let me look at your prisoners. Cemetery John may be among them."

One day Jafsie bustled on to a Bronx bus. After scrutinizing the driver and all the male passengers, as had become his wont, he settled down and gazed out the window. "Stop this bus!" he shouted. "Stop this bus! I am Jafsie. I see the Lindbergh kidnaper—there, across the street!"

By the time the bus stopped and Jafsie dodged his way through heavy traffic to the other side of a busy thoroughfare, Cemetery John had disappeared. J. Edgar Hoover, for one, wondered how it was possible that only Jafsie had noticed Cemetery John. Hoover couldn't understand why everybody in the Bronx, not to mention talent scouts for the Ringling Brothers side show, hadn't singled out the man. According to Jafsie's own descriptions of John, given at various times to various interested parties, Cemetery John was 6 feet tall and 5 feet 8 inches tall, square-chinned and pointed-chinned, the possessor of large brown eyes and small blue eyes, big-nosed and small-nosed, high-browed and low-browed, and big-chested and small-chested, though not three-legged. Lindbergh said to a G-man after the bus incident, "If Condon were a younger man, I'd be very suspicious of him."

Other men of talent similar to Jafsie's were doing fast and slow burns over the old man's ability to steal the show. Senator William E. Borah, the Lion of Idaho, shook his shaggy mane and growled, "Justice will triumph in the end. It always does."

An unctious-voiced ex-jailbird named Taylor, who was knocking out a quarter of a million dollars a year by pontificating on the kilocycles as the Voice of Experience, was, between writing out checks to blackmailers to clam up about his past, trying to hedge against eventual exposure by solving the Lindbergh case.

He invited his fans to send him tips. As a result, the cops spent thousands of man hours on blind-alley marathons.

Few men were made by trying to get into the Lindbergh act. Several were ruined. The Voice of Experience was one. The cops grew so weary of running down his tips that they took a good look at the man himself and dusted off his past. *Time,* the news magazine, lowered the boom on Taylor and, since his strength derived from his supposed holiness, he disintegrated into his own ether, later to turn up in California, where he died.

Up along the New Jersey Palisades, a youngish, round-faced minister given to cream-colored flannels and blue blazers —the Reverend Vincent Godfrey Burns —had been badly bitten by the spotlight bug. Burns was a brother of Robert Eliott Burns, the original fugitive from the Georgia chain gang. The minister had arranged the deal whereby his brother, who had abandoned the chain gang and made his way to New York, was locked up with a ghost writer and a case of rye in a Broadway fleabag to turn out his story, which Warner Brothers bought for a movie. After the sale was made, the Reverend Burns approached Jacob Wilk, a Warner official in New York, and inquired, "Who have you got in mind to play the role of my brother in the picture?"

"Paul Muni," said Wilk sourly. "Why?"

"Have you signed Muni yet?" asked the parson.

"No. Why?"

"*I,*" said the Reverend Burns, "could give that part just what it *needs.*"

"Go away," said Wilk.

Burns had a visit one night from a nut-type man, as Abe Burrows would say. The caller announced he had snatched the Lindbergh child. The confession season was at its height. Jailbirds, exhibitionists and wheels the country over wanted to get into the act. That cut no ice with Reverend Burns. Daily, he emerged from the protective fastness of the Palisades to journey across the Hudson and make the rounds of Manhattan book publishers and magazine offices. Ten grand, he suggested, would be about right as an advance for his story of the desperado who had come out of the night to unburden his conscience to a man of God. "Golly," the minister would say to an editor, "can't you just *see* that thing as a movie—with *me* in the leading role?"

Of the clues in the case itself—the ransom notes, the ransom money, the ladder and the chisel—the chisel had by now dropped by the wayside. It was of the dime-store variety.

Samples of the ladder wood—pine—had been identified by microscopic analysis as indigenous to a certain section of South Carolina. There it was traced, through distinctive markings in the saws that had cut it, to a specific planing mill. The mill had shipped to just one northern firm the particular type and cut of wood used in the ladder. The firm was the Great National Millwork and Lumber Company in the Bronx.

There the luck ran out. Any one of thousands of customers could have come in, a year and a half previously, and purchased for cash enough of the wood to make a ladder.

Ransom bills began to turn up regularly in gas stations and other small businesses in the Bronx. Pins stuck in the spots on a map where the bills appeared disclosed that the passer was operating on the perimeter of a circular area where not a single bill had shown up. The supposition was that the passer lived in the center of this circle, which was several blocks in diameter, and was taking the precaution of not passing any of the money in his immediate neighborhood, where he might be recognized.

The bills, subjected to chemical analysis, disclosed traces of emery dust, indicating proximity to a machine shop or a carpenter's bench. They had a musty odor, indicating that they had been buried or kept where air was not circulating.

From a psychological analysis of the ransom notes, and from descriptions of the voice of Cemetery John, as supplied by both Jafsie and Colonel Lindbergh, it was decided, beyond doubt, that Cemetery John was a German. The night the ransom was paid, Cemetery John had seen Jafsie coming and had shouted to him, "Hey, Doctor!" Lindbergh, who had good ears, had heard the two words although he had been sitting in a car almost a block away. He was certain, as was Jafsie, that Cemetery John was a German.

The cops built a replica of the ladder. A rung broke under a total weight of two hundred ten pounds. The deduction was that the rung of the actual kidnap ladder that had been broken had given way when the kidnaper was descending with the thirty-pound baby in his arms. Thus the man would have weighed around one hundred eighty pounds. After a bad start, the cops were now cooking with gas. There even began to emerge some semblance of cooperation between the state cops, the New York cops and the G-men. Everybody was hunting for a German mechanic or carpenter who lived in the center of the ransom-bill circle.

One night in November, 1933, at about nine-thirty, a man appeared at the ticket window of Loew's Sheridan Square Theater, in Greenwich Village, and bought one admission for a gangster film entitled *Broadway Through a Keyhole*, written by Walter Winchell. He paid for his ticket with a five-dollar bill. After the man had gone into the darkened theater, there to become swallowed up in the audience, the ticket seller, Mrs. Cecilia Barr, decided that he had acted very furtively. She re-examined the bill he had given her, thinking it might be counterfeit. She found it to be a Lindbergh ransom note. Mrs. Barr called the cops. The money passer wasn't found.

This was the first instance in which a description of a passer was available. Police sketch artists translated the impressions of the man in the cashier's mind to black and white on paper. A sullen-looking individual of about thirty-five, with flat cheeks, a pointed chin and narrow eyes, emerged.

The following summer—1934—when the case was more than two years old—Jafsie put it back on the front pages. He was on a bus again, he saw Cemetery John again, and once more Cemetery John had vanished before Jafsie could cross a thoroughfare thick with fast-moving traffic.

One day in September of 1934—two and a half years after the snatch—a man drove up to a filling station in the Bronx and bought some gas with a ransom bill. The gas-station attendant, impressed by the customer's furtive manner, checked the bill against the Treasury's list of ransom serial numbers while there was still time to take down the customer's license. That was how a thirty-six-year-old Bronx carpenter named Bruno Richard Hauptmann suddenly found his outlook limited by jail bars.

Hauptmann lived in the center of the ransom-bill circle. He was a German. He weighed one hundred eighty pounds —the weight that broke the kidnap ladder. He was married and had a small son, who had been expected at the time of the snatch in the Sourlands. He had been convicted, at the age of twenty, in Germany, as a thief and a stick-up artist. He had broken jail and come to the United States illegally.

Bruno Hauptmann was the spit and image of the pictures that police artists had drawn following the theater incident ten months previously. He had frequently made purchases at the Bronx lumberyard from which the wood in the kidnap ladder had come.

Almost fifteen thousand dollars of ransom money was found buried and otherwise hidden in the garage back of the carpenter's home in the Bronx. Five thousand in ransom money had already been passed. That left thirty thousand dollars unaccounted for.

Hauptmann said that a friend—one Isadore Fisch—had turned over to him, Hauptmann, personal belongings while he, Fisch, took a trip to Germany following the snatch. Fisch had died in Germany. Hauptmann had discovered the money among Fisch's belongings following the man's death. Fisch, a fur dealer who had frequently done business in the Sourland mountains, had owed Hauptmann several thousand dollars. Hauptmann, to collect the debt, had begun to pass the money. He hadn't known it was Lindbergh money, though he considered it illegal money inasmuch as it was gold-seal stuff, long since called in by the government. Thus he had passed it surreptitiously.

A grand jury in the Bronx began listening to testimony looking toward an extortion case against Hauptmann while the State of New Jersey was trying to figure out a way to link him, by means of direct evidence, to the actual snatch. Jafsie took a look at Hauptmann and told Special Agent Leon Turrou of the FBI, "That is not the man. Cemetery John was much heavier." In view of the testimony that Jafsie was to give at Hauptmann's trial—a trial conducted on the premise not of kidnaping but of murder—it has always been a source of fascination to students of the case that the old man, *after* having looked at Hauptmann and talked to him a dozen times in the days following the carpenter's arrest in the Bronx, went running down to Florida, there to examine, in the hope of finding Cemetery John, a Brooklyn boy jugged at the prison camp at Raiford.

Mrs. Barr, the theater cashier, identified Hauptmann as the passer of a ransom bill. One of the taxi drivers who had been utilized by Cemetery John during the ransom negotiations—a fellow named John Perrone—identified Hauptmann as the man who had given him a letter to take to Jafsie's home. Perrone picked Hauptmann out of a line-up. There were just three men in the line-up —the suspect and two flatfeet in uniform.

Lindbergh himself, asked before the Bronx grand jury whether he would be able to identify Hauptmann as the man he had heard calling "Hey, Doctor!" the night the ransom was paid, replied, "It would be very difficult for me to sit here and say that I could pick a man by that voice." That remark, too, was to interest thoughtful spectators at Hauptmann's trial.

A few days after the pinch, the New Jersey state cops announced that Hauptmann had definitely been placed on the Lindbergh property by two residents of the vicinity—a woodsman named Millard Whited, and a man of eighty-seven named Amandus Hochmuth. Both Whited and Hochmuth had come under routine police questioning at the time of the snatch. Then they had been stout in their denials that they had seen any suspicious strangers in the vicinity of the Lindbergh home. Now, Whited, the woodsman, whose own relatives were one day to testify that he had a bad reputation, said that he had seen Hauptmann loitering around the Lindbergh estate on several occasions just prior to the kidnaping. Old Hochmuth identified Hauptmann as the driver of an automobile, with a three-section ladder strapped to its side, that he had observed on the edge of the Lindbergh estate the day of the crime. Hochmuth, a social-security man, seems to have had a sudden deterioration in his eyesight within a short time after having observed Hauptmann. On June 29, 1932—four months after his observation—the Division of Old Age Security had made this report about Hochmuth:

Health is very poor, applicant partly blind.

On August 4, little more than a month later, an Old Age Security investigator had made this further written notation:

Frail. Failing eyesight due to cataracts.

For several days after Hauptmann's arrest, more than thirty state cops, New York dicks, and G-men went over every inch of the Hauptmann house, including the attic. More than a dozen official reports stated that there was nothing in the attic that bore any relationship to the case. Suddenly, however, the state cops made not one but two very incriminating discoveries. They found Jafsie's name and phone number written in pencil on the inside of a closet. They found that a piece of the board flooring in the attic had been removed, presumably some time previously. There was one rail in the kidnap ladder that had been made not of Carolina pine but of another kind of wood. It turned out now that the rail in question matched precisely, even to the grain, with the wood in the attic flooring.

A battalion of handwriting experts compared Hauptmann's penmanship with that on the ransom letters. The experts split down the middle—par for the course. Those who disagreed that Hauptmann was the ransom author were told to go away. Albert S. Osborn, a leading authority, said he believed Hauptmann wrote the letters. Osborn joined the act.

Hauptmann had bank accounts and brokerage accounts. He had little money, when pinched, except the ransom dough. Accountants for the State, however, started toting up figures and arrived at the conclusion that, including the money found in the garage, fifty thousand dollars, almost to the penny, had passed through the carpenter's hands since the snatch. Hauptmann explained that he had frequently transferred money from a bank to a brokerage account, then back to the bank again, then back to the brokerage account, then back to the bank. What the accountants were doing, he maintained, was counting the same money several times.

That splendid volume of autobiographical reference, Who's Who in America, has, in its time, in addition to listing a ghost and quite a few three-alarm phonies, fallen for misleading information supplied by some of its subjects. Several editions listed, among the accomplishments of ex-Governor Harold Giles Hoffman of New Jersey, authorship of a one-thousand-word article, to which Hoffman's name was signed but which was written by a newspaperman.

The article was submitted to a national magazine. It was not accepted; moreover, it was lost, and neither Hoffman nor his ghost ever saw it again. Still, the ex-Governor listed the nonexistent one-thousand-word work written by somebody else as Arnold Toynbee might list A Study of History. Critics of Hoffman find a rewarding irony in the title of his listed accomplishment. It is "Getting Away With Murder."

The Harold Hoffman who wrote "Getting Away With Murder" which was an account of how a hit-and-run killer escaped justice, was one of the twentieth century's outstanding authorities on how to get away with murder. This was the same Hoffman who was to be revealed, following his death in 1954, as one of the cleverest crooks ever to darken the American political horizon. Hoffman, who was also a banker, had started taking home samples early in his political career, and by the time he horned into the Lindbergh case, he had juggled bank and state funds until he had made off with, and successfully covered, about a third of a million dollars.

At the time of Hauptmann's arrest, Harold Hoffman was a chubby thirty-eight-year-old personality boy who was serving as New Jersey's Commissioner of Motor Vehicles. He paused in his breathless pursuit of the Governorship, for which he was at the moment running, to cast a weather eye northward toward the Bronx. Word had filtered through to Hoffman that the plan now was to abandon the gang theory and custom-tailor a case that would fit the conception that Hauptmann was the sole and absolute proprietor of the crime of the century.

Hoffman—a fellow who looked ahead —figured that if he won the election, he would be Governor by the time Hauptmann went on trial in New Jersey. He telephoned to Ellis Parker, the Old Fox of Burlington County, to drop into the State House next time he was up in Trenton.

"Ellis," said Hoffman, "how do you have this Lindbergh case doped out?"

"The man they got in the Bronx ain't guilty of stealin' that kid," said Parker. "Extortin' money from old Jafsie, maybe. But stealin' the kid, never."

"Why are you so sure, Ellis?"

"Because," said Parker, "I'm shadowin' the feller that did steal the kid."

"What!"

"Now don't go astin' me who it is, Harold," said the Old Fox. "I ain't talkin' 'til I make a pinch."

When Hauptmann was pinched, his wife—a harassed, *hausfrau* type—retained, at the suggestion of friends, a conservative attorney named Fawcett. Attorney Fawcett had hardly banked the retainer fee when a representative of the *Daily Mirror*, competitor of the *Daily News* in the New York sex-and-crime field, approached her and announced, "Mrs. Hauptmann, you are getting rid of the lawyer you have. We have hired a lawyer for you." That's what the man said. The *Mirror* wanted a hippodrome in New Jersey when Hauptmann went on trial, and it had located just the fellow to put it on—a Brooklyn barrister by the name of Edward J. Reilly.

Brother Reilly—a huge, earthy man with sandy hair, horn-rimmed glasses and a face like red flannel—had, because of a unique talent for alienating juries in capital cases, become known around Borough Hall in Brooklyn as Death House Reilly. Big Ed, as he was also called, conveyed the impression that he moved in an envelope of impending fraud although he had never actually been seen fraternizing with a juror while a case was on. He dearly loved to roam

the corridors of the Brooklyn Museum of Art, there to contemplate the nudes while getting starched on a flaskful of orange blossoms.

The trial was set for the day after New Year, 1935, in the town of Flemington, seat of the county in which the Lindbergh home was situated. Three local lawyers—among them C. Lloyd Fischer, who had defended Commodore Curtis, the man who had obstructed justice by being in touch with the kidnap gang—were to be associated with Big Ed in an advisory capacity. "This," Big Ed announced at the first conference with his associates, "is going to be the Goddamnedest trial you ever saw."

As Fischer and the two other local lawyers—conservative men all—saw it, the big point for the defense would be to dispute the identification of the body that had been found. The Jersey lawyers had amassed considerable evidence along the lines that Detective Parker had originally developed. "Good idea," said Big Ed. "Not only that, we'll pin the crime itself on that maid who committed suicide and Whatley, the butler, who was in the house the night of the crime. Whatley did die, didn't he?"

"Yes," said Fischer. "But Mr. Reilly—"

"If they're dead," boomed Big Ed, "who the hell's going to know the difference?"

Big Ed reached into a new fifty-dollar brief case he had stuck a Fifth Avenue leather dealer for. He hauled out some stationery he had just had made up. The legend read:

The Hauptmann-Lindbergh Trial
Edward J. Reilly
Chief Counsel

Running down the left-hand margin of the paper was a drawing, reproduced in bright red, of the kidnap ladder.

Big Ed demanded personal privacy in Flemington, where, in anticipation of the trial throngs, they were already renting pool tables as beds. Fischer got him a room in the home of a college chum and his wife. The couple didn't run a rooming house; they were willing to put up the distinguished Brooklyn gentleman, free of charge, as a favor to Fischer.

In the middle of the first night, Reilly spent on the premises, the doorbell rang. A blonde in a mink coat stood at the threshold. "I have come," she announced to the lady of the house, holding up a stenographer's notebook, "to take dictation from Mr. Reilly."

When the Hauptmann trial opened, Flemington took on a mood somewhere between that of a Mardi Gras and a World Series. Tickets were printed for the various performances in the ancient courtroom and peddled like black-market circus ducats. A newsreel camera was hid in the rear courtroom wall, with a synchronized microphone hidden in a broken electric fan near the witness stand. Bookies and B-girls arrived in large numbers, the former laying odds on the outcome of the trial.

Jafsie and Lindbergh, by virtue of fat parts and long rehearsals, were the co-stars of the act by now. Hauptmann, the man who should really have been the star, was reduced to a supporting role, along with such other performers as Betty Gow, the baby's nurse, and Colonel Schwarzkopf of the state cops. Hauptmann lacked experience, audience appeal and a build-up.

Big Ed Reilly spent his nights drinking and dictating. He arrived in court each morning thoroughly bushed, afraid to lean over, and reluctant to open his eyes for fear of bleeding to death. He was never fully awake until after lunch, when he drank eight or ten orange blossoms out of a coffee cup in a hotel across the street.

At one trial session, while the little men with the hammers were at work on the inside of Big Ed's temples, the question of the identification of the body came up. Lloyd Fischer, Reilly's associate counsel, was supposed to arise at that point and begin introducing evidence to dispute the State's claim that the body of the Lindbergh child had really been found. Reilly was on his feet first, "We concede," he said, "that the corpse that was found was that of the Lindbergh baby." The State's lawyers could hardly believe their ears. Fischer left the courtroom to give his temperature a chance to drop.

The case against Hauptmann embraced all of the previously announced evidence: the wood in the ladder, the piece of missing floor board from his attic, Jafsie's phone number in the closet, the accounting wizardry tracing $50,000 —$30,000 of which had never turned up —to him; authorship of the ransom letters, and identification by the theater cashier, the taxi driver, and the two local men who had, in 1932, been certain they had seen nobody around the Lindbergh property.

There were three important additional identification witnesses. A Miss Hildegarde Alexander—a model who introduced the sole touch of sex appeal at the trial—said that one night almost three years previously, while Jafsie's secret ransom negotiations were in progress, she had happened to observe a man loitering at a telegraph desk in a Bronx railroad station, and noticed another man watching him. Both men, said Miss Alexander —a lady with an extraordinary memory for strange faces—were in the courtroom. The loiterer was Jafsie and the watcher was Hauptmann.

Jafsie himself seemed to find the Flemington visibility and acoustics far more conducive to certainty than he had found them in the Bronx. The old man identified Hauptmann as Cemetery John. Hauptmann blew a gasket right in the courtroom. He began calling Jafsie names. Hauptmann's performance was regarded as a cheap attempt by an ambitious amateur to detract from the smooth professionalism of the co-star. Nobody took him seriously.

Colonel Lindbergh made an identification of Hauptmann merely from having heard the man uttering two words in the dark a block away almost three years previously. Big Ed Reilly had before him the minutes of the Bronx grand jury, which quoted Lindbergh in direct contradiction to the testimony he was now giving. When Reilly let *that* go by, too, his associate Fischer whispered to another associate, "It wouldn't be so bad if the big bum was just lousy, but he's *prosecuting* the client."

Reilly was by that time barely on speaking terms with his associate counsel. All they knew about the defense was what they heard in the courtroom and what they read in the *Daily Mirror,* the paper that had hired Reilly. Big Ed wasn't too interested in cross-examining the state's witnesses, such as old Hochmuth, the almost-blind identification witness. He would sit with his head in his hands, wondering if it wouldn't be better to swear-off the sauce altogether, and yell out a name—the name of his next witness. Fischer and the other defense lawyers, hearing the name for the first time and not recognizing it, would wince, fearing the worst.

The fears were well founded. Reilly began a parade to the stand of the most incredible collection of perjurers ever to offer testimony in a major trial. Several

of them said that they had seen Violet Sharpe, the maid who had committed suicide, and Isadore Fisch, Hauptmann's furrier friend, on a Hudson River ferry late the night of the kidnaping with—you guessed it—the little eaglet. Another Reilly witness said that he had seen Isadore Fisch running like hell away from the cemetery the night Jafsie paid the ransom.

Next on the program was a Reilly-produced memory act. The performers in this turn all recalled having seen Hauptmann in a Bronx bakery, drinking coffee and eating strudel, at the hour of the snatch. There were so many witnesses who testified that they had just happened to drop into the pastry shop that night almost three years previously, and see a stranger they now remembered as Hauptmann, that spectators conjured up the picture of a bakery shop approximately as busy as Grand Central Terminal and catering exclusively to memory experts.

One day, after he ran out of liars, Reilly's gaze came to rest on Betty Gow, the nurse. "Boy," he muttered, "if *you* were only dead."

As the trial neared its end, a crisis approached in several lives. Detective Ellis Parker, who had often slapped murderers in the can without the formality of an arraignment, was pondering a plan to take the law into his own hands again. This time he was going to grab a man and put him in irons and have the hell beaten out of him by way of cleaning up the case.

The best radio coverage of the trial was being given several times a day, over Station WOR, by an obscure ex-Brooklyn reporter named Gabriel Heatter, who talked like a minister. Good-News-Tonight can thank a man named Hauptmann, as he would put it, for his financial success in radio. Heatter's meat was

Hauptmann's poison. Heatter's shining hour was at hand.

The Reverend Vincent Godfrey Burns, who had not yet unloaded his psychopath as a Lindbergh kidnaper, brooded among the trial spectators, wondering if he could peddle his nut to the judge. He decided to try. "Stop, Your Honor!" screamed the parson. He paused for a hot moment to glance in the direction of a couple of theatrical producers in the audience. "Stop, in the name of God! This man Hauptmann is innocent! I can name the *real* criminal!" The cops removed the Barrymore of the exhibitionist circuit with what untalented vaudeville performers once referred to as the hook.

There were several Hauptmann trials, all going on simultaneously, but separate and distinct from one another. There was the one in the courtroom. There was the one in the newspapers, in which experts, some of whom never laid eyes on Hauptmann, explained the man's mental processes. There was the Hauptmann radio trial, at which hacks of the air waves were able to load or angle the evidence by vocal nuances. There was the curbstone trial, right in Flemington, wherein Hauptmann was almost completely ignored, as he was led from the courtroom to jail between sessions, and Lindbergh, packing a gat, was cheered as he darted from the courthouse to a limousine.

All four trials had one thing in common—an arresting switch applied to the tenet of American jurisprudence that holds that a man is innocent until proved guilty. Hauptmann was presumed guilty unless proved innocent. The only question was: how guilty was he? The suspense over the outcome of the four trials was confined to speculation as to whether Hauptmann would get the chair or life imprisonment. When the defendant himself took the stand, to explain his posses-

sion of the money, everybody cried, "Ah, the *Fisch* story!"

The verdict in the courtroom trial was awaited throughout the United States and several European countries with approximately the same interest as word of the cessation of hostilities in a world war. The Associated Press, remembering its fluke Pulitzer Prize and not unmindful of the possibility of lightning striking twice in the same kind of place, laid elaborate plans to scoop its chief competitors—United Press and International News Service.

In the movies, demon representatives of the Fourth Estate, curiously immune to contempt of court, tear the verdict from the jury foreman's hand, trample over the defendant, his counsel and several bailiffs, and bolt from the courtroom to flash the word to their papers. In actuality, everybody, including the press, is usually locked in the courtroom when the verdict in a major trial is brought in. This is to assure the judge an audience while he reaches for, slices and hands out to the jurors the thank-you-for-your-services bologna—an anticlimactic act roughly comparable to the acrobats who used to close vaudeville shows while the audience filed out. That was how things were to be handled when eight good men and four true women on the Hauptmann jury lugged in the carpenter's fate.

The AP, fixing to beat its competitors by the number of minutes that would elapse between the announcement of the verdict and the opening of the courtroom doors, devised a system of flashlight signals whereby a man at a window in the courtroom would blink the verdict to a man in an alley, who would relay the flash to another AP man at the mouth of the alley, who would flash it on to a man leaning out of a second-story window up the street, who in turn would pass it on by word of mouth to a telegrapher in the same room.

Paul Revere, the Boston minute man, had a pipe compared to what the Flemington split-second men were up against. Revere worked with lights of only one color, a maximum of two lamps, his signal did not have to pass through other and possibly incompetent hands, and he was obliged to let the public know merely whether the British were coming by land or by sea. Each of the Flemington signalers, however, had to work with lights of three colors—red, green and amber—a flashlight for each color, had to deal with three possible verdicts—death, life imprisonment and acquittal—and had five men in the act compared to the North Church solo turn.

Largely because of Brother Reilly's performance as defense counsel of Hauptmann, the men in the AP act were hardly anticipating use of the amber flashlights, amber being the color decided upon for acquittal. They were anticipating red for the chair or green for life imprisonment.

When the verdict came in, the man in the courtroom blinked his light. The man in the alley blinked his, and the man at the mouth of the alley blinked his, and the fellow with his head sticking out of the window up the street passed the word along to the telegrapher. The AP flash—life imprisonment—went around the world by radio, and extra editions of papers on the Pacific Coast were spilling off the presses with it almost before the doors of the courtroom in Flemington were opened.

But when the doors *were* opened, there was hell to pay. International News and United Press flashed the verdict of death in the chair, which was the jury verdict.

Somebody in the AP act had either flashed green for red or been color-blind or mistaken the face of a jealous competitor for a green flash or heard wrong or something. Whatever had happened, it added up to one of the major bloomers in journalistic history—one of a stature commensurate with the Lindbergh case as a whole. When anybody, in later years, would mention the Flemington signal system to the late Joe Connolly, chief of International News Service, Connolly would look quizzically at his auditor for a moment, then say, "Oh, *that*," and start laughing until the tears rolled down his cheeks.

The AP boner was the final touch to a legal proceeding of which *Editor and Publisher*, a mouthpiece of the newspaper profession itself, had this to say:

> No trial in this country has so degraded the administration of justice. If the life of one man and the unhappiness of hundreds are to be commercialized for the benefit of entertainment, of radio broadcasters, newspaper publishers, newsreel producers; if a public trial means protection from star-chamber tyranny but not from the indignities of the mob, then the ancient institution of trial by a jury of peers is without meaning.

There was little disagreement that the German carpenter had received woefully inadequate representation by Death House Reilly. Students of jurisprudence, looking at the trial in retrospect, wondered how it had been possible for Reilly to defend his client so ineptly. The simple explanation was that Big Ed just didn't give a damn. He had his *Mirror* dough in advance, and his mind, the entire time he was in Flemington, was concerned with orange blossoms and dictating. On top of that, Reilly could very well have been in the first stages of insanity during the trial; less than two years later he became an inmate of the Brooklyn State Hospital for the Insane.

In the death house, Hauptmann, broke since the ransom money was taken from him, issued an appeal to the public for funds with which to fight his conviction. The *Daily News* made him a proposition which would have given him ample funds, although it was difficult to see how Hauptmann could have conscientiously employed the money for what he had in mind. The *News* offered him one hundred fifty thousand dollars for a series of articles under his name to be entitled, How I Killed the Lindbergh Baby.

Hoffman, who had meanwhile been sworn in as Governor of New Jersey, made a three-dimensional probe of the case and concluded that Hauptmann had not been in the Lindbergh crime alone, if indeed he had been in it at all. It was Hoffman who learned that Hochmuth, the old man who placed Hauptmann at the crime scene, had not only been practically blind in 1932 but had, like Whited, the other placement witness, sworn to the cops that he had seen no suspicious strangers.

Hoffman, a tough guy with a lot of guts, got Whited, the woodsman, into a room in a Trenton hotel and made him admit that the state cops had given him dough. Hoffman hauled in old man Hochmuth, seated him in a chair, and pointed to a silver loving cup filled with red roses exactly ten feet away. "Dad," he said to the old boy, pointing to the vase, "what is that?"

"A picture," said Hochmuth. "A picture of a woman."

Hoffman got mental indigestion every time he considered that a score of investigators had fine-tooth-combed Hauptmann's house for several days before coming upon the cut floor board and Jafsie's telephone number. He began to see the faint outlines of a case that had been partially constructed with carefully cultivated evidence. Dr. Erasmus Hudson, the fingerprint expert who had found half a thousand prints on the kidnap ladder, none of which turned out to be Hauptmann's, told Hoffman that Captain Lamb of the state cops had asked him if it was possible to fake a print.

Certainly the two witnesses who placed Hauptmann at the crime scene did not belong in the same room with Caesar's wife. Then, suppose that the state cops, really convinced that Hauptmann was the kidnaper, and enthusiastic in their belief that the end justified the means, had nudged the case along a little, such as by planting the evidence in Hauptmann's attic. What remained of the case against Hauptmann as the actual snatcher after that? As the cynical tourist said, when traveling through Oregon, "Take away the scenery and what have you got?"

If Hauptmann had made the kidnap ladder, Hoffman wondered, would he, a carpenter, have made a ladder that would give way under the weight of himself and the baby? And would anybody clever enough to have conceived and executed the snatch all alone, and then successfully conducted the ransom negotiations, been stupid enough to fashion one rail of the crime instrument out of a floor board in his own attic, let alone write down Jafsie's phone number and leave it there?

Every ransom bill that was passed, though undetected in other channels, was eventually spotted when retired by the Treasury because of old age. Only two-fifths of the dough ever showed up. If Hauptmann had spent all of the ransom money except that which was found in his garage, as the state contended, where was the other thirty thousand dollars?

There wasn't a single handwriting expert in the country who was willing to say that Hauptmann's writing was that of J. J. Faulkner, the mysterious one who had disposed of almost three thousand dollars of the ransom money when gold certificates were called in. If Hauptmann wasn't Faulkner, who was Faulkner? Accountants had carefully ascribed to Hauptmann, through their interpretation of his bank and brokerage accounts, fifty thousand dollars, almost to the penny, of money he had not earned in legitimate endeavors. They had completely overlooked the Faulkner deposit, which brought the figure closer to fifty-three thousand dollars than the fifty thousand dollars that Hauptmann went away on.

It wasn't the stand that Hoffman took in the Lindbergh case that got him in wrong so much as the way he took it. He had a publicity man who dished out the latest developments with an eye to maximum newspaper space. The hippodrome tradition of Flemington was being followed out in a place where there should have been some dignity. Mysterious callers were ushered into the executive offices in the dead of night. Everything was dramatized to the hilt. Hoffman saw everybody. He sat and listened, gravely, to the publisher of an astrology magazine, who assured him that Hauptmann's horoscope proved that he could not have committed the crime. Things like that.

Hoffman called on Hauptmann in the death house, again late at night. He was accompanied by Ellis Parker's secretary, dressed in an evening gown. Hauptmann didn't say anything except that he was innocent of any wrongdoing and that he was a victim of circumstances. He insisted that the ransom money—twenty thousand dollars of it—had come into his possession through the dead Isadore Fisch.

There seemed to exist, on the part of Colonel Schwarzkopf of the state cops and others who had been active in the prosecution of Hauptmann, a desire to resort to what has been described as indecent haste to seat the carpenter in the electric chair. Governor Hoffman, in his melodramatic way, pretty definitely established for a large portion of the thoughtful public that evidence not fitting the lone-wolf theory had mysteriously disappeared from the state police files.

Schwarzkopf, who had grown in social stature by virtue of infrequent invitations to dine with the Lindberghs, was impatient with anyone who suggested that the case was not 100 per cent cleaned up. The ex-floorwalker particularly resented Hoffman. The Governor, now his superior, instructed him to turn over anything new and hot in connection with the case. One day Schwarzkopf sent a special messenger to the Governor with a letter from a screwball that stated:

I know who done the Lindbergh job. Gov. Hoffman done it.

Hoffman learned that Schwarzkopf, who, in addition to his ten thousand dollar annual salary, was allowed expenses when away from home base, had put the bite on the state for the maximum daily allowance during the months he had received free room and board at the Lindbergh home. That cooked the colonel's goose. Hoffman said he would not reappoint him—a little failure that dealt Schwarzkopf out of a five thousand dollar-a-year life pension.

Schwarzkopf might have been in a bad way had it not been for the man who was rapidly becoming America's unofficial chief of police—Phillips H. Lord, the proprietor of a mid-Manhattan carnage factory turning out such radio crime programs as Gang Busters. Lord, who always had a weather eye cocked for a cop with a front-page name, signed Schwarzkopf at his old state police salary to comment, by proxy, from a mythical room at New York police headquarters on a weekly cops-and-robbers opera of the type that has been accused of making a major contribution to the sum total of the country's juvenile delinquency. By virtue of Lord's by-proxy gimmick, which misleads many listeners into believing that they are hearing something extra-official instead of an actor pinch-hitting for an authentic individual, Schwarzkopf was able to be in Europe with the Army in the last war at the same time he was inhabiting the American radio crime waves.

A number of observant critics who believed that Hauptmann could not have pulled the snatch all by himself pointed out that both Commodore Curtis, of the Three Virginians, and Gaston Means had, at a time when Jafsie was still negotiating with Cemetery John in secrecy, called some of the turns. The commodore had turned up with an accurate and unpublished plan of the inside of the Lindbergh home, for instance, and Means had come through with the correct description of the sleeping suit and with the latest news on the rising ransom price. How could they have known these things, the argument ran, unless they really had been in touch with someone implicated in the job? The anti-Hauptmannites, however, brushed this sort of thing aside. Maybe the commodore's house plan hadn't been published in the newspapers, they said, but it could easily have been bootlegged around, as copies of the top-secret ransom note were. As

for Means, he was a shrewd guesser with a personal knowledge of police procedure; he could logically have surmised that the published information on the crime would include at least one false tip, the most likely description to falsify would have been that of the child's clothing, and the sleeping suit was the only item of clothing he had. The increase in the ransom demand could have been guessed, too. Or Means might have got his information through underworld connections he was known to have, which might have linked up with somebody at headquarters like Mickey Rosner.

Most of the twenty-five thousand dollars reward money offered by the state was paid to the gas-station attendant who had turned up Hauptmann. The Supreme Court of the United States, in March, 1936—four years after the snatch —refused to rule on the case. It wasn't within the power of a New Jersey Governor to commute a death sentence to life imprisonment. A board of pardons had to do that, and it wouldn't.

The night of March 31, 1936, was the one set for Hauptmann's execution. Good-News-Tonight Heatter was at a microphone across the street from the big house in Trenton. The execution was set for eight o'clock. Heatter was on the air, momentarily expecting the flash that the man named Hauptmann had paid for the Lindbergh crime tonight. It didn't come and it didn't come. At half past eight, Heatter was still talking, now extemporaneously, for he had long since used up his prepared script. At nine o'clock he was still talking. He talked for almost two solid hours before word came through that Hauptmann had been granted a stay of execution. He had the whole country hanging on to every word. No radio commentator had ever accomplished a feat like that before, and with such a mighty audience. Good-News-Tonight left the five-thousand-dollar-a-year brackets for the five-thousand-dollar-a-week brackets.

The reason for Hauptmann's reprieve, it turned out, was that Ellis Parker, the Old Fox, had brought in *his* candidate for the Lindbergh job at the eleventh hour. The thing was getting cornier and cornier. Eliza crossing the ice in *Uncle Tom's Cabin* seemed, by comparison, austere.

Parker's man, who had confessed the crime, was Paul Wendel, a notorious Trenton ex-jailbird who had, in his time, practiced law and pharmacy. Wendel—a pious-looking big character with a flair for making his accusers feel guilty and himself feel innocent—quickly became the star of the Lindbergh act. He convinced a grand jury in Brooklyn that Ellis Parker had, in that city, tortured him into falsely confessing the Lindbergh job. Hauptmann's execution—and to hell with *him*—four nights after it had been stayed was just one more anticlimax.

Wendel, who had not been doing so well financially before some Parker-directed punks had snatched him on a New York street and taken him to a dungeon, did all right now. As the star of the epilogue of the great Lindbergh act, he was ensconced in a luxurious Brooklyn hotel for months with Brooklyn footing the bill, while he was filling in law-enforcement officials on the details of his snatch. Between times, he told his story to a ghost-writer for a magazine and picked up a little change that way.

The prosecution of a big case is hungrily sought by publicity-conscious lawyers. There was an undignified scramble among state and federal prosecutors to try Ellis Parker. Parker, in his dotage, and his co-conspirators were finally tried in Federal Court in Newark, New Jersey —almost eight years after the kidnaping case—and sent to prison for kidnaping Wendel. "I know," said Parker as they took him away to prison, where he died, "where the Lindbergh kid is. He's a big boy now, you know—going on ten years old."

So long as the records of the Lindbergh case exist, there will remain the questions:

Was the body of the Lindbergh baby ever found?

Why were no fingerprints found in the child's nursery?

Was Hauptmann the sole perpetrator of the snatch? If not, who were his co-conspirators?

Was Isadore Fisch the real leader of the kidnap gang?

Was Commodore Curtis in touch with the real kidnapers?

Who was J. J. Faulkner?

Three-fifths of the ransom money has never turned up to this day, more than a quarter of a century later. Why?

No matter how guilty or how innocent Hauptmann really was, he surely got a rough ride to the death house. As one observer said, though, it was just as well that they did execute him in the end. Had he somehow been sprung, he would have faced something just as inexorable as death. He had not paid income taxes on all that dough that the accounting wizards ascribed to him. Mr. Whiskers was all ready with an income-tax rap against him.

The Case of the Curious Cubs

*Here is the step-by-step account of how a couple of smart reporters kept
ahead of the detectives and snared Dickie Loeb and Nathan Leopold
as the authors of one of the most heinous crimes on record.*

Once upon a time, two cub reporters
—a pair of raw but smart kids on the
Chicago *Daily News*—made chimps of
the cops and unpeeled a doozer. Their
names were James Mulroy and Alvin
Goldstein—an Irishman and a Jew—and
they were, in 1924, two years after their
graduation from the University of Chicago, devoting their talents mainly to
running out for coffee, cigarets and hard
apples for the city editor. When, on the
afternoon of Wednesday, May 21, 1924,
one of the biggest stories in Chicago's
journalistic history began to unfold, it
looked as if all Mulroy and Goldstein
would know about it was what they read
in the papers.

A fifteen-year-old-boy named Bobby
Franks, the son of a prominent multimillionaire real-estate man and ex-money-
lender, dropped from sight. Bobby, a
quiet, sensitive kid, had left the Harvard
School, a nobby knowledge foundry a
few blocks from his sumptuous home on
fashionable Ellis Avenue, when classes
broke at three in the afternoon, and
never turned up for dinner.

At nine o'clock that night a man who
gave the name of Johnson telephoned the
Franks home. The boy's mother took
the call. "Your son has been kidnaped
for ransom," said Johnson. "You will receive a letter in the morning telling you
how to proceed." The caller hung up
before the woman could question him.

Jacob Franks, father of the victim,
consulted with Chief of Detectives
Michael (Get-'Em-Mike) Hughes, a fair-
to-middling man hunter who thought
that a length of rubber hose was a pretty
good substitute for brains—which, in
fact, it often was. Get-'Em-Mike was all
for turning the town inside out.

"No," said Franks, whose money
talked, "I want you to work secretly.
Trace all phone calls coming into my
house, and whatever else occurs to you.
But not a word to the papers; I don't
want to antagonize the kidnapers. They
might take it out on Bobby."

"You got any ideas who done this, Mr.
Franks?" asked Get-'Em-Mike.

"I made a few enemies in the old
days," said Franks, who wore a perpetual
squint from his long years of examining
suspicious collateral. "I had to press some
people for money I loaned them."

"Who, for instance?"

Franks, it developed, had in his time
pressed enough debtors to fill a neighborhood movie house.

Next morning at nine o'clock, a spe-
cial-delivery letter arrived for Franks.
The envelope was addressed by hand—
in letters that were printed to disguise
the writer's natural penmanship—but
the letter inside was typewritten. And in
the classic ransom tradition it demanded
ten thousand dollars in old, unmarked
twenties and fifties, and warned against
a squeal to the cops. It told Franks to
put the dough in a cigar box and stand
by for another phone call. It bore a
typed signature, "George Johnson."

Johnson, whoever he was, was obvi-

47

ously a cultivated character. His letter mentioned the "futility" of summoning the police, the "execution" of his plans, and threatened death for Bobby upon the slightest "infraction" of his instructions. Unquestionably here was a clue of sorts—Johnson's education. No ignoramus could have composed the letter. An educated man can simulate ignorance, but an ignorant one can not simulate learning.

At the very hour that the ransom letter was being delivered, Mulroy and Goldstein, the *Daily News* cubs, were warming up a couple of chairs in the rear of the city room when the city editor barked at them. A boy's body had just been discovered in a culvert near some open fields in the Hegewisch section of the city. The papers did not yet know about Bobby Franks, and all the good reporters on the *Daily News* were out on other assignments; the city editor had no choice but to tell his two cubs to hightail it out to Hegewisch.

"Just ask the coroner if he suspects foul play," said the city editor, "and phone in."

Mulroy and Goldstein were the first reporters to reach the culvert. The body, that of a boy in his early teens, was still there, but the cubs weren't allowed to look at it. A representative of the coroner's office and a couple of coroner's investigators were guarding it. Mulroy and Goldstein learned that the corpse had been completely stripped.

"It ain't been here only since yesterday," one of the investigators disclosed.

"Murder?" asked Goldstein, a quick, dark fellow.

"We ain't found no marks yet."

Mulroy and Goldstein poked around. Mulroy, who had guileless blue eyes in a moonlike face, suddenly began to act furtive. He made sure the cops weren't looking, then leaned down, picked up something and stuck it in his pocket.

"What'd you just do?" asked Goldstein.

Mulroy shushed his brother cub—so loudly that one of the cops asked what was doing. "Nothing," said Mulroy, "only we gotta get out of here." What Mulroy had picked up was a pair of horn-rim eyeglasses.

"Maybe," said Goldstein, "they belong to the kid who was found in the culvert."

"And maybe they don't," said Mulroy.

As the morning progressed, news of Bobby Franks' disappearance began to seep to the lower levels of the police department, but the press was still in the dark. The coroner's office, which had custody of the corpse, didn't then maintain a very close diplomatic relationship with the cops—so that Get-'Em-Mike Hughes didn't know any more about the body in the culvert than the coroner did about the name of Bobby Franks.

Get-'Em-Mike and other thinkers on the cops, who were working the case and who weren't working it, were poring over the ransom letter. It bore the postmark of the Hyde Park postal substation, only a few blocks from the Franks home. It had been mailed the night previously, several hours after Bobby Franks had been snatched. The dicks wondered why the kidnaper had written the ransom letter itself on a typewriter, then used pen and ink to address the envelope.

One dick, smarter than the others, pointed out that the letter itself did not bear a date or the name of Jacob Franks, but bore the salutation, "Dear Sir."

"Maybe," he reasoned, "it was written some time ago—before the kidnaper knew who he was going to send it to. Then, after the victim was decided on, the kidnaper used pen and ink to address the envelope because he had already gotten rid of the typewriter."

Get-'Em-Mike glowered at the dick. He had never heard of such behavior on the part of a criminal. "Let's stick," said Get-'Em-Mike, "to *facks*."

Get-'Em-Mike summoned a typewriter expert. "What make of machine do you figure this was?" he asked.

"An Underwood."

"You sure?"

"Well, pretty sure. It *could* be a Corona."

Jacob Franks made a trip to the bank, then settled himself at the telephone with a cigar box containing ten thousand dollars at his elbow.

Mulroy and Goldstein had phoned in to their city editor, not breathing a word about the horn-rim glasses but whetting his appetite by informing him that they wouldn't be a bit surprised if they had run smack into a murder. The city editor had a knotty sensation in the pit of his stomach. His good reporters were still out; he had no alternative but to tell his cubs to stick with the coroner's office and find out if any signs of foul play turned up.

Late in the morning Goldstein phoned in again. He and Mulroy had followed the body to the morgue.

"This could be a murder, boss. The coroner thinks maybe this kid was hit on the head to make him unconscious and then poisoned."

"Why does the coroner suspect poison?"

"There are acid burns or something around the mouth."

Just then an assistant high-signed the city editor that there was something hot on another phone. What was hot was a tip from a cop on the *Daily News* payroll that Bobby Franks was being held for ransom. The city editor got a description

of the Franks boy, then got on Goldstein's phone again and asked the cub what this boy in the morgue looked like. Goldstein spilled a description.

"That sounds like it could be Bobby Franks," said the city editor.

"Bobby *who*?"

"Franks. He lives in the five-thousand block on Ellis Avenue. Being held for ransom."

"We'll go right over there, boss, and—"

The city editor, loath to send two boys on a man's errand, was about to tell them to stay the hell where they were when Goldstein, two thinks ahead of him, hung up. The cubs climbed into a hack and drove over to the Franks home. No admittance. They beat the bushes, flushed an uncle of the missing boy, shoved him into the hack and headed back to the morgue.

At one o'clock in the afternoon the Franks phone rang. Johnson, the kidnaper, asked Franks if he had the money in a cigar box. Franks said he had. The kidnaper thereupon informed Franks that a cab would shortly draw up to his door. Franks was to take the cab to a drugstore at the intersection of Sixty-third Street and another thoroughfare. He was to tell the cab to wait, go into the drugstore and ask for a letter in a plain envelope that had been left for him there. The letter contained further instructions as to where and how Franks was to deliver the ransom.

The kidnaper was talking fast. Franks, straining to catch every syllable, missed one word completely—the most important—the name of the street that intersected Sixty-third at the corner where the drugstore was located. Sixty-third was a long thoroughfare, with many corner drugstores. Before Franks could ask him to repeat the location, the kidnaper, no doubt fearing the call was being traced, hung up.

Franks called Get-'Em-Mike Hughes, who was supposed to be on top of all incoming calls to the Franks home.

"Where," he asked, "did that call just come from?"

"What call?" asked Get-'Em-Mike who, along with the phone company, had muffed the thing completely.

A Yellow cab drew up on Ellis Avenue. Franks rushed out. "Where are you supposed to take me?" he asked the driver.

"Search me," said the driver. "Don't *you* know where you're going?"

Franks partially explained. "Who sent you?" he asked.

"We got a phone call to send a cab over here."

"Where are you from?"

"The Cottage Grove Avenue branch." That was right in the neighborhood. Now the phone in the Franks home rang again. The taxi raced off as Franks went inside. The uncle of the missing boy— the man the two reporters had taken to the morgue—was calling. He had news for Jacob Franks; dreadful news. He had identified the body from the culvert as Bobby Franks. At the same time that the uncle was phoning, the cubs were phoning their scoop to their paper.

Now, of course, the lid was off. Some acid, apparently hydrochloric, had been poured over the genitals of Bobby Franks. This suggested abnormality of some sort on the part of the acid pourer. It appeared that Bobby Franks had not been poisoned, but had been suffocated. The marks of poison on his mouth were also found on other parts of his face; the deduction was that his killer had begun to pour hydrochloric acid on his face to thwart identification, then had either abandoned the idea or run out of acid.

Mulroy and Goldstein were on fire when they walked into the city room. Mulroy tossed the horn-rim glasses on the city editor's desk.

"What are these?"

"Another scoop, boss. We swiped 'em right from under the noses of the men guarding the body at the culvert."

"Maybe they belonged to Bobby Franks."

"Huh-uh, boss," chimed in Goldstein. "I asked Bobby's uncle if Bobby wore glasses and he said no. Positively no."

The city editor looked at his cubs with new respect. "You're sure of this?"

"Absolutely."

The city editor was behind two eight balls. Should he entrust these two green kids to track down the owner of the glasses, an assignment that any reporter in Chicago would have willingly gone on the water wagon for? The city editor had a heart of fine Italian marble, but it wasn't hard enough to cause him to take the glasses away from the kids.

"Go to it," he said. "Run these down, but don't let *anybody* know why you're doing it."

The cubs hit a big optical store. A man there became interested in the hinges on the horn-rim frame.

"This hinge here," he said, "is a new patent held by a New York firm. It's the best hinge on the market. I wish we had it."

"Whadda you mean, you wish you had it?" asked Goldstein.

"The patent is exclusive in Chicago with Almer, Coe and Company."

Almer, Coe and Company, a prominent retail optical house, immediately identified the glasses as their product. They had sold more than one hundred frames with the new hinges during the preceding month. The cubs wanted to know if the company would be kind enough to check the lenses in the glasses against their prescription records and thus narrow the search at the source. Glad to oblige; but it would take overnight. Detectives and reporters were traveling in useless circles all over Chicago. The two cubs had the only lead worth while.

In the morning—Friday morning, the second day after the kidnaping—the curious cubs learned that just three persons in all Chicago had purchased glasses with both frame and lenses exactly the same as those found at the crime scene. One customer was a woman, another an engineer and another a young man named Nathan Leopold of the 4700-block of ultra-exclusive Greenwood Avenue.

"Nathan Leopold," repeated Goldstein to Mulroy. "Look, Jim, wasn't there a guy named Nathan Leopold in college with us?"

"Yeah, come to think of it, there was. He was a year behind us."

"Sure. He would of graduated last year. A very smart fellow and richer'n hell. His old man has a lot of Sears Roebuck stock. And that address is right in the same neighborhood as the Franks home."

The Leopold family, like the Franks family, drew a lot of water in Chicago. "What a place!" muttered Goldstein as he and Mulroy leaned against a mansion that had cost more than one hundred thousand dollars.

"We want to see Nate," said Goldstein to a butler. "We're old friends." The ruse opened the door. The butler showed the visitors to a paneled library, heavy with burnng incense.

Nathan Leopold walked into the library wearing gray slacks, a checked sports jacket and brown suede shoes. He was twenty years old, slim, of medium height and moved with the measured grace of a jungle beast. His skin was white, his brow high and his hair blue-black.

"To what," he asked with a quick smile, "do I owe the honor?" His voice struck his visitors as being effeminately high.

Goldstein didn't horse around. "These glasses," he said, holding them up, "were found near Bobby Franks' body yesterday. We want to know if they're yours."

Leopold reached for the glasses. "Yes," he said, "these are mine. I lost them."

"When," Goldstein asked, grabbing the glasses, "did you lose them?"

"Let's see; it must have been last Saturday. Yes, it *was* last Saturday."

Mulroy was at a window. "I can see the Franks home from here," he said to Leopold. "Did you know Bobby?"

"Slightly. He was five years younger than I, but our parents are good friends. Why do you ask?"

"Doesn't it strike you that maybe you got some explaining to do, seeing your glasses were found near the body?"

"Not at all. I've been going out to Hegewisch, to the very place where Bobby was found, for several years now, regularly."

"For what?"

"Why, to watch birds. Ornithology is my hobby. Didn't you know that?" Leopold crossed the room. Mulroy and Goldstein exchanged glances—glances that implied exactly the same thing: if this fellow knew anything about the kidnaping and murder of Bobby Franks, he was by all odds the coolest customer they had ever met. "Here," said Leopold, pointing to one section of the library shelves. "I have quite a collection of books on ornithology."

For the next fifteen minutes Nathan

Leopold talked birds. He showed his visitors some monographs of his authorship. He showed them newspaper and magazine clippings mentioning his status as an ornithologist. He took from a shelf a can containing a reel of movie film and held portions of it up to the light and under a magnifying glass for Mulroy and Goldstein to see. "That is I," Leopold said, pointing to a figure in the film, "taken in the Michigan woods last summer. That speck on my shoulder is the Kirtland warbler. The Kirtland warbler is such a shy bird that few people have even seen it, yet there it is, perched on my shoulder."

Leopold detached himself from his ornithology with what seemed to be an effort. "You can see that when I tell you I go to Hegewisch to watch birds, I speak the truth."

Leopold pulled a wine-colored bell rope. A petite maid entered the room. He asked his guests if they would join him in a drink. The boys said they didn't mind if they did. Leopold addressed the maid in French.

"Are you a linguist, too?" asked Mulroy. "I speak fifteen languages," said Leopold. He went to the incense burner and put on another cone.

"Will you do us a favor?" Mulroy asked Leopold.

"Certainly, if it's in my power."

"You know Mr. Franks. Call him and ask him what the kidnaper said to him when he called him on the phone yesterday. We know the kidnaper called, but the cops won't tell us what he said."

"I'll be glad to," said Leopold.

The two cubs sat in while Leopold got the slain boy's father. Leopold asked Franks what the kidnaper had said. Then he listened. Then he thanked Franks. Then he hung up and told the cubs the story about Franks not catching

the exact location of the drugstore on Sixty-third Street where he was supposed to play out the next act of the drama the kidnaper had written.

A crisis was at hand for Mulroy and Goldstein. The boys had a dollar-sixty between them—not enough for much more riding around in cabs. They didn't want to put the slug on the office for expense money; they were afraid even to get in touch with the office and fill in the city editor for fear he would decide their assignment had outgrown them and pull them off it. They explained their predicament to Leopold, then asked him if he would mind driving them around while they hunted for the drugstore where the kidnaper had left the letter for Franks. Leopold, amused, consented. He got out a bright red sports job and the three young graduates of the University of Chicago were off.

If Goldstein and Mulroy had acumen and brass, they were also hung with horseshoes. The third drugstore they tried—at the corner of Sixty-third and Cottage Grove Avenue, not far from the Franks' home—was holding the letter. A young man had come into the place the previous morning—the morning after the snatch—and left the letter with the proprietor. "A man carrying a cigar box will come in for this about half past one," the young man had said. "Will you be good enough to give it to him?"

Leopold was sitting outside in the red car. "Take a look at that fellow out there," said Mulroy to the druggist. "Is he the one who gave you this letter?"

"No. He doesn't look anything like the fellow who was in here."

The letter, in a plain envelope, again saluted "Dear Sir," not Franks by name, and instructed the recipient to proceed at once to the Sixty-third Street station of the Illinois Central Railway, close at hand. There he was to inquire at the Pullman window for an envelope bearing the name of George Johnson. The envelope would contain a ticket for a Pullman chair on a southbound train leaving at two-five o'clock, and still another letter, this one giving final instructions for payment of the ransom.

It was shortly after noon when Nathan Leopold dropped Goldstein and Mulroy at the Illinois Central. "You know," Leopold said just before he drove off, "if *I* were going to kidnap and kill a kid, I'd choose a snotty little kid like Bobby Franks."

The two cubs stood on the sidewalk looking after the red car. "You know," said Mulroy, "something about the way he made that remark about Bobby Franks sent a chill up my spine."

"I was going to say the same thing," said Goldstein.

"You know something, Alvin—I'll bet that guy's in on this, at that."

"But the druggist said he wasn't the one who came in with the letter."

"No—because he had somebody else in it with him."

The cubs got the letter at the Pullman window. It had been typed on the same machine as the letter left in the drugstore; the small letter *t* in each communication was distinctively defective. The second letter instructed the ransom payer, again addressed as "Dear Sir," to go to the rear of the two-five train, watch for certain landmarks a few miles out of town, then toss the cigar box alongside the tracks parallel to a factory with a huge red smokestack bearing in white letters the word CHAMPION.

The city editor almost choked on an apple when Goldstein and Mulroy checked in with their tale. "Great!" he said. "Simply great! Tell you what we'll do. We'll give the police the information

about Leopold, as soon as we get an extra on the presses with it, but we'll hold out these letters while we try to run down their source."

"Who's goin' to run down the letters, boss?" asked Goldstein.

The city editor grinned. "You two *stars*, of course. Who else? Look. We have information that the police think the letter Franks got was written on an Underwood or Corona. Find out if Leopold has an Underwood or a Corona."

Get-'Em-Mike Hughes had been slowly going out of his mind. He had been given just one thing to work on—the story that one of the instructors at the Harvard School had at least a dash of lavender in his make-up. Get-'Em-Mike saw a connection between the lavender and the acid on Bobby Franks' genitals. The instructor was entering his twelfth hour under the rubber hose when the *Daily News* told Get-'Em-Mike about Nathan Leopold.

The dicks hit the Leopold mansion with all the ebullience of a battalion of ax-wielding firemen hitting a house known to contain a grand piano. State's Attorney Robert Crowe, a lantern-jawed gent with 20-20 vision for publicity, got hep and hit the place, too. Mulroy and Goldstein, having struck pay dirt once in the Leopold mansion, decided to try for another vein in the same place. Nathan Leopold, the cool intellectual, was being passed around like a volley ball from questioner to questioner. He excused himself to go to the bathroom, and the cubs nailed him.

"Nate," said Goldstein, familiar-like, "have you got an Underwood or a Corona typewriter?"

"I own only a Hammond," said Leopold.

An elderly Irish maid was going through the motions of industry within earshot of the reporters. When Leopold left them, the maid beckoned to the boys. "I heard what the young master told you," she said. "He wasn't telling the truth."

"You mean he *has* an Underwood or a Corona typewriter?"

"He had an Underwood machine as well as his Hammond until a few weeks ago."

"How do you know?"

"I do his rooms."

"Where's the machine now?"

"I think young Mr. Loeb took it away."

"Young Mr. *who*?"

"Loeb. Dickie Loeb. He's the young master's very close friend."

"Not the Loebs," asked Goldstein, "who are also part owners of Sears Roebuck?"

"That's them."

"How close to here do they live?"

The maid led the cubs to a window and pointed to the Loeb mansion.

Richard Loeb—tall and attractive, icy and snobbish—was eighteen, two years younger than Leopold. He had graduated the previous year from the University of Michigan, the youngest graduate up to then in the college's history. Neither linguist nor ornithologist, he was just blindingly brilliant. His visitors bluntly asked Dickie, as he was called, what he had done with the Underwood typewriter he had taken from the Leopold home. He didn't know what the reporters were talking about. Had he heard that his friend Leopold had his tail in a sling? No, he hadn't. . . . What about? About the Franks kidnaping. Oh, *that*! Whoever thought Nate had anything to do with that was a Grade-B moron.

Mulroy and Goldstein raced to the drugstore where the kidnaper's letter had

been left, took the proprietor to the Loeb home, and asked him if Dickie Loeb had been the fellow who had left the letter.

"Positively not," said the druggist.

"And now," said Dickie Loeb to the reporters, "if you are through trying to incriminate me in something I know nothing about, I'd appreciate your getting to hell out of here."

By that night—the second night after the snatch—the case had Chicago by the ears. State's Attorney Crowe was trying to get another kind of grip on Nathan Leopold, and on Richard Loeb. He had set up shop in a suite in the fashionable Drake Hotel where, between times, he and a large staff of assistants, who normally ate in a greasy spoon near the Criminal Courts Building, enjoyed plenty of the best food in Chicago at the expense of the taxpayers.

Leopold and Loeb were at the Drake, too, dwelling in a twilight zone somewhere between incarceration and freedom. They turned out to be devoted students of Nietzsche, apostle of the superman. They also seemed to be part lavender, but they went for dames, too.

The suspects claimed to have been out in Leopold's red sports car during the critical hours between two and ten P.M. the date of the crime—out necking and drinking with a couple of girls they had picked up. If the boys couldn't substantiate their story, the state's attorney couldn't disprove it. Leopold and Loeb simply weren't having any part of a crack-up. Their intellects fitted the educated kidnaper who had talked to Franks and his wife, and who had written the kidnap letters and planned a crime clever enough to have put several layers of insulation between themselves and the police. The fact that Leopold's glasses had been found at the crime scene proved almost nothing because of the youth's established standing as an ornithologist. From where Crowe sat, it began to look as if a smart lawyer might make any charges against Leopold and Loeb look ridiculous unless the Underwood typewriter was found.

Next night, Saturday, when the newspapers were beginning to inquire why Crowe was functioning in the Drake instead of his own office, the state's attorney shifted to the Criminal Courts Building. He was like a man digging a hole for himself, sinking with every move.

Then came news—bad news for Crowe —in the form of an unkempt, unpleasant-looking little man who shuffled through the dirty corridors of the Criminal Courts Building just after midnight on Sunday morning. The man was Clarence Darrow, one of the trickiest characters ever to earn a livelihood at the practice of law. He was entering the case as counsel for Leopold and Loeb.

Darrow, although honest, might as well have been crooked; he could find loopholes in the law that had precisely the same effect on justice as a purchased juror. Somehow, the man gained a wide reputation as the champion of the little man, the defender of the underdog. Actually, what he liked was a case, whether the defendant was an underdog or an overdog, that would pay well and lend itself to skillful courtroom maneuvering and to the front page. He sure had a couple for page one in Leopold and Loeb. As for remuneration, their families had told Darrow that he could practically have the combined bank accounts if he got the boys off, and that, if Nate and Dickie *were* guilty, he could write his own ticket if he wangled anything short of the hangman's hemp.

Darrow started to grumble about habeas corpus. "Make a charge against my clients," he said to Crowe, "or I'll proceed against your office."

Crowe was sweating out a decision behind a locked door when somebody on the other side of the door almost broke it down trying to get in. "Open up!" yelled Goldstein. "Yeah, Mr. Crowe," chimed in Mulroy, "we got your case solved for you!"

And be danged if the boys hadn't done just that. They had infiltrated themselves among Leopold's college classmates, who were scattered throughout the city, mostly lined up at employment offices. They learned that Leopold, while in his senior year, had sometimes volunteered to type up class lessons for his fellow students. Goldstein and Mulroy got hold of some of this typing, still in the possession of the now-graduated students, and compared it with the typing of the kidnap letters. It was identical; in all of Leopold's college typing, as in the kidnaper's letters, was that distinctively defective letter *t*.

Leopold and Loeb had been friends since childhood. Their "intellectual drive" had led them to experiment in unnatural sexual practices. Despite their later interest in girls, these practices continued. One of the ruling motives of Nathan Leopold's existence was to do things that would impress the younger Loeb. Thus, many months before the Franks crime, Leopold conceived the perfect crime—the thrill murder that would never be solved. The two young supermen would be too clever for the police.

Together, on Leopold's Underwood typewriter, they wrote the ransom letters, without having the slightest idea who would eventually get them. This was part of the detachment that supplied much of the thrill in the murder project.

After the ransom letters were written, the typewriter was tossed into a lagoon in a Chicago park.

On the day chosen for the crime, the pair hired a drive-it-yourself car and hung around the Harvard School, where they had decided to pick their victim. By this time they had a couple of boys in mind, but the kids didn't show up when classes broke. Along came Bobby Franks. "He'll do," said Loeb to Leopold.

Bobby was offered a ride in the car. He got in, quite unsuspectingly. Loeb drove while Leopold knocked Bobby unconscious with blows on the head from the heavy end of a chisel; then he suffocated the boy. After darkness fell, they deposited the body in the culvert. That's when Leopold, leaning down, dropped his glasses, which had been in the handkerchief pocket of his jacket. Later, after burning the boy's clothing, calling Franks on the phone and mailing the first kidnap letter, Leopold and Loeb picked up a couple of prostitutes and had themselves a time.

Next day the killers had hired a youth on the street to go into the drugstore with the ransom letter; that's why the druggist couldn't identify either of them. They hung around the vicinity, waiting to see Franks go into the drugstore. When Franks didn't show up, they knew the plot had curdled. Then they heard that the body had been found.

The typewriter was retrieved from the lagoon and linked to the killers. Darrow pleaded his clients guilty before Criminal Courts Judge John R. Caverly. Thus he removed the boys from exposure to a jury that would have been drawn from a citizenry thirsty for blood. Now Darrow resorted to a rare legal maneuver;

he began to introduce witnesses so that Judge Caverly could determine, as Darrow so delicately put it, the degree of guilt. Many of Darrow's witnesses were dome doctors who claimed Leopold and Loeb had cerebral Charley horses that made them irresponsible for their deed. The state's attorney also produced witnesses. For all practical purposes, this was a trial, but without a jury; the verdict would be up to the judge.

"What blind, cruel forces drove these boys to their horrible crime?" Darrow orated in his closing address. "How can you expect man to overcome some insuperable will that moves him as a pawn? What I am pleading for here is life—and charity, kindness and infinite mercy. I am pleading to overcome cruelty and hate with kindness and love."

The state's attorney, a politician, hardly alienated the voters when he said, "The only useful thing that remains for Leopold and Loeb in life is to get out of it as quickly as possible."

Judge Caverly mulled over his decision for thirteen days. Then, with charity, kindness and infinite mercy, he spared Leopold and Loeb. He gave them life in the big cage at Joliet for murder and ninety-nine years for kidnaping, the sentences to run concurrently.

Mulroy and Goldstein won the Pulitzer Prize for solving the case; brilliant careers in the newspaper business loomed ahead of them. Dickie Loeb was assigned to the rattan factory in Joliet, and Nathan Leopold to the prison library. Some years ago, Dickie ratted on a rattan worker and got himself scragged.

Nathan Leopold was released from prison in 1958.

The Man They Couldn't Kill

*Here's another case from the official files that outstrips fiction—the
incredible account of the man they couldn't kill.*

Tony Marino's speakeasy on Third
Avenue in New York's sprawling Bronx
was, in the dismal month of December
in the year of 1932, a sort of poor man's
Duffy's Tavern. It was a long and narrow
dark hole behind a frosted, flyspecked
front window, and the *décor* featured
cherry-stained plywood. There was, at
the far end of the bar, something that
was referred to, for want of a better
name, as free lunch. The odoriferous
character of the free lunch, acting in
concert with the fragrance given off by
Tony Marino's patrons, has prompted
one survivor of the establishment—a
newspaperman who just happened into
the place one day—to suggest that what
Tony's place, as the joint was called,
needed most was a decaying herring to
act as an Air-Wick. The habitués of the
place were so inured to the atmosphere
in Tony's, however, that the only time
they were ever aware of anything unpleasant assailing their nostrils was
when, after closing hours, they found
themselves out in the fresh air.

Marino himself, unlike the owner of
Duffy's Tavern, did not function by remote control. A dark, sharply dressed
little man, he was a highly sharpened
product of a bitterly competitive society,
a great man for elbowing at the turns.
He sat at a small round table behind a
beaded curtain in the rear of the establishment, there to cast a knowing eye on
what went on out front. Although Tony's
bar didn't, in those days, have a TV set,
there were, just the same, fights every
night. A character named Daniel

Murphy, a fumbling wise guy with
greenish teeth and a heart overflowing
with larceny, was the bartender and so-
called manager—a sort of real-life counterpart of the Archie of Duffy's place.
Murphy, who was called "Red" because
he had hair the color of whisky, was
constantly on the *qui vive* for signals
from Tony, sitting there behind the
beaded curtain, by which the proprietor
instructed him as to which patrons were
to be, in the language of the era, mick-
eyed and rolled. It was an article of faith
with Tony that a man who lost consciousness on the premises forfeited all
claim to any cash or hockable possessions
he happened to have on his person.

Not that Tony didn't have sufficient
motivation for his approach to living. A
great depression was on the land and the
streets were filled with shaken men. Although, as President Hoover, the great
engineer, put it, prosperity was just
around the corner, nobody could seem
to locate the corner. Speakeasies like
Tony's, which in some parts of the Bronx
were a dozen to the square block, were
engaged in a lethal price war. A mixture
of raw alcohol and colored water was re-
tailing at fifteen cents a shot, or two
jolts for a quarter. Tony, sitting there
in the back room, was really up against
it. Some weeks he didn't take in fifty
dollars.

Tony's closest friend was the neighborhood undertaker—a blubbery little
man named Frank Pasqua, who was so
devoted to drink that he sometimes all
but fell into the grave ahead of the cof-

fin. Pasqua was filled with nostalgia for what he called the good old days—the influenza epidemic of 1918 when residents of the Bronx had died like flies and Pasqua and some of his professional colleagues were able to stow some of the victims in crude pine boxes, hustle them underground in the dead of night, then charge the survivors for expensive mahogany caskets.

"Why can't we," Pasqua asked Tony one night, "have a plague or something?"

The only plague that Tony Marino could think of—apropos his gloomy friend's question repeated that December evening of 1932—was a one-man pestilence by the name of Michael Malloy. This gentleman was a graying, leathery little County Donegal Irishman of uncertain years who had long since exhausted his credit in at least 10 per cent of the Bronx speakeasies. So far as was ever learned, Malloy devoted his daylight hours to the studious avoidance of gainful employment and spent his nights in speakeasies, cadging drinks in return for hoary jokes that took on a semblance of originality because of the teller's brogue, and agreeing to sweep up in the morning in return for a night's lodging on the floor. Michael Malloy, looking at the world through the bottom of a glass, agreed with the poet who observed that life is a lying dream and that he only wakes who casts the world aside. Bravo, Malloy!

"You know," said Marino to Pasqua, "Malloy don't have no relations."

"He don't?" said Pasqua.

For several days and nights Tony and Pasqua, sitting there in the back room, devoted the kind of attention to Malloy that Newton is reputed to have devoted to the apple. Then, in response to their summons, there appeared in the back room a commission-happy insurance agent who waived certain formalities commonly practiced by members of his profession, such as the physical presence and the personal signature of an applicant for the company's protection. The result was that Michael Malloy, without knowing it, became an actuarial risk to the extent of twelve hundred dollars. Malloy's age was recorded as forty-five years, although the man was probably nearer sixty. Tony Marino was named beneficiary. Pasqua, in return for putting up part of the first quarterly premium payment, was to get the burial job. Red Murphy, the bartender, was now consulted.

"This Malloy," said Marino. "We gonna knock him off. Didn' you used to study chemistry? What could you slip in his drinks?"

The problem, as Murphy saw it, was to get some kind of liquid that tasted much the same as the stuff regularly dispensed at Tony's but which contained a deadly poison. Automobile-radiator antifreeze mixture, which was practically pure wood alcohol, would be, it was decided, just the thing. Murphy was promised a hundred dollars out of the insurance money, upon certification of the corpse.

Christmas was approaching. Good cheer superimposed itself upon the depression. Street-corner Santa Clauses, some of them with breaths that practically singed their false beards, were making outrageous promises to demanding kids. An unidentified speakeasy started the insane practice of every fourth round on the house, and competitors had to follow suit. The only saving grace to the yuletide, the way Marino looked at it, was that Murphy the bartender could shove free drinks at Malloy without arousing the Irishman's suspicion.

On the night that the plotters got down to business, Murphy quickly anesthetized Malloy with the regular stuff. Then Marino, looking on from the back room, nodded. Murphy slipped Malloy a drink of antifreeze. Malloy was still on his feet five minutes later. Murphy, on a signal from Marino, gave it to Malloy again.

It took five shots of antifreeze to send Malloy crashing to the floor. Protocol in Tony's demanded that other patrons ignore recumbent figures on the floor. Thus, when Tony's closed up, around three A.M., Malloy was still lying exactly where he had fallen. His heart was barely beating.

"It won't be long now," said Pasqua, who, by virtue of his profession, was something of an authority on the workings of the human body. The lights were switched off in the bar, and Pasqua, Marino and Murphy went to the back room where they devoted themselves to a bottle of paint-remover and sat around to wait for death.

Occasionally Pasqua would get up and go out to the bar and feel Malloy's pulse. It wasn't until daylight began to show through the flyspecked frosted-glass front of Tony's that the undertaker returned to the back room with bad news.

"He just opened his eyes," said Pasqua. "His heartbeat's normal. He's all right."

Marino blamed Murphy for the failure. "You didn't give him enough antifreeze."

During the ensuing week, Michael Malloy, whose taste buds had obviously long since lost all sensitivity, consumed enough radiator mixture to have killed and blinded himself ten times over. All that happened was that he lost consciousness. The only scientific explanation for this would seem to be that Malloy had consumed wood alcohol in small doses

in bootleg liquor over a long period of time and thus developed a tolerance for it.

It was Murphy the bartender who conceived the next step in what the Bronx district attorney, Samuel J. Foley, was later to call the most grotesque chain of events in New York criminal history. Murphy, falling back on his knowledge of chemistry, took the lid off a can of sardines and set the fish out to putrefy.

"When they get bad enough, we'll make Malloy a sandwich," he explained. "He'll die of ptomaine poisoning."

After several days, the sardines, which were kept off by themselves under the bar, alongside the cop's bottle, were suspected of causing a foul odor. This suspicion was confirmed when Murphy took the can outside, into an alley, and smelled the contents in the fresh air. He made a sandwich for Malloy and put it under the bar, awaiting Malloy's nightly appearance.

"What did you do with the can?" asked Marino. "I want the can. I want to make sure of things this time." What Marino did was duck out to a Bronx machine shop and get the can reduced to small slivers of metal. He blended the shavings with the rotten fish in the sandwich. "This'll cut his guts to pieces," he announced with satisfaction.

Malloy, who had been repeatedly warned to keep away from the free-lunch end of the bar, a section reserved for paying clients, was practically overcome with emotion when Murphy offered him the sandwich.

"Red, me boy," said Malloy, whose speech was that of a low comedian, "it's a foine, generous lad ye are." Marino and Pasqua, in the back room, watched the gentleman from County Donegal munching the ptomaine-and-tin sandwich and washing it down with anti-freeze.

"You ever see anything like that?" Marino inquired. Pasqua had not.

The sandwich had no effect whatsoever on Malloy.

There is no scientific explanation for this. And no unscientific explanation—unless hopping from speakeasy to speakeasy over the years had given Malloy the stomach a goat is popularly supposed to have.

During the week between Christmas and New Year's, Pasqua had a suggestion. He had once buried a man who had come to his end after mixing raw oysters with whisky.

"The whisky is supposed to turn the oysters to stone in your stomach," Pasqua explained. Marino, who felt a quiet desperation creeping over him, approved Pasqua's suggestion, and added a touch of his own.

"We'll soak the oysters in antifreeze before we give them to him," he said.

The oysters and antifreeze killed Malloy like caviar and champagne kills a chorus girl.

One night during the first week of the new year, 1933, Malloy was soundly unconscious on the floor of Tony's bar when the place closed up. A violent sleet storm was pelting the city. A taxicab was parked at the door of Tony's. Marino and Pasqua carried Malloy outside and put him in the cab. They got in with him, and the cab driver—Hershey Green, a friend of Marino's—shoved off.

The cab came to a stop in a lonely stretch of Claremont Park. While Green kept an eye peeled for cops and other cars, Marino and Pasqua carried Malloy off the road twenty or thirty feet and, screened by shrubbery, laid him on the ground face up. Malloy didn't own an overcoat. The plotters removed his jacket. Then they opened his shirt and undershirt so that his bare chest was exposed. The idea was for Malloy to freeze, or at least contract pneumonia.

The sleet was bouncing off Malloy's chest and the temperature was about fourteen degrees below freezing, but that wasn't enough to suit Marino. He went back to the taxicab and got a five-gallon demijohn, filled with water, and poured the water over Malloy's head.

Next afternoon Hershey Green came in to report that he had driven past the spot where Malloy had been left and that Malloy positively was not there. Marino telephoned to Pasqua, who had had a funeral that morning, and asked him to bring the afternoon papers with him when he arrived for the evening. When Pasqua showed up, his eyes were watering, his nose was running and he croaked when he talked. He had caught cold while trying to kill Malloy.

"I don't feel so good myself," said Marino. "I feel hot, then cold, then hot again. Let's see the papers you brought."

There was nothing in the papers about a man being found either dead or ill in Claremont Park. Marino and Pasqua were wondering precisely what their next move would be when the front door opened and in walked Malloy.

"The funniest thing happened, Red, me lad," they heard Malloy telling Murphy. "I woke up this mornin' in Claremont Park. I wonder how I got way over there?"

Murphy shrugged. "How do you feel?" he asked.

"I got a bit of a chill in the park, but nothin' a shot or two won't fix."

While Malloy was conversing with Murphy, an old friend of Marino's—Anthony Bastone—lumbered in. Tough Tony, as Bastone called himself, was a hairy character with practically no fore-head, and somehow gave the impression that his natural habitat was a cave. Strangers meeting him for the first time seemed faintly surprised that he could talk.

"How," Tough Tony wanted to know of Marino, "is every little thing?"

"Not," said Marino, "so good." He nodded toward Malloy. "We're trying to bump him off and it's a hell of a job. We give him wood alcohol and poison sardines and ground-up tin and put him outside practically stripped in a sleet storm and nothin' happens."

Tough Tony addressed himself to the problem. The element that was lacking in the plot against Malloy, he decided, was violence.

"But we don't want to make it look like a murder," Marino said.

Tough Tony grew impatient. "You don't get it," he said. "Make it look like a accident."

"What you got in mind?" asked Pasqua.

"You just get this bum drunk. Then you take him out somewhere nice and quiet and hold him up in front of a automobile and let the automobile hit him."

Marino and Pasqua looked at each other. Tough Tony had something. Hershey Green was summoned and asked if he would be willing to hit Malloy if the gent were held up in front of his cab.

"I'll hit anything," said Green, "if there's enough in it for me." Green was promised a hundred dollars out of the insurance proceeds. "Who's goin' to hold him in front of the cab?" he asked.

"I will," volunteered Tough Tony.

"For how much?" asked Marino.

"For a hunnert," said Tough Tony. It was a deal. Holding a man close

enough to a charging car to shove him in front of it, so that he would be hit full force while still upright, called for a certain amount of dexterity.

At three o'clock in the morning the plotters were on a deserted thorough-fare called Gun Hill Road. Pasqua was in the cab with Green, and Marino was out in the road with Tough Tony and Malloy, who had passed out a couple of hours previously. Green drove a few hundred feet up Gun Hill Road, turned around and poised his hack for the charge. It was very dark. Just so there would be no slip, such as Malloy being held up for the wrong car, Green was to toot his horn twice as he bore down on the spot where he was to hit the Irish-man.

There was only one house in the vicinity and it was completely dark. Everything was set. Green got a good start and was going about forty miles an hour when he tooted his horn. Just after the horn tooted, Pasqua noticed a light snap on in the neighborhood's one house. Green just had time to swerve and avoid hitting Malloy. Tough Tony and Ma-rino, whose backs were to the house, didn't know what had gone wrong until Green and Pasqua returned and ex-plained.

"Let's get out of here and try some-where else," said Green. "We don't want no witnesses to a murder."

Marino paused to kick Malloy in the ribs. "I never seen such a lucky bum as this bum," he said.

The plotters by now were beginning to feel as futile as the little boy in Aus-tralia who, wanting a new boomerang, tried to throw the old one away. They set up shop again half an hour later on a street called Baychester Avenue. This time the cab, hitting forty-five, caught Malloy flush and upright. Next morning the conspirators stationed themselves at the plants of the city's afternoon newspapers to catch the early editions fresh off the presses.

There was not a line in any of the papers about a hit-and-run victim in any part of the Bronx. There was nothing in The Bronx *Home News,* either. Murphy the bartender was dispatched on a round of the city's morgues, with specific instructions from Marino to get a look at all unidentified male bodies under the pretext that his brother had gone missing. Murphy hit all the dead houses and he saw stiffs in his dreams for weeks thereafter, but he did not lay eyes on Michael Malloy.

"Maybe," suggested Tough Tony, "he ain't dead. Maybe he's in a hospital somewheres. It could be. People fall off buildings and live sometimes."

The plotters went out and bought a pocket directory of Greater New York and systematically covered the hospitals by telephone. No Michael Malloy. A week passed. Still no Malloy.

"I wonder where the old bastard is," Marino inquired of Pasqua. "He's got to be *somewhere*. He's not still on Baychester Avenue. Hershey Green drove past there day before yesterday."

Another week passed. Action of some kind was imperative. An alcohol-dealer was putting the screws on Marino for an unpaid bill, and Pasqua was being pressed by a coffin company. Tough Tony, the Neanderthal Man, contributed an original thought.

"Leave us," he said, "get a substitute for Malloy and kill him and say he's Malloy."

Getting a substitute for Malloy would be a problem, but not too much of a problem. Since Malloy's general physical characteristics were recorded in the insurance policy, a man of his general

specifications was needed. The substitute would also have to be a man without family or close friends and, of course, a drinking man. The plotters fanned out and covered the Bronx bars in the roles of talent scouts.

Tough Tony was in a Harlem dive when he came upon just the man the boys in the back room were looking for. The actor who was to portray Malloy was a fifty-year-old Irishman named McCarthy. Tough Tony offered McCarthy a job as sweeper-upper in Tony's speakeasy at a dollar a day and all he could hold. McCarthy grabbed what struck him as the chance of a lifetime, and in a way he was right.

Tough Tony went to a printing establishment and had a few name-cards run off. The cards bore the name Michael Malloy. The caper was to plant one of the cards on McCarthy when he was killed so as to establish his identity for the insurance company. It never occurred to any of the plotters that a man with no seat in his pants would hardly be likely to go in for calling cards.

McCarthy had an aroma all his own, but he soon lost his individuality when he went to work at Tony's. He wasn't in Tony's long—just a few days. Marino gave the sign to Murphy one night and soon McCarthy was thoroughly starched. He was removed to the bleak reaches of a road winding through Claremont Park and there hit so hard by Hershey Green's cab that the radiator was dented. To make assurance doubly sure, as Shakespeare would say, Green turned around and ran over him. Pasqua, the authority on the human system, bent over McCarthy.

"He's gone," he said. "Gimme one of them name cards to put in his pocket."

Next day the conspirators had a sense of living part of the recent past all over again. They went to the newspaper plants for the early editions but found nothing about a Bronx hit-and-run victim.

"I hear," said Tough Tony, who was now practically running the plot, "that sometimes the papers don't have room for everything that happens. Let's find out what morgue he's in." McCarthy didn't seem to be in any morgue.

Marino asked Pasqua, "You sure he was dead?"

Pasqua's professional pride was hurt. "Look," he said, "I know a stiff when I handle one."

That night Tough Tony entered Tony's speakeasy breathing hard. "I got bad news," he told Marino and Pasqua. "This bum is alive. He's in Fordham Hospital." McCarthy had a compound fracture of the skull, two broken arms, a compound fracture of the left leg, twelve broken ribs and assorted internal injuries. "The hospital says he's hangin' on."

Marino turned on Pasqua. "Why you fat dog! We coulda' run over him all night and made sure. But no. *You* know all about bodies. *You* say he's dead. We ought to kill *you*."

McCarthy continued to hang on, but the prognosis was not hopeful. Marino sent him some oranges. Then word came from the hospital that McCarthy was sinking; he couldn't last out the night. The gloom in the back room of Tony's was dissipated. Pasqua, staring out into the bar, almost choked on his drink.

"What's the matter with you?" asked Tough Tony.

Pasqua couldn't talk; he just nodded toward the bar. There stood Malloy— the one, the only, the original.

Marino rushed out into the bar to get an explanation of where the man had been; it was about three weeks now since he had been hit by the cab. Malloy had been in a hospital.

"Banged up a bit, me lad, but I'm foine now." Through a clerical slip-up, his name had not appeared on the list of accident patients when the plotters had checked the hospitals.

Michael Malloy's status had, of course, undergone a basic change. McCarthy was the man whose death would pay off now, not Malloy. Marino said to Murphy the bartender, "Throw the bum out." Malloy's reaction was that of a collie kicked in the ribs by Albert Payson Terhune; he was purely and simply astonished. He couldn't understand cruel treatment from people who had lately been so openhanded with him. Malloy picked himself up off the pavement and told Murphy not to worry.

The suspense in Tony's was all but visible next day. McCarthy was still alive. That night there were black tidings. McCarthy had emerged from a crisis; he now stood a chance to recover. A few days later, Malloy's double was pronounced out of danger. The plotters couldn't have been more depressed.

A dilemma posed itself. Should the boys in the back room await McCarthy's release from the hospital, which might be a matter of weeks, to try their luck on him again, or should they hunt down the real Malloy and put everything they had into one grand final attempt to kill him? It was decided to go to work again on Michael Malloy—if he could be found.

Marino located him sweeping out a rooming house a few blocks from Tony's. Malloy had sunk to employment to get money to buy drink. Work had vested the man with a certain dignity. He wanted no part of Marino or any of the other boys in the back room. It thus became necessary for the plotters to summon help. They called in a broken-down fruit dealer named Daniel Kreisberg, who had become embittered at the world because corner apple-sellers had ruined his business. Kreisberg, a friend of Tough Tony's, was open to any proposition that entailed the elements of an easy buck and somebody getting hurt.

Kreisberg roped Malloy at a new hangout of the Hibernian's. On the afternoon of Washington's Birthday, some three months after the plot had originally gotten under way, he invited him to his room in a Fulton Street roach trap, not far from the Pasqua Memorial Home. Kreisberg got Malloy stiff, then phoned Tony's for instructions. Marino sent Murphy the bartender to Kreisberg's room with a length of rubber hose. Kreisberg and Murphy attached one end of the hose to a gas jet, held the other end in Malloy's mouth, and turned on the gas.

That did it.

There was joy in the back room of Tony's that night. Pasqua conned a careless doctor friend into signing a death certificate ascribing Malloy's demise to pneumonia. Next morning the durable Irishman was packed in a pine box and laid away in a twelve-dollar plot in a Bronx cemetery.

The insurance company paid off. What with all the characters in the plot and the time and expense devoted to achieving the end of Michael Malloy, twelve hundred dollars didn't go far. The boys in the back room began to quarrel among themselves over the importance of their individual roles in the scragging. It was hardly surprising that the members of a coterie that numbered a melon-head psychologist who planted a name-card on a derelict would, finally, leak at the mouth.

Tough Tony, for example, began to pester one habitué of Tony's speakeasy for a written opinion as to how much of the murder money he was entitled to. This precipitated an argument and Tough Tony himself got killed. Hershey Green went around telling people that he had damaged his taxi hitting a guy for a friend and then the friend had refused to pay for the damage even after collecting insurance on the hit guy. Kreisberg, the Johnny-come-lately of the plot, went around asking perfect strangers if they thought the cops would suspect him of giving the gas pipe to a man who had died of pneumonia in his room on Washington's Birthday.

Talk like that gets around and, if it reaches police stations, is often taken seriously. It reached a Bronx police station in May. A couple of nosy detectives began to thumb through the death records for Washington's Birthday. They found that a Michael Malloy had died that day. They wrote to all the insurance companies, asking if Michael Malloy had been insured. Thus they unearthed the transaction involving Marino.

Malloy was secretly dug up. The body was almost as well preserved as a brandied peach or cherry . . . a beautiful cherry-red hue that gas poisoning gives to a body.

The boys in the back room were put under the magnifying glass. Pasqua had paid the casket company something on account the day after the insurance money had been paid. Marino had settled an alky bill at the same time. Red Murphy had bought a new suit. The law lowered the boom. The plotters outdid each other filling the detectives in on every detail of what had gone on. They thought that talk would be mistaken for cooperation and that by being cooperative they would escape the big burn. Hershey Green, the cabby, was the only one to get off with a prison stretch. Marino, Pasqua, Murphy, and Kreisberg died seated in Sing Sing.

The Stiffs in the Old Folks' Home

Sister Amy Archer ran a retreat for old folks on a quiet, tree-shaded street in a little Connecticut town. She gave them a jumbo life contract for a fixed fee. It wasn't until a snoopy reporter decided to look into the hasty departures of several of Sister Amy's charges—in coffins—that the lid blew off.

Prospect Street, in the village of Windsor, Connecticut, was, in the month of April, 1907, a sedate tree-lined thoroughfare where the white Victorian houses were the habitats of socially-minded wing-collared gentlemen and bustled ladies who, having long since come out on top in life's little struggle, dwelled in righteous complacency. Morals were at a premium on Prospect Street, elderberry wine was the strongest drink that darkened the doors, and the loudest sound that reached sensitive ears was the clatter of horses' hoofs on the cobblestones.

Little wonder, then, that the quiet tenor of the ways in one particular block on Prospect Street was rudely shattered when a dark-haired little lady of thirty-three by the name of Amy Archer purchased a three-story architectural monstrosity, whose owner had just settled permanently in the village burial grounds, for the announced purpose of opening a home for old folks. Mrs. Archer, before arriving in Windsor, where, in the years ahead, she was to make an historic contribution to the gallery of premeditated murder, had been a nurse in New York's Bellevue Hospital. The gilt legend on a big black sign tacked up on the front door read:

THE ARCHER HOME
FOR ELDERLY PEOPLE
AND CHRONIC INVALIDS

Directly across the street from The Archer Home lived two little old ladies —lavender-and-old-lace busybodies named Bliss—who, sitting behind Irish lace curtains in a green plush parlor, peered through bifocals at the comings and goings on the street. The morning after four moving vans had deposited in The Archer Home For Elderly People And Chronic Invalids enough second-hand furniture to equip a hotel containing ten bedrooms, Mrs. Archer, accompanied by her husband, James, walked across the street and pulled the porcelain door bell of the Bliss domicile.

"We thought it would be nice if we introduced ourselves," said Mrs. Archer, smiling briskly as the Bliss sisters invited the callers into the parlor. Mrs. Archer, who weighed only ninety pounds, had a pinched, rather pretty little face, small brown eyes that reflected a very active mind, and she was all starched out in a nurse's uniform.

Amy Archer was garrulous but Big Jim, as some people were soon calling her husband, was a silent type who just sat there on a black mohair chair twiddling his thumbs and staring at the floor while his spouse chattered away. Archer, a huge lump of a man dressed in a light brown suit and black blucher shoes, had a fat whitish face, a handsome chestnut walrus moustache that acted as a perfect host for beer foam and small eyes that

69

reminded some observers of a couple of pinkish marbles.

Mrs. Archer informed the Bliss sisters that she was going to accommodate ten persons, both men and women, in her institution. Her guests were to get life contracts, for a fixed fee, including, as a jumbo bonus, at the end of the bargain, a fine funeral and a choice grave in the local cemetery. "It'll be kind of like insurance," piped up Big Jim, speaking for the first time though not raising his gaze from the floor. "If some of them live long enough they'll put us in the poorhouse."

"It's not the money," chimed in Mrs. Archer, tilting her head slightly, a righteous glint in her eyes. "It's the privilege of serving the Lord."

One of the old maids asked Mrs. Archer if she and Mr. Archer would like a glass of elderberry wine. "Gracious no!" said Mrs. Archer. "We never let alcohol touch our lips." The sisters were to say later that they could well believe Mrs. Archer, but that Big Jim, glancing up for the first time, seemed to be sorry that he hadn't had the chance to speak for himself.

The Archer Home For Elderly People And Chronic Invalids was soon off and winging. Populated by five elderly men, four elderly women, and one youngish man who looked so thin, white and shaky that he was obviously on the brink of eternity, the Home was a happy place. Sister Amy, as Mrs. Archer preferred to be called, resembled a blur as, starched out in her white uniform, she darted through the murky hallways with medicine and nourishment for her charges. A glutton for work, Sister Amy, who wanted no part of servants, did all the nursing and cooking herself while Big Jim made the beds, emptied the bed

pans, and kept the dirt from piling up.

When the weather was salubrious, Sister Amy shepherded the contractees out onto a big portico that stretched across the entire front of the house and half way around the side, clapped them in rocking chairs and left them to play checkers and cribbage and swap whoppers. At nights, Sister Amy played a wheezy organ in the red-plush parlor and the more wakeful of the guests joined her in singing old-fashioned hymns.

The Archer Home had been functioning for only three weeks when, one night when the moon was full and the street was silent and an owl was hooting in the distance, the Bliss sisters were awakened by the clatter of hoofbeats on the cobblestones. Jumping out of bed, they saw a shiny black hearse, drawn by a span of coal-black horses, pulling up to the Archer Home. Two figures got out of the hearse, went into the Home with a box, came out with the box, which seemed heavier than when it had been taken in, stacked it in the hearse, and clattered away.

Next morning, around breakfast time, the old maids, sitting there behind those lace curtains, the window open, could hear Sister Amy's organ. She was leading her charges in a rendition of *Nearer, My God, To Thee.*

Along toward noon, Big Jim came out to putter around and one of the Bliss sisters went to the front door, called over to him and inquired if they could be of any help in the Home's bereavement.

"No thank you," answered Big Jim.

"Who was it left during the night?"

"The young man."

"What did he die from?"

"Complications."

Although Sister Amy's neighbors knew practically nothing about what was going on inside the Home, the habitués of

Paddy's, a fine Irish saloon a couple of streets away, soon glimpsed part of the picture. This was no rowdy saloon, Paddy's, but a domain of respectable neighborhood citizens who foregathered of a night to partake of a pipe, a glass and gentle talk. Big Jim was wont to sneak around to Paddy's, hoist a few whiskies with beer chasers, peer solemnly at his reflection in the mirror behind the bar, pop some cloves into his mouth, and sneak back. One night a fellow bar fly who had come to be friendly with Jim drew him into conversation by remarking: "You don't look like a happy man, Mr. Archer."

Big Jim turned, blinked at the man, and wiped the foam off his moustache. "And indeed I'm not a happy man," he said, in a County Mayo brogue as thick as the smoke in the air. "You appear to be a friendly soul and I'd like, if I may, to tell you my troubles."

Archer's troubles were Sister Amy. "I can't satisfy the woman at nights," he said. "A little's all right but my wife would be a terrible drain on any man."

"They tell me," said the bar fly, "that your wife is very opposed to drink. If that's the case, how do you deceive her? Surely the cloves you chew are not enough."

"She'll overlook practically *anything* so long as I take care of her at night. But I tell you, my friend, I don't know how long I'll be able to keep it up."

One night in June, two months after Sister Amy had set up shop, the old maids across the street were awakened by the thudding of hoof beats. The hearse was making another call at The Archer Home. Next morning one of the Bliss girls learned from Big Jim that a male octogenarian had bit the dust. "The poor man just run down like a clock," Big Jim hollered over, "and stopped."

Everything rocked along without untoward event for a couple of weeks, with the old folks playing checkers and cribbage and chattering on the porch by day and singing hymns in the parlor by night. Some of the tony neighbors, who knew good singing when they heard it, couldn't think of a good word to say about the sounds that floated through the open windows of Amy's place.

Mrs. Archer's charges were great letter writers and their communications to friends on the outside, carefully edited by Sister Amy before being posted, all dwelled on the fine food, the delightful comforts, and the loving care that characterized the Home. As a result, by the time the institution was a year old, it had earned a reputation that extended up and down the Atlantic Seaboard, and the old folks were practically battering down the doors to get in. When a resident involuntarily forfeited the franchise —and the old men and the old ladies were entering that night hearse in boxes at the rate of one a month, almost like clockwork—Sister Amy, leaving the Home in charge of Big Jim, would pack a bag and bustle off to some distant point to audition applicants. An average of a dozen applicants were interviewed and researched before the lucky one was selected.

Although the death rate of the population in The Archer Home was about four times as great as the average reflected in the actuarial tables of the big insurance companies in nearby Hartford, nary a suspicious eyebrow was raised. It just wouldn't have been natural for anybody to have been suspicious of Sister Amy.

When one of the Bliss girls came down with a bad cold that threatened to turn into pneumonia, Sister Amy practically knocked herself out running across the street every hour or so to minister to the patient. When a beggar shuffled up to the back door of The Home he was not only given a coin but invited inside for a hot meal. At Christmas time, Sister Amy bought a fine plaid muffler for the cop on the beat, a guileless man whose service revolver had long since rusted in his pants pocket.

Sometimes, when one of her charges was at death's door, Sister Amy would summon one of three doctors who had staked out the block. These followers of Hippocrates, who wore wing collars and smelled of pills, were not only unsuspicious men but they were far from whizzes in the field of diagnostics. When, then, Sister Amy diagnosed an illness of a doomed patient, a sawbones, respecting the opinion of an experienced nurse, went right along with it and signed the death certificate.

One day in February of 1912, almost five years and more than fifty deaths after Sister Amy had first come to Windsor, there appeared at the back door of The Archer Home a man who wanted a hand-out. Big Jim was giving the caller the bum's rush when Sister Amy happened along and put a frail white hand on Jim's hammy arm. Sizing up the caller, she saw that he was an impressive-looking man in his late thirties. His named turned out to be Michael Gilligan. He had red hair, a bulbous nose, wore a checkered vest and baggy pants and altogether resembled a top banana in a burlesque show. He had roguish eyes, a ready smile and a charming voice.

"Come in," said Sister Amy to Gilligan. "Come right in and I'll fix you something to eat." Gilligan blinked at Archer, standing there with his mouth open, and walked right in.

After a hearty repast, Gilligan said he would like to make a tour of the premises. "I'm good with tools," he told Sister Amy after looking things over. "I could fix this place up if you gave me board and lodging." Sister Amy, taking another good look at the man, signed him up.

Presently, The Archer Home was loud with hammering and sawing as Gilligan, bending to his task like a dedicated man, ripped up flooring and knocked down partitions. Gilligan, both a drinker and a tobacco chewer, usually had a cud in his mouth and a breath that would wither a geranium. Big Jim couldn't understand this. In all the years he had been married to Sister Amy he had been forced to drink on the sly and now along comes a red-headed, baggy-pants stranger who does as he pleases.

Big Jim, his pride pricked and his jealousy aroused, decided that Gilligan had to go. So one afternoon, when Sister Amy was out shopping, he interrupted Gilligan while the man was doing some repair work around the front door.

"We won't be needin' you around here any more," Big Jim said to Gilligan.

"Who says so?" asked Gilligan.

"I do." Big Jim pointed to the black-and-gilt sign a couple of feet from where the dialogue was developing. "The sign there says this is The Archer Home and don't forget I'm Archer."

Gilligan studied the sign briefly, shifted the tobacco cud in his mouth, flexed his lips, and let go with a swift stream of brown juice that splattered the sign. "That," he said, "is what I think of your goddam sign."

One fine morning in April, when Gilligan had been around The Home for a couple of months and when the sap was flowing, Sister Amy dropped in on the Bliss girls, far from her cheerful self.

"What on earth's the matter, Sister Amy?" asked one of the sisters.

"It's my husband."

"Big Jim? Why, what's the matter with him?"

"He's not long for this world."

"Oh, how awful! What on earth's wrong with the man?"

"He's all gone from drink." Sister Amy had been staring at the floor. Now she looked up into the faces of the sisters. "He's been a secret drinker."

"You mean you never knew he drank?"

"Never. Why, did *you?*"

"Oh, yes, Sister Amy. We've known it all along."

"Well, no matter. He's done for now, poor man. He has those terrible stomach hemorrhages."

"How often?"

"Practically every night."

"Have you called in a doctor?"

"It's no use," said Sister Amy, sighing, and biting her lower lip. "I'm a nurse and I know when a person's too far gone." Sister Amy arose, clenched her hands at her sides, and stared over the heads of the sisters, looking very noble. "Oh," she said, "if poor dear Jim had only let me know in time."

For about a month after Big Jim had departed in the night for that undiscovered bourn from which no traveller returns, Sister Amy was inconsolable. She walked around The Home loudly inquiring of the Lord why He had taken Big Jim and she was at that wheezy organ every hour or so playing *Nearer, My God, To Thee* over and over again.

But every cloud has its silver lining. Sister Amy suddenly emerged from the doldrums and one sunny morning she hustled across the street. "Oh!" she said, hugging one of the Bliss girls. "Congratulate me! I'm the happiest woman in the world."

"What on earth has happened, Sister Amy?"

"Mr. Gilligan has asked me to be his wife."

"No!"

"Yes!"

Brother Gilligan, as Sister Amy now began to call the groom, had a lot more gumption than Big Jim Archer had ever had. He continued to drink openly, carrying a pint bottle in his hip pocket and swigging it whenever he had a mind to. Some of the guests, knowing of Sister Amy's opposition to strong drink, wondered why she was putting up with such shenanigans. "He needs it for his health," Sister Amy explained to a couple of the cribbage players one day. "In his case it's like medicine." But the boys at the bar in Paddy's got the real explanation. Brother Gilligan had quickly smelled out the watering hole and had by now accumulated quite a coterie of confidants there. A boastful type, he had divulged to his cronies that, after years of wandering around as a hobo, he had finally fallen into a soft berth. "And do you know why the little woman allows me to drink—she being opposed to liquor as she is?" he said at the bar one night.

"No, why?"

"My manhood!" Gilligan thumped his chest. "She's quite a little woman to take care of nights. But Michael Gilligan's the man for the job."

The months wore on and then the years. Hardly a month passed but that hearse didn't draw up to The Archer-Gilligan Home, as the place was now named. By the spring of 1913, six years after Sister Amy had first come over the horizon, more than seventy life-contract guests had bit the dust and left in a box in the night. Still nobody gave all those deaths a second thought; it seemed quite natural that the old folks should, in the normal course of events, come apart at the seams and die. The life span half a century ago was considerably less than it is today and most of Sister Amy's guests were, when they checked in, already living on borrowed time.

One night, Brother Gilligan dropped into the saloon a very downcast man. A great tragedy had befallen him. Years of over-indulgence in alcohol, not to mention over-exercise of the marital franchise with Sister Amy, had taken their toll. Red-haired, baggy-panted Michael Gilligan had, with devastating suddenness, been stricken by impotency.

"Gee whizz," said a fellow bar fly, "you ought to see one of them doctors who fix up things like that."

Gilligan turned to look at the bar fly, his eyes sad as a doe's. "That's just it," he said. "I have and the doctor can't do a thing for me."

Now, as fortune would have it, there checked into The Archer-Gilligan Home one fine day a nattily-dressed gentleman by the name of Andrews who was fifty-one years of age but who was so well preserved that he looked to be a vigorous forty—clear skin, snapping blue eyes, springy step. Andrews used heady perfume, walked around reading poetry and had a vague sort of a past and an uncertain present. Nobody in the house could quite make the man out.

Since the appearance of Andrews coincided with the arrival of Gilligan's affliction it was but natural that Sister Amy should begin to pay particular attention to him. Andrews, unlike the other contractees, had most of his teeth and could chew practically anything, so Sister Amy began to cook special fare for him. Within a few weeks of his arrival in The Home, Andrews was looked upon by one and all as a privileged character.

One night, less than a month after Brother Gilligan had disclosed his affliction to his friend at Paddy's, his status in the saloon had changed from that of a crony to that of a memory.

"Too bad about Gilligan," the bartender said to a fly.

"Wasn't it, though. A finer man never lived."

"You at the funeral?"

"No. The burial was private. His wife's wishes."

"We'll sure miss him around here."

"We sure will. They say he just went to sleep and never woke up. The heart."

The bartender swept the bar with a swivel gaze. "What'll it be, men? In memory of Brother Gilligan this round's on the house."

The next arrival at The Archer-Gilligan Home was a twinkly-eyed, flannel-faced old gentleman named Runyon who had, somehow or other, succeeded in deceiving Sister Amy when, in undergoing his entrance examination, he had palmed himself off as a teetotaler. Runyon, a childless widower from New Jersey, was an old soak. He used to sneak around to Paddy's, get a royal load on, lurch back to The Home along toward midnight, sit on the porch with his feet up on the railing, and, in a belligerent baritone, sing old Irish songs and wake up the neighborhood.

It was Runyon who now briefed the boys at the bar about what was happening in The Home. Sister Amy, following the demise of Brother Gilligan, was beginning to make goo-goo eyes at the polished, mysterious Andrews. Early one evening, Runyon hustled around to the saloon bursting with news. "That Andrews man!" he began. "The funniest thing has happened."

"What?" asked the bartender.

"He's an odd one."

"How do you mean, odd?"

"He's queer."

"You mean he's a fairy?"

"Nothing else."

"How do you know?"

It seemed that Runyon had been walking through a second-floor hallway, on his way to the bathroom, late the night before. As he was passing Andrews' room, he heard the sound of low talking. Stopping to get an earful, he identified the voices of Sister Amy and Andrews.

"You're a very attractive man," Sister Amy was saying to Andrews.

"Oh, please, Sister Amy," Andrews said. "Don't touch me like that."

"Why, what's the matter? Don't you consider me attractive?"

"It's not that, Sister Amy. Not that at all."

"What is it, then?"

"Well, to tell you the truth, I've never bothered with women."

"You haven't? Why?"

"I just haven't."

"But why? For goodness sakes, why?"

"I prefer men."

"You mean—you mean you're not *natural?*"

"If you want to put it that way, yes."

"W-e-l-l!" said Sister Amy. "I seem to have made a *dreadful* mistake!"

Runyon, recounting the episode, told the bartender that he had hastened down the hallway after that. Poor Runyon didn't last long after carrying the tale about Andrews. The vacancy caused by his departure was no sooner filled than the Bliss girls saw an elderly couple hobbling into The Home one blustery afternoon. The old folks were in The Home for more than an hour and when they came out they stood on the sidewalk, supporting one another and looking around. Then they crossed the street and pulled at the door bell of the old maids' home.

The callers—a Mr. and Mrs. Gowdy of another part of Connecticut—told the Bliss sisters that they had heard so much about The Archer-Gilligan Home that they had taken it upon themselves to personally call and apply for membership. "We're well fixed," said the old man, "but we have no kin and we would like a nice place to live for the rest of our days."

"But you must have found The Home all filled up," said one of the Bliss sisters.

"Yes," said Mr. Gowdy, "but there's going to be a vacancy soon."

"Who?"

"The young gentleman. The one who reads poetry."

"Mr. Andrews?"

"Yes, I believe that is his name."

"What's wrong with him?"

Gowdy tapped his heart.

"But," said the Bliss sisters, "Mr. Andrews is the picture of health."

"It just goes to show you," said Gowdy, "that appearances are deceiving."

When Mr. Andrews, neatly boxed, rode away in the hearse a few nights later, the Bliss sisters, after all these years, began to feel vaguely uneasy. Putting two and two together, they were puzzled by the fact that young residents of The Archer-Gilligan Home seemed to pop off as soon after entering as the old folks. "It just does seem kind of funny, doesn't it, Sister?" one of them said, biting the fingernails of one hand while, with the other hand, she parted the lace curtains and looked over at The Home.

The Gowdys—the well-fixed Gowdys—moved in to the Andrews room but didn't live very long to enjoy it. Less than three weeks after they checked in they checked out—the same night, within three hours of one another.

"My," said one of the Bliss girls to Sister Amy when Amy dropped over for tea the day after the Gowdys left, "but your people are dying off awful fast, aren't they?"

Sister Amy sipped her tea before answering. "It's God's will," she said. "The Lord works in mysterious ways His wonders to perform."

One day in the spring of 1914, seven years after Sister Amy had first come over the horizon, a reporter on The Hartford *Courant*—a real Front-Page type character named Mike Toughy, pipe, cynicism, battered hat and all—was thumbing through some Hartford County records, hoping to pull together some statistics of some kind that might form the basis of a Sunday feature story. When Mike Toughy discovered that the population of The Archer-Gilligan Home had undergone a complete population replacement through death every twelve months he felt his pulse quicken. He wondered if those juicy life contracts that Sister Amy offered her charges were, unbeknown to the charges, being abruptly abrogated.

Checking the mortality rate at the Old Peoples Home in Hartford, Toughy learned that the death rate was only one-sixth, on the average, of what it was at Sister Amy's. Next he dropped in on an actuary in the home office of one of the big insurance companies in Hartford. The actuary, a mirthless little man with rimless eyeglasses and thinning blond hair, began to scribble some figures on a pad. Finished, he sighed, leaned back in his swivel chair, clasped his hands behind his head, and studied Toughy. "I think," he said, contributing to the literature of understatements, "you can feel perfectly safe in assuming that some unnatural element is hastening the deaths of many of those people at The Archer-Gilligan Home."

Toughy got in touch with the doctors who had signed the death certificates. Nothing suspicious. Now he tried to reach kin of the deceased. Kin simply didn't exist. Next, definitely taking the tack that Mrs. Archer had killed for profit, Toughy canvassed the insurance companies to find out if the little lady in white had tried to insure any of her charges. She had, it developed, attempted to take out policies on several of the ladies and gentlemen but only one had been in sufficiently young or sound enough to pass the examination.

"And who was that?"

"The name's Andrews. He died of a heart attack right after the policy was taken out."

Mike Toughy, like many reporters of the era, didn't have too much respect for the law when it interfered with a probe into a suspected violation of the law. So he simply went out and greased the palms of a couple of grave diggers, dug up Andrews in the dark of the moon, got an intern friend to take out the man's insides, then tucked Andrews back in the grave.

The news that Toughy got from a Boston laboratory where he sent part of Andrews was quick and discouraging. Andrews had not, as Toughy hoped, been poisoned.

Deciding that while Andrews might have died a natural death, some of the others hadn't, Toughy dug up two more bodies. Neither had been poisoned and neither had been clubbed, shot or otherwise lethally dealt with.

By now Mike Toughy was discouraged but by no means through. The still, small voice that all the nothing-sacred reporters of the old school had urged him to keep at it. While other *Courant* reporters began to examine the poison books of every drug store in Hartford County, Toughy, posing as a door-to-door canvasser, began to ring doorbells in Sister Amy's block.

When Toughy rang the bell at the Bliss sisters' house and was invited into the parlor something told him he had come to a good place. Divulging his identity and his mission, the reporter got the Bliss sisters talking. When he learned that they, too, had become uneasy about the happenings in The Home he felt encouraged for the first time. Toughy quietly holed into a second-floor room in the girls' house that afforded a view of The Archer-Gilligan Home. Peering across the street through field glasses, Toughy got several good looks at Sister Amy and marked her down as a real sly one.

Nothing much happened for a week. Then one night that hearse appeared again. Toughy followed it and arranged for a quick secret autopsy of the stiff— that of an elderly woman—before it went underground. The woman had died from the infirmities of age.

Although he was beginning to feel a quiet desperation creeping over him, Toughy called on Hugh Alcorn, Sr., the clever, ambitious State's Attorney of Hartford County, and laid his suspicions on Alcorn's desk. Alcorn sat there considering things, then wheeled around in his swivel chair and looked out the window. "Not only do you not have any evidence that I could take into court, Mike," said Alcorn, "but you might get the *Courant* in hot water."

"How?"

Alcorn wheeled around in his chair. "Mrs. Archer-Gilligan," he said, "has been in here to see me."

"She *has*. What for?"

"She claims you've been persecuting her."

"Why, the little fiend! How could she possibly say a thing like that?"

Alcorn shrugged. "All I know is she knows you've been investigating her. And she says if you don't stop it she'll have your paper sued for persecution."

Toughy holed into that room in the Bliss home again, this time accompanied by a *Courant* artist. The artist drew a sketch of Sister Amy as she darted around that big porch.

Toughy hit the drug stores with the sketch. That did it. Sister Amy had used assumed names in buying rat poison. Her poison purchases had usually preceded, by a few days, the date of a death in The Home.

With Toughy's evidence on his desk, Alcorn rolled up his official sleeves. He dug up not one, not two, not three but four gentlemen who had kicked off a few days after the most recent of the arsenic purchases. All of them were shot through with the stuff.

Sister Amy, placed on trial for the last of the arsenic deaths—that of a middle-aged man—was a demure little figure, dressed in black and carrying a small Bible, as Alcorn pictured her as a twentieth-century Borgia. In his enthusiasm, Alcorn introduced evidence that Sister Amy had not only killed the man for whose death she had been placed on trial, but twenty-three others over a period of eighteen months.

Sister Amy was convicted and sentenced to hang. But her mouthpiece, appealing the case on the grounds that Alcorn, itching for Sister's neck, had introduced evidence of poisonings not relating to the case at bar, got the little lady a new trial. Pleading guilty when the second trial got under way twelve years after she had first opened that Home on Prospect Street, Sister Amy Archer-Gilligan got off with life. A few years later, she went off her rocker and spent the next third of a century in a squirrel cage.

"Big Jim," Sister Amy used to mutter in the squirrel cage. "Big Jim." Nobody ever knew whether Big Jim had collaborated with one of the arch-fiends of modern American criminal history, or whether Sister Amy continued to mention his name because the man with the handsome walrus moustache had, before being disenfranchised by Gilligan, been the answer to Amy's nocturnal prayers.

New York's Easter Murders

*When the Mad Sculptor went to live with the Gedeon family, little did the
Gedeons realize how mad the fellow really was. Had they suspected the
truth, the cops would have been spared a king-size headache.*

The Gedeon household was that kind
of place where something, sooner or
later, was bound to happen. It had considerable of the full-moon qualities of
the Sycamore household in *You Can't
Take It With You* without having any
of the Sycamore charm.

The Gedeons were a family of four—
father, mother and two pretty grown
daughters. They lived in various apartments on New York's upper East Side,
in districts where one block marked the
difference between swank and slum. The
family usually, somehow, located in a
building that was under suspicion of the
fire department, if not the board of
health, but which bore a street number
that sounded, at a distance, very flossy.

Joseph Gedeon, head of the household, was a small and thin Hungarian.
Fiftyish, he didn't weigh more than 125
pounds even if full of beer. He had a
large shock of graying hair and a thin,
guileless-looking face. He wore pince-
nez glasses and white piping on his vests.
For a man who looked so utterly inoffen-
sive, he had a surprisingly sharp tongue.
He ran a little upholstery shop on Thirty-
fourth Street, near Third Avenue, and
was a great hand at turning out a really
tasty job in tufted velvet. At nights,
Gedeon devoted himself to skee ball and
a few mugs of Pilsner-type beer in a
Third Avenue saloon called Corrigan's
Bar and Grill but which (being in the
town where the Fifth Avenue Flower
Shop was located on Madison Avenue and
the North River is due west of the East

River) was owned and operated by a
gentleman named Caligero Parlapiano.

Gedeon's wife, Mary, a naïve woman
who had been a gorgeous Magyar beauty
in her youth, and who, in her forties,
was still a comely person, had an affinity
for trouble. If the corner grocery store
had one bad egg in a case, Mrs. Gedeon
was sure to get it. She was a short woman
and, when she attended the theater, an
ex-member of a Washington State row-
ing crew or somebody just as tall was
bound to have the seat directly in front
of her. Once a man named Fitten, employed by a government bureau, called
to ask Mrs. Gedeon some very simple
questions about a relatively simple matter. Complications piled up until Fitten
found himself standing before a judge,
being sentenced for attempting to extort
some cheap jewelry from Mrs. Gedeon.
Things like that.

The daughters—Ethel and Veronica—
were as different as the poles. Ethel, a
couple of years older than Veronica,
was a placid brunette with impeccable
morals. Veronica, on the other hand,
was a blonde with a low boiling point.
Ethel went to business and was engaged
to a serious young man. Veronica, who
preferred to be called Ronnie, was an
artists' model. At the age of sixteen she
had married a fellow named Bobby
Flower, a hot-dog concessionaire. Life
among the frankfurters proved not very
exhilarating, and Ronnie had obtained
an annulment.

Ronnie, turning eighteen, was beautiful, voluptuous and exciting. She wanted to be a movie star. She wasn't too intelligent, but she was shrewd for her years. Whether she took the high road or the low road evidently didn't concern her so much as the distance ahead. One day she met a prominent city official in a Greenwich Village attic with north light. The man, hearing of her Hollywood ambitions, led her to the erroneous impression that he and Cecil B. DeMille wore each other's socks, and proceeded to other matters.

A few weeks later, upon receipt of an unpleasant lunar surprise, Ronnie confided in her mother.

"Who is the man?" asked Mrs. Gedeon.

Ronnie identified the city father.

Mrs. Gedeon was delighted. "Now," she said, "you can be somebody. We'll make him marry you."

The politician was already married. A divorce wouldn't have been compatible with his career. Besides, his wife wouldn't give him one. So Ronnie underwent an operation.

Papa Gedeon, getting secondhand wind of Ronnie's predicament, inquired of his daughter, "Sometime, just for a change, why don't you try having fun with your clothes on?" Ronnie threw a humidor at Papa. The mother sided with her and home life for Gedeon wasn't the same after that.

The Gedeons took in male roomers to make ends meet—one or two at a time. Mrs. Gedeon's affinity for trouble was never better reflected than in the type of people who appeared in response to her newspaper ads. Something was wrong with most of them. Ranging from actors, through blind piano tuners to short-order cooks in lunch wagons, the boys were apt to be either deadbeats, eccentrics, drunks or wolves. The result was

that Mama Gedeon dwelled in a state of almost constant flutter.

One night in 1935, Mama, the eternal optimist, told her daughters, "Girls, we have the most *charming* gentleman coming to take the back room tomorrow."

"Young or old?" asked Ronnie.

"Young and very handsome," Mama replied.

The subject of the conversation was Robert Irwin, a sculptor. Irwin—dark, earnest and good-looking—had a deceptively normal appearance. He looked like one of those fellows in the clothing ads, peering determinedly into a glorious future with an empty pipe clenched in his teeth.

Irwin hadn't been around long until the girls knew that Mama had let in another wheel. Irwin couldn't decide whether to continue with art or drop it and become a minister.

Irwin was one man who remained unstirred by Ronnie. Ronnie didn't care about him particularly, but her pride was hurt. And she was just female enough to do something about it. One day she contrived to be alone in the flat with Irwin. He was in his room, she in hers. She called to him. When he walked into her room she was sitting on the bed —naked.

Irwin's eyes popped. "Oh, boy!" he said, "wait till I get some clay!"

Ronnie went around telling people that Bob Irwin was a homo. That, of course, wasn't true. What Ronnie didn't know at the time was that Irwin was carrying a terrific torch for Ethel. Irwin confessed to Mrs. Gedeon that since he couldn't have Ethel he didn't want anybody. "Poor boy," said Mrs. Gedeon.

Irwin tried to perform a self-emasculation on himself and was sent to an asylum. "Poor, *poor* boy," said Mrs. Gedeon. By the spring of 1937, Ethel had married and left home. Papa Gedeon, too, had removed himself from the family fireside. After repeated quarrels with Ronnie about her wildness, and with Mama Gedeon because she always took Ronnie's part, Gedeon had moved into a cubbyhole sort of room in the rear of his upholstery shop. Ronnie and her mother took a fourth-floor walk-up flat on East Fiftieth Street. They had two roomers, a young girl model and an Englishman named Frank Byrnes—an attendant at the exclusive Racquet and Tennis Club who somehow gave the impression of having stayed too long in a steam room.

Saturday night, March 27th, was the night before Easter. The model who roomed with the Gedeons was out of town for the holidays, and lucky for her. Byrnes, the Englishman, returned to his room in the Gedeon flat about nine o'clock, pooped from a hard day among the swells at the Racquet and Tennis Club, and went directly to bed. Mrs. Gedeon was alone in the place with Byrnes. Ronnie was out on the town with a fellow named Butter—Stephen Butter, Jr., a Wall Street runner. Mrs. Gedeon got undressed and sat around in her night clothes, reading a magazine.

A gentleman by the name of Cosmon Cambinias, who was in residence in the second-floor rear of the building where the Gedeon apartment was located, heard a woman's scream almost on the stroke of eleven P.M. Cambinias had become something of a connoisseur of screams, the tenants in the building being what they were. The scream he heard was definitely not associated with anything amatory or alcoholic. It was born of sheer terror. It was short, as if stopped by a hand clapped over a mouth. Cambinias marked it down to a routine incident between an incompatible hus-

band and wife, shrugged, and went to the icebox for a bottle of beer.

At about three o'clock on Easter afternoon, the former Ethel Gedeon and her husband, in from the suburbs, approached the East Fiftieth Street apartment building and were surprised to see Papa Gedeon lounging out front, holding a huge bouquet of roses.

"What are you standing here with those flowers for, Father?" asked Ethel, smelling the old man's breath.

"I thought since it was Easter," said Gedeon, "I would try to make up with Mama."

"Well, you'll never do it standing down here."

"I was there but nobody answers the bell. I thought I would wait around until Mama or Ronnie or one of the roomers showed up."

"Mama's *got* to be home," said Ethel. "She invited us to dinner at three. Chicken paprika."

"Maybe she was in the bathroom or something," said Gedeon, "and didn't hear the bell. I'll go up and try again."

Ethel and her husband waited on the sidewalk. In a few minutes, Gedeon came out the door much differently—and faster—than he had gone in.

"They're dead!" he said. "Ronnie and that fellow Byrnes!"

"Where's Mama?" asked Ethel.

Gedeon shook his head in agitation. "Over telling the police, I guess."

Mrs. Gedeon wasn't over telling the police anything. She was upstairs under a bed, murdered.

The Gedeon flat consisted of three bedrooms—two of which were not a great deal larger than piano boxes—a small living room, a kitchenette and a bathroom. By actual count, there were twenty-two persons in this modest layout within twenty minutes after the murders were discovered, not counting the bodies.

Thrown in for good measure was Mrs. Gedeon's Pekingese dog, Touchi, a particularly snotty little animal even for a Pekingese. Aside from Ethel and her husband, and Gedeon, there were two fingerprint men, two men from the Medical Examiner's office, a police photographer, a man from the D.A.'s office, two flatfeet and eleven dicks, headed by the department's fashion plate—Inspector Francis Kear, chief of all detectives in Manhattan. Here was the convention in a telephone booth you've heard about. Everybody was there but the killer—they hoped.

Byrnes, the boarder, had been neatly dispatched in his sleep. The murdermaster had inserted a sharp instrument —an ice pick or something similar—into the canal of his right ear, thence into his brain. Ronnie and her mother had been strangled—strangled by somebody's bare hands. Ronnie was completely nude, lying on a bed. Her mother had been stuffed under the bed. That, Gedeon explained, was why he hadn't seen her when he discovered the other bodies.

One of the dicks—Tom Tunney, a brother of Gene, the Connecticut squire —asked Gedeon how it was that he had not been able to get into the apartment the first time, yet had obtained admittance the second try. "The door was ajar," said Gedeon. "I didn't notice it the first time."

The phone rang. Inspector Kear grabbed it. A male voice asked for Ronnie. A guy had put a nickel in a coin box and bought himself a bargain in trouble.

"Who is this?" asked Kear, a deceptively soft-spoken man.

"Steve."

"Steve who?"

"Steve Butter."

"Where are you, Steve?"

"Home."

"Where is that?"

Butter told Kear.

"You just stay there, Steve. Somebody will be right over. Now don't go away."

The apartment wasn't disordered. Kear was under the impression that the killer had known the place pretty well. The ladies had not been raped; just strangled. Kear's hunch was that the killer had burned with a monumental hatred for either Ronnie or her mother, and that two of the murders had been committed to make way for the third.

Three cakes of plain Castile soap, in block form, were found on the floor of the bedroom, where Ronnie and her mother had died. The soap, a quick checkup revealed, wasn't like any in other parts of the flat. The only inference to be drawn was that the killer had dropped it. What he or she had been carrying soap around for, however, wasn't so easily inferred.

Cosmon Cambinias, the sound collector and second-floor tenant, told the dicks about the eleven-o'clock scream he had heard. That was interesting. It also brought up something else; neither Cambinias nor anybody else available for questioning had heard so much as a low growl out of Touchi, the Gedeon dog, all night long. The fact that the Peke had been silent all night, then, meant that he not only knew the killer but might even have liked the character.

By nightfall, Inspector Kear was in possession of all the facts necessary to dope out the sequence of the murders. Mrs. Gedeon had eaten a blue-plate special in a neighborhood restaurant around five o'clock Saturday afternoon. An examination of the food in her stomach disclosed that it had been subject to digestive processes for about six hours.

That meant she had been killed around eleven o'clock, which in turn checked with the time Cambinias had heard the scream. A similar yardstick was applied to the time of Byrnes' death.

Steve Butter, the fellow who had telephoned to Ronnie and drawn Inspector Kear, said he had dropped Ronnie at her door about three A.M. Steve and Ronnie had eaten a night club meal about eleven o'clock on the Saturday night in question. Ronnie's stomach had digested food for about four hours before her death, so *that* checked.

The lodger and Mrs. Gedeon, obviously enough, had been slain at eleven o'clock. The killer had thereupon lain in wait for Ronnie for four hours.

The dicks, learning from Sister Ethel that Ronnie and her father had not hit it off any too well, began to get interested in Papa Gedeon. He had been seen in Corrigan's Bar and Grill—a fifteen-minute walk from the murder flat—intermittently from eight o'clock Saturday night until closing time, three A.M. Sunday. As the evening in Corrigan's had worn along, the place had become more smoky and more beery, not to say louder and funnier and more crowded. It would have been entirely possible for Gedeon to have absented himself from the saloon for an hour or so and scarcely have been missed. He could thus have been in the flat on Fiftieth Street at eleven o'clock. He could also have returned there after Corrigan's closing hour.

Kear was mildly surprised to find Gedeon at work in his shop the night of that corpse-strewn Sunday, finishing up a chair for a customer.

"Don't you have any feelings in this matter?" asked the Inspector, mixing dramatics with business. "Doesn't it do anything to you when you realize that

your wife and your own flesh and blood are on cold slabs in the morgue?"

Gedeon studied the man briefly. "I see you don't understand Hungarians," he said. "We don't blubber; we keep our feelings to ourselves."

Kear walked back to the cubbyhole that Gedeon now called home. The walls were plastered with nude and might-as-well-be-nude pin-ups. "Quite a hobby you have," he commented. Gedeon removed a pipe from his mouth and pointed with the stem to one particular picture. "That's the type of girl I want for my next wife," he said.

"Your next *wife*?"

"Life goes on," said Gedeon, "and we must live it."

Kear reached into his pocket, extracted a cheap gray cloth glove, size 8, and handed it to Gedeon. "Try this on for size," he said. The glove, for the right hand, fitted Gedeon. Kear took the glove back and put it in his pocket.

"What goes on here?" asked Gedeon.

"We picked that glove up in the bedroom where your wife and daughter were found," said Kear. "There was no mate to it. We figure the murderer dropped it."

Gedeon's eyes sparkled. "Just because that glove fits me don't make me the murderer!"

"Nobody said it did."

The murder flat was still heavily populated with assorted investigators late on Sunday night. The boys were in each other's hair largely because opportunity was knocking. In a big case like this there always was the chance for a dick to pick up a clue that would save the department a pother of time, trouble and expense. Such a feat might earn a promotion—if somebody above the detective didn't plant a heel in his face while walking away with all the credit.

The Gedeon flat was a gritty monument to bad housekeeping. Mrs. Gedeon
had been a stanch advocate of the once-
over-lightly technique in dusting. The
result was that a good type of detecting
dust, like in novels, outlined objects
that weren't frequently moved. One investigator noticed a small clean area on
a bureau scarf in the room of the girl
lodger who had gone away for the week
end. The deduction was that a clock had
rested on this clean area and that the
girl had taken the timepiece with her.

The girl lodger, having heard about
the murders on the radio, returned to
the scene twenty-four hours ahead of
schedule. She owned a Baby Ben alarm
clock, which she seldom used and which
had stood on the bureau scarf's clean
area. She had not taken the clock with
her, nor could she account for its absence. That meant the murderer had
taken the clock, didn't it?

Ronnie Gedeon had kept a diary.
What she hadn't known about syntax she
had compensated for by selectivity in
subject matter and devotion to detail.
The incident about Bob Irwin, the
screwball sculptor, who had been artisti-
cally rather than amorously aroused by
the sight of Ronnie in the nude, had
been painstakingly recorded. Dimen-
sional and staminal intelligence about
some of the town's prominent wolves
was all down, in black and white, to fascinate the official readers.

Diary characters like Irwin, the sculptor, who had had no apparent personal
interest in Ronnie, were passed up in
favor of men who could have had classic
reasons to kill the model—jealousy, hatred, the removal of an obstacle, and so
on. Ronnie could well have fallen into
the obstacle class; certain people were
unkind enough to classify some of her
activities as modified blackmail now and

then, only she called it gold-digging.
Running down the leads in the diary
might well consume weeks or months.

The fingerprint men were coming up
with prints other than those of the dead
trio and the live girl lodger. As a matter
of fact, it was to turn out that the pow-
der-and-brush boys were developing
more than one set of loops and whorls
that had been left on flat surfaces by
some of the dicks themselves. There
were not, however, any prints—even
smudged ones—on the three cakes of Castile soap found on the bedroom floor.
This indicated, beyond much doubt, that
the killer had worn gloves, and buttressed
the belief that the gray glove found in
the murder room was a real clue.

The Medical Examiner's office arrived
at two tentative conclusions. The sharp
murder instrument, whatever it was,
that had been inserted in the ear and
brain of Byrnes, the lodger, had been
handled with skill that reflected a professional knowledge of anatomy. And
the strangler must have had remarkably
strong hands, at least during those moments of passion. You ordinarily do not
associate strong hands with a woman.

It is a truism that there are always sufficient divergent facts obtainable about
any given man to make him out a prince
or a slob, depending upon which is
wanted at any given time. The cops
wanted a murderer in the Gedeon case
and they were running true to form when
they gathered suspicious facts and ignored unsuspicious ones. They were
aided in their work by the usual assortment of citizens who materialize in this
kind of investigation—some intelligent,
observant people, others fruit-cakes who
want to see their names in the papers.
The rub is that the dicks can't always
immediately distinguish a high-grade
moron from a smart citizen.

Somebody had seen a man waving an ice pick walking under a street lamp near the murder building shortly before dawn on Easter morning. The man was described as short and stocky, and in his late forties. Period. It was one of those tips that cops both dread and hope for.

The description fitted a character in the diary—Georges Guiret, a chef of French extraction who had once boarded with the Gedeons. Frenchy, as the man was called, now lived in a rooming house diagonally across the street. He wasn't at home when the cops called on the Monday morning. They gave his room a good toss—and came up with two blood-stained handkerchiefs.

Frenchy, picked up, said that he had been asleep at the time of the murders. He couldn't prove his statement, nor could the cops disprove it. He explained the handkerchiefs by saying he'd had a nosebleed.

Every murder, the dicks say, is preceded by an epidemic of nosebleeds among possible suspects.

Frenchy had strong hands. As a chef, he probably knew plenty about animal anatomy, if not human. He was adept, in the course of his work, at strangling chickens. The cops began to shove him around a little. The guy may have been eccentric, but no dope. "It says in the papers," he said, "you found a glove size eight. I take nine. Ha!"

The detectives preferred to ignore the glove for the time being. Frenchy was taken to the murder flat so that his reactions could be studied. Touchi, the dog, was still in the place. He took one look and quickly was skidding toward the chef's ankles, barking his head off. If the glove could be ignored, the Peke couldn't. The dog hated Frenchy. Frenchy simply couldn't have been in the murder apartment long enough to commit one mur-

der, let alone three, without the dog raising so much hell it would have been heard all over the building.

Late on Monday, a detective was snooping around Gedeon's upholstery shop. "Where is your regulator needle?" he asked Gedeon. "I don't see no regulator needle." A regulator needle is a long, thin steel shaft with an eye and a blunt end. It is about as essential to an upholsterer as a brace and bit to a carpenter. Detectives are supposed to know these things, or find them out.

Gedeon shrugged. "It seems to be missing," he said. "I must have mislaid it."

The detective went out and phoned Inspector Kear. "That needle could have been the murder instrument used on the roomer," said Kear.

"Yeah," agreed the dick. "And Gedeon could of picked up some information about anatomy on account of his daughter was a model."

The detective went back to Gedeon's shop. He drifted into the man's living quarters. In a little while he reappeared in the shop. "You only got one suit?" he asked.

"No," said Gedeon. "Two."

"Well, where's the other one? It's not in your clothes closet."

"I sent it out to be cleaned."

"When? Where?"

Gedeon seemed to be amused as he answered.

The sleuth promptly went outside and called the establishment which Gedeon named. The suit had been thrown into a chemical solution at the cleaners, and the detective cursed to himself.

The dicks dug up a man who knew Gedeon well. "A very strong little man," said Gedeon's acquaintance.

"How do you mean?"

"Ask him to show you what he does with a beer-bottle cap."

"You mean he can crush it in his fingers?"

"I've seen him do it dozens of times. It's remarkable."

Somebody else popped up to say that Gedeon had been observed walking eastward from his upholstery shop, carrying a package, just after daylight on Easter morning.

Gedeon was taken to the murder flat. The dog began to lick his hands. "That's funny," he said. "Touchi never used to like me."

"He likes you now," said a detective with a gold badge in his pants pocket. "We're taking you in for questioning."

Papa Gedeon didn't bruise easily. Near the end of the maximum time the cops could hold him without preferring a specific charge, he looked a good deal fresher than the men who had been working on him in relays.

The cops got a break. They found a snub-nosed automatic in the room that Gedeon called home. How they had overlooked it for several days may or may not be a commentary on police work. They had the weapon now, and that was the important thing. Gedeon didn't have a gun permit, which is a serious offense in New York State. He was held on the no-permit charge, under ten thousand dollars bail, and this gave the cops more time to move.

They were still kicking the case around the Friday after the murders. Papa Gedeon's bail on the no-permit charge had been reduced and he was free again. He seemed to be getting very weary of the whole business, especially of newspaper reporters. A certain elemental question posed to him by the representative of a great tabloid prompted Papa Gedeon to throw some beer in the scribe's face.

It had been Inspector Kear's experience that murderers often hang around town after doing their dirt, just to keep an eye on how things are progressing, and then light out for elsewhere. When a man thus takes it on the lam, Kear knew, he often checks some belongings in a public checkroom, preferring not to be encumbered by anything he can't run with. On the off chance that the Easter killer fell into the check-it-and-beat-it category, Kear ordered the city's big checkrooms combed.

In New York, investigating like that, you can come upon a few hundred pieces of baggage with sounds inside that seldom mean a bomb but, not to bore you, the boys struck pay dirt in Grand Central Terminal. They singled out a small black valise which first attracted their attention because something was ticking inside. What was ticking was a Baby Ben alarm, a thirty-hour clock—and it was far from run down, indicating that whoever had checked the valise had done so within the previous twenty-four hours.

There was an assortment of men's old clothing in the valise. Included was a pair of blue-denim trousers, with a number stamped on the seat. "These pants look like they come from a state institution somewhere," said a dick.

The girl lodger in the Gedeon flat identified the Baby Ben as the clock that had been taken from her bureau. It was an old-timer, and it had been scratched and otherwise marked up, so she was sure.

The positive identification of the clock made the blue-denim pants vitally important. The pants, it quickly turned out, were from the Rockland State Hospital, an institution for the mentally unbalanced. The serial number on the seat of the pants had been that of Robert Irwin, the odd-minded sculptor who had wound up in the asylum a couple of years previously on the occasion of his attempted self-emasculation. Released, he had taken the pants with him.

If the cops do dumb things, murderers can do dumber things. Irwin needed that pair of pants and a cheap alarm clock as much as he needed a hole in his head. Yet, had he not gone out of his way to fasten those clues to himself the cops might have passed him up indefinitely.

The pieces fell into place quickly now. A sculptor usually has strong, capable hands. Sculptors use a tool which could have been the murder weapon. Sculptors know anatomy. Sculptors often carry blocks of soap around with them, to do carving in their spare moments.

Now that Irwin was in the sights, his motive emerged. He had told acquaintances that he felt like killing Mrs. Gedeon, Ronnie and the sister Ethel. Ronnie and Mama Gedeon, he felt, had queered him with Ethel, and, so long as he couldn't have Ethel, he didn't want her husband to have her. Byrnes had been killed just incidentally.

Irwin, probably getting tired of looking at his own picture in the papers, gave himself up in Chicago a couple of weeks later. He was carrying the mate to the glove found at the murder scene.

The Mad Sculptor, as some highly unoriginal reporter called Irwin, was a disappointed man. He had hoped to find his dream love, Ethel, present in the Fiftieth Street flat the night he had gone to kill. "Four is such a nice round number," Irwin told the cops, "and Ethel would have made four."

Irwin escaped the electric chair after the expected legal circus and was given a life ticket to an asylum. Papa Gedeon, a much-abused and quite innocent little man who had admitted the enormous crime of having a gun without a permit, had known Irwin. He once asked of a news reporter why Irwin had taken that damnable alarm clock.

"He says," said the reporter, "that he wanted the clock because he never knew what time it was."

94   NEW YORK'S FATAL MURDER

of the parts had been that of Robert, who insisted to have his. Brgus had

The Worm That Turned

All little Warren Lincoln asked for in life was to be left alone so that he could putter with his sweet peas. Then his wife's big bully of a brother came on for a visit and not only trampled the sweet peas but got the white meat of the chicken. Then little Warren Lincoln, who knew his statutes, committed the almost-perfect crime.

The neighbors pegged Mr. and Mrs. Warren Lincoln as an odd pair from the day in the spring of 1921 when they took up residence in a modest bungalow on the outskirts of Aurora, Illinois. Mr. Lincoln, a man nearing fifty, was small, frail, and timid-looking—a sort of in-the-flesh Milquetoast. His wife was a solid big woman, half a head taller than he; she had a square jaw and wore rimless eyeglasses pinched to her nose. Mr. Lincoln was a Chicago criminal lawyer who had withdrawn from the turmoil of the courtroom because of faltering health; comfortably fixed, he now planned to indulge his hobby, raising sweet peas. Mrs. Lincoln, a woman who wanted everybody to be happy—her way—immediately identified herself with the local chapter of the Women's Christian Temperance Union, thus continuing a cause to which she had for many years devoted her ample energies. The Lincolns were, it goes without saying, childless.

It soon became obvious to even the more astigmatic observers that Mrs. Lincoln wore the pants in the family. Once, when Lincoln was puttering in the sweet-pea beds behind the house, meanwhile smoking a cigaret, his wife appeared at the back door and bellowed "War-*ren!*" Lincoln, without looking up, dropped the cigaret as if it were a live wire. Liquor and tobacco were forbidden to him, both

on and off the premises. Furthermore, every Sunday morning he was marched off to church, where Mrs. Lincoln contributed a rich alto to the choir, and each Wednesday night to prayer meeting.

Travelers to Chicago, some thirty miles to the east, brought back tales of Warren Lincoln's courtroom feats. He had specialized in murder cases. Once, not long prior to his retirement, he had scored six acquittals in a row; reporters around the old Criminal Courts Building had begun to call him Scott Free Lincoln. It was hard to reconcile the clever courtroom strategist with the timid soul of the sweet-pea beds, but a fact is a fact. Warren Lincoln may have been a lion in a courtroom, but he was a mouse in his own home.

Some months after the Lincolns first appeared in Aurora, they had a visitor— a 220-pound, grinning, non-smoking total abstainer named Byron Shoup, who turned out to be Mrs. Lincoln's younger brother from Nebraska. Shoup, who had once been a Boy Scout leader, was a great fellow for keeping in shape. He got up at dawn and ran practically around Aurora; he shadow-boxed and did calisthenics behind the bungalow at intervals throughout the day.

Shoup was a man of highly accented tastes; he was either nuts about things or

91

couldn't stand them. For some reason or other, he was crazy about Aurora. He decided to stay with the Lincolns indefinitely. He sent to Nebraska for his athletic paraphernalia—punching-bag stand, exercise bars and rings, and Indian clubs. When the stuff arrived and Shoup set it up behind the bungalow, the place looked like an outdoor gymnasium. Shoup had a few thousand clams in the bank, and, since his wants were simple and inexpensive, he didn't have to work. Thus he was around the house all day.

In his pursuit of the athletic life, Shoup frequently trampled his brother-in-law's flower beds. Lincoln remonstrated mildly, but his wife told him to stop picking quarrels with her brother. Lincoln sighed and built a little greenhouse behind the bungalow where his flowers would be safe from Shoup's big feet.

The winter of 1921–22 came on. It was cold outside. Shoup moved his paraphernalia into the greenhouse. The big fellow, concentrating on the leathery rhythm of his punching bag, made a mess of the greenhouse flowers; every once in a while, an Indian club would fly through a pane of glass. Shoup appropriated the most comfortable chair in the living room, the white meat of any chicken that was served, and the daily and Sunday newspapers. Life in his own home became increasingly untenable for little Warren Lincoln.

Mrs. Lincoln had meantime become the spearhead of a white-ribbon crusade to close up Aurora's speakeasies. She and her co-crusaders would smell out one of the evil places, turn their information over to the cops, then lend a hand during a raid.

It so happened that at the very time that his wife was hell-bent for total aridity, Warren Lincoln turned to the back rooms of speakeasies in quest of asylum from his home life. Never a drinker, he was content to sit around over a couple of beers and fan the breeze with the boys. Then, before going home, he would pop some whole cloves or coffee beans into his mouth to kill his breath. He was fairly safe from detection by his wife, so long as he didn't actually stagger; she considered kissing promiscuous and was so busy with her temperance work that she hardly noticed him.

As time passed, Lincoln discovered, as have so many men, that a happy saloon has it all over an unhappy home. He became attached to certain speakeasy proprietors. He began to tip them off when the little woman was drawing a bead on them. Thus the valuable inventory of a happiness exchange would be removed to the safety of a cyclone cellar before a raid; when the law crashed in, everybody would be sitting around drinking ginger ale in an aura of innocence. Mrs. Lincoln was quick to sense a traitor within the ranks; the trouble was, she didn't know who it was.

One day, Byron Shoup happened to be passing a joint when whom did he see identifying himself at the peephole but his little brother-in-law. Shoup couldn't wait to run home and tell sister. When Lincoln got home, he found his wife making a supreme effort to conceal the fact that she was exhaling fire.

"Byron wants to see you," she said. "He's out in the greenhouse."

Shoup had a couple of pairs of boxing gloves in the greenhouse.

"Put on a pair," he said to Lincoln, "and we'll go a few rounds."

"But I don't want to box," said Lincoln.

"Yes, you do," said Shoup. He stuffed Lincoln's hands into the gloves and proceeded to belt him around. Shoup could, of course, have finished Lincoln with one punch, but he was a sadistic man. He preferred to torture Lincoln. When the retired barrister collapsed, Shoup threw him over his shoulder and carried him into the house. Lincoln was in bed for three days. He never went in for counter-espionage work again.

Warren Lincoln was deep in despair when, in the spring of 1922—a year after he had moved to Aurora—a local flower shop, having heard about his wonderful sweet peas, asked him if he could supply the blooms commercially. The prospect of putting his hobby on a paying basis made life worth living again for Lincoln. He took on a helper, a naïve fellow named Frank, and lost himself in seeds, lime, and fertilizer. On Sundays and holidays, cars would draw up to the greenhouse for Warren Lincoln's sweet peas. Business was so good that it was necessary to enlarge the greenhouse.

Mrs. Lincoln suggested to her husband —and a suggestion from her was the equivalent of a command—that the profits from the sweet-pea enterprise be kept in a separate account in a local bank. She shared the account and bought expensive gifts for her brother. Shoup began to dress better than Lincoln; his sartorial superiority increased his disdain for his little brother-in-law.

Then it developed, in January, 1923, that Mrs. Lincoln, of all people, had a boy friend. Lincoln confided this to one of his favorite bartenders. He even showed the man a note which his wife had carelessly misplaced. The boy friend's name was George; it appeared that he and Mrs. Lincoln met at frequent intervals in Chicago. Lincoln sure was on the horns of a dilemma, the horns being his wife and brother-in-law.

"I wish," he said to the bartender, "I had the courage to ask the two of them to leave."

"Why don't you try it, Mr. Lincoln?" said the barkeep. "You can't be no worse off than you are right now."

Lincoln studied a freshly drawn glass of beer. He shoved it aside. "Let me have some of your rye," he said.

That evening, when Warren Lincoln hove into sight of his house, he saw a light in the greenhouse. That would mean that Frank, the helper, was working late, as he often did. Frank was a bear for work. He was always hustling loads of earth and barrels of lime from place to place, anything to keep busy.

Lincoln appeared in the greenhouse toward eleven o'clock that night. "Frank," he said, "I might need your help. I'm going to tell my wife and her brother to go packing. I want you to come and stand outside the living-room window and listen to what goes on. If a fight starts and I yell for help, go get the police."

Frank heard Warren Lincoln—a new and masterful Warren Lincoln, born out of a rye bottle—ordering his wife and Shoup out of the house. "And I mean this very night—right now!" He heard Mrs. Lincoln beginning to protest, in that bellowing voice of hers, then he heard Shoup uttering a threat. "Just a moment!" shouted Lincoln. "Just a minute while I read you a love letter I have found and then tell me if either of you can face your neighbors here again." Shoup and his sister lapsed into silence when Lincoln started to read the letter to Mrs. Lincoln from her lover.

In a little while, Lincoln appeared outside. "It's all right, Frank," he said. "Go on with your work or go home or whatever you want to do. They're packing up." Frank returned to the greenhouse and puttered around for another hour. When he left to go home, all the lights in the bungalow were out.

Warren Lincoln, the worm who had turned into a dragon, became the hero of the peephole set. Then there fell a shadow over his happy bachelor establishment. One night, while Lincoln was downtown at the movies, Frank was working alone in the greenhouse when he became conscious of a face peering through one of the panes. He rushed outside and chased a figure fleeing through some fields that stretched behind the greenhouse. He lost the figure in the darkness and went back to his work.

Late the second night following, Lincoln, wearing night clothes, appeared in the greenhouse. "Frank," he said, "I'm scared. I just saw a prowler looking in my bedroom window."

"That's funny, Mr. Lincoln. There was one around here a couple of nights ago. I didn't say nothin' to you because I didn't want to worry you."

The whole black business was clear enough to Lincoln, the man with the legal mind. After his wife's departure, he had found more letters to her from her lover George; the letters had been in a small bundle secreted in a broom closet. Mrs. Lincoln had apparently forgotten them in her haste to pack up and get out. Now she had obviously hired a gumshoe to see what he could do about getting the letters.

Lincoln called on the chief of police of Aurora, one Frank Michels, a casual man of middle age with a stringy mustache and a glazed uniform. He filled Chief Michels in on events leading up to the prowler, then tossed the bundle of love letters on the chief's desk. The letters, neatly typewritten, had all been postmarked Chicago and sent to Mrs. Lincoln care of a box in a Chicago postoffice substation. They bore no return address. Mrs. Lincoln had apparently been meeting George secretly over a period of months.

The chief asked what he could do. Lincoln wanted special protection against the gumshoe. The Aurora police budget couldn't stand the strain of special protection. "You police are all alike," Lincoln said to the chief. "You always wait until it's too late."

Three months passed. Then, one morning late in April, almost two years from the time the Lincolns had moved to Aurora, Frank, the greenhouse helper, had the feeling that things in the bungalow were ominously quiet. As the morning wore on and Lincoln didn't appear, Frank climbed in an open bedroom window. The place was a shambles. Furniture was overturned and there was blood on the bed clothes and on the walls. Frank called the cops.

Chief Michels found three sets of footprints—two of men and one of a woman—leading from under the bedroom window to a roadway a few hundred feet behind the greenhouse. Near the roadway, where the prints ended, presumably because those who had made them got into a car, Chief Michels picked up a calling card.

Milo Durand
Private Detective
Chicago, Illinois

The sizes of the men's shoes that had made the prints were 9 and 11; the woman had worn a woman's size 12. Chief Michels canvassed shoe stores in Aurora and learned the foot sizes of those in the Lincoln household. Warren Lincoln himself had taken a size 7, small for a man. Shoup had worn an 11, and Mrs. Lincoln had taken a 12. The way the chief figured it, the prints had been made by Shoup, Mrs. Lincoln, and the private detective, who had dropped his card during the operation.

The Chicago police went on the prowl for Milo Durand. They couldn't find any such private eye in the city. That was not to say he didn't exist; the Chicago cops have hunted for a lot of people they either couldn't or didn't want to find.

The Midwest was scoured for Warren Lincoln. Not so much as a grease spot was turned up. Then, one lovely morning in June, six weeks after Lincoln had vanished, a neighbor of Lincoln's looked over toward the bungalow and saw a little man working around the grounds. He thought he was looking at a ghost; what he was looking at was Warren Lincoln.

When intelligence of Lincoln's reappearance reached Chief Michels, the chief sauntered over. Lincoln looked like a model for an accident advertisement. He took the chief inside and stripped; he was bruised and welted from head to foot. His wife and Shoup, in company with a third man, presumably private-eye Milo Durand, had come to the house in search of the love letters Mrs. Lincoln had left behind. Not finding them, they had beaten him into unconsciousness and abducted him. When he came to, his eyes were taped. Eventually he found himself in a windowless room. Three hired strong-arm men went to work on him, operating with brass knuckles and buggy whips around the clock in eight-hour shifts. One night, one of the captors got drunk and fell asleep. Lincoln escaped and returned to Aurora.

Chief Michels wanted to know where Lincoln had been held prisoner.

"In Cleveland."

"What address there?"

"I wouldn't know the house. I only know the street. When I got outside, I didn't stop running until I was blocks away." The chief could understand that.

The George letters to Mrs. Lincoln now took on a new significance. Lincoln had long since placed them in a safe-deposit box in a Chicago bank. Chief Michels accompanied Lincoln to the bank for another look at the letters. The chief hoped for some clue to George's identity through which he might get on the trail of Mrs. Lincoln and hence her brother and the private eye. But there was no such clue in the letters. Lincoln put them back in the safe-deposit box.

The lawyer again lost himself in the culture of sweet peas. He began to experiment with some plants in a big flower box on his front porch. He used to sit in a rocker on the porch, smoking a cigaret, his feet up on the edge of the flower box, and pass the time of day with neighbors—a happy, emancipated little man.

"Chief," he said to Michels one evening, nodding toward the box, "did you ever see prettier sweet peas in all your life?"

"Can't say that I have, Mr. Lincoln. You doing something special?"

"New kind of fertilizer."

Chief Michels made no pretensions to being a double dome, but he was a very thoughtful man. He began to brood over the high incidence of carelessness by the principals in the mystery. Mrs. Lincoln had left a single letter from her lover where her husband could come upon it. Then she had left a whole bundle of letters behind when ousted from the bungalow. Then Durand, the gumshoe, had carelessly left his calling card at the scene of a crime.

Chief Michels felt a compulsion to make another trip to Chicago, this time alone. He went to the post-office substation where Mrs. Lincoln had kept a box and examined the application that she had signed. The chief had samples of the woman's penmanship, obtained when she had signed complaints against speakeasies. A comparison convinced him that the signature on the post-office application was false.

Michels was walking out of the substation when he realized that the bank where Warren Lincoln had placed the love letters for safekeeping was less than a block away. The chief went to the bank and asked how long Lincoln had maintained an account there. Lincoln had never had an account at the bank; his only dealings had been the rental of the safe-deposit box.

The chief began to poke around printing establishments in the locality. He found the one that had printed the Milo Durand card dropped the night Lincoln had been kidnaped. The previous December, a month before Mrs. Lincoln and Byron Shoup had left Aurora, a customer had come in and ordered the printing of one card—just one solitary card. He wished to play a joke on somebody, so he would have use for only one card. And so the single card was printed and this was it. The clerk who handled the transaction recalled the practical joker: man about fifty, small and frail of stature.

The chief, cooking with gas now, called at Chicago police headquarters. There he talked with some detectives who had known Warren Lincoln the lawyer. One detective had once spent an uncomfortable half hour on the witness stand during the trial of a murderer Lincoln was derapping. In cross-examining the dick, Lincoln had grown sarcastic; his sarcasm took the form of mimicking the voices of male and female informants of the sleuth. "Why," the dick

told Michels, "that little son of a bitch could imitate *anybody*."

Lincoln was finishing some minor repairs to his bungalow when the chief dropped in on him again. He had just fixed up a sagging end of his front porch. By way of buttressing the porch, he had used a flower box, covered with concrete, as a prop. He was quite pleased with his handiwork; the once-sagging end of the porch was as solid as new. "I was sitting looking at that flower box where I was growing those beautiful sweet peas I showed you," he said to the chief, "and I asked myself what would be wrong with covering it with concrete and using it as a pillar. Pretty clever, eh, for a man who is not supposed to be a mechanic?"

Lincoln was going off on a little vacation. He would be back in a few weeks or a few months. "I'm going to be a regular gypsy," he told Michels. "Go wherever I please and stay as long as I like."

When Lincoln departed, Michels had a talk with Frank, the greenhouse helper. About that night, now some six months past, when Mr. Lincoln had ordered his wife and brother-in-law out of the house: was Frank certain that it had been Mrs. Lincoln and Mr. Shoup he had heard talking with Mr. Lincoln? Oh, very sure. "It couldn't of been nobody else, Chief. It sounded just like them."

"But you didn't actually *see* either of them that night—when you were standing outside the window or, later, when they left?" Frank, of course, had not.

The chief still had the bed clothing that had been stained by blood the night Lincoln was abducted. Stained by chicken blood? Hardly anything so obvious. The stains proved to be human blood, all right.

Michels was talking to himself. Here he was, right on top of the biggest case of his career, yet he couldn't lay hands on it. He fell to thinking about the George letters. He remembered that they had been typed on a typewriter with a faulty capital I. Michels had noticed and remembered that because the personal pronoun had been used so much in the letters. He asked Frank if Lincoln owned a typewriter. "He did," Frank said, "but he sold it."

"Where did he sell it?"

Frank didn't know; Lincoln took it with him one morning when he drove into Aurora and didn't have it when he came back. A pawnshop? Yep. The three-ball emporium had sold the machine only a few weeks previously. Michels ran down the purchaser and examined the machine. It had the same faulty capital I as the machine that had typed the letters to Mrs. Lincoln.

Michels got a crew of workmen and dug up the Lincoln grounds. Nothing doing. There was a huge furnace in the greenhouse.

The way Michels now doped things out, without being able to prove a thing, was this: little Warren Lincoln, living a miserable life at the hands of his wife and his brother-in-law, had set his legal mind to work. The only way really to rid himself of two menaces would be to murder them.

Warren Lincoln conceived a fictitious love affair between his wife and the man called George. He typed out several letters and had them pass through the mails to the post-office box that he had rented in his wife's name. Thus he came into possession of a batch of authentic-looking letters to integrate into the over-all plot.

When, that night in January, he approached Frank and told him to listen in while he ordered his wife and Shoup out of the house, his wife and brother-in-law were already slain. The voices Frank heard were not the voices of Mrs.

Lincoln and big Shoup, but of Lincoln mimicking them. The murderer could have taken his time disposing of the remains, probably in the greenhouse furnace. The remains of ground-up bones would have excited no suspicion where so much fertilizer was used.

It had evidently occurred to Lincoln, even before he committed the murders, that there might be somebody who would suspect that the vanished Mrs. Lincoln and Shoup were no longer among the living. Therefore, Lincoln had staged his own abduction to make it appear that his wife and brother-in-law, enlisting the services of Milo Durand, the nonexistent private eye, were still very much alive. The man whom Frank, the greenhouse helper, had seen peering at him one night had been Lincoln. When his boss had announced two nights later that he had seen a prowler, Frank believed him. Lincoln, methodically working on the mind of Frank, had been conditioning the man for the spurious abduction.

Lincoln had been able to simulate footprints of his wife and Byron Shoup by saving, for that very purpose, the shoes from the feet of the pair after he murdered them. He had obtained a third pair of shoes somewhere to produce the footprints of Durand, the fictitious dick. Lincoln's bruises and welts, exhibited after his return, had been self-inflicted.

Quite obviously, Mrs. Lincoln and Shoup had ended up as fertilizer—perhaps that new fertilizer that had produced such gorgeous sweet peas in the box on the front porch.

Lincoln returned from his vacation in the fall, nine months after his wife and brother-in-law had vanished. The chief let him have it straight. "I think you killed your wife and her brother."

"Why?" asked Lincoln.

"Because they made life miserable for you."

"Let's say you're right," said Lincoln, "just for the sake of argument. How did I do it?"

The chief outlined his theory. Lincoln studied him for a time. "By God, Chief," he said, "you're not as dumb as you look. You're absolutely right. That's *just* how I did it."

"Then I charge you with murder."

The little man's answer was to become memorable in the annals of crime. "Sure I'm guilty," he said, "but go ahead and prove it. You've got to have a corpse to prove murder."

Lincoln was proud of himself, and not, perhaps, without reason. He wanted the chief to know just how clever he had been. So he told him.

After shooting his wife and Shoup with a gun equipped with a silencer, he had beheaded them and then cut up the bodies at his leisure and burned them in the greenhouse furnace. He had retrieved the bullets, then ground the burned human remains into fertilizer.

The heads, kept separate, he had put in the bottom of the flower box he kept on the porch. He had covered them with quicklime, then placed earth, into which he had mixed the human fertilizer, on top of the lime, and had planted sweet peas in the earth. He had watered the sweet peas regularly and the water had acted on the quicklime and the quicklime had acted on the heads, so that there wouldn't be enough of them now to identify even as human heads.

"Then the heads," said the chief, "are in that flower box you covered with cement and used to fix your porch." Lincoln nodded. The chief said he was going to open up the box.

"Go ahead," said Lincoln. "A hell of a lot of good opening the box would do, with the quicklime having had nine months to work."

The chief opened the box anyway. Lincoln was, shall we say, embarrassed.

There were the heads far from disintegrated. They were in an excellent state of preservation. The corpus delicti was proved. Lincoln was sent up for life in Joliet, where he died in 1941.

During his years in prison, Warren Lincoln had ample opportunity to ponder the caprices of fate. His perfect crime had backfired because Frank, the greenhouse helper, always hustling barrels around to keep busy, had transposed a barrel of quicklime and a barrel of slaked lime. Lincoln, instead of covering the heads with quicklime that would disintegrate them, had, with magnificent irony, covered them with a substance that was practically a preservative.

The Case of the Resurrected Girl

Introducing Grant Williams, the man who was known to the New York Police Department as the Skeleton Specialist. All Grant Williams ever asked was a rag, a bone and a hank 'o hair and he could reach into the infinite, there to wrest secrets that sent killers to their doom.

Once, on the Island of Manhattan, there was a man known as the skeleton specialist. His name was Grant Williams, and he was on the cops. Long before, as a kid, Williams had liked to study the reconstructions of prehistoric life in the Museum of Natural History. He had thus come to realize that, everything else being equal, the skeletal structure of an animal predisposed not only the amount of flesh on the frame but the outward contours of the flesh. Going on from there, Williams found that the same intimate relationship between bone and flesh held true with humans, particularly regarding their faces.

Now this discovery was by no means new. Sculptors, doctors and scientific men had known the same thing for generations. Two features of the Williams discovery, however, took it out of the ordinary. Williams came upon it all by himself; nobody pointed it out to him. And he was, after deciding to make police work his lifetime career, to put his discovery to use in the solution of crime.

On April 13 in the year 1922, an Empire State hillbilly was clambering toward the summit of a lofty elevation known as Cheesecock Mountain, located in Rockland County, an hour's travel north of New York City. The hillbilly was looking for trailing arbutus. Instead, he came upon a skeleton in a shallow grave that had been opened by animals or vultures.

The local law-enforcement authorities in the Rockland County of a quarter century ago were tobacco-chewing characters with satchel seats who, left to their own inexperienced devices in crime detection, would probably have kicked the skeleton around until it got lost. This particular collection of bones, however, became important because a man named Richard Enright, who happened to be Police Commissioner of New York City, had social aspirations. The New York Police Department had no jurisdiction whatsoever in rural Rockland County, but the connection was that Commissioner Enright, dressed to kill and his red face shining, frequently visited Tuxedo Park, a renowned citadel of the aristocracy which lay in the shadow of the mountain where the skeleton was found.

The socialites were unnerved, not to say outraged, that anything so common and vulgar as murder had been done in their very midst. Commissioner Enright was quick to look upon the skeleton as a ladder to social acceptance. His department, he announced, would be glad to take over the investigation. The local hawkshaws, who had accomplished nothing save to bring the skeleton down the mountain to a country undertaking parlor, wiped the sweat of futile toil from their weatherbeaten brows, and everybody was happy—except possibly the person who had committed the murder.

That was how the skeleton specialist entered the picture. Grant Williams—he was Captain Williams—had recently retired from the department after reaching the pension age. But when Enright told him about the skeleton he was like an old fire horse getting a whiff of smoke.

Captain Williams, a tall, lean, benevolent-looking man with mild blue eyes, gold-rimmed glasses and gray hair, stood in the undertaking parlor in the valley beneath Cheesecock Mountain, measuring the skeleton.

"Five feet six," he said to a county official.

"He wasn't very tall," said the official.

"It wasn't a he. It was a woman," said Williams. "A woman under thirty."

"How can you tell?"

"From the bone structure and the obvious age of the bones themselves."

"How long you reckon she was up on the mountain before that kid found her?"

"Judging from the bleached condition of the bones, six months at least. Maybe even longer."

"It's funny about her hair. None of it around."

"Not necessarily funny. The scalp probably dried and hardened, then loosened. The winter winds could have blown it away. It's possible that it's still in one piece, somewhere, holding all the hair together, like a wig. It will help a lot if we can find it."

Williams began to manipulate the skeleton at the base of the spine. There was a snapping sound—as of two bones coming together. The victim had had curvature of the spine. That would have cut down her height. Allowing for the spinal curvature, and the fact that the skeletal structure would have been more compact when held together by flesh,

Williams now deduced that the victim had been five feet tall and had weighed about one hundred pounds.

The skull had been fractured in three places—on the left temple, on the left side of the forehead and on the left side of the crown. The size of each fracture indicated the ball of a small hammer. The depth of the fractures indicated that the hammer had been used by a person gripped by fury. Williams further deduced, just from studying the three fractures, that the murderer was left-handed, had been behind his victim when the blows were struck, and that the crime had been committed in the dark.

The angle of each blow indicated that it had been inflicted by a person standing behind the victim and holding a hammer in the left hand. If, reasoned Williams, a maddened killer holding a hammer stood behind a victim in daylight, he or she would never have inflicted widely separated wounds on the side, front and crown of the head, and missed the back of the head entirely. The chances were all in favor of concentrating on the back of the head. These three fractures, then, had been inflicted by someone who struck wildly in the dark. Elementary, Watson.

It was one hell of a climb from the valley to the point up on Cheesecock Mountain where the skeleton had been found. Near the spot Williams discovered a grotto which overlooked the valley below, including Tuxedo Park. There was some evidence in and around the grotto that it had been used, over a long period of time, by moonlight spooners who were just as willing to dispense with the moonlight. The grotto was almost inaccessible, being reached only by passage across a narrow ledge above a sheer drop of a thousand feet, and it had taken on a natural sort of protective coloration which kept it hidden from anyone who didn't know just where to look for it.

Thus, while it was tabbed as a lovers' bower by the looks of things, it was a place that meant obtaining privacy the hard way and not a parking lane such as any villager can point out around the country. There was no beaten path to the grotto and its frequent use did not mean it was popular—few couples really wishing to risk their necks for a spot of necking—giving rise to the theory that a very few men, perhaps only one, with several girl friends willing to risk all, had made it a trysting place.

Letchworth Village, a state institution for the mentally deficient which housed more than a thousand inmates of both sexes, was visible from the mountain grotto. None of the Village inmates was missing. Nor was there any record in Rockland County of any missing girl resident. The only answer seemed that one of the nurses or other female employes of Letchworth Village, among whom there had been a large turnover, may have been the victim. Many of these employes had their homes in distant points, so there would have been no local record of one having dropped from sight.

There was a long pole near the grotto. Fastened to one end of it was a large piece of white cloth. Apparently the pole had been used by the grotto lover for the purpose of sending signals down into the valley. That, Captain Williams decided, would bear looking into.

Williams noticed an arrow, at eye level on the trunk of a tree, pointing straight to the grotto. He backtracked all the way down the mountain, picking out eye-level blaze-marks on tree trunks. They marked a path from the base of the mountain right to the grotto.

Williams had spent vacations in the Maine woods. He knew that the Cheesecock Mountain signs had been slashed into the tree trunks with the swift, practiced hand of a woodsman.

Some people in the valley—in the towns of Garnersville and Thiels, and in Tuxedo Park—had seen a moving white signal from atop Cheesecock the previous summer and fall. They had not known what it meant, and paid it little attention. *Somebody* had paid attention to it, though.

Captain Williams suggested to Commissioner Enright that he assign enough men to question everybody who lived within sight of the signals, on the theory that more than one girl had followed the arrows and that one of them might be able to identify the frequenters of the grotto. Enright was outraged at the suggestion. The residents of Tuxedo Park, he pointed out, had been able to see the signals. It was unthinkable that a lady from Tuxedo Park would have been interested in a man who waved from a mountain when he wanted a woman to come to him.

Williams put the skull of the skeleton in a paper hat box, went to New York and holed up in a workroom on West Fifteenth Street, hard by the Hudson River. He began to perform his magic at seven o'clock the morning of April 15 —two days after the skeleton had been discovered.

First Williams cleaned and sterilized the skull by treating it with a formaldehyde solution. The body of the Cheesecock Mountain murder victim had been buried face down. As a result, a small patch of dried and hardened skin had remained on the chin. This Williams carefully preserved.

The skeleton specialist covered the entire head with a thin coating of sculptors' clay. Then he began to reproduce the nose. The direction and character of the nasal bone, as it comes from the forehead, more often than not determines whether a nose is straight, hooked, concave or convex. This was a concave nose. It had a thick, knobby end. That meant the fleshy part of the girl's nose probably had been prominent and turned up at the end.

Williams applied sculptors' clay accordingly; he knew just how much to use. The bottom of the nose is always on a direct line with the top of the roots of the teeth, and the teeth roots were still in the skull. When he was through making the nose, Williams said to himself, "Irish, maybe."

The lips were easily reproduced. They were determined by the oral bone structure. The lips turned out to be thin, and not very attractive.

The chin was as easy as the brow. It practically shaped itself. Williams noticed now that the girl had been lantern-jawed. He observed also that the jaw was not exactly the same on both sides; he had the impression that the jaw had been dislocated. He could not determine, of course, whether such a dislocation might have taken place during the murder or before.

The cheeks came next. Other things being equal, the amount of flesh on cheeks and the contours of the flesh are determined by a mathematical relationship between the chin, cheekbones and eye sockets. After certain precise measurements, Williams gave the girl fairly prominent, fleshy cheeks.

You can tell about a thing like this in a fraction of the time required to accomplish the task. Williams had been on the job for thirty-six hours, with only a few hours' sleep, by the time he finished the cheeks. He was almost out on his feet, for he was no longer a young man.

The specialist tackled the eyes in the early evening of his second day in the Fifteenth Street room. A specific scientific relationship between the cheekbones and the bony structure of the eye sockets determines whether the eyes are deep-set or bulging. Williams supplied the skull with bulging blue glass eyes. The color was tentative.

The eyebrows followed an easily determined course, beginning at the inside corners of the sockets, then upward and along the edges of the sockets to thinning-out points at their outer ends.

Williams was trying to guess what color the victim's eyebrows had been, and of course he could do no more than guess with what he had, when a cop came down from Rockland County with a positive answer. The cop handed him what at first glance looked like a jet-black wig. What it was, however, was the murder victim's dried and hardened scalp which had come loose from the skull and which, still holding every hair in place, had been found up on Cheesecock Mountain. There were even rusty hairpins still in it.

When Williams fitted the scalp to the skull, the hair fell naturally into a certain type of dress. Now he saw that the hair had probably been held in place by a ribbon running horizontally across the brow, then along the sides to be tied in a knot at the back of the head. He obtained a ribbon and tied it in such a fashion. Next he made eyebrows and eyelashes from the hair of the head.

Commissioner Enright, anxious to tell his friends in Tuxedo Park how his department was progressing, dropped in just as Williams finished putting on the eyelashes and brows. Enright studied the thing that seemed to be coming slowly to life.

"You got blue eyes in that skull," the

Commissioner said. "How do you know they were blue?"

"I put blue in temporarily," said Williams, "but now I'm sticking with that color. I'm sure of it." Williams took a pointer and indicated certain features of the gray face.

"Take a look at that jaw, Commissioner," he said. "It's the kind an Irish girl could have. The nose is definitely Irish. The hair could be typically Irish, too. All that being so, the eyes would almost have to be blue. There aren't very many brown-eyed Irishmen, as I don't have to tell you, Commissioner."

"I see what you mean," said Enright. "What color you going to make her face?"

"Red cheeks, white skin and pimples on her chin."

Enright wanted to know how the skeleton specialist figured *that*. Dark-haired Irish girls, Williams pointed out, frequently had highly colored cheeks in contrast to very white skin. This girl probably had red cheeks anyway, for she had been the athletic type. Any girl who made the arduous climb to the grotto near the summit of Cheesecock Mountain, as this girl presumably had done numerous times, was surely athletic. The pimples were elemental; Williams had detected them on the piece of skin he had taken from the chin.

On the third day of his labors, the skeleton specialist applied coloring, then coated the face with paraffin. This gave it a life-like quality. Enright stopped by again. Williams had his handiwork in a sort of stage setting now, behind a curtain, against a black velvet backdrop, with a spotlight playing on it.

When he drew the curtain aside, Enright said, "My God! You've *resurrected* that girl!"

The thing that Williams had wrought

was photographed. Copies of the photo were passed around Rockland County, and among the staff of Letchworth Village, the mental institution. The likeness of the resurrected girl was recognized instantly. The murder victim had been a waitress in Letchworth Village named Lillian White.

Nobody there knew Lillian White's home address or anything much about her. She had worked at the institution for about six months and quit her job the previous September 15th—seven months before her skeleton was found on Cheesecock Mountain. The first pieces of evidence to corroborate the Williams deductions bobbed to light. A Village staff doctor had treated Lillian White for pains in her back, caused by a combination of hiking and curvature of the spine. The waitress's medical record disclosed that she had been twenty-six years old, five feet in height and had weighed ninety-eight pounds. She had once suffered a dislocated jaw, the result of a skating accident. She was Irish.

There entered the picture at this stage of the proceedings a woman by the name of Mrs. Mary Hamilton. Mrs. Hamilton was the first and, up to that time, the only policewoman in the history of the New York Department. Commissioner Enright put her on the case because it now developed that the investigation was going to touch Tuxedo Park after all, and he didn't want any tough-talking bulls on the prowl among the elite. The reason the Park now came into the investigation orbit was that an ex-waitress at Letchworth Village named Mabel, who had been Lillian White's roommate, had often expressed a desire to better herself. Mabel's idea of bettering herself had been to get a job as a domestic in a Tuxedo Park mansion. Policewoman Hamilton soon came upon Mabel in a canvass of the Park's below-stairs world.

Lillian White, Mabel disclosed, had, the previous summer, been running around with a fellow whom Mabel had never seen and whose name had been John. Lillian had been startled to learn, early the previous August, that she was going to become a mother. She and John had thereupon become engaged "informally." Lillian had quit her job in September, presumably to get John to an altar and become an honest woman. Instead, John had obviously prevailed upon her to climb the mountain again, to be murdered.

When departing from the Village, Lillian White had left behind her a shoe box, bound with pink ribbon. Mabel had kept the box, thinking that Lillian would get in touch with her and ask for it. Now she turned it over to Mrs. Hamilton.

The box contained a bunch of letters addressed to Lillian, from a man who signed himself John. The letters reflected what had undoubtedly been a very earthy relationship. Judging from the spelling and the grammar in them, John had not been too well equipped educationally, but he was quite a lover.

There was a small prayer book among the letters. In a flyleaf was a quotation from Browning having to do with love, but a less physical type of love than that indicated in the "John" letters. The Browning quotation was unaddressed and unsigned. The writing was distinctly feminine.

Mrs. Hamilton was puzzled. She considered the possibility that Lillian White had written the inscription and had been murdered by John before she had a chance to give him the prayer book. Then it occurred to her that the pale kind of love Browning wrote about wouldn't have greatly interested the waitress or her boy friend. That posed the possibility that someone else had written the inscription, which in turn raised the question as to how and why the prayer book had come into Lillian White's possession.

Mrs. Hamilton consulted with handwriting experts. The practitioners of this inexact science circulated in an even wider area of disagreement back in those days than they do today. Even so, three of them were in complete agreement on two points. One, the Browning inscription had been written by a young woman other than Lillian White. Two, the "John" letters had *not* been written by a left-handed man.

In one way these findings suggested the scenario behind the crime, but in another way they ran counter to the Williams' theory of a left-handed killer. The crime picture that Mrs. Hamilton saw was this: John had never intended to get seriously involved with Lillian White. When she found she was pregnant she pressed him to marry her. Meantime, another girl had engaged John's romantic interest. This was the girl who had written the Browning inscription. Lillian White had somehow come into possession of the prayer book. That had precipitated a quarrel and perhaps the waitress had threatened John with exposure. He had pretended to patch things up, then lured her up to the mountain grotto to consummate the reconciliation, and there murdered her.

Mabel had once heard Lillian White say that she had a sister who lived over a restaurant on Bergen Street in Brooklyn. The cops covered flats over restaurants on Bergen Street like a blizzard and quickly came up with the sister.

The sister was taken to the room on West Fifteenth Street. She took one look at the thing with the spotlight playing on it, screamed and fainted. The skeleton specialist had not realized when he was resurrecting the girl how accurately he was doing his job. The blue eyes and the hair-do were correct, and so were the highly colored cheeks and very white skin. For years afterward, the New York Police Department kept a picture of a full-face view of Lillian White herself, and a similar view of the Williams work. At first glance it was practically impossible to tell which was which.

Lillian White had once told her sister that one of the Letchworth Village male attendants was sweet on her. That had been all. The girl had not mentioned the attendant's name.

There were more than fifty male attendants at the Village. They were, on the whole, an occupational hazard to the nurses and waitresses. Their attitude was that a job as hard and dirty as an attendant's should have compensation of pleasure over and above fifty bucks a month and keep.

Several of the attendants bore the name of John. All were amorously inclined. All were bad spellers. None was left-handed, and none was a woodsman.

Williams, his work done, and well, faded back into retirement. Mrs. Hamilton learned of a former attendant named Jim Crawford. He interested her for two reasons. He had quit his job at Letchworth Village the day Lillian White had quit hers. He had been a native of Maine, and an expert woodsman. That sounded good. But his name was Jim, not John. He had been that *rara avis* among attendants—a university graduate, hardly the type to spell with a "k" instead of a "c." Moreover, Jim Crawford had been right-handed. Still, Mrs. Hamilton was a smart cop. She knew that seemingly irreconcilable facts can often be reconciled.

An old friend of Williams, she called on the skeleton specialist. She had a theory about the murderer, and she told him what it was. "So you see," concluded the policewoman, "when you say that John the killer was left-handed, and the handwriting experts say that John the killer was right-handed, you could both be right."

Mrs. Hamilton returned to the Village. She questioned nurses and waitresses on just one point: Did they know any girl who had worked in the Village the previous summer who had been very fond of poetry, especially the poetry of Robert Browning? That kind of question could very well have drawn a blank. A cop figures on ninety-five blanks out of a hundred questions; it's the five that pay off that count.

The figure of a former Village nurse named Ruby Miller emerged. Ruby Miller had been a poetry addict. She had walked starry-eyed through the corridors, saying, "God's in His Heaven and all's right with the world." The other nurses had got sick of it. But they had one thing to say for Ruby: she had been a looker.

Ruby had left the previous September to get married. She had been secretive about who the man was. Nobody at the Village had heard from her since.

Mrs. Hamilton dug into the marriage records. She found that Ruby Miller had married a James Crawford in Nyack, New York, September 17th—two days after the presumed time of Lillian White's murder. So Ruby, the pretty nurse, had married an attendant? That accounted for her secrecy about her husband's identity. There is a caste system in hospitals, too. A sample of Ruby Miller's handwriting, on the application for a marriage license, bore the same characteristics as that on the flyleaf of the prayer book found in Lillian White's effects. Mrs. Hamilton was getting hot.

The minister who had married Ruby Miller and James Crawford clearly recalled Crawford. "He was worried about his hand," the minister told the woman cop. "It was an infected hand."

"Which hand?"

"The right one."

That tied everything up in a neat but grim package. Crawford's right hand had been infected when he had killed Lillian White. Thus, he had been temporarily left-handed at the time of the murder. Crawford's middle name was John, and that's what he had told Lillian White to call him. It was part of a cover-up. The misspelled letters, bordering on the illiterate, had been part of a cover-up, too. But Crawford hadn't been able to completely disguise his handwriting. Enough of his own characteristics had escaped into the simulated penmanship of the "John" letters to damn him.

Crawford had flown the coop very successfully. Months went by and there was no trace of him. Captain Williams, talking to himself because his resurrection girl appeared to count for nothing, came out of retirement a second time. He went to Maine, Crawford's home state, and hunted doggedly until an old license application in the Maine Motor Vehicle Department put him on the trail.

Williams headed for the little town of Biddeford, near Old Orchard. Crawford and the former Ruby Miller were living in a rooming house there. Crawford had that sixth sense that animals have when they are being hunted. He deserted his bride, who of course knew nothing about the murder, just as Williams was getting in. Williams returned to New York with some fingerprints taken from articles Crawford had handled.

Three years went by. In Lake Maranocook, Maine, a girl named Aida Hayward got herself in trouble with a young wolf named Harry Kirby. Then she got herself shot dead by the same Kirby. Kirby got away, but he left some fingerprints behind. When they reached New York, they matched with the prints that Williams had obtained three years previously.

They caught up with Kirby, or Crawford, this time. The resurrected girl had paid off after all. While in jail in Winthrop, Maine, facing two murder raps, the killer confessed to the skeleton specialist's Holmesian deductions about using a hammer on Lillian White, while behind her, while furious, with his left hand, and in the dark. He committed suicide in jail.

"All I have to say," said the skeleton specialist, when he heard about the suicide, "is that he killed the right man."

Oregon's Riddle of the Bodies That Weren't There

What, exactly, is a corpus delicti? When you have read this fascinating account of an infamous Oregon murder case you may find yourself in for a surprise.

As the proprietor of the Fashion Livery Stables in the town of Hood River, Oregon, Bert Stranahan, a knowing man of Hibernian antecedents, thought, in the year of 1904, that he had seen just about everything. What went on immediately behind Stranahan's back as he drove friends, acquaintances and total strangers around the Hood River Valley, especially after the fall of dark, eventually turned the man into one of those people who go around telling other people they could write a book. Stranahan became so inured to transporting male fares in varying degrees of intoxication and female ones on graduating registers of moral delinquency that it would have taken at least the birth of triplets in the back seat to disturb his aplomb.

When, then, one unseasonably warm day in February, 1904, a stranger who had arrived in town on the morning train from Portland walked into the Fashion Livery Stables and announced that he had come to prospect for gold in a region long noted not for minerals but for fruit, Stranahan took the stranger in stride. The newcomer—a chap of about thirty with yellow shoes, an open, shining face, and a straw suitcase—announced, as if he had to, that he was fresh from the tall-corn country in Iowa. His name, he said, was Jackson. He knew exactly where he wanted to begin prospecting; in the open homestead country some twenty miles northwest of Hood River. Stranahan pointed out that the trip would cost quite a lot of money. Money, said Jackson, was no object. He borrowed a spade from Stranahan and the two were off.

Stranahan inquired of Jackson if he would mind answering a question. No, Jackson wouldn't mind. "What gives you the idea there is gold out here?"

That, said Jackson, was a funny thing. "Back in Iowa I would wake up in the night and something would tell me to come out here and dig, dig, dig." Stranahan fell into silence for the balance of the trip; the only wheels in close proximity to him weren't, he decided, all on his rig.

Early in the afternoon, as the travelers approached a hamlet called Parkdale, in the shadow of Mount Hood, Jackson asked Stranahan if he had ever heard of a woman named Mrs. Louisa Nesbitt, or of her daughter, Alma. Sure, Stranahan had heard of the Nesbitts. Alma Nesbitt, an attractive black-haired girl of about twenty-five, had come from the East some five years previously and staked out a claim for some homestead land. Her mother, a silver-haired widow, had, not long afterward, come out to join the daughter. The pair had worked the land for a while, then left for parts unknown.

"Were they nice people, the Nesbitts?" asked Jackson.

111

"The old lady was a fine woman," answered the liveryman, "but I did hear the girl run around some. She was supposed to marry a man named Norman Williams but she run out on him."

What, Jackson wanted to know, did Stranahan know about Norman Williams?

"He was a homesteader, too. Had the next ranch to Mrs. Nesbitt and her daughter."

"What happened to him?"

"Norman Williams had a broken heart when the girl didn't marry him. He left and went away somewheres around the time the Nesbitts left—either right after they left or right before." Williams had been a mild big man of perhaps fifty-five, with silver hair and a lined, benevolent face, who could, had he worn a clerical collar, easily have been mistaken for an Episcopalian bishop. "This is his place we're comin' to," Stranahan told his fare. "Nobody lives there now."

The Williams acres yawned with desolation. The lean-to that Williams had called a homestead seemed to be disproving the laws of gravity by the mere act of standing. Behind it was a barn, a henhouse and a comfort station. Jackson's eyes were wide and his breath was coming to him in short excited spurts as he jumped from Stranahan's rig and surveyed the property. Then he grabbed a spade and ran toward the barn.

Stranahan, remaining in the rig, crossed his legs, lit his pipe and began talking to himself about the vagaries of human nature. In a little while curiosity drove him into the barn. Jackson was furiously digging into the dirt flooring—here, there, and all over the place. He would dig for a few minutes, then look up, spot another place, and begin digging there. "Let's go into the hen-house," he said to Stranahan. "Maybe I'll find something there."

In the henhouse, Jackson, who could make a spade do everything but talk, was down more than three feet in no time at all. "It's getting dark," said Stranahan. "What do you intend to do—stay here all night?"

"Why not?" said Jackson. "I know I'll find something here in the morning."

"It won't be gold, Jackson," said Stranahan.

"Maybe I ain't huntin' for gold—and maybe my name ain't Jackson."

Next day, Jackson popped out of the henhouse holding a large piece of gunnysack. He had, he told Stranahan, come upon the gunnysack six feet down. "Somebody's been buried where I been diggin'," he said to Stranahan. "Look! Look at the dark splotches on this gunnysack. And look at them hairs." A dozen or more hairs, some silver, some black, were stuck to the splotches in the cloth.

Jackson left Hood River as mysteriously as he had come, carrying his piece of gunnysack with him. Next stop: the office of District Attorney Frank Menefee of Wasco County in The Dalles, not far east of Hood River. There the young man whom Stranahan knew as Jackson presented himself as George R. Nesbitt. He informed Deputy District Attorney Fred Wilson, an up-and-coming local lawyer, that Louisa Nesbitt was his mother and Alma Nesbitt his sister. "They both disappeared four years ago," the visitor told the deputy district attorney. "Here! Here's proof they were murdered."

Wilson examined the gunnysack. The splotches on it may or may not have been human blood. The hairs may or may not have been human hairs; they may have come from foxes, horses or dogs, which abounded in the region; and so might the blood.

"What," asked Wilson, "about bones or other remains? You can't prove a murder with a piece of gunnysack and some dried blood and a few hairs."

"He probably *burned* the bones and the flesh and their clothes," said Nesbitt.

"*He?* Who do you mean by *he?*"

"Williams. Norman Williams."

The stranger was going too fast for the deputy district attorney. Wilson applied the brakes and asked for a fill-in on the backgrounds and relationships of Louisa Nesbitt, Alma Nesbitt, and Norman Williams.

Norman Williams and the Nesbitt family were neighboring farmers back in Shelby County, Iowa. Williams, an aging bachelor, was a regular old tomcat; he was constantly off on the prowl. The more attractive housewives of the region barred their doors when they saw him coming, or at least *said* they did. The young bucks of the region, who got an occasional look at Williams in the old swimmin' hole, gazed upon the older man in awe, admiration and envy. They could well foresee what would happen to *them* in open competition with Williams.

Norman Williams had first cast his connoisseur's eye on pretty Alma Nesbitt when she was only fifteen; he was exactly thirty years the girl's senior, making him forty-five at the time. When Alma was twenty and Williams was fifty, and still going strong, he began a campaign for the girl. Since she was a highly moral young lady, Williams was not able to show his best side. Finally he abandoned the project and left for Oregon. That was in 1897—seven years before George Nesbitt showed up in Hood

River and borrowed a spade from the liveryman.

In the Hood River Valley, Williams filed a homesteader's claim, took possession of one hundred wild acres, and set about taming them. He began to write to Alma Nesbitt, and to her mother, telling them how well he was making out, what a wonderfully romantic country Oregon was, and suggesting that they, too, come out and be homesteaders. Alma, who had come to look upon Williams in a different light, now that he had gone, decided in the spring of 1899, when she was twenty-five, to strike out for the pioneer country.

Alma began to write back to her mother saying that she had filed for and been granted one hundred sixty acres right next to Norman Williams' place. The mother, who knew of Williams' reputation, began to get concerned over the possibility of her daughter suffering, as it was called in those days, a fate worse than death. So she, too, struck out on the Oregon trail.

After Mrs. Nesbitt arrived in Oregon she wrote periodically to her son George back in Iowa. Life was rugged, but interesting. Norman Williams, the old tomcat, wasn't such a bad character, after all. It had been through Williams, Mrs. Nesbitt disclosed, that Alma had obtained the rights to particularly choice land. Norm, as the mother was now calling Williams, was neglecting his own property to help Alma get hers cleared. He was paying for the hire of men to grub the trees and throw up a shack for Alma and her mother. Mrs. Nesbitt seemed to be cupping hand to ear, listening for a future that was to bring wedding bells.

As time passed, and as the year of 1900 dawned, there was less and less mention of Norm in Mrs. Nesbitt's letters home. Finally, Norm, so far as the woman was concerned, dropped through a hole into space. Then Mrs. Nesbitt and her daughter did likewise. The mother wrote to the son, on March 8, 1900, some ten months after her daughter had originally gone West, saying that she and Alma were coming home. They could be expected back in Iowa, she said, within a month. The letter had been sent from a rooming house in Portland, some fifty miles west of Hood River.

"That," said George Nesbitt to Deputy District Attorney Wilson as he completed his fill-in for Wilson in The Dalles four years later, "is the last I ever heard from Mama or Sister."

Nesbitt said he had written to Williams after his kin had dropped from sight. Williams replied that Alma had gone off and married a younger man whom she had met in a Portland rooming house. He appended the shocking intelligence that Alma had turned into a dissolute woman.

Young Nesbitt couldn't supply a motive for the murders he said had taken place—except that maybe Williams had decided to see Alma Nesbitt dead rather than married to somebody else, and had been forced to commit a second murder, that of the mother, to cover up the first.

Why, Wilson wanted to know, had it taken four years for Nesbitt to come West to investigate the disappearance of his mother and sister? The farmer said he had spent the time in correspondence with police departments, sheriffs, postmasters, hotels and boarding-houses throughout the Pacific Northwest. "And besides, I always thought Mama and Sister would turn up. Then I started having this strong feeling to come out here and dig, dig, dig."

"Why did you pick Williams' place—

and the particular spot where you found this gunnysack?"

The Williams acres had seemed a natural place to dig, in view of Nesbitt's suspicions; the spot in the henhouse where Nesbitt had started digging had, he said, appeared comparatively soft, as if the earth had been turned over before. "He built a fire on that spot, Williams did," the farmer added. "There's black ashes mixed with the dirt."

The sheriff of Wasco County, a painstaking official named F. C. Sexton, put the ground under the henhouse, and other parts of the Norman Williams homestead, through a sieve, hunting for bones, teeth, buttons—anything, in fact, that might lend some support to the stranger's tale. He found nothing. Then he set out for the rooming house in Portland where Louisa and Alma Nesbitt had last been heard from.

Mrs. Nesbitt and her daughter had lived at the Portland rooming house off and on during the winter of 1900—four years before. They had occasionally gone up to the Hood River Valley to spend a night or two on the girl's land, time put in on homestead property being a requisite to holding it. They had checked out of the rooming house, for good, March 8, 1900—the date on which George Nesbitt had last heard from them. The proprietor, an observant man named Winters, recalled that the Nesbitts had had a visitor, a man about forty. There had been some unfriendly words between the man and the Nesbitts about love and property and duplicity, but Winters, separated from the quarrelers by a door, hadn't been able to determine who was accusing whom.

The investigators pointed out to George Nesbitt that the man who had been seen with his mother and sister had been described as at least fifteen years younger than Norman Williams. Nesbitt had an answer for that. "I don't know why," he said, "but Norman Williams don't look his age. Everybody will tell you he don't look his age."

Norman Williams had once been employed in a sawmill back in Iowa. Sheriff Sexton sent handmade fliers to sawmills throughout Oregon and Washington. One mill in Bellingham, Washington, three hundred miles away, was employing a Norman Williams—a man about sixty, formerly a homesteader in the Hood River Valley, before that a native of Shelby County, Iowa. The district attorney's office was assailed by doubts. If a man had fled after committing two murders was it likely he would go under his own name and make no attempt to cover his tracks?

When Norman Williams was brought to The Dalles for questioning he turned out to be a man who looked every one of his sixty years, and maybe a few more. George Nesbitt, who had insisted Williams did not look his years, explained it all away. He said the man had probably aged because he had murder on his conscience. Williams was a mild, righteous-looking character of soft voice and gentle mien. He might have been, as Bert Stranahan, the liveryman, had said, taken for a preacher. He behaved like a preacher, too. He bore no malice toward anyone; his heart overflowed with understanding and forgiveness. When young George Nesbitt, young enough to be Williams' son, bluntly accused him of having murdered his mother and sister, Williams seemed to fill up with sorrow rather than anger. "George," he said, "if Alma would come back to me I would be the happiest man in the world to have her for my wife."

Williams examined the gunnysack, with its splotches and its gray and black hairs. A piece of gunnysack was a piece of gunnysack. Williams allowed as how the splotches could be blood—the blood of a mare that had foaled a colt. The hairs? Gray horses and black horses and dogs of all colors had roamed the ranch.

But how, District Attorney Menefee and Sheriff Sexton wanted to know, would a piece of gunnysack wind up as deep as six feet underneath the henhouse unless it had been hidden there? Williams had a simple explanation. The henhouse was built over a spot originally occupied by a two-seater chicsale. Before building the henhouse Williams had thrown trash down the chicsale; when he built the henhouse he filled in the excavation below the chicsale with the remains of a trash fire and other debris.

Williams studied his accuser and those who were questioning him. He had answered quite a few questions; now it was his turn to ask one. Were the gentlemen sure that the gunnysack had been found on his property? There had been only one witness to the excavation operations of George Nesbitt on the Williams acres —Stranahan, the liveryman—and he had not actually seen Nesbitt find the gunnysack. Was it possible that George Nesbitt, for obscure reasons known only to himself, had planted the so-called evidence?

Nesbitt didn't miss the significance of the query. "He's just trying to wiggle out of it!" he said. "Ask him when he last seen Mama and Sister."

Williams had last seen the Nesbitts after Alma, on a two-day visit from Portland to her property to put some time in on it, had come over to his ranch. She said she was going to marry another man, and asked him if he would drive her and her mother to the railroad station in Hood River where they could get a train back to Portland. Williams had pleaded with Alma to reconsider. "The man was younger than me," he said. "I was too old for her. That's what she said."

"Who was the man, did she say?" Williams didn't know.

"And you drove them to the railroad station?"

"Yes. I hired a rig at the Fashion Livery Stables to take them into Hood River."

"When was that, do you remember?"

"Along in March, four years ago."

Bert Stranahan, the man who could have written a book, hadn't owned the Fashion Livery Stables four years previously but a dispatch book in the stables antedated Stranahan. The dispatch book was thoroughly detailed. Norman Williams had taken a rig out at eight o'clock on the night of March 8, 1900—the date the Nesbitts had last written home to Iowa—and returned it at nine o'clock on the morning of March 9. Williams said he had driven the Nesbitts from Alma's ranch into Hood River on the morning of March 9 in time for the nine o'clock train for Portland. What happened to them after that Norman Williams had no way of knowing.

Fred Wilson, the young deputy district attorney, became caught up in the improbable atmosphere of the case when, for no reason he could explain, he became suddenly imbued with the suspicion that Norman Williams had married Alma Nesbitt. And, certainly enough, marriage records in Vancouver, Washington, just across the Columbia River from Portland, disclosed that Williams and Alma Nesbitt had been married in July of 1899—two months after Alma Nesbitt had gone West from Iowa. "That's funny," said George Nesbitt. "You would think Alma or Mama would

of mentioned a thing like that. I can't understand it."

Neither could the district attorney. Then, in keeping with the strange turns the case was taking, somebody in the D.A.'s office had a rather strange thought. "I wonder," asked this somebody, "if Williams was married to somebody else *before* he was married to this Alma Nesbitt."

Norman Williams had indeed been married to somebody else. He had taken a wife, in the town of Dufar, Oregon, only a year previous to his marriage to Alma Nesbitt. Located, the lady was asked where she and Williams had been divorced. "We ain't never been divorced," she said. She had just one wish for Normie, as she called him—that he get his neck caught between her hands.

Norman Williams, then, was not only a liar; he was a bigamist. Was he also a murderer?

Reaching back into time, there to grasp evidence, is frustrating business at best. People die, memories of the living dim, and the inexorable law of change gets in its work on physical things. But a little group of intelligent investigators found themselves in luck when they set out to see what they could lay hands on to support a rapidly deepening suspicion against Norman Williams. They found memories sharp; they found that people had noticed many small and seemingly unrelated things that were now to be woven into a large and meaningful pattern.

The first fact of significance to be developed dissipated Norman Williams' explanation of how a piece of blood-stained, hair-matted gunnysack could normally have found its way six feet underground. Neighboring ranchers and hands who had once worked on the Williams property said there had never been a privy on the spot where the henhouse now stood. The henhouse had been built *after* the Nesbitts had vanished—and on a spot where nothing had stood before.

The probers next developed what came to be known as the oat story and the fire story. Four springs previously, just after the Nesbitts had vanished, a neighboring rancher dropped in to pass the time of day with Norman Williams. Several big gunnysacks of oats were piled on top of one another in the spot where Williams later threw up the henhouse. While Williams and the rancher talked, a violent rainstorm blew out of the Cascades.

"Hey!" said the rancher, looking at the gunnysacks, "you better get them oats into the barn yonder outa this here rain."

"Oh," said Williams, "to hell with the oats!" Homesteaders just didn't say to hell with oats back in the days before the United States government paid farmers to plow pigs under.

A laborer named Reese, a man very capable with profanity, cut down some trees and pulled up some stumps for Williams. "Pile all the stuff right there on top of the oats," Williams instructed Reese.

" 'Twas the goddamdest pile of stuff you ever did see in your goddam born days," Reese now told Sheriff Sexton. "It made the goddamdest fire these goddam old eyes ever did look at."

"He burned the trees and the stumps and the oats?"

"You're goddam right he did."

The one hundred sixty acres that Alma Nesbitt had homesteaded were better property than Williams' acres. The sheriff recalled that Winters, proprietor of the Portland rooming house, had overheard loud words about property

between the Nesbitts and the man who had called on them before they disappeared. That man, it was now believed, had been Norman Williams. The rooming house proprietor, in stating that the Nesbitts' visitor had been about forty, whereas Williams had been fifty-five at the time, had been in error.

Homestead records on file with the United States Attorney in Portland disclosed that Norman Williams had appeared there, shortly after Alma Nesbitt had left the Oregon scene, with a document bearing the signature of Miss Nesbitt and relinquishing her one hundred sixty homestead acres in his favor. The document had been accepted at the time and the property turned over to Williams. Then a conscientious clerk in the United States Attorney's office fell to speculating on the transaction. How could he be sure that Alma Nesbitt had signed the paper that Williams had brought in? He wrote to Washington and obtained the original claim that the Iowa girl had filed. Her signature didn't look anything like the one on the paper that Williams had brought in.

The United States Attorney sent a deputy over to the Hood River Valley to pick up Williams for forgery. Williams had seen the deputy first and fled. He was, at the moment that the probers from the Hood River Valley came upon the intelligence, wanted by the government for forgery.

By this time the law was placing a new and sinister accent on the splotched gunnysack with the hairs on it. As luck would have it, there dwelled in Portland at the time a very remarkable young woman—remarkable because she was a ravishing brunette beauty and because she had brains enough to be a professional chemist. Her name was Victoria Hampton—*Doctor* Hampton, if one pleased. District Attorney Menefee tossed the gunnysack in her lap. "Suppose," he said, "you tell us if that's human blood on there and if those hairs are from a person's head or from an animal."

Although laboratories today take in their stride such questions as whether a bloodstain is of human or animal origin, science was only beginning to resolve such problems back in 1904. Doctor Hampton had put practically everything she had into laboratory equipment that would determine the basic differences between human and animal blood.

There was no question about the origin of the blood on the gunnysack. It was human. Not only that, but the hairs found on the gunnysack were, like the blood, of human origin. Moreover, they had been pulled from the heads of persons still alive. The microscope revealed that roots were still clinging to the hairs. Roots clung to hairs only when hairs were pulled from a living head; after death the hairs come away without roots.

The probers determined to learn more about the movements of Williams and the Nesbitts between the time Williams had hired the rig from the Fashion Livery Stables that March night four years previously, and the time he had returned it the following morning. A man named Langille had operated the stables at the time. He was a man of kind heart and long memory—two factors, plus a series of small coincidences, that were to prove of prime import.

The night Williams hired the rig had been dark and stormy. Langille was just reporting on duty when Williams drove out of the stables. Right after Williams left, it occurred to Langille that the man might have use for a lantern on a night such as this. He lit a lantern, left his stables, and went through the town looking for Williams. He found his rig in front of a rooming house on the main street. Williams was taking on two passengers—both women. Langille got a look at the women in the rays of his lantern; not a good look but a look nonetheless. One was elderly, with silver hair; the other young, dark-haired and pretty.

Langille tarried on the street, in front of the rooming house, and watched Williams and his two passengers drive off into the darkness. There weren't many roads leading out of Hood River in those days; if a traveler took a certain road, he had committed himself to a certain destination. There was only one road leading to the Parkdale region, where the Williams and Nesbitt homesteads were located. Williams took it. Langille stood watching the rig, with the lighted lantern he had lent Williams, until it was out of sight.

Normally, when Langille worked at his stables at night he didn't report on until afternoon of the following day. The morning after Williams had rented the rig, however, one of Langille's workers reported sick, so Langille was at the stables bright and early. From the stables he could see the Parkdale road. Along toward nine o'clock he saw, in the distance, Norman Williams and the rented rig—coming from Parkdale. Williams was alone. He returned the rig, paid for its hire, and went on about his business —whatever, precisely, his business was that morning.

Langille's story riddled Williams' account of the movements of Louisa Nesbitt and his bigamous wife just before they dropped from sight. There was little doubt that the two women Langille saw getting into the rig with Williams that night four years previously had been the Nesbitts. Williams had hired the rig the night of the day Mrs. Nesbitt had mailed, from Portland, the last letter her son ever received from her. Thus the inference was that the Nesbitts had arrived in Hood River from Portland, on an early evening train, contradicting Williams' story that the two women had been at the younger one's homestead for two days.

When last seen, the Nesbitts had been headed toward the Williams property at night—not for Portland, on a train, next day. In point of cold fact, there had been no nine o'clock train out of Hood River for Portland the morning Williams returned the rig to the Fashion Livery Stables, as Williams claimed there had been. Railroad records disclosed that the only train that had gone from Hood River to Portland that particular morning had left Hood River shortly after five o'clock—almost four hours before Williams had arrived back in town, alone, on the Parkdale road.

District Attorney Menefee and Deputy Wilson got their heads together. There was no doubt, they concluded, that Norman Williams had murdered the two women. The motive could have been a combination of factors. Perhaps Alma Nesbitt had discovered Williams had another wife and threatened him with exposure. No doubt he coveted her land. After luring the women back from Portland, perhaps under the pretext of settling a disagreement that had arisen over the younger woman's land, Williams had driven the two out to the lonely reaches of his homestead and murdered them in the night. He had thereupon dug a hole in the earth behind his lean-to and covered the bodies with the sacks of oats as a temporary measure. Subsequently he had built a funeral pyre that had destroyed the remains—all but the piece of gunnysack that had somehow escaped the flames.

Then he had buried everything in a six-foot hole. When George Nesbitt came along four years later and found the gunnysack, Williams invented the story about the henhouse having been built on the site of a privy. The story about Alma Nesbitt having become enamored of a younger man had been pure invention on Williams' part; so had the rumor that the girl had turned into a doxie.

Menefee and Wilson decided they had a pretty good circumstantial case against Williams. All they needed was a corpus delicti. Repeated searches of the Williams property failed to turn up so much as a filling from a tooth. The man had built a very hot fire. Now Menefee and Wilson began to look in a new light at the gunnysack with the blood that the woman scientist said was human and the hairs that she said had come from living heads. What, they asked each other, was a corpus delicti, anyway? Nothing, more or less, than physical proof of death. Who had ever legally determined the extent of such proof? What was wrong, then, with the bloodstained, hair-matted gunnysack as proof of death? What indeed! What, in combination with the circumstantial evidence, could a couple of skeletons prove that couldn't as well be proved with the bloodstained, hair-matted gunnysack?

Since Williams had married Alma Nesbitt, and since he had forged her name to a document that gave him possession of her homestead property, the law decided to charge Williams with the murder of the younger woman. It would use the disappearance of the older woman, and the silver hairs on the gunnysack, as supporting evidence.

The nature of the state's case snared for the defense Oregon's greatest devil's advocate—Henry McGinn, a rotund,

moon-faced Irishman who knew a loop-
hole when he saw one. When the evidence against Williams, topped by the
scientific testimony of pretty Doctor
Hampton, was in, McGinn refused to
put a single witness on the stand. Why,
he demanded in a flood of purple oratory, should he? The state of Oregon
was accusing a man of a murder that had
not been committed. How, in view of
mere circumstantial evidence, and a
piece of gunnysack, could twelve good
men and true send a man to the gallows?

The jury was quite impressed by Mc-
Ginn's oratory. But it had been more impressed by Doctor Hampton. It took the
jurors just four hours to decide that
Norman Williams should go to the gallows. He did, with this now legally renowned blessing of the Oregon Supreme
Court:

> The strict rule contended for by defend-
> ant would operate completely to shield a
> criminal from punishment for the most
> atrocious crime, and afford him absolute

immunity if he were cunning enough to
consume or destroy the body or completely
hide it away or otherwise destroy its identity. But the death of the person alleged
to have been killed is a distinct ingredient
in the case of the prosecution for murder
and must be established by direct testimony or presumptive evidence of the most
cogent and irresistible kind. Where, as
here, the circumstances point with one accord to the death of the person alleged to
have been murdered, the finding of frag-
ments of a human body, which are identified as part of the body of the alleged
victim, will be sufficient, if believed by the
jury, to establish the fact of death, when
this is the best evidence that can be obtained under the circumstances. . . . No
universal rule can be laid down in regard
to the proof of the corpus delicti. The
body of the crime may be proved by the
best evidence that is capable of being ad-
duced, if it is sufficient for the purpose.
There was sufficient evidence, without
commenting on it, in the case at bar, in
our opinion, to establish the death of the
alleged victim within the rules of the law
referred to.

Who Killed Sir Harry Oakes?

Here's the fascinating account of the murder that set the glamorous international set on its ear—the story for which the author has been banned from the Bahamas.

Sometime between the dark and the daylight, known in the Bahama Islands as the carnal hours, a murder was committed in Nassau, the Bahama capital, in the second week of June 1943—a murder that has taken its place as one of the most baffling mysteries in the annals of crime. Not since the kidnapping of the Lindbergh baby has there been a crime that, for its strange and bewildering aspects, compares with the murder of Sir Harry Oakes.

Although the Oakes case is officially dormant, many reputable law-enforcement authorities who have studied the evidence, including Homer S. Cummings, former Attorney General of the United States, think it still wide open and that the mastermind may be walking the streets of Nassau today, if he hasn't faded into the fastness of some secluded and half-civilized Bahama island. Just as the investigation of the Lindbergh kidnapping was bungled by the New Jersey State Police, then an organization chiefly concerned with traffic regulations, so was the Oakes case messed up by a police department that didn't even possess modern fingerprint equipment.

There are several theories as to who murdered Sir Harry Oakes, and there is a motive to fit each theory. But the only theory that is openly discussed in Nassau, even at this late date, is the one that was officially embraced. All other theories are discussed guardedly, if at all. It is not healthy in Nassau to talk too freely

about some of the less well publicized aspects of the mystery of Sir Harry Oakes' death. A man was officially accused of the crime and tried for it. The case against him turned out to be as full of holes as a screen door, but as far as the local authorities seem to be concerned, the case ended there anyway. If he didn't do it, apparently nobody did.

The Bahama crime, like the one in New Jersey, was populated with a distinguished and colorful cast of characters. Sir Harry Oakes himself, who was the star of the cast that set Nassau on its ear and enchanted newspaper readers throughout the world, was a belligerent, barrel-chested man of sixty-eight who had more enemies per square foot of Bahama real estate than any other man in the islands. The fact that Sir Harry had attained his sixty-eighth birthday without being knocked off was as much of a mystery as the murder itself. He had, all his life, been asking for it.

Oakes was a notable character not only in the Bahamas, but in the United States, England, and South America too —an authentic international celebrity. He was one of the richest men in the world, the best estimate of his fortune being in the neighborhood of two hundred million dollars. He circulated only in the more rarefied precincts of the social world and participated in taffy pulls with such ultra-ultra figures as the Duke and Duchess of Windsor, who were particularly close friends. His death by malice aforethought thus became a world-wide

123

sensation even in the midst of a global war.

The prominence of the victim was but one of two factors that made the Oakes murder a world wonder. A peculiar weapon, even today only guessed at, was used by the slayer. And after death, Sir Harry's body was blow-torched and sprinkled with feathers. All of which added up to a combination of factors that remains unique, so far as the records reveal, in the history of modern crime.

The murder was committed in Sir Harry's twenty-bedroom estate, Westbourne, a fabulous place once owned by Maxine Elliott, the celebrated American actress. The property faced the sea in the western part of Nassau. On the night the crime was committed, there were no servants in the main house. The only other person on the premises was one of Sir Harry's closest friends, Harold Christie, a governing official of Nassau and one of the island's wealthiest and best-known citizens. Christie, who had spent the night with Sir Harry to wrap up some business transactions in which they were jointly associated, discovered the body about seven o'clock in the morning. He put through telephone calls to the police and Dr. Hugh Arnley Quackenbush, a prominent Nassau physician. The Doctor arrived at Westbourne about seven-thirty.

Sir Harry lay on a bed in a second-floor chamber, face up. There were four wounds behind his left ear—triangular in shape and about half an inch wide at the greatest dimension. It was apparent to Dr. Quackenbush that the wounds had been made by the end of an instrument of some kind. Whoever had handled the instrument, whatever it had been, had probably been a person of unusual strength. Each wound was more than a quarter of an inch in depth.

Obviously the four wounds had been the cause of quick death. Oakes had been dead between two and a half and five hours, which fixed his demise as having occurred between two-thirty and five o'clock in the morning.

The bedchamber was heavy with smoke. Part of a rug was smoldering. The head of the bed and part of the mattress had been burned. Sir Harry himself had been the target of an intense flame, particularly around the eyes and the seat of his manhood. He had been burned both before and after death; for his body contained wet blisters, which arise only when a person is still alive, and dry ones, which result only after death.

As if all this weren't enough, the corpse on the bed had been sprinkled with feathers taken from the pillows. As the feathers were not burned, it was plain that they must have been put there after the fire was out.

The Superintendent of Police, Colonel R. A. Erskine-Lindop, who reached the scene shortly after Dr. Quackenbush, knew at a glance that he was facing a genuine poser. The concentrated flame that had been applied around the eyes and the genitals smacked of an uncivilized hatred; the feather business gave the crime a touch of witchcraft. The islands around Nassau were thick with black men whose familiarity with jungle ritual of one kind or another was far from extinct.

At about eleven o'clock, some four hours after Harold Christie had reported the finding of Sir Harry Oakes' body, His Royal Highness the Duke of Windsor, Governor of the Bahamas, having been notified of his close friend's untimely death, sat in Government House trying to arrive at a grave decision. The Duke was somewhat rusty in arriving at decisions, having been free of the necessity of making any important ones since he decided to forego his crown six years previously. His problem in this affair was whether to entrust the local constabulary with the formalities to be performed in connection with the passing of an important citizen or to call in out-of-the-country cops.

With a few exceptions, the Bahama cops would have warmed the heart of Mack Sennett, the old-time Hollywood movie maker whose Keystone Kops supplied nickelodeon patrons with belly laughs a third of a century ago. About the only act of stupidity some of them had not been suspected of, at one time or another, was falling victim of mistaken identity and pinching one another. The Duke decided that the local boys might need some help. He picked up a piece of royal telephone equipment and put through a call to Miami, where, according to the Nassau Daily *Tribune,* in an editorial calling the Oakes case a comedy of errors, His Royal Highness apparently got the wrong number. The wrong number in question was the Miami Police Department. There the Duke was put through to Captain Edward Melchen, chief of the Homicide Department. The Duke was personally acquainted with Captain Melchen, who had previously arranged special guards for him when Windsor had passed through Miami.

"A very prominent citizen is dead here," said the Duke to Melchen, "and it might be suicide. Can you come at once?" The Duke, for reasons to this day unexplained, was apparently not in possession of much clear information about the discovery of Sir Harry's body when he made the call; obviously, this was no suicide. Captain Melchen said he would catch the next plane.

The Duke's mistake in reporting Sir Harry's death as a suicide rather than a murder proved to be, as the Duke himself later put it, most unfortunate. A cop lights out with considerably more equipment to investigate a murder than he takes with him to look into a suicide. Most suicides are caused by gas, poison, or shooting. So when Captain Melchen, accompanied by Captain James Barker, head of the Miami Police Identification Department, left on the eleven-fifty plane, they were carrying with them equipment for investigating only those three methods of self-destruction. Fingerprints, as it was to turn out, were to be of the utmost importance in the investigation, but Captain Barker was carrying only a small portable fingerprint outfit and no fingerprint camera.

Melchen and Barker landed in Nassau at one-thirty-five in the afternoon and were driven directly to Westbourne. As soon as they saw the murder room, of course, they realized the Duke's message had started them off on the wrong foot. That wasn't all. Though the murder room and the immediate vicinity were jumping with bloody finger- and handprints, everything was so damp from a heavy storm of the night before that dusting for prints was out of the question. A print is comprised of 1 per cent body oil and 99 per cent water. The body oils do not show up under conditions of extreme dampness. Barker decided to wait until the following day, when he hoped to be able to develop prints.

The Miami cops took a good look at Sir Harry's body, which had not been left in place pending their arrival. They decided that somebody must have poured some highly inflammable agent over Oakes; and in the process, they figured, he might well have received some burns himself, because of close proximity to the blaze. They thought in terms of the male sex exclusively; the force of the blows on the skull ruled out from the beginning all likelihood that the crime had been committed by a woman.

As a matter of normal police routine, Harold Christie, as the only other known occupant of Westbourne at the time of the murder, was subjected to a microscopic examination to determine whether he had any singed hairs on his head, his face, or his hands and arms. He hadn't.

In the course of the examination Christie informed the police on the situation at Westbourne. Lady Oakes and the five Oakes children were in the United States, having gone North sometime before, as they usually did at that time of year, to escape the heat of the summer months in Nassau. Christie, at the invitation of Sir Harry, had come over to Westbourne to stay with him, while cleaning up some business matters, until Sir Harry was ready to go to South America—which he had been planning to do, in fact, that very morning.

On the previous evening Sir Harry had thrown a party for himself at Westbourne—ironically, a farewell party. It was a comparatively small get-together of friends, including the Duke and Duchess of Windsor, and broke up more or less sedately about midnight. Then Sir Harry and Christie had another drink or two by themselves while the servants cleared away the debris left after the festivities. The servants had finished putting the house to rights by about one o'clock, and left for the nearby cabins in which they lived. Shortly afterward, Christie and Sir Harry had said goodnight to each other and gone to their respective rooms.

The Miami dicks, endowed with official police powers, began looking around for a suspect. They quickly filled themselves in on local scuttlebutt. They learned that Sir Harry Oakes was an autocratic old buzzard who had enough enemies to populate a fair-sized island.

Oakes had looked upon the world as his oyster and he had a Gargantuan appetite. He was a ham-fisted gent and, despite his age, he packed a pile-driver wallop. He seemed to delight in knocking his inferiors around. A sporting instinct caused him to look upon Negroes, who constitute the bulk of the population of Nassau and the other Bahama islands, as a form of life best used as punching bags or footballs. If a shopkeeper did something to displease him, he would clear his throat and spit on the man. His servant turnover, both colored and white, was heavy.

Oakes seemed to have come equipped with a built-in aphrodisiac. He used to go down to the wharves, wearing white pants and a loud sports jacket, and cast a gimlet eye on the stuff that came down the gangplanks from the tourist ships. When he saw something tasty, the chase was on. It was hardly a secret in Nassau that more than one fair tourist, after being spotted by the old huntsman, had had experiences not mentioned in the tourist literature.

The talk around Nassau was that Sir Harry had dished out both financial and amatory favors to certain ladies in permanent residence on the island. Some of these biscuits were married to men somewhat less broad-minded than they. If many of the residents of Nassau would have liked to have a hand on a rope to hang Sir Harry, some of the betrayed husbands would have liked to have *both* hands on the rope. Any one of these men would have been a logical suspect.

The more the cops listened, the clearer it became to them that if they were going to try to do a thorough checking job on everybody who might have had a motive for bumping off Sir Harry, they would be at it the rest of their lives. Besides motives, opportunity had been virtually unlimited. Despite the palatial aspect of the Oakes home, guardianship of it was entrusted to a local watchman or two, casually making rounds through the night hours. The security furnished by this arrangement was such that a prowler would practically have had to make an appointment with the watchman in order to get caught entering the place. Sir Harry, who could have afforded to maintain a standing army of guards, had never bothered; he had never had the slightest doubt that he was well able to take care of himself.

Conveniently in the foreground of their inquiries, however, was one suspect who might have been called a natural. He was Count Marie Alfred Fouquereaux de Marigny, a tall, thin, handsome fellow of thirty-seven, and Sir Harry's son-in-law. Less than a year before the murder, he had married eighteen-year-old Nancy Oakes, the oldest of Sir Harry's five children and the apple of Papa's eye. The Count, a French native of the island of Mauritius in the Indian Ocean, had never been Sir Harry's boy. He was not at all Sir Harry's type. Nancy Oakes was his third wife. Before his second wife divorced him he had borrowed a big chunk of money from her—reputed to have been in excess of a hundred grand —and had never got around to returning it. In the eyes of the cops, the Count was a classic example of the no-good fortune hunter.

At the time of his murder, Oakes had been concentrating on some way to see that de Marigny would never lay hands on any of his two hundred million dollars. This project, naturally, did nothing to inspire the Count with affection

for his father-in-law. The Count and Oakes had not been on speaking terms for several months. At the time of the murder, de Marigny was living in a cottage about five miles from Westbourne. In another part of the island, he had a farm where he raised chickens.

The two Miami cops, pondering the intelligence about de Marigny, became excited. But not nearly so excited as when they heard about a remark the Count had made the morning the news of the murder spread through Nassau. "It's about time that somebody killed the old bastard," the Count said to a local man who informed him that Sir Harry had been murdered.

From that moment forward, Count de Marigny's goose was in the oven and the imported and local flatfeet began to turn up the gas. They not only ignored everything else on the stove; they threw it to hell in the garbage can.

Melchen and Barker and a couple of Nassau cops leaned on the Count. What, they wanted to know, did the Count know about the murder of his father-in-law? The Count said he knew nothing. Why, he countered, should he? Where, the dicks wanted to know, had the Count been during the time span in which the murder had been committed—between two-thirty and five in the morning? Asleep, said de Marigny, in his cottage.

One of the cops noticed that the hair on the Count's hands looked singed. De Marigny was asked to roll up his shirt sleeves. When he did, it was apparent that the hair on his arms was singed, too. The Count had a little pointed beard of the type that some dolls consider cute. That, too, was singed at the point. Would de Marigny be kind enough to explain how he had come to get his hands, arms, and beard singed? And while he was at it, would he oblige with an alibi—one that could be corroborated—for his whereabouts during the vital time span? De Marigny favored the cops with what one of them later described as a sneer. But he would be glad to explain everything so long as they were so damned insistent. This, then, was how De Marigny explained:

Early on the evening before the murder, de Marigny, not having been invited to Sir Harry's party, was busy preparing to throw a small party of his own. He and a house guest of his—a thirtyish matinee idol, a marquis by the name of Maxim Louis Georges de Visdelou-Guimbeau, a friend of de Marigny's from their native island in the Indian Ocean—were going to have a quiet dinner for a few friends de Marigny had made on the island. Two of the guests were to be ladies who were married to Englishmen training in Nassau for the Royal Air Force. De Marigny's bride, the former Nancy Oakes, was in the States with her mother and the other Oakes children.

The party was to be held on the lawn behind the de Marigny cottage, and by way of preparing for it the Count went out and lit four hurricane lamps. In the process, he singed the point of his beard and the hair on the backs of his hands and on his forearms—both hands and both forearms, since he was ambidextrous. But after de Marigny lit the lamps, he noticed the mosquitoes were particularly bad, and decided to entertain indoors.

Three guests remained after midnight —the two wives of the R.A.F. pilots and a young blonde movie-theatre cashier named Betty Roberts. The Count's friend, the Marquis, was attentive to Miss Roberts, who, any way one looked

at her, was well worth attention. She was an authentic dish.

The five of them sat around talking and lifting a couple until ten minutes after one. The fliers' wives said they must be going. De Marigny offered to drive them home. The Count had three cars—a Lincoln, a Packard, and a Chevrolet. He got the Chevvy out of a garage behind the cottage and drove off with the fliers' wives, leaving Miss Roberts and the Marquis alone in the cottage.

The fliers' wives were staying a ten-minute drive from de Marigny's cottage and fairly near Westbourne. The Count, in fact, had to pass Westbourne to take them to where they were staying. As they passed the Oakes property, the two ladies noticed that it was in total darkness.

De Marigny dropped the women at their door, then returned to his cottage, getting back there about one-thirty or a little later, some twenty or twenty-five minutes after he had left. The Marquis and the blonde were nowhere in sight.

The Marquis owned a black male Persian cat, a very intelligent-looking animal that the Count had given him. The cat was roaming around, having left the Marquis' rooms, where it usually stayed, either of its own accord or by request. The Count retired to his own apartment, but the cat followed him in and began to annoy him. It continued to annoy him, and at three in the morning the Count knocked on the door of the Marquis' apartment and asked him to take the cat. Miss Roberts was there. The Marquis explained that he had been taking a little nap and that he was now going to drive the girl back to the home where she was staying. "Use the Chevrolet," said the Count. "It's in the driveway."

That was about three-thirty. When the Marquis returned, shortly before four o'clock, he left the Chevvy right at the cottage, alongside a door leading to a flight of stairs to the second floor.

The Count said the Marquis de Visdelou-Guimbeau would back him up. But the Marquis didn't back him up— not entirely, anyway. The Marquis didn't mention the blonde at all in accounting for his actions and observations of the previous night. He said that De Marigny had come in around one-thirty, after taking the two ladies home, and that that had been the last he had seen of him until he saw him driving away in the Chevrothe murder had been committed between two-thirty and five o'clock, that left the let around seven in the morning. Since Count with no alibi whatever for the important time area. That, plus the fact that his hands, forearms, and beard were singed, looked very bad.

There are four different kinds, or degrees, of burned hair. In the first stage, the hair becomes more brilliant than usual. This is caused by the natural oil's coming to the surface. The second stage causes the hair to curl. In the third stage the tip of the hair, thinner than the base, crusts, while the part near the base becomes either curly or brilliant. The fourth stage, caused by intense heat, causes the hair to burn, leaving only a carbon ash. The Count had all four degrees on his beard, hands, and forearms.

By way of buttressing his claim that his singed hair had come about under noncriminal circumstances, de Marigny said he could have acquired some of the burns while working in scalding water at his chicken farm. The cops pointed out that that would hardly account for the burned hair on his beard. The Count seemed stumped, but only for a moment. Brightening up, he said he had had the Van Dyke singed by a barber. Just what barber? And when had the singeing been done to the beard? De Marigny couldn't recall. He was a busy man, what with one thing and another, and he didn't keep an account of visits to barbers.

A local cop—a Lieutenant John Douglas—was assigned to keep an eye on the Count, twenty-four hours a day, from this point on. The Miami cops came right back at de Marigny. They had talked with every barber in Nassau and none of the tonsorial artists recalled singeing the Count's beard. "This begins to look pretty bad for you," said Captain Melchen. The Count was in no position to argue.

In the meantime, Westbourne was alive with police. The place had dried out somewhat and Captain Barker was busy dusting for fingerprints in and around the murder chamber on the second floor. De Marigny was told to sit in a drawing room on the first floor, to await the attention of the cops. Lieutenant Douglas, the man assigned to keep an eye on the Count, was sticking with it—except, of course, to make an occasional trip to a bathroom. The Count had to go to the bathroom once in a while, too. As the day wore on, Westbourne became busier and busier and things began to loosen up a bit.

There was a large five-paneled folding screen in the murder chamber. Sir Harry had frequently used this screen close to his bed to protect himself from drafts. It had been put to such use the night of the murder. The screen, made of paper with a floral design, was smudged with smoke from the fire in the room.

In the afternoon, de Marigny was taken to a room on the second floor—not the murder chamber—and fingerprinted by Captain Barker. Presently the Captain announced that a print of the little finger of de Marigny's right hand had been found on the screen in Sir Harry's room. The Captain explained that he had removed the print from the screen by means of applying a strip of Scotch tape to it and then transferring the print from the Scotch tape to a piece of portable surface. After removing the print from the screen, the Captain further explained, he circled with a pencil the spot on the screen—the *approximate* spot, he was later to admit—from which he had removed the print. Things were beginning to heat up for de Marigny.

The two Miami detectives were now convinced that de Marigny had murdered his father-in-law. He could have done it, they decided, out of sheer hatred for Sir Harry. Or he could have done it to protect his interests in the Oakes estate before Sir Harry completed legal steps to make sure that his son-in-law would never get a pound of his money.

The Miami sleuths could not find the murder weapon—a somewhat important piece of evidence in a homicide such as this. They were not even certain what kind of lethal instrument had been used. The case was by no means open and shut. If the Count had given a true account of his movements the night of the crime, he would have had to be something of a magician to transport himself from his cottage to Westbourne to commit the crime. Moreover, was a fellow like the Count the type to slug and burn Sir Harry, then stick around to sprinkle him with feathers, with Sir Harry's good friend Harold Christie sleeping in another room? And what about the feathers, anyway? That feather business was strictly dark-of-the-moon stuff, and the Count was a light-of-the-moon character.

Nonetheless, the Miami boys went before Police Superintendent Colonel Erskine-Lindop and placed the facts—their facts—before him. Colonel Erskine-Lindop ordered Count Marie Alfred Fouquereaux de Marigny arrested for the murder of Sir Harry Oakes in the name of His Majesty, the King.

Upon receipt of the news of Sir Harry's death, Lady Oakes, Nancy Oakes de Marigny, and the rest of the slain baronet's family had come to Nassau to remain with friends. Now Lady Oakes took the body of her husband to the United States for burial. Nancy Oakes was permitted to talk with de Marigny in jail. He convinced her of his innocence. The girl was in a real dilemma. She had loved her father and she loved her husband. One of her loves was charged with taking the life of the other. She couldn't believe that her husband was guilty of the crime, or that he even had the slightest knowledge of it.

Dr. Paul Zahl, a New York physician and an acquaintance of Nancy's, dropped into the Manhattan offices of Raymond C. Schindler, the country's number-one private eye, and asked him to get into the case on behalf of de Marigny.

Schindler, a smooth, ruddy man in his early sixties, with quite a paunch from the better life, was a natural enough recommendation, considering the circles in which Nancy Oakes moved. Schindler is known in investigative circles as the society detective. The title is not altogether incorrect. Although Ray Schindler will handle any kind of investigation, provided it is strictly legal and the remuneration is well worth while, he prefers to operate in high-level social, sporting, and theatrical circles. The man makes a hobby of collecting celebrities. There is probably nobody in the United States today, with the possible exception of ex-Postmaster General Jim Farley, who can call more celebrated persons by their first names than Schindler. It was scarcely remarkable that the person to whom Nancy Oakes turned for help suggested him.

Schindler, who had been reading about the murder in the papers, didn't jump at the proposition offered him by Dr. Zahl on behalf of the slain man's daughter. "First," Schindler told Zahl, "I'd have to got a letter from Nancy de Marigny saying that if, in investigating the case, I find her husband guilty instead of innocent, I have permission to turn the results of my investigation over to the Nassau authorities."

Dr. Zahl flew to Nassau and returned with such a letter. Then the question of fee was discussed with Schindler's brother, the late Walter Scott Schindler. Ray Schindler comes high, but Nancy de Marigny had it. Ray Schindler, who had meanwhile gone to the Pacific Coast on another case, thereupon flew to Nassau and got to work.

Harry Oakes was not, as many people thought, an Englishman. He was a Yankee from Sangerville, Maine, the son of a surveyor in modest circumstances. He was made a baronet—a cut above a knight and one below a baron—when, after having become a subject of Great Britain, he was included in the King's Birthday List in 1937, at the age of sixty-two. The Oakes career up to that time was pluck-and-luck stuff in the Horatio Alger tradition—with one exception. The Alger heroes who climbed from the bottom to the top, snagging a pretty dish during the ascent, were tough, and sometimes rough, but never nasty. Oakes, on the other hand, bore more than a passing resemblance to the storied bachelor who was despondent because he didn't have a daughter to throw out into a raging snowstorm. Oakes never forgot a score even years after it had been piled up against him.

As Oakes grew into his teens—a big-boned fellow with a barrel chest—he decided that Maine was not for him; he didn't like potatoes or lobster and he wasn't particularly fond of hunting or fishing. He saw a possible escape through a sound education at Bowdoin College, where he earned expenses by playing semipro baseball and waiting on table at the Mount Pleasant House in Bretton Woods during summer vacations.

He was graduated in 1896, at the age of twenty-one, but the best he could do by way of starting on a career of some sort was to latch onto a minor clerkship. The emolument was such that by the time he would have been in a position to go into a restaurant and order a meal without worrying about the price, his teeth would long since have fallen out. After two years of hunching over a desk, Oakes quit.

Like everyone else in the civilized world who could read or hear, he had become interested in the fortunes that were being made by prospectors for gold in the Klondike. He kissed Maine good-by and set out to burn up the trail north, to a land that made Maine in the winter look like a summer resort. He encountered everything the Klondike and Alaska had to offer—except gold. The dogs pulling his supply sled died in the white wilderness and Oakes had to snowshoe it for uncounted days. His feet froze. He lost his moneybag. Men with less moxie had cracked up under tests far less severe. Oakes emerged from the crucible with flinty eyes and a jutting jaw. He had hit the North too late to get his share of the shiny stuff but, by God, he would find it someplace else. He was young and the world was wide.

The scuttlebutt around the camps was that the Philippines were loaded and just pining for smart diggers with or without divining rods. He bummed his way to San Francisco, looking and smelling like a fugitive from a garbage dump, and shipped to Manila as a galley cook. As in Alaska, he arrived too late; the Philippine gravy train had come and gone. Next stop: West Africa. It was the same story there; the pay-dirt fields had already been staked out.

Harry Oakes was twenty-eight when, in 1903, he showed up in Australia, still on the prowl for the yellow stuff. He didn't find it, but he found something else. In Sydney, where he took odd jobs to meet living expenses, he stayed at a boardinghouse where a pretty girl who sat across the groaning board began to put him off his feed. He wondered why. He came to the realization that, for the first time in his life, the cute little guy with the bow and arrow had shot him straight through the heart.

The girl, who was almost ten years younger than Oakes, was an attractive doll by the name of Eunice MacIntyre; she worked in a jewelry store. She was gentle and sweet and, caught up in the law of attraction of opposites, she was completely enchanted by the stony, barrel-chested adventurer.

The only thing that dealt a sky pilot out of a job was the fact that Oakes didn't have the cash to get a knot tied. For the first time in his life, the lad from Maine found himself ridden by indecision. He wanted to marry Eunice MacIntyre and he wanted to lay hands on a quick fortune in gold. He couldn't have both, for there wasn't any gold in Australia—at least, not for him.

While he was trying to decide what to do, his board bill began to pile up. He couldn't find a job anywhere in Sydney. Oakes had a lumberman's appetite, and the woman who ran the boardinghouse, sensing that he would eventually eat her

into insolvency, lowered the boom on him. He would either pay up, she informed him, or get the old heave-ho.

Miss MacIntyre paid up for him; moreover, she lent him money for passage back to America. "I'll never forget you for this," he assured her. "When I make a strike I'll come back and marry you." It was to be twenty years, when he was a man almost fifty, before he set foot on the land down under again.

For several years after leaving Australia, Oakes followed the will-o'-the-wisp. Then, in 1911, when he was thirty-six and as far as ever from the end of the rainbow, he got wind of gold deposits in northern Ontario, in the vicinity of Porcupine Lake. He was in Nevada at the time, clean out at the pockets, so he bummed his way to the Middle West, then struck north toward his destination.

He was riding in a rattler in Ontario, bound for Porcupine Lake, with no money and no ticket. When the conductor came through and asked for his ticket, Oakes went through the motions of searching his pockets for it. "Well, what do you know about that?" he said. "I seem to have lost it."

That was no dandruff out of the conductor's hair. The passenger could pay cash. But the passenger didn't have any cash. The conductor studied Oakes with all the enthusiasm of a loan shark studying questionable collateral, left the car, and returned with two brakemen. The train came to a stop and the man who one day was to be knighted by the King of England was tossed to hell off. Oakes stood in the Ontario wilderness watching the train disappearing into the distance and loudly reflecting on the ancestry of three members of the crew.

Oakes walked many miles to the nearest settlement—a place called Kirkland Lake. He gave the landlady of a boardinghouse there a song and dance, moved in, then went out on the town to rustle up something—anything. He fell into converse with some natives and heard tales about gold thought to be in the vicinity. Oakes rubbed his chin. By God, maybe this was it. He went into the local hardware store and began a pitch to the proprietor to let him have some digging equipment on credit. The proprietor, a large and powerful man, tossed Oakes out the door—the future baronet's second heave-ho of the day.

The proprietor of the local laundry, a Chinese bearing the celebrated Oriental moniker of Lee, happened to be passing as Oakes flew into the street. He helped Oakes to his feet and inquired as to the nature of the difficulty. The Oriental was fascinated by Oakes' recital of the long string of events leading up to the tossola. He offered to grubstake Oakes. Oakes accepted.

On the shores of Kirkland Lake, Oakes struck gold. Almost overnight he was transformed from a bum into a man worth more than three hundred thousand dollars. He sold his holdings, pocketed his cash, and then promptly did three things.

First, he went to the Chinese who had grubstaked him, paid him off in full, and then asked him what it was he would like to have more than anything else. The Chinese, for some obscure Oriental reason, had all his life dearly wished to own a movie theatre. Oakes may have been somewhat startled to hear of this unusual ambition, but he didn't let that stand in his way. He ordered construction begun at once, and as soon as the theatre was finished he made a present of it, free and clear, to his benefactor.

Second, he built a hardware store right next to that of the man who had so enthusiastically thrown him out into the

fresh air, and made a policy of selling everything below cost. In about three months his enemy was out of business.

Third, he looked up the conductor who had tossed him off the train and, for a switch, put him on a pension for life. By the Oakes reasoning, if this conductor had not had him bounced off the train at that point, he would have ridden past the town where he struck his first gold. As the limeys in London were one day to say, upon hearing the history of the new baronet, " 'E was quite a lad, Sir 'arry."

With his grudge settled and his debts paid, Oakes went on the prowl for another and bigger strike. Soon the lightning struck again. He found gold in another Canadian spot, christened the mine the Lake Shore, and, almost before he realized it, was a multimillionaire. The Lake Shore soon became the second largest gold-producing mine in the world.

Now, in 1923, at the age of forty-eight, Harry Oakes lit out for Australia. In Sydney he headed straight for Eunice MacIntyre, the girl who had, two decades before, given him enough money to get out of the boardinghouse, out of town, and out of the country. He had corresponded with her all that time. She had, in storybook fashion, waited for him. They were married.

As a wedding present, Oakes presented his wife with a half-million-dollar mansion on the Canadian side of Niagra Falls. But one address, even though it was a mansion, was not enough for Harry Oakes. He built a house in Newport and another in Palm Beach, and began to circulate among the swells. He learned to sip tea with the little finger of his right hand stiffly perpendicular, to carry on a conversation without swearing, and to give his seat to a lady. At heart he was still a roughneck, but he was a most acceptable gentleman in circles where money was more important than anything else, for by this time he was worth several million dollars.

By 1935, after he had been married for twelve years, Harry Oakes, sixty years old, had sired five children—two daughters, of whom Nancy was the elder, and three sons, all younger. Although Oakes, everything considered, was a loving father, he was especially devoted to his eldest child, Nancy.

Now, with millions piling upon millions from the gold mine, with a devoted wife and a fine family, plus the home in Canada and the two in the United States, Harry Oakes, never a satisfied man, decided, for reasons best known to himself, to go to England. There he purchased a magnificent town house in London, a country estate, and a hunting lodge in Scotland. He began to make lavish gifts to English charities. Then, in June of 1937, when he was sixty-two, he was created a baronet on the King's Birthday Honours List. Thus the onetime boy from the backwoods of Maine became Sir Harry Oakes.

Early in 1938, Sir Harry received a visitor at his town house in London. The caller was a dark-eyed, moon-faced man of middle years by the name of Harold Christie. Christie, by this time a highly successful real-estate operator in the Bahamas, boasted that he could accommodate a land buyer with anything from a lot to an island. This meeting between Oakes and Christie was to be the beginning of a fine and lucrative friendship.

It was real estate that Christie had come to see Sir Harry about. Real estate and income taxes. The Second World War was already looming pretty clearly. Income taxes in Britain were becoming increasingly tough and were very likely to become even tougher. Sir Harry's in-come was in the neighborhood of three million dollars a year and as a British subject, he was wide open to taxes that would take practically all of it. While Sir Harry by this time had perhaps fifty million dollars scattered around here and there, he still turned purple every time he thought of the amount of dough he was forking over every year to the Chancellor of the Exchequer.

Christie pointed out all this to Sir Harry, as if Sir Harry were not already painfully aware of it. What, asked Sir Harry, did Christie have in mind?

"Why not come to Nassau, become a resident, and take advantage of a practically nonexistent tax on large incomes there?" Christie said. Sir Harry was more than interested.

Christie had just the property to sell to Sir Harry—a twenty-bedroom estate once owned by Maxine Elliott, the noted American actress. Brother Christie could let Sir Harry have the place for a song— say the equivalent of five hundred thousand dollars. Sir Harry and Lady Oakes took off for Nassau to look the place over. They were enchanted by it, and bought it for cash. That was in 1939.

Once in Nassau, Sir Harry and Lady Oakes quickly became top social leaders in a very society-minded neck of the world. They tossed lavish parties, with buckets of champagne, tubs of caviar, and everything else to match. Sir Harry's belligerent attitude, however, had not diminished with the years. One night he went into the British Colonial Hotel, Nassau's largest, and became incensed at the headwaiter because the headwaiter, new and not familiar with Sir Harry's little ways, seated the Oakes party at an inferior table.

Now Sir Harry, according to Lady Oakes, did something that many men have wished they could do to even a score. He made a telephone call to New York next morning, to the Munson Steamship Company, owners of the hostelry. He closed a deal for the purchase of the hotel for one million dollars in cash. That night he went back to the hotel, deliberately late so that the best tables were already taken, and ran into the same headwaiter. Sir Harry pointed to a choice table. "Seat me there," he said.

"But that table is occupied, Sir Harry," said the waiter.

"So what?" said Sir Harry. "Throw those people out." The headwaiter said he couldn't do that. "Oh, you can't!" said Oakes. "Well, I bought this damned place this morning and you're fired!"

The longer Sir Harry Oakes lived in Nassau, the better he liked the place. Although he made occasional trips out of the country, he spent as much time as possible at Westbourne, even in the hot summer months. All the while, he was engaging in various business enterprises, mostly real estate, with Harold Christie. Christie, rising in power and importance, became one of the governors of the Bahamas. Eventually the two men—Sir Harry with his tremendous wealth and Christie with his official position and general know-how—were, between them, practically running the islands.

It was but natural, then, for the Duke of Windsor and his wife, the former Wallis Warfield Simpson of Baltimore, to become friendly with Sir Harry when the Duke arrived to take over his chores as governor general of the islands. The Duke, in fact, became so chummy with Sir Harry that he and the Duchess stayed at Westbourne while Government House, the Duke's official residence, was undergoing repairs. There were some big balls at Westbourne during the Duke's residence there. His Royal High-

ness had a swell time except on those occasions when the Duchess, focusing a cold glare on her husband's tenth champagne refill, would say to him, "That will be quite enough, David!"

At one of these parties at Westbourne there appeared a tall, slim fellow in his middle thirties. When things had reached the high-decibel level, Sir Harry pointed toward the fellow and inquired of Lady Oakes, "Who the hell's that?"

"I'm sure I don't know," said Lady Oakes. "I thought perhaps *you* knew."

"Never saw him before in my life," said Sir Harry. "He's spending an awful lot of time with Nancy. Find out who he is."

Nancy, seventeen now, heiress to more money than she would ever be able to count, and within a year of the age when she could marry without parental consent, had eyes filled with stars. Her friend, she told her mother, was Freddie —or, to be more specific, Count Marie Alfred Fouquereaux de Marigny. Freddie was staying with friends in Nassau. She had been introduced to Freddie quite properly, she assured her mother, but just hadn't got around to introducing him to her parents.

Freddie, it turned out, had a voice strikingly like that of the movie actor Charles Boyer, both in timbre and in accent; he was handsomely turned out and altogether gave the impression of a lad who had a way with women, and knew it. When Lady Oakes passed this intelligence along to Sir Harry, the baronet was all for throwing the Count out. Lady Oakes restrained him. "All right," said Sir Harry, "but I'm looking the sonofabitch up first thing in the morning."

What Sir Harry found out about Count Alfred de Marigny wasn't at all to his liking. He learned about the Count's two divorces and the hundred grand that his second wife had given him at the time her knot with him was untied.

Lady Oakes told her daughter about this. Nancy was unimpressed. "Your father never wants you to see that man again," said the mother. Nancy was still unimpressed.

Nancy said she thought she would take a trip to New York to visit friends. She didn't expect to see the Count again, she told her mother. So she left for New York. De Marigny left a couple of days later.

Sir Harry put detectives on the trail of the two. The dicks sniffed out their quarry too late. Nancy and de Marigny had left for California with a young married couple as chaperons. By the time the gumshoes got to California, the quartet had lit out for Mexico. In Mexico City, Nancy ate some food that proved to be tainted. She came down with typhoid fever. She almost died.

Upon her recovery, she and de Marigny went to New York. There, in January 1943, the day after Nancy's eighteenth birthday, she and de Marigny were married by a magistrate.

Not long after the marriage, Nancy de Marigny discovered that she was pregnant. She was not a robust girl and she was in an especially run-down condition after her siege of illness in Mexico. Several doctors decided that if the pregnancy continued, her life might be endangered. An immediate operation was recommended. The Count went to Florida with Nancy. She checked into the Good Samaritan Hospital in West Palm Beach.

De Marigny took a room next to his wife's and decided, as long as he was in the hospital anyway, that he would have his tonsils removed. The day after the Count had his operation, Sir Harry and Lady Oakes came over from Nassau to see their daughter. While Sir Harry was

about it, he stopped into the next room to voice his opinion of the Count for getting his daughter into a pregnant condition right after her siege of typhoid.

It was far from flattering. "And if you don't get out of this room, away from Nancy," declared Sir Harry in closing, "I'll throw you to hell out."

The Count quietly got out. Burning up, he wrote a letter to Sydney Oakes, Sir Harry's eldest son, then only fifteen —a letter that has never been made public, but which Lady Oakes was one day to describe as "the most diabolical letter a man could write to a child of fifteen about his parents."

While Sir Harry was in West Palm Beach he consulted his attorney, a prominent and highly ethical lawyer named Walter Foskett. Foskett drew up a new will. Precisely what was in that will has never become publicly known, but Lady Oakes was to say later that the document was prepared "to protect Nancy against herself until she reached the age of discretion."

Somehow or other, de Marigny got wind of the change. He stormed into Attorney Foskett's office and demanded to know precisely what was up. Foskett, of course, wouldn't tell him.

De Marigny had found out something else. His second wife, Ruth Fahnestock, of New York's Horse Show set, upon hearing that de Marigny was interested in Nancy Oakes, had written a letter to Sir Harry and Lady Oakes, putting the blast on the Count. Not knowing precisely where Sir Harry and his wife were when she wrote the letter, she had sent it to Attorney Foskett. Foskett, who was authorized to open Oakes' mail, opened the letter, read it, and sent it along to Sir Harry. Naturally, the lawyer wouldn't disclose the contents of the letter to the Count. It turned out later, however, that

Miss Fahnestock had, among other things, dwelt on the Count's habit of getting rid of large sums of money. All this hardly improved Sir Harry's feelings toward de Marigny.

Nancy's illness, however, somehow changed conditions, at least for a time. In love with her husband, she made her parents promise that they would let bygones be bygones if she got better. They promised. And so after a time, everybody returned to Nassau together, one big, almost happy family.

Sir Harry asked the Count what he could do except chase girls with money. The Count said he had a chicken farm. It was five miles from Westbourne, and he and Nancy took up residence there.

Sydney, the Oakes' eldest boy, had taken quite a liking to the Count. He often visited the chicken farm and remained overnight with the Count and his sister at the cottage. Sir Harry, violently objecting to his eldest son's attachment to the worldly Count, went to the cottage one night while Sydney was there. He ordered Sydney off the premises. "And if you ever set foot in this place again," Sir Harry roared, "I'll disinherit you. One in the family's enough to have anything to do with this character." That wrapped it up, but good.

By the time Schindler had filled himself in on the past of Sir Harry Oakes, arrangements had been completed for his entrance into Nassau. So he went to Miami, caught a Clipper, and set foot on the British possession six days after Nancy de Marigny had first asked him to enter the case. The built-in antenna that all good detectives have—that which enables them to pick things out of the air —told him that he was, in certain circles at least (notably official circles), about as welcome in Nassau as a good island-wide

outbreak of bubonic plague. Schindler shrugged it off. Private eyes get used to things like that.

Schindler checked into luxurious quarters in the home of the Baroness de Trolle and her husband, who were friends of Nancy's, and began reading the local newspaper accounts of the case. The newspaper stories didn't make things look any too good for the Count. Then Schindler called at the offices of a handsome fellow by the name of Godfrey Higgs, one of Nassau's top lawyers. Higgs had been engaged by Nancy de Marigny to defend her husband. Schindler liked Higgs and Higgs liked Schindler at their very first meeting. Whatever the outcome of the whole business, these two would get along fine.

Higgs was already in possession of most of the data that the police had picked up before putting the collar on the Count—the data that disclosed the fact that there were many people on the island who had a motive for killing Sir Harry. The way Higgs saw it (and Schindler was presently to see it the same way), the cops had gone out and found a suspect whom they fitted to the evidence rather than finding evidence and then fitting it to a suspect. Higgs told Schindler that as he saw the picture, the Count's reputation was against him. In logic the Count's reputation, no matter what it was, should have had no influence on the investigation of the case. But obviously it had. The boys had gone to work building a gallows for the Count, throwing away all the wood that might have been used to build one for somebody else.

Higgs showed Schindler the official photographs of the corpse of Sir Harry. The pictures made it doubly clear to the detective that this had not been a murder for profit. When a man kills for money, as de Marigny was now accused of having done, he commits the crime as quickly and simply as possible and then gets away.

This killer had not been in a hurry; he had deliberately taken time to stick around and concentrate an intense flame on Oakes' eyes and genitals. This suggested hatred—perhaps over a woman. The sprinkling of feathers over the corpse after death suggested a cultlike ritual of some kind. The feather-sprinkling might have been done by a crazed Bahama native—or by someone who wanted to make the crime look as if it had been committed by a native. Either way, though, it was plainly no hit-and-run job.

Schindler now devoted his attention to the time element in de Marigny's alibi. If everything de Marigny said was true, it would have been just about impossible for him to be at Westbourne between two-thirty and five o'clock in the morning.

According to the Count, the only time he would have had to leave his cottage, commit the crime, and return, without being observed by anyone or at least heard by the Marquis, would have been during the approximate half hour when the Marquis had taken the blonde home. But more than half an hour would have been needed, the way Schindler figured it, for the Count to have done everything the murderer had done.

It had been storming violently during the night of the crime. Fast driving had been out of the question. But even if the Count had needed only ten minutes to cover the five miles between his cottage and Westbourne, the round trip would have eaten up twenty minutes of the half hour. That would have left less than ten minutes to commit the crime. It seemed to Schindler that more than ten min-

utes—perhaps a good deal more—would have been required to do everything that had been done in the Oakes mansion. If the Count had done it, he would have had to move extremely fast for that half hour—and even at that, his timing would have had to be desperately close.

The trouble was that the Marquis' story of the night's events differed from that of the Count. De Marigny said Miss Roberts had spent some two hours in the Marquis' rooms, leaving only after three A.M. The Marquis said nothing of the kind. Schindler figured that the Marquis was chivalrously shielding the good name of the blonde. Schindler put it up to the Marquis in clear terms. Which was more important, a blonde's good name or a friend's life? The Marquis decided the life was more important. He corroborated everything the Count had stated about his movements the night of the crime.

It thus seemed more and more unlikely that the Count could have committed the crime. If he hadn't committed it while the Marquis was taking the blonde home, he would have run a chance of being detected by the Marquis had he left in a car after the Marquis returned. Schindler established the fact that the Marquis was a very light sleeper.

Now Schindler, who wanted to fill himself in on everything possible before talking to De Marigny, decided it was time to go through Westbourne. Bahama regulations called for him to be accompanied by several cops. Schindler thought as much of that as he would have of a mickey in his drink. But he had no choice. The flatfeet buzzed around him like native mosquitoes.

The whole area of the crime struck Schindler as having been torched, rather than merely burned. The bed on which the Baronet was found had definitely been subjected to a flame so intense that it could have come only from a torch. There were marks on the rugs, on the floor, and on doors and woodwork between the murder rooms and the first floor that looked as if they had been made by a torch carried by the killer.

Every time Schindler turned his head he saw bloody finger- and handprints—either intact or mussed up. Even the French telephone in Sir Harry's room (the one that Christie had used to summon aid) and a phone book near it were bloodstained. There was a big bloody fingerprint on a door leading to Christie's room. This, of course, was understandable. Christie had touched his friend's body in an attempt to determine whether Oakes was really dead and, in his excitement, had naturally picked up some blood.

There were bloody hand marks on the wall of the murder room that had not been of any particular interest to the police. The marks were near two windows, as if the killer, after the first phase of the murder, had gone to the windows to look out to see that nobody was around, placing his bloody hands on the wall while he did so. The prints had obviously been made made a short, stubby hand. The Count's hands were long and thin.

Now it was time for Schindler to talk to the man he was to prove either innocent or guilty. Schindler had measured a good many murderers in his time. Murderers run to types. Schindler's first impression of the Count was that he just wasn't the type to take to murder. The Count may have been a slayer of the ladies, but he didn't impress Schindler as a killer of men. He was too fond of life ever to do anything, for whatever reason, that would lay that life on the line. Moreover, he sounded sincere to a man who had been measuring sincerity for a third of a century.

Schindler learned that the Count had asked one of the cops guarding him at Westbourne if a man could be hanged on circumstantial evidence. What about that? Schindler wanted to know. The Count just smiled and shrugged. Wasn't it, considering his position, a natural question?

The singed hairs on his hands, arms, and Van Dyke? His friend the Marquis would corroborate the Count's story of hand and arm burns from the hurricane lamps, and/or the chicken-singeing chores. No barber could remember singeing his beard? Well, perhaps not. He might have singed it the last time himself and have been confused when the police were pummeling him with questions. The fingerprint the Miami cop had come up with? He had not been in the room during or after the murder. The print of his little finger on the screen in Sir Harry's room might have been faked. Yes, *faked*. Those two American cops, and most of the local cops, had just been too damned eager to pin the rap on him. Why didn't they look around a bit? The Count could name a dozen people who had a lot to explain but hadn't even been questioned.

Schindler went back to his hotel and conferred with himself. He decided to seek some advice, to orient himself for his next moves. He flew back to the United States. He went to Washington and called on an old friend—Homer S. Cummings, Attorney General of the United States.

Schlinder wanted Cummings' advice about what he had found. Cummings was just the man to give it. Years before, when he was a prosecuting attorney in Connecticut, the Attorney General had found himself in a unique situation. A young fellow was accused of a murder. Although it was up to Cummings to prosecute, he was convinced that the fellow had not committed the crime. So instead of prosecuting, Cummings set out to prove that the defendant was innocent. And he did prove the fellow's innocence; the defendant had been a victim of mistaken identity. The story of that case was later made into an outstanding movie—*Boomerang*.

When Cummings heard Schindler's story, he said, "Ray, I think Count de Marigny is innocent. If there's anything I can do to help, just let me know."

Upon his return to Nassau after his conference with Attorney General Cummings, Schindler learned that the Nassau police had committed themselves to a program of getting him up in the morning and putting him to bed at night.

Realizing the importance that fingerprint evidence was to assume in the investigation, Schindler made trips to New Orleans and Chicago to get the best talent possible. Then there appeared in Nassau two gentlemen who, like Schindler, were as welcome to the Nassau police as ants in a picnic sandwich—Captain Maurice B. O'Neil, chief of the Bureau of Identification of the New Orleans Police Department, and Professor Leonard B. Keeler, executive director of the State of Illinois Crime Bureau. Captain O'Neil was recognized in official circles throughout the United States as one of the country's top fingerprint experts. Keeler, a quiet, handsome man in his early forties, who knew how to wear casual clothes, was the inventor of the lie detector and an authority on scientific crime detection. Both were old friends of Schindler.

Schindler studied a copy of the Crown's picture of De Marigny's fingerprint that had been developed by the Miami cop. He noticed that the print had been developed against a background of circles. The circles looked to Schindler as if they had come from a glass surface rather than a paper one. The screen from which the print had supposedly come had a smooth surface; there were no circles, at least that Schindler could see with the naked eye, on that screen. He showed the fingerprint photograph to Professor Keeler and Captain O'Neil. "There's not one chance in ten million," said Keeler, "that this print came from that screen." O'Neil agreed. Just to make sure, Keeler took a photograph of that part of the screen where the Miami cop said he had developed the Count's print. Sometimes a photo will show up something not visible to the naked eye. But not in this case. "Bring me a pile of Bibles," Keeler said to Schindler, "and I'll swear on them that that print did not come from this screen."

So far as Schindler was able to learn, that fingerprint was the most important piece of physical evidence that the Crown had against the Count. Schindler had a couple of Scotches on that.

The day the murder was discovered, and the following day, *some*body had washed the walls of the murder room, thus removing fingerprints and handprints. The phone book in Sir Harry's chamber had not been removed, and it had blood splotches all over it. But, prior to Schindler's arrival to begin his probe, dozens of persons had picked up that phone book, so that it was not possible to get a print that meant anything.

Schindler, picking up pieces of information as he went along, now learned that when the Nassau police had first arrived on the murder scene they had found a loaded revolver lying on top of a pile of bills on a dresser. The weapon had since vanished. From all Schindler was able to learn, Sir Harry had not owned a revolver. The sleuth made an attempt to get the gun so that he could trace its origin. But an official in the police department informed him that the weapon had been done away with. "Keeping it," this official informed the sleuth, "would only have confused the whole investigation. After all, Sir Harry was not shot." Confused the issue, indeed!

Schindler figured Oakes might have carried the gun as part of his personal equipment. If that were so, it might indicate that the Baronet had had some potent reason to fear for his personal safety, since he had still been a good man with his fists. Interesting. Had Oakes feared somebody—man or woman— enough to think that his life was in immediate danger? If so, who? Schindler would have paid a high price for that gun. He could have run down its origin from its serial number. Thus he could have established where and when and under what conditions Oakes had come into possession of it. If Oakes had acquired it recently, that would point pretty clearly to some definite threat.

It would have been very easy for anyone to reach Sir Harry's bed that night. A violent rain—and windstorm with lightning and thunder blasted away most of the night. Outside stairs led to the upper porches that practically surrounded the house. All one had to do was walk upstairs and open the door. No one could have heard an approach and the doors were not locked.

The bedrooms were furnished, but the mattresses and covers were not on the beds. Schindler never learned why Sir Harry, on two or three occasions during the week before he was murdered, walked along the upper porch to go into one of these bedrooms and sleep on a mattress on the floor. The servants found his bedcovers in each of these rooms. Sir Harry would carry them with him without the knowledge of anyone. It was obvious to Schindler that the man had been in mortal fear and was hiding out in case someone came to his bedroom.

Moreover, it was within the realm of possibility that Sir Harry could have been drugged before going to bed. If Oakes had not been drugged, and had been awakened by his attacker, Sir Harry, although sixty-eight, would have been capable of putting up one hell of a fight. He could have yelled for his friend and business associate in the other bedroom. Christie was a powerful man, too.

But it hadn't worked that way. The intruder had reached the bed without waking Oakes and killed him, then remained to torch him and sprinkle him with feathers.

Schindler would have given a year of his life to have had a good look at the corpse of Sir Harry Oakes right after the murder. He could have followed through, by way of an autopsy and a scientific examination of the vital organs, on the possibility that Oakes had been drugged before death. He could have had a good look at the Baronet's head, particularly at those four wounds. But things could have been worse. The police had done one thing well; they had taken excellent photographs of that part of the victim's head containing the wounds. Schindler got hold of copies of the photographs and the medical reports.

The pattern of the four wounds was rectangular in shape—about two inches wide and a little longer. The police hadn't the slightest idea what sort of instrument had been used by the murderer. Neither did Schindler. Although the wound pattern formed a sort of rectangle, it was not possible to determine whether the four wounds had been made by four separate blows, each blow making one mark, or by two blows with a two-pronged instrument.

One end of the cradle of a European telephone, if brought down four times on a man's head, could have produced the murder wounds. Although there was such a telephone in the murder bedroom, it was too far from the Baronet's bed to have been used for such a purpose. Schindler searched through Westbourne for the possibility that any other French phone had been yanked from a wall. Nothing doing.

In the garage behind Westbourne, Schindler found a stack of short wooden railings, two inches by two inches in thickness. He learned from an Oakes servant that such a railing had been found, the morning after the murder, leaning against one of Sir Harry's cars, which he had left parked in a driveway behind the house. Out of curiosity, the servant had kept the railing. Schindler examined it. There were no indications of blood on the wood. Schindler questioned the servant closely as to just how the railing had been leaning against the car when it was found. It had been leaning against one of the wheels.

Schindler figured the railing business as this possibility: The murderer, going into the garage in search of a weapon of some kind—a weapon that could not be traced to him—had picked up a couple of railings. On his way to the house itself, the murderer had decided that one railing would be enough for his purpose. So he had discarded the second railing. In landing on the ground, it had struck the wheel of the car while still in an upright position, and it had stayed that

way until the servant came across it the next morning.

Although in one respect the railing (one point of the end of it used four times) sounded good to Schindler, in another it didn't. The superior investigator has a singular digestive apparatus; he can't, somehow, stomach a piece of evidence that, however attractive it looks, just doesn't seem appetizing. A murderer armed with a piece of railing would be likely to use it as a club, rather than poke the end of it at his victim, like a sword. Schindler was not discarding the railing, but he wasn't swallowing it, either.

Keeler, the Chicago criminologist, was meanwhile devoting himself to the development of scientific clues. He took pieces of the rug in the murder room, and pieces of the burned woodwork at the head of the bed, and began to conduct experiments in the home of the Baroness de Trolle. He concluded definitely that the killer had used a torch while going about his grisly business. De Marigny didn't own a torch and had never had reason to use one on the chicken farm. The Baroness de Trolle, eager to see Schindler and Keeler develop any evidence favorable to the Count, nonetheless must have looked on the discoveries of the two dicks with mixed feelings. Keeler, experimenting with different kinds of flame produced by different kinds of fuel, stank up her home. To top thinks off, one shaft of flame got out of control and ruined a piece of priceless furniture. Schindler is still apologizing for bringing Keeler into that house.

Since a blowtorch had been used in the crime, Schindler wanted to check the entire island to find out who owned blowtorches. Such equipment was rare on the island except in one place—where wartime building operations were going on. Schindler wanted permission to question the workmen on such projects. Permission was denied. Schindler began to bite his nails and sprinkle a little more profanity than usual into his speech.

Every person arriving at or leaving Nassau had his name and address recorded in official records, along with his reason for coming or going, and the dates of his arrival and departure. Schindler wanted a look at those records. Permission was denied.

Schindler took to gnashing his teeth. What with the revised testimony of the Marquis and the evidence he and O'Neil had developed in regard to the fingerprint, Schindler was confident that the case against De Marigny could be smashed to splinters when it came to trial. As that was what he had been hired for, he had already earned his fee. But he wanted to do more. Having satisfied himself on the basis of provable facts that De Marigny did not commit the murder, Schindler at this point was aiming to find out who did.

Schindler learned that Oakes had another home in another part of Nassau—not as large or pretentious as Westbourne. Sir Harry had sometimes entertained dolls at this other home.

Sir Harry liked to tinker with tools. In the rear of this second residence was a tool house. Schindler found a detailed list of the equipment supposed to be in the house. He began to check the tools against the list. Everything was there except one thing—a prospector's pick.

Now, a prospector's pick is a heavy, short-handled piece of hardware with an odd triangular point. Prospectors use it to take samples from veins of ore. A prospector's pick could have been just the thing to do in the one-time prospector. Its triangular point would have produced just the kind of wounds that had been found in Sir Harry.

Sir Harry didn't occupy this second home very often, and when he wasn't there, it was completely deserted. A watchman kept an eye on it at night. But it would have been possible for anybody, studying the watchman's movements, to go into the tool house and come out with the pick.

In moving around Nassau, Schindler traveled both on foot and in a hired automobile, which he drove himself. He knew he was being followed, whether he was on foot or on wheels. Sometimes he saw his shadows, sometimes he felt them, but they were always there.

For years Schindler had been an exponent of the practical joke. He first became addicted to practical joking through his friendship with Joe Cook, the comedian, whose estate at Lake Hopatcong, New Jersey, aptly named Sleepless Hollow, was long celebrated as a testing ground for outrageous practical jokes. So Schindler decided to have some fun with the Nassau cops. One night he stopped his car in the center of town, ran into an alleyway, studied a blank wall with a magnifying glass, placed a chalk circle around a small spot, ran out of the alley, jumped into his car, and drove away. One member of the Nassau cops spent a week in the alley, trying to figure out what the hell the circle on the wall indicated.

Schindler became a fairly well-known figure in Nassau. That was just the way he wanted it. His reasoning was that somebody in the city, feeling that the cards were being stacked against De Marigny, would eventually contact him with some interesting information. And sure enough, while he was taking a walk one night, a woman walking behind him drew abreast of him and, in appearing to brush against him, slipped a note into his hand and hastened on her way.

Schindler, knowing he was being followed but not knowing whether the tails had seen the woman slipping him the note, played it smart. He sauntered around town for fully an hour, then got into his car and drove back to the villa of the Baroness. It was only then that he read the note that had been slipped to him. It was from a prominent woman in Nassau whose name Schindler had come to know. He was to come to her home the following night at ten o'clock.

The next night Schindler gave his tails the slip. He thus arrived at his destination undetected. He found the note passer a conservative person, very intelligent, and not, he judged, given to going off half-cocked.

"Did you know," she asked Schindler, "that Sir Harry Oakes had a gold cache on the island of Eleuthera?"

Schindler had heard about such a gold cache, but had not learned any details—particularly the detail of the precise island where the stuff was reputedly cached. Gold was hot stuff; it had been called in by the British government and also by the United States government.

"Yes," the woman continued, "Sir Harry had several millions buried on Eleuthera."

Eleuthera is one of the largest of the Bahama islands, some seventy miles east of Nassau. Schindler wanted to know how his informant had come into possession of the information.

"Why," she said, "practically everybody in Nassau knows it."

Schindler was hardly in a position to check that statement. Suddenly Schindler became conscious of the fact that the women was telling him that Oakes *had* had gold cached on Eleuthera. He asked the woman to explain.

"Draw your own conclusions, Mr. Schindler," she said. "But I think if you go over there you will find natives selling gold coins at about half their face value."

Schindler was later to learn in Nassau that Oakes had, shortly before his death, made several trips to Eleuthera. Such trips by a man of Sir Harry's prominence would have excited suspicion both in Nassau and on Eleuthera itself. It would have been entirely possible for the Negroes of Eleuthera—cunning men who were half savage, although some of them spoke with an English accent—to have become curious about the Baronet's visits and followed him. Discovering the gold cache, they could have taken it into their little heads to help themselves to it. Then, being discovered by Sir Harry, they might have feared he would use his influence to have them imprisoned (despite the fact that he had violated the law by not declaring the gold when gold had been called in by the British government). Fearing Oakes' reprisal, the culprits could have crossed to Nassau by boat in the night, crept into Westbourne, and done Sir Harry in. The savagery of the crime—the burning of the eyes and the sex organs—had distinct overtones of primitive ritual. The circle of possible suspects was getting bigger all the time.

There were, Schindler learned, five escapees from Devil's Island, the notorious penal colony off the coast of French Guiana, three of whom were thought to be hiding on one of the Bahama islands. It was possible that this group of convicts had discovered the gold cache in Eleuthera, helped themselves to it, then learned that Sir Harry was after them. Knowing of the man's power in the islands, they would have had ample reason to do him in.

Schindler located all three of the escapees. He met them secretly and put it right up to them: Did they know anything about the murder of Sir Harry Oakes? Through long experience, Schindler is usually able to satisfy himself as to the truth or falsity of a person's statements. He decided that the men from Devil's Island had had nothing to do with the murder.

Late in August—several weeks after he had first come to Nassau and shortly before the trial of Count de Marigny was to get under way—Schindler began to recapitulate what he had found since his arrival. He had satisfied himself that De Marigny had not committed the crime. He had further satisfied himself that the job could have been done by any one of a number of enemies Sir Harry had acquired before or after he took up residence in Nassau. It could have been done by dark-of-the-moon characters from the outer islands.

Schindler had in the meantime been filling himself in on the local gossip. Thus he had learned the identities of the husbands of women whom Sir Harry had successfully and unsuccessfully made passes at. Schindler had, in fact, met some of these men at parties he had been invited to because of his connection with the Baron and Baroness de Trolle. None of the wronged husbands seemed to fill the bill as suspects.

Now Schindler decided to go back to the beginning—or to a few days before the beginning. If he took things step by step, he figured he might come across something he had not so much as considered. Investigations are that way.

A week before the murder, Sir Harry's friend Christie moved into Westbourne to keep him company. The two men were alone in the big place at night, as the servants slept out. Christie occupied a room on the second floor, about eighteen feet from the nearest wall of Sir Harry's room. In that eighteen feet were

two other rooms—a small dressing room and a bathroom. It was thus possible for someone to walk from Christie's room into Sir Harry's by passing through a door that led from Christie's room into the small adjoining room and from there through a door leading into the bathroom, then out another bathroom door into Sir Harry's room. There was also another way of going from Christie's room into Sir Harry's. A screen door led from Christie's room onto a veranda that ran the entire width of the house. A similar door in Sir Harry's room led onto this veranda. It was the habit of the two men, when they alone remained at Westbourne, to go out through the screen doors of their respective rooms and meet on the veranda for breakfast in the morning.

On the night of the sixth, Sir Harry and Christie sat out on this veranda sipping drinks made of native rum, sugar, and fresh lime juice—a pleasant nightcap. Then the two men retired.

In the morning—the morning of the seventh—they had breakfast on the veranda. Then they spent a busy day together, preparing for Sir Harry's departure the next day on a business trip to South America.

They got back to Westbourne around five in the afternoon, played a couple of games of tennis, had some drinks, and got bathed and dressed for Sir Harry's farewell party that night. The party broke up about midnight and the servants straightened up and left Westbourne for the night. Christie and Sir Harry had a couple of more drinks and then went to their respective rooms. All during the night it stormed like hell. In the morning, when Sir Harry did not show up on the veranda for breakfast, Christie walked into his chamber and discovered the body.

Schindler wondered all over again exactly what had happened between the time Christie and Oakes parted for the night and the time Christie walked from the veranda into the Baronet's chamber in the morning.

Since his arrival in Nassau, Schindler had run into Christie occasionally—in the street and once in a while at a party. The two men had never really spoken to each other, just nodded in a stiff sort of way. After all, they were on opposite sides of the official fence—Christie to be a witness for the Crown and Schindler trying to knock down the Crown's case. But even had they not been on opposite sides of the fence, they probably wouldn't have liked one another. It was a case of chemistry; the two men just didn't click.

Now Schindler began to drop a few questions about Christie. Everyone on the island had a good word for the man —or so it seemed. Yet nobody seemed to know much about his background. He had, apparently, just materialized in Nassau and over the years come to be a power in the place. But Schindler began to catch whispers. Some residents of the island who had come from far places and bought property from Christie weren't satisfied with it. Some of Christie's real-estate clients were, in fact, downright dissatisfied with their purchases. But they didn't complain very loudly. For some reason or other, some people seemed to be afraid of Harold Christie. Schindler began getting interested.

Just about this time, a man walked into the Schindler offices in New York. He introduced himself as Harry Phillips, formerly a sleuth in the United States Treasury Department. He talked with Walter Schindler. He had, he said, been reading in the papers that Ray Schindler was working on the Oakes case. True,

and what? "Well," said Phillips, "I thought perhaps you would like to know something about this man Christie."

What did Phillips know about Christie? Well, for one thing, Christie was something less than the lily-white character that the upper-bracket citizens of Nassau held him to be. Christie, Phillips explained, had a shady background. He had been a rumrunner during prohibition days, reputedly palsy-walsy with the Capone mob in Chicago, and had been in some sort of trouble with the federals around Boston in the early twenties. As Phillips recalled, there had been a body attachment out for Christie in connection with false registry of a ship, but the attachment had never been served.

The Boston offices of the Schindler organization examined the federal records there but drew a blank. Walter Schindler told Phillips that he must be mistaken. "The hell I am," said Phillips. "I'll go up to Boston and get the record myself."

Phillips was in for a surprise. There was nothing in the federal indexes in Boston to indicate that Harold Christie had ever been accused of any infraction of a federal law there at any time. This simply didn't add up. Phillips was dead certain that a body attachment for Harold Christie had been issued in the early 1920's.

All federal records bear numbers—numbers that are recorded on federal indexes that give the names of persons accused. So now Phillips set himself to the tedious task of going through every number in the indexes beginning in 1920. What he hoped to find was that one number in the indexes was missing. And sure enough, it was.

Now Phillips asked to see the records that the missing number referred to.

The records related to Harold Christie and his alleged infraction of a federal statute. Included in the records was the unserved body attachment. Somebody had removed from the indexes the number leading to the record and the attachment, which is similar to a warrant. If it hadn't been for Phillips' search, the records in the Christie case might have been overlooked till doomsday.

Phillips had a copy of the federal record made and took it to New York, where Walter Schindler mailed it to Raymond in Nassau. The copy of the federal record could be an important piece of paper at the trial. If Christie, a principal witness for the Crown, were to be revealed as something less than a knight in armor by the disclosure of his past, the Crown's case might well begin to look fairly sickly.

As the trial was about to begin, Colonel R. A. Erskine-Lindop, the Superintendent of Police—one of the first to reach the scene of the murder and reputed to have his doubts about the guilt of the Count—was transferred to the island of Trinidad. There he was to become Assistant Commissioner of Police. Although the transfer had been in the works prior to the murder of Sir Harry Oakes, certain observers of what was taking place thought it was somewhat queer that Erskine-Lindop was not to be called as a witness at the trial.

Schindler didn't exactly expect fast delivery of the envelope containing the dope on Harold Christie once it reached Nassau. The envelope, like all other mail arriving at the island, would be subjected to wartime censorship. But he didn't suspect that the envelope wouldn't get to him in time for the trial.

Schindler knew it was against regulations to try to contact the censors directly. He could have contacted Harold Christie to see if Christie could look into the matter for him, since Christie, who was practically running the island, had certain powers over the censors. But asking Christie to investigate the fate of an envelope loaded with a blast against himself was out of the question.

So the trial of Alfred de Marigny for the murder of Sir Harry Oakes, which began in October and which was to last twenty-two days and receive more newspaper space than any trial since that of Bruno Hauptmann for the kidnapping and murder of the Lindbergh baby, got under way with the dope about Christie not in Schindler's possession. It was not possible to go through the legal machinery and other time-consuming steps necessary to get another certified copy of Christie's federal record in time. Schindler didn't get the Christie dope until after the trial was over.

Everybody in the courtroom wondered just how Harold Christie was going to make out. He made out all right. He gave a simple account of his discovery of the murder. If there had been any commotion in Westbourne during the commission of the crime, he had not heard it because he had been fast asleep. Anyway, the noise of the tropical storm would have drowned out any disturbance in the chamber of his long-time friend and business associate.

The defense, in attempting to contradict Christie's contention that he had not been out of Westbourne after he and Sir Harry had gone to bed, placed on the stand a police officer who had known Christie since both were boys—Captain Edward Sears. Captain Sears testified that he had seen Christie driving a station wagon not far from Westbourne around midnight on the night of the murder. This observation by a police official seemed strange. It had been made as a station wagon he was driving passed one going in the opposite direction. It was in this second station wagon that Sears claimed he saw Christie. Both cars, Sears estimated, were traveling at about fifteen miles an hour. The observation had been made when the two vehicles passed each other under a street lamp.

The Sears testimony made Christie burn. Sears had apparently made a mistake. Curiously enough, nobody brought out the fact that Christie had a brother who looked very much like him—enough like him, in fact, to pass for a twin in the conditions under which the cop saw the man in the station wagon.

The Marquis de Visdelou-Guimbeau and the blonde Betty Roberts pulled the Count away from the murder time span. The all-male jury, getting an eyeful of the blonde, began to get ideas. They were locked up in a hotel each night and the nights were long. One of them sent a written request to the prosecutor: "Send up six blondes."

It was when Captain Barker, the Miami cop, got into the witness box that Godfrey Higgs, chief defense counsel, opened up with ammunition supplied by Schindler, Captain O'Neil of the New Orleans Police Department, and Keeler. The principal piece of evidence against the Count was the fingerprint developed by Barker. The defense convinced the jury that the print of the Count's, allegedly found on a screen in the murder room, couldn't possibly have been taken from the screen.

The screen was of a grainy substance, and a photograph of the print showed no such grain in the background. Higgs convinced the jury that Barker had faked the print—lifted it with Scotch tape from something De Marigny had touched after his arrest.

Alfred de Marigny, then, was quickly

acquitted. Barker, who turned out to be a dope addict, went back to the States and got himself shot to death.

Not that the boy was completely out of trouble, at least in Nassau. The jury recommended his deportation. The Count moved fast. It seemed that he had, among other things, been guilty of violating the wartime gas-rationing regulations. He and his wife lit out for Cuba. But before he went he attended a little party at the estate of the Baron and Baroness de Trolle. Keeler was there with his polygraph.

"Say," the Count said to Keeler, "how about giving me a lie-detector test about the murder of Sir Harry Oakes? I'd like to take such a test. You know, I asked the Crown for such a test when I was arrested, but was refused."

So the test was made, with a stenographer present, and here are the questions and answers:

Q. Is your name Alfred de Marigny?
A. Yes.
Q. Did you know Sir Harry Oakes?
A. Yes.
Q. Do you know who killed Sir Harry Oakes?
A. No.
Q. Have you had something to eat today?
A. Yes.
Q. Did you kill Sir Harry yourself?
A. No.

De Marigny's answers to the key questions brought no more of a reaction in the mechanism of the lie detector than his replies to the unimportant queries. The lie detector has long been a reliable instrument in recording a guilty reaction. The fact that De Marigny's answers did not produce reactions of guilt convinced many crime-detection authorities throughout the civilized world that the man knew nothing about the murder of Oakes.

Now everybody packed up and went home. But Raymond Schindler, sitting in his office in New York, was not through with the Oakes case yet. He went through the whole business with Attorney General Cummings. The Attorney General pondered the matter, then wrote Schindler this letter:

From what I can see from the record, the police in Nassau fell into a mistake common to inexperienced officers everywhere. They found their logical suspect first and then proceeded to search for facts to fit him. From this first step it was easy to fall into a state of mind where the investigator makes himself blind to every bit of evidence except that which he can apply to the preconceived theory he has created in his own mind.

Next Schindler dictated this letter to the Duke of Windsor:

Knowing your deep concern for the welfare of the citizens of the Bahamas, I take the liberty of addressing you on a matter of great importance. It is my considered opinion that the murderer of Sir Harry Oakes can be found, identified, convicted and brought to justice. During the incarceration and trial of Alfred de Marigny no adequate investigation was possible. Statements which failed to point toward the defendant were ignored. It goes without saying that I, and my associate, Leonard Keeler, would welcome an opportunity to work on the case. We would willingly offer our services without compensation.

No less a personage than President Franklin D. Roosevelt, an old detective-mystery fan, had been following the Oakes case. He had, as a matter of fact, formed his own theories about the mystery—and De Marigny definitely was not his boy. The President, like practically everybody else in possession of the salient facts, had the definite feeling that the investigation into the scragging of the Baronet had been handsomely fouled up. Attorney General Cummings, in discussing the case with the President one day, received a tacit nod at his suggestion that the Federal Bureau of Investigation, busy as it was turning up spies, might be able to send a few men down to Nassau and take the mystery apart. Scotland Yard could have done the same thing. But His Royal Highness the Duke of Windsor wanted none of it. One of his secretaries sent Schindler a form letter saying thank you, no.

The Duke had done one thing, though. He ordered an investigation of law-enforcement in the islands. The probe accomplished approximately as much as a probe into the gambling situation in practically any American city.

The Nassau Daily *Tribune* had this to say:

Nassau can now relax after witnessing nearly a month of the tensest possible emotions engendered by the trial of Alfred de Marigny. . . .

Before the trial had progressed very far it was aptly described as "The Tragedy of Errors." The first—and perhaps the greatest—error was made when His Royal Highness the Governor called long distance and obviously got the wrong number. But in passing judgment on this action it must be conceded that His Royal Highness acted in good faith, doing what he believed to be in the best interest of the Colony. . . .

It is pleasing that, in the closing chapter of this case, the cloud which threatened to obscure the life work and career of the Honorable Harold Christie was completely lifted by the defense, the prosecution and the bench. Mr. Christie has served this country well and its citizens owe him a large measure of good will.

Today, Harold Christie, whose life work and career were temporarily clouded, is still a power in the islands. The Count and Nancy Oakes de Marigny have long since been divorced. The Count himself is circulating in the fashionable watering places, the same as ever. Raymond Schindler sits in his office in New York after a busy day at his desk, pondering the mysteries of the Oakes case. Schindler still believes that he could crack the mystery if he went down to Nassau and were given a free hand. But time is running out. Raymond Schindler, although you would never know it to look at him, is well into his seventies.

One thing is officially certain: Marie Alfred Fouquereaux de Marigny was not guilty of the murder. Another thing is equally certain: Officials of Nassau have demonstrated that they don't want Schindler, or anybody else, to prove guilty the real killer of Sir Harry Oakes.

The Pied Piper of Boston

When Charles Ponzi hit Boston, he didn't have a pot to bake beans in.
Then he thought up a money-making dodge that brought the
dough in faster than he could count it.

One sweltering afternoon late in June, 1919, Charles Ponzi, a thirty-six-year-old clerk in the employ of J. P. Poole, a Boston import-and-export brokerage house, opened an envelope from Spain and made a fascinating discovery. The envelope contained a postal-reply coupon—something Ponzi had never even heard of. The coupon, which the writer in Spain had enclosed to cover the postage for a letter of reply from the brokerage house, had, Ponzi saw as he examined it, been purchased in Madrid for the equivalent of one cent in United States currency. Yet it was redeemable at any post office or bank in the United States for five cents.

Charlie Ponzi pursed his lips and looked off into space. Here, he decided, was something worthy of serious investigation.

During the next few days, Ponzi boned up on postal-reply coupons. Such coupons had for years been part of the international postal systems of most large countries. Gathering data on the prevailing monetary rates in various European countries, Charlie got busy with pencil and paper. His eyes must have glowed as he decided how a smart operator could go into the business of buying the coupons in countries where the currency was depressed, then cashing them in in countries, such as the United States, where they would bring up to five times their purchase price, such as had happened with that coupon that the man in Madrid had sent to Poole's.

On paper, the scheme looked to be not only foolproof but promised unlimited possibilities. Ponzi, seized by his own fertile imagination, could foresee the day when he would have dozens of agents wafted hither and yon by the changing winds of international financial fluctuation. Thus he would be making anywhere from 100 to 500 per cent on a given investment in a batch of coupons.

The morning after he had completed his preliminary research, Ponzi, the soul of servility and punctuality during the two years he had been a counting house slave at Poole's, was an hour late for work. A toy fox-faced man, standing five feet two and weighing only one hundred and ten pounds, wearing a shiny double-breasted blue serge suit that pinched his wasp-like waist, Ponzi strode to his desk exuding a suddenly acquired belligerence. His boss, standing off to one side, arms folded and tapping his foot, bore down on him. "You're late, Ponzi," said the boss, consulting his watch. "An hour and three minutes late."

"What about it?" answered Ponzi, a sneer on his oversized lips, his little dark brown eyes shooting out sparks of defiance between high cheek bones.

"I've a good mind to discharge you for such impertinence!"

Ponzi shifted his gaze to the other counting house slaves, hunched over their desks. "I'm quitting," he said. "I don't like it here anyway."

It was, as it turned out, a black day for Bostonians when Charles Ponzi quit his job with J. P. Poole, soon to strike out for himself as the head of an outfit bearing the high-sounding name of The Securities Exchange Company. For Charles Ponzi, on the basis of the score he ran up in a racket unique in all the annals of crime, was one of the most successful con men in the history of criminal misrepresentation.

Operating out of a one-room office in a shabby five-story building on a side street for a period of thirty-two weeks and a few days—from December 20, 1919 until the law clamped down on him on Friday the thirteenth of August, 1920—Ponzi bilked the suckers for approximately fifteen million dollars. It was somehow congruous that the thoroughfare where Ponzi held forth was named School Street. For Charlie certainly taught everybody a lesson. He was, without realizing it, his own star pupil. When the dust had settled in Boston poor Ponzi, who had handled all those millions, didn't have a pot to bake beans in.

Promising investors 50 per cent interest on their money in ninety days—and, later, when he was really rolling, 50 per cent in forty-five days—Charlie simply robbed Peter to pay Paul, using the money of new investors to take care of the old ones. It was the simplicity of Charlie's racket that made it possible. While bankers, whose resources were being drained by depositors who were turning over their savings to Charlie, were trying to figure out just how Charlie was paying all that interest, he was simply playing one of the oldest con games in the books. But he was playing it on such an enormous scale that it looked as mysterious as it was simple.

At the height of his fraudulent operation, Ponzi was the most popular man in Boston. One scorching July day he was travelling through Washington Street in a chauffeur-driven dark blue Locomobile limousine when a mob of admirers surrounded the car. "Ponzi! Ponzi! Ponzi!" shouted one investor. "You are the greatest Italian in history!"

Charlie, sitting there with his little hands folded over the head of a walking stick, a ten-carat diamond glittering in a stickpin, just beamed on the speaker for a few moments. Then he said, "My friend, Columbus was the greatest Italian. He discovered America."

"But you, Ponzi," shouted the admirer, "discovered money!"

After quitting his job in the brokerage house that morning, Ponzi went home to a two-room flat he shared with his wife of two years in an Italian district in Boston's teeming North End. Mrs. Ponzi, the former Rose Guecco, the plump, thirtyish daughter of a wholesale fruit merchant, knew little about her husband. He had, a few years before, suddenly materialized out of thin air and, with those penetrating brown eyes of his, a glib tongue and some vague wartime cloak-and-dagger story to account for his immediate past, wooed, won and wed Rose over the apoplectic protests of her old man.

After marrying Rose, Charlie had conned her pater into letting him manage the wholesale fruit business. Within nine months he wrecked the enterprise, driving it into bankruptcy. Then, at the age of thirty-four he went to work for J. P. Poole as a fourteen-dollar-a-week stock boy. When he threw up his job as a clerk with Poole, he had been making sixteen dollars a week.

"But what will we do now?" inquired Rose as Charlie broke the bad news to her that morning he quit Poole's. "The rent will be due next week."

Little Ponzi, Rose was one day to tell investigators, was stalking around the room waving his hands wildly in the air. "Next week!" He snapped his fingers. *"Poof* to next week," he said, his voice rich, under perfect control and practically without an accent. "In a month we'll be rich."

It was now, now that he had quit his job and really got down to earth and the business of actually entering the postal coupon game, that Charlie discovered he had gone off half cocked. He had neglected to check one salient point. The sum total of postal-reply coupons used all over the world in any one year seldom exceeded seventy-five thousand dollars. There were certain rules, regulations and formalities to the postal-coupon business, Charlie now discovered, that took the bloom off the rose. A man attempting to make a living out of dealing in the coupons would be put to an expense exceeding the profits and would eventually run into the law of diminishing returns.

Charlie, disillusioned but not discouraged—and assailed by quiet desperation—sent five dollars to the man in Madrid, requesting the Spaniard to invest it in postal-reply coupons and forward them to him. When the coupons arrived Charlie, flashing the coupons, began to circulate among his friends in the North End. In a wise sort of way, Charlie asked his friends if they had ever heard of postal-reply coupons. None of them had. The general ignorance on the subject of postal-reply coupons was, Ponzi decided, refreshing.

One night in September—a hot night in Indian Summer when the Italians in the North End were leaning out of the tenement windows for a breath of fresh air and when Charlie saw no hopes of a job—Charlie was sitting on the front stoop of his tenement when a couple of hod-carrier friends stopped to chat. "Gee," remarked one of the hod carriers, having put in a tough day lugging wet concrete, "I sure wish I was rich."

"Me, too," said the other.

Right then something snapped in little Charlie. He was never able to explain, later when the official dome doctors were pumping him, just why he said what he did. But he found himself sparking the following chunk of dialogue. "What," Charlie asked his two friends, "would you do if you was rich?"

One of the hod carriers said he would drink himself to death and the other said he would chase women.

"How would both of you like to invest a little money with me—say fifty dollars?" asked Charlie. "In three months you would get seventy-five back."

"How?"

Ponzi smiled sagely. "Oh, it's a little secret I learned at that place I worked. I'm the only one knows about it outside of Rockefeller and men like that."

"Any chance of gettin' stuck?"

Charlie laughed. "No more than if you lent your fifty dollars to Morgan or Rockefeller."

Ponzi showed the postal-reply coupons to the hod carriers and, imaginative fellow, got off a likely whopper about how he had contacts with agents who bought postal-reply coupons in various European countries dirt cheap with American money and later converted the coupons for cash in New York for a killing. He might as well have been talking Greek to his two friends but what he was saying sounded as authentic as a race-track tip from the horse's mouth.

Next night, the two men met Ponzi on the stoop and each handed him fifty dollars, practically their life's savings. Ponzi wrote out receipts for the money, promising, in each receipt, to repay the sum of seventy-five dollars in ninety days.

Ponzi must have realized come ninety days he would have to get up that money or get out of town. So he conned a couple of other neighbors into investing in the non-existent coupons—a couple of Peters who would be robbed to pay the two Pauls. Then he had to dig up somebody to pay *them*. Before he realized it, Charlie had his monumental swindle going.

We might attempt to look into Ponzi's psychological processes at this point. How did Charlie expect to get away with it? He was cunning, if not highly intelligent, although he was intelligent enough to know the simple rules of mathematics. He must have realized that his scheme had to keep growing bigger to cover him up but that the bigger it grew the greater would be the risk of eventual detection.

The most plausible explanation of Ponzi seems to be that he had a screw loose somewhere and that he had his feet firmly planted on a cloud. Then, too, the streak of the confidence man was strong in him. And, to the confidence man, there is no thrill on earth, dames and liquor and skiing and mountain climbing included, that compares to the charge that comes from taking a sucker.

Ponzi also seems to have been strongly afflicted by egomania. He had a genuine thirst for power, as indicated by his statement to the press, when he was at the summit of his fraudulent scheme, that he thought he might run for Mayor, that he imagined he might make a good movie star, and by his willingness to be compared with Columbus as the greatest Italian in history.

Whatever the errant springs that flowed within him, Charles Ponzi quickly became a new and fascinating man to his tenement neighbors in the North End.

One of the first things he did with the profits of his initial transactions was to walk into a clothing store, wearing his glazed blue serge suit, leave it behind him and walk out of the place decked out in a double-breasted coca number with wide white stripes, pinched at the waist and with no cuffs on the pants. Then he stopped into a couple of other stores and bought a cane and a pair of two-toned high shoes—black patent leather bottoms and brown calfskin uppers.

The word began to get around that Charlie, while working in the financial house, had discovered a remarkable secret that could make people rich. Charlie stuck a sign in the front window of his flat reading:

Charles Ponzi
Foreign Exchange
Investments

Most of the neighbors couldn't read English but Ponzi was always darting in and out so that he was available to interpret the sign for them. When they asked him just what the nature of the foreign-exchange investments was he was glad to elucidate—with all that authentically-sounding gabble about international manipulation in coupons.

It was during the first week of December, when the skies were leaden and there was the feel of snow in the air, that the lightning struck. Ponzi's two original investors—the hod carriers—walked up to his flat after supper one evening and presented their receipts for fifty dollars. In a little while they bounced out of the tenement glowing.

"That man Ponzi!" one of them said to a neighbor. "He is a miracle man!" The hod carriers disclosed that Ponzi had been sitting there waiting for them, not only with their fifty dollars but with 50 per cent interest.

"Let me see the money," said their auditors.

"*See* it! Why, we give it back to Ponzi. He's goin' to do the same thing all over again."

"You give him the profits, too?"

"Sure. We're goin' to make a *profit* on the profits."

A couple of days later, when the second pair of Pauls got theirs from the money the third group of Peters had turned over to Charlie, and reinvested the money with Ponzi, practically everybody in the block heard about it.

Now Ponzi's neighbors began to open tin cans in kitchen cupboards and turn up bed mattresses and hustle down the street to hand over their cash to Charlie. Ponzi, growing in stature, was now settled behind a little oak desk acquired in a second-hand furniture store, and he sat there writing out promissory notes guaranteeing the return of principal and 50 per cent interest in ninety days. Each eager investor pressed anywhere from five dollars to a couple of hundred on Charlie and he, with an impressive show of scorn for cash, was tossing the stuff in paper bags.

During the second week of December, quite a few notes fell due. Little Charlie, dressed in his loud striped suit and looking like a fox that had just outwitted a pack of hounds, sat there at the oak desk, paying off. Some of his customers were grabbing the principal and the profits but others were forcing the money back on Charlie. Every once in a while, though, especially when there were three or four new investors in the room, Charlie would refuse to accept money for reinvestment. "Take it," he would urge a client. "Christmas is coming on and you'll need this to buy presents with."

The sight of Ponzi not only handing over the principal and the profit, but occasionally refusing to take the money back for reinvestment, had a pronounced psychological effect on the new investors. They considered themselves fortunate to get in on the good thing, whatever, precisely, it was, and went around crowing about their luck.

By mid-December, four months after he had severed his connections with Poole's, Charlie's snowball had gathered sufficient momentum for him to rent an office in downtown Boston. So, on December 20, we find him in a second-floor-front room, about twenty feet square and with two windows in it, in a shabby five-story gray stone office building on School Street.

The furnishings in Charlie's new office consisted simply of a second-hand oak desk and a chair in one corner of the room, facing the door, an ink well, a pen and a batch of blank receipts. The floor was without a carpet and there wasn't a hat rack, so Charlie, sitting there in his striped suit, had to put his hat and his cane on the desk.

Charlie went around the corner and had a sign painter make him a couple of signs reading:

FOREIGN EXCHANGE COMPANY
CHARLES PONZI, PRES.

He stuck one sign in a window facing School Street and the other in the vestibule on the ground floor, with an arrow pointing to a stairway leading to the second floor.

The very first day Ponzi opened up on School Street, several clients came to town from the North End, both to collect and to invest. Ponzi, sitting there at the desk, reaching for one of those ninety-day notes, would study the note, glance up at the investor, flash a quick smile, then ask, "Do you wish to take the cash, or shall I reinvest it for you?"

The replies were about fifty-fifty. When Ponzi was asked to pay off, he made a production of reaching into a drawer of the desk, where the long green had been tossed with an impressive abandon. "Don't forget to tell your friends about your good fortune," he would tell the lucky investor as he forked over the money. "There's plenty of this stuff"— he'd pat the drawer where the money was—"to go around."

The first four days he was on School Street Charlie took in about twelve hundred dollars and handed out about seven hundred and fifty. He locked up late on the afternoon before Christmas, went around to Filene's department store and bought his wife a handsome wine-colored silk dressing gown. When he took it home at supper time and handed it to her she was practically delirious with joy. "Oh, Charlie," she said, "it's wonderful."

Ponzi brushed the whole thing off. He had brought himself a cigarette holder and now he lit up and walked up and down the room, holding the holder at shoulder level. "What has happened so far," he said to Rose, who was lost in admiration, "is nothing. Positively nothing. One of these days—and not long from now, either—I'm going to buy you a mansion out in one of those swell suburbs. Will you like that, Rose?"

Now let's take a look at the background of this little man who stood at the threshold of a career unique in the annals of crime. Charles Ponzi first opened his dark little eyes on the world that was to be his oyster in the town of Parma in the Province of Emilia in Northern Italy. The Province of Emilia was noted for the manufacture of silk and the produc-tion of cheese and it was not far from Bologna. It would seem that the locale of Ponzi's birth could hardly have been more congruous since the little man turned out to be a big cheese, smooth as silk, specializing in handing out bologna.

Charlie was in his seventeenth year when, in 1899, he sailed from Naples for New York with savings of approximately two hundred and fifty dollars. His parents had been farmers, raising their own help. Charlie, quick-witted and impatient, could see no future out plowing in a sun-baked field, the horizon shut off by the rear end of a beast of burden.

On the way over on the boat, Charlie, his little eyes wide with wonder, sneaked past the barricades that separated the immigrants in the steerage from those travelling second- and first-class. It was while roaming the first-class deck one moonlit night, with the music playing and men in tails waltzing around with beautiful dolls, that little Ponzi became enchanted by the high life.

Hanging around the first-class smoking room the last night out, Charlie was lured into a game of cards by two well-dressed strangers. It was the old story of a couple of sharpers taking a sucker. When Charlie walked off the boat next morning he had only two dollars and a half left in his pocket—a conspicuously unauspicious entrance into the land of milk and honey.

Ponzi, clutching his remaining cash in one hand and a knapsack in the other, walked from the docks up Broadway, craning his neck at the tall buildings. He had heard stories in Italy about the wealth in America and how easily it was acquired. But he was in for a jolt. He found himself swinging a pick on a construction project where the Irish foreman and practically everybody else called him not by his right name but "John."

Charlie, who had a gift for languages, and who already spoke some French and some German, found English a cinch to master. He wandered to Pittsburgh. Somebody had told him that the pickings were easy in the steel mills there but he found out differently. He became a pick-and-shovel man in the Smoky City.

Two years after he had first hit New York, Charlie, now nineteen and now speaking English with hardly a trace of an accent, turned up as a bus boy at Rector's fabulous restaurant in New York. This was the blue-sky era, when a man could commit financial murder and get away with it. Charlie, a foxy, under-sized fellow, used to stand there on the red carpeting, looking off into space but eavesdropping on the plots that the male diners, over after-dinner brandy, cooked up to rob the widows and orphans.

From all Charlie had been able to observe in his two years in this country, honesty may have been the best policy but it sure as hell wasn't paying off. The honest men were digging ditches, sweeping floors or breaking their backs in the mills and the crooks were wallowing in wealth.

A few years passed and Ponzi rose in the world. He became a waiter at Delmonico's. All the while he was living in a hall bedroom and dreaming of the day when he, dressed to kill, would be sitting at a table in one of those tony joints instead of waiting on it.

One day, when he was twenty-three, Charlie heard a group of Wall Street men in Delmonico's discussing a big killing they were about to execute. Charlie decided that here was his golden opportunity. He had saved his tips and had several hundred dollars salted away. If

he could get a piece of this deal he'd be on the way.

Approaching the table where the financiers were in a huddle, Charlie smiled, bowed and said, "Pardon me, gentlemen, but I couldn't help overhearing your conversation. I have several hundred dollars that I would like to invest in your project."

The silence was dreadful. The financiers just sat there looking at Charlie, then at each other. When at length one of them spoke it was not to Charlie but to bark for the head waiter. "Discharge this impudent fellow! He has been eavesdropping on our private conversation."

So there was Charlie, out in the street. Jobs were hard to come by in New York restaurants in those days. Not only that, but when a fellow got himself canned the word went along a restaurant grapevine. Charlie soon saw that the future in New York was hopeless. Having heard that the people in Canada were a softer touch than those in America, he lit out for Montreal.

There were snow flurries in the air when Ponzi opened for business in that second-floor office on School Street the day after New Year's, 1920. Late in the afternoon, Charlie, sitting there behind the desk, was writing out a ten-dollar receipt for a North End Italian laborer when he got a hot flash. He looked up at the laborer, squinted his eyes and asked, "How would you like to stop digging ditches and go to work for me?"

"What I got to do?" the laborer wanted to know.

"Go around and get your friends to invest," said Ponzi, handing the son of toil a book of blank receipts. "I'll pay you ten cents for every dollar you collect."

Charlie's deal with the laborer was one of those little acorns out of which great oaks grow. Within a week the laborer was not only rounding up investors for Charlie but was getting a friend to corral investors for *him*.

Ponzi was quick to realize that he had struck gold. So, every time he raked in money from a new investor he would toss out the same proposition as he had put up to the laborer. Practically everybody went for it.

By the middle of February, some two months after Charlie had opened up in School Street, he was really off the ground. His agents had infiltrated the stevedore gangs on the Charlestown docks and were circulating among waiters, elevator boys, barbers and bartenders in speakeasies in downtown Boston and among the French-Canadians in Worcester and Providence, the Italian millworkers in Lawrence, and even down to the Poles in Bridgeport, Connecticut.

By the middle of March, the flow of investors and the volume of mail from agents coming into that office on School Street became too much for Charlie to handle alone. So Rose left her mop and scrubbrush in the North End tenement and came into town to act as a sort of secretary to her husband.

Charlie called in a carpenter and installed a plywood partition, complete with a couple of windows, separating the front of his office from the rear. Then he plucked a couple of Italian friends from his home neighborhood—men who were as honest as they were stupid—and planted them as receiving tellers at the windows. Charlie, sitting there at the desk, with Rose on a chair alongside of him, doubled in brass as President of the Foreign Exchange Company and paying teller.

Most of Ponzi's investors were bringing in small sums—anywhere from a dollar to five dollars. Not a soul asked a single question. Everybody seemed to know or have heard of somebody who had actually collected and nobody was in a mood to look a gift horse in the mouth.

The bulk of the suckers showed up on their lunch hours. Thus from noon until about two o'clock the line out in front of the gray building on School Street stretched around the corner into Washington Street. Charlie, shifting into high gear, was taking in sometimes as much as three thousand dollars a day—mostly in one- and five-dollar bills.

A born showman, Charlie made a production of his intake. Each of the two window tellers had a big wire waste paper basket on a counter at his elbow. When accepting an investment the teller would, on instructions from Charlie, simply toss the money into the wire basket so that the investor could stand there and be impressed while the teller was writing out a receipt.

Charlie kept his records in a small safe. A great man for avoiding complications, he simply marked down on a little white card the name and address of an investor, the amount invested and the date the principal and interest were due. Then, a couple of days before pay-off time, Charlie's wife would send a postcard to the lucky client, advising that payment date was approaching.

By mid-April, four months after he had opened up in School Street, and one month after he had paid off the first batch of School Street investors, practically half of Boston was talking about Charlie. By now there were six clerks busy behind the beaverboard partition, raking in the money, tossing the stuff in wire baskets, and writing out receipts. Charlie was still sitting out front at his desk, with Rose alongside of him, both very busy, Rose mailing notices to investors, Charlie paying out the cash when he had to and keeping it for re-investment when he could.

By now Charlie had a stock way of dealing with the customers. He would flash the old smile and, if the sucker took his advice and reinvested, he would get up and shake hands or clap the man on the back. But if the sucker insisted on making off with the loot, Charlie would just sit there, waiting until the man got to the door, then shout, "Don't forget to tell your friends about your good fortune!"

After locking up for the night, Charlie would stuff the day's take into a straw suitcase and, accompanied by Rose, drop into a downtown Italian restaurant. Charlie loved spaghetti; in fact he ate it for dinner practically every night. He and Rose would sit there eating, the suitcase lying flat on the floor under the table, Charlie's feet up on it.

After dinner, Charlie and Rose, and the suitcase, would take a street car to their tenement flat in the North End. Charlie was open for business in the flat, too. On the fine spring nights there were always anywhere from a dozen to fifty investors waiting for him.

First thing in the morning, Charlie would show up at the Hanover Trust Company, on Washington Street directly across from The Boston *Post,* and deposit the take from the previous day. During one week late in April, Charlie deposited thirty thousand, three hundred and eighty-six dollars in his account in the Hanover Trust.

Came the day when the office on School Street was no longer big enough to accommodate the customers. The work of paying off investors had by this time grown too burdensome even for Charlie. So he took over an abandoned saloon in Pi Alley, a narrow thoroughfare that ran off Washington Street in a stretch of the thoroughfare that housed both The Boston *Post* and The Boston *Globe.* There he installed six clerks who did nothing but issue checks to investors who wanted to cash in. Thus when a man or a woman or a boy or a girl showed up at the School Street office and asked for cash, Charlie would send them around to the Pi Alley branch to get a check.

By this time Charlie had opened accounts in half a dozen Boston banks. But his biggest account was in that jug across the street from The *Post.* Sometimes, during the lunch hour, there were so many investors crowding into Pi Alley and into The Hanover Trust Company that traffic in Washington Street ground to an absolute standstill.

Ponzi's name began to supplant the weather as a conversational opener, not only in Boston but in the New England hinterlands. There were only two kinds of people in The Hub now—those who had invested with Ponzi and those who needed their heads examined. Loan sharks were doing a land office business with suckers who were willing to pay them exorbitant interest rates to get money with which to make even more exorbitant profits with Ponzi.

Curiously enough, the press—every paper in Boston, and there were six of them—ignored Charlie as it would have ignored an elevator accident in a department store. Reporters on The *Post* and The *Globe,* going to and from work and out on assignments, had to fight their way through crowds of Ponzi investors, completely muffing the biggest story New England had known since Paul Revere rode through the countryside tipping the populace to the lantern signals in the Old North Church.

One morning in June, Ponzi, sitting at the desk in School Street with Rose, told his wife to mind the store while he went out and did something. He returned late in the afternoon, looking like a tabby that had just swallowed a sparrow.

"What have you been doing all day, Charlie?" asked Rose.

"Ah, Rose," said Ponzi, putting his arm around his wife, "remember what I told you one night when I left Poole's?"

"About the mansion?"

Ponzi nodded.

"What about the mansion?" asked Rose.

"Come and see."

Closing up shop, Ponzi hustled Rose into a waiting taxi. "To Lexington," he told the driver.

"But Charlie," said Rose. "The taxi fare to Lexington will cost a fortune." Poor Rose. On those rare occasions when she had been in a taxicab she had worried herself sick over the mounting figures on the meter. "Poof," said Charlie, snapping his fingers and still sticking to his favorite expression of contempt for a monetary problem.

The place in Lexington was not so much as mansions went but it was a dream for people like Charlie and Rose, who had always lived in tenements. It was a large rambling brown house, in the Victorian tradition, set in the middle of sweeping lawns and fine shrubbery. "Oh, goodness, Charlie," said Rose, standing on the lawn and looking up at the house, "it's wonderful. But it'll keep me awful busy doing the housework."

"Poof," said Charlie. "We'll get servants."

After Charlie had shown Rose around the house, she asked him how much the place had cost. "Thirty thousand dollars," said Charlie. "I paid for it this morning—cash."

A minute later, Charlie was racing over the lawn to the waiting taxi. "Hey," he shouted to the driver. "Come help me carry my wife out and get her to a doctor."

"What's the matter with her?" asked the driver.

"She's fainted," said Charlie.

Rose of course recovered. And a good thing, too. A few nights later, when she was leaving the School Street office with Charlie, she stopped to admire a handsome big blue Locomobile limousine parked at the curb. "Gee, Charlie," she said, "just look at that big car."

"Some car, isn't it?" said Charlie. The vehicle was so long and so wide that one astigmatic observer estimated that it was a morning's march from the radiator cap to the spare tire in the rear.

"I never seen one so long. I bet it cost a fortune."

"Twelve thousand dollars," said Charlie. "Custom built. I paid cash for it this morning."

Rose looked at Charlie, saw he wasn't kidding, and said she felt faint. Charlie snapped his fingers to a chauffeur, who had been standing at attention clad in a uniform to match the car. "Open the door for the lady, Joe," Charlie said to the chauffeur, helping Rose into the car. Now Charlie got in, settled himself with his hands folded over the head of his cane, and said, "Home, Joe."

As the big blue Locomobile swung through the streets of Boston and then into the outskirts Rose gradually recovered from her shock. "Hey Charlie," she said, "he's not taking us home. He's goin' someplace else."

"We're on the way to Lexington," Charlie explained. "We're not going back to the North End anymore."

"But what about furniture, Charlie? We can't live in an empty house."

"Wait," said Charlie, "and see."

What Rose saw, when she stepped out of the blue limousine and entered a door opened by a liveried butler, was an interior decorator's nightmare. The house was a bad dream of costly Oriental rugs, antique furniture of various periods, billowing pea-green silk chair coverings and royal blue and cardinal red velvet draperies. Charlie took Rose by the arm and led her from room to room. When the tour was almost complete Rose asked, "What did all this cost, Charlie?"

"One hundred and six thousand dollars," Charlie replied. "Now don't you go fainting again, Rose."

"Where's the furniture from our flat?" asked Rose. "I don't see the furniture from our flat."

Charlie snapped his fingers. "I gave it away," he said, "to some poor people."

One morning in the middle of June, six months after Ponzi had opened that office in School Street, there was a meeting of the board of directors of the Hanover Trust Company. Little Charlie, his hands folded over the top of that cane, was sitting outside of the directors' room as the directors filed in. Two of the directors stopped to say "Hello" to Ponzi; the others either gave him a refrigerated glare or ignored him altogether.

Ponzi just sat there, looking off into space, occasionally tapping one foot on the marble floor. In about an hour the door of the directors' room opened and a man sweating under a heavy black worsted suit beckoned to Charlie. "Mr. Ponzi," said the man, "the directors would be pleased to see you."

Charlie minced in, paused dramatically near the head of the directors' table and searched each face. Then he smiled and said, "Yes, gentlemen?"

One of the directors cleared his throat. "Mr. Ponzi," he said, "it would seem that you have purchased a good deal of the stock of this bank. It would appear, in fact, that you have purchased controlling interest."

"That," said Ponzi, "comes as no surprise to me. I have long wished to control a bank, gentleman."

"What," asked the spokesman for the directors, "are your wishes, Mr. Ponzi?"

"I want," said Ponzi, smiling, "to be president."

The spokesman just looked at the other directors. Then, raising his eyebrows, he said, "Gentlemen, I hereby propose Mr. Charles Ponzi for the presidency of this bank. All in favor will signify by raising their hands; all opposed need not raise their hands."

Ponzi ran his tongue over his upper lip as his little dark eyes swept the faces of the men at the table. All of the faces were frozen, in the best Boston tradition, but the right hand of every man at that table shot up. "The vote being unanimous," said the spokesman, "I hereby declare Mr. Ponzi our new president."

Ponzi got up and approached the man he had just succeeded. "How long will it take you to clean out your desk?" he asked.

"I can be out of here in an hour, Mr. Ponzi," said the deposed official.

"Fine," said Charlie.

Upon assuming the presidency of the Hanover Trust Company, Charlie checked into the jug first thing every morning, before the night watchman had gone off duty, and was the last man out nights. Between times he darted across the street to the office in Pi Alley and over to the main office on School Street.

One morning, not long after taking over the Hanover Trust, Charlie walked into the Poole brokerage house—the very place where he had left, practically by request, only twelve months before. Just inside the door, he stopped, folded his arms, began tapping his foot, and searched the place with an unfriendly gaze. Finally, he spotted the man who had once been his boss. Charlie smiled and beckoned to the man. "Yes, Mr. Ponzi?" said Charlie's ex-boss, all oil and subservience.

"So," said Charlie, "you remember me."

"Indeed I do. You were one of our most valued employees."

"That wasn't what you thought that day I came in late." Charlie, never a man who failed to extract the most from a situation, just stood there, a fixed little smile on his face, while his ex-boss ran his index finger under his tightening collar. "Now," said Charlie, "you can go to the cashier and get your pay."

"But I don't understand, Char—Mr. Ponzi."

Charlie tapped the floor with his cane. "I said go and get your pay. I purchased controlling interest in this company last night and you, my friend, are fired."

It was along about now that the key men in Boston's financial circles began to take serious notice of Ponzi. At first, the bankers and brokers and big business men had considered Charlie beneath notice, a flash in the pan. Nobody had known, or cared, just what his scheme was, but nobody in the loftier financial circles had thought it could last. But now, now that Charlie had been operating for half a year, the big-time money changers began to grow apprehensive.

One noontime seven Boston bankers met in a private dining room of Loch Ober's, perhaps the finest restaurant in The Hub, and, over clam chowder and lobster thermidor, discussed Ponzi. "For the life of me," said one banker, "I can't see how this man Ponzi is doing what he is doing. It just runs counter to every-

thing I've learned in thirty years in the banking business."

"Is it possible," asked another banker, "that the man is a crook?"

"He couldn't be," said a third banker. "Why?"

"I don't know. But I don't think it's possible that the man could be crooked. Why, if he were, he'd be bound to be found out."

"What worries me," chimed in another money man, "is that our depositors are drawing their savings out to give to Ponzi."

"Are any of them putting the money back at the end of ninety days?"

"That's just it. Some of them are. They're getting 50 per cent interest. I *wish* I knew how he was doing it." The speaker looked earnestly at the faces of the other men. "Gentlemen," he said, "I'll tell you one thing: if this man Ponzi continues he'll drain the resources of every bank in the city."

Boston's Police Commissioner—a bulky man by the name of Michael J. Crowley—was a good cop but he seems not to have known the limits of his authority. Wondering what, precisely, Ponzi was up to, Crowley sent a sergeant and two flatfeet around to the Hanover Trust to have a talk with Charlie.

The trio of gendarmes barged into the jug right at opening time one morning and asked to speak to the president. Charlie must have felt a twinge or two when a secretary entered his office and told him there were three policemen outside to see him. But if he did he never let on. "Send them in," said Charlie.

Ponzi sat there listening to the cops asking him how he ran his business. "I'll tell you what," said Charlie. "Let's go around to my School Street office and I'll explain everything to you."

At School Street, Charlie opened his little safe and brought out some of those coupons that the man in Spain had bought for him a year before. The cops, not wishing to appear stupid, nodded as Charlie went through his spiel about fluctuations in foreign exchange. When he was through explaining, the cops were still sitting there, nodding. Now they began to look at one another.

A little while later, the sergeant and the two flatfeet walked into Commissioner Crowley's office. "Well," asked Crowley, "what'd you find out?"

"The man's positively on the level," said the Sergeant. "Ain't he, fellows?" The two flatfeet nodded.

"How do you know?" asked Crowley.

"Why, we invested ourselves."

"What!"

"We're puttin' in fifty dollars apiece. Ponzi says we'd be crazy if we didn't."

Charlie sure had come a long way in that year since he had quit Poole's. His dodge was now running more or less on its own momentum so that Charlie was enabled to spend more and more time at the brokerage house and at the bank.

Ponzi was at his best at the bank when he presided over a directors' meeting. He was the toughest bank president in town when it came to passing on loans. Charlie had a fishy eye for questionable collateral. The only time any of his associates in the board room of the jug ever heard him raise his voice was when he refused to okay a loan to some business because of the collateral offered. "Why," Charlie would say, screwing up his face and flicking the ashes from his cigarette, "this collateral is *shaky*."

Ponzi's interests were by no means confined to business, now that he had that place out in Lexington. Like many men who come into the big money from the wrong side of the railroad tracks,

Ponzi had social aspirations. He went to a printer and had the man make up engraved invitations to a house warming. He sent the invitations to about fifty of his fashionable neighbors in Lexington.

Ponzi planned well for the house-warming, which was scheduled to begin at two o'clock on a Sunday afternoon. He hired a caterer and there were tables out on the lawn, groaning with smoked hams, cold turkeys, whole cheeses, and off to one side, cases of bootleg beer and whiskies. Charlie was prancing around the lawn, awaiting the first arrivals, decked out in a summer suit and a new pair of two-toned shoes. Rose was sweating under the hot sun in a long purple satin dress. A corps of waiters, wearing white duck suits, stood at attention behind the host and hostess.

By two-thirty nobody had showed up. At a little after three, when none of the guests had arrived, Charlie put his watch back in his vest pocket and glanced into space. "There must be a mistake," Charlie said to Rose. "I'll go in and phone."

In about twenty minutes Charlie came out again. "I can't understand it," he told Rose. "Nobody I invited's come." He walked around in a small circle, his hands in his pockets, shaking his head. "I simply can't understand it." Rose started to cry. "*I* can understand it, Charlie," she said. "We ain't good enough for the people who live here."

Ponzi looked at Rose, his eyes wide. "Do you really think so, Rose! But why not?" He fingered the lapels of his jacket, then pointed to Rose's purple gown. "Nobody wears better clothes than us, Rose," he was saying. He waved a little hand at the food tables. "Look at all that food. Who eats better than that?"

Charlie began to walk around in a little circle again. "Charlie," said Rose, "what are we going to do with all that food and nobody to eat it?"

Charlie thought for a few minutes, then said he had an idea. Presently he was being whisked away in the blue Locomobile. An hour or so later Rose and the waiters, still standing out there on the lawn in the hot sun, saw the Locomobile approaching. Behind it were five taxicabs.

When the cars drew into the grounds and disgorged their passengers the joint really began to jump. Charlie had gone back to his old neighborhood in the North End and rounded up his former neighbors for a big bust.

If the Lexington neighbors had ignored Charlie's invitation they certainly couldn't ignore his party. The thing was still going strong at midnight with most of the male guests drunk. A couple of the guests happened to be piano movers and they moved a piano out onto the lawn. The gendarmes arrived a little before two o'clock on the Monday morning and broke things up.

By now the most inquiring mind in Boston inhabited the skull of Edward J. Dunn, the forty-one-year-old city editor of The Boston *Post*. Eddie Dunn, a hefty, soft-voiced man with inquiring blue eyes behind gold-rimmed glasses, held forth in a swivel chair behind an old-fashioned roll-top desk in a second-floor cubbyhole that looked out on Washington Street across the street from the Hanover Trust Company.

Sitting at his desk, Dunn had frequently seen Ponzi darting in and out of the Hanover Trust Company across the street. And now in June, Eddie Dunn found himself waking up in the middle of the night, wondering about Ponzi. No man living knew more about what was going on in Boston's high and low places,

and all places in between, than Eddie Dunn. As the dusk was deepening one sultry evening, Dunn was sitting in his cubbyhole wondering why it was that if Ponzi's system were on the level it had been overlooked by the proprietors of Boston's staid old counting houses.

And so Eddie Dunn summoned one of his reporters. "I want you to look into one particular angle of this Ponzi business," Dunn said to the scribe. "Find out how it is *possible* that Ponzi is making all that money simply by dealing in postal-reply coupons." Dunn had a way of looking at a reporter and, in a flat New England tone, placing emphasis on certain words that saved himself and the reporter a great deal of time. Thus when he emphasized the word *possible* he and the reporter were in perfect rapport.

Twenty-four hours later Eddie Dunn had his first facts. In an average year, there were less than $75,000 worth of the coupons printed. In the calendar year of 1919—the year when Ponzi had begun operations—there had been a total of $58,560 coupons issued. Dunn sat at his desk studying the figures. When he had digested them, he looked up at the reporter, squinted his eyes, and said in a strained tone, "What Mister Ponzi claims to be doing just isn't possible." This time Dunn put a low connotation on the word *Mister*.

Dunn, perhaps the most astute man in all Boston at collaring a reluctant fact, was a great hand for a telephone. Sometimes he used it by the hour, calling contacts he had built up over a period of years. He had a way of crouching over a phone and talking into it so that somebody sitting right alongside of him couldn't hear a word he was saying.

And so, on a sticky June night, Eddie Dunn took to the phone. He telephoned to tipsters that he had all over Boston—

THE PIED PIPER OF BOSTON

tipsters who walked around their bailiwicks, ears and eyes wide open, and getting paid anywhere from twenty-five to a hundred dollars when they turned in an exclusive story to Eddie Dunn.

This particular June night, along toward ten o'clock, Eddie Dunn was talking on the telephone to a man who lived in the Italian district of Boston's North End. "Have you invested any money with Ponzi, Tony?" Dunn asked.

"Not a cent, Mr. Dunn. Not a cent."

"Why, Tony?"

"I don't trust that man Ponzi."

"You don't say. And why don't you trust him, Tony?"

"He's been in trouble somewhere."

"What kind of trouble?"

"Trouble with the law."

"Keep talking, Tony. This will be worth money to you."

The trouble was Tony didn't seem to know any more than what he had already told Dunn. All he knew was rumor. He had heard, somewhere, sometime, that Charlie Ponzi had been in trouble with the law.

Dunn hunched closer to the phone, and, with an effort, keeping his voice low and calm, kept pressing Tony. Where had Ponzi been in trouble? In New York? In San Francisco?

At length, Tony said, "No, I think Ponzi was in trouble somewhere not in this country."

"In Italy, perhaps?"

"No, closer." Dunn, whose roots were in Ireland, where the little men cavort in the glens, heard the little men speaking to him now. "Canada?"

"Yes! Canada. Now it comes back to me."

"What part of Canada, Tony?"

Tony didn't know. This time, when Eddie Dunn pressed, he didn't get anywhere.

When Dunn hung up, he motioned to an office boy. "Go to the morgue," he said, meaning the paper's library, "and bring me a map of Canada."

Poring over the map, Dunn summoned several reporters. "I want you fellows to take a map of Canada," he said, "and divide it up among you. Cover every law enforcement agency from Vancouver to Nova Scotia and find out if Charles Ponzi has ever been arrested. Use the phone. Use the telegraph. Use *anything*. But get hold of everybody. Get 'em all. Don't miss a single one."

A week went by. Dunn's boys drew nothing but blanks. He had them double check and triple check the police and prosecutors in such populous cities as Montreal, Toronto and Vancouver, where there were sizeable Italian populations. But nobody knew anything about Charles Ponzi. Yet something in Eddie Dunn's bones—or perhaps it was the little men—assured him that the tipster had been right when he said Charles Ponzi had once been in trouble in Canada.

Dunn assigned reporters to go around town and have off-the-record talks with men highly placed in financial circles. One banker suggested that a reporter interview Clarence W. Barron, publisher of *Barron's Weekly*, a financial bible. The reporter asked Barron what he thought of Ponzi's business. "Not much," said Barron. "If his scheme—whatever it is—is so good, why doesn't he invest in it himself?"

One night, when his reporters had reported in, Eddie Dunn taxied across the Charles River to the Cambridge home of Richard Grozier, son of the publisher of The *Post*, who was taking over in his father's absence. Eddie Dunn sat in a big leather chair, in Grozier's library, insisting to the publisher that it was in the interests of justice to draw a bead on

Ponzi. Grozier gave the go-ahead for a series on Ponzi—a series that wasn't to say much but which was to hint that The *Post* questioned the whole Ponzi operation.

The first headline in The *Post*, two columns on page one of the issue of Saturday, July 17, 1920, read:

DOUBLES THE MONEY
WITHIN THREE MONTHS

----

50 Per Cent Interest Paid in 90 Days
By Ponzi—Has Thousands of
Investors

Deals In International Coupons Taking
Advantage of Low Rates
Of Exchange

That first story didn't say very much, except that there was a financial wizard operating out of School Street and that the lines of investors were getting bigger every day. But in subsequent stories in the series, Barron was quoted. And then The *Post* ran a box showing how it was impossible that Ponzi's profits were accruing from dealings in postal-reply coupons.

If Eddie Dunn thought that series in The *Post* was going to put the paper in right with the populace he missed his guess. By mid-week, after the fourth article hit the streets, crowds began to gather in Washington Street, outside The *Post*. Dark-skinned men in yellow high button shoes and women wearing bushkas stood there in Washington Street, in the midsummer heat, sweating and hurling imprecations up at the editorial rooms. Eddie Dunn, sitting there in his cubbyhole, would look down on the street scene and sigh.

One afternoon Dunn summoned one of his reporters—a fellow named Jim Dempsey—and told him to try and get an interview out of Ponzi. Dempsey went around to School Street and found the great man sitting at his desk in front of the money cages. Ponzi, one hand resting on the head of his cane, just glared at Dempsey. "I should sue that paper of yours for what you've been printing about me," Ponzi said.

"If that's the way you feel, Mr. Ponzi," said Dempsey, "why don't you come around and have a talk with our city editor? He'd like to meet you."

Ponzi gripped the end of his cane until his knuckles showed white. "That's a good idea," he said. "Come on. We'll walk around right now."

A crowd began to collect as Dempsey and Ponzi started out on the short walk to The *Post*. By the time they entered the stairway leading up to the editorial rooms, there were probably a thousand people milling around Washington Street.

Dunn, sitting back there in his cubbyhole, didn't bat an eyelash as Dempsey appeared in front of his roll-top desk with Ponzi in the flesh. But he did get up to greet the little man. Ponzi extended his hand and Dunn took it half-heartedly. "I should sue you," Ponzi said to Dunn.

"That, Mr. Ponzi, is certainly your privilege." Dunn's voice was deceptively soft. The two men were standing face to face with their faces not eighteen inches apart. "Mr. Ponzi," Dunn said, his voice down to practically a whisper, "tell me about that trouble you were in up in Canada."

Ponzi's face hardened and Dunn could see his body stiffening under the summer suit. "Oh, that Montreal business," Ponzi said. "It amounted to nothing. Nothing at all."

"Tell me about it," said Dunn. Ponzi, caught off base by the first question, now quickly recovered. "It is a closed issue," he said. "Absolutely closed and unimportant."

That was all there was to the little talk. The two men just stood there glaring at each other. Then Ponzi relaxed, smiled, shook hands with Dunn and left.

The moment Ponzi was out of sight, Dunn summoned his star reporter—Herbert L. Baldwin. "Baldy," he said, "Ponzi has just admitted to me that he was once in trouble in Montreal. I want you to go up there and find out all about it."

Baldwin, later to become head of a public-relations firm in Boston, was a tall, faultlessly-tailored fellow of twenty-six, given to brown suits. He frightened information out of people by firing questions at them in stentorian tones, the while boring right through them with large, quizzical brown eyes. He ambled into the paper's morgue and stuck in his pocket several recent pictures of Ponzi that had been snapped by *Post* photographers, dropped into the cashier's office for expense money, then caught the night train for Montreal.

Baldwin's first stop in Montreal was at the Identification Bureau of the Police Department. He flashed Ponzi's pictures on Eugene Laflamme, head of the bureau. Laflamme, a dark, excitable Frenchman, studied the photos for several minutes, saying nothing as his eyes alternately widened and narrowed. Then he looked up at Baldwin. "Wait," he said. He went into another room and Baldwin saw him opening a green cabinet and riffling through some files. Then Laflamme returned. "No," he said. "We have no record of your Mister Ponzi."

"I thought," said Baldwin, "when you told me to wait that perhaps you recognized him."

"He did look somewhat familiar," said Laflamme, "but now I realize why he looked familiar. I have been looking at his pictures in the newspapers." Laflamme smiled mirthlessly. "Better luck next time, Monsieur. Yes?"

"Uh-huh," grunted Baldwin.

Standing on the pavement outside Police Headquarters, Baldwin went in for a little deduction. First, he assumed that Charles Ponzi in Boston was a crook. If, before appearing in Boston, Ponzi had been in Montreal, and been up to some crooked work, but the police had no record of him, he had perhaps used another name when in Montreal.

What kind of crooked work had Ponzi, under another name, been up to in Montreal? If his suspected track record in Boston was any clue, he had probably been up to the same kind of work—a get-rich-scheme of some kind.

By an extension of his theory, Baldwin decided that Ponzi had, while in Montreal, taken his own people—those of Italian extraction—in his scheme, whatever it had been. And so Baldwin, emerging from his speculations there in front of Police Headquarters, flagged a taxi. "Take me," he said to the bi-lingual driver, "to the Italian district—wherever it is."

On Friday, July 23, Ponzi, decked out in a new cream-colored suit and swinging a malacca walking stick, paid a call at the offices of Judge Dominick Leveroni, his counsel. "Judge," he said, "I want to do something about these stories that have been running in The *Post*."

"Just what do you want to do, Charlie?" asked the Judge.

"I want to set the record in order. I want to clear my good name."

The Judge thought things over. "I have an idea, Charlie," he said. "There's a publicity man here in Boston who might be just the man for you. Fellow

by the name of McMasters. He's been
handling some political campaigns in
fine shape." The Judge leaned back in
his swivel chair. "Yes, the more I think
of it the more I'm sure McMasters is the
man for you."

William McMasters—a tall, slim man
in his early forties who had worked on
The *Post* as a nothing-sacred reporter—
strode into the Judge's office within half
an hour. Ponzi, sitting there with Judge
Leveroni, jumped to his feet and pumped
McMasters' hand.

"Just what can I do for you, Mr.
Ponzi?" asked McMasters.

Ponzi said he wanted, somehow, to
counteract the stories in The *Post*. Mc-
Masters had been reading the stories and
had begun to wonder if Ponzi were on
the level. But now, as he searched the
face of the Judge he found it suffused
with complete trust. "All right," said Mc-
Masters, "how far do you want me to
go?"

"What about money?" asked Ponzi.
"We haven't discussed money."

"We can get to that later," said Mc-
Masters. "First let's see what I can do for
you."

McMasters phoned The *Post* and was
put through to Eddie Dunn. "Eddie," he
said, "if you send one of your reporters
over to Judge Leveroni's office you'll get
an exclusive interview with Charles
Ponzi."

"I'll have a man right over," said
Dunn. "You say this is exclusive, Bill?"

"I'll guarantee it. I'm handling publicity for Mr. Ponzi."

Ponzi, calling all the turns and giving
himself the best of it, gave out quite an
interview to The *Post* reporter. He lam-
basted his critics, calling them green-
eyed with jealousy because he had come
upon a financial secret that was giving

the little man a share of some of the
gravy.

Eddie Dunn had given the reporter a
loaded question. "How," the reporter
asked Ponzi, "can you invest in postal-
reply coupons all the money that you are
obviously taking in when there aren't
enough postal-reply coupons in the world
to match such sums?"

Ponzi, flicking the ashes off his cigarette, was glad the reporter had asked the
question. "I can now divulge," he said,
"that only a small percentage of the
money I take in goes into postal-reply
coupons. Just *where* I invest the bulk of
the money must remain my secret." He
leaned close to the scribe and looked
him straight in the eyes. "Do you think
I am going to divulge my secret—the secret that is giving my investors such a
handsome return on their investment—
so that Morgan and Rockefeller and
those men will get hold of it? I should
say *not*."

But if Charlie was keeping one thing
secret, he had something else to divulge.
Figuring that The *Post* would hardly
give him the best of it, he had thought
up something by which to beat The
Post at its own game. Charlie told the
reporter that he was no longer going
to give a 50 per cent return on invested
money in ninety days. "You're not!" said
the reporter. McMasters, sitting there
listening, gulped. "No," Charlie went
on, smiling and walking around the
room. "You can put this in your paper
tomorrow morning: Ponzi is *now* going
to pay fifty per cent in *forty-five* days."

"Really!" said the scribe.

"Yes, really. From now on, all investors will be paid their principal and
interest in half the previous time."

"What about those who now hold
ninety-day notes?" McMasters broke in
to ask.

"Beginning tomorrow morning," replied Charlie, "I shall honor all ninety-day notes that are forty-five days old."

The interview with Ponzi broke under a two-column headline on the front page of The *Post* on the Saturday morning. W-e-l-l. When the people read that remark of Ponzi's to the effect that he would honor the ninety-day notes in forty-five days, it seemed as if the whole town put down The *Post* and made a rush for School Street.

At nine o'clock, when Ponzi's offices opened for business, the line of investors was four blocks long. Ponzi drew up in his limousine, got out, waved his straw katie to the crowd, and pushed his way to his office. There he took a seat at his desk. He took one look at the crush of people at the windows, practically all of them waving cash and begging the tellers to take it, then picked up the phone and called the police. "I need protection," he told the police. Six cops hustled right around.

As the morning wore on, the line down in School Street grew longer. By noon there were a dozen police in School Street and around the corner, in Washington Street, for almost three blocks. A second line, stemming from the pay-off office in Pi Alley, had also snaked out into Washington Street. Charlie's clerks there were wearing out pens writing checks to lucky investors. After getting their checks, the investors rushed across Washington Street to the Hanover Trust to cash in. What with the lines in Washington Street from School Street and Pi Alley and the clusters of investors rushing in and out of the bank, the thoroughfare was a shambles.

Up in his School Street office, Ponzi sat at his desk, his little legs crossed, his hand on the head of his cane, the diamond in his stickpin glistening, observing what was going on at the six windows. The clerks were taking in and handing out money so fast that what Ponzi observed, as he sat there, must have resembled a pleasant green-and-gold blur. Every once in a while there would be a slight dispute between an investor and a clerk in the School Street office as to the age of one of Ponzi's notes. Ponzi would get up from his chair, examine the note and, finding it not quite forty-five days old, but almost, he would smile at the investor, then turn to the clerk behind the wicket and say, "Pay this good man."

Charles Ponzi was now like the Pied Piper of Hamelin, who led the children to the sea. Ponzi's children were grown-up suckers enchanted by the lovely rustle of crisp new bills and begging to be led to the deep waters of financial disaster.

What made Ponzi possible was that he arrived in just the right place at just the right time with just the right dodge. He had popped up in conservative Boston in an era when there was no such thing as a Securities Exchange Commission and when the little man felt that he was not getting his share of the gravy.

Charlie had something else in his favor, too—public opinion. Not a single one of tens of thousands of his investors uttered a word of complaint against him. While he was shearing the sheep the newspapers and the law-enforcement authorities engaged in a conspiracy of silence, not daring to raise a hue and a cry. Politicians and editors, although trembling at the inevitability of a judgment day, considered it foolhardy to take a stand against a man who was a hero to the voters and to the readers. It was no trifling matter to step in and muss up a project that was paying 50 per cent interest in six weeks to laborers, school teachers, butchers, office boys and old ladies in sewing circles.

It was shortly after noon that there came to pass an untoward development. A gentleman with a little waxed moustache and wearing a sharp shepherd's-plaid suit pushed his way through the crowd with three male companions, walked up to the third floor and let himself into a vacant office immediately above Ponzi's. In a little while a couple of men appeared with a desk and three chairs and went up to the office on the third floor. Then some men arrived carrying signs.

Then, from a window of the room on the third floor the crowd down below saw one of the signs being put in place. It read:

OLD COLONIAL FOREIGN EXCHANGE CO.
CHARLES BRIGHTWELL
PRES. AND TREAS.

Now the gentleman in the checkered suit appeared at the window and fingered his waxed moustache as he looked down at the crowd with honest-looking blue eyes. "The name's Brightwell," he shouted, shaking his hands like a victor in a prize ring. "Ponzi's offering you only 50 per cent in forty-five days. I'll give you 50 per cent in *thirty* days."

The suckers, broiling in the midsummer sun, just stood there gawking up at Brightwell. "Come on!" shouted Brightwell. "What are we waiting for!"

"I'm going up," said one man in line. Now some of the investors in the Ponzi line began to fall out, one by one, to straggle up to Brightwell's. But most of Ponzi's suckers remained faithful to the

one, the only, the original. There were, though, so many suckers to go around that by mid-afternoon Brightwell and his three associates had stuffed their pockets with bills.

Along toward three-thirty Bill McMasters ambled into School Street to see how things were going. Shocked to see that Brightwell had opened for business, he rushed up to the second floor, draped himself over Ponzi's desk, and inquired of his employer: "Did you know about the people above you?"

"No. What about people above me?"

McMasters briefed his client on Brightwell. Ponzi arose and drew himself up to his full five feet two. "Why," he shouted, "what an unethical thing to do! I must counteract this, McMasters!"

Ponzi went downstairs, stood on the steps of the entrance of the building and clapped his hands for attention. "Beware of imitators!" he shouted. "Beware, my friends of *impostors!*" Now he jerked a thumb toward the sign in Brightwell's window. "Brightwell," he rasped. "Brightwell. Who among you has ever heard of the man before?" Nobody had. "But who has heard of Ponzi?" A great yell went up.

"My friends," said Ponzi, "you have proved that you are wise people. You have demonstrated by your applause that you know the genuine from the imitation." He paused dramatically. Then: "I thank you." Now he rushed back upstairs. The line that had snaked its way from the street to Brightwell's office on the third floor began to thin out to a trickle.

"Well," Ponzi said to McMasters. "I guess that fixed Brightwell—the c-h-e-a-p c-r-o-o-k."

The suckers kept coming until nightfall that wonderful Saturday. When the last investor straggled away and the clerks staggered off, leaving McMasters and Ponzi alone in the room, Charlie locked the door. He and McMasters went behind the cages. Several wastepaper baskets were filled with bills and money was piled up in a corner, on the floor. Ponzi phoned for the police. Several cops came. "Help me with this stuff," he told the cops, grabbing a fistful of money to give to each cop. "I'm going to take it home over the weekend."

Early on the Sunday afternoon, McMasters went out to Ponzi's estate in Lexington and found the little wizard on the lawn. "Boy, am I happy!" Charlie told McMasters. "Do you know how much money changed hands yesterday? More than a million dollars. *That's* how much." Ponzi was rubbing his little hands together.

"I've arranged for a Pathe newsreel cameraman to come out today," he told Ponzi.

"Wonderful," said Ponzi. "When will he be here?"

McMasters looked out into the street. "Any minute."

"I must go and change my clothes," said Ponzi. "I must look my best for my investors."

When the cameraman arrived Charlie appeared decked out in a freshly-pressed summer suit, a red carnation in his lapel, and wearing a pair of two-tone shoes—black patent-leather bottoms and white canvas uppers. He strutted and hammed it for the cameraman for twenty minutes. When the shooting was over, the cameraman said, "Some place you got here."

"Yes," said Ponzi, "it serves its purpose."

"Say," said the cameraman, "I'd like to get in on this 50 per cent thing. I got fifty dollars on me."

"You'll have seventy-five in forty-five days," said Charlie, grabbing the money and scribbling out a receipt. McMasters, looking on, felt there was something somehow disenchanting about the transaction.

When the newsreel men left, Ponzi invited McMasters into his mansion. "I have a problem, Bill," he said. "I want to send for my mother in Italy. What's the best way to send her a thousand dollars that she can quickly cash over there —American Express Travellers Checks?"

McMasters blinked; he thought Ponzi was kidding. But Ponzi wasn't kidding. He actually was in need of information as to exactly how to transfer passage money to his mother. This struck McMasters as peculiar. Here was a man, dealing in millions, and supposedly with connections in high international money circles, who simply didn't know the A.B.C.'s of transferring a thousand dollars from Boston to Italy.

"It's funny," said McMasters, "that you should be asking a guy like me a question like that—you with your connections."

Ponzi managed a tired smile. "I've got too many big things up here"—he tapped his forehead with his forefinger—"to worry about a small thing."

That Sunday night, McMasters was sitting with Ponzi in the great man's panelled library while Ponzi was going through a batch of accumulated mail. "Boy," Charlie said, "here's something!" He handed a letter to McMasters. It was from a shoe store offering Ponzi his choice of a pair of expensive shoes, free of charge. "I always did like nice shoes. I'm going around to that store first thing in the morning."

McMasters was squinting at Charlie as he handed the letter back to him. He saw by the expression on Ponzi's face, somewhat to his surprise, that Ponzi wasn't kidding about the offer of a free pair of shoes. This, like Ponzi's ignorance of the simple mechanics of a money transfer, simply didn't add up. When Bill McMasters left Ponzi's estate early that Sunday night he had begun to entertain serious doubts about the man.

First thing next morning McMasters walked in on Simon Swig, the president of the Tremont Trust Company. Swig—a gentleman with white piping on the vest of his black suit—was known to have just about the sharpest eye in Boston for questionable collateral.

"What do you think of Ponzi?" McMasters asked the banker.

"I think the man's a dead beat."

"Exactly why, Mr. Swig?"

Swig said he had learned that Ponzi, who claimed to have foreign connections, actually had no connections abroad—a statement that McMasters, in view of Ponzi's ignorance about sending money to his mother, was quick to believe.

McMasters recalls that Swig got up from his desk, went to a window and stuck his hands in his hip pockets as he stood with his back to him. "Consider this, McMasters," Swig was saying. "Here is a man who makes 50 per cent for his investors in forty-five days—or claims to —and yet what does he do with his *own* money? Why, he has a third of a million dollars lying around here at four and a half per cent. He's doing the same thing with his money at other banks. If the man's on the level why doesn't he invest his own money in that 50 per cent stuff?" Swig turned around now and stared at McMasters. "Why *doesn't* he, McMasters?"

After he left Swig's office, McMasters telephoned to District Attorney Joseph C. Pelletier—a man he knew from his newspaper days. "Mr. Pelletier," he said, "I'm going to bring Charles Ponzi over to your office if I may. I'd like you to

have a talk with him. Perhaps it would be in the public interest if you convinced him that he should not take any more of the people's money until you have some accountants go over his books."

"Why, Bill, you don't for a minute think there's anything *wrong*, do you?"

"That's for your accountants to judge."

McMasters ambled into Ponzi's office at the Hanover Trust Company at half past ten that Monday morning and draped himself over the great man's desk. "I've arranged for you to have a talk with the District Attorney," said McMasters.

Ponzi stiffened. "What for?"

"To counteract those stories in The *Post*."

"But those stories *have* been counteracted," said Ponzi. He pointed out the window to Washington Street. "Look at those lines there—one from School Street and one from Pi Alley."

"Yes," said McMasters, "I see the lines. But I've been tipped off that Pelletier would like to have a chat with you. We'd better keep the appointment."

Ponzi drummed his fingers on his desk and looked out the window. "All right," he said. "I've got nothing to hide."

Ponzi got up and left his office. When he came back he was carrying that straw suitcase. "What's in there?" asked McMasters. Ponzi smiled. "You'll see," he said. "You'll see."

District Attorney Pelletier, a great man for a bottle and a bird, was shaped like a top as he entered the middle years. Unlike most Boston politicians of the era, Pelletier was a highly erudite man. Able and keen, he was, among other things, an authority on the works of Shakespeare—or, as Pelletier used to put it, the works Shakespeare got the credit for. Joe Pelletier belonged to that group of scholars who believed that Bacon wrote

Shakespeare's stuff. The trouble was Joe Pelletier had a naïve streak in him.

Pelletier got up and shook hands with Ponzi when Charlie walked into his office with McMasters. Ponzi, lugging that straw suitcase, put it down on the District Attorney's desk. "What's in there, Mr. Ponzi?" Pelletier asked. "A couple of million dollars," said Charlie, unstrapping the suitcase and opening it. And there, sure enough, were stacks and stacks of gold-backs. Pelletier examined the money briefly. All of the bills, fresh off the presses, were hundred-dollar gold-backs.

"I just wanted to show you," Ponzi said to the D.A., "that I'm pretty liquid."

So there they were, the little knave with no education and the big scholar with little talent for intrigue. McMasters, standing there looking at that straw suitcase filled with money, suddenly arrived at the unshakable conclusion that Charles Ponzi was one of the biggest crooks in the history of fraudulent misrepresentation.

Ponzi, one hand in his pocket, the other one free to wave around, started to pace up and down. "I love the little people, Mr. Pelletier," Charlie said, the words gushing from his mouth. "The little people should have some of the good things in life, Mr. Pelletier. Don't you think so?" Charlie was staring at the D.A. with a semi-religious glint in his eyes. Pelletier cleared his throat, smiled and nodded.

McMasters figured it was time to break in. "I would suggest, Mr. Pelletier," McMasters said, "that Mr. Ponzi, as a gesture of good faith, temporarily abstain from taking in any more money—until one of your auditors goes over his books."

Out of the corner of his eye McMasters saw Ponzi stiffen. "Mr. Ponzi," McMasters went on, "is a highly ethical man. He has nothing to hide. He insists that he take in no more money—only pay out money to those clients whose notes are due—until he has been officially investigated."

"But I am perfectly happy," said Pelletier.

"I know," said McMasters, feeling like punching the D.A. in the nose for his gullibility, "but Mr. Ponzi here isn't happy." McMasters turned to Ponzi and said, "Are you, Mr. Ponzi?" Then, before giving Ponzi a chance to answer, McMasters caught Pelletier's eye and winked.

Now Pelletier seemed to catch on. "Fine," he said. "A great suggestion, McMasters. You will agree, then, Mr. Ponzi, not to take in any more money until an auditor goes over your books."

"Yes, Mr. Ponzi will agree to that," said McMasters, knowing Ponzi couldn't very well disagree without arousing the D.A.'s suspicions. "In fact, Mr. Ponzi will shake hands on it." Turning to Ponzi, McMasters said, "Won't you, Mr. Ponzi?"

"Yes," said Ponzi, having no other course.

Out on the street, after the meeting, Ponzi said to McMasters, "What did you do a thing like *that* for?"

"Oh, it was just a little scheme of mine to see that you take in more money than ever. Don't you see, Mr. Ponzi, that after the District Attorney announces that you are completely solvent that you will draw more business than ever?"

Ponzi didn't answer for a few seconds. "S-a-y," he said. "I think you're right!"

Before Ponzi realized it, he was sitting with McMasters in the office of United States Attorney Francis Gallagher. Gallagher, like Pelletier, was a highly cultivated man. Short and plump, he had a voice that reminded some courtroom observers of an organ.

Ponzi, lugging that suitcase with the two million in it, gave Gallagher the same production and spiel as he had given Pelletier. The result was the same. Gallagher didn't understand much of what Ponzi was explaining (and no wonder) but when Ponzi was through talking the United States Attorney was simply enchanted.

"You're doing great, Mr. Ponzi," McMasters said to Charlie when they left Gallagher. "Boy, what an impression you're making!"

"You really think so?" asked Ponzi.

"Do I?" said McMasters, who was now out-conning the con man. "Why, after you show your books to Pelletier's accountants you'll be a cinch to clean up several million dollars and then run for Mayor."

Ponzi smiled and lapsed into thought. "Bill," he said, "you know I'd make a great Mayor."

Late in the afternoon, McMasters made a third stop with his client—this time in the office of Attorney General J. Weston Allen in the State House. Charlie was still carrying that suitcase. Allen—a gruff big faker—refused to see Ponzi and McMasters. He was too busy at the moment. He wanted no part of putting the boots to a man who was a hero to so many voters.

McMasters told Ponzi to wait in the Attorney General's anteroom. Then he dashed off to the office of the Governor.

Governor Calvin Coolidge—tall, reddish of hair and with a calculating glint in his eyes—looked up from a neat pile of papers when McMasters was shown into his office. "What's on your mind, McMasters?" asked Coolidge, who knew McMasters from his newspaper days.

"Your Attorney General refuses to see Charles Ponzi and me."

McMasters recalls that Coolidge made a tent with the fingers of his two hands and peered over it at him before speaking. "Where is Mr. Ponzi now?" asked Coolidge.

"Waiting for me in Mr. Allen's outer office."

"You can go right back," said Silent Cal. "Mr. Allen will see you and Mr. Ponzi."

When he got in to see the Attorney General Ponzi made more of a production of the audience than he had with either Pelletier or even Gallagher. When the interview was over, Allen grabbed Ponzi's hand and the little swindler walked out of the office in a shimmering envelope of confidence.

When, on the Monday after lunch, District Attorney Pelletier called in the press and announced that Mr. Ponzi had agreed to accept no more money until accountants went over his books, Boston reacted as it probably would today if a hydrogen bomb was dropped on the outskirts. Heeding the newspaper extras, practically everybody who held Charlie's notes dropped what they were doing and rushed to School Street or into Pi Alley.

But Charlie was right on the job, right there to cope with the situation. And he was in a royal position to do so. Directing operations from his desk in the president's office of the Hanover Trust, he was dispatching armed guards with bags of bills across to Pi Alley and around to School Street every half hour or so. Every once in a while he would leave his office in the bank and, giving the crowd the old hello, look in on the Pi Alley office, then get into the blue Locomobile, parked in front of the bank, and be driven around to School Street. He was the eye of the hurricane, calm as the furies swirled about him.

Late in the afternoon, Ponzi was getting out of the Locomobile at School

Street when somebody in the mob yelled to him. Ponzi, standing on the running board of the car to get a better look at the man who called to him, spotted the fellow and said, "What's on your mind, my friend?"

"Ponzi," shouted the fellow, "you're a crook. A dead beat!"

Ponzi, the master at diluting any irritation he might have brewed, just fixed the fellow with that prop smile. "Do you have one of my notes?" he asked. The fellow did. "For how much?" Fifty dollars. When was it due? Not for more than a month. "Never mind," said Charlie. "If that's how you feel, I'll pay you not only your principal but your interest." Charlie peeled seventy-five dollars off a roll in his pocket, gave the man the money, took the note and then, looking at the crowd, asked, "Can I be of service to anybody else?"

Charlie had a bagful of money in the back seat of the car. He sat there in the back seat, personally accepting notes not yet due and paying off until the money in the bag was gone. Then he stood on the running board of the car, waved at the crowd, and headed for his office, shaking hands and clapping people on the back as he made his way through the mob. The sight of Charlie sitting there in the car paying off before he had to had a salutary effect on practically everybody. Practically everybody, that is, except McMasters. McMasters, circulating in the crowd, saw what Charlie was up to. The problem was to bring him down, but good, before he got going again.

On the Tuesday morning at eight o'clock, an hour before opening time, there was a line five blocks long at Ponzi's. Promptly at nine o'clock, the little man wheeled into School Street in his blue Locomobile. While the faces of some of the investors were dark, the morning was

bright and so was Charlie. He gave the crowd the old hello and then asked for volunteers to help him carry six suitcases of money to the second floor. Several eager helpers crowded around the Locomobile, grabbed the bags containing the dough, and carried it upstairs. "You can see," Ponzi shouted to the crowd, "that Ponzi's words are as good as gold."

"Hurray for Ponzi!" shouted a hard-faced man up near the front. McMasters, hanging around, tilted his head as he looked at the fellow. "Yeah," shouted another character, "hurray for Ponzi! I don't want my money. Ponzi gives me more than the banks do. I'm leavin' my dough with Ponzi."

McMasters waited until Ponzi disappeared into the building, then approached the man who said he was leaving his dough with Ponzi. "I'm representing Mr. Ponzi," McMasters said to the fellow. "Mr. Ponzi wants to know if you can come back tomorrow at the same price."

"Sure," said the man. "Same time?"

"Yes," said McMasters. "I've forgotten how much Mr. Ponzi is paying you."

"Ten bucks."

"Beat it, you bum," said McMasters.

McMasters found Ponzi sitting at his desk, hands folded over his cane, beaming at everybody. "Did you hear that fellow down there who said he didn't want his money back?" McMasters asked Ponzi.

"Yes," said Ponzi, beaming. "Wasn't that a splendid show of confidence?"

"He tells me you paid ten dollars to do what he did."

Ponzi just blinked up at McMasters and he was still blinking when he was saved by the bell. A commotion at one of the windows gave him an excuse to get up. At the window one of the clerks told Ponzi that a lady investor had raised one of his notes to double its face value. Examining the note, Charlie made a ticking sound with his tongue, then looked at the woman. "Madam," he said, "always remember: honesty is the best policy."

It was along toward noon before a couple of auditors from District Attorney Pelletier's office showed up and asked Ponzi for his books. Charlie, glad to oblige, went to his little safe, twirled the dial, and pulled out a couple of black books. Thumbing through the records, the auditors looked puzzled. "Is this all the records you keep?" one of them asked Charlie. Yes, that was all. Ponzi explained that it wasn't necessary for him to keep complicated books since his business was always in such a liquid state.

All of the notes that Ponzi gave out contained serial numbers. The lower the number the older the note was, the higher the number the more recent the vintage. McMasters, deciding that Pelletier's accountants wouldn't get very far, determined to do a little investigating on his own. "By this time," says McMasters, "I felt that I would have to carry the whole burden of exposing Ponzi. The public officials were too stupid to see through him and the press was half afraid of him."

McMasters got to work on the Wednesday morning, the second day since the District Attorney, without knowing exactly why, had temporarily shut down on Ponzi. The crowds were still coming. But Ponzi, arriving every few hours with a new load of money and a broad smile, was still paying off.

McMasters, circulating among the crowd, and posing as an investor, began to swap information with the more talkative suckers. Thus he got the numbers on the notes they held. He got a hundred numbers within a few hours.

McMasters got more numbers on the Thursday, when the mob was still being paid off, and still more on Friday, when Ponzi was continuing to shell out. What McMasters was after was enough serial numbers to work out a geometric ratio that would convince even somebody who didn't understand geometry that Ponzi was a crook who was simply robbing Peter to pay Paul.

But McMasters knew that he would have to hurry. Time was of the essence. The District Attorney was already getting poison pen letters from people who resented his casting doubt on Charlie. And Charlie, the sly one, had come up with a new dodge. He hired confederates to infiltrate the lines of investors. Other confederates would come along and approach the confederates in the line and engage in some dialogue written by Ponzi. "You cashing in your notes at face value?" one sharper would ask the other sharper in a loud voice. "Yeah," would come the reply, "I'm gettin' out while the gettin's good."

"I'll tell you what, Mister," the first sharper would say, "I'll just give you 25 per cent interest on that note you have there in your hand."

"You will?"

"Uh-huh. Here's the money." Whereupon the sharper would dig into his pocket for a fat roll of bills and close the deal. After this would go on five or six times, a planted man in the line would refuse the offer of the speculator. "Like hell I'll sell to you," this man would say. "I'm hangin' on to mine."

All this had a very salutary effect on others in the line. The result was that by the Saturday—four days after the run on Ponzi had begun—the line was down to a trickle.

Bill McMasters shut himself up at home early on the Friday night with the figures he had collected from the investors. He worked through the night. By dawn, when he hit the hay for a couple of hours' sleep, he had come up with a geometric ratio confirming his suspicions that Ponzi had been robbing Peter to pay Paul.

It was shortly after noon on Saturday, July 31—exactly one week after Ponzi's own con-man's story had come out in The *Post* and really got the ball rolling—that Bill McMasters walked into the dining room of Young's Hotel and approached Richard Grozier, the acting publisher of The *Post,* who always lunched at Young's on Saturdays.

"How would you like a story for Monday morning proving that Charles Ponzi is absolutely insolvent?" McMasters asked Grozier.

"Have you got the facts and figures to prove it?" Grozier wanted to know.

McMasters had.

McMasters briefed Grozier on the incongruities he had encountered out at Ponzi's estate the previous Sunday—Ponzi's ignorance of the mechanics of money transfer to his mother in Italy, and his jumping at the offer of a free pair of shoes. Next McMasters showed Grozier some figures he had worked out—figures that McMasters felt indicated that if Ponzi were to meet every obligation outstanding without paying interest he would be roughly two million dollars in the red.

Grozier sat studying the figures for several minutes. Then he drummed his fingers on the tablecloth and looked at a distant wall. His jaw was set and there was anger in his eyes. "I want you to do the story, Bill," Grozier said at length. "Can you turn it in to the city desk by the middle of tomorrow afternoon so that our lawyers can get a chance to go over it before we print it?" McMasters could. It was Grozier who brought up the mat-

ter of compensation. "Will five thousand dollars be satisfactory?" he asked. McMasters, who would have been willing to settle for half that, gulped and nodded.

McMasters went home and shut himself in a room with a typewriter, some paper and a basketful of notes. He wrote and rewrote the story from early evening until dawn. Then he went to bed for a few hours, got up and polished the thing, copied it and went into The *Post* with it. It was twenty-seven hundred words in length and Grozier and The *Post* lawyers were so pleased with it that Grozier gave McMasters an extra thousand—for a word rate that Huntsman Hemingway is still shooting at.

Ponzi got up shortly before seven o'clock on the morning of Monday, August 2. He stepped into a pair of fur-lined bedroom slippers, threw a blue silk dressing gown over his green silk pajamas, and padded down to the front door. Picking up his copy of The *Post,* which had been dropped at the door a couple of hours before, he stood there unfolding it. There, splashed all over the front page, was the beginning of the McMasters story.

A slight drizzle began to fall, but Ponzi, engrossed in the story, stood there, turned to an inside page, and read every word of the story. He was still standing there, the paper at his side, looking off into space, when Rose appeared at an upstairs window. "Charlie," she called, "come on inside out of the rain. You want to catch a cold?"

Charlie, who had caught considerably more than a cold, got dressed, passed up breakfast, got into the Locomobile and was driven to the bank. It was shortly before half-past eight when he let himself in. "Nice morning except for that drizzle, Mr. Ponzi," said the night watchman. "Yes," said Charlie, "it's a nice morning."

Ponzi picked up a telephone and called McMasters at his home. "Bill," he said, "what on earth ever prompted you to write such a story as The *Post* has this morning?" Charlie, McMasters recalls, was speaking more in sorrow than anger.

"I have to tell the truth as I see it, Mr. Ponzi," said McMasters. "Too much is at stake here. Why, I understand schemes like yours are springing up all over the country."

"Bill," said Charlie, "all I can say is that you will live to regret your action." Then Charlie hung up.

There was one thing in Ponzi's favor —time. About four million dollars in notes and interest wouldn't yet be due for a month or more. We know, in retrospect, what Ponzi did. As president of the Hanover Trust Company, he had access to millions of dollars in cash. There was nobody to dispute his going into a big safe and taking practically anything he wanted to take to his office. He had already plastered the bank with his personal notes and had created a virtual flurry of paper between the Hanover Trust and the other banks in the city so that nobody, Charlie included, really knew what the score was.

Shortly after the big vault was opened at nine o'clock that Monday morning, Charlie went in and took two million dollars in hundred-dollar bills, leaving an I.O.U. in the place of the money. Putting the money into a suitcase, he instructed his chauffeur to drive him around to School Street just to see what was going on. The mob in School Street was something big and something fierce. It seemed that practically everybody in Boston had read that story in The *Post*. The suckers were really growing suspicious of Charlie now. So, ever a man with his finger on the public pulse, Charlie got out of School Street fast.

Charlie had his chauffeur drive him down to Saratoga Springs, in New York State. There, after checking into the United States Hotel as Charles Bianchi, he started to plunge at the gaming tables.

When he checked into Saratoga Ponzi had a dream—the dream of that many a crook has had before and since although not on such a large scale. He hoped to run that two million up to perhaps ten million by betting not only at Saratoga but with bookies who would lay his money at race tracks all over the country. Thus he could go back to Boston, pay off, and still be in the clear. But of course nothing like that happened. Three days after he left, Ponzi was back in Boston, completely cleaned out of that two million.

But Charlie was still paying off his investors. The Peters whose money he was using to pay the Pauls held notes that were not yet due. Charlie, as president of the Hanover Trust, decided that he would take another fling at gambling. But now the directors stepped in. They advised him not to drop any more I.O.U.'s in the bank. Charlie just blinked and nodded.

For several days, Ponzi just sat at the bank, or in his office at Poole's, twiddling his thumbs. He was living in a state of suspended animation. Boston was divided into two camps—those who thought Charlie was a dead beat and those who thought he was wonderful.

After all, up to now not a man, woman or child who had handed their money over to Charlie had lost a cent. The worst that had happened to anybody— after Pelletier had issued that injunction against Charlie and McMasters had come out with his blast—was that they had gotten their principal back without interest.

Thousands of little people were walking around Boston displaying that 50 per cent that Charlie had paid them. Street fights were breaking out all over town when a non-investor would impinge on Charlie's honesty to a lucky speculator. Pelletier was waiting for his accountants to unearth some clue to what Ponzi was really up to, the bankers were sitting back waiting for the bomb to go off, and Governor Coolidge was sitting under the bronze dome of the State House, swathed in cold silence, as he peered into space over that little tent that he made with his fingers.

Meantime, in Canada, Herbert Baldwin was trudging through the twisted streets of Montreal's Little Italy from early morning till late at night. He flashed the Ponzi pictures on men holding up lampposts on the street corners, on housewives, on street-car conductors and on the proprietors of small shops. Late one afternoon he happened into the offices of a man named Cordasco, a steamship agent on St. James Street. Cordasco, a taciturn little man, rubbed his chin as he looked at the pictures of Ponzi. "Yes," he said. "Yes and No."

"Just what does that mean?" asked Baldwin.

"The face is somehow familiar. But I just cannot seem to place it."

"From the newspapers?" asked Baldwin, hoping the answer would be No. It was. The pictures rang a distant bell in the mind of the steamship agent. How distant? Oh, ten years or more maybe.

Baldwin, sure that he was now closing in, kept pressing Cordasco for just what was familiar, and what was unfamiliar, about the face. "Something about the mouth is not right," said Cordasco.

"Maybe you knew this man when he had a moustache," Baldwin suggested.

Cordasco looked up at him and blinked. "Perhaps. Perhaps."

Next morning, Baldwin was back at Cordasco's. "Take a look at these pictures now," he said. Baldy had been in the art department at the Montreal *Star* and had an artist paint a moustache on the Ponzi pictures. Cordasco's eyes lighted up. "To be sure!" he said. "That's Bianchi."

"Who?"

"Charles Bianchi."

"Spell that last name."

"B-i-a-n-c-h-i. And a clever devil he was, too!"

The little steamship agent was greatly excited. Baldwin placed a hand on his shoulder. "Take your time," he said, "and tell me all about it."

There had been, thirteen years before, in 1907, a sharpshooter by the name of Zarrossi who had operated a loan company at the corner of St. James and Inspector Streets. All the Italians in the neighborhood had implicit trust in Zarrossi. When any of them had a tale of woe they ran to Zarrossi with it. When one of them got in the wine and beat up his wife and kids, and/or strayed from the connubial couch, Zarrossi straightened things out.

And then one day there appeared in Zarrossi's office a little moustached-fellow by the name of Charles Bianchi—a fellow about twenty-five, mincing of step, bright of eye, glib of tongue. Presently changes began to take place in Zarrossi's. Zarrossi branched out. He began to accept money from the Montreal Italians to be sent to their relatives in Italy—with interest. His own partner, Bianchi, was in charge of this branch of the business. "The Italians here got the interest," the steamship man was explaining to Baldwin, "and their relatives in Italy got the principal— or were supposed to."

Of course the relatives never got the principal. Letters began to cross the Atlantic, between Montreal and Italy, and soon the bubble burst. Zarrossi fled to Mexico, there eventually to lose himself in thin air. Bianchi was left holding the bag. And so, for being engaged in a scheme whereby he and Zarrossi kept money belonging to the suckers, Bianchi was sent to prison—the St. Vincent de Paul Prison—for three years. He was released in 1910, when he was twenty-eight.

Now, back at Police Headquarters, Herbert Baldwin officially established that Ponzi and Bianchi were one and the same. And so, on Wednesday, August 11, The *Post* broke the story.

Eddie Dunn, breathing hard at his desk in that cubbyhole at The *Post,* sent a man over to the bank to have a talk with Ponzi. Charlie, smoking a cigarette, just blinked at the reporter when the scribe told him what Baldwin had uncovered. "Let him who is without sin," said the little scoundrel, "cast the first stone."

Charlie had no sooner been revealed as Bianchi than another chapter of his life came to light—a chapter when he had told Rose he had been engaged in some cloak-and-dagger work. After being released from jail in Canada, Charlie, to make ends meet, had smuggled a couple of aliens across the border into the United States. Nailed for the caper, he had been given a three-year jolt in Atlanta. So now The *Post* broke *that* story.

It was all over for Ponzi now. Everybody—the city authorities, the county authorities, the State authorities and the Government authorities moved at once. Everything Charlie owned, including the house and furnishings in Lexington, was attached. He was locked out of the Hanover Trust Company and the doors at Poole's were barred against him. He wasn't allowed to set foot in his office on School Street or in the one-time restaurant in Pi Alley.

The cops kept an eye on Charlie to make sure he didn't get away. It took the authorities nine days to make enough sense out of the shambles to learn exactly what Charlie had been up to. The best estimate was that Charlie had raked in about fifteen million dollars and paid back practically that much. There were about five million of his notes still outstanding. All of his assets were so heavily mortgaged that they were worthless as security.

One fine morning two hard-faced deputy United States Marshals called at Ponzi's place in Lexington. Charlie personally answered the door. "You are under arrest for violating the Postal statutes," said one of the Marshals. The postal law is one of the most elastic on the books, covering a multitude of sins. Charlie, in notifying his investors that their money was due, had violated the law by notifying them by postal card to come in and collect money that had been obtained by fraudulent misrepresentation.

Charlie smiled sadly at the two deputies. "All right," he said, "I'll come with you without making trouble."

Things happened fast during the ensuing years. Charlie got five years from Uncle Sam and was sprung after doing three and a half. Then Massachusetts gave him a seven-to-nine jolt for grand larceny.

Rose met Charlie at the prison gate when he was released in February, 1934. Fourteen years had passed since Ponzi had taken Boston. His appearance had changed; he had put on quite a lot of weight. But several thousand investors still remembered him—the investors who had missed the boat and lost their savings. They met Charlie and Rose when they pulled into South Station. The gendarmes had to be called out to whisk Charlie and Rose away to a little hotel.

Now Charlie's official past, which he considered a bucket of ashes, suddenly burst into flame. Uncle Sam decided that since Charlie had never taken out citizenship papers he was still an Italian citizen—and an undesirable one, at that. So Charlie was hustled into court and officially banished from the country. "I'll never forget you," he told Rose as he said good-bye to her one afternoon when the sunset was on the purplish windowpanes of Beacon Hill. She handed him a couple of hundred dollars she had saved during his prison term. "I'll either send for you or I'll be back."

It was a gray day in October, 1934—just thirty-five years from the time he had first landed in New York from his native Italy—that Charles Ponzi, now fifty-one, balding and suety around the middle, stepped out of a taxi cab onto the dock of a New York pier in company with two sober-faced men. Handcuffed to one of the men, for his two companions were deputy United States Marshals, Charlie minced toward the steerage gangplank of the *Vulcania*. Charles Ponzi had come full circle; he was going back to Italy.

In his white iron stateroom, which he was to share with three other passengers, Ponzi received the press. He sat on his bunk, his little legs dangling over the side, holding a cigarette in a holder, cocked his head to one side, and said, "Well, gentlemen, I suppose you want to know if I have a statement to make."

The gentlemen of the press indeed wanted a statement.

"You can say," said Charlie, flipping some cigarette ashes on the iron floor,

"that I'm going to start all over again in Italy."

"Doing what?" asked a man from The *Daily News*.

"That," said Ponzi, "is my secret. But you'll hear about it. Mark my words."

Arriving in Italy, Ponzi headed for Rome. He rented a furnished room on the Via Brescia, a thoroughfare of cheap new dwellings on the outskirts. There Signor Ponzi arose at dawn each morning, went downstairs to the kitchen to make himself some black coffee, and returned to his room to work. He was working on two books—one, his autobiography, which he was calling "The Rise Of Charles Ponzi," and the other, "Boston Merry-Go-Round." This latter work, the title of which derived from an American best-seller called *Washington Merry-Go-Round*, was designed to rattle a few skeletons in Boston closets. Sitting at a table by a window that looked down on the street, Ponzi wrote for hours on end, using a pencil on a tablet of cheap yellow paper.

The months began to roll by, quicker than Ponzi would have preferred. His funds were running low. He was in correspondence with several New York publishing houses about the autobiography and the expose he was projecting. He didn't get a nibble. He was getting bored. He craved action.

At nights, Ponzi would stroll through the middle-class neighborhood and drop into a cafe and play scopa, a game in which the loser pays for a round of sweet vermouth or caffe espresso. Ponzi missed, most of all, the attention he had gotten in Massachusetts, before and after his downfall. The humdrum men he now associated with either didn't really know who he was or, if they did, didn't care. At any rate they never asked him anything about himself—what he was doing or what things had been like in America. No, it was all very depressing.

Every time a big trans-Atlantic boat was due at Naples and the mail from the United States would come up to Rome, Ponzi would hang around the American Express Company's office in Rome, where his wife always sent his mail. At first Rose was a faithful correspondent, telling him how things were in Boston and how she was making out in her job as a stenographer. But as the months wore on, Rose's letters became less frequent and when she did write she had less to say.

Something told Ponzi, with that instinct of his, that his marriage was coming apart at the seams and that there was not a grain of truth in the sayings that distance lends enchantment and that absence makes the heart grow fonder. As a matter of fact, every once in a while, Ponzi, dipping into his frail reserve, would go into Rome, sneak into the red light district, and have himself a time.

There was, operating out of Rome while Ponzi was in residence there, a man with whom he had much in common—a man by the name of Benito Mussolini. Mussolini, exactly the same age as Ponzi, was at the height of his power, standing on balconies, his chin out, conning the peasants with promises of something for nothing. Ponzi used to join the crowds listening to Mussolini when the great man got up on his balcony in Rome. It seemed in the cards that these two boys should get together and, sure enough, they did.

It was in 1936, when Mussolini seized Ethiopia, that Ponzi saw his chance to get on the bandwagon. He holed up in his room and spent two days laboriously composing a letter to Mussolini—a letter in which he stated that he would be just the man to handle relations with the foreign press in Ethiopia if His Excellency thought he could be of value. Ponzi took the letter to a girl he knew who owned a typewriter and together they got the thing off to the Dictator.

Three days later, a man in a Fascist uniform walked into Ponzi's little room. "You are to come with me, Signor," said the visitor. "What for?" asked Ponzi, a little apprehensive that he might be being arrested. The man in the uniform smiled. "You have been summoned by His Excellency," he told Ponzi.

So there they were, the biggest fraud in Italy and the man who had been the biggest fraud in America, face to face in that private office of Mussolini's—the biggest thing Ponzi could recall since he had that Locomobile. The two were together for almost thirty minutes—an important chunk of time in the life of Mussolini, what with the affairs of state and the affairs with women. Mussolini seemed more interested in what Charlie had done in America than in sending him to Ethiopia. In fact, Ethiopia was hardly discussed. "If I need you to go there I shall command you," said Mussolini.

When Charlie went back to his rooming house, he found a crowd waiting for him. His landlady had heard the soldier telling Ponzi that Mussolini had sent for him and blabbed the word all over the neighborhood. Ponzi, with a fine display of mock modesty, informed his listeners that Mussolini might send him to Ethiopia to handle press relations for Italy.

But days passed, and weeks, and no word from Mussolini. Ponzi wrote two letters to Mussolini, inquiring if he could be of any service. But he didn't get an answer.

By now Ponzi was broke. He was not only broke but desperate. So he took to a form of blackmail. He sat down and got off a number of letters to some pretty well-heeled men in Boston, some of them high in politics, others of no prominence. Ponzi knew something about every one of the addressees—tidbits that he had picked up while engaged in the big caper in Boston. Each letter was quite clever. It stated that he, Ponzi, was writing an expose of life in Boston and it inquired as to certain details of a certain crooked or illicit episode—an episode in which the recipient of the letter had been a participant.

W-e-l-l. Nothing happened but that there was literally a flood of money to Ponzi care of The American Express Company in Rome. It came by cash, check and draft. Within the space of a couple of months, Charlie must have taken in about five thousand dollars—enough to supply his modest wants indefinitely in the Italy of those days.

But one day came a letter of another kind. It was a letter from Rose. Rose was suing for divorce. There wasn't any other man. Rose just wanted her freedom. Ponzi never attempted to fight the action and the divorce went through on the statutory grounds that Ponzi had served more than five years in prison.

Ponzi, his vanity hit, took Rose's action pretty hard. He began to lose his grip and drop things on the floor. He used to go around the wine shops in his neighborhood, getting drunk and babbling about how cruel life had been to him. Charles Ponzi became an alcoholic. He abandoned his writing and his trans-Atlantic blackmail, and drank wine from early morning till late at night. Then his cronies, with whom he still played scopa when he was sober enough, would carry him up to his cheap little room.

One day a Fascist soldier called at Charlie's room. "His Excellency commands you," the soldier told Charlie.

Mussolini sent Ponzi to Rio de Janeiro as the business manager for the Latin Airlines, a pet project of the Dictator's. In Rio, Ponzi, at the age of sixty, seemed to take on his old bounce. Bald, with tufts of gray at the temples, he lived in a flossy apartment, acquired a couple of mistresses, and had a New York tailor send suits down to him.

Then, Mussolini fell, and so did Charlie Ponzi. He began to drink heavily again. He suffered a stroke that left him partially paralyzed and blind in one eye. He was taken to a charity ward. There, one day in January, 1949, Charles Ponzi died in poverty.

How Oscar Reaped the Farmers

It has long been axiomatic that when a tall stranger tells a tall story in the tall corn country he winds up on cordial terms with the receiving teller at the bank. Oscar (The Great) Hartzell for years reaffirmed that great truth. Even after Uncle Sam's Postal sleuths finally caught up with him and put him in durance vile, Oscar's victims simply couldn't brings themselves around to the belief that the man had, although bilking them of their life's savings, done them any wrong.

The sun was setting on the baked brown earth of Madison County, Iowa, one summer afternoon in 1901 when a dark-moustached stranger in top hat and frock coat rapped on the front door of the ramshackle Hartzell farmhouse. Flashing a toothy smile at widow Hartzell and her two grown sons, Oscar and Canfield, the visitor talked his way into the parlor. There he settled on a horsehair sofa, opened a satchel containing a pile of imposing documents bearing red seals and blue ribbons, and began to question the woman about her family tree. Suddenly the visitor flashed his smile again and snapped his fingers.

"Just as I thought," he said. "Madam, you are one of the Drake heirs."

"One of the *what*?" asked Oscar, a big raw-boned fellow of twenty-four.

"One of the Drake heirs. Your mother, young man, is a descendant of Sir Francis Drake, who died three hundred years ago without leaving a will. Now she will share in his huge fortune."

"When do we get the money?" asked Canfield, who was five years Oscar's junior, and not exactly a card.

The stranger blinked and cleared his throat. There were, he explained, certain legal obstacles to be hurdled before the estate could be settled. Naturally,

widow Hartzell and the other heirs would be required to foot the bill for legal expenses.

"But," the stranger went on, "you'll get back ten times what you put up, you lucky people."

Although Oscar Hartzell had only a little-red-schoolhouse education, he knew a wooden nutmeg when he saw one. But his mama, a strong-willed woman who took no guff from her boys, mortgaged the old homestead anyway, and turned the proceeds over to the stranger. That was the last she or the boys ever saw of the man. One glimpse was enough for Oscar, however, because if mama lost her chemise, Oscar got on the track of millions in real dough.

It took a few years, but then Oscar was to grab the Drake estate swindle and take the suckers as they had never been taken before. Dossiers on Oscar Merril Hartzell still fatten the files of the United States Post Office Department. They reveal that between 1924 and 1932 Oscar clipped more than seventy thousand people in seven mid-western states for over two million dollars.

To sell shares in the vast estate that existed only in his imagination, Oscar and a little band of hand-picked henchmen, spreading over the tall-corn country like a plague of locusts, told a fascinating story. The germ of Oscar's plot was that Sir Francis Drake, the English buccaneer, had, while not roving the seas, collaborated in an affair of state with Queen Elizabeth. The supposed fruit of this liaison was a bouncing bundle of male illegitimacy which had been clothed in a fictitious identity to avoid historic scandal.

When Drake died, in 1596, his impressive fortune, Oscar's yarn went, should have been inherited by his bastard son, but the British government, loathe to admit his presence, had held onto the money. Despite this injustice, the boy had married and propagated his kind, and the inheritance rightfully belonged, Oscar said, to the bastard's descendants, now scattered all over the American Middle West.

How big was the fortune? Oscar had it figured out nicely, with interest to date. Twenty-two billion dollars.

To back up his story, Oscar declared he had unearthed ancient documents in England substantiating his claim. He fast-talked the suckers into buying shares in the fortune, promising one hundred dollars back for every dollar invested against the day that his English lawyers, secretly slashing their way through a jungle of legal obstacles and greasing the palms of highly placed British government officials, could wrest those billions from John Bull.

When Oscar first started making his pitch, he had wondered only briefly how an upright Iowa farmer, reaping the golden fields under a blue sky, would react to the word that he was tainted by illegitimacy. He got his answer right off the bat when, one humid summer day, he bore down on Number 1, a tiller of the soil named Jones. After telling Jones that research had revealed him to be a

Drake heir, Oscar disclosed the scandalous origin of the good news. Jones thought things over for a minute, then squinted at Oscar.

"You mean to say," he asked, "that I'm a kind of a bastard?"

Oscar nodded.

"But you say," went on Jones, "that if I put maybe fifty dollars into this thing I'd get five thousand back?"

"Yup," said Oscar. "A hundred for one."

Jones looked off into the distances. "Come on into the house," he said, "and I'll get you the money. For that kind of a profit I don't much care if I *am* a bastard."

One day Oscar dropped in on a banker in a Nebraska whistle stop. The banker, a bald, round little man whose thinking processes were soon stopped by Oscar's hundred-for-one proposition, had only one question to ask.

"Why," he demanded, "is the English government still holding onto that money?"

Oscar, whose blue eyes, behind heavy horn-rimmed glasses, sparkled with integrity, said he was glad the man had asked the question.

"Just think," he declared, "what the transfer of twenty-two billion dollars from England to this country will do to the international money balance. Why, it will raise holy hell."

This conversation took place even before the Roosevelt administration stunned financial circles by raising the annual federal budget to five billion dollars.

"Twenty-two billion," repeated the banker, looking hard at Oscar. "Sa-a-ay, the transfer of that much sure *would* raise hell. Count me in for five thousand."

Once Oscar got rolling, the donators (as he called the suckers) among the so-called descendants of Sir Francis were so enthusiastic that Oscar suspected the non-descendants, or those of other than English ancestry, would be simply crazy to get in on the good thing. He couldn't have been more right.

One Saturday night in the summer of 1924, when an electrical storm was lashing the countryside, Oscar barged in on a Lutheran minister named Schmidt, who had a household of children, a bare cupboard and a leaky roof. Amid the patter of raindrops and little feet, Oscar shook the rafters with his booming offer to let the pastor ride the gravy train.

Schmidt pondered Oscar's hundred-for-one proposition, then, his voice throbbing with emotion, intoned, "God has sent you here."

Next morning, Oscar was sitting in the rear pew of a little white church, listening to Schmidt inform his flock that good fortune had descended upon it. When the service was over, the parishioners hustled home to examine their bankbooks and lay plans to mortgage their farms. A few nights later Oscar blew into town again, scooped up more than five thousand dollars, scribbled receipts, and blew out.

But it had taken a long time for Oscar to get his pitch to this sharp a tone, and he had plenty of time for improvising along the way.

It all began when the moustached stranger had walked off with mama's mortgage money. Pretty soon, when mama couldn't keep up the interest, the bank snapped up her farm, and sons Oscar and Canfield hit the road. They wandered through Iowa, Wisconsin, the Dakotas, Minnesota, Nebraska and Illinois, selling feed and grain and farm implements. Everywhere Oscar went he ran into the same old story: the moustached stranger had come and gone. But the lad was such

a smooth operator that apparently not a single victim could bring himself to believe he was a fraud.

Canfield, a dopey joe with an open face and a saucer haircut, just about made out on this tour. Oscar, however, developed into a real personality boy, a great handshaker, backslapper, and story-teller who killed himself with his own jokes, and he accumulated a large circle of friends as he moved through the sucker belt. He had a fantastic appetite for food, liquor, and dames. When he was thirty, he met a girl who said no, so he married her and settled down in Madison County, Iowa.

Giving up the road, Oscar backslapped his way into an appointment as deputy sheriff. He picked up quite a knowledge of law hanging around courtrooms watching clever lawyers confuse witnesses and fool jurors. It soon became an article of faith with Oscar that the entire Middle West was populated by citizens who were suckers for a tall story.

Oscar's marriage finally came apart at the seams, and his wife divorced him in 1918, when he was forty-one. He ran for sheriff on the Democratic ticket, lost at the polls, and was looking around for a new project when the lightning struck.

One night he was visited by a sharply dressed, fast-talking little man and a woman with buck teeth and crafty brown eyes. Introducing themselves as Milo Lewis and Mrs. Sudie Whiteaker, they divulged to Oscar that research had disclosed he was one of the heirs to the Sir Francis Drake fortune.

"You don't say," said Oscar, biting the tip off a fresh cigar. He let them ramble on for a while, then lowered the boom.

"My mother," he announced, "was swindled on this same damned thing years ago."

Milo and Sudie looked at each other and made for the door.

"Wait a minute," Oscar cried. "Maybe we can get together."

"What do you mean?" asked Lewis.

"Well, I happen to know a lot of people around here who might be interested in your proposition."

Supplied with sales-talk data by Sudie and Milo, Oscar drove around Madison County selling shares in the Drake estate on a commission basis. Calling on a farmer, he'd cross-examine the man about his family tree, then slap his knee and say, "Golly, but ain't you the lucky one, though. Why, you're one of them there Drake heirs."

By this time Oscar was a big, bluff man with a red-flannel booze face, a pot belly, and a booming laugh, and his circle of contacts in Iowa and his home-spun personality opened doors to him that would otherwise have been closed. Quick to exploit his advantage, and coming out the victor in every struggle with his conscience, Oscar laid it on with a trowel.

"Friend," he'd say to a sucker, looking the man straight in the eye, "you can go to bed and sleep sound tonight knowin' your money's safe with old Oscar."

After Sudie and Milo had signed up several agents in the area, they pulled out for London. Foxy Oscar, with an eye cocked on the future, said he'd like to go along.

"It'll make a good impression on the folks back here," he explained, "me bein' over there lookin' after things."

So Sudie and Milo took Oscar along as a kind of handyman. They checked into London's Savoy Hotel, Sudie and Milo taking a suite together and Oscar occupying a two-by-four in the servant's wing. One evening Oscar slipped into the suite and went through Milo's desk. He discovered that several hundred dollars a

month was coming over from the bush-beaters in the Midwest, and this bit of knowledge fascinated him so much that he copied the names and addresses of the salesmen. Then he got off a poison-pen letter to Scotland Yard, advising it that Sudie and Milo were illegal cohabitants. The couple, who had a whole catalog of good reasons for not returning to the United States, managed to get booted into France instead.

Oscar, taking over, returned to the Midwest and contacted the agents of Sudie and Milo.

"How much commission are they paying you?" he asked each.

"Ten per cent."

"Shucks. That ain't enough. I'll pay you twenty."

With Sudie and Milo thus left high and dry in France, Oscar set out to sign up some live wires. The first man he contacted was a traveling salesman named Joe Kirkendall, who lived in the town of Spencer, seventy-five miles northeast of Des Moines. Kirkendall, a shifty citizen in his middle forties with a long horse face and black hair parted in the middle, listened attentively as Oscar played it straight. While in London, Oscar said, he had discovered records establishing the birth of the illegitimate Drake baby and needed some key men to organize sales of claiming shares to the descendants.

"I don't think," said Kirkendall, blinking at Oscar, "there's any such thing as a Drake estate. But so long as there's people who believe there is, I ought to be able to unload some shares. When do I start?"

The next executive Oscar signed up was another salesman who also lived in Spencer—a fellow named Joe Hauber. Joe, a chunky middle-aged man with a round face, bald head and rimless eyeglasses, was an amateur actor who gave impersonations at smokers.

Oscar's third lieutenant was Otto Yant, a beaten-looking guy with a wispy mustache and a far-away look in his eyes. Otto, an ex-barber who was to clip 'em proper in the years ahead, was the teller in the lone bank of Mallard, Iowa. Oscar wanted him to correspond with tellers in other banks, get lists of highly liquid depositors, and turn the names over to the boys on the road.

The fourth man Oscar signed up was Delmar Short, a traveling salesman who looked a lot like Lou Costello, the comedian, and always left them laughing, if broke.

Oscar, Kirkendall, Short and Hauber hit the road, selling shares and hiring sub-agents on a commission basis. Yant began to supply so many prospects that the sub-agents hired sub-sub-agents. Oscar's racket mushroomed.

Finding the pickings easier than he had imagined, Oscar now branched out into the states around Iowa. And after his eager reception by the good Pastor Schmidt he also decided to let non-descendants join the happy contributors.

A regular caste system began to spring up in the prairies: people were either descendants of Sir Francis Drake and Queen Elizabeth, and bastards, or they were commoners, and legitimate. Oscar, quick to exploit the situation, began to play both ends against the middle.

"Your neighbor down the road," he'd say to a prospect with the off-color purple blood, "ain't fit to shine your boots, you bein' a descendant of Queen Elizabeth of England and everything."

Then, after palming off a few shares in the Drake estate and scribbling a receipt, Oscar would call on the neighbor for another sale.

"You ought to be glad," he'd say, "that your kids ain't in the same fix as them kids up the road—illegitimate and everything."

Every other Sunday, Oscar held a meeting with Kirkendall, Hauber, Yant and Short in a Des Moines hotel suite. At one such meeting he announced that he would shortly be leaving for England.

"Why?" asked Kirkendall.

"It'll look better with me over there," said Oscar. "You can tell the donators that I'm attending to things for them—lookin' out for their interests. We'll keep in touch by cable—never mail, you understand?"

"Okay," said Kirkendall. "How do we get the money to you?"

Oscar had that all figured out. He was bringing his brother Canfield in on the scheme. Canfield was going to live in New York. Kirkendall, Hauber and Short were to gather the boodle and ship a load of cash by express to Canfield each week. Canfield would then run up to Canada and send the stuff to Oscar in London by American Express money order. Oscar had learned about the mail-fraud statutes while a law-enforcement officer, and he wanted no part of a tangle with the Post Office Department.

In London, assuming the guise of a retired Texas cattleman, Oscar set himself up in a handsome flat, decked himself out in Bond Street clothes, hired a valet named Stewart, and began to drink and chase women. The stream of money gathered by his agents in the corn belt came into the American Express office every week. Nobody ever had it better than good old Oscar.

Even in the late 1920's, several years after his game had begun, the Drake fever in the Middle West was still rising. Every couple of weeks Oscar shot a cable to the boys advising them that things were progressing satisfactorily and sending his best wishes to the donators. These pep cables were copied and read by the agents swarming the countryside and infiltrating church suppers, prayer meetings, strawberry festivals and quilting bees.

About that time Oscar walked into a pub one night for an 'arf and 'arf. He took a table in a corner and waited for something to emerge from the smoke and babble around him. When she did, she turned out to be a buxom blond bar maid. Her name was Maggie, she was only twenty, and Oscar was just the man she'd been looking for. She lived around the corner in a cold-water flat with her widowed father, a window washer named Alf.

Oscar checked on his supply of aphrodisiacs and took the girl home. When Old Alf, a stubby little man with a walrus mustache, sized up Oscar, the first thought to cross his mind was that his daughter had trapped a millionaire.

A couple of months after she met Oscar, Maggie discovered an unpleasant development.

"'E's got to do the right thing," Alf said hopefully to Maggie. "I'll go and see him."

Oscar seems to have been at his best when Old Alf called on him. He not only convinced papa that somebody else had seduced Maggie, but he sent the old boy hustling to his bank to invest in the Drake estate.

Not long afterward Oscar ran across the newspaper advertisement of a South Kensington medium who called herself Madam St. John Montague. Curious to see what the future held in store for him, he took a run out to her address.

Madam Montague held forth in a faded brick house, functioning in a dark second-floor room complete with heavy red drapes, incense and a crystal ball.

The madam, swathed in billowing green satin, was a fat old frump with a suety face and pig eyes. When Oscar clumped in, she quickly discounted his Bond Street clothes and, her practiced eye spotting the hayseed still sticking out of his ears, knew she had a live one.

Playing for time, Madam Montague told Oscar that her crystal ball seemed a bit foggy that day, but it was clear enough for her to advise him to come back the following week. Then, she said, she would have interesting news for him. She didn't mention that, to dig up the news, she had in her kennel a private detective named T. W. Barnard, who ferreted out scuttlebutt about her clients.

Barnard chased down Old Alf, roped him, and got the story of what had happened when Alf called at Hartzell's apartment. Next, tailing Oscar, Barnard shadowed him to the American Express office, and there learned that Oscar was receiving large weekly drafts from Canada.

Next time Oscar called at Madam Montague's, the crystal ball was practically issuing bulletins.

"I see here," said Madam, "a man with a large mustache accusing you of some misdeed. Ah, yes, here it is: he is accusing you of being the father of his daughter's unborn child. But you convince him that you are not the father. Now I see an exchange of money. The old man is handing you some money."

Barnard, behind a curtain taking everything in, peeked out to see Oscar listening intently, leaning forward in his chair, hands on knees, a dead cigar clenched in his teeth.

"You're wonderful," he said to the Madam, utterly flabbergasted. "Simply wonderful. What do I owe you?"

"Ten pounds," said the Madam modestly. "And I think it might be to your benefit to come here at least once a week."

Oscar took the advice and stuck to it the rest of the time he was in London.

Barnard contrived a bar-room acquaintance with Oscar. Late one raw afternoon, they were bellying up to the Savoy bar, safely out of the fog, when the detective, studying Oscar's reflection in the mirror behind the bar, decided the time was ripe to find out more. Steering the talk around to money, Barnard began, "I never told you what I did for a living, did I?"

"No," said Oscar, "you didn't."

"I don't have to work any more," said Barnard. "I made several million selling stocks in the United States."

"What kind of stocks?"

"Not very good stuff," said Barnard, chuckling. "As a matter of fact, the stock I cleaned up on was so bad I had to get out of the country. That's why I'm back over here."

Oscar, already half in his cups, boomed out a laugh. Now he had to top Barnard's story. Sparing no details, he disclosed the racket he was in. One day in the future, sitting in an Iowa courtroom, he was to wish he had bitten his tongue off before growing so confidential.

Curiously enough, Oscar wasn't salting away any of his boodle. He had taken up gambling. Half the gyppo boys in London got their clutches on him in one way or another and were taking the money from Oscar almost as fast as he laid hands on it. As shrewd as he was when it came to pulling the wool over the eyes of American farmers, Oscar was a real pushover for the English sharpies.

As time passed, Oscar, to keep his midwestern donators from growing restless, seized on newspaper headlines and gave them phony hidden meanings supposedly relating to the Drake estate. Then he sent his lieutenants galloping through the sucker belt to cry the latest developments.

A public official couldn't open his mouth without having Oscar grab his words and rearrange their meaning. The result was that the peasants actually believed Louisiana's Senator Huey Long was referring to the Drake estate when he constructed his share-the-wealth platform. They were told to keep an eye on that underslung pipe of Vice President Charley Dawes, the Chicago financier. If Dawes appeared in a newspaper photograph lighting the pipe, that would be the tip to the insiders that settlement of the estate was imminent.

In 1931, after Oscar had been at it for seven years, the depression shook the midwesterners down and donations began to fall off. Oscar, with his eyes peeled for a headline that would jack things up, got just what he was looking for when President Hoover announced prosperity was just around the corner. Hoover's words were still ringing in the national ear when Oscar's team of Kirkendall, Hauber, Short and Yant set out to fire the prairies with pep talks.

"You've all read what our President said about prosperity being just around the corner," Yant told a congress of boobs near Des Moines one night. "Do you know what he *really* meant? He meant *our* proposition. *That's* what he meant."

One yokel at the rally spoke for them all when, rubbing the stubble of his chin and squinting at the leaden sky, he announced that he was going to sell the old spotted cow and take his setting hens right off their nests and hustle them to market.

By the time the boys completed their tour everything had boomed back to normal for Oscar.

For several years law-enforcement officials and newspaper reporters in Oscar's Spanish Main had been pretty sure the gang was engaged in a racket although they had had no idea of the magnitude of the operation. But Oscar kept a step ahead of trouble by having his lieutenants swear donators to an oath of "silence and non-disturbance" under pain of being red-inked out of participation in the estate. This threw the fear of God into the suckers, who had only scribbled receipts saying "Received $50," or some such amount, to show for their money.

The attorney general of Iowa issued a statement saying there was no such thing as a Sir Francis Drake estate, and that people investing in such a project could kiss their money goodby. All he got for his trouble was a sackful of poison-pen letters accusing him of being in cahoots with the forces dedicated to keeping the Drake billions from the rightful heirs. When the Des Moines *Register & Tribune* ran an editorial saying the whole Drake business was a swindle, the phones in the city room jangled with calls from outraged Drakers and rocks began to fly through the windows.

The man who was *really* fascinated by Oscar's operations, however, was Kilroy P. Aldrich, Chief United States Post Office inspector. Aldrich, a smallish, mild-mannered man with gold-rimmed glasses, thinning hair, and the persistence of a permanent magnet, assigned inspectors to the corn belt to see whether they could lay hands on evidence of using the mails to defraud.

The mail-fraud statute is an elastic one —so elastic, in fact, that it can almost snap up a crook who so much as thinks of something illegal while in the shadow of a mail box. But Aldrich's inspectors, fanning out through the Midwest, soon discovered that Oscar was well aware of the dangers of fraud by mail. He had not only sealed the lips of his victims but had carefully circumvented the law by using the cables instead of the mails, and by having the boodle shipped by express.

One day, though, the Post Office men ran into a piece of luck. A hick sheriff, wanting to make a name for himself, hit the barn of a farmer named Amos Hartsock in Pocahontas, Iowa. Hartsock, functioning as a sub-agent of Oscar's, had violated the rules and engaged in elaborate correspondence with hundreds of donators. The sheriff confiscated a wagonload of Drake stuff that had gone through the mails, but after taking it to his office didn't know what to do with it. Aldrich's men, hearing about the seizure, grabbed it and realized that they had, at long last, struck a gusher. The Hartsock correspondence was admissible as court evidence against Oscar because, while he himself had not written it, he had, in the legal view, *caused* it to go through the mails.

Now Aldrich sent inspectors to London. There they reconstructed the whole story of Hartzell's activities during the preceding years. Their prize catch in London was Barnard, the private eye to whom Oscar had spilled the details of his racket. Barnard agreed to come to America to testify.

Indicted in Iowa for using the mails to defraud, Oscar was booted out of England in January 1933 as an undesirable alien. Back in his home state again, he was hailed not as a criminal brought to justice, but as a conquering hero who, tripped up by powerful forces, had come a temporary cropper.

Released on bail pending trial, Oscar got together with his four lieutenants and spread the word that he would address a jumbo conclave to be held on a farm outside Spencer, Iowa, the first Saturday night in June. The farmers came in from the fields early that day, scrubbed their faces, put on their best duds and drove off by buggy and car. As the dusk thickened, the streams of rubes converging on the meeting ground were visible to the horizon.

Oscar was hiding in the barn, awaiting the moment of his grand entrance. His four con-men were posted around the farm at strategic points, holding lanterns and peering into the faces of every arrival, eyes alert for the law. The Drakers were directed to a cow pasture, where they flopped on the grass facing a wagon lit up by red flares, which was to serve as Oscar's speaking platform. There was a commotion in the darkness at the edge of the crowd.

"Here he is now!" somebody shouted.

A yell to wake the dead went up as Oscar, bringing the crowd to its feet, elbowed his way to the wagon. Nimbly jumping up, he displayed a get-up of white pants, two-tone shoes, blue jacket and flaming red necktie. He gave the crowd the old prize-ring handshake and touched off another thunderous ovation. Oscar was in rare form that night.

"Donators," he cried, his voice throbbing with emotion, "are we goin' to let the Interests rob us—take the money right outa our pockets?"

"No!" came an ear-splitting roar.

"Do you know," Oscar asked, "who's behind this indictment of me? The King of England, who wants to rob you of your rights. *That's* who! But don't worry. We've only begun to fight!"

As the sweat rolled off the faces and down the backs of the suckers, Oscar rambled on, spouting some high-sounding mumbo-jumbo about the international plotters in Washington and London who were conspiring against the good folk of the Middle West. After orating for more than an hour, Oscar made a production of pulling his pants pockets inside out.

"You can see," he yelled, "that his fight against the Interests has left old Oscar broke."

With the crowd in a frenzy, Yant, Hauber, Short and Kirkendall began circulating, putting on the bite for what they were calling the Oscar Hartzell Defense Fund. While the collection was in progress, two harmonica players got up on the wagon and, flanking Oscar, who was looking on benignly, they began to play hill-billy music.

"Dig! Dig! Dig!" Oscar shouted every minute or so. "Dig deep. Put another mortgage on the old homestead if you have to. Remember, you're goin' to get a hundred for one."

When everybody had gone home and only the stars looked down on the cow pasture, Oscar had taken the boobs for another twelve thousand dollars.

The wind was whipping over the prairies on a slate-gray morning in November, 1933 when Oscar Hartzell went on trial in the United States District Court in Sioux City, Iowa. The charge was furthering a scheme to defraud. A carnival atmosphere pervaded the town. The plowboys, in from the fields, were wearing shiny blue serge suits, their hair slicked down and their faces shining with wonder.

The trial lasted three weeks. Uncle Sam produced English legal lights who explained to the jury that there never had been such a thing as an unsettled Drake estate. Barnard, the private eye, repeated the incriminating bar-room conversation he had had with Oscar. Then the government went through an intricate maze of mail that linked our boy to the fraud. Oscar, who didn't dare take the stand in his own defense, was found guilty. His lawyers appealed, however, and he was released on bail.

The verdict didn't have the effect on

the suckers that the government thought it would. Harry M. Reed, the United States attorney who handled the case, was besieged by threatening calls from the donators.

"They still thought," Reed recalls today, "that Oscar had been framed by unseen interests."

Oscar had no sooner been sprung on bail than he skipped Iowa. He went to Chicago, where, in an office on Rush Street, Yant, Short, Hauber and Kirkendall had set up shop. They showed Oscar a basketful of letters that the faithful had sent in, asking how they could help the martyr.

"Isn't it wonderful," said Oscar, "what trust these good people have in me!"

"You bet it is," said Short. "Let's not disappoint them."

"All right, boys," said Oscar. "Carry on—but don't put nuthin' in writing."

Eventually, however, good old Oscar lost his appeal and checked into Leavenworth. Undismayed, the lieutenants kept going strong at the Chicago office. Then one day there developed one of those untoward coincidences that sometimes thwart the best-laid plans of swindlers. A yokel in Wisconsin who had sent fifty dollars to Kirkendall grew restless when he didn't get a receipt. He wrote to a nephew in Chicago asking him to go to the office for a receipt. The nephew misunderstood the letter and went instead to the police, where Detective James Zegar lent him an ear.

All four of Oscar's con men were on the premises when Zegar, palming himself off as the Wisconsin donator, dropped in. After getting the missing receipt, the dick said he thought he might interest a friend in the proposition and would be back the next day.

He was back, all right. The trouble was that he was accompanied by several co-workers who rushed the Rush Street files. They cleaned out the place lock, stock and barrel. When they were hustling the boys out to the wagon, Hauber, the amateur actor, drew Zegar aside.

"Secret Service," Hauber whispered, flashing a phony badge. "I've had my eye on this crowd for months. Well, I've got to be getting back to Washington now."

"Wait a minute!" yelled Zegar. "Let's have another look at that badge."

Now the Post Office sleuths moved into the picture. They found, in the welter of stuff which the Chicago cops had seized, the makings of mail-fraud indictments not only against the four lieutenants, but also against Oscar's brother Canfield. All five got jail jolts.

Oscar Hartzell cracked up in prison and was transferred to a booby hatch, where he died. But he left a legacy to the United States Post Office Department. Oscar worked the Drake swindle to such a fare-thee-well that it has never got off the ground since. Still, most of Oscar's victims believed in him to their dying day.

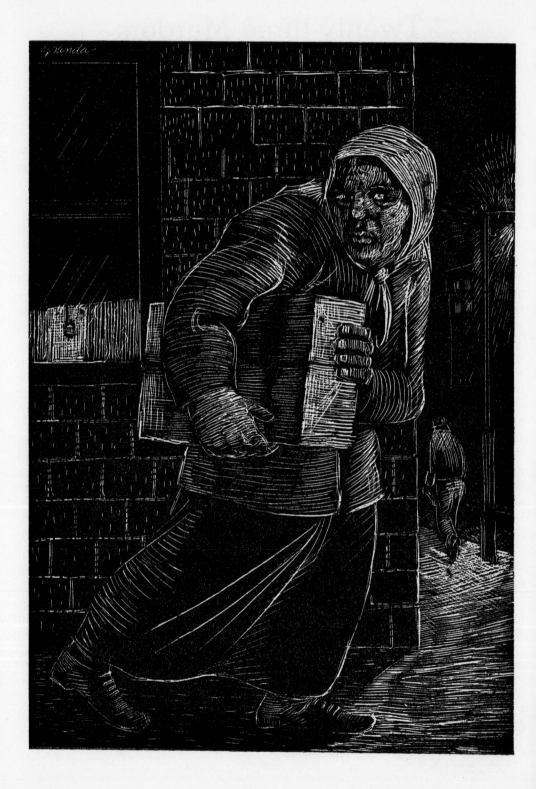

Twenty-three Murders

Meet Edmond Chasse, the French Canadian story-book reporter, who was ahead of the Royal Canadian Mounted Police in getting to the core of one of the most infamous crimes on record.

The newspapers (as well as motion pictures, radio, and, lately, television) have long been under indictment by psychiatrists, educators and other authorities as stimulants to criminal deeds. Whenever the police locate some moronic murderer and are startled to learn that he can talk, and he says, in answer to a question about what lodged the idea for the caper in his head, "I seen it in the papers," the fourth estate is charged with another overt act.

In May of 1949 the papers carried a story about a lady in the Philippines who, supposedly wearying of her husband and taking a lover, allegedly got rid of the husband by way of hustling him off on an airplane trip and hiring some gangsters to plant a time bomb on the plane so that neither the husband nor anybody else on the plane ever came back. The lady in the Philippines had allegedly been guilty of an oversight in that she had been seen, before her husband had departed on the trip that was to take him into another dimension, in some highly questionable company—namely with some gentlemen who had for some time been under surveillance by the National Bureau of Investigation. Result: wholesale arrests.

Of all the millions of readers of the newspaper story that came out of the Philippines, one reader—a reader who lived on a sordid street in the ancient French Quarter, or Lower Town, of Quebec, Canada—was influenced by it. This reader was, after a fashion, a pla-

giarist—an unoriginal author who appropriated the plot of the alleged Far Eastern authors. As a result, twenty-three persons perished when a time bomb went off in an airplane in what the Royal Canadian Mounted Police have called the cruelest crime in the history of the Dominion.

As if by way of compensation for what it had done—putting the pattern of a crime in the head of the plotter—the fourth estate itself helped furnish the means in the form of a reporter for the great Montreal daily, *Le Canada*. Well, not *exactly* a reporter; more of a journalist. The difference between a reporter and a journalist is, as any newspaperman knows, that a journalist carries a cane. *This* journalist—a sixty-one-year-old French Canadian by the name of Edmond Chasse, the Quebec correspondent for *Le Canada*—not only carried a cane; he wore spats.

Chasse, then, was not, as the late Alexander Woollcott was fond of calling all newspapermen, an ink-stained wretch; he was, rather, a highly polished fashion plate—an alert, smallish man with sharply cut clothes and graying hair, at whom you would have looked twice had you happened upon him hastening through the lobby of the Château Frontenac, or taking his morning constitutional near his home on Quebec's handsome and sedate Grande-Allée, where he lived only two blocks from his good friend Louis St. Laurent, Canada's prime minister.

It was Monsieur Chasse, cane, spats and all, who heard the first meaningful rumor, who ran down the first clue, who leveled the original finger of suspicion, at a time when even the renowned Royal Canadian Mounted Police, one of several law-enforcement agencies working on the case of the twenty-three murders, was, while not exactly fumbling the ball, still behind its own goal line.

It seems that Monsieur Chasse fell to talking to a taxi driver, and that the taxi driver had heard another taxi driver speaking of a third taxi driver who had in turn spoken of having driven an ugly-looking woman in black, carrying a mysterious package, to l'Ancienne Lorette airport, about five miles by taxi from the Château Frontenac, on the morning of Friday, September 9, 1949—a fateful date, as shall be seen.

The ugly-looking woman (Monsieur Chasse was to learn) got into a taxi driven by one Henri-Paul Pelletier at the Palais Station of the Canadian Pacific Railway in Quebec's Lower Town—the section of old, quaint and sordid streets as contrasted with the city's Upper Town, with its Château Frontenac, its sleek shops and its socially conscious residential addresses. Pelletier's passenger was a squat and fortyish woman with a hard, square face and small black pig eyes—a sort of female Rasputin. She said she wanted to get the package she was carrying on a northbound Quebec Airways plane that left at ten o'clock. It was now about nine-twenty. The woman, settling herself in the cab, cautioned Pelletier not to drive fast. Her package was very fragile; she didn't want it to be jounced.

At the airport, the woman in black told Pelletier to wait. She waddled into the express office, checked the package, which weighed twenty-seven pounds and cost her $2.72, and inquired twice of the express clerk if he was certain that it would go out on the ten o'clock plane. When assured that it would, she got back into the taxi and left the airport.

The ten o'clock plane, incoming from Montreal, was bound for the northeastern reaches of Quebec Province, with a stop at the town of Baie Comeau, between Quebec City and its destination. It was a DC-3 with a crew of two—pilot and stewardess—and a passenger list that included the president, a vice-president, and the president-elect of the Kennecott Copper Company, en route on an inspection of mining properties; two executives of a Canadian paper mill, and ordinary men and women and three small children. Several passengers were to get aboard at Quebec, bringing the total number of persons in flight up to twenty-three.

During the first part of its flight after taking off from Quebec, the plane would be flying over long stretches of primeval wilderness; then its route would take it out over the St. Lawrence River at about ten-twenty-five.

The DC-3, which made the round trip from Montreal to upper Province three times weekly—Mondays, Wednesdays, and Fridays—was usually prompt in arrivals and departures. This particular morning, though, it had been delayed getting out of Montreal so that it came down late at Quebec and left late—seven minutes late. That seven minutes was to make a great difference all around; it meant that at ten-thirty the plane, which normally would have been out over the St. Lawrence River, was, instead, still over land.

The hour of ten-thirty was important because that was the moment when the ship, traveling at about five thousand feet altitude near a stretch of desolation known as Mount Torment, was rocked by an explosion. Several lumbermen, a gang of railroad section workers and an eel fisherman in the region, who had glanced up to watch the ship in flight, now saw it begin plummeting toward a slope of Mount Torment. Then, seconds later, the observers heard the sound of the explosion that had caused the ship to plummet.

It was afternoon before the first eyewitnesses could make their way through the evergreen fastness to the crash scene. The plane had landed into the mountain, but it had not, singularly enough, caught fire; its gas tanks had not exploded although the pilot had not shut off the ignition. Everybody on board was dead, of course, but although the bodies were mangled they were not burned.

The odor of fire was, therefore, not present to obliterate another odor—that of dynamite. The men who stood around the wreckage of the plane that September afternoon, especially the lumbermen, had worked with dynamite all their adult lives. They knew dynamite when they smelled it, and they were smelling it now. That's where those seven minutes came in; had the plane not been delayed it would have been out over the St. Lawrence when the explosion took place and dropped into the water, and nobody would have had a chance to smell anything.

The tragedy occurred about forty miles north of Quebec City and it wasn't too long after the natives reached the spot that the law arrived and took over —the law in the form of the National Transport Authority, The Royal Canadian Mounted Police, the Quebec Provincial Police, and investigators of the Canadian Pacific Railway, which operated Quebec Airways. The law smelled that dynamite, too, then imposed a censorship on the natives. The natives were not to breathe a word about the smell of dynamite to *anybody*—least of all to newspapermen.

The censorship had no sooner been imposed than there materialized, out of the fastness surrounding the tableau of doom, Monsieur Chasse of *Le Canada*, spats, cane, and snapping brown eyes. The law forthwith set up a layer of insulation between what Chasse had come to look at and Chasse himself. But the law could not establish such insulation between Chasse and the lumbermen, railroad section hands, and the eel fishermen who dwelled in that primeval region. Chasse's heart beat to the same rhythm as the hearts of these simple men; Chasse was far from simple, but he, too, had been born in Quebec. The affinity of one French Canadian native of Quebec for another French Canadian native is a unique and wonderful thing.

And so it was that Edmond Chasse returned to Quebec City that Friday evening, to file his story for his paper in Montreal, in possession of the information that what had caused the ship to plummet into the face of Mount Torment had been a dynamite explosion. The law must have known the same thing. Yet the law was saying nothing about it. Very well, then; Chasse would not tip his hand, either.

What the law was doing was bringing pieces of the interior of the ship and the clothing of some of the victims to a make-shift laboratory in one of the rooms in the Château Frontenac. There it was definitely determined that a dynamite blast of intensity great enough to instantly kill everybody in the ship had taken place in the skies above Mount Torment. This explained why the pilot had not shut off the ignition. It is instinctive with a pilot to shut off the ignition at the first sign of trouble that might cause the gas tanks to explode; the fact that this pilot, a wartime veteran, had not done so indicated that he had been killed before he could obey his instinct.

In checking the airport records of freight aboard the plane, the detectives came across a phony. A twenty-seven-pound package placed aboard at Quebec, and supposed to have contained a piece of religious statuary, had borne the name of a nonexistent addressee. Since a package weighing twenty-seven pounds could have held just what a fiend would have needed to blow up a DC-3, the police fell to the task of laying hands on whoever had dropped it at the airport.

The airport express clerk—a man by the name of Willy Lamonde—recalled the person who had sent the package. The sender had been a woman, a particularly ugly woman, a regular dragon —a five-by-five with a square, mean face and pig eyes. Woman about forty to forty-five. Dressed in black. Lamonde had no way of knowing whether the woman had been a passenger on the plane. The police figured she had not.

If the woman in black had come to the airport for the sole purpose of placing a package of dynamite aboard the DC-3, she had probably come by car, had the car wait, and departed in it, since private car or taxi was the most accessible means of reaching the airport. On the chance that the car the woman had traveled in had been a taxi, the detectives began to question taxi drivers. Inasmuch as taxis arrived at the airport from any one of a number of starting points, this procedure was a roundabout one at best —a task harder than it would seem to be.

Meantime, Monsieur Chasse of *Le Canada* was going around Quebec City, sniffing here, sniffing there, like any man with a nose for news is supposed to do. Frequently, in the Château Frontenac, he would run into his good friend, Inspector René Belec of the Mounties—a lean, fortyish French Canadian with tight lips—as Inspector Belec was entering or leaving the room where the investigators were headquartering. Inspector Belec would smile mirthlessly to Monsieur Chasse, shake his head from side to side, and say he was sorry but he had no news to give out. But somehow, Chasse got wind of what was coming to light inside that room and elsewhere. He learned that the law was on the prowl for an ugly woman in black who had sent a package on the plane. He learned that pieces of metal and other component parts of an alarm clock had been found. Since an alarm clock is to an infernal machine what a trigger is to a gun, Chasse now had corroboration, as if he needed it, that those twenty-three persons aboard that plane over Mount Torment had been murdered.

But who among the twenty-three had been the target of the murder? The pilot? The stewardess? Some individual passenger, or group of passengers? Those three officials of the Kennecott Copper Company looked mighty interesting. The men were Americans, bent on business involving millions of dollars. Was it possible that their deaths were the end result of some superplot such as one would normally encounter only in fiction? South of the border, the Federal Bureau of Investigation started an investigative ball rolling to find out.

Edmond Chasse, however, was thinking in more domestic terms. He had a hunch that some individual in either Montreal or Quebec (but probably Quebec because the plane had blown up after leaving there) had wanted to get rid of one of the passengers on that ship and had killed the other twenty-two persons on board in the process. That being so, there was no telling where a good journalist might turn up a clue that would pay off. Chasse engaged everyone with whom he came in contact—taxi drivers, waiters, other reporters, people on the street, but especially taxi drivers —in conversation about the tragedy.

It was on the Monday following the Friday of the explosion that Chasse was taxiing around Quebec in the course of what he elegantly chose to call his inquiry. "Tell me," he said to the taxi driver, "what do you make of the accident?" The driver had no opinion. What, he asked Chasse, did Chasse make of it? A fair enough question.

"I think," said Chasse, "that was no accident. That was a *crime*." The taxi driver turned around. A crime? A *deliberate* crime? Why did Monsieur Chasse think such a thing? "Because nothing was wrong with that plane mechanically. It was blown up by dynamite." The taxi driver was silent for a block or so.

"What you say," he said finally, "makes me think of something that happened Friday morning at the Palais Station." And what, Chasse quickly demanded, before the man could change his mind and close his mouth, was that?

What had happened Friday morning, half an hour or more before the plane with the Indian sign on it had been due to take off, was that a woman—a singularly ugly woman in black—had appeared in the Palais Station carrying a heavy package and asked one of several taxi drivers standing around waiting for fares to take the package to the airport and check it for her on the ten o'clock plane for Seven Islands. For some reason or other, none of the taxi drivers would accept the commission. This resulted in the woman getting into a cab herself—

the cab of Henri-Paul Pelletier—and going to the airport.

Chasse lost no time in getting to the taxi stand at the Palais Station. He learned that Pelletier had, after taking the woman in black to the airport, dropped her at a street intersection along the Rue Monsignor Gauvreau, in the ancient French Lower Town. Chasse began to sniff around the Rue Monsignor Gauvreau—a neighborhood of small, shabby, and rickety houses. Chasse, with his affinity for the natives, learned of a character in the thoroughfare whose name was Mrs. Marguerite Pitre (pronounced *Peetr*) but better known to neighbors as the Raven. Mrs. Pitre had fallen heiress to this appellation by virtue of her penchant for black—black everything, from shoes to hat.

Mme. Pitre was just the woman to intrigue a newspaperman, murder or no murder. She was, Chasse soon learned without so much as laying eyes on the woman, a many-faceted individual. She kept a couple of roomers in the little two-story dirty-gray frame house where she lived, she worked occasionally as a waitress in Lower Town indigestion traps, and, on the side, was reputed to function as a procurer. This latter fact was of particular interest to Chasse. He knew that if he threaded into Mme. Pitre's past as a procurer that, while he might not necessarily uncover the answer to the infernal machine on the DC-3, he at least wouldn't find the work monotonous.

Instinct told Chasse that he would learn something about a woman such as Mme. Pitre in either the court or the law-enforcement records of the Lower Town. Chasse's instinct was right. The name of Mme. Pitre bobbed up in the records of a court proceeding that had arisen out of a disturbance in a Lower

Town restaurant three months previously. It appeared that a waitress in the restaurant—a sassy little character named Marie-Ange Robitaille, twenty years old, provocative of face and figure—had gotten into an altercation with a patron by the name of Joseph Albert Guay, and that Guay, all wined up, had whipped out a revolver, then saved the young lady's life by not firing at her. Guay, a man of thirty-two, who had described himself as a jewelry salesman, had been arrested for the disturbance, whereupon Mme. Pitre had furnished his bail, hustled up a mouthpiece and been a character witness for him. The result was that Guay wriggled off the hook with a small fine when he might well have gone into the deep freeze for a somewhat extended period.

Chasse's eyes were really snapping as he digested the intelligence from the court proceeding. For Joseph Albert Guay, the man who had quarreled with the pretty waitress, was, after a fashion, a somewhat distinguished widower. He had been a widower for four days now. His twenty-seven-year-old wife, Rita Morel Guay, had been one of the passengers on the plane. The connection between the woman who had gone to the airport with the mysterious package and a man whose wife had perished on the plane constituted, to Edmond Chasse, so much smoke that there just had to be beneath that smoke a roaring fire.

Edmond Chasse was just the man to lose himself in the Lower Town and compile, with incredible speed, a private dossier on Joseph Albert Guay. The little widower was one of those characters indigenous to the Lower Town— part of the mean streets and fulsome alleys of the old city. He had been weaned on wine, and had quit school after learning to read, write, and count; strictly a city boy, the only green he had ever seen until maturity was, as the saying goes, the baize on a pool table. Yet Joseph Albert Guay was a fellow with ambitions. He had, after living by his wits through his teens, risen above his surroundings because he wanted to be a flashy dresser with money in his pocket, the better to have fun with girls. He began to inhale his own perfume.

For, despite the fact that he stood only five feet six inches and weighed only about one hundred and twenty pounds, Guay seems to have been equipped with steel wool on his chest. He had long been known as a character with eyes in the back of his head, the better to scout talent in the rear, and ears reputed to be able to detect the rustle of a skirt around a corner.

It wasn't until 1939, when he was twenty-two and the Second World War broke out, that Guay really began to hit his stride financially. A real patriot, he went to work in a Quebec munitions factory to help supply the boys on the fighting fronts. He had himself a field day with the widows and detached wives and unmarried girls in his neighborhood. He paused during the hunt to do a strange thing. He got married. His wife was a girl by the name of Rita Morel; she was a plain, prim little thing, not at all the type Guay had preferred; nobody could understand the union except that the bride's parents were reported to be well fixed.

While working in the munitions factory, Guay earned extra money by peddling watches and other jewelry to fellow workers. When the war ended in 1945, he became a full-time jewelry salesman. He was enterprising. He soon carved out a lucrative route for himself in the scores of small towns along the north shore of the St. Lawrence above

Quebec. In order to cover ground quickly, he frequently traveled by plane —the thrice-weekly DC-3 that made the run between Montreal, Quebec, Baie Comeau, and northeastern Quebec Province.

It was in 1946, five years after his marriage, that Guay met Marie-Ange Robitaille, the waitress he later threatened three months before the plane blew up. Marie-Ange was only seventeen at the time; the talk in the Lower Town was that Mme. Pitre, functioning as a procurer, delivered the girl, whose father was a neighborhood contractor, to Guay in a room on the second floor of her little house on the Rue Monsignor Gauvreau. Whatever the precise circumstances of the meeting between Guay and Mlle. Robitaille, it was lust at first sight. If Guay's wife had not been able to slow him down, this seventeen-year-old girl had what it took. She had it in such abundance that Guay was sometimes unable to go off on scheduled selling trips. He just didn't have the strength.

Eventually Guay's wife found out. She went to the girl's father. There was an acrimonious scene. Then the girl left home. She lived with Guay in various hovels in the Lower Town and for a while set up light housekeeping with him in Seven Islands, in the northeastern part of the province. Then, along in the spring of 1949, in the third year of her relationship with Guay, she apparently felt the need of a change. She told Guay she wanted to go to Montreal to visit friends.

She had been absent from him for about two months when, one night, he chanced to go into a restaurant in the Lower Town. There he saw Mlle. Robitaille, working as a waitress. He asked her how long she had been back. She had not, she informed him, ever been away.

He pulled the gun and was arrested. That was when his friend Mme. Pitre came into the picture to furnish his bail and hire him a lawyer. Afterward, he had apparently resumed activity with Mlle. Robitaille because, Chasse learned, the two had frequently been seen visiting Mme. Pitre together.

All this was, needless to say, simply fascinating to Chasse. Meantime, Inspector Belec of the Mounties, officers of the Provincial Police, and investigators for the Canadian Pacific had also become intrigued by the small, drawn figure of Joseph Albert Guay. Where Chasse had come upon Guay through tracing Mme. Pitre through the taxi ride from the Palais Station to the airport, the detectives, who had not yet learned the identity of the woman in black who had taken the package to the airport, got on Guay's trail at the ticket desk of Quebec Airways in the lobby of the Château Frontenac. They got on his trail for the simple reason that they had to consider every possibility in examining the theory that *somebody* had wanted to get rid of one or more of the twenty-three persons aboard the plane. Joseph Albert Guay had purchased a round trip ticket for his wife two days before the flight. The girl at the ticket counter remembered Guay for two reasons. He had showed an inclination to flirt and she was a nice girl. He had occasionally bought tickets from her before. This had been the first time that Guay had ever bought a ticket for anybody but himself.

Guay had, in purchasing a round-trip passage at Baie Comeau for his spouse, inquired about insurance—something he had never done previously. He took out ten thousand dollars' worth of travelers' insurance—good during the trip either way—in his wife's name, naming himself as the beneficiary. The policy cost him fifty cents. The girl at the desk told him that it would be necessary that his wife sign the insurance application.

On the morning of the flight, Guay and his wife appeared at the Château Frontenac, to take the air-line taxi out to the airport. Guay took his wife over to the air-line desk and had her sign the insurance application. Just a formality. There seemed to be a misunderstanding between Guay and his wife about when she was returning. She had been under the impression that there would be a plane out of Baie Comeau that evening which would return her to Quebec. The ticketseller said there would be no such plane. Mrs. Guay, who didn't want to be away from her five-year-old daughter overnight, balked. She didn't, she said, think she would go.

"Why," she asked Guay, "don't *you* go, Albert?" Guay was persuasive, even charming. His wife needed a rest. She had relatives in Baie Comeau. She could stay with them over the weekend and return the first of the week. He would take care of the little girl. The woman seemed still in the throes of misgivings when he took her by the arm and propelled her toward the taxi for the airport.

In holding Guay's past up to the light, the detectives came upon Mme. Pitre. They came, too, upon the story of the relationship between Guay and Marie-Ange Robitaille. They thus arrived, several days after the twenty-three murders, at the same point as the journalist Chasse, but from opposite directions, like tunnel workers beginning to dig at opposite points and meeting in the middle. From there on in, Chasse and the detectives engaged in a grimly good-natured race to see who would be first to wrap up the bundle.

The detectives were getting Mme.

Pitre and Guay up in the morning and putting them to bed at night—in separate beds, to be sure. Mme. Pitre was sticking close to her dirty little gray house; Guay was bent by grief. "Our last contact," he was going around telling acquaintances, "was a kiss at the airport." The Robitaille girl had gone back to live with her parents. The investigators were impatient for the three to start contacting one another. So was Chasse. Up to Wednesday morning, September 14—five days after the explosion —not a newspaper had peeped that there was so much as a suspicion of foul play. Chasse knew by now that the detectives on the job knew substantially what he did; knew, too, why they weren't moving in on Guay and Mme. Pitre. They didn't have any direct evidence on which to make an arrest.

Chasse liked action. He went to Inspector Belec of the Mounties and demanded action of some kind. It wasn't forthcoming. Very well, then. Chasse would create his own action. He would force Guay and Mme. Pitre to somehow betray themselves. The best way to do that would be to scare the hell out of them. And the best way to do *that* would be to drop a little infernal machine of his own in the columns of *Le Canada,* which, he knew from his prowling around in the Lower Town, both Guay and Mme. Pitre read. And so, on the sixth morning after the explosion, Chasse disclosed in *Le Canada* that the authorities suspected a woman of having shipped an infernal machine on the plane.

That did it. Guay, with a copy of *Le Canada* under his arm, rushed over to Mme. Pitre's. Mme. Pitre rushed over to the Robitaille dame's. Mlle. Robitaille rushed over to Mme. Pitre's. Guay rushed home. Mlle. Robitaille rushed home. Mme. Pitre rushed over to a little hole-in-the-wall in François Street, a few blocks from home. What was the hole-in-the-wall but a watch-and-clock repair shop. And who ran the watch-and-clock-repair shop but a brother of Mme. Pitre —a fifty-one-year-old neighborhood character by the name of Généreaux Ruest.

Ruest was straight out of Victor Hugo. He was afflicted with tuberculosis of the bones and had, for most of his life, been confined to a wheel chair. He had facial skin of the tautness and color of that on a drum, thin purple lips, large brown eyes and small brown teeth. His hands and forearms were massively out of proportion to the rest of him. There he sat in the hole-in-the-wall, a one-room combination home and place of business, day after day, sometimes deep into the dark hours, working away at his watches and his clocks. One look at Ruest and the detectives suspected he had been just the one to have fixed up a timepiece for an infernal machine. But *proof*? Where, again, was proof? None of *these* characters—Guay, Mme. Pitre, or Ruest—looked like vocal types, and the law, in the absence of anything more than a circumstantial case up to this point, could hardly expect any of them to suddenly develop voices. The Robitaille girl looked like she would talk, but the chances were she didn't know anything.

On September 20—eleven days after the blast—the law, canvassing all sources of dynamite, learned that an ugly woman in black had, a few days before the blast, gone into the hardware store of Samson and Filion, on St. John Street, in Upper Town, and bought ten pounds of dynamite, ten caps, and fifteen rat-tail fuses.

On that same day, September 20, Joseph Albert Guay made another visit to Mme. Pitre's house. He went from there to the hole-in-the-wall of Généreaux Ruest. Ruest impressed detectives, watch-ing him through spyglasses from hidden vantage points, as a badly shaken character after Guay left. The detectives watching Mme. Pitre's house couldn't see what her reaction to Guay's visit was; when they did lay gaze on the woman it looked as if it might be too late. An ambulance appeared in the Rue Monsignor Gauvreau and Mme. Pitre was hustled off to an infirmary. She had, it seemed, gone on a diet of sleeping pills.

For seventy-two hours the detectives sat by her bedside. Finally she opened her eyes. Then she opened her mouth. She had quite a story to tell. The detectives, and Chasse, had made substantially correct deductions from the very beginning. Guay had wanted to get rid of his wife and collect enough insurance to go to the end of the earth, or somewhere, with Marie-Ange Robitaille. Généreaux Ruest had made the infernal machine for Guay, but had not known that it was designed for murder. "My brother thought it was to be used to set off some dynamite to blow up a fish hole."

Mme. Pitre had bought the dynamite for Guay. Then, later, at Guay's behest, she had delivered the package—the package she now realized had contained the infernal machine—to the airport. Guay had told her the package contained a religious statue and to be very careful that it wasn't jounced. But, after Chasse's story in *Le Canada*, when Guay saw that the law was on the trail of Mme. Pitre, and that she might incriminate him, he called on her and set about selling her on the idea that the best thing she could do would be to commit suicide. He had come prepared to help her; he gave her a box of sleeping pills. Mme. Pitre at first thought the suggestion was ridiculous; then she saw the angle when Guay pointed out that he himself had neither purchased the dynamite nor delivered the infernal machine to the airport. Somehow, that part of Mme. Pitre's story about why she tried suicide gave the detectives mental indigestion. Would an authentic dupe have tried suicide—or was there a deeper reason for the woman's act?

Joseph Albert Guay was arrested on the basis of Mme. Pitre's story. Mme. Pitre, Généreaux Ruest, and Marie-Ange Robitaille, whose only sin had been loving a man with a wife, helped send Guay to the gallows. But before the little man died, he confessed. He had first thought of dispatching his wife by putting poison in her favorite drink, cherry wine. Then, in May of 1949, he had read in the press about the alleged Far East plotters who had placed the bomb aboard the plane to get rid of the husband. The more Guay thought about the plot alleged in the East, the more it appealed to him. He decided to appropriate it and have *his* plane blow up over the waters of the St. Lawrence so that the remains of the blast would never be recovered. By way of preparing for murder, Guay made a special trip from Quebec to Baie Comeau holding a watch in his hand. He noted that the plane was out over the St. Lawrence for fifteen minutes beginning at about ten-twenty-five. An infernal machine set to go off at ten-thirty, then, would do the trick. But the plane ran seven minutes late and Guay's machine went off before the ship was out over the river.

Judging from Guay's confession, Mme. Pitre and Généreaux Ruest had not been the innocent dupes they had pretended to be; they had, on the contrary, been up to their eyeballs in guilt and had been declared in on the insurance that Guay was to have collected. As a result, Généreaux Ruest was tried for murder, found guilty, and sentenced to hang. Mme. Pitre was tried for the same thing and was also found guilty and sentenced to hang. Both appealed but got the rope.

And Edmond Chasse? Ah, Edmond Chasse was a most happy man after the case was solved. The case of the twenty-three murders had become a personal thing with him; he would never have rested until not only Guay, but Ruest and Mme. Pitre were found guilty. Yes, Edmond Chasse was a very happy man—happy as only a reporter—pardon, *journalist*—can be after an assignment well covered. It was only now that Edmond Chasse began to think of himself. He hadn't been feeling too well for some time. Maybe it was because he was now sixty-three, maybe because of something else. So he went into a hospital for a checkup. There it was found that all the while Edmond Chasse had been stalking his killers, a killer had been stalking him. Cancer finished him on, of all days, Good Friday.

The Pink Ducks

*Moralists may say that Willie Guldensuppe got, in the end, exactly
what was coming to him. Willie was a great man for the ladies.
But there came the day when he ran up against a big hunk
of masculine opposition who not only collaborated
with Willie's sweetheart in cutting him out but in
cutting him up.*

One fine June morning a man named
Jake Wahle, who occupied an ugly little
house in the New York city suburb of
Woodside, Long Island, called the attention of a neighbor to the fact that
some white domestic ducks that he owned
had, overnight, taken on a decidedly
pinkish hue. "Come into the back yard
and take a look at them," Wahle said to
the neighbor. "It's the damnedest thing
you ever seen."

The neighbor, looking at the birds,
agreed with Wahle, adding that he had
seen white ducks, brown ducks, speckled
ducks and mallard drakes with green
heads, but never in his life had he seen
pink ducks.

That afternoon Captain Stephen
O'Brien, the middle-aged chief of the
detective bureau of the New York Police
Department, bit his lower lip as he
scanned a report that three kids, swimming in the refuse-littered oil slick of the
East River, near Eleventh Street, had
come upon the upper part of a man's
body, minus the head. The discovery had
been wrapped in oilcloth.

The curtain was up on a true horror
mystery which, although it happened
long ago—in the year 1897, to be precise
—the boys still talk about between gin
rummy and pinochle games in the side
rooms of the station houses.

Captain O'Brien made a ticking sound
with his tongue when he absorbed the
torso news. "I suppose," he said to one
of his men, "that this means we'll have to
send somebody else to the electric chair."

Captain O'Brien was something of a
curiosity in the department in that it
pained him to track a man down for
murder. The captain himself wouldn't
have harmed anybody, and he simply
couldn't understand why one man should
take the life of another. He did understand, however, what was required in
carrying out his official duties, so here
he was, off on another distasteful man
hunt.

Between that afternoon—it was Saturday, June 26th—and the succeeding Sunday afternoon, berry pickers in the High-
bridge section of the city and sailors at
the Brooklyn Navy Yard came upon other
parts of the same body—almost everything, in fact, except the head—and the
parts were matched up in the city morgue.

A particularly discerning coroner's
physician, Dr. Philip O'Hanlon, noticed
that the feet of the corpse were excep-
tionally large, as if they had spread beyond their normal size, and that they
were callused on the bottom. "Whatever
this man did," Doc O'Hanlon explained
to Captain O'Brien at headquarters, "his
job didn't require shoes. He worked in
his bare feet."

"Did he have an outside job or an inside job?" asked Captain O'Brien.

"He worked inside somewhere. Now if

211

you'll come down to the morgue with me and—"

"Bless me, no!" interrupted the detective chief. "You *know* I don't like to look at things like that."

"Well, this man was so pale that it's obvious he never got much sunlight."

Captain O'Brien went to a mirror over the washstand in his office and began to comb out his handsome brown handlebar mustache. "Doc," he asked, "what were this man's hands like?"

"No calluses at all. Very clean and white. Didn't do hard work."

"Any dirt under the fingernails?"

"Nope."

"It sounds to me," said O'Brien, putting his comb away, "like maybe he worked in a Turkish bath."

There were other leads that Doctor O'Hanlon had picked up from the slab in the city morgue. A large patch of skin in the middle of the chest had been cut away. There was a distinctive scar on the left index finger. The dead man had, in one virile particular, been anatomically abnormal.

His flesh had been cut with an exceedingly sharp instrument and his bones carefully sawed by someone who, in the opinion of Doctor O'Hanlon, possessed a certain degree of skill.

"What kind of skill?" asked O'Brien. "Skill in cutting or knowledge of the human body?"

"Perhaps both," replied the coroner's physician.

"Could it be a physician or a medical student is involved?"

Doctor O'Hanlon bristled. "Why the hell," he snapped, "do detectives always think of a doctor or medical student just because a body hasn't been *torn* apart? Doctors and medical students aren't necessarily addicted to murder."

"I didn't mean to hurt your feelings, Doc," said O'Brien.

"Oh, that's all right," said O'Hanlon. "But you might consider a butcher, a barber, or an undertaker in a case like this." O'Hanlon added as an afterthought, "Or an artist. An artist knows all about anatomy."

While the first part of the body to be found had been wrapped in red oilcloth of distinctive pattern, the other discoveries had been encased in white oilcloth and canvas duck. The coverings of all three finds had something in common: they were new. Perhaps they had been purchased exclusively for the purpose to which they had been put. O'Brien decided that a routine but relentless check of every store on Manhattan Island that sold oilcloth and duck would be in order.

On Sunday evening, O'Brien's men, visiting Turkish-bath establishments as a result of the detective chief's first deduction, learned that a man named William Guldensuppe, employed as a rubber at the Murray Hill Baths, on Forty-second Street near Sixth Avenue, had been absent from work since Friday. When that intelligence was forwarded to O'Brien, he went immediately to the baths himself to conduct the questioning.

William Guldensuppe was a middle-aged German who for several years had padded about the Murray Hill Baths, from early morning to early evening, wearing only a towel around his midriff. Guldensuppe, a bachelor, boarded on Ninth Avenue, his boss told O'Brien. On the previous Thursday, he had asked for and obtained a day off on Friday, saying that he was going out of town on business, but his absence on Saturday was only partly accounted for and his absence on Sunday was unexplained.

On Saturday morning, according to Guldensuppe's boss, the rubber's landlady, a Mrs. Gussie Nack, had appeared in the baths with a telegram from her roomer which asked her to notify his employer that he would be out that day, too. Mrs. Nack lived in the 400 block on Ninth Avenue, the record at the baths showed, and O'Brien dispatched two detectives to question the woman about the missing man.

When O'Brien divulged to Guldensuppe's boss that pieces of a body had been found around Manhattan Island, the boss immediately suspected the worst. "Why are you so sure the man in the morgue is Guldensuppe?" asked O'Brien.

"Because it ain't like Guldensuppe to miss work three days straight. He thinks too much of his pay and his tips. Why, he practically never takes a day off and seldom takes a vacation."

Guldensuppe, O'Brien learned, had the bust of a naked woman tattooed on his chest. The size and location of the tattoo corresponded to the patch of miss-ink skin on the chest in the morgue. O'Brien brooded on the cunning of the criminal. With the head missing, and perhaps weighted so that it would never be found, the removal of the tattoo on the chest might have thwarted identification indefinitely, or at least long enough for the killer to smudge his tracks and get away, had not O'Brien deduced the victim's occupation. There was no doubt now in O'Brien's mind that Guldensuppe was the victim.

The fact that the tattooed woman on Guldensuppe's chest had been naked, considered with the anatomical distinction of the man in the morgue, caused Captain O'Brien to suspect that Guldensuppe had been inordinately fond of women. If that were so, a woman may have been part of the motive for the crime.

It happened that a prominent man-about-town was in the Murray Hill Baths this Sunday night, groping his way out of a hang-over; he was said to know Guldensuppe quite well. When O'Brien told him, as a prelude to asking some questions, about the dismembered body in the morgue that was believed to be Guldensuppe, the man-about-town excused himself hurriedly. O'Brien saw him go to a locker to get a hair of the dog that had bitten him. The shock of O'Brien's news now counteracted, the man who had known Guldensuppe was ready to be of whatever help he could.

"Guldensuppe," said the man-about-town, "lived for women. I like women myself, but Guldensuppe was really off his head about them."

"You don't say," said Captain O'Brien, who frowned on promiscuity. "Please tell me more."

"There's nothing more to tell. It's just that Guldensuppe could never get enough of women."

The German rubber, O'Brien gleaned from his informant, had been attached to no particular woman. His tastes in women, food and liquor had been decidedly comprehensive. Quantity, not quality, had interested Guldensuppe. The man had been heavy-set, square-faced, good-natured and earthy. He had been given to grunting and belching, and O'Brien decided that his women, whoever they had been, couldn't have been very fastidious.

The man-about-town asked a certain question about the body in the morgue. Captain O'Brien gave an affirmative answer. "That's Guldensuppe, all right," said the man-about-town.

O'Brien was back at his office in headquarters, combing his mustache, when the dicks who had gone to question Mrs. Nack, Guldensuppe's landlady, reported in. They said that her roomer seemed to occupy a place in the lady's opinion, somewhat below esteem, inasmuch as he had, prior to departing for an unannounced destination the previous Thursday, borrowed fifty dollars from her. The landlady appeared to be more upset about her monetary loss than about Guldensuppe's suddenly abbreviated end.

The detectives had brought back the telegram delivered to Mrs. Nack on Saturday morning requesting her to notify Guldensuppe's employer that he would not be at work that day. O'Brien ordered that the original of the telegram be tracked down within the Western Union organization so that he could determine whether Guldensuppe had actually written the message.

After acquainting the two dicks with the fact that Guldensuppe had been overly fond of women, O'Brien inquired if there was a possibility that the rubber had been romantically attached to Mrs. Nack. He was greeted with a burst of laughter from each man.

"You ought to see her, Captain," said one of the dicks. "Her husband left her a couple of years ago. No wonder." Mrs. Nack, a huge woman in her forties, the detectives said, had three chins, cross-eyes and a bad breath that had caused them to back away from her early during the questioning.

Gussie Nack was a midwife. She had taken Guldensuppe in to board with her when her husband, Herman, had left for parts unknown.

"Just why'd the husband leave?" O'Brien wanted to know.

"She admits he couldn't stand the sight of her."

"Was Guldensuppe the only boarder she had?" asked O'Brien.

The sleuths nodded.

"And you're sure he wasn't carrying on with her?"

The dicks were sure.

O'Brien slept on the case. By noon on Monday there were three major developments.

On Saturday a man with remarkably rosy cheeks had been seen on an East River ferryboat, en route from Long Island to Manhattan Island, carrying a huge bundle in patterned red oilcloth. The man had been accompanied by a woman—a woman whose description was not yet in focus—and he had, according to several observers, behaved in a furtive manner and showed a preference for the stern of the boat. The hour at which the observation had been made was earlier than the time when the swimming kids found the first part of William Guldensuppe.

The proprietor of a dry goods and notions store in the Dutch Hills district of Long Island City, reading in the papers a description of the oilcloth and canvas wrappings, volunteered the information that a strange man had, on Saturday, purchased the very wrappings found around the dismembered Turkish-bath rubber. The chief characteristic of the purchaser was that his cheeks were remarkably rosy, as if he spent considerable time out of doors. O'Brien recalled Dr. O'Hanlon's remark that the killer could possibly have been an artist, and he pondered whether outdoor sign and billboard painting was a form of art.

The original of the telegram that had been sent to Mrs. Nack was located in a Western Union office on Sixth Avenue, around the corner a short distance from the Murray Hill Baths. Although O'Brien turned the original of the message over to penmanship experts for confirmation, it was obvious to him that William Guldensuppe had not written it. Samples of Guldensuppe's handwriting, obtained from the Murray Hill

Baths, disclosed a weak hand, whereas the penmanship on the yellow Western Union blank was that of a man who wrote with bold and decisive strokes.

Since two of the three Monday developments—the story of the man on the ferryboat and the disclosure of the origin of the murder wrappings—pointed to Long Island, O'Brien's men were soon swarming over the locale like locusts.

O'Brien, as Shakespeare would say, always made assurance double sure. He had good men around him, but he knew the best of them were capable of muffing one now and then. It was with this thought that he sent for Mrs. Gussie Nack.

The detective chief saw what his men had meant when Mrs. Nack walked in. In addition to her other unattractive features, she had a natural bustle and oily skin. Now that he saw the woman with his own eyes, O'Brien told himself that no man with eyesight good enough to distinguish between dark and daylight would have been attracted by the big midwife.

Mrs. Nack took out a dirty handkerchief and blew her nose. She fastened an uncertain stare on Captain O'Brien. O'Brien, a very intuitive man, felt his stomach muscles tightening. He wondered why. He looked away from Mrs. Nack, and then at her again. He felt sure suddenly that no matter what the physical evidence, or lack of it, he was in the presence of a woman who was dripping with guilt.

O'Brien didn't know how Mrs. Nack fitted into the murder picture, but he believed, as certainly as if the woman had admitted it, that she was deeply involved in the murder of William Guldensuppe.

O'Brien didn't let on that Mrs. Nack had aroused his suspicion. Instead, he quietly asked her some routine questions about Guldensuppe. Then he thanked her for coming down to headquarters. When she walked into Center Street, a couple of O'Brien's men were not far behind her.

That night, after supper at home, O'Brien sat with his elbows on the table, fingering his mustache.

"Steve," said his wife, "just what is it you're worrying about?"

"Tell me," said O'Brien, "is it possible for two men to want the same woman if the woman is the ugliest thing the Good Lord ever put breath into?"

"You know as well as I do, Steve," said Mrs. O'Brien, "there's no accounting for taste." She went about the business of clearing the table. Then she asked, "Are there two men jealous of an ugly woman in that murder you're trying to solve, Steve?"

"It seems like the only answer," said the captain, rising to return to headquarters. "Still, I saw the woman, and I can't for the life of me— Oh, well."

Late that night, when O'Brien was getting ready to leave headquarters, three detectives—a team and a lone wolf— reached his office simultaneously from several hours of sleuthing along Ninth Avenue. The first man's report was as simple as it was exciting. On the previous Friday—supposedly the day of the murder—a woman with cross-eyes and other characteristics similar to those of Mrs. Nack had hired a horse and surrey from a livery stable on Ninth Avenue. She had said that a man would call for the rig the following day. A man *had* called for the rig—a man with rosy cheeks. He had called for the rig before noon and had returned it near dusk.

"The horse was covered with sweat and dust, Captain," the detective concluded. "Seems like it was taken to the country somewhere and worked hard. The liveryman was sore as hell."

"But he doesn't know who the man was?"

"No."

"See him in the morning again," O'Brien instructed. "Take him to Mrs. Nack's neighborhood and have him get a look at her without her knowing it."

The team of dicks now spoke up. From a newsy neighbor of Mrs. Nack they had learned that the woman's husband had left her, not, as she had told two other detectives, because of her personal appearance, but because William Guldensuppe had taken his place in her affections.

O'Brien blinked. "Certain of that, boys?" he asked.

"Absolutely, Captain. Our informant knows what she's talking about."

"Go on."

"Guldensuppe wasn't the only boarder she had. She lied about that, too."

"She did?"

"Sure. A barber boarded there, too, until last winter. He had rosy cheeks."

O'Brien's mind went back to Dr. O'Hanlon's report about the sharp instrument that had been used to cut Guldensuppe's flesh, and the skill with which it had been employed. A razor, O'Brien wondered, in the hand of a barber?

"Did you get the barber's name?"

"Not yet. There was a hell of a fight in this Nack woman's house one night last winter and it wound up with Guldensuppe beating up the barber and throwing him out on Ninth Avenue."

Captain O'Brien sat at his desk long after his men had gone, trying to fit all the pieces together. He couldn't, quite.

The next day—while Mrs. Nack was under surveillance, although she didn't know it—O'Brien's human locusts, swarming over Long Island, happened upon Jake Wahle, the man in Woodside who owned the pink ducks and was still

surprised enough to want to talk about it to all comers. The detectives were immediately interested when they learned that the ducks had taken on the pinkish hue sometimes just prior to Saturday morning.

"Come on inta the back yard," said Wahle, having his hour in the sun. "Damnedest thing you ever seen."

The dicks went beyond the back yard. They went to a ditch where the ducks did their swimming. The ditch, the sleuths learned, caught the drainage from a two-story cottage behind Wahle's house.

The cottage seemed unoccupied. Two of O'Brien's men shouldered open a door. Everything was neat, cheap and orderly on the first floor. When they entered a bedroom on the second floor, though, the sleuths thought for a moment that they had wandered into a slaughter house. A murder had been committed in that bedroom. Either that, or a body had been taken there to be carved up.

There was evidence in the bathroom that the carver had grappled with certain phases of his grisly chore there.

"That's why them ducks is pink," said the dick. "The blood went down the drain to the ditch where the ducks was swimmin'."

"We might not 'a' come into this here cottage for a year if it wasn't for them pink ducks," said the dick's partner. "Now all we gotta do is find out if anybody rented this place recent. If somebody did, that's goin' to make the captain very happy."

Neighbors said the cottage had been vacant all summer. On the previous Friday, however, they had observed a man and a woman going into the place. Had the man had rosy cheeks? No. He had been pallid.

Other details convinced the probers that it was Guldensuppe who had been seen going into the cottage with the woman.

And what had the woman looked like? The neighbors hadn't got a very good look at her. But she had been huge.

The owner of the cottage, a woman, lived in Manhattan. She said that she had rented the place, only the previous week, to a man named Fred Braun. Captain O'Brien went through a list of barbers working in Greater New York. The name of Fred Braun, employed in a midtown shop, was included in the list.

The fly in the ointment was that Braun had vanished like a figure rubbed from a blackboard. The proprietor of the tonsorial parlor where he was employed had not seen him, or heard from him, since the previous Thursday—the day before the murder. Braun, his employer revealed, was a dapper fellow in his thirties whose rosy cheeks had proved attractive to ladies. His last-known address at the barber shop was on Ninth Avenue—the house of Gussie Nack.

From a neighbor of the Woodside pinkduck owner came the information that a man and a woman had appeared at the vacant cottage, in a surrey answering the description of the one rented on Ninth Avenue, on Saturday.

Mrs. Nack left her home to go up the street to buy some sauerkraut. The liveryman who had supplied the horse and surrey showed no hesitation in identifying her as the woman who, on Friday, had arranged for the rig.

O'Brien ordered Mrs. Nack brought to his office and her house gone over meanwhile with the official magnifying glass.

"You said Guldensuppe borrowed money from you when he left last Thursday," O'Brien said to the woman. "What you were doing when you said that, Mrs. Nack, was trying to establish that you severed your connection with Guldensuppe a day before he was murdered. You thought that story would throw us off the track." O'Brien waited until Mrs. Nack blew her nose. "Well," he said, "it didn't at all. We know about Fred Braun, too." O'Brien's intuition told him that he had hit a bull's-eye.

Mrs. Nack was still being detained at headquarters when one of the detectives who had been assigned to examine her house returned. He had in his possession a love note, written to Mrs. Nack and signed "Fred." When O'Brien looked at the handwriting he knew that the note had been written by the same man who had sent the fake Guldensuppe telegram.

It all added up, circumstantially. Yet, O'Brien realized, he was without a shred of direct evidence. All he had was legal identification of the body, which had been achieved, in the absence of the head, only by a finger scar. A doctor who had treated a felon on Guldensuppe's left index finger positively identified the left index finger of the corpse as the member he had treated.

Mrs. Nack was charged with the murder. She was surly but silent. Captain O'Brien regarded her as the most evil woman he had ever seen.

The whole case hinged now on the hunt for Fred Braun, the rosy-cheeked barber. Day after day passed. Captain O'Brien wasn't sleeping well. The gory crime had attracted more public attention than any murder in years. The heat was on O'Brien as long as Braun was uncaught, and that dreaded specter of all police officials, a department shake-up, haunted him.

Police departments don't like to admit it, but a large percentage of major crimes in big cities are brought to final solution through information volunteered by stool pigeons, by decent people, or by luck. It was the combination of a respectable citizen—one Jack Gotha, a barber who worked in a shop on Eighth Avenue—and a lucky break that took the place of headache powders in police headquarters on July 6—eleven days after the murder of Guldensuppe.

Gotha walked into headquarters and stated, none too articulately, that he wished to speak to Captain O'Brien and nobody else on a matter of extreme importance.

Yesterday morning, Gotha said, he had been lathering a customer when in walked a man who for years had been a close friend. The friend's name was Fred Braun.

O'Brien almost jumped out of his pants. He wanted to know where Braun was right then. Gotha didn't know. He would, he said, come to that if O'Brien would let him tell his story.

Braun, a man with a load on his mind, had asked Gotha to meet him that same afternoon at a street corner uptown. The two met. Chiefly because he was scared stiff and had to talk to somebody, which is where the lucky break came in, Braun unfolded this tale:

After Gussie Nack's husband, Herman, had left her because of Guldensuppe, Gussie, a creature of habit who had been used to buying and cooking for three, advertised for another boarder and Braun moved into the house on Ninth Avenue. He was quick to notice that Gussie, who was a whale of a cook, obviously had other attractions for Guldensuppe, although they didn't meet the eye. More out of curiosity than anything else, he decided on a personal investigation. He was pleasantly surprised, and he and Gussie soon reached a sordid understanding. Everything was going along all right until one night Guldensuppe investigated suspicious sounds emanating

from Gussie's room, gave Braun a shellacking and threw him out on the grounds that he had seen Gussie first and therefore had priority rights.

Gussie met Braun on the outside after that, still preferring him to Guldensuppe. But the Turkish-bath rubber insisted upon including Gussie's affection in the price of board and lodging, and simply refused to move out of the house.

The solution to the whole problem was cooked up by Braun, who not only wanted the exclusive rights to Gussie's amatory services, but revenge on Guldensuppe. He rented the cottage in Woodside and hid in an upstairs closet on Friday, June 25, while Gussie lured Guldensuppe out to the place with a story that she had a chance to buy it cheap.

Braun shot Guldensuppe between the eyes and, when Gussie went back to New York, spent Friday night sawing the bones and cutting the flesh with his razor, and embedding the head in a plaster-of-Paris mixture.

On Saturday, Braun went into New York and sent Gussie the fake telegram. Then he picked up the rig and took Gussie out to Long Island. The wrappings for the pieces of the torso were purchased, and then the pieces were bundled at the cottage, placed in the surrey, and the trip back to New York was begun.

From the ferryboat, Braun dumped some of the pieces, including the weighted head, which was never found. He had planned well, but not well enough. Guldensuppe's remains had soon been discovered and an intelligent coroner and an intelligent cop had quickly established identification. Then had come the clues, including the clue of the pink ducks.

The barber Gotha, ending his tale to Captain O'Brien, said that Braun had pleaded with him for assistance . . . assistance of any kind.

"And—?" asked O'Brien.

"I'm to meet him tonight at eight o'clock at the same place where I met him yesterday afternoon."

The rest was anticlimax. Braun was nailed when he kept his rendezvous with Gotha. Gussie, to save her own neck, turned state's evidence against him and got off with fifteen years.

On a sultry night in August in the year following the crime, Captain O'Brien stood in front of the mirror in his office, combing his mustache and pondering two things about Fred Braun. How had the man such rosy cheeks when he had been employed indoors and had seldom gone into the sun? And how on earth could Braun, and Guldensuppe too, for that matter, have overlooked Gussie Nack's three chins, cross-eyes and bad breath? Captain O'Brien put his comb away. He told himself that he couldn't be speculating. There was other work to be done, and Fred Braun had just been put to death in the electric chair.

The Coronary Con Men

Take a crooked lawyer, a crooked doctor and a crooked insurance salesman. Put them all together, and you have the ingredients for a monumental headache for the big insurance companies.

Snow was in the air that slate-gray afternoon in December, 1933, as the three men gathered in a shabby office in the unfashionable part of New York's Fifth Avenue, glasses at their elbows, and earnestly addressed themselves to a plot that was to make criminal history.

"There's a fortune in this if we handle it right," said a natty little man of thirty-four, his feet propped up on a battered oak desk. Joseph J. Weiss, who had a small foxy face and a withered right arm, was an attorney-at-law who handled disability claims against the big insurance companies.

"I sure could use some money," said Dr. Hirsch L. Messman, who had modest offices on Central Park West and who examined policy holders represented by Weiss. Doctor Messman, a chunky, well-dressed man of forty-five who wore horn-rim glasses and sported a brush mustache, was married but had recently acquired a taste for blondes. Turning to the third man in the room, he said: "I guess you could use some extra money, too, couldn't you, Marty?"

Martin Gross, a forty-two-year-old salesman for The Maccabees, an old and respected insurance company, just nodded and grunted. Gross, a real hustler, was built like a top and had a blubbery face, thick lips and half-closed eyes. Fountain pen clipped to the handkerchief pocket of his coat and his coat pockets stuffed with blanks, he bustled around the five boroughs of Greater New York badgering prospects until, just to get rid of him, they signed on the dotted line.

Attorney Weiss, who had a knack for alienating juries and losing verdicts and was thus fighting a delaying action with the wolf at the door, had conceived a plot for gypping the insurance companies that was so fool-proof that he wondered why nobody had ever put it on a mass-production basis. The idea had first begun to inhabit the little lawyer's skull when he represented a client who, carrying fifty-thousand-dollars worth of life insurance with provisions for permanent disability, had suffered a coronary thrombosis. Recovering, the insured man had, under the permanent-disability provisions, begun to collect one per cent of the face value of the policy, or five hundred dollars, every month for the duration of the disability without having to fork over another dollar in premium payments. Should he have died, his widow would have collected the full face amount of the policy less whatever monthly payments had been made.

"A lot of business men are having trouble meeting their premium payments these days with the depression and everything," Weiss said to Doctor Messman and Marty Gross, "and it wouldn't surprise me one bit if many of them would welcome a good heart attack." Weiss made a little tent with his fingers, looked over it, and grinned. "Not a *real* heart attack, you understand."

"Go on, Joe," said Doctor Messman, pouring himself another drink.

"You've had experience with coronary cases, Doc," said Weiss. "How's the best way to fix a man up with a fake heart attack?"

Messman, out of the richness of his professional experience, had an answer on the tip of his tongue. "The electrocardiograph."

The electrocardiograph, a complicated instrument then practically in its infancy, reduced to ink graphs the behavior and condition of the human heart. The trouble was, Doctor Messman said, that very few doctors, even heart specialists, were yet able to interpret with any degree of positiveness an electrocardiogram." They're disagreeing all the time," Messman continued. "One reads an electrocardiogram one way, somebody else another way."

The best way to make practically every doctor agree that a man with a sound heart was on the brink of death, Messman said, would be to surreptitiously administer digitalis, a drug widely used to stimulate the human pump. The graph that showed up on the heart-detecting instrument after digitalis had been administered looked so much like a coronary-thrombosis graph that not one doctor in a hundred could tell the difference.

"All you'd have to do," said Messman, "would be to give digitalis pills to a patient, tell him to keep his mouth shut, and then get an electrocardiogram made for the insurance people. There are other factors, of course, such as telling the patient how to fake certain symptoms, but fooling that instrument with digitalis would be the big thing."

Little Joe Weiss, who thought big, said that if Marty Gross, with his access to home-office insurance files, could eventually dig up a total of fifty policy holders carrying an average of $50,000 each,

total monthly payments under the disability provisions would amount to $25,-000. "We would," said Joe, "take a third of that twenty-five grand each month, for services rendered, and split it three ways. Once we got this thing going the three of us would be on easy street."

The immediate order of business, as Weiss saw it, was to nominate the first prospect, sell him on the idea, and turn him into a guinea pig—a sort of a trial run over the fraud track. "I got just the man," piped up Gross.

Marty's man was a belligerent forty-two-year-old wholesale butter-and-egg dealer named Jake Harrison, who lived in Brooklyn, and who was good and sore at Marty's insurance company because it was quibbling over a two hundred dollars claim for a sprained back. Harrison carried sixty thousand dollars in disability insurance.

The December wind was whipping through the quiet streets of Brooklyn that night when Marty Gross stepped out of a taxi in front of a brownstone house, hustled up the steps and jammed his thumb against Jake Harrison's door bell. "Hello, Marty," said Harrison. "Got the two hundred?"

"I got better than that, Jake," said Gross, brushing past the man and into his cozy parlor. "I'm gonna make you a happy man.

"You're pressed for money, Jake," Gross went on, pacing up and down while Harrison sat on a sofa. "You work like a slave. Up in the morning ahead of the damned sun liftin' hunnert-pound tubs of butter an' everything." Harrison nodded.

"And you ain't gettin' no younger."

Harrison shook his head, his eyes riveted on the insurance salesman. Gross stopped, tilted his head to one side, and fixed Harrison with a dark stare. "What would happen to your wife and kids, Jake, if your business got even worse and you couldn't keep up your insurance and then—God forbid—you kicked off?"

The mere thought of the picture Gross was painting made the sweat pop out on Harrison's brow.

"Listen, Jake," said Gross, easing himself onto the sofa, "we're gonna fix you up with a nice case of fake heart trouble and you're gonna get six hundred dollars a month for the rest of your life without payin' one cent more on premiums."

After Gross had explained how the thing could be worked, Harrison thought for a little while, then asked: "Will I have to go to a hospital?"

"I imagine. Why?"

"I was just thinking," said Harrison. "I could use a good rest."

Doctor Messman went out to Brooklyn the first week in January, slipped Harrison a bottle of digitalis pills and then, a week later, acting as the man's personal physician, took him to an honest heart specialist in Manhattan. The heart specialist made an electrocardiogram of Harrison, studied it briefly, and said to Messman: "This man has had a coronary. He should be hospitalized."

The guinea pig was checked into a private room in Sydenham Hospital, where the cardiac division was headed up by a cooperative colleague of Messman's named Maximilian Goldstein, and Messman kept slipping digitalis to Harrison. Electrocardiograms made at the hospital confirmed the original diagnosis of a coronary.

One day an insurance doctor walked into Harrison's room. While Messman stood by, the insurance sawbones drew a chair up to the patient's bed. "How do you feel?"

"Rotten," said Harrison. "Rotten all over."

Harrison, carefully coached by Doctor Messman, recited the classic symptoms of a serious heart condition: shortness of breath, general exhaustion, mental depression and fear of impending death.

Harrison lay there in the hospital for five weeks, Messman regularly slipping him digitalis. The day he was being carried out on a stretcher, on his way back to Brooklyn, Messman was standing in the corridor with the insurance doctor. "How long would you give him?" Messman asked.

"With luck," said the insurance doctor, "a month."

One night Gross and Weiss went out to Brooklyn to Harrison's house and Harrison, lying there in bed, faking for the benefit of his family, saw a flurry of white papers and a flashing fountain pen. Weiss didn't give Harrison a chance to look at the fine print and Harrison, without realizing it, signed over to the little mouthpiece one-third of any settlement Weiss made with the insurance company.

At the Maccabees offices, Little Joe dealt with the same lawyer who had quibbled over Harrison's claim for the sprained back. Although the insurance lawyer had balked at an honest claim for two hundred dollars, he never flinched in putting his John Hancock on the fake claim for six hundred dollars every month.

When Harrison learned that Weiss, Gross and Messman were going to take two hundred dollars out of his six hundred dollars payment he squawked—but not too loudly. "You're gettin' four hundred dollars every month, Jake," said Gross, fixing the man in bed with a fishy stare. "What you got to kick about?"

Flushed with the success of their first

effort, the three plotters rolled up their sleeves to go to work in earnest. At nights, when the Maccabees offices were closed, Marty Gross let himself in, explaining to the watchman that he was catching up on some work (which indeed he was) and began to riffle through the company records. He soon compiled a list of more than a score of big policy holders who, the records reflected, were having trouble keeping up premium payments.

The second prospect nominated by the plotters was a man named Watson—a puffy, red-faced citizen of forty-one who ran a small construction business out on Long Island. Watson, loaded up with seventy-five thousand dollars worth of insurance with The Maccabees, The Prudential and New York Life, would be eligible for seven hundred and fifty dollars a month in disability payments.

By this time, Weiss had thought of a couple of wrinkles for the plot. The guinea pig would have to put on a pre-attack show for his family and friends so that the attack would come as no surprise. "And we can't have our attacks look as serious as Harrison's," Weiss said to Gross and Messman, "or the insurance companies'll begin wondering why the hell nobody kicks off."

Gross barged into Watson's office one rainy afternoon and Watson, chewing a dead cigar, just glared at him. "You needn't try to sell me any more insurance," Watson said. "Things are tough."

Gross maneuvered the talk around to the plot and when he unfolded it. Watson wanted to know if anybody else was participating in it.

"I got a list this long," said Marty, spreading his hands apart.

"I got to talk to one of them," Watson said cautiously.

Gross called on Harrison, whose anger had somewhat subsided, and slipped him a hundred to tell Watson how simple the whole thing was. Then he took Watson to Harrison's house and acted as a sort of master of ceremonies as the two men discussed things. When Watson said he was willing to participate, Gross took him to Doctor Messman's office and Messman coached him on the build-up.

Next day, Watson said to his wife: "I don't think I'll go to work today. I got a funny sort of pain in my shoulder."

For the next couple of weeks, Watson, complaining of pains in his shoulder, stomach and chest, worried his wife and his friends. Then, one morning, he slumped over his desk, gasping for breath and dramatically clutching his chest. "Get me to a doctor," he moaned. "I'm dying."

The fraud machinery meshed into high gear. Watson was surreptitiously dosed with digitalis, hospitalized and the insurance-company doctors hoodwinked by the electrocardiograms. Within six weeks, he was back home in bed collecting five hundred dollars a month for the rest of his unnatural life, while Gross, Weiss and Doctor Messman were splitting two hundred and fifty dollars a month three ways.

Gross, bustling around Greater New York so fast that he must have resembled an over-fed blur, was working practically around the clock flushing new prospects. He found a very fertile field right in his home bailiwick of the Bronx, and Long Island, too, was lucrative territory. Many once-prosperous and still heavily-insured dairy farmers in the reaches of the Island could hardly *give* their milk and dairy products away and were having a tough time digging up the scratch for their insurance premiums. Marty, materializing over the horizon, his eyes wide and his mouth agape, was like the answer to a prayer.

One afternoon in December, 1934, a year after the plotting had begun, Weiss, Gross and Doctor Messman were sitting around the little lawyer's office—and sitting pretty. They had by now run a total of eighteen policy holders through the fraud mill. Five companies—The Maccabees, The Prudential, The Metropolitan, Pacific Mutual and New York Life—had suspended premium collections on a total of $540,000 in policies of the eighteen digitalis-fed guinea pigs so that the gross monthly take was now $5,400. Since all the money was filtering through Weiss and he was skimming the top third off the take, to be split three ways, the attorney, the chaser and the doctor were now each salting away six hundred dollars a month—and they had, as Weiss so aptly put it, just scratched the surface.

Meantime, there wasn't so much as a raised eyebrow in any of the insurance companies. The eighteen insured men had, up until now, been lying around the house all day, seldom openly exerting themselves to a greater extent than going down to the corner to buy a loaf of bread for the wife. Gross kept bustling around, dropping in with monthly checks for his policy holders and auditioning new prospects.

The only problem the disabled boys had, except for the boredom that set in with lack of activity, was keeping an eye peeled for the insurance docs, who dropped in every now and then to make a check up. Jake Harrison, the original guinea pig, went through an act typical of that put on by the others. Hearing the doorbell, Jake would peer through the front window and, spying a man with a black bag, would summon his wife. "Answer it!" he'd whisper. "Tell him I'm in the bathroom but I'll be right down."

Harrison would then bound upstairs, take off his clothes, get into pajamas and bathrobe, and begin to do nip-ups to increase his heart action and work up a sweat. Then, coming down to the parlor, he would shuffle in, looking hot and breathing hard. Extending a limp hand to the doctor and smiling wanly, he would drop into a chair.

The doctor, getting out his stethoscope, would listen to the man's heart, which would be going like a trip hammer. "Still short of breath and getting these sweats, eh?" said the sawbones.

"All the time, Doc. All the time."

"I'll be damned," the doctor would mutter to himself as he left Harrison's house, "if I know what's keeping that man alive." It is typical of the entire medical profession that none of the doctors suspected that anything was wrong. For all their vast knowledge of science, doctors are probably the most unsuspicious and gullible men in any of the professions.

By the spring of 1936, two years and a few months after the caper got under way, it was rolling smoothly along on its own momentum. The three master plotters had by this time branched out. Some of the spurious heart patients, intoxicated by the sweet smell of easy money, were supplying Gross with leads and getting a cut of the take. Weiss had, by way of diverting suspicion from himself, drawn half a dozen other crooked barristers into the plot to front for him in the settlement of the disability claims. Doctor Messman, also growing cautious, had now enlisted the aid of several colleagues who had long since kissed goodby to the Hippocratic oath.

All told, the scheme now embraced one hundred and six policy holders, carrying an aggregate of $3,180,000 in insurance, in six companies. The monthly take had risen to more than $30,000. Even after cutting in other physicians, lawyers, doctors, insurance agents and policy holders, the three plotters-in-chief were stashing away about $7,000 each. But were they happy? You bet they were!

Neither Weiss nor Gross changed his mode of living, Weiss sticking to his crummy office and Gross, living in a rented house in the Bronx, deliberately falling behind in the rent and letting the neighbors know about it. Only Doctor Messman changed. Doc filled a closet with custom-made suits, stuck a red carnation in his lapel and became a Good Time Charley in the night spots, buying a blonde for each arm and champagne for the house.

Up until now, the guinea pigs, following instructions, had stuck pretty close to their homes, always on the alert for insurance doctors. Now, though, the visits of the doctors became increasingly infrequent and the boys were beginning to grow restless. Sitting around the house all day, not being able to go out to a ball game or around the corner to a saloon, wasn't all it had been cracked up to be.

One day in late April of 1936, Gross, delivering the monthly check to Harrison in Brooklyn, accidentally dropped an envelope on the parlor sofa and left it behind. Examining it, Harrison saw a list of names, addresses and phone numbers, with figures alongside of each phone number. The names were obviously those of other men who were faking illness and, the figures indicated, turning over a third of the insurance take.

Harrison was startled to find that there were more than one hundred names, and that some of the proprietors of the names were carrying as much as a hundred grand in insurance. Before Gross came back to pick it up, Harrison made himself a copy of the list.

Spring was in the air, Harrison hadn't been any farther than the corner grocery in two years, he was a Dodger fan and the repulsive Giants were coming across the river for a three-game set at Ebbets Field. Obeying an impulse, Harrison picked up the phone and called Watson, the Long Island construction man who had, in company with Gross, visited him two years previously.

"Remember me?" Harrison asked Watson. "You were at my house with Marty Gross."

"Oh, sure," said Watson. "How the hell are you?"

"Damn sick and tired of hanging around the house," Harrison muttered. The two men found they were in total agreement and, by the next afternoon, they were sitting in a box along the third base line, drinking beer and munching hot dogs, and talking over their common experience. "Can you imagine that little sonofabitch Weiss," Harrison grumbled, "getting a third of the insurance from more than a hundred guys like us? He must be piling up a fortune."

"Yeah," Watson said. "Somebody ought to put a stop to that."

"Just what I was thinking," Harrison said. "I'm going to call a meeting at my house for Saturday night. I'll get every guy on that list. My family's away for the weekend, and we won't be bothered."

Next, talking in a whisper so his wife couldn't overhear, Harrison hunched over the phone and began calling the names on Marty Gross's list. "We have a mutual friend," he'd say when he got his man on the line. "Marty Gross."

"Yeah?" the man would say warily.

"Well, some of the rest of us heart

cases are getting together at my house Saturday night. I figured maybe you'd like to join us. It might be to your financial advantage."

Most of the policy holders were either cautious or downright suspicious, suspecting that the police were somehow involved, and declined the invitation. But, by the time he had finished combing the list, Harrison had seven acceptances.

Counting the host and Watson, there were, then, nine men gathered in Harrison's house that Saturday night. Four of the visitors were cloak-and-suit men from the Bronx; one ran a furniture store in Manhattan; one operated a stationery store in Brooklyn, and the seventh was a wholesale butter-and-egg man from Long Island.

The boys beat a path to the refrigerator, then sat around the parlor eating pastrami sandwiches and drinking beer and generally letting their hair down. Harrison, calling the meeting to order, took a poll to determine what everybody thought of Joe Weiss. Acquainted, for the first time, with the scope of Joe's operations, everybody present thought Joe was a little weasel and agreed that steps should be taken to curb his greed.

Bright and early on Monday morning, Weiss had barely settled himself at the desk of his crummy little office when his secretary announced the arrival of the nine-man delegation. Before the lawyer could brace himself, the guinea pigs trooped in and grouped themselves in a semi-circle around his desk. "What the hell," Weiss asked, "does this mean?"

Harrison, the spokesman, was brief and to the point: Weiss was ladling off too much of the gravy. "So," said Joe, "*that's* it." The lawyer, his head on a swivel, measured the visitors, one by one. Then, running his tongue over his lips,

he began to talk. "Let me tell you bastards something. Do you realize you could all go to prison for what you've done—taking money from the insurance companies under false pretenses?"

"Ha! Ha!" piped up a butter-and-egg man, "*Us* takin' the money. *That's* a good one."

"All I did," said Weiss, "was handle your claims. Why, if I picked up this phone here and called the insurance companies and told them that I've grown suspicious of those heart attacks you're collecting on, you'd all be in jail within six months."

"But you thought up the whole thing, Weiss," said Harrison. "You and Marty Gross and that doctor up on Central Park West."

"Me?" said Weiss, pointing to his chest with his good index finger. "Why, I don't know what you're talking about. And that goes for Marty Gross and Doc Messman. You've deceived them, too." The Weiss eyes were mere slits of cunning. "See what I mean, boys? Don't you see that you don't have a leg to stand on?"

Now Weiss got up. "There's the door," he said, pointing. "Now get out of here —you dirty little crooks."

Harrison turned to the other complainants. "I guess," he said, "we better be going."

One bleak afternoon in January 1937 —three years almost to the day, after Doc Messman had gone out to Brooklyn and begun to dose the first guinea pig with digitalis—a little man in a blue serge suit sat in an office of The Prudential Insurance Company in Newark, New Jersey, poring over some papers. His name was Phipps and he was an actuary—an expert at calculating risks for the company. Busy with his calculations, Phipps didn't finish his figuring until almost closing time. Then he leaned back in his chair, took off his glasses, closed his eyes and pinched the bridge of his nose.

Phipps' boss popped his head in to say good night. "Got a minute?" asked Phipps. "I've just run across something interesting."

What Phipps had run across was fifty-eight coronary cases in the Bronx and on Long Island on which the Prudential was paying permanent disability and which had been handled by Attorney Joseph J. Weiss.

"What about it?" asked Phipps' boss. "That lawyer probably specializes in handling disability."

"Yes," said Phipps, "but none of his coronaries seem to die. They're all still alive—every single one of them—running counter to every actuarial and medical statistic I've ever heard about in thirty years."

Bright and early the next morning, Phipps was on the phone to brother actuaries with New York Life. The Maccabees and the other big companies. Little men with cold blue eyes and flying pencils ate their lunches at their desks for several days. In the end they came up with corroboration of the Phipps disturbance; there was something damned suspicious emanating from the office of Joseph J. Weiss. In all the companies, not a single Weiss coronary had kicked off.

Several investigators from the various companies gathered in The Prudential offices. Since the records revealed that Weiss had begun to handle disability claims on a large scale three years previously, the initial strategy was simple. Detectives would merely loiter around the homes of several of Little Joe's disability clients to see what they could see.

Harrison and Watson, the two original guinea pigs, and seven others who had gone to the office of Weiss that day, had by now become close friends. The insurance dicks, tailing Harrison and Watson, saw them meeting the others around Times Square, then spending the day in bars and at burlesque shows—hardly the behavior of men in the shadow of eternity.

By early March, two months after the shadow work had begun, the insurance sleuths had drawn a bead on almost 50 permanent-disability cases who were chasing around the Bronx, Manhattan, Brooklyn and Long Island and having a high old time.

Meantime, attorneys for the insurance companies had engaged the services of the top man in the country at interpreting electrocardiograms—Dr. Arthur M. Master of New York. Dr. Master shut himself up in his office on East Seventy-second Street, poring over the electrocardiograms of Harrison and more than fifty other guinea pigs. His scrutiny over, he picked up the phone and called a Prudential official. "Not a damned one of these cases," said the specialist, "is a coronary. These so-called coronary patients have all been dosed with digitalis."

In negotiating with the insurance companies, Weiss had written hundreds of letters, thus running afoul of the elastic statute making it a Federal offense to use the mails in the furtherance of a fraudulent scheme. This brought about the entrance into the case of Post Office Inspector Frank E. Shay, an elderly man of benevolent mien who had, in his youth, studied for the priesthood.

"What we'll have to do here," said Shay, "is put taps on the telephone wire of this man Weiss."

The taps were no sooner on Little Joe's wire than he called Gross. "Marty," he said, "what you got lined up?"

"Fellow named Joseph. I'm sending him to Doc Messman's in the morning."

"How much does he carry?"

"Forty thousand."

"Where?"

"New York Life."

"Good boy, Marty. Every little bit counts."

By the time Joseph called at Messman's, taps were on Messman's and Marty's phones. When Joseph left Messman's office, the physician phoned Weiss. "I gave that fellow some of those pills, Joe," said Messman. "He'll be ready for the insurance people in a few days."

Dr. Master, the specialist with the eagle eye, was waiting for Joseph when the guinea pig arrived at the offices of the New York Life Insurance Company for an examination. He was panting for breath and little wonder. A detective tailing him observed that he had run up several flights of stairs to the offices instead of taking the elevator.

"Been running or something?" Dr. Master asked the faker.

"No, Doc. Just go off the elevator."

Master took Joseph's pulse. "A hundred and thirty," he said. "Better lie down on the couch there for a while."

Master let Joseph lie there for an hour, and the pulse rate dropped to 75.

Now Master attached the electrocardiograph to Joseph and began to observe the ink graph of the fellow's heartbeats. The needle began to move up and down at a steady clip, indicating to the specialist, that Joseph was shot full of digitalis.

"When," asked Dr. Master, looking at the graph, "did you take your last digitalis pill?"

"My what?" asked Joseph, and the needle began to reflect a suddenly excited heart. "I don't know what you're talking about, Doctor."

When Joseph left the insurance offices, he phoned Gross. "I had one hell of a time with that insurance doctor," the listeners on the Gross tap heard him saying. "He knew damned well I've been takin' that stuff." The listeners heard Gross passing the word to Messman and Messman passing it to Weiss.

Next, to stir things up, a doctor for The Maccabees went out to Brooklyn, dropped in on Harrison unexpectedly, and examined the original guinea pig. "Well, well, well," said the sawbones, "I have good news for you. You can go back to work."

"I can *what*?"

Placing his hand on Harrison's shoulder, the physician said: "My good man, you can go off disability now. You're as sound as a dollar."

Other coronary cases began receiving visits from their doctors, who told them the same discouraging news, and the phones of Weiss, Gross and Messman began to sizzle with outraged calls. And, then as if they didn't have enough trouble, the law swung into action.

On the morning of May 18, 1937, just three years and five months after the plot had been hatched, some fifty detectives and post office inspectors left their headquarters and fanned out through Manhattan, Brooklyn, the Bronx and Long Island, starting to make the arrests which eventually led to the capture of the three master plotters, thirteen co-conspirators and thirty-six guinea pigs.

The prisoners were taken to the offices of the United States attorney in Manhattan where the guinea pigs and the co-conspirators were separated from the three master plotters. Postal Inspector Shay took Weiss, Gross and Messman into his private office. A door leading into the next room was ajar as Shay, courteously offering his guests comfortable leather chairs, settled himself at his desk and pretended to read some reports.

There was only silence for a minute or

so, then some talk began to come through from the next room. "Is that you, Joe?" came a voice.

"Yes," came the answer. "That you, Doc?"

"Yes. Marty just sent me another one and I've given him some digitalis."

Messman cocked his head and stared wide-eyed toward the source of the sounds. "What the hell's that?"

"That's you, Doctor," said Shay. "You and Mr. Weiss here. We'll hear from Mr. Gross in a minute."

Messman got up and rushed into the next room. There he saw two men at a recording machine and several stacks of records that the investigators had, over a period of weeks, made from conversations coming over the Weiss, Messman and Gross phones.

Messman rushed back into Shay's office, glowering at Gross and Weiss. "I don't know what you two are going to do," Messman said, "but I'm going to confess."

The other two men refused to talk and received, for their trouble, sentences of three years each. Messman, blurting out every detail of the complicated plot, got

off with a suspended sentence for turning government's witness against Weiss and Gross. Two other physicians, Dr. Goldstein of Sydenham Hospital and Dr. George Krupp of the Tremont Sanitarium, both of whom had labored long and hard for the fake coronary factory, got a year and a day each. Harrison, the original guinea pig, and the six men who got the bum's rush from the Weiss office that day, also became government witnesses. All of them, plus most of the other plotters, got off either with light or suspended sentences and some slipped through the net entirely.

One of the mysteries of the case that puzzled the investigators was what had become of all that money that Weiss, Messman and Gross had split among themselves. The trio were quite embarrassed about it at first. Then Messman, who had babbled on about everything else, finally explained. The boys had taken up big-time gambling. The Broadway bookies had taken them, along toward the end, almost as fast as the dough came in, and when they were pinched they had nothing to show for all their efforts.

The Yellow Kid

Meet Joe Weil, the Yellow Kid, who proved, year in and year out, that dishonesty was the best policy. When Joe conned the suckers, they stayed conned, some of them refusing to believe, even after Joe had taken them, that the man had done any wrong.

Charitably-inclined Chicagoans, solicited over the telephone for several years now by a honey-voiced gentleman raising funds for various authentic causes, would be surprised to learn that they have been talking to Joseph R. Weil, alias the Yellow Kid, perhaps the most versatile confidence man in the history of human cupidity. Weil has reformed, perhaps for the last time. He is strictly legitimate. He sits at a telephone in a modestly furnished office in the Loop, from ten in the morning until five in the afternoon, Monday through Friday, and calls subscribers in the Chicago telephone directory on behalf of church and hospital building funds, children's societies, benevolent associations, and unwed mothers. He works on a commission basis, sometimes netting one hundred dollars a week, which is minor scratch for the Kid but a living nonetheless. It somehow makes sense that in the late autumn of his life, the Yellow Kid, whose once golden whiskers are now frosted clear through, is, although straight, still separating people from money.

For more than a third of a century—from 1905, when he was twenty-eight, until 1939, when he was sixty-two—Joe Weil grossed one hundred thousand dollars a year, year in and year out, except for comparatively brief periods when he was in the sneezer, from assorted confidence games in this country, on the high seas, and in Europe. Although many of the dodges practiced by Weil are old hat today, they were daisy-fresh when he perpetrated them. The Yellow Kid, in fact, was the creator of many original and unique touches to basic confidence schemes, mostly in the fields of real estate, the horse parlor and the race course, that are still in wide and lucrative use today.

Weil, although a fugitive from justice in one place or another for practically the entire span of his notable career as a confidence worker, never once went into hiding. A man of prepossessing appearance, he lived openly and in taste and luxury in apartments, hotels and houses on Chicago's Gold Coast. Although often arrested, and sometimes even imprisoned, the Yellow Kid was never looked upon as either a common or an uncommon criminal. He was, rather, a celebrity. Head waiters in the nobby Drake Hotel deferred to him, the exclusive boot and shirt makers and tailors on Michigan Avenue were flattered to have his patronage, and people pointed him out on the street. Weil commanded such respect in certain levels of the police department that a traffic cop who ticketed his Rolls-Royce was practically requesting banishment to some unattractive post.

The more naive portion of Chicago's populace often wondered how it was that such a notorious rascal as Joe Weil could go about as he pleased at times when the

Chicago police were supposed to be hunting for him on behalf of an out-of-town cop force or, for that matter, on behalf of themselves. It didn't seem possible that there could be such a high incidence of astigmatism in one police department. The answer was that Weil peeled 10 per cent off the top of his take in every operation perpetrated in the Middle West and paid it out as courtesy money to officials of the Chicago police department and the Cook County state's attorney's office. "In my record," Weil told a reporter for the Chicago *Sun* in 1947, "you will find many a nolle prosequi, many a dismissal for want of evidence, and even verdicts contrary to the evidence. All those were the result of well-spent protection money."

There were, of course, times when even protection money could not save Weil. Sometimes—on an occasion, for instance, when the Yellow Kid sold the toll rights to the Chicago River, accepted a one hundred thousand dollar down payment on the Palmolive Building, or leased the information booth of the Northwestern railroad station for a fruit stand—the power of the press packed more weight than protection money. Then a dick would call at Weil's home, give his hat to the butler, and clump into a panelled library lined with authentic first editions, there to impart to the master of the manse the tidings, "We're sorry, Joe, but we'll have to take you in."

A pinch inconvenienced Weil, but it didn't worry him. He was arrested exactly twenty-five times between 1905 and 1939 and beat the rap twenty times, for a batting average of .800 in a league where .333 is terrific. An actual pinch merely penetrated Weil's outermost line of defense. There remained to be dealt with the D. A.'s office, the complainant, the witnesses, the evidence, the judge, and the jury. Somewhere along the line, four times out of five, the Yellow Kid wangled the fix.

When a complaint against the Yellow Kid progressed as far as a trial, Weil sometimes acted as his own counsel. Old-timers in Chicago say that a trial at which Weil, accused of operating a confidence game, conducted his own defense, was really something to see. The Yellow Kid would show up late for the beginning of a court session, keeping the prosecutor, the witnesses and the jurors waiting. Then, when he swept in, carrying a cane in one hand and a hand-stitched morocco briefcase in the other, he was the star of the show, making the grand entrance. Invariably, he was a symphony in gray, fawn or lavender, from spats to Homburg. He was below medium height, slender, and quick, gracious and impressive of movement. His eyes, behind the ever-present pince-nez, were light blue and suffused with a combination of humor, intelligence and guile. A carefully nurtured mustache and Van Dyke, pink in those early days, when he was in his forties and at the height of his powers, acted as a perfect balance for a magnificent forehead. His hair was fine and lay fairly flat on his head, like that of Monty Woolley, whom he resembled except that he was quiet where Woolley is bombastic.

When Weil, acting as his own counsel, began to cross-examine the state's witnesses—particularly the complainant, whom he had swindled—he always put on a memorable performance. Weil, who had studied law in his spare time and who knew the rules of evidence and cross-examination, was always deceptively gentle, and very much the underdog, when he opened a cross-examination. He would make outrageous little statements

—"Do you mean to sit there and tell these intelligent jurors that you have never told a lie in all your life?"—that would cause the witness to redden and shift uncomfortably in his chair. Then the Kid, ever the master at embracing the psychological moment, would maneuver the witness into a major or minor trap. As the witness sat there sputtering, feeling like biting his tongue off for having made a contradictory statement, the Kid would look at the jurors, finger his mustache, and wink. He and the jurors became thirteen men apart from everybody else in the courtroom, sharing little jokes and secrets. The Yellow Kid thus beat several raps that he could have been caged for.

There were, of course, times when Weil didn't have to work on the jurors. When the fix was in at the state's attorney's office, the custodian of the public trust who was sent into the courtroom on behalf of the state of Illinois deliberately flubbed the case. On occasion, when a disagreement was as good as an acquittal, the Kid or one of his representatives rendezvoused with a juror in an area of faulty illumination and paid off the man's mortgage. At least one Chicago judge was so fascinated by the personality of Joseph R. Weil that he continually threatened the prosecutor with contempt of court for hampering, by way of angry objections, the buttery flow of Weil's rhetoric. The Kid is perhaps the only man on record who, on trial for a crime, offered the alibi that he was in a distant city, committing another crime. This was on the occasion, a quarter of a century ago, when he put himself on the stand to deny swindling the complainant out of ninety thousand dollars in a stock deal.

"Do you deny," asked Weil the lawyer of Weil the defendant, "that you were in the city of Chicago at the hour when the state's attorney charges the crime for which you are now on trial was committed?"

"I do," answered Weil the defendant. "I wasn't in the city of Chicago all that day."

"You weren't?" went on Weil the cross-examiner. "Well, where were you?"

"I was in Decatur, Illinois."

"What were you doing in Decatur?"

"I was," answered the man on trial for perpetrating a confidence game, "in Decatur selling forty thousand dollars' worth of fake stocks to a bank president."

The jury box began to rock with laughter. The jurors were still laughing when they brought in the verdict; so was the Yellow Kid.

Although Weil applies himself to his present fund-raising work with the sober diligence of a man who has been honest all his life, students of the man maintain that if his present reformation sticks it will be only because of his advanced age. Joe Weil has staged as many public reformations as Harry Lauder made farewell appearances. After every one of his five jail or prison stretches, the Kid would emerge a chastened man, choking with remorse over the evil life, eager to hit the trail to strict legitimacy. He would go straight for a while, monetizing his reformation by lecturing on his exploits. Then his enthusiasm for the platform would noticeably diminish. Invariably there would follow a yelp from some fat sheep who had been skillfully sheared, and the cops and everybody else would know that the Yellow Kid had resumed the practice of his profession.

The man who has been called Chicago's minister of human cupidity was born in 1877 near Harrison and Clark streets in Chicago. His parents, Mr. and

Mrs. Otto Weil, were German-Americans who ran a corner grocery store. The parents used to get up at five in the morning and work until practically midnight, seven days a week, and when Joe was old enough to figure things out for himself he figured out that such hard work and long hours were not for him.

The neighborhood where Joe was brought up and went to school contributed to the molding of his character. Harrison and Clark was strictly brass-knuckle territory in the eighties and nineties. This was post-fire Chicago, with its rough-and-ready opportunists operating against a backdrop of gaslights, hansom cabs, horse cars and new indoor plumbing. The smells of quick money and larceny were in the air; the kids on the street corners, with sensitive nostrils, went out and got what they could with their fists. Joe Weil was undersized and frail; if somebody in the next block sneezed, Joe caught cold. He simply couldn't hold his own against other kids physically. He fell back on his brain. He discovered that while he couldn't punch his way out of a paper bag, he could talk his way out of anything.

By the time Joe was sixteen he had developed a craving for luxury—fine clothes, fine foods, and, precocious lad, beautifully gowned women. This was no doubt a reflex action resulting from the sordidness of the neighborhood where he had been raised. The smart people, Joe noticed, the people who had lots of money—saloonkeepers, gamblers, politicians, and bookmakers—didn't work very hard. Moreover, the most successful men seemed to be partly or wholly fraudulent. Perforce, it became an article of faith with Joe that hard work bore no relationship to wealth and ease but that fraud did.

Joe was always so far ahead of his classmates in school that he grew bored and quit at sixteen. He got a job collecting horse bets in saloons and running them to the headquarters of a small syndicate. The pay was three dollars a week and Joe, gazing ahead, detected the faint outlines of a bleak future. Then he conceived an angle. Most of the money he collected was bet on horses that later lost at the track. Why not, Joe asked himself, pocket for himself money laid on horses that were obviously going to lose?

Joe submerged himself in performance charts, the better to determine which horses wouldn't be likely to win. Then he subjected the syndicate to an involuntary withholding tax. He began to average fifty dollars a week—a fortune for a kid of sixteen in 1893. Once in a while Joe got stuck with a winner, but his cushion from losers was great enough to absorb the shock.

What should have happened to Joe—getting caught with a big pay-off he couldn't meet—didn't happen. But it might as well have. As Joe approached his seventeenth birthday, he was a walking clotheshorse with a decided predilection for French champagne and Clark Street dolls. His employers, curious as to how he accomplished all that on three dollars a week, checked up on his collections. By way of dispensing with Joe's services, the syndicate operators gave him such a shellacking that, for one dark and terrible moment, Joe actually contemplated an honest future.

Joe's next job, which was to furnish him with invaluable experience for the future, was as a shill and assistant to a frock-coated, goateed old humbug known throughout the Middle West as Doc Meriwether. Doc was a medicine man. He rode the country-fair and carnival circuit dispensing something called Doc Meriwether's Elixir—guaranteed to cure tapeworm, gall stones, kidney trouble, cancer, consumption, Bright's disease, rheumatism, indigestion, boils, and general debility. Joe decided that if people believed what Doc Meriwether told them —and they did—they could be made to believe almost anything. It was all in how a thing was presented.

By the time he was nineteen, Joe was sincerely dedicated to the proposition that there were only two kinds of people in the world—those who were suckers and those who weren't. Everything he did from now on he did with an eye to how it could be monetized. He got a job as a legman for the City News Bureau, which supplied the Chicago newspapers with local coverage. Joe got six dollars a week for ferreting out news and phoning in the information to the Bureau, where a regular rewrite man would put it into shape for transmission to the Bureau's clients.

Joe's salary with the City News Bureau was practically beneath his notice; he would have *paid* $6 a week for the opportunity that the job afforded for locating skeletons in closets—particularly closets along the Gold Coast, which was practically rattling with them. Joe began to wire the skeletons for a pay-off.

It wasn't long before Joe had sixty thousand dollars in the bank. He began to wear spats, carry a cane and flash jewelry. He had an apartment of his own and began to take up with actresses. He became something of a character around town. He was free with his money; he bought expensive gifts of jewelry for his girls, and the head waiters in the lobster palaces of the Chicago of the nineties knew young Joe Weil of the City News Bureau as a lavish tipper and a fellow who knew his way through a wine list. And Joe was still a year too young to vote.

Eventually, the City News Bureau got wind of what its dandy young legman was up to. Joe was canned. In looking around for a new connection, where the work would not be too arduous but the remuneration sufficient to maintain his luxurious standard of living, Joe turned to horses.

At the turn of the century, when he was twenty-three, Joe began touting at the race tracks in the vicinity of Chicago. All it took to be a tout was the ability to convince clients that one had just had a private conversation with a horse that was hot or a jockey who was crooked. This was not as difficult as it may sound. Horse players were then, as they are today, the biggest suckers in the world. Joe began to specialize in fixed races. The races weren't really fixed, but Joe represented them to be and collected varying sums from bettors eager to get in on a sure thing. Joe's racket entailed the occupational hazard of getting the hell beat out of him on occasion by plungers who got laundered. By way of reducing to a minimum the chances of being hospitalized, he resorted to various forms of disguise. He began to carry a collection of false mustaches, thick-lensed and dark eyeglasses, wigs and costume changes as standard touting equipment.

Joe spent many a convivial evening at one of Chicago's most celebrated watering holes—the saloon of Bath House John Coughlin, a massive Irish politician who wore brocaded vests and who sold asylum to criminals on the lam. Bath House John's place was located on Madison Street, near LaSalle, and was a sort of early-day Stork Club in that it was a focal point for the town's celebrities, semi-celebrities, and phonies. Bath House John, known simply as the Bath, had been a rubber in a Turkish bath before attaining his Billingsleyesque stature.

Joe liked to keep his hand in things, even while relaxing at the Bath's, by perpetrating small frauds on other customers at the bar. One such trick had to do with betting that he could make an egg stand on end, then, after applying a gummy substance to the egg, winning the bet. One night Joe tried the egg trick on the wrong customer. When the customer discovered the fraud, he reached for a large glass bowl filled with fresh eggs (an adjunct of every strip of mahogany in those days), and crowned Joe. Joe became highly visible as the yolks of the eggs began to ooze down over his face and clothing. "Ho! Ho! Ho!" bellowed the Bath. "Look at the Yellow Kid!" From that night on, Joe Weil was the Yellow Kid.

As the Yellow Kid passed farther into his twenties, the die for his future became definitely cast. Chicago was one of the favorite spots for confidence men; this was because there was so much cattle money around and in the hands of men who wanted to double or quadruple it quick. The con men frequented the same places that Joe Weil frequented— the back rooms of spots such as Bath House John's, the lobster palaces, and the sporting houses. Joe got to know the con men, first in a casual way, then more intimately. Joe the tout and the con men had much in common; Joe was taking the suckers and so were the con men. The bunco artists and Joe used to talk shop and laugh at each other's tales until the tears rolled down their cheeks. As he was taken farther into the confidence of the confidence men, Joe learned the identities of the law-enforcement officials in Chicago and Cook County who were selling protection.

Joe's debut into the confidence profession came in 1902, when he was twenty-five. A couple of veteran confidence men, getting ready to take a sucker in a hotel room by pretending to be big racing men making a fortune on fixed events, had a spot for a sharp-looking young man who was to enter the hotel room in the presence of the sucker, carrying a bag of money from a betting commissioner who had supposedly just been taken in a fixed race. Joe, by virtue of his friendship with the two confidence men, and his obvious qualifications, was selected for the role. It entailed a few lines of dialogue. Joe was to enter the hotel room, carrying the money, and, in turning over the dough, say to the two confidence men who were essaying the roles of big-time race fixers, "The commissioner wants to know where you gentlemen are getting your information, anyway." To which one of the con men was to laugh and reply, "That's our secret," the while winking to the sucker, who was being readied to make a big bet with his life's savings. Joe was thereupon to counter with, "Well, seriously, gentlemen, I'm afraid you have to find another commissioner to take your bets. My boss says to tell you that he won't be able to handle any more of your bets if you win again tomorrow." This last remark was to have the effect of hastening the sucker to get his money down before it was too late for a killing.

The two confidence men rehearsed Joe in the part—right in the back room of Bath House John's. Joe had the briskness and authenticity of a representative of a betting commissioner. He needed little coaching; he was a natural actor. When he made his entrance on the real confidence scene, the Yellow Kid carried his part off perfectly. The sucker was subsequently taken, and Joe was paid one thousand dollars for his services.

Joe was like an alcoholic who tasted liquor for the first time. This, he said to himself, was for him. He braced other confidence men of his acquaintance for roles to play. He began to devote less and less time to touting and more and more time to confidence work. He soon established himself in the confidence profession as an actor of notable virtuosity. Sometimes he went to other cities—St. Louis, Detroit, Denver—to fulfill engagements. His parts included those of a betting commissioner in a fake horse room; a message sender in a fake Western Union office; a physician attending a supposedly fatally ill principal in a con game whose death would keep a sucker from getting suspicious; a floor manager in a fake stock-brokerage office, and a repetition of his first con-game role, that of a representative of a betting commissioner delivering the pay-off on a fixed race. For three years the Yellow Kid climbed the confidence ladder, playing larger and more important roles until, in 1905, when he was twenty-eight, he was ready to begin big-time operations on his own.

Joe chose as his medium into the confidence field the so-called wire game—one of the three big basic swindles in all confidence history. The wire game was then enjoying quite a vogue in Chicago. Joe was by this time not only well-acquainted with the members of the talent pool who played the minor but important roles in various confidence schemes, but he had also formed an opinion of their respective merits. He knew, then, before beginning operations, just about whom he would cast in the various parts. There remained but one step before going into production; a visit to the police department and the state's at-torney's office. There he introduced himself to certain contact men for higher-ups, whose identities he had learned from other confidence men, submitted a prospectus of his plans, agreed to pay 10 per cent protection, and got a go-ahead.

The basic fraud in the wire game centered about supposed collusion between the confidence man and a telegrapher employed by the Western Union Telegraph Company. In those days, Western Union supplied Chicago horse parlors with race results. The results from the eastern and southern tracks came into WU's main offices on the eighth floor of a building on South Clark Street; they were disseminated from there to telegraph operators who sat in the horse rooms throughout the city and audibly translated the intelligence that came over their instruments in Morse code. Nowadays, no bet is accepted after post time; in those days, bets were accepted until the results began to come in over the WU wires.

The supposed collusion was represented as taking the form of a crooked Western Union telegrapher in a horse room slipping the result of a race to a con man in the horse room, then withholding the same result from others in the horse room until the con man and his victim could place a bet on the race that had already been run. The victim, getting his feet wet by placing small bets, gradually got so enthused about the potential of betting on a sure thing that he converted all his holdings into cash for the grand plunge, only to strike his head on the bottom and never see the surface again.

In the furtherance of the wire game, the confidence man had to establish one or more stores, as false fronts are called in the profession. One store sometimes took the form of a Western Union office, and a second store was a horse room. A store in a confidence game often looks more authentic than the real thing, yet has all the permanence of a smoke ring. A Western Union store looked so real that many a passer-by stopped in to send a telegram, later to find the office abandoned when calling to complain that the message had never reached its destination.

The fake horse room of the wire game was the same masterpiece of production as the Western Union store. The manager of the joint functioned behind a wicket, sometimes up to his eyeballs in money, a telegrapher sat at a genuine Western Union wire, and the main part of the room was populated by likely-looking frauds essaying the roles of odds makers, bettors and spectators. A genuine Western Union wire was necessary in the wire game because authentic, up-to-the-second racing information was essential to taking the sucker.

The establishment of a store required of a confidence man abilities and talents somewhat similar to those required of a theatrical producer. A store was, in fact, a theatrical production. The audience was limited to one person at a time—the sucker—but the performances of everybody concerned had to be flawless. Sometimes unemployed actors were recruited to play such roles as messenger boys in Western Union stores and bettors and spectators in horse-parlor stores. The players for the more important roles —managers of stores, odds makers and spectacular plungers in horse rooms, roles such as the Yellow Kid had played while serving his apprenticeship—were of course recruited from the swelling ranks of the confidence profession.

The producer of a confidence game— a man like Joe Weil—would, in addition to casting the production, writing the script and rehearsing the players, essay a principal role himself and finance the production. The outlay in preparing a major con such as the wire room frequently entailed upward of ten thousand dollars for such items as scenery and actors' salaries while the production was in rehearsal. Joe had long since enjoyed enough affluence to finance such a con.

Although Weil was to play practically every role in the confidence repertoire during the course of his career, he specialized in being a roper—the man who goes out and strikes up an acquaintanceship with the lamb, or sucker, then leads him to the slaughter. He was always the roper when he put on the wire game.

In going into production with the wire game, Joe Weil decided against opening a Western Union store. He settled on something even better—the real Western Union offices on South Clark Street. For this purpose, he needed a man to play the part of an underpaid, undernourished and overworried Western Union telegrapher. He interviewed various applicants in the back room of Bath House John's. He finally settled upon a young con man named Billy Wall. When Wall tried on a green celluloid eye shade and a black alpaca coat that constituted the costume for the role, Joe knew he had the perfect man for the part.

After placing Billy Wall under contract, Weil began to cast about for his first sucker. The Yellow Kid, thanks to his native shrewdness and his experience at reading character while shilling for Doc Meriwether, soon spotted his man— a blubbery big German named Weinholt, the proprietor of a prosperous delicatessen. Weinholt hung around Bath House John's. He was a horse player; he was, moreover, a very greedy man. Other things being equal, the greedier a mark is, the easier he is to take.

Joe hired another confidence man to help him rope Weinholt. All the other confidence man had to do was to carry on conversations with Joe, in the back room of Bath House John's, within earshot of the prospective mark. "How much did you win on the races today?" Joe would ask his confederate. "I didn't make out so well," the confederate would say. Joe would sympathize with the confederate. "I bet only on fixed races," he would say. "Right now I'm working on a plan that is even better than a fixed race." "How," the confederate would ask, "could there be a better plan than a fixed race?" "It's a plan to bet on a horse after it has already won the race." The confederate would look incredulous. So, at the next table, would Weinholt. "How is such a thing possible?" the confederate would ask. "It's possible, all right," Joe would say. "All it needs is financing."

Joe had a way of looking up at a stranger, blinking and smiling. He gave Weinholt this business one night after he had been talking again about his mysterious scheme for betting on races that had already been run. Joe's confederate got up and left; Joe looked up, just happening to look in Weinholt's direction. "Will you," he asked Weinholt, "join me in a drink?"

Weinholt asked what Joe's scheme was. Joe acted surprised that Weinholt knew about it. He played hard to get. It took Weinholt several nights to get him to divulge what he had in mind. Joe's scheme could probably be put into operation, he disclosed, if somebody—Weinholt, for example—was willing to put up two thousand dollars for medical and sanitarium care for a sick woman. "What," Weinholt wanted to know, "has

a sick woman got to do with the horse races?"

"It's the wife of this telegraph operator who works at Western Union headquarters," the Kid explained. "He works on the golden wire and—"

What, Weinholt interrupted to ask, was the golden wire? The golden wire, Weil explained, impatient to be on with the story, was the wire that carried racing information from Saratoga and other eastern tracks to Chicago, from which point the operator with the sick wife put it on another wire that relayed it to the Chicago horse parlors. Weil, it developed, had already sounded out the golden-wire operator on the possibility of his participating in a scheme whereby he would tip off insiders in Chicago horse parlors to the winners of certain races by relaying one sentence of code information, then withholding the result until the insiders got their bets down. The code sentence was to contain the name of the winner of the race.

Weinholt got excited. Weil cautioned against overenthusiasm. "This operator at Western Union hasn't said definitely that he will agree to all this," said Joe. "But I think he can be persuaded."

"Could we see him to talk to him?" asked Weinholt.

Next day, the Yellow Kid and the sucker went to the building on South Clark Street where WU was located. They went up to the seventh floor, the floor below the WU offices. "Wait here," said Joe, "and I'll go up and bring him down." Billy Wall had been sitting for an hour in a booth in the eighth-floor washroom, waiting for Joe. He came out wearing the green eyeshade and the alpaca coat. When he reached the seventh floor by way of a flight of stairs he was arguing with Weil. "You shouldn't of come here," he said. "You should of come to my house at night."

"I brought a man who is willing to pay for your wife's operation," Weil explained to the harassed dot-and-dash man. Wall viewed Weinholt with suspicion. Here was basic con-man technique. The sucker was placed on the defensive; in fighting his way to a position equal to Wall his normally alert mind was distracted from what was going on. The WU telegrapher was hard to get. There were several subsequent meetings, all at Wall's home.

The home was something. It was a rented place in a low-class section of the city. Weil had hired a broken-down actress to play Wall's sick wife. While the sucker, Wall and Weil talked over the plot in whispers in the parlor, the actress, upstairs, moaned constantly in what seemed to be the last hours of her life. Wall was torn between fear of getting caught and losing his job and love for his sick wife. He finally consented to the plot. Weinholt paid over the two thousand in cash and readied himself for the kill. Weil took him to the horse-parlor store established for the occasion.

The plan was for Billy Wall, the harassed operator at the Chicago end of the golden wire, to withhold the result of the fifth race at Saratoga, then slip the name of the winner into a piece of phony delayed-start information. Weinholt and Weil arrived at the parlor just as the third race was getting under way. The place was jumping with crooks and actors poring over performance charts, arguing with each other, and placing bets with both real and stage money. The telegrapher was droning out everything coming in over the wire—authentic information that the sucker could check in the next day's newspapers.

As post time for the fifth race approached, Weil maneuvered Weinholt to the rear of the room. The idea was to get him as far from the betting window as possible. The telegraph instrument began to clack. Actually the running of the fifth race at Saratoga was coming in. "The start is being delayed by two horses at the post," the telegrapher announced. The clacking continued. When the race was actually over, the telegrapher announced, "The delay at the post is being caused by Fickle."

Weil and Weinholt glanced at a blackboard giving the odds. Fickle, a filly, was three to one. "How much are you going to bet?" asked Weil of the sucker. "A thousand dollars," said the German.

There was a sudden rush to the betting window. Weil and Weinholt found themselves sixth in line. Then an argument—carefully rehearsed—broke out at the window. One of the actors was accusing the actor behind the window of short-changing him. "Please hurry up!" shouted Weil. "My friend and I wish to place a bet on the fifth race before it begins." The participants in the argument ignored Weil and Weinholt and went on with their fight. The telegrapher began to announce the running of the race. The argument continued. It continued until the race was over. Fickle, of course, won, as Weinholt saw in the paper next day. "Oh well," said the Yellow Kid, "they'll be running again tomorrow."

Next day Weinholt got his thousand dollars down on a horse that paid even money. That night he began to compare sure-thing horse betting with the profits on slicing liverwurst. Weinholt sold his delicatessen.

The German went to the horse parlor with the proceeds of the sale—twelve thousand dollars. The telegrapher announced that Honey Boy was holding things up at the post. Weinholt forked his dough through the betting cage. Honey Boy didn't even show. Weinholt began to turn blue. What had happened? Weil thought he knew. Billy Wall, who hadn't been feeling well, had probably been taken sick and had to leave the golden wire before the race was run. "We'll find out," said Weil. The Kid and the sucker went to the seventh floor of the building where WU was located on the eighth floor. Weil went up to the eighth floor and came down again. "Just as I thought," he said. "He collapsed and they took him home. Worry over his wife. She's not expected to live, you know."

The Kid took the sucker out to Wall's house. Wall was seriously ill. He was not, in fact, expected to live. A fake doctor assured Weil, in Weinholt's presence, that the end was a matter of days. Weinholt asked Weil what would happen to the betting scheme now. "How," Weil inquired, "can you think about money at a time like this?"

A few days later, Weil called for Weinholt. "Our friend is dead," he said. "I thought you would like to pay your last respects." Wall's home was populated with phony mourners. In a room filled with floral pieces was a casket containing a wax replica of the WU telegrapher. Weinholt left Wall's house resigned to the fact that his bank roll of twelve thousand dollars had gone not because of a swindle but by a combination of unfortunate circumstances culminating in an act of God. He kept after Weil for a time, beseeching Weil to find somebody else at WU headquarters who would participate in the scheme. The Yellow Kid was unsuccessful in finding anybody.

The swindle that had paid off so nicely in the case of Weinholt was repeated on other suckers for several years. Billy Wall

died on an average of twice a month. The plot never varied, from the time the sucker was first taken to the seventh floor of the building on South Clark Street until the moment he gazed at the wax replica of Billy Wall in the coffin. The only precaution that was necessary was to make certain that none of the suckers knew one another. Then one day one of the suckers saw Billy Wall, who had been buried four months previously, at the Washington Park race track. This time he very nearly got laid out in a coffin for sure. Joe Weil, who had 20-20 vision when it came to reading handwriting on a wall, closed up his long-run production. There would be other suckers, and other productions.

Joe Weil was thirty-three when he closed up the wire game. He was now living in a suite in the nobby Blackstone Hotel. He sprouted his Van Dyke, pink and luxurious, along about this time. The management of the Blackstone knew him as a prominent young market speculator, or pretended to, but the bellboys knew him, and respected him, for what he was. Joe never attempted to deceive what he called the smart people and he considered hotel bellboys in that category. The bellhops were always welcome in Joe's suite; he was good for a drink or a touch any old time. This was all by way of maintaining good public relations and it paid off. Once, a mark who knew that Joe lived in the Blackstone appeared in the lobby and began yelping. A bellboy to whom Joe had loaned twenty dollars got on a house phone and tipped him off. Joe left the hostelry by a service entrance.

Joe was by now very much the man about town. His small, slim figure was the delight of Chicago's custom tailors. He wore spats, an Ascot cravat studded with a pearl, and piping on his vest. He would spend hours in front of the mirrors at a tailor's, fussing about the hang of a trousers, the length of a jacket, or the lie of a lapel. He was by way of becoming a gourmet. His natural curiosity was leading him into the riches of the classics in literature and into the realm of art. Slowly, there were developing two Joseph R. Weils—one the crooked sharper, the other the cultivated gentleman.

Students of Joe Weil are all agreed on one point—the man would have made a superb actor. The confidence man has to possess histrionic ability to a marked degree. He has to play his part flawlessly; if he muffs his lines, or if his timing is off, his scheme might go out the window and he might go to jail. Joe Weil realized the value of authentic characterization.

The old Essanay movie studios were in Chicago, grinding out comedies, tragedies and cliff-hangers, and utilizing for the purpose some pretty good authorities on timing, make-up and characterization —fellows named Charlie Chaplin, Bronco Billy Anderson, Douglas Fairbanks and William S. Hart. The actors used to eat in a restaurant near the studio. Weil, desirous of getting acquainted with them, began to patronize the restaurant. He soon achieved his objective. He became particularly friendly with Chaplin and Fairbanks. Neither actor knew what Joe was up to. When, then, Joe expressed a desire to watch them make pictures, Chaplin and Fairbanks assented.

As the acquaintanceship between the con man and the movie stars ripened, Joe was invited into the dressing rooms of Chaplin and Fairbanks as they made up for their roles. He asked questions, very intelligent questions, about make-up, timing and characterization, and he received intelligent and highly valuable replies. When Chaplin and Fairbanks

left Chicago for Hollywood and worldwide fame, Joe Weil, due in part to tips he had picked up from them, was ready to embark on that phase of his career that made him unique. He became, in confidence circles, the great impersonator. All confidence men are, of course, impersonators, but most of them specialize in one role, or play two or three at the most. Joe was different; to him characterization was a high art. He was, by virtue of his versatility, to get a double bang out of taking a sucker. He was not only to know the thrill of the take but the satisfaction of having essayed a difficult role to perfection.

The first of Joe's notable characterizations was that of Colonel Rutherford B. Lehigh, a querulous horse breeder from the blue-grass country. Since has was only in his early thirties, Joe had to add at least twenty years to his age. This he accomplished by growing whiskers and mustache which, together with his Van Dyke, all but obscured his youthful countenance. He wore thick-lensed glasses that dulled the vigor of his eyes, walked with a pronounced stoop, and partially depended on a gnarled cane. His costume consisted of a large black hat, frock coat, string tie and boots. Joe had a little trouble mastering the authentic Kentucky dialect but he worked hard at it. By the time the curtain went up, his audience thought the man had been born with a mint julep in his right hand.

Colonel Lehigh put in his first appearance at the Washington Park track in Chicago. There he rented a box for the entire meet. He traveled with a retinue, including a colored valet and a younger colored lad who looked as if he might be a stable boy. The butler was in constant evidence. When the colonel entered his box for the afternoon, the butler would take up a position on the infield, just below the box. The colonel's slightest whim was a command. He had only to clear his throat and the butler would produce a long cigar, snip off the end of it with a gold knife, reach up, place it in the colonel's mouth, and light it. The colonel had but to run his tongue over his lips and the butler, who carried a small suitcase, complete with shaved ice, would produce a mint julep.

The colonel was, for the most part, occupied by making studious notations on a small pad. Occasionally, somebody—a member of his supporting cast of sharpers—would drift up to his box, wait until the colonel gave a sign of recognition, then whisper something in his ear. The colonel would nod and the whisperers would go away. Then, just before the start of a race, the colonel would make a mysterious sign with his hand, and the colored boy would materialize from the crowd on the infield. The colonel would thereupon scratch something on his pad, hand it to the boy, and then peel off a few gold-seal bills from a wad he packed. The boy would disappear. After the race the boy would come back, smiling, and hand the colonel a roll of bills big enough permanently to halt the respiration of the winner of the race that had just been run.

All this attracted attention. As the meet progressed, Colonel Rutherford B. Lehigh became not only an object of curiosity and speculation; he became an individual to cultivate at all costs. The colonel, however, was aloof. He was courteous enough when spoken to by strangers, but there was something in his manner that discouraged further attempts at intercourse with him. This made his acquaintanceship all the more desirable.

It was usually during the last couple of days of the meet that the colonel broke down and had his man servant whip up some juleps for the other boxholders and pass them around with his compliments. The ice thus broken, the suckers tumbled over one another in the scramble to offer large sums of money for the colonel to bet for them. The build-up, over a period of weeks, all climaxed into a single race. The colonel accepted almost thirty thousand dollars from other bettors to place for them the last afternoon of the Washington Park meet. Nobody made so bold as to inquire of the colonel what was hot in the race the money was going down on. The colonel's past performance was enough for the suckers. They just saw the colored boy coming up to the box, the colonel scratching something on the pad, handing it to the boy with the money, and the boy disappearing—to meet a trusted confederate of Weil's outside the track and turn over the take.

When the race started, Colonel Lehigh casually kept abreast of developments through his glasses. There was no point in being tense; the thing was in the bag. At the three-quarter turn the colonel was on his feet—something nobody had ever seen him doing. He had a julep in his hand and he let it crash to his feet. He began to shake his fist toward the track. He began shouting above the roar of the crowd.

Just what Colonel Rutherford B. Lehigh was shouting was not too intelligible to the bettors who had entrusted their money to him, but they could make out an occasional, "Damned Yankee crooks!" Joe had learned how to hold his breath and force the blood into his face. Now, as the horses crossed the finish line, his face was crimson under the whiskers. The colonel was speechless with rage. When at last he found his tongue, he turned to face those behind him in the stands. Then he began to fight the Civil War all over again. He didn't care about his own money, but as a Southern gentleman he had been disgraced to lose money that had been entrusted to him by his new-found friends. He had lost that money because of a damned Yankee plot right down there on the track. He now revealed, for the first time, the name of the horse he had wagered on; it had come in second. The colonel was so loud in his outrage, and so partisan in his regional feelings, that the suckers temporarily forgot their losses in the fear that Lehigh would topple right out of his box with a stroke. Later, in the cold black light of night, most of them didn't even realize they had been swindled.

Joe would get together with other confidence men at night, in his suite at the Blackstone. Cards were played. The game was honest. The stakes were terrific. Sometimes Joe would lose all that Colonel Lehigh had made; sometimes he would win. By now, over a fifty-two-week stretch, Joe was grossing two thousand dollars a week. But expenses were high. Two hundred went off the top for protection. Confederates' salaries had to be paid. If there was one thing that Joe liked almost as well as taking a sucker, it was spending money. He gave lavish parties at roadhouses around Chicago. Sometimes he invited the entire choruses of musical shows playing in Chicago. He would get high and give waiters one-hundred-dollar tips. Worst of all, he began to speculate in the stock market— the real stock market. He was as bad at picking a stock as he was good at picking a mark. What was left in his boodle after graft, salaries, parties, luxurious daily living, dolls, and market losses was so little that Joe, like many another big-money operator outside the law, was usu-ally pressed to get another operation under way.

The Yellow Kid, as Colonel Lehigh, held boxes at tracks in various parts of the country for several years. Finally, Joe ran afoul of the law of diminishing returns. Suckers from his previous operations began to recognize him. Then the Pinkertons, who were by now guarding many of the big tracks, and who could see through a pair of spurious whiskers, cut Joe off at the pockets. He couldn't get close enough to a Pinkerton track to hear the roar of the crowd.

Colonel Lehigh continued to operate at non-Pinkerton tracks, especially those courses where horses made trial runs in the early morning. He originated a cute trial-run dodge later copied by Wilson Mizner and other confidence men—and, for that matter, still being worked. He bought a fair-to-middling horse and turned it over to a ringing expert so that its own mother couldn't recognize it. Then he had confederates spread the word around among other owners that Colonel Lehigh owned a new wonder horse—the secret son of an early-day Man o' War.

Joe's confederates, obliging fellows, would agree to sneak rival owners—the type of owners more interested in the improvement of their financial status than in the improvement of the breed— into the trial track to get a hinge at the wonder horse in a secret workout. Colonel Lehigh and several colored stable hands would appear in the dawn's early light, dramatically sniff around for any eavesdroppers, then unwrap the supernag. Morning after morning the eavesdropping rival owners, holding stop watches in their hands, would see, with their own astonished eyes, the wonder horse clipping anywhere from half a second to a second from the record for the three-quarter mile.

The bidding for Colonel Lehigh's horse soon got under way and became progressively frantic. Colonel Lehigh would finally agree to part with the horse for whatever the traffic would bear. The horse turned out to be something like the talking dog that was sold by the indigent ventriloquist and who got so sore at what it considered betrayal on the part of its master that it announced, in the presence of the new owner, that it would never say another word as long as it lived. Colonel Lehigh's horse was no threat to any track record once the sale was consummated. It now reminded clockers of a pot of glue rather than a ball of fire when it did the three-quarter mile. The answer lay in the fact that the horse had never run the three-quarter mile in its secret workouts. Joe Weil had cut down the track distance by the simple device of moving the finish post just far enough inside of the true three-quarter mile mark so as not to be noticeable to the eavesdropping clockers but sufficient to impressively cut the horse's apparent running time.

The Yellow Kid's fame began to spread among the ranks of confidence men in all parts of the country. Big-time bunco artists passing through Chicago stopped off at the Blackstone to get acquainted with Joe Weil. Joe had by now hired a combination valet-butler—a distinguished-looking gray-haired colored man—who answered the door to callers. As often as not, a visitor would come upon Joe, in a wine-colored smoking jacket, in the library of his suite, seriously immersed in a volume of Thackeray, Dumas, Balzac or Hugo. Joe would lay aside his book, take a cigaret in a long holder from his mouth, and rise to greet the caller in soft, cultured tones.

He had by now added a mustache to his Van Dyke, and had discarded his gold-rimmed glasses for the pince-nez, attached to a black ribbon, with the result that a visiting confidence man, seeing Weil for the first time, was not always sure whether this was the real Weil or some distinguished character the Yellow Kid was playing.

Being accepted into the confidence fraternity as a brother operator was considered a great distinction. The brotherhood was an exclusive organization comprising upward of one hundred men who have been aptly called the aristocrats of the underworld. These men were, circa 1912, approaching their golden age. Back in those days a dime was a dime instead of a dollar with the taxes taken out and a businessman could turn over a fast million and keep it instead of kicking most of it back to Mr. Whiskers. The result was there was more cash around. The more loose cash, the greater the opportunity for the confidence man. Killings of a quarter of a million dollars were, while not exactly common, not uncommon, either.

The confidence man wants no part of the legitimate life, with its security, its constrictions, and its monotony. If a man like Joe Weil had his life to live over again, he'd live it over, time in the cage and all. To the confidence man, there is no thrill on earth like taking a sucker. The golfer can have his hole in one, the fisherman his strike, and the huntsman his buck or his first tiger. Give the confidence man a good fat sucker and his joy is supreme. Nothing in life equals, for a Yellow Kid, the excitement that is inherent in the matching of wits, in the cumulative suspense during the build-up, and in the thrill of the take—not even a woman. To many men, work is secondary to dames in general, a mistress, or even a wife. To the confidence man, distaff stuff is strictly subordinate to work.

Joe Weil was getting an occasional jolt in jail along about now. Once he suffered the humiliation of spending seventy-five days in an Illinois county sneezer for misjudging the influence of a sucker. Occasionally, he would find himself picked up and charged with larceny in one degree or another. Joe took such things philosophically. Getting pinched was, after all, an occupational hazard. Moreover, Joe was learning the ropes; he knew what law-enforcement officials had their hands out, and how to measure a juror if the worst came to the worst.

It was around 1913 that Joseph R. Weil, now thirty-six, really got rolling. He was on speaking terms with virtually everybody engaged in confidence work by this time and, when he let out the word that he was going to establish a fake stockbroker's office in New York, he had more applicants for minor roles than he could make jobs for. Joe himself was going to play the part of V. Timkin Farnsworth, the roper. In casting about in his mind for a substantial-looking character to play the insideman, who was to be known as H. Dixon Grenfell, member of the New York Stock Exchange, Joe decided upon a man named Fred Buckminster. Buck, who had once been a Chicago policeman, was in his early forties, prematurely gray, portly and ruddy of complexion. He had a certain pious quality that later earned him the sobriquet of the Deacon. He exuded honesty and inspired confidence. He was just the hearty, solid type of citizen who would be a member of the New York Stock Exchange.

There was a branch bank on upper Broadway that made available to its cus-

tomers desks on the floor, near those of the officers of the bank. A customer could sit at one of these desks, and clip coupons or do small business chores, or even write letters. A person walking into the bank, glancing at the customers sitting at the desks, could not always distinguish between a customer and an officer of the jug.

Joe opened a substantial account at the bank under the name of V. Timkin Farnsworth and made it his business to ingratiate himself with everybody from the brass to the floor cop. He began to look around behind the wickets for a worried-looking teller. Being a keen student of character, he soon spotted his man, contrived to run into him during a lunch hour, and found that the fellow was living at the rate of twenty-five dollars a week and making only twenty dollars. Joe offered him one hundred dollars for a list of twenty of the bank's biggest depositors and records of some of the securities they had purchased through the bank. It was a deal.

Joe cased the list of depositors over a period of months until he finally selected his mark—a shrewd, loud and greedy businessman of middle age named Wilson. What happened to Wilson is typical of what happens to practically any con-man victim. He entered a pleasant, exciting world that seemed as authentic as it was spurious, and wherein lay the opportunity of a lifetime. When a mark is concentrating on laying hands on a fast lump, and drooling when he thinks what he is going to do after he has it, he is so beset by such emotions as greed, fear that the deal might not go through, and vengeance by way of planning to tell somebody off after he is rich, that his normal reasoning processes simply aren't functioning.

Joe Weil, alias V. Timkin Farnsworth,

and Fred Buckminster, alias H. Dixon Grenfell, raised the curtain by which they were to take Wilson, the businessman, with a phone call. Wilson was in his office late one afternoon when he got the call. "Good afternoon, sir," said the caller. "This is Mr. Farnsworth at the bank. As a good-will gesture, we are letting a few of our choice depositors in on a new stock issue that will assure them of a two-hundred-per-cent turnover within sixty days of when it goes on the market. We thought if you'd like to drop down at your convenience and discuss the matter that you might feel constrained to sell some of your American Tel and Tel."

Wilson said he'd be down at ten in the morning. "What did you say your name was?"

"Farnsworth." The caller laughed. "There are so many of us vice-presidents here at the bank the president can't even remember all of us. I'm new at the branch here; I'm from the main office downtown. Just ask for me when you come in."

Wilson walked into the bank in the morning and looked around. He went to a cluster of desks where the officers sat. "Where is Mr. Farnsworth?" he asked a vice-president. The officer pointed to a gentleman with a pink Van Dyke, busy at a desk. Mr. Farnsworth rose and grasped Wilson's hand. "Sorry, but I was busy with some papers here," he said. "Here, take a chair."

In low tones, Farnsworth explained that there had been a new gold strike in California. "It's highly secret as yet," he went on, "but I can tell you that it will make the previous California strikes—the Klondike, for that matter—look sick. The samples of ore recently taken from one of the mines are simply unbelievable." Farnsworth opened his desk and rummaged around. "I thought I had a sample here, but I just remembered I returned it to Mr. Grenfell." Farnsworth looked around, to make certain he was not being overheard. "What we are doing," he said, "is advising certain of our customers to buy heavily of the stock in the new strike. The common stock is selling for fifty dollars a share; it will undoubtedly open at a hundred when it goes on the market next month and should be selling at a hundred and fifty within sixty days."

Two hundred per cent in sixty days was Wilson's dish. Who, he asked, was handling the stock. "Grenfell," said Farnsworth.

"Grenfell. Grenfell. Who is Grenfell?"

Farnsworth blinked at Wilson. "H. Dixon Grenfell, member of the New York Stock Exchange."

"Oh," said Wilson, "of course."

Farnsworth suggested that Wilson accompany him to the offices of H. Dixon Grenfell, right in the building. As he got up to go, he summoned the bank's floor cop. "If anybody calls for me," he told the cop, "tell them I've gone out for twenty minutes or so. I'm taking Mr. Wilson here up to the Grenfell offices." "Yes, Mr. Farnsworth," said the cop.

The offices of H. Dixon Grenfell and Company were jumping when Farnsworth and Wilson walked in. Tickers were spouting quotation tapes, blackboard boys were posting prices, phones were ringing and clerks were frantically executing buy and sell orders. Several prosperous-looking men, puffing on aromatic Havanas, sat in front of the blackboard. Off to one side was a door bearing the legend:

H. Dixon Grenfell
Private

A pretty secretary sat just outside of Mr. Grenfell's office. She greeted Farnsworth pleasantly. "I've brought one of our depositors to meet Mr. Grenfell," said Farnsworth. "H. D. is on the phone at the moment," said the secretary. "He is talking to Mr. Livermore." The mere mention of the word Livermore excited a market speculator. Jesse Livermore, a pale blond young man who had once been a blackboard boy in a Boston brokerage house, was the most spectacular plunger Wall Street had known for thirty years.

When, presently, Farnsworth and Wilson were ushered into Mr. Grenfell's presence, Mr. Grenfell was licking an envelope. He handed it to his secretary. "Have a boy rush this down to J. P. Morgan and Company at once."

Mr. Grenfell turned to his visitors; he was a courteous but extremely busy man. After Farnsworth introduced Wilson, Mr. Grenfell asked, "And what can I do for you, Mr. Farnsworth?" Before Farnsworth got a chance to reply, Mr. Grenfell's secretary knocked gently and entered. "Mr. Otto H. Kahn is on the wire, sir," she announced. Mr. Grenfell seemed to hesitate momentarily as to whether to talk to the celebrated partner in Kuhn, Loeb and Company, noted private international bankers. When he picked up the phone, he said, "Hello, Otto. Say, before discussing whatever it is you have in mind, let me apologize for Mrs. Grenfell. She hasn't gotten around to writing to Mrs. Kahn to say what a simply wonderful time we had at your place last weekend. I don't know when we've enjoyed ourselves more thoroughly. . . . Thank you, Otto. Now what was it you had in mind?"

Mr. Grenfell listened while the international banker talked. All he said was an occasional "uh-huh." At times he would reach out to scratch some figures on a pad. Finally, he said, "It sounds wonderful, Otto. Hold on a second, will you?" Mr. Grenfell added up a column of figures. "Count me in for a hundred, Otto. I'll send a check immediately. I certainly appreciate this. Good-by, Otto." When he hung up, Mr. Grenfell summoned his secretary. "Draw a check payable to Kuhn, Loeb and Company from my personal account for one hundred thousand dollars."

Mr. Grenfell was again turning his attention to Farnsworth and Wilson when there was a knock on the door. It was Mr. Grenfell's floor manager. "Pardon, sir, but that stock you told me to keep an eye on has hit ninety-two." The floor manager consulted a slip of paper. "Your personal profit is fifty-six thousand dollars as of the moment. Do you wish me to execute a sell order?" "Just a moment," said Mr. Grenfell. He picked up a phone and called a number. "This is H. Dixon Grenfell," he said. "Let me talk to Mr. Livermore. . . . Jesse, this is Dix again. I forgot to ask you. My floor man tells me that stock we talked about has hit ninety-two. Do you still plan to dump it at ninety-five or take it higher? Uh-huh. . . . Uh-huh. . . . I see. All right, thanks a lot, Jesse." Grenfell addressed his floor manager. "Hold on. The plans have been changed. The issue is going to be taken to a hundred and thirteen. I'll get out at a hundred and ten."

Mr. Grenfell just couldn't seem to get around to his two visitors. There were a number of incoming and outgoing calls relating to stock manipulation and social activities, decisions to be made and checks and letters to be signed. Finally Mr. Grenfell's secretary announced that the editor of the New York *World*, one of the country's most influential papers, was on the wire. "What does *he* want?" asked Mr. Grenfell as he reached for the phone.

Wilson gathered that the editor of the *World* was inquiring if Mr. Grenfell knew anything about a new and secret gold strike in California. Mr. Grenfell seemed to be denying knowledge of any such thing. When he hung up, he turned to Farnsworth and asked, "Has anybody in your bank been talking about this California business—the president or anybody?" "Not so far as I know, Mr. Grenfell. Why do you ask?"

"There's been a leak somewhere. The *World*'s got wind of it. I had to lie like a gentleman and deny I knew anything about it."

"Speaking of the strike, Mr. Grenfell," said Farnsworth, "Mr. Wilson here is very anxious to buy some of the stock before it goes on the market." Wilson had expressed no such desire, yet he realized that Farnsworth's statement accurately represented his views.

The Grenfell features, harassed but pleasant up to now, darkened. "Mr. Farnsworth, I told you only the day before yesterday when I let that other depositor of yours—whatever his name was —have seventy-five thousand dollars' worth of the stock that the issue was practically all sold out. Why, there's less than two hundred thousand dollars' worth left —and, after all, I've got to take care of any personal friends who might want to get in at the last minute."

"I'm sorry, Mr. Grenfell," said Farnsworth, "but I must have misunderstood you. I understood you to say that you had about three hundred thousand open and that we could have most of it for one or two more of our depositors. Mr. Wilson here wouldn't want very much of the stock. He'd be happy with any amount you could spare—say fifty thousand or so. Right, Mr. Wilson?"

Wilson, who had been exposed now for almost half an hour to the tremendous excitement of close proximity to the insiders of Wall Street—the men who, by a nod of the head, could make fortunes for other people—stammered that he would be glad to get whatever he could of the new gold stock. Mr. Grenfell wasn't at all hopeful. "After all," he pointed out to Farnsworth, "just because your bank was kind enough to lend me three million dollars for forty-eight hours when I was a little tight for cash eighteen months ago hardly obligates me to the bank's customers. Or, for that matter, to the bank, either. I paid interest on the loan, you know!"

Finally, as a call came in from Bernard M. Baruch, Grenfell seemed to soften. "Let me think this over," he said to Farnsworth. "I might be able to arrange a little something."

"Tell you what," said Farnsworth to Wilson when they got outside, "give me a ring at the bank tomorrow afternoon and I'll let you know if there's any word." It was left at that. Late that afternoon, Farnsworth phoned Wilson at his office. "I've got to go to Boston on business for the bank," he said, "so I won't be in tomorrow if you call. But I'll only be gone a couple of days. I'll ring you the minute I get back. Oh, by the way; just a suggestion, but if I were you I'd liquidate some of your holdings so as to have fifty to a hundred thousand in cash on hand so you can take Mr. Grenfell right up on whatever he might let you have."

"Do you think there's a chance of my getting in for as much as a hundred thousand?"

"No, I think fifty is the most we can hope for. But we could be very lucky."

Farnsworth had a word of caution. "When you dispose of your stock, don't let on to anybody at the bank that I've let you in on this. Some of the other vice-presidents haven't been able to take care of their customers." Farnsworth added as an after-thought, "As a matter of fact, it will probably be just as well if you don't mention to *anybody* at the bank that I called you in."

Three days later, Wilson got a call from Farnsworth. "I'm just back from Boston. Say, you wouldn't have fifty or seventy-five thousand dollars lying around loose that you would like to invest in a nice gold stock, would you?"

"You mean Mr. Grenfell is going to let me in?"

Farnsworth laughed. "How did you guess?" Then he grew serious. "I had the opportunity to do Mr. Grenfell a good turn up in Boston. That was the straw that broke the camel's back."

Wilson went for seventy-five grand. He received for that sum some handsomely printed certificates in a company that existed only in Joe Weil's imagination. Joe and Buck now went to work on another mark. They took him and went to work on a third mark. While taking the third mark, Joe strung Wilson and the second mark along by saying the stock hadn't been placed on the market yet. Joe kept the marks away from the bank by saying he was out of town. By the time he and Buck really left town, abandoning the handsome offices of H. Dixon Grenfell, they had, after paying the actors, netted almost two hundred thousand dollars.

The taking of Wilson is illustrative of the amount of preparation that goes on before the sucker is even approached. It took Joe Weil weeks to ingratiate himself with the workers in the branch bank. It took him weeks more to investigate the prospective suckers before deciding on Wilson. More time was spent constructing the stockbroker's store, writing the script, casting the production, and rehearsing the actors. It all climaxed by Wilson spending about a half an hour in the office occupied by the substantial-looking Buckminster. The build-up is the big thing in any confidence game; the actual take is in the nature of an anticlimax.

Joe Weil and Fred Buckminster became close friends—a friendship that was to last many years. Although they were dissimilar in appearance—Joe being on the small size, spare and fastidious in appearance, and Buck being big, portly and, while neat, not given to sartorial elegance—they were strikingly similar in mental and emotional make-up. Each was practically nerveless, had a mind that moved with the speed of light, and had a congenital scorn for a mark. Each was a character reader par excellence. In fact, Joe and Buck used to sit around hotel lobbies betting with each other as to the occupation of other lobby sitters.

Joe and Buck were dining in the Plaza Hotel in New York one night when they noticed a mark they had taken more than a year previously settling himself at the next table. "Let's get out of here," said Joe. As Joe and Buck rose to go, the mark spotted them. He began to squeal, right in front of the other diners. Joe and Buck left the dining room fast, but the sucker was right at their heels.

In a corridor off the dining room, which was practically deserted, Joe stopped in his flight, turned to face the sucker, and grabbed him by the lapels. "Listen, you," he said. "Go ahead and squeal. Squeal your god-damned head off. You've already lost fifty thousand. Do you want to lose some more?" The question stymied the sucker. "You've got everything to lose and nothing to gain," Joe went on, "by squealing. You're running an important business. How do you think the other businessmen you do business would feel about you if they knew you were a chump? Think it over, sucker."

The sucker had never thought of the swindle in that light. Now that he did, he cooled out in a hurry. *He* was the one who left the hotel; Joe and Buck went back to the dining room and had their dinner.

As he neared forty, the Yellow Kid was living like a prince. He not only maintained his apartment at the Blackstone in Chicago, but he now had quarters on Riverside Drive in New York, then the town's most fashionable street. He began to go in for custom-built automobiles; he took on a Rolls-Royce and a Fiat. He hired a Filipino chauffeur and became something to see in Chicago as he rolled around the city in his town car, behind a cigaret in a twelve-inch ivory holder. When the Kid made a trip anywhere by train, he traveled only in a drawing room and always sent one of his cars and the chauffeur on ahead so that he would have distinctive transportation at his disposal during his stay.

The Kid became a familiar figure at the big prize fights, at the World Series, and at the Memorial Day races at the Indianapolis Speedway. There was only one type of sport he couldn't stand—college football. He couldn't for the life of him understand how people could get steamed up about a bunch of kids playing only for glory.

The Kid practically had to fight off women. He was so distinguished-looking, so witty, so free with his money, and reportedly such a virile character, that the dames practically sent *him* roses. He regarded women as he regarded food and wine—something that was necessary every so often, and to be selected with discrimination. The Kid's choice was invariably a blonde. He always made it plain to the girl that she was nothing more than a passing frenzy; he kept out of trouble with girls all his life except for one occasion in Chicago in 1929 when a couple of dames got into a hair-pulling and eye-scratching match about the Kid and the rumpus got into the papers.

Joe read the newspapers and the magazines as assiduously as he read the classics. He was always looking for an angle, a way in which to monetize an existing situation. He once came upon an article about confidence men which stated that, next to horse players, doctors were the biggest suckers in the world. Joe knew that to be true. He decided, therefore, to harvest the medical field. What better way to do it, he inquired of himself, than to pose as a physician? Joe, the thorough one, went into seclusion for several weeks and did practically nothing but read medical books. By the end of that time, he could hold his conversational own in any clinic or operating room. Next Joe went to an acquaintance who was operating a medical diploma mill and got some authentic X-rays of a fractured right shin bone of a small male adult.

Joe emerged as Dr. Richard T. Dorrance, general practitioner of Lexington, Kentucky. Dr. Dorrance, a pink-whiskered character, well turned out but smelling of pills, walked into the office of a bone specialist on New York's Park Avenue. He was, he said, the personal physician to Colonel Edward R. Bradley, the operator of Bradley's gambling casino at Palm Beach and the owner of the famed Idle Hour Farms in Lexington, Kentucky. "The colonel," Dr. Dorrance explained in a fragrant blue-grass accent, "has a jockey who is worrying both of us. One of the Idle Hour colts kicked him in the right patella six months ago and the injury doesn't respond to treatment. Here, doctor," went on Joe, opening a little black medical kit, "I have some X-rays of the injury."

Joe could see the mind of the fee-happy specialist working. Could the specialist go to Kentucky, expense no object? *Could* he!

"The colonel will be very happy," said Joe. "He is just like a father to all his jockeys. Do you mind if I telephone him now—collect, of course?"

Buckminster was planted at a phone in a rented house in Lexington. Dr. Dorrance gave the telephone number of the house to the bone specialist's nurse and asked her to put a collect person-to-person call through for Colonel Bradley. The nurse heard Buckminster answering the phone in Kentucky and identifying himself as Colonel Bradley's butler. Then Buck changed his voice and came to the phone as Colonel Bradley. Colonel Bradley asked to speak to the bone man. Money, he said, was no object.

The bone man invited Dr. Dorrance to dinner that night. Over brandy and cigars, Dorrance disclosed that Colonel Bradley made so much money on horse betting that he could hardly count it. As a matter of fact, the colonel had given him a tip on a horse that was running at Belmont Park next day. He scribbled something down on a slip of paper, put it in a sealed envelope, handed it to his host and said, "Give this to your nurse in the morning. Tell her not to open it until I tell her to."

Late the next afternoon, Joe breezed into the bone man's office, all smiles. He asked the nurse for the envelope. He opened it, pulled out the slip of paper,

palmed the paper and handed the doctor another piece exactly like it, upon which he had written the name of a long shot that had come in at Belmont a couple of hours previously. "That," he said, "is the kind of information Colonel Bradley gives to his close friends."

Joe let the bone man win a couple of comparatively small bets. Then, when the specialist had twelve thousand dollars—a favorite sum of Joe's—down on a race, something went wrong. "That," said Joe with a shrug, "is racing for you." Then something else happened in Lexington. Colonel Bradley, a notoriously changeable character, according to Dr. Dorrance, had decided to get another bone man for his jockey.

The Yellow Kid was not invulnerable. He fell in love. Joe fell in love with precisely the kind of girl he wouldn't have been expected to fall in love with. Her name was Jesse Brooks, and she was a plain little girl from a middle-class Middle West family. Joe had known her since he had first become conscious of the rustle of a skirt; her parents had lived near his people in Chicago. He hadn't seen her for years. During those years he had seen, and holed up with, many women quite unlike Jesse. When, then, he met Jesse again, after the years, in an infinitely respectable Chicago chop house, he fell in love. Maybe it was because Jesse was so different. Joe palmed himself off as a traveling salesman—which, in a way, he was. His con-man friends were sure he had gone completely out of his head.

Joe suddenly underwent a great change. He began to save his money. He bought his fiancee a little wedding present—an apartment house on Pratt Boulevard, in the Rogers Park section of Chicago. Joe had no use for stocks and bonds, but he was a firm believer in income-producing real estate. Joe and Jesse went shopping for furniture. Then they were married. They went to Europe on their honeymoon. When they came back, they took up residence in one of the apartments in Jesse's building and rented the rest. The other tenants had no idea that their charming, bewhiskered landlord was a prominent young confidence man.

Joe's wife liked Chicago, and Joe didn't want to be separated from her. He decided to get into something that would enable him to remain in Chicago for a while and still not generate too much heat. Buckminster, Joe's closest friend, used to come to dinner at the house. Mrs. Weil thought Buck was a stockbroker. One night Buck said to Joe, in Jesse presence, "I was told by a friend today that almost a thousand Chicago people have lost money investing in building lots in northern Michigan."

"Is that so, Buck?" said Joe.

"Yes," Buck went on. "These poor people paid two hundred dollars apiece for lots in this place on the strength of some photographs that were very deceptive. The lots are completely worthless. They are either covered with trees or under water."

"What a terrible thing," said Mrs. Weil. "Isn't it," said Joe.

"I saw a list of the owners of the lots today," said Buck, looking past Mrs. Weil at Joe. "I wish there was something that could be done about it."

Thus was born a swindle that was original with Joe, and which is still in use today. It is known as the abstract racket. All the con man needs to begin operations is two offices, in close proximity to one another, a couple of stenographers not necessarily in on the plot, and a list of people who have invested in worthless lots. Joe stuck an ad in the classified columns of the Chicago papers stating that it would be to the advantage of all purchasers of the supposedly worthless lots in northern Michigan to get in touch with the North American Asset Realization Corporation in the Alhambra Theater Building. Suckers who answered the ad found the office of the asset-realization outfit austere but impressive. Joe, using the name of T. Raymond Manningham, sat behind a desk dictating letters to a stenographer—letters that were never mailed but which led the waiting callers to believe that Mr. Manningham was up to his whiskers in important business transactions of various sorts. Mr. Manningham was too busy to give more than a minute or two to those who called. Briefly he stated that he represented a syndicate that wished to buy up the property in northern Michigan for a purpose he was not at liberty to disclose. "We are willing to pay you exactly what you paid for the property," Joe would explain. "All we ask is that you supply us with an absolutely clear title to the lot we purchase from you."

The sucker, elated at the chance to get off the hook, was more than willing to supply an abstract. Mr. Manningham suggested that the Universal Title, Abstract and Guarantee Company, right down the hall, was in a position to give prompt service. "The sooner you have the abstract, the sooner we can close the deal."

Buckminster presided over the Universal Title, Abstract and Guarantee Company. The charge for an abstract on the northern Michigan property should have been not more than ten dollars a lot. Joe and Buck tapped the suckers for up to fifty dollars an abstract. It was a whirlwind campaign; in ten days the pair took more than five hundred suckers for a total of twenty thousand dollars. When it came time for Mr. Manningham to buy up the suckers' lots, he had bad news for them. His syndicate had decided not to go through with the purchase of the Michigan land. Too many clouded titles. "But you can feel easy," he would explain to the unhappy though unsuspicious bag-holder. "Your title is nice and clear. Nothing to prevent you from selling if you get an offer."

Joe and Buck took the abstract racket on tour. They played as far west as Oregon, and as far east as New York City. They never left a city with less than fifteen thousand dollars for a two-weeks stand.

The confidence man is ever the opportunist; a basic swindle that is beginning to grow a beard can be rejuvenated if linked to a news development or to an existent local, national or international situation. Early in 1920, several months after a defeated Germany had signed an armistice with the Allies, Joe appeared in Cleveland as Herr Doktor Tourneur Saint-Harriot, purchasing agent for a group of influential Prussian business men anxious to rebuild their Fatherland. Herr Doktor, who had been a submarine commander in the war, was stiffly correct, gray at the temples and monocled; he exuded the ego and arrogance of a Baltic baron. He received the press in his hotel suite and explained, in his limited English, that he had come to the Middle West to let contracts to American factories to supply Germany with the materials that would rebuild the areas damaged by the late conflict. Herr Doktor, gallant in defeat, paid the highest respect to our fighting men. The American Navy, the reporters gathered, had caused him some bad moments during the course of the war. "Many times," he reminisced, "id loog lag der end."

From Cleveland, Herr Doktor fanned out into various Middle West cities and towns, with copies of the newspaper interview, and called on manufacturers of all products that could be utilized for reconstruction purposes. His syndicate, which had unlimited millions at its disposal, was particularly interested in street lamps, concrete, lumber, hardware, and bricks. He told each manufacturer that he was interested not in part of their output. "We vant *eferyting*," he would say, with an autocratic wave of the arms, "for fife year." Such a prospect called for a bit of figuring. There was no urgency; Herr Doktor would be back. At the end of six weeks, after Joe had hit some fifty cities and towns, he had practically become a one-man boom. Production cutbacks that had gone into effect with the armistice were now brought up for reconsideration at boards of directors' meetings; the arrogant gentleman from the Fatherland stood in a fair way to reverse the downward plunge of employment charts.

Herr Doktor Saint-Harriot began to grow a trifle difficult when it came to actually signing the contract for a factory's output for five years. The president of one appliance company found himself in a typical hassle with the Herr Doktor when Saint-Harriot, despite his limited knowledge of English, insisted that first one clause then another in the contract being prepared by the manufacturer's lawyers be reworded. Then, after the contract had finally been reworded to the Herr Doktor's liking, Saint-Harriot just couldn't seem to bring himself to put his signature on the dotted line.

Finally, the president of the appliance concern, which stood to sell about three million dollars' worth of merchandise, grasped, from the maze of Herr Doktor's broken English and double talk, the fact that Saint-Harriot had his hand out. That simplified everything. Just what was it, the manufacturer asked, that the Herr Doktor wanted? Saint-Harriot's proposition was stunning in its larcenous simplicity. He would permit the manufacturer to hike the price of his five-year output by 10 per cent, which would net the manufacturer an added profit of almost a third of a million dollars, in return for a little advance kickback—say fifty thousand dollars, as Herr Doktor pronounced it, gash.

That sounded like a good deal from any angle. Joe took fifty thousand here, fifteen there, forty another place, and continued until he had collected almost a quarter of a million in pure, cool green.

Some of the manufacturers never caught on to the swindle until after they had sent their first shipment to Germany, under terms of the contract Saint-Harriot had made so difficult, only to learn that the consignee was nonexistent. Most of the victims kept the swindle to themselves; to have gone after Joe would have meant exposing themselves to ridicule and loss of business prestige. The handful who did squawk got nowhere. Joe had peeled 10 per cent off the top for protection to cops and prosecutors and sunk the rest into Rogers Park real estate in Chicago—and in his wife's name.

Chicago has always had an affinity for sharp operators. Men who would be clinked in other cities, or at least treated like lepers, have been lionized in Chicago. Fame and notoriety are often the same thing in the lusty metropolis on the shore of Lake Michigan. Joseph R. Weil was, in the year of 1923, when he was forty-six years of age, one of the city's fullblown celebrities. The newspapers began to consult him for technical information relating to swindles and swindlers. The Yellow Kid numbered among his favored friends reporters such as Charles MacArthur, Ben Hecht and others who were making such valuable contributions to the rowdy and flavorful journalism of the city.

Joe's wife, the former Jesse Brooks, knew by now, of course, that Joe was not a traveling salesman. Joe was, however, a pretty good husband, as men go, and Jesse was quite happy. After all, she might have married a steamfitter's helper, and in those days the practical artisan did not enjoy the prestige and affluence that he enjoys today. As it was, Jesse Weil had a whole mansionful of servants to slap around, and, not having been used to servants before marriage, she sometimes did just that.

Jesse's salient characteristic turned out to be love of money. With Joe, it was easy come, easy go; Jesse squeezed a silver dollar until she choked the eagle. She maintained the most cordial of relations with the receiving tellers in a half a dozen Chicago banks. One night, while Joe was browsing through the first editions in his paneled library, Jesse walked in and said, "Joe, somebody was telling me there's a lot of money in the hotel business. Why don't we buy a hotel?"

Up until that moment, the Yellow Kid had looked upon a hotel as a place to rope a sucker or take a woman. Now he realized for the first time that a hotel could also be a place where a man could turn a dollar. Joe thought it would be kind of fun to go legitimate; there would be a certain novelty in it. He began to shop around. He bought a 200-room hostelry on the North Side called the Hotel Huntington. Joe changed the name of the hotel to the Hotel Martinique and put in many improvements. By the time he opened for business, he had an investment of three-quarters of a million dollars—other people's money but money nonetheless.

Joe was, despite frequent parties of belching, freeloading police, building up a nice business when the underworld embraced the place. Hoodlums, stick-up artists, blackmailers and lamsters from other cities began to make the Martinique their stopping or holing-up place on the theory that any establishment operated by the Yellow Kid was out of bounds for the cops. Joe tried to explain that the hotel was not under official protection, but the hot guests wouldn't believe him. The fact that there was usually at least one cop in the dining room or elsewhere on the premises convinced the hotties that Joe had bought protection. The joker was that the cops were having such a good time, what with the free food and some Clark Street dolls who had taken up residence in the Martinique, that they never noticed the other guests.

The Martinique finally began to resemble the hotel where the management sounded a gong at six in the morning to suggest to guests that they return to their own rooms. The police caught on eventually and Joe found himself paying protection money again. These were dreary days for Joe. He began to speculate in the stock market for the first time since his marriage. He went in whole hog. Joe sometimes dropped twenty thousand dollars in a single day.

In the summer of 1924, a year after Joe had taken over the hotel, there was a sensational two-million-dollar mail robbery on a train at Rondout, Illinois, thirty odd miles southwest of Chicago. Most of the loot was in negotiable securities. William Fahy, a handsome Irishman who was the ace of the postal inspection service in the Chicago area, spearheaded the probe into the crime. As it turned out, Fahy himself had masterminded the job, and he went to the big cage for it.

Some months after the Rondout robbery, one of Joe's guests at the Martinique, hearing that he was losing the monograms from his silk shirts in the market, suggested a sure thing. He would let Joe have some hot paper for one-third of its face value. Joe has always claimed that he didn't know the bonds were from the Rondout job. He just could have been telling the truth; the Rondout job was a federal offense and Joe was certainly acquainted with the fact that, even in 1924, federal dicks manifested a quaint aversion to protection money. Joe was caught stuck to the paper. His hotel, already in hock from his market plunges, sank deeper into the mortgage mire as he tossed money in every conceivable direction trying to extricate himself from the Rondout jam. The Yellow Kid was completely busted when, one day in 1926, he was dropped behind the high wall at Leavenworth holding a five-year ticket.

After he had settled in Leavenworth and sized things up, Joe went to the warden. "I would like to give a little talk to the prison population," said Joe, a ham at heart. "What about?" asked the warden. "On the evil life, and how it doesn't pay." The warden arranged for the talk. The prison population included such celebrated malefactors as Dr. Frederick A. Cook, the physician-impostor who had claimed to be the discoverer of the North Pole. Doc was in for a Texas oil dodge. When he saw and heard Joe Weil, Doc Cook knew he had met a kindred soul.

Cook, being a physician, had, probably because of a breakdown in normal bureaucratic mental processes, been assigned to the practice of medicine in Leavenworth. He asked the warden to let him have Joe Weil as an assistant. Joe was quick to wire his job for sound. A prisoner up for parole had to meet certain medical requirements. Joe would go to a prisoner ripe for springing, divulge to him the spurious information that his medical record was against him, but add that for a fee he'd fix it up. Here was a new type of confidence game. Joe didn't get rich on it, but when he came out of prison in 1930, he wasn't worried about the immediate future.

Joe announced that he had reformed; this was the first of many such announcements. He took to the lecture platform. He appeared in Chicago and other cities in the Middle West, crusading against the evil life. He spiced his lectures with inside information about confidence games. As he stood on the platform, looking down at the open, shining faces in the audience, he was struck once again, as he had been while a shill for Doc Meriwether, the medicine man, more than a third of a century before, with the basic truth that people, properly approached, will go for anything.

Certain peace-enforcement officials in and around Cook County were saddened at the spectacle of Joe Weil going straight. Joe's legitimacy was cheating them of a pay-off. They propositioned Joe; why didn't he resume the practice of his profession? Joe resented the avarice of the public servants. He continued with his lectures. A couple of high-level Chicago cops got sore and began invoking various technicalities which enabled them to shutter Joe's Chicago lectures.

Joe teamed up with Fred Buckminster again and opened a chain of brokerage stores from coast to coast. He began making money faster than he could count it. The con varied according to the personalities of the suckers. On several occasions, Joe and Buck took bankers. Joe would blow into a town, posing as H. Jefferson Warrington, a partner of J. P. Morgan and Company, inform a bank president that he was interested in secretly buying up an entire city block for a purpose that he was not at liberty to disclose, and then, after a preliminary conference with the mark, leave behind him a letter, apparently accidentally dropped from his briefcase. The letter was on the stationery of J. P. Morgan and Company, and was a personal message from J. P. himself to H. Jefferson Warrington. The letter hinted at a big killing soon to be made in the market. Joe always obliged the banker by letting him in on the killing.

In the early thirties, when a great depression was on the land and when cash was scarce, Joe went into production with a fresh and original version of a con known as a green-goods game. He became Professor Von Chopnick, a criminally inclined German scientist who manufactured hundred- and thousand-dollar bills in a basement laboratory in New York's Greenwich Village. Von Chopnick in this case was the inside man. Buck and other ropers steered the suckers to the professor.

What the professor had was a wondrous scientific device of German origin, that *duplicated* money. He would place a bill in the device, pour chemicals over it, and, some hours later, take out two bills. Each genuine bill could be duplicated only once; a new genuine bill was needed for every duplicate.

The sucker would know that a specific bill had been duplicated because both bills coming from the machine bore the same serial number. The catch was that Weil functioned with new bills, straight from a bank, with serial numbers that ran consecutively. It was a simple matter to convert one numeral in one bill from a 3 to an 8, so that when both bills were taken from the machine one did indeed appear to be an exact duplicate of the other.

A Broadway bookmaker, of all people, was the first victim Buck steered to the Greenwich Village basement. The bookie was a wise guy who knew all about the green-goods game. The fact that he was such a wise guy made him an ideal mark; he held himself in such esteem that he couldn't imagine anybody trying to slip one over on him.

Professor Von Chopnick was puttering around the basement in the acid-stained smock when Buck steered in the bookie. The professor squinted briefly at the visitor through thick-lensed eye-glasses, then went about his business at a foul-smelling bench filled with bottles. The professor, who spoke only a few words of English, seemed like a malevolent character. "He had to get out of Germany," Buck whispered to the bookie. "You remember when Germany changed its currency?" The bookie vaguely remembered something of the sort. "It was on account of the professor here," said Buck. "He flooded the country with so much duplicate stuff that the German money became practically worthless."

"Is that why he had to get out?"

"No," said Buck. "He murdered a man."

The professor made a C note for the bookie. "Let's take it to a bank," said Buck, "and test it."

"But it smells," said the bookie, sniffing the bill. "It'll attract attention." The bill gave off a strong odor—the odor of a disinfectant that had been poured over it and which didn't harm it in any

way. Buck shoved the bill through the wicket of a teller in a branch of the Corn Exchange Bank. "Break this up into fives for me." The teller noticed the odor of the bill. He sniffed it and gave Buck and the bookie a suspicious hinge. "What's the matter," snapped Buck, supremely confident of Professor Von Chopnick's handiwork, "do you think it's a counterfeit or something?" The teller disappeared with the bill. The bookie was all for getting to hell out of there. "Don't be a sap," said Buck. "They'll never detect it in a million years." The teller came back in a little while, riffled twenty fives from a stack and shoved them through the wicket.

When Buck and the bookie returned to the counterfeiter's basement, Von Chopnick was in a rage. He held up his thumbs; they were stained by green ink. He sputtered something in bad English about having run out of the chemical required for the fixing bath into which the bills were placed after coming from the machine so that the color would not run. "This is bad," Buck told the bookie. "We can't take a chance on laying any of the professor's money, good as it is, unless he gets more of the fixing bath."

"Where do you get that?" asked the bookie.

"That's just it," said Buck. "It's a secret formula. It comes from Germany."

The bookie, used to action, wanted action. He wanted either a machine, and all the chemicals that went with it, or he wanted to buy bills, preferably in denominations of one thousand dollars from the professor at a discount. "We'll have to cable to Germany," said Buck. "That's the only way we can get the stuff for the fixing bath."

"Who do you cable to?"

"To a friend of the professor's. He'll have to bring the stuff over himself."

"Why can't he send it?"

"The customs people would be tipped off if they saw it."

"How will the professor's friend get it past the customs?"

"In a trunk with a false bottom. He did it that way when he went into England once."

"England?"

"The professor made some fifty-pound notes there two years ago."

Buck sat down and wrote a cable addressed to a Jacob Ludwig at an address in Hamburg. The cable was in German. Buck handed it to the bookie. "Send this for me when you go uptown, will you?"

The bookie, wise guy, had the cable translated before he sent it. The message asked Jacob Ludwig to get the first ship for the United States and to bring his violin in the special case. The bookie interpreted the violin and the case to mean the fixing bath in the trunk with the false bottom.

There was, in Hamburg, a man by the name of Jacob Ludwig. There were, in fact, half a dozen men going under the name of Jacob Ludwig, all of them ready to start shuttling back and forth across the Atlantic—one by one, one for each swindle, each to meet a different roper and victim at the Hamburg-American Line's pier in Hoboken, New Jersey, across the Hudson River from New York. The first Jacob Ludwig answered Buck's cable, saying he would arrive in the U. S. A. eight days later. Buck let the bookie see the cable and take it up to Broadway for translation. What could have appeared more genuine?

Buck and the bookie met the ship. Jacob Ludwig, played by an ex-actor who had worked for the Yellow Kid in various cons, walked down the gangplank, in European-cut clothes, and greeted Buck in broken English. Buck

and the bookie stuck around while Ludwig had his baggage examined by customs. Ludwig acted so nervous that Buck began to act nervous, too. "If they ever find that false bottom," whispered Buck to the bookie, "we're sunk."

The false bottom, however, wasn't found. Everybody got together in Professor Von Chopnick's basement. The trunk was opened and there, in the false bottom, was about twenty pounds of white crystals—the priceless secret mixing bath. Von Chopnick, usually dour, showed signs of joy.

Next day the bookie appeared with twenty-five one thousand dollar bills; he wanted the professor to duplicate each of them. The professor made some calculations, based on his equipment and the amount of chemicals he had. The job would take three days. That was fine with the bookie, until he called three days later to find the basement laboratory deserted.

The Kid moved around town for months, taking men in practically every walk of life with the wondrous money-duplicating device. In every instance, the clincher was the arrival of the German with the secret fixing-bath crystals in the false-bottom trunk. The crystals, as it turned out, would have been of more benefit to a victim, if taken internally, than in the mixing bath. The crystals were Bromo Seltzer.

After Hitler came to power in Germany, Joe Weil was the first of the confidence men to put the wealthy refugee on a paying basis. In 1937, Joe emerged on the Pacific Coast as H. Huntington Black, former attache of the American Embassy in Berlin. His package this time was an up-to-date version of the Spanish Prisoner game. A wealthy German refugee, Joe would explain to a loaded mark, preferably a small-town banker, had gotten as far as Mexico but lacked the proper papers to get into the United States. The gimmick was that the refugee, a woman named Hortense, had in her possession a trunkful of American securities worth two million dollars. There were, the former state-department attache explained, certain technicalities that made the securities worthless unless the refugee personally reached the United States with them and endorsed them in the presence of an American treasury official.

H. Huntington Black had with him a letter from Hortense, which a confederate had mailed from the classy Reforma Hotel in Mexico City. Hortense was willing to part with a million dollars to unfreeze two million. H. Huntington Black would suggest to the mark that a small expenditure—fifty thousand, say—would bring Hortense, and a profit of a million dollars, to the U. S. A. The expenditure would entail the purchase of a boat of some kind, and the hiring of a crew. Hortense, and her two million dollars' worth of securities, were to be smuggled into the United States.

The mark was never able to say later that Joe Weil didn't give him a show for his dough. Joe would take the mark to water-front dives after the fall of night, there to proposition tough-looking sea-

men who were part of the Weil stock company. The owners of seagoing craft —other Weil actors—would be contacted. At length, the mark would go down to a wharf and see Joe going off on a fast, small boat—off to Mexico presumably, but actually to come back with the boat, a hired one, return it to its owner, then vanish in the direction of another mark.

When the European war broke out in September, 1939, Joe went to New York and opened a brokerage store. In clipping one sucker, he made the serious error of writing a letter. That was using the mails to defraud. The Federals sent Joe to Atlanta for twenty-seven months. When he came out, early in 1942, at the age of sixty-five, Joe's health, never robust, had begun to go. He didn't feel up to the rigors and suspense of a big con or a short con. He announced another reformation. He picked up living money on the lecture platform. His wife had died. He took a modest little flat in the 400 block on Melrose Avenue in Chicago. There he dwells today, with a police dog and his memories, while he goes about his legitimate business of soliciting Chicagoans on the phone on behalf of charity. The name over Joe's mail box in the lobby of the apartment building where he lives is somehow curiously fitting. It is Dr. James Wilson.

Prophet Joshua and His Holy Rollers

*The revival meetings of this phony evangel broke up early in the
morning and broke up many a happy home as the spurious
Prophet put religion on a sex-and-business basis.*

A unique man emerged from the ever-green fastness outside the town of Corvallis, Oregon, one sunny day in the spring of 1903, and, as a result, things in and around Corvallis were not to return to normalcy for some time. The man, barefooted, in tatters, and carrying a staff, had hidden his identity behind a crop of golden-brown whiskers and a beard that flowed to his elbows. His hair, glistening in the sun, hung down to his shoulders. His eyes were wide, dark-brown and piercing.

As the man shuffled along the middle of the town's main street, inducing nightmares in little children, he announced, in rich, organlike tones, that he was a Divine Messenger, come to Corvallis to save the citizens from eternal residence in the fires of hell.

It was a saloonkeeper, of all people, who had the effrontery to approach the Messenger and inquire just who he was. "I am the Prophet Joshua the Second," announced the visitor, looking up at the sky. "I am come to found the Church of the Bride of Christ."

That night, after the prophet had gone back into the evergreen fastness, the saloonkeeper submerged himself in deep thought. He was wondering where he had seen the prophet before. "It's them eyes of his," he said as he drew a beer for a client. "I've seen them eyes somewheres before."

Next day Joshua appeared again and, as he shuffled along the middle of the main street, he turned his face skyward and bellowed for guidance as to how best to reap a bumper crop of community souls. Occasionally, he would lower his gaze, the better to peer at the townsfolk standing gaping at him from the sidewalk—especially, it seemed, those townsfolk who were female, young and anatomically interesting.

The prophet's visitations occurred daily. On the seventh day he was accompanied by a second tattered man who walked immediately behind him—a gaunt, gangling character who was, like the ecclesiastic, wearing a hair chest protector. As Joshua trudged along, this second man would occasionally dart to the sidewalk, whip out pencil and paper and take down the name of some female.

The saloonkeeper asked this second man who he was. "Brother Brooks," came the answer. "Just call me Brother Brooks."

"It's a funny thing," the saloonkeeper remarked one night, "but this Brother Brooks only takes down the names of women. He never takes down nobody's name who's a man."

By now many of the citizens of Corvallis were wondering where the prophet and Brother Brooks slept at night—in a cabin, in a tent, or, what seemed quite possible, in a cave. Another puzzling question was just where Joshua was going to hold forth, once he got going with the Church of the Bride of Christ. Then the word got around that the prophet would conduct services in the homes of parishioners and that Brother Brooks

265

would take up collections to be put away in a fund to build an edifice.

The prophet's first service was held one night in the home of an old maid on the edge of town. About twenty women, ranging in age from sixteen to about fifty, attended. Next day none of the communicants would discuss what the service had been like, but they began to walk around town with an unearthly glow suffusing their faces.

One warm night in June, after Joshua and Brother Brooks had emerged from their protective coloration to conduct several services, a jumbo revival was held in the home of a middle-aged married woman whose husband was away on a trip. Although the people who lived right next door couldn't see anything, the window shades being drawn, they could hear everything.

Services began with a prayer by the prophet. Then Brother Brooks, a handy man with a phrase, exhorted the parishioners to dig deeply—to dig, in fact, until it hurt—for the privilege of contributing to the erection of an edifice.

As the collection was taken up, the neighbors next door could hear Brother Brooks saying, "Thank you, Sister. *Thank* you!" and Joshua vibrating with "Praise the Lord! *Praise* the Lord!"

Then Joshua began to chant. Gradually the parishioners joined in. The chanting swelled in volume and intensity and continued for several minutes. Then, as if somebody, probably Joshua, waved his hands, it stopped abruptly.

Now the prophet began to exhort his parishioners to cast out sin. "Cast it *all* out!" he bellowed. "Be *done* with vile earthly things! Take off your *clothes*!"

The people next door began to hear moaning, screaming and hysterical laughter as the ladies started to divest themselves of their vile garments. Getting un-dressed was a production back in those days, what with the girls wearing bustles, whalebone corsets and layers of petticoats. Many a man, come wedding night, was chagrined to learn that he had been cruelly betrayed.

"Roll, Sisters!" the neighbors now heard the prophet exhorting the parishioners. "Roll!" While the sisters rolled, apparently on the floor, the neighbors could hear them moaning high and moaning low.

The moaning and rolling and exhortations by Joshua and "hallelujahs!" by the parishioners went on for about three-quarters of an hour. Then, with the devil apparently cast out, at least for the night, things quieted down. In a little while, everybody left and the shades were pulled up in the home of the communicant.

The story about this particular service soon got all around town. Even the unbelievers began to express interest in knowing where and when the next service would be held. But Joshua was too shrewd for the curious. He staged one revival after another, here and there in and around Corvallis, but nobody except the faithful ever knew where one was to be held, just as nobody except the players ever knew in advance the location of a floating crap game.

The saloonkeeper—the man who had a vague suspicion that he had seen Joshua somewhere before—informed a reporter for the local paper, the Corvallis *Times,* that the prophet's meetings had cast a blight on three homes that he knew of, and probably more. It seemed that certain married women had, after rolling with Joshua, declined certain connubial services to their husbands. "Them men," the bartender informed the scribe, "are awful mad."

In midsummer Joshua divined that it was time to get out of town. Well, not *exactly* out of town. Just *partly* out. He decided to settle on Kiger Island, out in the Wilmette River, which divided Corvallis from the eastern banks of the stream. Kiger Island was densely wooded and thus an ideal spot for an evangel who wanted to perform his miracles safe from the prying eyes of unbelievers.

About thirty of the faithful set out from Corvallis in rowboats, and things began to hum on Kiger Island. Everybody gathered logs, branches and twigs and built a big wigwam for the prophet. Once the wigwam was up, it was covered by mud, the better to make it peek-proof. Presently the communicants were in full cry. Although nobody in Corvallis, or on the opposite shore, could see anything, they could hear plenty coming from the little wooded island in the middle of the river. When the wind was right, it carried the sounds of the prophet's exhortations and the squeals and the moans of the faithful as they rolled in ecstasy. People began to call the prophet's parishioners the Holy Rollers.

Along toward the middle of September, a female Judas emerged from the fastness of Kiger Island to spread details of just what was going on there. Joshua, it developed, had received divine instructions to find a communicant who would collaborate with him in bringing forth what he said would be a second Christ. He began to audition applicants in his peek-proof wigwam and turned out to be a hard man to please, though a robust one.

When the woman was invited into the wigwam she was shocked when the prophet informed her what was expected of her. So she handed in her letter and rowed back to shore determined to tell all.

The tale of the talkative backslider quickly crystalized scattered resentment against the bearded prophet. Several men whose wives had suddenly switched from hot to cold after becoming Holy Rollers got up a water posse and rowed out to Kiger Island on the prowl for the evangel. But Joshua and Brother Brooks had taken on protective coloration and couldn't be located. There were mumblings and grumblings around Corvallis for a few days, then things quieted down.

People around Corvallis began to wonder what had become of the prophet. They didn't wonder long. Around Thanksgiving time he turned up, in company with Brother Brooks, in the home of a man named O. P. Hunt, one of the town's most respected citizens, who seems to have been a Casper Milquetoast-type man. Hunt's wife, a strong-willed woman with a jutting jaw, and his pretty and pliable seventeen-year-old daughter, Maude, were two of the holy man's most devout disciples. Hunt himself, who could take Joshua's shenanigans or leave them alone, was out of town when the prophet moved in. When the word got around that Joshua was holed up in the Hunt home, the curious began coming around the place. But Joshua quickly stopped that. He put up a sign on the gate:

NO ADMITTANCE
EXCEPT ON GOD'S BUSINESS

One night, while Hunt was still away, there was a huge bonfire in the man's back yard. The prophet wasn't burning anything except most of Hunt's household furnishings—the devil's goods, as he called it. There he stood, in the reflection of the bonfire, with pretty Maude Hunt holding his right hand, and her mother holding his left, and Brother Brooks standing behind him, and his bronze chest protector getting singed by the heat. "Be gone, vile things!" he roared at the crackling furnishings, his eyes lifted to heaven. "Be *gone!*"

After the fire died out the Hunt home came alive with a great revival meeting. Dispensing with caution, the revivalists put on all the lights in the house and didn't bother to pull down the shades and screamed and yelled as they cavorted around stark naked.

When Hunt, the nominal master of the manse, stepped off the train at the Corvallis railroad station from wherever he had been, at least twenty people stopped him before he got home to fill him in on what had taken place during his absence.

If poor Hunt had any idea of calling the cops and having the two bums thrown out, his wife quickly dislodged such a notion from his head. "My dear," said Hunt's wife, as he surveyed the shambles, "the most *wonderful* thing happened while you were gone."

"What?" asked Hunt.

"Our darling Maude is going to be the bride of the prophet!"

If Hunt was on the verge of uttering a protest, however feeble, his wife stuffed the words right back into his throat. The prophet and Brother Brooks were ensconced in the master bedroom and Hunt had to sleep on a couch downstairs. He succeeded in asserting himself only to the extent of removing the No Admittance sign from the front gate.

Hunt, very unhappy in his home but incapable of doing anything about it, started spending some time in saloons. The story of the prophet having literally taken over Hunt's home was, of course, all over town and the saloonkeeper who had the vague feeling that he could recognize the prophet if only he could get a look at him kept pressing Hunt for details about the holy man.

One night Hunt told the saloonkeeper that he had overheard Brooks addressing the prophet by the name of Franz. The saloonkeeper thought for a moment. "Now I know!" he said. "That bum's nobody else but Franz Creffield. Why, don't you remember, we run him outa town two years ago!"

Franz Edmund Creffield had been a mild-looking, clean-shaven little German-American who first appeared in Corvallis beating the drum for the Salvation Army. He had lent a rich alto to the hymn singing as he paraded through the streets.

Nobody, the Salvation Army included, had known anything about the past of little Franz Edmund Creffield. He had just appeared in the Portland headquarters of the Army one day and, saying that he could sing and beat a drum, was signed up as a soldier in the war against sin in general and drink in particular.

On a notable occasion two years before Franz Edmund Creffield went into hiding behind his whiskers and his long beard and came down out of the hills as the Prophet Joshua, he had overextended himself in his drive for righteousness. One night, on his own time, he had called at the home of a Corvallis matron whose husband was out at a lodge meeting. Creffield had heard that the matron not only drank cocktails but smoked cigarettes in private. In his zeal to reform the lady, Creffield seems to have removed his uniform and was not able to get it back on before the husband came home unexpectedly.

The husband gave little Creffield a terrible beating and the story of the whole sordid affair got all around town. When the news reached the ears of Creffield's superior officer in the Army, Creffield was cashiered out of the Christian service. It seemed that even before his downfall in Corvallis, he had been under suspicion of having short-circuited some of the collection money dropped into the tambourines.

Such, then, was the background of the man now calling himself the prophet who, with Brother Brooks, had moved into the home of O. P. Hunt. The saloon-keeper was quick to disseminate the news. On New Year's Eve several robust gentlemen, in the saloon and filled with the spirit of brotherly love, began feeling sorry for O. P. Hunt. That was how the gentlemen came to make a resolution at the stroke of midnight—a resolution to get the prophet and Brother Brooks to hell out of town.

Three nights later a little band of citizens popped up at the Hunt home and invited the prophet and his collection-taker outside. The holy men were escorted to a quiet wooded spot on the edge of town. There they were informally introduced to some other citizens who had meantime been heating up a big pot of tar. The two were stripped, tarred and feathered. Then they ran screaming into the woods.

That was the last that Corvallis was ever to see of Brother Brooks, whoever he was and wherever he had come from. But not so with the Prophet Joshua.

Hunt, no doubt feeling that his domicile was now comparatively secure, went away on another trip somewhere. The minute his train pulled out Mrs. Hunt and Maude lit out for the woods from whence Joshua had originally appeared. They found him living in a cave. They sneaked him back into the Hunt home. They removed the tar from him and cut off his magnificent beard because the tar had ruined it. Then they gave him a bath and bought him a suit of store clothes. Presently the prophet and Maude Hunt were to be seen walking arm and arm around town, like any other happily

engaged couple. Creffield had arisen, phoenixlike, from his own ashes and the citizenry was too startled to do anything about it.

One day the happy couple went down to the railroad station and boarded a northbound train. When they returned a few days later they announced that they had gone to Portland and been married by a justice of the peace.

The bride, though visibly enamored of the groom, liked to sleep on a mattress rather than on a bed of pine needles. But the groom was unable to support her in the manner to which she had been accustomed. He refused to stoop to ordinary employment.

It was the prophet's mother-in-law who resolved the problem. She thought it would be a wonderful idea to have the newlyweds living right in the Hunt home. So they moved in.

When Hunt, the Milquetoast, returned to town he was met at the railroad station by a group of friends who couldn't wait to give him the news. But Hunt didn't react the way his informants hoped he would. He just sighed, shrugged, and said, "I guess everything will turn out for the best. My wife and daughter must know what they are doing."

"But ain't you goin' to do nothin'?" asked one man.

"All I want," said Hunt, "is peace."

If the prophet availed himself of the personal possessions of his father-in-law, there was one thing of Hunt's that he didn't use and that was a razor. Franz Edmund Creffield began a slow retreat behind a new crop of facial spinach.

Came spring, with the sap beginning to flow, and the prophet grew restless. One day he took a trip to Portland for the purpose, he told his wife and mother-in-law, of laying the groundwork for a new band of followers. Whether the prophet spoke the truth was to remain a debatable point for he was in bed with a married woman when the lady's husband came home. Discovering the prophet in his rightful place, the husband made a contribution to the gallery of useless questions. "What," he inquired, "is going *on* here?"

Instead of beating the devil out of Joshua, the husband ran out of the house yelling for a cop. By the time a cop arrived Joshua had dressed and gone. The prophet's visitation to the Portland bed chamber made the front page of the Portland *Oregonian* and received official recognition. Joshua was indicted on a morals charge.

But the prophet had vanished. Then, a short time later, back in Corvallis, a young son of the Hunts, hunting for worms to go fishing, crawled under the house to find some. Instead he found the prophet, wrapped in an old quilt, lying in a cave of his own digging. The kid shot out from under the house screaming. A few minutes later Joshua was intercepted running down a street covered only by a quilt.

O. P. Hunt, the timid soul, made a statement to the press. "My wife and I," he said, "have decided to ask our daughter Maude to seek a divorce from Mr. Creffield."

The Prophet Joshua, abandoned by his wife, his in-laws and his followers, drew two years in jail for the statutory offense in Portland. He reaped an abundant harvest of souls in the state pen in Salem. As the result of his good works, he was sprung in December of 1905 after serving little more than half his term. His wife had meantime divorced him.

Joshua, looking around for an opening, went down to Los Angeles, which even in those days was a magnet for assorted nuts, bolts and wheels. For some reason, though, he never got off the ground in the City of the Angels.

The prophet still had a yen for his ex-wife. He moved north to San Francisco and there began a correspondence with some of his ex-parishioners in Corvallis. Thus he learned that Maude Hunt was living in Seattle with relatives.

Joshua wrote to Maude. The young lady, who had found the prophet endowed with certain qualities that she could not forget, answered right back, saying she still loved him. What, then, asked the prophet, would prevent them from getting remarried? "Nothing," said Maude. "Come right up."

That was in March 1906. The city by the Golden Gate had, Joshua decided, treated him shabbily. For one thing, the cops had been inclined to draw a bead on him when, seeing something tasty standing on a street corner, he had approached with a proposition. "May the curses of heaven fall upon all of you!" Joshua roared to a reporter on the San Francisco *Chronicle* before taking off for Seattle. "May the wrath of the Almighty visit your wicked metropolis and destroy it!"

Arriving in Seattle, Joshua and Maude Hunt had a joyous reunion. Then they rushed off to a minister and got remarried. The bride's parents, getting second-hand news of the wedding, packed for Seattle. Hunt seemed pretty mad when he left Corvallis but by the time he reached Seattle his wife had not only talked him out of being mad at Joshua but talked him into accepting the prophet all over again.

Poor Hunt walked right into a bear trap in Seattle. His wife and his daughter insisted that he sit down in a hotel room and listen to a great idea that his son-in-law had. What the prophet had in mind was establishing a new Garden of Eden.

"The world is all wrong," he told his father-in-law, "and I'm going to make it over."

The prophet walked up and down the hotel room, roaring and gesticulating about what was wrong with the world while Hunt just sat there looking at him, utterly fascinated at the ambitiousness of the project. Hunt couldn't have moved because his wife and his daughter were standing alongside of his chair with their hands on his shoulders.

The prophet went on to inform Hunt that he had found the very spot to establish the new Garden of Eden—a stretch of wilderness facing the Pacific Ocean near the town of Waldport, southwest of Corvallis.

"Don't you think it's a *wonderful* idea, Father?" asked Maude.

"I guess so," said Hunt.

"It *is* a wonderful idea," Mrs. Hunt informed her husband. "And you're going to help Joshua."

"How?" Hunt timidly inquired.

"You're going to buy the land."

"I *am?*"

"Yes, you are! Now give Joshua a check for the money to buy the land with."

"How much?" asked Hunt.

"Two thousand dollars."

Joshua and his twice-wed wife and a little hard core of followers went to the Seattle railroad station on the morning of April 17, to get a train to take them toward the Garden of Eden. The prophet borrowed a box from a bootblack, mounted it, and made a little speech to a group that was seeing him off. Still rankled by the treatment accorded him by the hateful cops of San Francisco, he ended his search with a dire prediction.

"A curse on San Francisco," he shouted. "A curse on that modern Sodom and Gomorrah! May it tumble into hell!"

The prophet and the faithful were on a train bound for the Garden of Eden, when San Francisco was visited by the great earthquake.

By the time Joshua arrived in Waldport, the nearest railroad point to the Garden of Eden, his renown had preceded him. Curious knots of people clustered about him and told him that his curse on San Francisco had come true: the city was in ruins. The prophet didn't speak and he couldn't have looked less surprised.

Joshua's stretch of wilderness on the shore of the Pacific came alive with the sounds of hammering and the screams, yells and shouts of religious fervor. The faithful threw up crude shacks to live in; Joshua and his two-time wife occupied a big tent.

Word of Joshua's prediction of the San Francisco 'quake convinced all the nuts in the Northwest that the man had something. For weeks the faithful of all ages, including a few men, burned or sold their worldly possessions and straggled into the Garden of Eden from all parts of the Pacific Coast. Eventually there were several score of women dwelling in tents and lean-tos in the Promised Land. Every new arrival was greeted by the same roar from the throat of the prophet—"Vile clothes, be gone!" Joshua would burn the clothes and supply the convert with a sackcloth garment that opened at the front. The prophet turned the older feminine converts over to the male parishioners, who rolled with them during services. Joshua personally rolled with the younger revivalists.

One of Joshua's new parishioners, freshly arrived from Corvallis, was a young lady of seventeen by the name of Esther Mitchell. Miss Mitchell was, from all available accounts, put together along the lines of Marilyn Monroe. She was quick to divest herself of her vile clothes, but in no particular haste to put on the sackcloth.

Soon word began to seep out of the Garden of Eden that Esther Mitchell had replaced the prophet's wife as the Number One Disciple. The scuttlebutt was that although Joshua had done his level best to make the former Maude Hunt bring forth a male child she had failed. And so now, while Maude was out in another part of the reservation, chopping down trees to make room for the new converts, Joshua and Esther were collaborating in the hope of achieving his objective.

This scandalous intelligence about the prophet and Esther Mitchell reached the large ears of George Mitchell, the young lady's hulking, ham-fisted brother. Mitchell began going around Corvallis telling people he had a damned good mind to knock off the prophet.

The let's-you-and-him-fight element of the town, comprising for the most part males who had reason to wish Joshua no good, goaded Mitchell on. And so one day, with a shooting iron in his pants pocket and a nervous trigger finger, Mitchell left for the Garden of Eden.

Mitchell found his sister in the Garden but not the prophet. Joshua and his wife had gone up to Portland to hustle up more converts. So Mitchell, grabbing his sister and plunking her off at Corvallis, kept right on going.

Spotting Joshua on the streets of Portland was made comparatively simple because the prophet was now in full beard again and when the sun was shining on the mattress it could be spotted a block away.

The sun was shining brightly on the seventh day of May in the year of 1906. Mitchell saw the prophet standing on the sidewalk, looking into a store window. He didn't do anything except walk up behind him, draw his shooting iron and send a slug through Joshua's brain.

The prophet's wife, who had been in a store, rushed out at the sound of the shot. There lay the prophet on the sidewalk as dead as he would ever be. And there stood Mitchell, holding his shooting iron, laughing so hard the tears were actually streaming down his face.

A cop approached and inquired, as if he had to, as to the nature of the trouble. "I just killed him," said Mitchell, handing his gun to the cop, the better to be able to hold his sides as he continued to laugh. "I just *killed* him."

"Don't *believe* him, officer," screamed the prophet's wife.

"Whadda ya mean?" asked the cop.

"He didn't kill Joshua."

"But he looks dead," said the cop.

"Joshua can't die," said his wife. "He will rise again on the third day."

The trial of George Mitchell for the murder of Franz Edmund Creffield was a two-ring circus—the defendant's sympathizers in one ring, the prophet's followers in the other. As the testimony developed, it seemed to some observers that the prophet, rather than Mitchell, was on trial. The defense introduced male witnesses who testified that their wives, sisters and mothers had fallen in lust with the prophet and that their homes had been in jeopardy ever since the day, more than three years before, when Creffield had walked down the main street of Corvallis, sounding the knell of the Judgment Day.

Creffield was, for the very first time, publicly revealed in his true light. The man had been an authentic fraud. He had used his Holy Rollers racket to make a living and to make the dolls. But one thing had to be said for him: He had a capacity for women that made him a man in a million.

George Mitchell himself testified that the prophet had seduced his sister. Esther Mitchell sat there, among the spectators, biting her lip and taking it all in. During most of the trial sessions, she sat alongside of the prophet's widow. The prophet's wife and his mistress had, for a reason not yet obvious, become fast friends. Jealousy did not seem to be part of their natures. The prophet, with his bountiful ability, had apparently possessed enough love to spread around.

The city of Portland would have been startled if George Mitchell had been found guilty. But it wasn't startled. Mitchell was acquitted on the grounds that his removal of the prophet had been in the nature of a state-wide improvement.

Mitchell was in the Portland railroad station, waiting for a train back to Corvallis, and taking bows from the peasants who crowded around him, when his sister Esther and the prophet's widow materialized out of the gathering. Esther didn't do anything to her brother that her brother hadn't done to the prophet. She just reached into a handbag for a little revolver and shot her brother right through the head. "Good for *you*, Dearie," the prophet's wife said to the prophet's mistress as she leaned down, the better to get a good look at Mitchell.

"Well, you can be sure *he* won't rise again."

It turned out that the prophet's mistress and the prophet's wife had collaborated on the murder of the prophet's murderer. Each girl, feeling that justice had miscarried when Mitchell was acquitted, had been so enthusiastic about the opportunity of dispatching Mitchell that they had consulted Joshua himself as to who should have the privilege.

Joshua had, from another dimension, selected Esther. Then the widow had purchased a little revolver, given it to Esther, and accompanied Esther to the railroad station.

Esther was acquitted of the murder on the grounds that she had been of unsound mind when she killed her brother, and committed to the Washington State Asylum. The prophet's wife, the former Maude Hunt, never did reach a courtroom. Before her trial for murder, she got hold of some strychnine in jail and poisoned herself.

A few years later, Esther Mitchell was released from the asylum, declared quite sane. But she, like so many other women, still had that old feeling for Joshua. She took up residence near the Garden of Eden, by then reclaimed by the wilderness, the habitat of the Prophet Joshua's broken dreams. There, not long afterward, she died, perhaps to take off to join the prophet and his wife in an everlasting three-cornered design for loving.

The Riddle of the Ragged Stranger

Here's another case of the cops flubbing a murder until the now-celebrated Ben Hecht, then a young nothing-scared news hawk, stepped in and put a noose around the killer's neck.

Carl Wanderer, a stubby, balding young man with an egg-shaped head and a faraway look in his china-blue eyes, was that *rara avis* of the First World War—a draftee who was simply nuts about the Army. When in October, 1919, Wanderer was returned to civilian life after service in France with the 17th Machine-Gun Battalion, he was like a cavalry general without a horse to sink his spurs into.

He had risen to a second lieutenancy in the Army as a result of heroism in battle, but he went to work in his father's North Side butcher shop in Chicago, cutting meat and delivering orders. He sorely missed the prestige that had gone with his wartime rank. There was a jarring discord between the whine of a drab housewife—"See that the chops are tender, Carl, and not too fat"—and the respectful "Yes, *s-i-rrr!*" of a buck private getting the lead out.

There was also a girl—an unsophisticated little clinging vine by the name of Ruth Johnson. Prior to his departure for overseas, Wanderer had presented to her a ring featuring a half-carat diamond, shot through with carbon spots; immediately upon his return, he married her, although he demonstrated little enthusiasm for what he was doing.

The couple went to live with the bride's mother, a quiet woman who lived on the second floor of a smoke-colored two-family house in the 4700 block of North Campbell Avenue. The routine of middle-class family life, a far cry from the

action and excitement of the Army, yawned ahead for Carl Wanderer.

Less than two months after the trip up the aisle, Ruth Wanderer, whose dream world was peopled exclusively with children, gleefully informed the war hero that he was going to be a father. The glad announcement not only left Wanderer cold; it depressed him. For one thing, he hadn't planned on being tied down with a kid so soon; for another, he conjured up a life-sized picture of himself pushing a baby-carriage through a park of a dull Sunday afternoon, and he didn't like it at all.

One day, while wiping suet off his hands in the butcher shop, he said to his father, "I feel trapped. I wish I was back in the Army." The old man thought his son was in need of an alienist, as they called psychiatrists in those days.

On Monday night, June 21, 1920—some six weeks before the baby was due—Wanderer and his wife went to a neighborhood movie to see *The Sea Wolf*. When they were walking home after the show, a little after ten o'clock, a neighbor, sitting on a front stoop fanning himself, saw them emerging from the hot, sticky gloom of North Campbell Avenue into the illumination of a street light, then ambling slowly into the gloom again. The neighbor noticed something else, too—some*one* else, rather—a tattered figure of a man who seemed to shuffle rather than walk in the wake of the Wanderers.

A few minutes later, the thoroughfare

came alive with the sounds of shots, screams and yells. The occupant of the ground floor of the house where the Wanderers lived—a man named James Williams—opened the front door of his apartment, flooding the vestibule with light. In the vestibule he saw Ruth Wanderer lying in a heap, moaning, and Carl Wanderer leaning over the prostrate form of a man, beating the man's head against the floor.

"You've killed her!" the war vet was shouting.

Ruth Wanderer, unconscious from bullet wounds, was carried upstairs, where she died in her husband's arms. The man whose head Wanderer had beaten against the floor was taken to Ravenswood Hospital, not far away, and there he lay, fatally shot and his head bashed in but still conscious, with a very strange look in his eyes. He was a young man, bearded, tattered and filthy. He seemed to want to say something, but the words wouldn't come out of his mouth.

Sergeant Michael Grady of the homicide squad, or Fearless Mike, as he was called, was assigned to the case. He picked up two automatics in the vestibule of the house on North Campbell Avenue. Both were .45-caliber Colts. One was stamped U.S. Army.

Ruth Wanderer had been shot twice; the ragged stranger, as he was to become known, three times. Five bullets had gone into the walls of the vestibule. That accounted for ten shots and checked with the number of spent cartridges Grady picked up.

Fearless Mike reached Ravenswood Hospital just in time to get a good look at the derelict before he died.

A doctor said, "He has an unusual expression in his eyes, Sergeant, as if he were mystified about something."

"Yeah," said Fearless Mike, "I been noticin' that."

Grady fired some questions at the fellow—his identity, how he had come to be on North Campbell Avenue that night, and why he had chosen the Wanderers as his stick-up victims. The bum just lay there, trying to speak with his eyes, and then he died.

Wanderer's story of the triple tragedy (one of the bullets had passed right through the unborn baby) was simple enough. As he and his wife had entered the vestibule, someone had jabbed a gun in his back, and said, "Stick 'em up." Ruth Wanderer had screamed. Her husband had seen red. He had drawn his Army Colt, which he always carried with him, and opened fire. The stick-up man had begun to shoot, too, there in the dark vestibule, and when it was all over, Ruth Wanderer and the stick-up man were fatally wounded.

There was employed on the Chicago *Daily News* in 1920 a twenty-six-year-old reporter named Ben Hecht—later to become rich and respectable as an author, playwright and motion-picture producer —who was one of the leading professors in Chicago's nothing-sacred school of journalism.

Hecht had a jaundiced eye for heroes. In studying the morning papers, he became intrigued by Carl Wanderer's face, especially the faraway look in the eyes, and some of the dramatic poses the fellow had struck for the photographers. He was equally fascinated by the veteran's speech and behavior, as recorded by fellow scribes—speech such as, "My honey has left me forever and ever," and Wanderer's reported use of the words of a current song hit, "Old pal, why don't you answer me?" while kneeling alongside the body of his wife.

Hecht went out to have a talk with

Wanderer. Chicago reporters in those days were considered sissies if they knocked on the door or rang the bell before entering a house, so Hecht didn't ring, but just tried the doors that led to the apartment of the dead girl's mother and found himself inside without the slightest trouble. He didn't see anybody, but he heard somebody in another room —whistling.

The unseen person was whistling the notes that accompanied the line, "Old pal, why don't you answer me?"

The whistler was Carl Wanderer. He was in the kitchen, pressing a pair of pants. He stopped short as he looked up to see Ben Hecht in the doorway. He glowered, then smiled, then looked sad.

Carl was having the time of his life in the glare of public attention. He was, to the astute Hecht, a ham actor who, after years of failure and neglect, had at last got a good part and was milking the role for all he could get out of it.

Hecht offered Wanderer a cigaret. "I don't smoke—or drink," said the hero.

Hecht asked Wanderer about his romance with Ruth Johnson. To hear Wanderer tell it, Ruth had been the lucky one out of about a dozen girls. "They were all nuts about me," said the hero, "but Ruth was the one I preferred."

Hecht gulped, then inquired about the hero's war experiences. He hit pay dirt there. Wanderer laid aside the iron he was pressing his pants with and acted out how he had personally killed several German soldiers.

"Would you like me to show you just what happened last night?" Wanderer asked. Hecht nodded. Wanderer went into what by this time had all the characteristics of a routine designed to be as dramatic as possible.

Now Hecht unfeelingly wanted to know how it was that none of the ten shots that had been fired in the inky-black vestibule had hit the hero. Also, was it customary for a husband to whistle a popular tune twelve hours after his wife had been murdered?

Hecht's needling got under Wanderer's skin. The hero had been standing at the ironing board, a fixed smile on his face, his eyes expressionless, while the reporter let go with the loaded questions. As he caught on to what Hecht was driving at, Wanderer clutched the iron and seemed on the verge of throwing it. Hecht, who had no earthly use for a dent in his head, backed toward the door, smiling and observed, "It wouldn't look very good if the *Daily News* said that you brained one of its reporters with an iron, now would it, Wanderer?"

The hero laid down the iron. Hecht left . . . he had a pip of a yarn.

When Wanderer got his pants pressed, he put them on and appeared before a coroner's jury. The jurors had contracted the hero-worship fever. After listening to the young butcher, they not only decided that he had been justified in murdering John Doe, as the ragged stranger was tagged; they complimented Carl Wanderer on his courage. And so Doe was consigned to Potter's Field.

Sentimental Chicago still couldn't get its fill of the details of the tragedy. Hecht's story of his interview with the hero struck the only sour note in the saccharine symphony. Smart readers saw, between the lines of Hecht's story, a somewhat different Carl Wanderer from the one Chicago had taken to its ample breast.

Among the between-the-lines readers was Fearless Mike Grady. Fearless Mike was a great brooder. He was brooding now, as he contemplated the Wanderer whom Hecht had seen—the man who whistled twelve hours after his wife's murder and had boasted of other girls in what should have been his hour of grief.

Grady began to argue with himself. Wanderer was an incurable ham . . . but did that make him a liar? The case was open and shut. Officially closed. Unquestioned. How could Wanderer's story have been false? The bum—the ragged stranger—had certainly been real enough.

As a matter of routine, the bullets taken from the two bodies had been checked against the two Colts in the vestibule. Nothing there. The bullets that had killed Mrs. Wanderer had been fired from the stick-up man's weapon, which bore the number C2282, and the bullets found in the tattered derelict had come from Wanderer's Army Colt.

Yet Mike Grady brooded. There had been that strange expression in the eyes of the ragged stranger before he had died.

While the hour of Ruth Wanderer's funeral drew near, Mike Grady quietly probed into the past lives of the veteran and his wife. Thus he came upon the remark that Wanderer had made to his father—that he felt trapped and wished he were back in the Army. A strange remark, in the opinion of Mike Grady. Even, possibly, an odd motive for murder.

A smart cop listens to everything, even if it seems to have no bearing on the subject at hand, and Mike Grady was a smart cop. (That was why he eventually rose to become the chief of the homicide squad.) He listened politely while a hatchet-faced neighbor of the Wanderers took the clothespins out of her mouth long enough to disclose that Ruth Wanderer had been a very stingy young woman. She had, in the language of the day, squeezed a coin until the Indian yelled. She had haggled with neighbor-

hood grocers and walked a mile to save carfare. That piece of intelligence seemed quite irrelevant at the time, but Grady mentally tagged it file-but-don't-forget and went on to other things.

At about that time, in the flat on North Campbell Avenue, Carl Wanderer was alone with his mother-in-law. He was hunting for something. He prowled the place, almost like a burglar, opening this drawer, slamming that one shut. His mother-in-law watched him through her bifocals, not knowing what to think.

Finally, the elderly woman asked Carl what he was hunting for. "None of your business!" he snapped. The woman, to whom Wanderer had always been very polite, was shocked. Her son-in-law apologized, explaining that his great loss had frayed his nerves. Somehow, his words didn't ring true. In a little while, when he went out for a walk, the old lady began to go through every drawer in the house, determined to learn what it was that Carl had been hunting for.

After searching for half an hour, she finally came upon two bills—one of $1,000 denomination and one of $500—secreted in some of her daughter's intimate bathroom effects. She stood holding the bills, examining them and hardly believing them to be real, when she became aware that someone was standing behind her. She turned, and there was Carl. He snatched the money out of her hands.

"That's what I was hunting for," he said. "It belongs to me!"

Carl Wanderer took the spotlight at his wife's funeral service. As the undertakers were closing the coffin, Wanderer attempted to climb right in. "I want to go with her!" he shouted. "Bury me with my honey!" At the cemetery, he made a move as if to jump into the grave—but not until, in the opinion of Mike Grady, who was watching him intently, he had assured himself that he was in close proximity to restraining hands.

A couple of days after the funeral, Grady found out from the girl's mother about the fifteen hundred dollars. The money, she had learned, had been drawn by Ruth Wanderer, two days before her death, from her account at the Lake View State Bank. It had represented almost the entire savings of the Wanderers, which Ruth had insisted upon depositing in her own name because she was so good at taking care of money. There was now less than one hundred dollars left in the bank.

Wanderer came in while the detective was talking to the old lady. He shot a look at his mother-in-law that was loaded with anything but best wishes. Grady asked why his wife had drawn the money from the bank. "We were going to put it down on a house," was the answer. Grady didn't pursue the point. He figured Wanderer was lying, but he didn't want to let him know.

The very fact that Ruth Wanderer had made the withdrawal when she had was significant to Grady. Had she left the money in the bank twelve days longer, it would have earned more than twenty dollars in semiannual interest, which was payable July 1. Even allowing for the fact that pregnant women do unpredictable things, Grady knew that a person who thought as much of a dollar as Ruth Wanderer had would never *voluntarily* have drawn interest-bearing money out of the bank at that time.

Mike Grady awoke in the middle of the night. Why hadn't he checked with the Colt arms people on that second automatic that had been found in the vestibule—Number C2282? And so next morning Mike Grady got off a letter to the Colt people in Hartford, Connecticut.

The days passed and Grady champed at the bit while waiting for a reply. Carl Wanderer had returned to his father's butcher shop where, at the request of customers, he would put down the implements of his trade and act out the tragedy of the vestibule.

And then, a couple of weeks after he had written to Hartford, Grady got his reply. C2282 had been shipped from the factory in Hartford in 1913—seven years previously—to Von Lengerke & Antoine, a prominent sporting-goods store in Chicago's Loop. Grady headed for Von Lengerke & Antoine's like an arrow for a target. The records of the store showed that a man named Hoffman had bought C2282 in 1913.

Grady spent a week locating Hoffman, who had moved several times in seven years. When he did find the man, Hoffman said he had sold the gun a couple of years previously. To whom? Why, to a neighbor. And what was the neigbor's name? Wanderer. Fred Wanderer. . . . Any relation to—?

Yes, Fred Wanderer was a cousin of Carl Wanderer. And Grady soon found that he was a nice, co-operative fellow, too. Now, about this gun, this C2282. When had it left Fred's possession, and to whom had he given it?

Cousin Carl had stopped around at Fred's house one evening and asked to borrow the gun. Fred hadn't asked Carl what he wanted the gun for. He had just given it to the butcher. And when had Cousin Carl stopped by and got the gun? Why, on the evening of June 21. That was the date of the stick-up shooting.

Mike Grady broke into a cold sweat, right in the middle of July weather in Chicago, as he realized that he had come within a whisper of passing up C2282.

Grady was now able to interpret that strange expression that had been in the ragged stranger's eyes. It had been the overwhelming bewilderment of a man who had been fatally betrayed. The stranger had lain there, hearing himself accused of murder, unable to talk and tell why he *couldn't* have been a murderer.

Grady was able to put together most of the story now, but not all of it. Only one man alive knew of the details, so detectives went around to North Campbell Avenue and told him they would like him to answer some questions at the police station.

Wanderer was tough. It took Mike Grady and half a dozen other cops, working in relays all night, to break the butcher down. And then he spilled this story:

While cutting meat, Carl Wanderer had reflected on a fate that he felt had been unkind to him. All his wife thought about was having a big family and saving pennies; all he thought about was the excitement and prestige that he had known in the Army. The murder of his wife seemed to be the only means of escape to freedom and adventure from the suffocating routine of life with a stingy woman and a raft of bawling brats.

Improvising as he went along, Wanderer got his wife to take the money out of the bank on the pretext that he had found a dream house at a big bargain. They had one hell of an argument about drawing the money before the semiannual interest date.

Ruth Wanderer took charge of the money after she brought it home. He wasn't worried about that; he could get it later, after the murder. He couldn't foretell that it would be so hard to find, and that his mother-in-law would get to it first, causing a scene that would prompt her to tell Mike Grady about it.

There had been a series of postwar stick-ups in Chicago. That was what decided him to utilize a nameless bum in his murder plot, taking the bum's life in the bargain.

A few days before the murders, Wanderer began to hang around Madison and Halsted streets—an intersection peopled by more than a normal share of derelicts. It wasn't until the fatal day of June 21 that he came across just the fellow he was looking for—a pliable, hungry, beaten young tramp who didn't seem very smart.

Wanderer asked the bum if he wanted a job. Sure, said the bum. Wanderer gave him a dollar on account. "I want you to meet me tonight," said Wanderer, "and I'll give you the details. Can you start work tomorrow?" The bum nodded. It was arranged that he was to wait at a certain point on North Campbell Avenue, in the 4700 block, that night at ten. "You'll see me walking home from the movies with my wife," said Wanderer. "Follow me to my house and after my wife goes upstairs I'll talk to you about the job."

Carl Wanderer left the bum and went to Cousin Fred's and borrowed C2282—the gun that he was to say the hold-up man used. That night, when he was on the way home from the movies with his wife, he saw the bum and gave him a sign of recognition.

When they got to the vestibule, he said to her, "Stand here, honey. I have a surprise for you." He motioned to the bum to come into the vestibule. Then he brought out both guns and let go with a surprise not only for his wife but for the ragged stranger.

When Wanderer went on trial for the murder of his wife, he repudiated his confession, and an impressionable jury, figuring he was nuts or something, let him off with twenty-five years in Joliet.

The aggressive prosecutor, Assistant State's Attorney James C. O'Brien—better known as Ropes because he had sent so many murderers to the gallows—felt deeply frustrated.

Ropes thereupon prepared another noose. He brought Wanderer back from Joliet, where he had been happily engaged in quarry work between re-enactments of his crime for his admiring coworkers, and put him on trial again, this time for the murder of the ragged stranger. Ropes wrapped up a tight case and Wanderer got the gallows.

A sentimental saloonkeeper, hearing that Carl Wanderer was a teetotaler, said, "Wouldn't you know it?" . . . and then put up the dough for a slab and a cemetery plot for the derelict. The slab read simply:

HERE LIES
THE RAGGED STRANGER

Before he went to the gallows, Wanderer admitted his guilt all over again. A reporter said to him, "Wanderer, if you wanted to get away from your wife so much and were so anxious to get back into the Army, why didn't you ask her for a divorce?"

Wanderer ran a freckled hand over his balding head and a look of staggering surprise suffused his face. "Good God," he said, "it never occurred to me to ask her." And then he added, "Anyway, I don't believe in divorce."

The Wife Who Got Boiled

Chicago's sausage king might have wound up all right in the end had it not been for his uncontrollable habit of straying from the connubial couch. And even that wouldn't have cooked his goose had he not taken it into his thick head to dispose of his wife by locking her in a sausage vat, alive, and turning up the steam.

The A. L. Luetgert Sausage Works—a sprawling, five-story brick-and-stone monstrosity—dominated a thickly settled German neighborhood on Chicago's North Side in the year 1897. Located at North Hermitage and Diversey Avenues, the factory employed some hundred men and women who lived in the immediate vicinity. Luetgert sausage—a tasty pork product put out in both link and loose form—was sold in Chicago and in various other cities of the Middle West. When business was brisk at the sausage works, the neighborhood enjoyed prosperity; when business was bad, despair mixed with the perpetual mists from the near-by Chicago River and permeated the ugly frame dwellings and the numerous taverns for many blocks around.

The A. L. Luetgert Sausage Works was a one-man proposition, and that man was Adolph Louis Luetgert himself. A German of fifty-three who had immigrated to Chicago as a boy, he was put together on Falstaffian lines. He stood 6-feet-1 and weighed around 275. He had a face of suet, puffy pig eyes and a large, untidy mustache that was a perfect host for beer foam. He wore his light-brown hair in pompadour fashion.

Mr. Luetgert was both respected and feared in the Hermitage-Diversey district. He personally did all the hiring and firing at the sausage works—and he combined the instincts of a dictator with an avid appetite for women.

Luetgert had a spouse of his own, a frail listless little woman of about one-third his weight. Her name was Louisa, and she was his second wife. She was pretty, but did little about it, being addicted to a brown flannel wrapper, cloth house slippers, blue cotton stockings and hair curlers. The effect could hardly fascinate a man of Luetgert's interests.

Therefore, when the news got around in January of 1897, that little Louisa Luetgert had a secret lover, the neighborhood was agog. The news came from a cop attached to the Sheffield Avenue station. He blabbed to a North Hermitage Avenue bartender that Mr. Luetgert had been in to see Captain Herman Schuettler, in charge of the precinct, about what a man could do to make his wife stop seeing another man. Captain Schuettler—who, like Luetgert, was a giant—had told the sausage-maker there was nothing the police could do about a situation like that. And then the captain, who knew everything that went on in his bailiwick had told Luetgert, in effect, that he was getting a dose of his own medicine.

Luetgert seemed crushed. He no longer played the benevolent neighborhood tyrant in the bars at night, roaring at the latest 1897 version about the farmer's daughter and the traveling salesman and quaffing seidels of lager till his eyes resembled pink marbles. He began to brood alone. His home, situated across an alley

283

from the sausage works, was a big, comfortable dwelling that smelled of good cooking. Luetgert left it. He put a cot in his office in the factory and slept there. He ate in taverns. He went home only for short periods late in the day to see that four Great Danes which he kept were properly fed. Eventually, in February, he moved the Great Danes into the sausage works with him. They slept in his office and, as one employee remarked, that made five dogs that bedded down in the office at night.

Mr. Luetgert, normally aloof with male employees, began to grow chummy with the night watchman—one Frank Bialk, a weird-looking character with a shiny bald head and a cadaverous face. He confided to Bialk what the entire neighborhood was now talking about— that his wife had a lover.

"Who is it?" asked Bialk.

"That's the trouble," said Luetgert. "I don't know."

"Well, how can you be sure there is such a man, Mr. Luetgert?"

"I found letters he wrote to her." Luetgert thrust a hand, which resembled a small ham in size and color, into his capacious coat pocket. The man seemed always to be hungry, and it was his habit to carry a string of the factory's cooked sausages on his person. He unstuck a grease-stained letter from some of his product and showed it to Bialk, biting into a sausage as he did so, and was gratified when Bialk lifted his eyebrows at the lurid words that he read.

Spring came early to Chicago that year, and with it a change in Luetgert's manner. It had been Bialk's habit to rap at the boss's office when starting his rounds, whereupon Luetgert would open the door and invite him in for a talk. Now Luetgert no longer answered when Bialk

knocked, although the watchman knew the boss was there.

The reason for his employer's change of attitude became visible to Bialk when, at dusk one evening, the watchman saw Luetgert leading a large woman with a built-in bustle through the gloom of the sausage works. Mr. Luetgert was forgetting his great sorrow. The lady appeared in the sausage works almost every night; sometimes she was still in the office when Bialk completed his twelve-hour shift at six o'clock in the morning. Frequently, during the late hours of the evening, Luetgert would summon Bialk, hand him a two-quart blue-enamel beer can and dispatch him to a saloon to get it filled— an operation that was known in that era as rushing the growler.

Bialk fell to speculating about the crowded conditions that must have prevailed in Luetgert's office. The place was hardly big enough to swing a cat in, yet it was accommodating four Great Danes, Mr. Luetgert and the lady.

Once Bialk asked Luetgert, "Is the lady fond of the dogs?"

Luetgert looked blank. "The lady?" he repeated. "*What* lady?"

Toward the end of April, the sausage works had visitors who boded no good. They appeared early one morning—a couple of flinty-faced gentlemen in striped trousers and braided cutaways—and sniffed around until noon, asking questions of the employees and making jottings in little black books, then took ten minutes for lunch and resumed until late afternoon, winding up in Luetgert's office, where loud words ensued. Presently the news seeped through the factory that Luetgert was in financial trouble and that a bank that held a big mortgage on the factory was threatening foreclosure.

On Friday, April 30, Luetgert summoned to him a veteran employee named

Oderofsky, better known as Smokehouse Frank, and led the way to the vat room in the basement. This chamber contained four wooden vats, each 8 feet long, 4 feet wide and deep, with lids that clamped on. Meat mixtures were brought to a boil in those vats with piped steam.

The boss pointed to some burlap bags containing several hundred pounds of a rough gray substance in chunk form. He instructed Smokehouse Frank to take the stuff and break it up into small pieces and put the pieces in a certain vat. "Wear gloves when you touch this stuff," he cautioned, "or it'll burn the hell out of your hands."

"What is it, Mr. Luetgert?"

"Never mind. Just break it up and call me when you got all of it in the vat."

Smokehouse Frank was one of the best sausage smokers in all Chicago, but he was never seen without a hat—a circumstance that may or may not have been due to the fact that his head came to a point at the top. Certainly he was far from bright, and he forgot to wear gloves and, just as Mr. Luetgert had said, the stuff he broke up and put into the vat burned the hell out of his hands.

Smokehouse Frank stood to one side, trying to shake off the pain, while Luetgert turned a valve that began to fill the vat with water. The resultant chemical reaction intrigued Smokehouse Frank. "*Smoke,* Mr. Luetgert," he wondered, "and on water, too!" Luetgert did not answer.

The following morning—Saturday, May 1—the bank sprang a *coup d'etat.* Somebody from the sheriff's office came around at the bank's behest and served Luetgert with a paper saying that the sheriff was, as of one minute past midnight Monday, May 3, taking over the sausage works and everything in it. At noon on Saturday, the factory workers were paid off. Luetgert, strangely enough, did not seem downcast.

That evening at six, when Bialk, the night watchman, checked in, he found Luetgert, in his shirt sleeves, working with the intensity of a beaver. Luetgert was firing up the furnace that supplied steam to the vats—a circumstance that was deeply puzzling to Bialk since there was no meat in the vats.

At ten that night, Luetgert called Bialk and sent him out for a growler of beer. "No hurry," he said, smiling. "Have a drink yourself while you're out —on me."

Bialk returned at half past ten. He found his employer perspiring and giving other evidence, such as fast breathing, of strenuous physical activity in his absence. Bialk handed Luetgert the growler of beer and the sausage manufacturer downed it in one series of gargantuan gulps. The beer seemed to have as little effect on him as a drop of water on top of a red-hot stove. He wiped the foam off his mustache with the back of his hand and sent Bialk for more beer. "Have another drink on me," he said. "Don't hurry back."

The watchman returned shortly after eleven o'clock. He found Luetgert just bolting down the lid of one of the vats. The manufacturer thereupon drew up a chair alongside the vat, accepted Bialk's can of beer and downed a pint or two. He put the can on the floor, got out a German-language newspaper and settled himself to read under the illumination of the overhead gas jet.

"What are you cooking, Mr. Luetgert?" asked the watchman.

"Cooking?" repeated Luetgert. "What do you mean, Bialk?"

The watchman nodded toward the vat. "Oh, *that,*" said Luetgert. "An experiment."

When Bialk went off at six A.M., the sausage magnate was still sitting there. Returning twelve hours later, the watchman found Luetgert busy removing ashes from the furnace. The vat in which the experiment had been made was open now, and a running hose was flushing it out. Luetgert made several trips outside with the ashes. In the middle of the evening, he said to Bialk, "Well, I have to get out of here before midnight."

"Where are you and the dogs going?" asked Bialk.

"Home, I guess. I only hope I don't find my wife's lover there."

Late Monday morning, Luetgert walked into the home of his wife's sister, Mrs. Wilhelmina Mueller, of Cleveland Avenue. "Is Louisa here?" he wanted to know. Mrs. Mueller, alarmed, demanded to know when Luetgert had last seen her. "Last night," he said. "We went to sleep together and this morning she was gone."

In the afternoon, Luetgert called at the Sheffield Avenue police station and reported his wife's disappearance to Captain Schuettler.

"She couldn't stand failure," said Luetgert.

"What do you mean by that?" asked Schuettler.

"Louisa is a proud woman. She thought people would make fun of her because I failed in my business."

"What do you want me to do?" asked Schuettler.

"Find her."

Captain Schuettler figured that Louisa Luetgert had finally had so much of the sausage executive that she had gone to live with relatives. Then, four days later, on Friday, May 7, there appeared in the Sheffield Avenue station a gentleman from less sophisticated precincts of Cook County. He was Diedrich Bickenese, a brother of Mrs. Luetgert, who operated a dairy farm on the outskirts of the city. He told the captain that his sister had been due to visit him the previous Monday, for a stay of at least two weeks, and that she had not shown up or communicated with him. "I can't get any satisfaction out of Adolph," said Bickenese.

The portly captain lumbered into the defunct sausage works and began a tour of inspection. When he reached the cellar room where the vats were, he detected an acrid, unpleasant odor. It seemed to emanate from one particular vat. The big cop wondered if it was due to the poor quality of the Luetgert pork product in recent months—a contributing factor to the failure of the business.

Schuettler came to the furnace room. On the floor in front of the furnace he saw about a score of burned matches. He leaned down and pocketed them, puffing slightly from the exertion. Somebody inexperienced in starting fires had started one in that furnace. Schuettler asked himself why.

In Luetgert's office, the cop riffled through a pay-roll book and jotted down some names and addresses. Then he scrutinized the place. Being a man of Teutonic thoroughness, he shifted the furniture from the walls to see what was behind it. From the floor between Luetgert's cot and the wall, he picked up a woman's change purse. It contained a few coins and a receipted grocery bill. The bill bore a woman's name and address.

That was how Schuettler came across the lady with the built-in bustle. She was a widow, and no lady. She admitted that she had recently spent her nights with Luetgert and the four Great Danes.

"When were you in Luetgert's office last?" Schuettler asked.

"Last Friday night."

"Were you usually there Saturday and Sunday nights?"

"Yes."

"Well, why weren't you there last Saturday night or last Sunday night?"

"Adolph said he would be busy."

"Busy doing what?"

"He didn't say, Captain."

Schuettler came upon Smokehouse Frank behind a pinochle hand in a Diversey Street saloon. "What are those marks on your hands?" Schuettler wanted to know.

"Burns," said Smokehouse Frank.

"Burns from what?"

"From some stuff I put in a vat last week."

"What kind of stuff?"

The other shrugged. "Something new. Something Mr. Luetgert was experimenting with." Smokehouse Frank described the stuff.

Schuettler made a guess and ordered a canvass of potash dealers and their recent customers. Potash was a poisonous corrosive that so far as he knew, should have had no part in the preparation of foodstuffs or the cleaning of utensils in a sausage factory.

While awaiting reports, he had an enlightening talk with Bialk, the night watchman.

That evening Schuettler puffed into the office of State's Attorney Charles S. Deneen, a conscientious public servant. "It's murder, Mr. Deneen," he was presently saying. "Mrs. Luetgert was last seen by neighbors about ten o'clock Saturday night. That's just the hour when Luetgert sent the night watchman out for beer and told him not to hurry back."

Deneen was pacing the floor, fingering the gray stubble on his chin. "About the potash," he said. "You say Luetgert bought almost four hundred pounds of it last week and that he had no possible legitimate use for potash?"

"That's right."

"And you think that this complaint Luetgert made to you in January—that his wife had another man—and the letter he showed to the night watchman . . . you think all that was part of a premeditated plan to account for his wife's subsequent disappearance?"

"Uh-huh. He wrote that letter himself."

"Captain," asked the State's Attorney, "just what do you think went on in the cellar of that sausage factory last Saturday night?"

"I think he boiled his wife to a pulp in one of them meat vats and then burned the bones in the furnace. That's what I think."

Deneen stopped his pacing and took off his rimless glasses and began to polish them. "I think so, too," he said. "But we've got to prove it."

On Sunday morning, Adolph Luetgert lumbered into the Sheffield Avenue station. Schuettler glowered at him.

"Captain," said Luetgert, "my wife has been gone a week now. I want a warrant sworn out."

"A warrant? What kind of a warrant?"

"For her arrest."

"Arrest! For what!"

"Desertion."

Schuettler couldn't talk right away. When he was able, he said, "Look, Luetgert, I don't blame your wife for deserting you, from the way you were carrying on with that widow."

"What widow?"

Schuettler mentioned the woman's name. "Be careful of your talk, Captain Schuettler!" Luetgert protested indignantly. "That's a serious thing you are saying about me and that widow woman. Why, I hardly know her."

Luetgert pulled a sausage from his pocket and munched it as he waddled off in outraged innocence.

Schuettler's problem now was to conduct an intensive investigation into Mrs. Luetgert's disappearance right under the nose of her husband without his being any the wiser. That night certain of the factory windows that faced the side of Luetgert's house across the alley were covered inside with black oilcloth so that the light of the gas jets and lanterns carried by roaming detectives would not be visible to Luetgert. Bialk, the watchman, and Smokehouse Frank were sneaked into the building. They singled out the vat where Luetgert had carried out his experiment; it was the one that Schuettler had previously noticed. A detective climbed into the vat, put on a glove and explored a drain in the bottom of the receptacle. He came up with a tiny piece of bone. Schuettler told him he would have to do better than that. A sausage factory was one place where pieces of bone might be explained away.

The ashpan beneath the firebox of the furnace was completely clean. That was significant to Schuettler. It meant that Luetgert had removed the ashes with great thoroughness for the probable reason that the ashes might contain something that would have incriminated him.

Schuettler wanted to lay hands on those ashes. Fritz Fiegel, the neighborhood ash collector, was dug out of a North Side saloon. He said that Luetgert himself must have disposed of the ashes that Bialk had seen him carry out on Sunday night, for the ash cans were empty when Fiegel made his usual call on Monday morning. However, he had noticed, strewn along the wall of the building, some gray matter that hadn't been there before. The side of the building in question was, fortunately, not visible from

the Luetgert domicile. Fiegel took detectives with lanterns to the spot. They found ashes, all right.

Inside, the ashes were sifted. More pieces of bone showed up. Schuettler, a difficult man to please, wasn't satisfied. Didn't his men realize that a clever defense attorney would say that these were pieces of animal bones? Ah, but a clever defense attorney could hardly contend that animals wore corsets, and here was a piece of corset steel among the sifted stuff.

Schuettler's massive features seemed to take on some of the pale yellow of the gas lights as dawn drew near. He dipped his pudgy hands into a bucket containing the slimy contents of a catch basin beneath the drain of the vat where Luetgert had experimented. His face creased in a smile. He held up a small shiny object. It was a wedding ring. Inside of the band were the initials L. L.—those of Louisa Luetgert.

Their last discovery was that part of a wall in the meat man's office seemed to have been quite thoroughly scrubbed, more than likely to remove bloodstains.

Putting his information and his surmises together, Schuettler conjectured that Luetgert had, on the night of Saturday, May 1, lured his wife to the sausage works by subterfuge during the time the watchman made the first trip to the saloon, felled the woman in the office, been interrupted by the return of the watchman, and had then sent the man away again. While Bialk had been absent the second time, the meat man had placed his wife in the potash solution, locked the vat lid and turned on the steam. Captain Schuettler hoped that Frau Luetgert hadn't, by any chance, been still alive.

There was an early visitor to the Sheffield Avenue station house a few hours after the investigators had returned wearily from their all-night search of the sausage works. The visitor was Mr. Luetgert himself. His purpose was to announce a reward of fifty dollars for information establishing his wife's whereabouts. They allowed him to depart in smug satisfaction. During the remainder of the day, he made several additional visits to the station house, each time hiking the reward until, at twilight, it had reached two hundred dollars. Mr. Luetgert had always been a hard man with a dollar.

Chemists agreed that potash, when mixed with water and brought to a boil, would have reduced the flesh of a woman of Mrs. Luetgert's weight to a pulp in about two and a half hours. The corrosive would also have acted on the bones, softening them to the extent that Luetgert could easily have reduced most of them to powder after subjecting them to the heat of a furnace fire.

When the police finally let Adolph Luetgert in on a little grand-jury secret, it became apparent that this was going to be a trying case. A murder charge based principally on a few pieces of indefinite bone, a wedding ring and circumstantial evidence, cried out for a particular type of defense counsel. A barrister by the name of Vincent—W. A. Vincent—rose to the occasion.

At the trial, the sausage maker became a man of many virtues. Mr. Vincent had an explanation for the state's most important piece of evidence—Mrs. Luetgert's wedding ring. The ring had dropped into the vat out of the defendant's vest pocket when Mr. Luetgert had leaned over during the course of his experiment. And why had Mr. Luetgert been carrying his wife's wedding ring in his vest pocket? As a symbol of his eternal devotion, that's why . . . his love for the woman who had fled with another man.

His client, Mr. Vincent pointed out, had been facing failure in his business. Wasn't it reasonable to suppose, then, that Mr. Luetgert had made plans to go into another business? Why, of course it was. And that's why he had been conducting the experiment with the potash. He had been trying to make a new kind of soap.

Testimony of this kind necessitated counter-witnesses for the state. Soap experts agreed that soap with a potash base would remove dirt all right, the trouble being that it would remove skin, too.

The state contended that Mrs. Luetgert had been boiled for two and a half hours. Mr. Vincent got an adjournment, went out to the sausage works and, in the presence of scientific witnesses, boiled a gentleman in a potash solution—an anonymous gentleman who had been a patient in a municipal infirmary and who had, to be sure, died before being taken to the sausage works. The gentleman had to be boiled for more than four hours before he was in proper condition to leave by way of the drain at the bottom of the vat, and this proved, Mr. Vincent contended, that Mrs. Luetgert couldn't have disintegrated in two and a half hours.

The State said that Mr. Vincent's test had been unfair. He had boiled a large man; Mrs. Luetgert had been a small woman. Mr. Vincent thereupon boiled a lady—a lady about the size of Mrs. Luetgert. The second experiment confirmed the State's argument so far as the time element went, but Mr. Vincent now raised new technical points about the bone remains, claiming proof of his contention that what the State was palming off on the jurors were bones from sheep, cows, dogs, elk and monkeys. The jurors looked interested, not to say confused.

Nonetheless, Adolph Louis Luetgert wound up in Joliet as a lifer, and died in a few years. What cooked him for cooking his wife was a comparatively simple thing. The defense had admitted the presence of the wedding ring in the vat drain. The State produced witnesses who testified that Mrs. Luetgert's knuckles had enlarged since her marriage and that for several years she had been unable to remove the wedding ring from the third finger of her left hand. Therefore, gentlemen of the jury. . . .

The "Burned-Up" Old Maid

Here was a killer who set a woman on fire—two ways. And he might have gotten away with both kindlings because the law-enforcement author- ities in the murder locale not only couldn't find stones in their own shoes but showed every disposition to kick the corpse around until it got lost. Then somebody was visited by the bright thought of calling in The Pinkertons . . .

Somebody set a woman on fire before dawn in a lonely neck of woods in Union County, New Jersey. The victim had been murdered with a single bullet shot into the crown of her head, so that it took a course straight downward inside her body and came to a stop in her stom- ach. Then she had been saturated with gasoline and turned into a human torch. When the cops found her she looked like a passenger in an airplane that had made a one-point landing; she was completely unrecognizable. Only parts of her shoes, a small piece of clothing here and there, some cheap costume jewelry, her bridge- work, and a small patch of skin on one cheek had escaped the flames. There were, nonetheless, certain physical clues, and, just as important, certain deduc- tions to be lifted from the scene of the crime, which, added up, were more than sufficient for a solution.

Yet, after ten days, all the prosecutor's detectives had succeeded in doing was transporting the remains from the spot where they had been found to a morgue in the nearby city of Elizabeth. The prosecutor—Abe J. David—sent out an SOS for the Pinkertons. The man who took over was William A. Wagner, assist- ant superintendent of the New York offices of Pinkerton's National Detective Agency—a sharp, clean-cut fellow in his middle thirties. Wagner spent an hour

with the corpse; at the end of that time he had reached certain tentative con- clusions. The victim was middle-aged. She was Polish. She had come from the coal regions of Pennsylvania, a few hours away. She had been involved in a romance.

"How," asked the prosecutor, "do you figure things like that?"

"This patch of skin from the woman's face," Wagner explained, "isn't exactly white; it's more on the yellowish side. The skin of Slavic people has a yellowish tinge. The contours of the woman's face bear me out. Her cheekbones were high and prominent—another characteristic of the Slavic races."

"So you figure," said the prosecutor, "if she's Slavic she comes from the coal regions because there are so many Poles over there."

"Exactly," said Wagner. "Now about the romance business. That patch of face skin was heavily rouged. A middle-aged, middle-class Polish woman from the coal regions wouldn't rouge her face heavily unless there was a man in the picture."

"Middle-class," said the prosecutor— "how do you figure she was middle- class?"

"From the cheap jewelry and shoes, and from the texture of remnants of her coat and dress. The jewelry's ten-cent- store stuff. Most of it's new. That's another thing that makes me believe this woman was interested in a man—all that new jewelry. She was making herself as attractive as possible."

The victim's shoes, black patent-leather oxfords, size 6-c, bore a complete serial number. Part of the hem of the woman's dress was intact. It bore evidence of having been repaired. "The stitches in the repair work," Wagner pointed out to the prosecutor, "are not the work of a tailor, but of a dressmaker or a seamstress. She could have repaired her own clothes." There was evidence that the victim's coat had been of black satin and monkey fur—one of the more revolting vogues of the twenties.

The serial number in the shoes turned out to be that of the Friedmann-Shelby Shoe Company of St. Louis. The shoes had been shipped to an unrecorded destination two years previously. The shoe company had long done business with wholesalers in the Pennsylvania coal regions, especially with its cheaper product. The first clue to be run down, then, was at least compatible with Wagner's broad theory.

Wagner got up a police flier. He incorporated in it all the known facts and deductions. Then he set out on a tour of the Pennsylvania coal region. He covered such towns as Reading, Scranton and Wilkes-Barre, with all stops in between. He papered the territory with his fliers. He talked twenty hours a day with police chiefs, sheriffs, dentists, shoe and clothing salesmen. When he had done everything he could think of, Wagner crossed his fingers and returned to New York to sweat it out.

Wagner was hardly damp when the chief of police of a little Pennsylvania coal-mining town—Greenville, not far from Wilkes-Barre—long-distanced the Pinkertons with a hot rumble. A couple of Greenville housewives had walked into the chief's office, after having taken a look at Wagner's flier posted on a local telegraph pole, and said that the flier seemed to describe a friend of theirs. The heavy rouge, the black satin and the monkey fur, the nonprofessional alterations to the clothing, and the romance, all seemed familiar to the two housewives. The friend of the women—a Mrs. Mildred Mowry, a middle-aged Polish widow—had dropped from sight after marrying a man she had located through an advertisement in a matrimonial magazine.

Wagner summoned the missing woman's friends—a Mrs. Dodds and a Mrs. Straub—to New Jersey. The remains of the torch victim were taken from the morgue icebox where they had lain for two months now. The ladies from Greenville made an immediate identification. Wagner had now reached the point where he was starting from scratch. The identification was the X factor that was to mark the difference between a solved and an unsolved case.

Wagner had the Greenville women fill him in on Mildred Mowry. The woman had been the widow of a miner named Jake Mowry, who had died ten years previously. Millie, as her friends called her, had come into a few thousand dollars in insurance upon her husband's death. She had sold her home, which netted her a few thousand more, and went to live in a rooming house. She earned her living by doing sewing, mending, and needlework for the townfolk; her little fortune, about six thousand dollars in all, remained intact.

As the years of widowhood passed, Mildred Mowry, reaching fifty, found herself in the grip of an overwhelming biological urge. She decided to insert an advertisement in a matrimonial magazine for a husband.

In her ad, which appeared in July, 1928—some seven months before she became a human torch—Mildred Mowry mentioned that she had about six thousand dollars. The ad drew an immediate response in the form of a well-dressed, fiftyish little man with prematurely white hair, parted severely in the middle, and rimless nose-glasses on a sensitive, almost feminine face. Mildred Mowry, rouged to the ears, introduced her prospective husband to her friends Mrs. Straub and Mrs. Dodds as Doctor Richard Campbell, a big New York surgeon. Doctor Campbell, who was in the habit of chewing cloves, disclosed that his specialty was intestinal surgery. "You might call me an inside man," he said to Mrs. Straub, laughing quickly, the while displaying a strong set of large, yellow teeth.

Some of Mrs. Mowry's acquaintances in Greenville were just a little suspicious of the doctor, who checked into a local inn while conducting his courtship. They wondered how it was that a big New York surgeon would come to the coal regions for a wife, and, more to the point, how any man with any sense of discrimination whatever could, after meeting Mildred Mowry in the flesh, remain interested in her.

There appeared to be, moreover, a basic incompatibility between Doctor Campbell and Mrs. Mowry. The lady, although taking an occasional sip of homemade elderberry wine, was bitterly opposed to overindulgence in strong drink. Dr. Campbell claimed that he was always chewing cloves to deaden a toothache. Mrs. Mowry, trusting soul, believed him. The more objective students of the doctor, however, questioned that even the most severe toothache

would cause him to lurch, as he frequently did late at night when making his way to his room in the inn.

Doctor Campbell's courtship was mercurial and spectacular. Although the inn where he was stopping was only down the street from where Mrs. Mowry lived, he sent her telegrams at all hours of the day and night. He woke her up in the morning with messengers bearing roses. He told friends of the bride-to-be that she set him on fire—a remark that caused them to wonder, on a later day, if they had heard him quite correctly. Mrs. Mowry flounced about town, intoxicated by the wine of her romance with—as she insisted upon calling Doctor Campbell—Dicky Boy.

She was a new woman. She was, for one thing, awake most of the day. That was unusual for her. Mildred Mowry loved to sleep. She was in the habit of dozing off in the middle of a parlor conversation.

Doctor Campbell turned out to be not only a man who knew his way around the alimentary canal but one who was making money hand over fist in Wall Street. The great Wall Street crash was, in the summer of 1928, more than a year away; there were only two types of people in the country—those who were cleaning up in the market and those who needed their heads examined. One rainy Sunday afternoon, Doctor Campbell, Mildred Mowry and her friends Mrs. Dodds and Mrs. Straub were in the living room of Millie's boardinghouse, sipping weak tea and munching homemade cookies, when the talk took a fiscal turn. Millie said that the bank was paying her three per cent on her savings.

"Why," said Doctor Campbell, "the bank ought to be *indicted* for *cheating* you! They're using your money to make anywhere from two to five hundred per cent in the market. You should be making that money yourself, Millie darling."

A few days later, Mrs. Mowry withdrew her cash from the bank and gave it to Dicky Boy to invest for her. Mrs. Mowry couldn't lose. "If anything *should* go wrong," she explained to Mrs. Straub, "Dicky Boy says he'll make it up to me himself."

Late in August, a month after Doctor Campbell had first integrated himself into the Greenville landscape, he and Mildred Mowry stole away in the night, if not like two Arabs at least like two fiftyish adults who weren't acting their age. Mrs. Mowry left a note for Mrs. Straub. "We couldn't wait," she said. "Will write."

A couple of weeks later Mildred Mowry-Campbell, as the lady was calling herself at the suggestion of the doctor, wrote to her Greenville friends from New York. Doctor Campbell had a large practice on fashionable Park Avenue. She and the doctor were, however, staying at a small residential hotel while his apartment, where he lived and practiced, was being redecorated. She saw very little of the doctor; he was busy from early morning to late night calling on patients, operating in several hospitals, and going out on consultations, often all night.

In October, some six weeks after her marriage, Mrs. Mowry-Campbell returned unexpectedly to Greenville to reoccupy her old room in the boarding-house. Her return, she went to great pains to explain, was temporary. Doctor Campbell had gone to California to take out the gall bladder of Tom Mix, the movie cowboy, and to perform an exploratory operation on Cecil B. DeMille, the spectacle maker. "Dicky Boy doesn't know exactly when he'll get back," his bride explained. "He says there's no tell-ing *what* he'll find when he opens up Mr. DeMille."

Two months later, toward the end of December, Dicky Boy was apparently still so busy looking around inside Mr. DeMille, and so intent on what he was seeing there, that he didn't get around to any Christmas shopping for his bride. Mrs. Mowry-Campbell was putting a brave face on things; her friends were sure that the doctor had done her wrong.

On the first day of February, 1929, some five months after her marriage, Mrs. Mowry-Campbell announced that Dicky Boy had returned to New York from California and sent for her. Mrs. Straub went to the train with her, doubting very much that her friend Millie had ever heard from Doctor Campbell and suspecting that she was going to New York to hunt for him. Two days later, on February 3, Mrs. Straub received a letter from Millie. Everything was all right, the letter stated; Millie would write again soon.

Mrs. Straub took the letter to Mrs. Dodds. "There's something mighty fishy going on," Mrs. Dodds said to Mrs. Straub. "The return address on this letter is 607 Hudson Street, New York. I thought Millie said the doctor lived on Park Avenue and that he was getting his apartment all fixed up right after they got married."

Mrs. Straub decided to keep the letter. She never heard from Millie again. Now, some three months after Millie had written, Detective Wagner studied the letter, which the addressee had brought to New Jersey with her.

The Hudson Street address on the letter turned out to be Laura Spelman Hall, a YWCA. The register there showed that Mrs. Mowry-Campbell, of Greenville, Pennsylvania, had checked in on the morning of February 2, and checked out on the afternoon of February 22. This latter date was the afternoon before the bride was found burning across the Hudson River in New Jersey. The deduction to be drawn from the register dates were simple: the bride had come to New York to hunt for her husband; she had, after almost three weeks, somehow located him.

A clerk at the YWCA practically corroborated Wagner's suspicion that Mrs. Mowry-Campbell had caught up with her husband before checking out. During her entire stay at Laura Spelman Hall, she had impressed the personnel there as an individual with a burden on her mind—until the afternoon she checked out. Then she had undergone a noticeable change; she had been smiling, lighthearted, unworried.

Wagner now resorted to a series of connected deductions, stemming from his theory that Mrs. Mowry-Campbell had left Laura Spelman Hall happy because she had found her husband. Campbell had put a face on things; somehow he had made an excuse to his bride for his long absence and silence and assured her that everything would be all right. That was why she had been so happy when checking out.

Now, putting himself in the position of a man who found himself in the spot where Campbell had found himself, Wagner tried to decide what he would have done between the time he had picked up the woman one afternoon and the time he had set fire to her before dawn the next morning. Wagner already knew certain things about Campbell. He knew he had told his bride he was a doctor. He knew he had told her he had an apartment on Park Avenue. Both of those statements had probably been lies. That being so, it would have been natural for the man to have ridden his bride

around in an automobile on the pretext that he had to call on patients, the while trying to make up his mind just how, where and when to murder her.

Wagner recalled that Mrs. Mowry-Campbell had been in the habit of dozing off. Campbell would have known that. He would have driven her around until she fell asleep. After she had dropped off, he had shot her, probably not far from where he later removed her body from the car and set fire to it.

The Pinkerton detective had, all along, been puzzled by the fact that the bullet that had killed the bride had been fired straight into the crown of her head, so that it had traveled a straight course and remained inside the body. The explanation for the path of the bullet now occurred to him. The woman had been shot, probably while dozing, while in Campbell's automobile. Her murderer had been careful to shoot her in such a way that there would be no bullet hole or bloodstains in his car after the job was done and the body removed.

Campbell had been a man in his fifties. He had probably been married. He quite possibly had a wife and family in or around New York. That would have accounted for his absences, on "consultations," all night just after he had brought the former Mildred Mowry to New York immediately following their marriage. His marital status would also have increased the ex-Mildred Mowry's stature as an obstacle.

The murderer, Wagner deduced, was no doubt well acquainted with the region where he had disposed of the body. There were, closer to New York than Union County, New Jersey, and far more accessible, spots in Westchester County, adjacent to New York City, and on Long Island and Staten Island, where a man could just as well have done to a woman what Campbell had done to the woman from Pennsylvania. Campbell, then, may even have lived in Union County.

Wagner got on the long-distance phone and called the chief of police in Greenville. Here was one small-town police chief who was on his toes. He had, after Mrs. Straub and Mrs. Dodds had departed for New Jersey to make an identification, gone to Mrs. Mowry-Campbell's room in the boardinghouse and examined it. He had found a series of letters to the bride from the groom—all written following the woman's return to Greenville after her marriage—and he was all ready with an intelligent digest of the communications when he heard Wagner's voice on the phone.

Doctor Campbell's letters to his wife bore two return addresses—office numbers in buildings on West 42nd Street and on Fifth Avenue, New York. The letters from West 42nd Street had been mailed in November and December, and the ones from Fifth Avenue during January—the month before Mrs. Campbell had come to New York. Through the doctor's purple prose of endearment ran one basic theme: don't come to New York. Dicky Boy had made one excuse after another, each one leaner than the preceding one, to keep his bride away from New York.

Wagner found the West 42nd Street and Fifth Avenue addresses to be those of mail-receiving services—outfits which, for a fee, permit use of their offices as mailing addresses for clients availing themselves of the service. The client calling himself Doctor Richard Campbell had been a furtive character. Just before terminating his arrangement at the West 42nd Street service in December, he had seemed to fear that somebody might call at the office of the service and ask for him. "If anybody comes," he told the

people who ran the place, "say you haven't seen me lately. Say I've left for China. Say anything."

Upon making arrangements to get his mail at the Fifth Avenue service in January, Doctor Campbell seemed even more fearful that somebody would come in and inquire for him. As a matter of fact, somebody did, several times in February —a woman who answered the description of the middle-aged bride. The caller had put in her appearance between the first part of the month and Washington's birthday—the period during which Mrs. Mowry-Campbell was registered at the YWCA. She had asked hopefully for Doctor Campbell at first, and then, as she continued to visit the place and found that she had missed him, she became visibly dejected.

Doctor Harvey Crippen, the London murderer, had been a very contained man, except for one thing. When he was excited, his Adam's apple bobbed up and down. Dr. Richard Campbell had an Adam's apple that did precisely the same thing. The doctor had worn high choker collars that covered his Adam's apple, but the apple had behaved like a bobbin on a sewing machine when the doctor was told that a middle-aged lady had been inquiring for him.

Another part of the picture was in focus for Detective Wagner now. Mrs. Mowry-Campbell had hung around the building on Fifth Avenue where her husband had received his mail and finally personally contacted him. Then he had driven her around until she fell asleep, and murdered her. But where was Doctor Campbell now? If Wagner couldn't find his man at the end of the trail, perhaps he would have more luck at the beginning of the trail.

Neither Doctor Campbell or Mildred Mowry had ever mentioned where they had been married. From all Wagner could gather about the woman, she wouldn't have stood for a relationship without benefit of clergy. Where, then, would a pair of middle-aged lovers, stealing away from the coal regions in the middle of the night, go to get married? The logical answer seemed to be Elkton, Maryland, a Gretna Green only a few hours distant.

Elkton it was. Wagner was interested in just one item on the application for the marriage license that the pair had filled in—Doctor Campbell's home address. The groom had given it as the 3700 block of Yosemite Street, in Baltimore.

The Baltimore address was a vacant lot. That in itself was a clue. A man had to know the neighborhood pretty well to know the number of a vacant lot. Pinkerton operatives canvassed several blocks of Yosemite Street. Finally there emerged in their minds the figure of a little man with sensitive face, pince-nez and prematurely white hair, parted severely in the middle. He had, a few years previously, lived in a rented house on Yosemite Street. He hadn't occupied the dwelling long. He had been a furtive sort of man.

His neighbors had never learned precisely what he had done for a living. His name had not been Campbell; it had been Close—Doctor Henry Colin Close. Wagner located the landlord who had rented the house to Doctor Close. The landlord knew but two things about Close: the man had previously lived in Salisbury, Maryland, not far from Baltimore; his Adam's apple had bobbed up and down when he was inwardly excited.

The town of Salisbury sounded vaguely familiar to Wagner. He had, sometime in the previous year or two, heard the name Salisbury, or read it in the papers, in connection with a murder case of some kind. Now a bell rang in Wagner's mind. He had read the name Salisbury in connec-

tion with another murder right in New Jersey—that of Margaret Brown, a New York governess, who, after being wooed and won by a stranger, had wound up, just like the woman from Greenville, as the hot core of a torch. All that had ever been learned about Margaret Brown's murderer was that he had represented himself to the governess as a Doctor Henry Ross, a practitioner of Salisbury, Maryland.

Wagner hunted out friends of Miss Brown's who had briefly glimpsed Doctor Ross during his courtship with the governess. Doctor Ross tallied to the eyelashes with Doctor Campbell. Even his Adam's apple had bobbed up and down. Wagner was on his way to clean up not one murder but two. He had started behind scratch; now he was about to wrest a killer from the thin blue air.

Wagner slept on his problem. He was shaving one morning when he was visited by the thought that a man who had committed two torch murders might very well have constructed some sort of an official record for himself before turning up in New Jersey with gun and gasoline.

Wagner's man, under half a dozen aliases, including his real name of Henry Colin Close, had a long record. The Chicago police department had a plump dossier on him. Close, a native of Colorado, was now in his fifty-ninth year. He had studied medicine as a young man, but had not gone through with it. Liquor and women were too attractive. He started out as a forger in California and wound up in Folsom. Then he came to New York, got a job as office manager for a construction firm, and maintained three different women in three different apartments simultaneously—quite an accomplishment even after being able to stand the expense. Close had been obliged to swindle his employer to hold up the fiscal side of his affairs and, caught, was sentenced to a term in Sing Sing.

Close was forty-two when he got out. He turned up in Omaha, loaded with fake credentials, and became educational director for the Union Pacific Railroad. He got himself engaged to five girls simultaneously in Omaha and left town when he saw feathers and smelled tar. After that he turned up in Chicago as a publicity and promotion expert. Some of the projects he promoted smacked so strongly of fraud that Close was, in a way, continuing his criminal career. A married woman probably saved Close's life in Chicago; she told him that her husband had just found out about them, and Close left the city.

Close's record stopped ten years short of 1929, when Wagner wanted him. Wagner searched vainly through telephone and city directories of every city and town in northern New Jersey for his man. He wondered if Close was still engaged in public relations work. Close's specialty had been promoting real estate developments.

Wagner looked through the New York papers for such developments. He began to canvass them by telephone. One of them employed a promotion expert named Campbell—Henry Campbell. As the man's description came over the phone, Wagner knew that, at long last, he had his man. Henry Campbell lived in Elizabeth, New Jersey. Wagner whistled when he heard Campbell's address. It was an apartment house right around the corner from the morgue where his bride's body had been identified.

Wagner called at the Elizabeth apartment. Campbell was in New York, handling a promotion of some sort. He had a wife—a fine woman who knew nothing of his criminal past and who considered him a devoted husband. She had been married to him for nine years and borne him two children. She knew that her husband had been in financial difficulties but it had never occurred to her that he had been engaged in criminal activity of any sort. Now that she thought of it, though, he had acted very strangely when the body of the torch victim had been brought to the morgue right around the corner. He had seemed overly interested in developments; he had sometimes phoned her from New York to ask her if there was anything new about the corpse around the corner. Then, when the body had been identified, Campbell had not been able to sleep.

They were waiting that night, Wagner and the detectives from the prosecutor's office, for the little slayer when he came home from work. His Adam's apple began bobbing when he saw the strangers. He wouldn't admit a thing about the first of the torch murders, but he couldn't unburden himself of the details of the second one quickly enough. Wagner's deductions had been correct. Campbell had married the woman from the coal regions for her cash. Mildred Mowry-Campbell had caught up with him at the second mailing address.

"Gentlemen," said Campbell, "you can imagine how I felt when, after trying to duck this old dame, I found her that afternoon tapping me on the shoulder in the lobby of the building where I got my mail, calling me *Dicky Boy*." A reluctant bridegroom, to be sure.

Campbell had driven his bigamous bride around the bleak New Jersey countryside all evening and late into the night, putting her off by saying he was calling on patients. Actually, he was stopping in to say hello to friends in various parts of Union County. Then, in the small hours of the morning, he did the lady in, just as he was done in himself, one night a year after the murder, in the chair where sitters sizzle in the big cage at Trenton.

The Case of the Extra Husband

This is the story of one of the most unique sex triangles of the twentieth century—a design for loving that pulled the long arm of coincidence right out of its socket. Many a wolf has paid dearly for seducing a maiden; here is the bizarre account, straight from the official court records in Los Angeles County, of a fellow who passed up a fortune for his failure to seduce a girl.

Back in the good old days—in 1924, to be precise—when the Mann Act was not mistaken for a male quartet or lightly fractured by a wolf transporting a blonde muffin between coasts in the luxury of a streamliner drawing room, but was soberly regarded as a piece of thoroughly formidable legislation, there came to pass in the thriving community of Jersey City, New Jersey, a unique situation, involving two fellows and a girl, that arose directly from the statute in question. The Mann Act, or White Slave Act, originally introduced in the House by Representative James Robert Mann, Republican, Illinois, in 1910, made it a prison offense to transport a woman across a State line for immoral purposes, and was regarded so seriously by young huntsmen throughout the land that their nightmares frequently took the form of their being in the back seat of an automobile with a young lady when the car began to roll down hill and, before it could be stopped, rolled across a State line.

Although the Mann Act is still invoked today, especially when the girl in the case is young, presumably innocent, and has an old man who swings a lot of weight, some authorities in the matter are of the opinion that if the Act were really enforced much of the male population of the country would be in jail. At least one Federal prosecutor thinks that the statute is old-fashioned. "I would hesitate to take a Mann Act case into Court before a modern jury," he says. "The chances are that at least one of the men on the panel would have violated it at some time or other and, for *that* matter, maybe one of the woman jurors would have once been a not-unwilling victim to such a violation."

But it wasn't always so. Back in the teens and the early twenties the mere thought of the consequences of getting caught sneaking a dame to an adjoining State for a little weekend holiday was practically a substitute for saltpeter. During the first few years that the Act was on the books, weekend traffic between New York, New York, and Atlantic City, New Jersey, slackened to the extent that the big boardwalk hotels in the Jersey resort missed the familiar faces of quite a few distinguished-looking middle-aged to elderly gentlemen and the pretty and shapely young ladies who had once been registered as their nieces and daughters.

There worked behind a receiving teller's cage in one of the Jersey City banks a naïve-type fellow of twenty-five by the name of Alexander Rhodes. Rhodes was a fairly average character—up to a point. He came from a nice, decent run-of-the-mill family which was untouched by the breath of scandal. He intended to get married some day, he supposed, but meantime he was playing the field and living at home with the folks. He made a hundred and fifty dollars a month in the jug and paid his mother ten dollars a week board so that he had about a hundred dollars a month left for himself— enough on which to have one hell of a time back in 1924 when you could take a doll out and show her the works for a double sawbuck.

Rhodes, a blondish, open-faced character who usually dressed in blue serge suits and white shirts and those high choker collars the boys wore in the twenties, began to hear stories all around him of people cleaning up in the stock market. He figured he might as well get a little of the gravy. What happened to Rhodes was in the classic tradition of bank employees who start taking home samples. First he lost his own money in the market, then he began to play with the bank's cabbage, hoping, of course, for that killing that would enable him to cover his finger work before the examiners came around.

Rhodes was, in January of 1924, an even thousand dollars on the sad side of the ledgers. He had borrowed twenty-five dollars from this account, thirty-five from another, sixty from another, and so on, until the bookkeeping of the project was keeping him up nights. He finally consolidated his peculations by borrowing a grand from the savings account of a depositor by the name of Jack Box, an automobile salesman. Box, whom Rhodes knew only by sight, carried about fifteen thousand dollars in his savings account, and never drew on it, so Rhodes knew he would be safe from the examiners, at least for a while.

Now Alexander Rhodes did a strange thing. The average fellow in his spot probably would have dipped farther into a comparatively inactive account, such as Box's, and tried to make a market cleanup and get ahead, or at least pull up even. But not Rhodes. Rhodes didn't have a great deal of moxie; he could hear the clang of a cell door behind him in the big cage down in Trenton, and he didn't like the sound at all. He decided to discuss his problem with, of all people, the man whose account he had dipped into.

Over a period of weeks, Rhodes forged an acquaintanceship with Box when Box called to make deposits. One noon Box, a sharply turned out, athletic man of thirty, with a hard square face and wavy black hair, suggested that Rhodes drop into a speakeasy for a drink. Rhodes, who didn't drink, jumped at the invitation.

The two fellows began to meet regularly at the speak. One day, while his foot was on the rail next to Box's, Rhodes got up enough steam to tell Box what he had been wanting to tell him along. He was, he confessed, a thousand dollars short at the bank and the thousand was, at the moment, charged against Box's account. Box studied Rhodes' reflection in the mirror behind the bar and downed a gin. "What you've done at the bank," he said, "is no concern of mine. The bank's responsible for any shortages in my account."

"What are you going to do about it, Jack?" asked Rhodes.

"I don't know yet. What do you intend to do about it? You're sure to be found out sooner or later."

"That's just it," said Rhodes. "I thought maybe *you* could help me out."

"You thought *what*?"

"That maybe you could help me out."

"*How* for Christ's sakes?"

"I thought seeing you had about fifteen thousand in your savings account that maybe you could lend me the thousand so I could put it back." Box was too fascinated to speak. Rhodes, the earnest eager beaver, pressed the point. "I'll pay you back, Jack. Honest I will," he said. "I'll do anything you want me to. You're the only one I can turn to."

Box lit a cigarette and fell into thought. "I'll think it over," he said. "I want to think this over for a couple of days."

"Then you won't tell the bank—at least not for a couple of days?" Box shook his head sideways. "That's a promise, Jack?" Sure it was a promise.

Jack Box had good news for Alexander Rhodes a couple of days later. He would lend him the money to square himself at the bank. But if he did, Rhodes would have to do him a favor in return. "Just say what it is, Jack," said Rhodes. "You're a true friend." The favor Box wanted was a little more complicated than something that could be put into a few words. "For one thing," said Box, "you'd have to quit your job at the bank." "Oh," said Rhodes, "I'll be *glad* to do *that*. I hate the place anyway."

"Then you'd have to go to California."

California! "Gee," said Rhodes, "this sounds too good to be true, Jack. Where does the favor come in?" And now Box got to the heart of the matter.

Box, a married man with a small child, had, about a year previously, fallen for a girl of nineteen. The two of them had been meeting secretly ever since. Box's wife didn't know anything about it, neither did the girl's father, a rich widower. "There'd be hell to pay if either my wife or my sweetheart's old man found out what was going on," said Box. "We want to start life all over again in California. I figure if we go out there, maybe while I'm gone my wife will meet somebody else she likes and give me a divorce, or that something will turn up to let us get married." Box said that remaining in

Jersey City was out of the question. His sweetheart's father, whom he did not identify, was a prominent and powerful citizen; if he found out that his daughter was having an affair with a married man he would ruin Box.

Rhodes, in his uncomplicated way, followed the narrative up to this point, then got lost. "I don't," he said, "see where *I* come in, Jack. Why don't the two of you just go to California? You could go separately and meet out there."

"Haven't you," Box asked, "ever heard of the Mann Act?" Rhodes had, of course, heard of it, but he had never paid much attention to it. Box, on the other hand, was an authority on the Mann Act. He explained that even if he and the girl went to California separately but got together out there they would be guilty of conspiracy to violate the Act.

That's where Rhodes came in. He was to marry Box's girl and take her to California as his wife. Box was to be best man at the wedding and accompany the honeymooners on the trip. "But you'll be a husband in name only," Box explained to Rhodes. "We'll switch places at night. See what I mean?"

"Yes, but from what you say about this Mann Act, Jack, couldn't we all get in trouble if we got found out?"

"Who would ever find out?" asked Box. "I'd never say anything and I know my sweetheart wouldn't. You wouldn't say anything because you'd be in trouble yourself the minute you did."

Rhodes seemed to be assailed by misgivings at this juncture. "It's better than going to prison," said Box. "Yes," said Rhodes, "I guess it is. How long would I have to stay married to your sweetheart?"

That, Box explained, presented another complication. Rhodes' tenure of matrimony would depend on an unpredictable factor—how quick Box could somehow get a divorce. Rhodes would have to remain married to Box's sweetheart until Box was legally free to marry the girl himself. Then Rhodes could get a divorce.

"What would the three of us do in California, Jack," asked Rhodes, "all live together in the same house or something?" Box nodded. The three of them would take a little bungalow in the Los Angeles area, where Box had an auto salesman's job all lined up. The bungalow would be rented under the name of Mr. and Mrs. Alexander Rhodes; Jack Box, their friend, would board with them. "And we'd switch at nights," asked Rhodes, "like you said?" Precisely.

But what, wondered Rhodes, would he do for a living in California? That, Box indicated, would be a bridge they would cross when they came to it. "You'll be able to pick up something," said Box. "Maybe you could get a job in the movie studios doing something." Box would, until Rhodes got situated, be glad to bear all expenses. "Even pocket money, Jack?" Yes, even pocket money.

Rhodes said he wanted to sleep on the thing. Box said there was no hurry. Rhodes could have until the next afternoon to make up his mind. Rhodes got to thinking of prison that night, and Box's power to put him there. He met Box in the speakeasy next day and told him he was ready to go ahead. "All right," said Box, "be right here tonight at eight o'clock and I'll introduce you to the girl you're going to marry."

What Rhodes saw that night was a genuinely pretty blonde—a well-stacked muffin who wasn't exactly sexy but who wasn't exactly innocent, either. Box introduced her as Jeanne Taylor. "Golly," said Rhodes, "not *the* Jeanne Taylor."

Miss Taylor smiled and nodded and ordered a Scotch and water.

The name of Jeanne Taylor had frequently been in the Jersey City newspapers—in the social columns and in the news columns. Her father was one of Jersey City's first citizens—an upstanding citizen, wealthy, socially prominent and politically powerful. Jeanne, an only daughter and the apple of papa's eye, had gone to the proper schools, travelled abroad, and been active in local civic and charity work. She was, everybody in Jersey City knew, especially the fortune hunters, heiress to a bequest from her late mother of four hundred thousand dollars, which she would come into on her twenty-first birthday. Her twenty-first birthday—and the four hundred thousand dollars—were, that night in April, 1924, when Jeanne Taylor and Jack Box and Alexander Rhodes sat in the speakeasy, about eleven months away.

Box had obviously talked the plot over with Jeanne in great detail. The only question to be settled at the speakeasy meeting was whether Jeanne approved of Rhodes as a husband in name only. She would, after all, have to be in close proximity to him for an indefinite period of time and the chemistry of the business had to be considered. The girl was so gone on Box, a character who apparently had what it took with the twists, that Rhodes could have been something out of Frankenstein's laboratory for all Jeanne Taylor noticed him. Of *course* he would do; *any*body would do.

Everything, then, was set. Box gave Rhodes the thousand dollars to square himself at the jug and the caper got under way. The plot called for Alexander Rhodes to start calling on Jeanne to take her out so that the elopement of the two, which Box was planning, would seem to be the logical outcome of a romance. Every fellow who buzzed around Jeanne was suspected by her old man of being a fortune hunter. When old Taylor found out that Rhodes worked in a bank, and as a mere teller, he looked upon the young man much as a Chinese mandarin might look upon a coolie. Taylor told Rhodes to get the hell out of the house and warned him that if he ever saw him within a block of the place he'd phone the president of the bank and get him canned. Rhodes, alarmed, reported this to Box. Box, the angle man, couldn't have been more pleased. "Don't you see," he said, "this makes it *perfect*. It gives you and Jeanne all the more excuse for running off and getting married."

Thus it was that Alexander Rhodes and Jeanne Taylor journeyed from Jersey City to Elkton, Maryland, and got themselves knotted by a fee-happy justice of the peace. Jack Box, who had meantime told his unsuspecting wife that he had landed something in California and would send for her if it panned out, was the best man.

The wedding took place in the afternoon. That evening, the newlyweds and the best man caught a Chicago-bound train at North Philadelphia for the first leg of their journey to never-never land. Box had not neglected a single detail. He had reserved a section—an upper and a lower berth—for Mr. and Mrs. Alexander Rhodes, and a lower berth, right across the aisle, for himself. When the porter came along to make up the berths, Box took Rhodes into the smoking compartment. "Now," he instructed, "when you go back into the car you get into *my* upper."

"But what about our *bags*, Jack?" Rhodes said. "I'll have your bags and you'll have my bags."

"Never mind about the bags," said Box. "To hell with the bags."

Jeanne and her husband-in-name-only sent a telegram to her father, advising the old boy of their marriage and asking his forgiveness. The father's telegraphic reply caught up with them in Arizona. He never wanted to lay eyes on either of them so long as he lived. Rhodes inquired of Box, in an academic sort of way, if there was anything Jeanne's father could do to block her inheritance. Box replied with what Samuel Goldwyn might call a two-word answer: "Nothing."

Arriving in California, the newlyweds and the best man registered at a hotel, in adjoining rooms, then set out to find a place to live and begin their new lives. They settled on a little white stucco torture chamber, with two bedrooms, on a bungalow court in Glendale, suburban to Los Angeles. The trap rented for forty dollars a month, complete with assembly-belt furniture.

When Mr. and Mrs. Alexander Rhodes, and their good friend and boarder, Jack Box, moved into the bungalow they soon impressed neighbors as three happy people, which indeed they were. Box and Mrs. Rhodes were sex-happy and Rhodes was adventure-happy. Rhodes had always dreamed of California, with its glamorous movie studios and even more glamorous movie stars and here, by golly, he was at last.

Box began his work as an auto salesman at once and Rhodes went job hunting. The two men would leave together in the morning and come back again about the same time in the evening. If Rhodes got home first, he would sit around the bungalow, reading the paper, while Jeanne prepared dinner. He and Jeanne became good friends, but it had never occurred to Rhodes to try anything funny with the girl. Rhodes felt too indebted to Jack Box for extricating him from the jam in the bank and bringing him out to California to even think of such a thing. Anyway, Jeanne was so enamored of Box that she looked upon Rhodes in such an impersonal way that she frequently ran around in front of him wearing considerably less than people usually wear around the house, even in Southern California.

A month passed. Box and Jeanne were fairly well settled into a pleasant routine, but Rhodes seemed to be having difficulty getting adjusted. For one thing, he couldn't find a job. While the deal had been that Box was to support him until he became self-sustaining, it now occurred to Box that maybe Rhodes wasn't exerting a maximum effort to get work. Box mentioned what was in his mind, trying to be delicate about it. Rhodes, a sensitive fellow, took offense. Things didn't move as fast in California as they did back East; it was unfair of Box to accuse him of soldiering on the job. Box laughed and told him to forget it; something was bound to turn up soon.

Another month passed and nothing turned up. Rhodes seemed somewhat discouraged. He was so discouraged, in fact, that some mornings he wouldn't leave the house with Box but remained behind to sit around and drink Box's gin until noon. That was another thing that Box and Jeanne had noticed—Rhodes' drinking. He seemed to have developed quite an affinity for Southern California prohibition sheep dip. This brought on little arguments. By the beginning of their third month in Glendale, Box, Rhodes and Jeanne were far from the happy people they had been upon their arrival—and the worst was yet to come.

Rhodes was spending more and more time around the house. When he did go out, he didn't hunt regular work. He went over to Hollywood and began to hang around the movie studios. He thought maybe he might get work as an extra. While he didn't succeed he struck up quite a few acquaintanceships among the crullers who hung around the offices of the casting directors. These girls were, for the most part, gorgeous little productions completely unlike anything Rhodes had ever seen back in Jersey City. Their morals were in inverse ratio to their beauty and who could blame them? They had left home and fireside in cities, towns and hamlets all over the country and come to Hollywood to be movie stars. Many of them had been victims of casting couches and still hadn't gotten jobs, so now they could be had for a drink, a meal, or even a few kind words.

Rhodes was at first shocked at these conditions, then delighted. A great new world had opened up for the lad from Jersey—a world he had never dreamed existed. Some of Rhodes' new-found girl friends lived six and eight in a bungalow but somehow they found room for Rhodes overnight when, after an afternoon and evening drinking paint remover bought with Jack Box's money, Rhodes was unable to negotiate the homeward trek to Glendale.

One morning, at breakfast with Box and Jeanne, Rhodes announced that he was bringing a guest home to dinner that night and hoped it would be all right. Of course it would be all right. Who was the guest? A young lady from pictures.

Rhodes and the actress were late in putting in their appearance for dinner. When they did arrive they were both loaded. Box, the authority on dames, knew what kind of an actress *this* dame was. Jeanne, who after all had had a fine raising, was shocked. When the evening was over, and Box sent the actress home in a cab, there was a hell of a row between Box and Rhodes. How dare

Rhodes to bring a girl like that into the house! Had he no self-respect—or at least respect for other people? What kind of a man was he, anyway?

Rhodes was drunk, but not too drunk to think. When Box was through talking, *he* started in. Listen, he pointed out, to who was talking. What, he wanted to know, was the basic difference between a girl who did it openly and one who did it on the sly—Jeanne, for instance?

Box was about to go for Rhodes at that crack when Jeanne went between them. Here, in real life, was a situation just as dramatic, and just as corny, as anything the boys were putting on celluloid over in Hollywood. In the morning, there were apologies all around. Rhodes was sorry he had done and said what he had done and said, and Box laughed the whole thing off—as if he had any choice in the matter.

Things might have gotten back on an even keel if only Rhodes had been able to find work. But he just couldn't seem to get anything. There had never been a specific agreement about just how much pocket money Rhodes was to get from Box and this indefiniteness became a source of trouble now. As Rhodes' social activities in Hollywood expanded his need for pocket money grew apace. Sometimes he needed twenty-five dollars a week. Box would complain about the amount but he had no choice but to come across.

Rhodes began to rationalize his position. After all, it was Jack Box who had brought him out here, using him to cover up an act for which Box could have gone to prison. Was it *his* fault if jobs were scarce? Rhodes just couldn't work up any sympathy for Box. When everything was eventually straightened out—when Box got a divorce from his wife, when Rhodes and Jeanne were di-

vorced, and when Box and Jeanne were married—Box would have a wife who would have four hundred thousand dollars. What was a little pocket money compared to a bundle like that?

Box, beginning to think in terms of getting his freedom from his wife, started a campaign to make the little woman sore at him. He made nasty little cracks in letters he sent home but the only effect they had on Mrs. Box was to make her love and miss her husband more than ever. She was a fine woman, true to her spouse, and apparently nothing was going to change her—and that was, from Box's point of view, bad.

Now Box, finding Rhodes increasingly difficult, began to digress from the original plot. He decided that Jeanne should get an immediate quick divorce from Rhodes in Nevada. He and Jeanne would then set up separate residences until such time as Box could somehow get a divorce. Meantime he would take his chances on being tripped up for conspiracy to violate the Mann Act.

Box slipped the dreary news to Rhodes one morning when he was giving him his pocket money. "This won't last much longer, Alec," he said. "Jeanne's going to Reno to divorce you. We'll all be splitting up."

"But I don't want to be divorced," said Rhodes. "I like everything just like it is."

Box laughed. Rhodes was just kidding.

Rhodes was like *hell* kidding. Box wasn't going to dump him off at this juncture of the journey, like a piece of excess baggage, so that he would be high and dry three thousand miles from home with no means of livelihood in sight. Rhodes' character had changed since he had come to California—or, perhaps, revealed itself. Although he had always been a conscientious worker back in Jersey City, the fellow seemed to have been a beachcomber at heart. The wonderful combination of the Hollywood chippies, the liquid pain killer, the pocket money, and the salubrious climate were, for the lad from Jersey, heaven. He had not the slightest intention of forfeiting all that by agreeing to a divorce from Jeanne.

Box got purple. "Why," he roared, "you double-crossing little son of a bitch! I got half a mind to get in touch with the bank and tell them what you did. Then you'll wind up in prison, where you damned well belong!"

Box, however, didn't have a thing on Rhodes. When Box had given Rhodes the thousand dollars to square things at the bank, Rhodes had merely replaced missing cash so that there was no more trace of what he had done than there would have been of a cupful of water removed from a bucketful and then put back.

But Box wasn't taking this lying down. "Jeanne's going to Reno," he insisted, "and there's nothing you can do about it."

"Oh yes there *is*, Jack. I can write to your wife. And I can write to Jeanne's father."

Box glowered, then sighed. "Look," he said, "I'll give you money to go home on and a thousand dollars besides."

"I don't want to go back to Jersey City. I like it out here."

Box, knowing Rhodes had him by the seat of his manhood, decided to bide his time. He would think of something—or something would turn up. Maybe Rhodes would get run over or fall off a cliff or drink himself permanently stiff some night.

Rhodes, the poodle who had become a mastiff, began to make increasingly large monetary demands on Box. He began to bring the Hollywood tramps to the Glendale bungalow. He had no particular interest in Jeanne, in a sexual way, but he now resented the fact that she had never given him so much as a tumble and he was determined to show her that he was an attractive fellow to other girls.

The presence of Rhodes' girls presented the neighbors with gossip fodder. Why was it, the neighbors wondered, that Mrs. Rhodes would stand for her husband bringing other women right into the house? *That* was going pretty far. Now the gossips began to wonder about Mrs. Rhodes and Box. Could it be that Box was one of those boarders known in those days as *star* boarders?

One night in February, 1925—after the travellers had been in Glendale for eight months—Mrs. Rhodes and Box had a neighbor couple in for a few rubbers of bridge and some drinks. Rhodes was out. He banged in about eleven o'clock, leaking at the gills and with a broad in tow. The new arrivals looked at the four bridge players, all eight of them, then staggered into one of the bedrooms and locked the door behind them. The neighbors, thinking they had wandered by mistake into a place, laid down their bridge hands and beat it.

Box broke down the bedroom door and threw Rhodes' dame out into the bungalow court. Then he tried to reason with Rhodes. Rhodes dropped into a stupor. Box and Jeanne waited until morning to try to make some sort of a deal with the ex-bank teller. Box offered Rhodes five thousand dollars cash if he would agree to let Jeanne divorce him and be quiet about it.

"Why should I take five thousand dollars," asked Rhodes, "when my wife will inherit four hundred thousand dollars in about six weeks?"

Box and Jeanne were stunned. They had figured Rhodes as a weakling, a mess, a piece of cumbersome baggage who had outlived his usefulness, but they had never figured him as a schemer.

Rhodes proceeded to develop his thoughts about Jeanne's inheritance. "I am going to take a trip around the world," he informed Box, "as soon as my wife comes into her money and makes a settlement on me. Then I'll decide what I am going to do." Rhodes added that one thing was certain; now that he had sampled high life and was married to an heiress, he never intended to do another tap of work so long as he lived.

That did it. Box went to work on Rhodes. Rhodes got loose and ran into the kitchen and grabbed a bread knife. Jeanne, caught in the middle, grew hysterical. Rhodes made a lunge at Box with the bread knife and just missed Jeanne. The girl began to scream. Neighbors called the cops.

Jeanne began to leak at the mouth. She spilled the whole story of the fantastic relationship between her and Alexander Rhodes and Jack Box—every detail of it that she knew from the moment when Box had first told her that he had hit upon a scheme to legally take her to California without marrying her and without violating the Mann Act.

The Glendale cops, who had heard a lot in their time, had never heard of anything like this. When Jeanne's story hit the papers, Federal officials found it fascinating reading. They questioned Jeanne. She repeated the story she had told to the Glendale cops.

Jeanne's marriage to Rhodes notwithstanding, the Mann Act had been violated. The marriage had been nothing but a conspiracy on the part of the girl, Rhodes and Box to violate the Mann Act. The unhappy trio were locked up in a Federal deep freeze. The two men, held without bail, got a mouthpiece. He advised them not to talk. The Federals would thus be obliged to rely on Jeanne's story as evidence against the two men. This would present a problem. The law forbade a wife to testify against her husband. If Jeanne couldn't testify against Rhodes the Government wouldn't have much of a case.

While Box and Rhodes, and Jeanne, were in jail, awaiting whatever action the Federals would finally decide to take, Jeanne came into her inheritance. Here she was, a pretty girl of twenty-one, with four hundred thousand dollars in the bank, and in the sneezer.

Her lawyer arranged bail. She didn't have any lipstick in jail. By way of prettying up for her release, she reddened her lips by moistening a paper poppy, made by one of the other inmates, and using it as a lipstick. She had a cold sore on her upper lip when she rubbed the red paper on her lips.

A few hours after her release, Jeanne's lip began to throb. Then it began to swell. She had developed poison from the red dye. She had contracted blood poison. She was removed to Glendale Hospital. The miracle drugs were unknown in 1925. Four days later Jeanne Taylor Rhodes died in agony.

Jack Box was a crushed man; he had really gone for the girl. Alexander Rhodes had had no feeling for Jeanne, one way or the other, toward the end. All that was in his mind now was that his wife, worth four hundred thousand dollars, was dead, and that the money would automatically come to him as her nearest heir. Pretty soft for a fellow who had faced prison a year before because he couldn't scrape up a thousand dollars.

The prospective inheritance made a great deal of difference to Rhodes. He decided to talk and get it over with. After all, he would probably draw only a cou-

ple of years in the Federal can; going to
the can with nothing to look forward to
when you get out and going with four
hundred thousand dollars to look forward to were two different things. Anyway, Rhodes hated Jack Box for Box's
general attitude toward him during the
final days in the little bungalow in Glendale. Turning Government witness and
testifying against Box, even though he
incriminated himself in so doing, would
be a pleasure.

Rhodes took the stand at Box's trial
and told in detail how he and Box had
conspired to beat the Mann Act. As proof
of his testimony that his marriage to
Jeanne Taylor had been a marriage in
name only, Rhodes swore that the marriage had never been consummated—a
statement which, in the light of other
facts, was undoubtedly the truth. Both

he and Box were found guilty of violating the Mann Act and got stiff jolts in
Leavenworth.

But Alexander Rhodes had a bigger
jolt coming. Relatives of his dead wife
went into court and contested his right to
the girl's fortune. Rhodes would have
been entitled to the money had he been
the girl's husband—but, since he had admitted that he had never consummated
the marriage, why, he had never really
been Jeanne's husband. The law was very
specific on a marriage that had never been
consummated. Alexander Rhodes had
never really been the husband of Jeanne
Taylor and so he was not entitled to a
cent of her money.

Many a man has paid dearly for making a girl. Alexander Rhodes paid four
hundred thousand dollars for *not* making one.

The Built-in Lover

*If this—the story of a woman who kept a lover in the attic—were fiction,
you would say it was overdrawn. But the whole incredible series
of events is a matter of cold official record.*

There were, back in the year of 1903, in the comfortable and robust city of Milwaukee, Wisconsin, three ill-assorted persons—a forty-year-old man, his thirty-six-year-old wife, and a seventeen-year-old boy—who, thrown into unique juxtaposition, became participants in a plot that not only lent impressive weight to the theory that truth is stranger than fiction but which twisted the long arm of coincidence all out of shape. The goings-on in which these three became involved lasted for nineteen long years and didn't come to light until after one of them shot the other one to death in the City of Los Angeles, a municipality that somehow seemed a most fitting place to serve as a backdrop for the climax of a bizarre series of events without counterpart in the annals of crime.

Fred Oesterreich, one of the three principals in our chronicle, was an arrogant, round-faced German who ran an apron factory in Milwaukee. He was in the habit of blustering through the factory, which employed about fifty men and women, verbally lashing the workers on to greater effort. Had the workers taken a poll to determine whom they hoped the factory would fall in on there is little doubt who would have won.

Oesterreich's wife, Walburga, was a well-stacked woman of medium height who, though mostly of German origin, had just enough Spanish in her to make her interesting. The lady was, as it turned out, what a certain Hollywood motion-picture producer might call an over-sexed nymphomaniac. Walburga had a low, musical voice, smouldering dark eyes and a Mona Lisa-type smile. She worked in the apron factory as a forelady and was very popular with the workers because, after her husband had blustered through the place balling out everybody, Mrs. Oesterreich would follow in his wake, picking up egos and returning them to their owners.

Fred and Walburga Oesterreich, who had been married for fifteen years and who were childless, were not a happy couple. Oesterreich had, from his wife's point of view, several failings. Although he was worth about a quarter of a million dollars in 1903, the man was, like many Germans, a careful custodian of a buck. The couple lived in an ugly mustard-colored frame house that was big enough to require the services of two maids but Oesterreich would not allow his wife even one servant. Worse yet, the man was a heavy drinker. Worst of all, he had come to be painfully deficient on the connubial couch.

It was this latter failing that Mrs. Oesterreich, what with that Spanish blood and all, simply couldn't overlook. She used to get into terrible battles with Fred in the watches of the night, taunt him about his unforgivable deficiency, and punctuate her remarks by throwing small articles of furniture at him. She raised enough racket several times for neighbors to call the police. If Fred was a lion in the apron factory, he was a mouse at

315

home; Walburga was by all odds the stronger personality of the two.

One day, when one of the sewing machines in the Oesterreich factory broke down, the third principal in our chronicle entered the scene—a 17-year-old youth by the name of Otto Sanhuber. Otto, who bore a striking resemblance to nobody in particular, was a wizened little fellow, not quite five feet tall, with rumpled brown hair, a receding chin, and watery blue eyes behind silver-rimmed glasses. He was so painfully shy that he blushed when a lady so much as spoke to him.

Just as Otto was completing his repair job, Mrs. Oesterreich spied him. What Walburga saw in little Otto is a tribute to the woman's powers of perception. Here was a nondescript youth, less than half the woman's age, who had never gotten so much as a second glance from the girls down by the Milwaukee beer vats. Yet, Mrs. Oesterreich saw in Otto exactly what she was searching for.

Mrs. Oesterreich, the sly one, saw to it that there was plenty of repair work at the factory for the bashful youth. In a few months Otto had grown to like and trust her.

One day a sewing machine that Mrs. Oesterreich kept in the master bedroom at home broke down, no doubt by design, and she asked her husband what she should do about it. "Why," said Oesterreich, "get that kid to fix it—that kid who's been coming around the factory."

It was a raw autumn morning when little Otto called at the Oesterreich home. Mrs. Oesterreich, who answered the door to the boy, was rouged to the ears, drenched in a bitchy perfume and, as it turned out, was wearing nothing but silk stockings, bedroom slippers and a fancy purple silk dressing gown.

Leading Otto to the bedroom, Mrs.

Oesterreich propped herself up on the bed while the boy addressed himself to the machine. As he labored, Otto got an occasional whiff of that perfume and, every once in a while, he would sneak a look at the voluptuous lady on the bed. Every time he looked it seemed that he saw less of the dressing gown and more of Mrs. Oesterreich.

W-e-l-l, as the outrageous facts in the office of the District Attorney of Los Angeles County were one day to disclose, a situation such as that in the Oesterreich bedroom that autumn morning could progress in only one direction. And it sure as hell did. By the time Otto Sanhuber left the house late in the afternoon he and the lady more than twice his age had put an intrigue in motion.

Otto, as Mrs. Oesterreich had so correctly divined, possessed the biological endowments that were the answer to a nymphomaniac's prayer. He would have been worth a chapter all by himself in the good Doctor Kinsey's *Sexual Behavior in the Human Male.*

Things rocked along very nicely for the next three years, with Otto, who still kept his job with the sewing-machine company, sneaking into the Oesterreich home when Mrs. Oesterreich made one excuse or another to be absent from her duties at the apron factory. Mrs. Oesterreich couldn't have been happier.

Somehow or other, probably through a neighbor, Fred Oesterreich got wind of the fact that his wife was receiving a visitor on those days she was not at the factory. The apron magnate questioned his wife and she, looking him straight in the eyes, assured him that there was nothing to the story.

Mrs. Oesterreich, fearful of discovery, was nonetheless reluctant to let go of little Otto, now that she had found him.

So she hit upon an inspired plan. She decided to have Otto move into the Oesterreich home, without her husband knowing it, as a permanent guest.

There was an unused cubbyhole in the attic, immediately above the master bedroom, which was entered through a trap door in the bedroom ceiling. Mrs. Oesterreich fixed the cubbyhole up with a cot, a rug, a small table, a couple of chairs, some candles and other necessities of life and, one day when Fred was at the factory, moved Otto, who had quit his job with the sewing-machine company, right in. She put a snap lock on Otto's side of the trap door so that if her husband should, for any reason, try to get into the attic cubbyhole he would think the trap door was stuck.

The arrangement went just fine. Mrs. Oesterreich, feigning one excuse or another, would remain home from the factory and, as the cold winter winds blew outside, would give her signal to Otto— three taps on the trap door—and he would open it up and descend into the bedroom.

Otto came out for exercise around the house only during the day, or when the Oesterreichs went out for the evening. Before going out at night with Fred, Walburga would give Otto the signal that it was all right to come down. But Otto never set foot off the premises.

Because of the demands that Walburga Oesterreich had made on him for almost four years now, Otto had hardly grown at all, still being under five feet and weighing only a hundred and five pounds. And what did Otto think of all this? He just loved it. Only a mixed-up character would have gone for such an arrangement but Otto was mixed up from 'way back. An orphan, he had had a hard raising. Because of his small stature and his nondescript face, nobody had

ever paid the slightest attention to him— until Mrs. Oesterreich had spied him.

Otto was living in a sort of dream world up there in the attic, not having to face the realities of life and with all his wants taken care of. Talk about social security! Mrs. Oesterreich supplied Otto with adventure books, which she obtained from a public library, and, as Otto read by daylight or by candlelight, he was transported into regions far removed from Milwaukee.

Sanhuber had by now developed a voracious appetite. The fellow could eat enough for three men. Mrs. Oesterreich kept him supplied with whole loaves of German rye bread, bottles of milk, and cheeses, liverwursts and bolognas, so that he could have snacks at night when the garment manufacturer was on the premises and Otto could not come down out of his hideaway.

There were just two precautionary measures that Otto had to abide by. One was that he was never to make the slightest sound at night, when Oesterreich himself might be just below him, there in the bedroom. The other was that he was never, under any circumstances, to go near a window in the cubbyhole that looked out on the back yard. The window was opaque with dust, and the light of a candle, which Otto kept at that end of the cubbyhole furthest from the window, was not visible after dark.

After a couple of years of reading adventure stories, Otto became something of a connoisseur of the stuff. Not only a connoisseur, but a critic. An urge to express himself, long bottled up, took the form of a decision to write adventure fiction for the pulp magazines.

So Otto began to scratch away with a quill pen, up there in the attic, turning out adventure stories laid, for the most part, in the South Seas and the Orient.

Mrs. Oesterreich bought a typewriter, learned how to peck away at it, and typed Otto's stories and sent them to the pulp magazines. She rented a post-office box under an assumed name and used the box for all correspondence on the literary level.

Otto, who was very prolific, turned out his stories pretty rapidly. During his first year as a writer, he drew nothing but rejection slips. Then, suddenly, he got the hang of the thing and his stories started selling. Although he used a nom de plume in the magazines, the checks were made out in his name. He endorsed them over to Mrs. Oesterreich and she opened a special bank account for him. Thus the little fellow became self-supporting.

Sometimes, while writing late at night, Otto would become so engrossed in his work that he would cough or clear his throat. "Where's that noise coming from?" Oesterreich would ask his wife. "Oh," Mrs. Oesterreich would answer, "it's probably a dog somewhere."

"It sounds closer than that. It sounds like it's coming from the attic."

"It's probably mice."

When the Oesterreichs were out for an evening to visit friends and drink schnapps, Otto liked to go down to the kitchen and raid the ice box. Oesterreich, coming home with his wife about midnight, was a great one for a snack before going to bed. He would go into the ice box, take out a roast, and look at it in a puzzled sort of way. "Whatever happened to all the meat on this thing?" he would ask his wife.

"We ate it at dinner."

"We didn't eat *that* much."

Mrs. Oesterreich would just look at her husband and make him feel foolish.

One Saturday afternoon, Oesterreich was out in the backyard, burning some rubbish. As chance would have it, Otto chose that very afternoon to disobey the injunction of his mistress never to go near that window in the attic. Otto not only went near the window, but he rubbed some of the accumulated grime away, the better to peer out. He was peering out when Oesterreich, down in the backyard, happened to look up. Otto ducked—but not quite in time.

Oesterreich ran into the house, yelling for his wife. "I *knew* there was something up in that attic!" he yelled. "I just *saw* something *move*."

Walburga Oesterreich, who was by now equal to practically any situation, feigned puzzlement. "If it'll make you feel any better, Fred, why don't you go up to the attic and look around." Oesterreich tried the trap door, but it wouldn't give. "The damned thing's stuck," he said.

"Fred," said Mrs. Oesterreich, "I want to have a serious talk with you."

"What about?"

"I think you should see a doctor."

"What for?"

Now Walburga Oesterreich came across with her master stroke. She tapped her forehead. "I think something's wrong in your head, Fred. You're imagining things. Maybe it's because you drink too much or maybe it's because you work too hard. But *some*thing's wrong, Fred. Promise me you'll see a doctor." Fred, fearing the woman might be speaking the truth, would promise nothing of the kind. But thereafter if he heard mice in the attic coughing and clearing their throats he kept his mouth shut about it.

Oesterreich was a great man for a cigar. There were always several humidors filled with cigars around the house. Now Otto (wouldn't you know it) took up smoking. When Oesterreich began to complain that his cigars were disappearing, his wife put her foot down. He would *have* to see a doctor.

The saw-bones just sat there in his office, looking at Fred Oesterreich while Mrs. Oesterreich did the talking. What she was saying was that her husband was imagining that somebody was smoking his cigars and raiding his ice box, that he was seeing things, like an imaginary face at the attic window, and that he thought he heard mice up in the attic, coughing and clearing their throats.

"Is this true?" the doctor asked the apron magnate. Oesterreich said it was. "Do you drink pretty heavily, Mr. Oesterreich?" asked the doctor. Oesterreich admitted that he did. "And you work very hard at your factory?" Yes.

The doctor wrote out a prescription. But the prescription didn't seem to do any good. Oesterreich began to brood about himself. He brooded so much, in fact, that he began to lose his grip. He was no longer the Simon Legree in his factory, no longer capable of lashing the slaves on to greater effort.

Mrs. Oesterreich, still carrying on great with her attic Romeo, took her husband to another doctor. The second saw-bones suggested a change of houses.

When the Oesterreichs changed houses, Otto went right along, being fixed up in the attic again. But Oesterreich continued to hear strange sounds every once in a while, and his cigars continued to vanish and edibles disappeared from the refrigerator.

In 1913, when Fred Oesterreich was fifty, his wife forty-six, and Otto twenty-seven, the Oesterreichs moved into still another house. Of course Otto went right along. The liaison between the little fellow and Walburga Oesterreich was still going strong, to the utter satisfaction of both, but Fred Oesterreich was rapidly

running down hill. He was still hearing things and imagining things.

Walburga Oesterreich was, at the age of forty-six, a remarkable woman—dripping with magnetism, buoyant of spirit, quick of mind. She was careful of her diet, kept her figure, and saw to it that she got out of a dress everything she put into it. Her dark, Spanish-type features made her age hard to figure out; sometimes, when she was well rested and well satisfied, she looked quite a few years younger than she really was.

Actually, the woman was leading two complete lives—one with her husband at night and one with Otto during the day. Fred Oesterreich, a methodical man, left the house at the same time in the morning and returned the same time at night. When Fred left in the morning, Otto would come down out of the attic, have breakfast in the kitchen, and then either go back to the attic to write or go to bed with Mrs. Oesterreich.

Otto and the lady hit the sack one morning and were making quite a racket when they heard a noise downstairs. Mrs. Oesterreich jumped out of bed, rushed to the open door of the bedroom, and listened. Sure enough, somebody was downstairs. "Who's there!" the lady cried out. "It's me," came Fred's voice. "Where are you, upstairs?"

"Yes."

"I'll be right up," called Fred.

"No," answered Walburga, "I'll be right down."

While Otto sneaked off to his attic hideaway, Mrs. Oesterreich put on bedroom slippers and dressing gown and got downstairs before her husband, who had come home not feeling good, got upstairs. Close—but no cigar.

One night, not long afterward, the Oesterreichs, who had gone out to play cards with friends, got into a drunken

fight with the friends and returned home
early. Fred, oiled to the gills, caught little
Otto in the kitchen, worrying at a leg of
lamb. Thinking Otto was an ordinary
intruder, he gave the little fellow a fright-
ful beating and tossed him out of the
house, little realizing that he was evict-
ing Otto from the only home he had.

Meeting Mrs. Oesterreich on the street
next day, Otto found that she had everything all planned. Afraid that her husband would suspect that Otto had been
considerably more than an ordinary intruder, put two and two together and
bust into that attic, Walburga told her
lover to go to Los Angeles. She would
keep in touch with him through a post-
office box, and soon join him in the City
of the Angels. She withdrew from the
bank the money he had made as a writer
and away he went.

Arriving in Los Angeles, Otto got a
job as a porter in an apartment house.
After all those years in the attic, he hated
all that California sunshine. Walburga
had no trouble talking Fred into selling
out and moving to California but it took
him two years to find somebody who
would give him half a million dollars for
his apron factory.

Landing in Los Angeles in 1918, the
Oesterreichs put up at a hotel while he
looked around for a business opportunity
and she looked around for a house. Walburga found just what she wanted on
North St. Andrews Place, one of the
city's tonier thoroughfares—a handsome
big residence that just happened to have
a walled-off portion of the attic right
above, of all places, the master bedroom.
While Oesterreich rushed around town,
investigating business opportunities, his
wife fixed up the attic quarters for Otto.

Oesterreich purchased controlling interest in a prosperous garment factory
specializing in aprons, dresses and lin-
gerie, and moved with his wife into the
residence on North St. Andrews Place.
Mrs. Oesterreich contacted Otto, met him
on a street corner one fine bright Southern California day and within the hour
the little fellow was ensconced in his new
quarters, safely in out of the sunshine.

Things rocked along for four years.
Then, on the night of August 22, 1922,
neighbors of the couple heard terrifying
sounds coming out of the open window,
and then they heard what sounded like
—and was—the sound of several shots.

The cops found Fred Oesterreich dead
on the living room floor, bullets through
his head and his chest. Then they heard
the widow yelling for help from a clothes
closet in the master bedroom. The closet
had been locked by a large, old-fashioned key, which was lying on the floor
just outside of the closet door.

Now there entered the scene a man
named Herman Cline, the Chief of Detectives of the Los Angeles Police Department—a hard-bitten man who, rumor
had it, each morning glanced into a mirror and looked with suspicion at his own
reflection. Cline looked at Mrs. Oesterreich, who was near hysteria, then at the
key that had locked the closet door, and
then at a space of about a quarter of an
inch between the bottom of the door and
the floor.

Mrs. Oesterreich told Cline that she
and her husband had come home and
surprised a burglar. After shooting her
husband the burglar had locked Mrs.
Oesterreich in the closet to prevent her
from phoning the police.

"What'd the burglar steal?" Cline
asked Mrs. Oesterreich.

Mrs. Oesterreich had seen the burglar
snatching her husband's watch—a handsome timepiece studded with diamonds.
The lady was carrying on at a great rate.
She volunteered the information that in

a third of a century of marriage she and dear Fred had never had a single quarrel.

The apron manufacturer had been slain by bullets from a .25-calibre weapon. "I think I'll go to Milwaukee and look into this Mrs. Oesterreich," Cline told his superior. "She could of locked her*self* in that closet and shoved that key back under the door. Not only that, but any woman who stands there with a straight face and says she's never even had a fight with her husband's a liar."

All Cline found out in Milwaukee was that Walburga and Fred Oesterreich had frequently quarrelled. Yet that was enough to establish that Walburga Oesterreich had lied to him. False in one thing, false in all?

Oesterreich had an estate of about a million dollars, but it was in such a tangled condition that his widow had to engage the services of one of Los Angeles' ablest civil attorneys—Herman Shapiro—to untangle it for her. As Walburga was leaving Shapiro's office the first day they met she presented him with a diamond-studded watch. "Here," she said, "this belonged to my dear husband. I want you to have it."

"Didn't I read something in the papers about that burglar stealing a watch like this one from your husband?" asked Shapiro.

"Yes," said Mrs. Oesterreich, "but apparently he didn't. I found this watch under the cushion of a window seat in the living room."

Mrs. Oesterreich put the house on St. Andrews Place up for sale and bought a smaller house on North Beachwood Drive. There was a nice, comfortable attic in this house, too, so Otto Sanhuber went right along.

Somewhere along the way, Mrs. Oesterreich had struck up an acquaintance-ship with an actor—a fellow named Bel-lows—and one day when they met for lunch in a Hollywood restaurant she reached into her handbag and handed him a large envelope. The envelope contained a .25-calibre revolver.

"What's this?" asked Bellows.

"I keep it for self-protection," said Mrs. Oesterreich. "But since dear Fred was also killed by a .25-calibre revolver, it might look suspicious if the police found this in my possession. So do me a favor, will you. Dispose of it somewhere for me."

Bellows tossed the gun into the LaBrea tar pits—a piece of Los Angeles real estate that holds more secrets than a Holly-wood casting couch.

One day about a year after the murder, Chief of Detectives Cline, still convinced that Mrs. Oesterreich had guilty knowl-edge of her husband's death, decided to drop into Shapiro's office. He happened to notice the diamond-studded watch. When Shapiro explained where Mrs. Oesterreich claimed to have found the watch, Cline clapped on his hat and headed for Beachwood Drive to arrest the woman and charge her with murder. A hold-up man, Cline knew, would not snatch a watch from a man he was mur-dering and then hide the watch under the cushion of a window seat.

What Cline was hoping for when he pinched Walburga Oesterreich was a confession. He didn't get it. The lady, held without bail, screamed for Shapiro. "Go up to the big bedroom in my home," Mrs. Oesterreich instructed Shapiro, "and tap three times on the trap door in the closet. There's somebody up there in the attic—a half brother of mine who's a sort of a vagabond. Please tell him I've gone to Milwaukee on business and will see him soon."

When Shapiro tapped three times on the trap door, the door opened and there was little Otto Sanhuber. Otto, now nearing his fortieth year, was the color of library paste but seemed to be in good health. When Shapiro, standing there in the closet and looking up, introduced himself and gave him Mrs. Oesterreich's message, Otto smiled and thanked him. Then, growing thoughtful, Otto said, "I feel as if I know you, Mr. Shapiro. Mrs. Oesterreich has spoken of you many times. It's too bad that she has been so upset over something that I did."

"That *you* did!"

"Yes, I shot Mr. Oesterreich. It was an accident."

"Tell me about it."

Shapiro sat down on the floor of the closet, got out a pencil and pad, and began to make notes. It seemed that on the night of the murder, the Oesterreichs had come home, quarreling as usual. Otto, who had been cavorting around the house after raiding the refrigerator, had, instead of going back to the attic, decided to get into the fight. He knew where Mrs. Oesterreich kept a little .25-calibre revolver, so he got it, then went downstairs and confronted Oesterreich. "Unhand this lovely woman!" said Otto, stealing a line of dialogue right out of one of his own stories. Oesterreich just glowered at little Otto and made a lunge for him. Otto, in a panic, pulled the trigger several times and the first thing he knew there was Fred Oesterreich lying on the floor dead.

Now Otto drew upon his talents as an author and concocted something to fool the police. He snatched Oesterreich's diamond-studded watch and gave it to Walburga. Then, he rushed to the second floor with Mrs. Oesterreich, told her to lock herself in the closet and shove the key through the crack between the bottom of the door and the floor, and disap-

peared into his hideaway in the attic.

It occurred to Shapiro that Otto had been pretty stupid. He should never have given that watch to Mrs. Oesterreich and he should have locked Mrs. Oesterreich in the closet himself, and left the key in the keyhole on the outside of the door. Then Chief of Detectives Cline would not have spotted the flaws in the whole business. But Otto, in a panic because he had just killed a man, hadn't been thinking clearly.

Otto, not having talked to a living soul save Walburga Oesterreich (and, briefly, Fred) for four years, couldn't dam up the flow of words. He lay on the floor of the attic and, looking down at the lawyer sitting in the closet, began to go over every phase of his long and unique relationship with Walburga Oesterreich.

Shapiro, deciding that Mrs. Oesterreich needed a good criminal lawyer, enlisted the services of Frank Dominquez, one of L. A.'s cagiest mouthpieces. "Go out to that house on Beachwood Drive," Dominquez said to Shapiro, "and get that man to hell out of that attic. In fact, tell him to get out of the country."

Sanhuber went north to Vancouver, British Columbia. Dominquez went to the District Attorney, and, since Otto was out of the country and the lethal weapon was in the LaBrea tar pits, demanded the release of Mrs. Oesterreich, and got it. Shortly thereafter Mrs. Oesterreich got her husband's inheritance and settled down to a comfortable life in the house on Beachwood Drive.

Seven years passed. Chief of Detectives Cline, now retired, wandered around Los Angeles, muttering in his beard. And then, one day in 1930, all hell broke loose. Shapiro, Mrs. Oesterreich's civil lawyer, went to the District Attorney. He and Mrs. Oesterreich had gotten into some fierce fights about money and the lawyer, fearing injury or possible death at the hands of the woman, wished to make public an affidavit about the death of Fred Oesterreich. And so Shapiro spilled the whole story.

Mrs. Oesterreich and Sanhuber were both in Los Angeles, but not seeing each other any more. The lady had found several new lovers, who were being paid well for their services. Otto, on the other hand, had married in Canada but, unable to find steady employment there, had returned to Los Angeles. He was working as a night porter in an apartment house so that he could sleep during the day when the sun was out.

When Mrs. Oesterreich and Sanhuber were pinched, she refused to talk, but Otto went before a grand jury and repeated everything that he had told to Shapiro that day seven years previously. Mrs. Oesterreich and Otto were both indicted for the murder of her husband.

Otto, tried first, had as his counsel Earl Seeley Wakeman, a man who had never lost a murder trial. Otto repudiated his confession so that the State was left with Shapiro's second-hand account of the murder. The jury didn't say Yes and it didn't say No. It found Otto Sanhuber guilty of manslaughter.

And maybe *that* didn't stir up a fascinating legal dust storm. The statute of limitations on manslaughter ran out after three years, and here was a man who was guilty of a manslaughter committed *eight* years previously. Simple arithmetic was all that was needed to establish the fact that little Otto Sanhuber was five

years on the laughing side of the limitations ledger. And so the little man was set free, to trail off, at the age of forty-four, into the silences, never to be heard from again.

Now Mrs. Oesterreich went to bat, having as her counsel, Jerry Geisler, the cagiest lawyer in California. Walburga, now sixty-three years old, got on the stand in her own defense and laid all the blame on little Otto. She had not come forward at the time of her husband's death and told the truth because she hadn't wanted to be embarrassed by public disclosure of her private life. Embarrassed indeed!

The jury couldn't quite make up its mind about Walburga; it disagreed. The murder indictment against the woman hung fire for six years and then, in 1936, the District Attorney, feeling he could never make the charge against the lady stick, moved to have the indictment nolle prossed.

Mrs. Oesterreich began to plunge in the stock market, with disastrous results. In the early forties, with only a few thousand dollars to her name, she took up residence over a garage in the Wilshire district of the city. Four years later, when a reporter for one of the Los Angeles papers sought to interview her, he found that she had, like Otto, trailed off into the silences, leaving no trace.

The Blind Goddess of Justice sure was taken for one hell of a sleigh ride. After all, a man *was* scragged. It does seem that *some*body should at least have been slapped by a good, stiff fine.

lawyer, fearing injury or possible death at the hands of the woman, wished to make public an affidavit about the death of Fred Oesterreich. And so Shapiro spilled the whole story.

Mrs. Oesterreich and Sanhuber were both in Los Angeles, but not seeing each other any more? The lady had found several new lovers, who were being paid well for their services. Otto, on the other hand, had married in Canada but, unable to find steady employment there, had returned to Los Angeles. He was working as a night porter in an apartment house so that he could sleep during the day when the sun was out.

When Mrs. Oesterreich and Sanhuber were pinched, she refused to talk, but Otto went before a grand jury and repeated everything that he had told to Shapiro that day seven years previously. Mrs. Oesterreich and Otto were both indicted for the murder of her husband.

Otto, tried first, had as his counsel Earl Seeley Wakeman, a man who had never lost a murder trial. Otto repudiated his confession so that the State was left with Shapiro's second hand account of the murder. The jury didn't say Yes and it didn't say No. It found Otto Sanhuber guilty of manslaughter.

And maybe that didn't stir up a fascinating legal storm. The statute of limitations on manslaughter ran out after three years, and here was a man who was guilty of a manslaughter committed eight years previously. Simple arithmetic was all that was needed to establish the fact that little Otto Sanhuber was free,

years on the laughing side of the limitations ledger. And so the little man was set free into the silence, never to be heard from again.

Now Mrs. Oesterreich went to bat, having as her counsel Jerry Geisler, the craftiest lawyer in California. Walburga, now sixty-three years old, got on the stand in her own defense and laid all the blame on little Otto. She had not come forward at the time of her husband's death and told the truth because she hadn't wanted to be embarrassed by public disclosure of her private life, Walburga reasoned indeed.

The jury couldn't quite make up its mind about Walburga it disagreed. The murder indictment against the woman hung fire for six years and then in 1936, the District Attorney, feeling he could never make the charge against the lady stick, moved to have the indictment nolle prossed.

Mrs. Oesterreich began to plunge in the stock market, with disastrous results. In the early forties, with only a few thousand dollars to her name, she took up residence over a garage in the Wilshire district of the city. Four years later, when a reporter for one of the Los Angeles papers sought to interview her, he found that she had, like Otto, trailed off into the silence, leaving no trace.

The blind Goddess of Justice sure was taken for one hell of a sleigh ride. After all, a man was scragged. It does seem that somebody should at least have been slapped by a good, stiff fine.

Mr. Coffey Buys—and Buries—
A Bride

*Here was a fine, upstanding man—a professional religious fund raiser
who took unto himself a bride with a little cash. It remained for an
unpedigreed dog to suspect that all was not gold that glittered.*

William N. Coffey was a big fiftyish
man with a round, pious face, a receding
hairline and a laugh that completely dis-
armed most people. His profession was
to raise funds for various charitable and
religious organizations, taking a percentage of the funds he raised as compensation for his worthy efforts. Mr. Coffey's
manner was charming, his bearing noble
and impressive, his expressed enthusiasm
for the Lord's work unbounded. And his
eyes were shrewd.

One summer day in 1926, Mr. Coffey
unpacked his clothing and Bibles in a
roach trap in La Crosse, Wisconsin, pre-
paratory to staging a fund-raising campaign. Discovering that his supply of
high stiff collars, size 17, had gone astray
somewhere along the charity trail, he
went to a local department store to buy
some more. That was how he came to
meet Mrs. Hattie Hales, a plump and
kittenish widow of fifty-five whose husband, a railroad engineer, had left her
with five thousand dollars when he had
gone around the last bend a few years
previously.

Mrs. Hales worked as a saleslady in the
department store; in conversation with
Mr. Coffey, however, she pridefully disclosed that she worked only to keep herself occupied, since her departed spouse
had left her well off.

Perhaps Mr. Coffey would have preferred a somewhat younger woman, but

he was a practical man. Mrs. Hale was
deeply religious. Mr. Coffey made it
clear to her that he was deeply religious,
too, and that he was unmarried. It was a
natural. In no time at all Mr. Coffey
eloped with the lady to Winona, Minnesota and then drove to Rockford, Illinois to spend an inexpensive honeymoon
at the home of relatives of the bride, including her mother.

All of Mrs. Coffey's Rockford relatives, near and distant, male and female,
were simply crazy about the groom, who
would never break bread without saying
grace, and who burst into psalms at odd
hours of the day and night. A bulldog
in the house where the Coffeys were staying struck the only discordant note in
this idyll of middle-aged romance. This
dog may have had his defects, but he
knew what he liked, and he didn't like
Mr. Coffey. When the animal growled at
the hearty fund raiser or showed an inclination to worry at his ankles or the
seat of his pants, Mr. Coffey forced a
smile and explained that the dog probably disliked him because he was a big
meat eater.

In Rockford, Mr. Coffey let it be
known that he engaged in fund raising
not to make a living, but for the inner
satisfaction that he felt when he helped
others. His commissions on funds he
raised, in fact, were something of a benevolent laugh to him because, he said

modestly, he gave them away, and then some, in private charities. From the new Mrs. Coffey Rockford learned that Mr. Coffey, despite his plain, middle-class appearance, was in reality a multimillionaire who went around hiding his good deeds. "You should just see the list of local charities that Billy Boy has marked down to make contributions to," the bride explained to a relative one day.

A fortnight after they had come to Rockford, the Coffeys left in his four-year-old low-price-range coupe. Friends and kin received several letters from the happy bride—from Dubuque, Iowa and other towns where the groom was raising funds. And then, in January of 1927—four months after the marriage—there came a letter not from Mrs. Coffey, but from Mr. Coffey. It was postmarked Chicago and addressed to the relatives with whom he had spent his honeymoon in Rockford.

Mr. Coffey said sadly that he had hardly known how to begin this letter: Hattie—his dear, beloved Hattie—had, he said, met a man named St. Claire and had run off with him. The name of St. Claire rang a bell in the minds of the folks in Rockford. Hattie had, in previous letters, been mentioning a Mr. St. Claire, presumably a fund-raiser too, with increasing frequency. Billy Boy, she had stated, had been busy with this or that charitable or religious drive and Mr. St. Claire—Billy Boy's most intimate friend, incidentally—had taken her out to dinner, or to the theater. It had all sounded perfectly above board and innocent, the bride's acquaintanceship with Mr. St. Claire—until now.

Mr. Coffey's woeful epistle divulged that he was going away. He was going into the silence to pray for Hattie and he was going to stay there until, as he put it, the great wound in his heart began, if

not to heal, to pain him less. His long letter ended on a highly religious pitch —"I ask God to forgive Hattie, for she knows not what she does"—and a postscript pleaded with the Rockford folks not to say anything to anybody about what Hattie had done, because Mr. Coffey's love for Hattie was, to quote him again, boundless. The recipients of the letter, including the bride's mother, who looked upon her new son-in-law as the salt of the earth, were outraged at what Hattie had done. They wanted to get in touch with Mr. Coffey and find out more, if they could, but, Mr. Coffey had put no return address on his letter and, now that they thought of it, the Rockford people never had found out just where where Mr. Coffey was from. Why, the addressees wondered, should they shield the actions of a woman who had left such a fine, noble husband to run off with another man? The bad news about Hattie was soon carried to her native Wisconsin, with the result that a male relative of Hattie—a man who lived in Wisconsin—walked into the office of Lyall Wright, the handsome and flamboyant twenty-seven-year-old sheriff of Juneau County one afternoon in the early part of January.

Wright, a quick-on-the-trigger young man who was known as the Boy Sheriff, listened to the tale of woe and then asked his visitor: "What am I supposed to do about it?"

"What are you supposed to *do* about it? Why, here's a woman who's broken the heart of the finest man God ever put breath into! *Find* her! Show her the error of her ways and reunite her with her husband."

Wright was an ambitious young man, but he couldn't see any grounds for legal action, at least by him, in the semi-comic marital affairs of the former Hattie

Hales. No crime was apparent, except perhaps a moral one committed against the philanthropic Mr. Coffey.

Then Mr. Coffey emerged from the silences in another letter to his wife's relatives in Rockford. This one had been mailed in Indianapolis. Mr. Coffey had been searching his soul and had come to the point of bitterly condemning himself for what Hattie had done. Had he not been so occupied with the Lord's work, he wailed, had he devoted more time and attention to Hattie, he was certain that she would never have run off with Mr. St. Claire. But he himself, alas, did not count: Hattie's happiness was all that mattered.

It was a touching effusion, this latest of Mr. Coffey's—up to a certain point. Then a sour and discordant note was struck in what had been a sweet symphony of charity and forgiveness. Hattie had, before departing with Mr. St. Claire, signed over to Mr. Coffey several hundred dollars' worth of shares in a small Wisconsin public utilities company—stock she had owned for several years. The stock, Mr. Coffey said, had been forced upon him by Hattie, apparently because she had wanted to do something tangible to recompense him for the loss of her companionship.

The transfer of this stock simply did not make sense. In the first place, Hattie Hales had been notorious as a collector of United States Treasury notes or their equivalent, and it just wouldn't have been natural for her to part voluntarily with anything of value. Also, according to Hattie herself, Mr. Coffey was a gentleman of considerable affluence, and a few hundred dollars to him would have meant little or nothing.

The couriers in gray again carried news of Mr. Coffey's latest communique into those reaches of Wisconsin where

Hattie was best known, and once again the Wisconsin relative of the missing woman journeyed to Mauston, the seat of Juneau County, and tackled the Boy Sheriff.

This time Wright was interested. He saw the possible outlines of a classic crime—a crime in which a high-powered impostor had married a skittish lady for her money, done away with her, and then created, out of whole cloth, a plausible reason for her disappearance.

Sheriff Wright decided to do some sleuthing by mail. He sent letters to officials of various religious and welfare organizations, with whom William N. Coffey had been associated in the past, and to various ministers and civic leaders in the Middle West and in the South, whose names Mr. Coffey had reeled off to friends and relatives of the former Hattie Hales.

The Boy Sheriff was hardly prepared for the result of his inquiries. To a man, those with whom Wright communicated stated that William N. Coffey was a flawless example of a perfect Christian gentleman. One city official of a community some distance from Wisconsin called Sheriff Wright long distance, frantic in the fear that the sheriff's inquiry about Mr. Coffey meant that some ill had befallen the esteemed fund raiser. A minister in the South telegraphed to Wright asking if he or his congregation, who had come to love the hearty big meat eater, could possibly be of any service to Mr. Coffey.

One former associate of Mr. Coffey in the fund-raising field, taking the sheriff's inquiry to mean that Mr. Coffey was in trouble of some sort, wrote to say that whatever Mr. Coffey was charged with, he was innocent. Mr. Coffey, this communicant disclosed, was simply incapable of harsh thoughts, let alone harsh actions, except in his battle against strong liquor. Mr. Coffey, it seemed, was so opposed to intoxicants of any kind that he was inclined to be unreasonable on the subject.

The male relative of the missing woman kept asking Wright how he was coming along with his investigation into Mr. Coffey. At last the Boy Sheriff said to the inquirer: "Go away."

This relative, however, had the persistence of a process server. The annual meeting of the little public utilities company in which Hattie had held stock—the stock now held by Mr. Coffey—was soon to be held. Mr. Coffey would more than likely know about the meeting, the relative told Sheriff Wright; what was more, Mr. Coffey might actually put in an appearance at the meeting for the express purpose of selling his stock.

The Boy Sheriff decided to attend the stockholders' meeting for the twin purposes of getting Hattie's relative off his official neck and of satisfying his own curiosity about an individual who was, on the word of just about everybody, a prince among men.

The meeting was held at night. Before it began, there was no sign of Mr. Coffey. But just as the chairman was banging for order, there was a commotion in the corridor outside the meeting room, and William N. Coffey, fighting foe of the demon rum, came into the room on legs made unsteady, Sheriff Wright could have sworn, by alcohol.

Mr. Coffey took a seat on the opposite side of the room from the sheriff, and a couple of hatchet-faced old ladies, sitting directly in front of him, arose and sought other seats, apparently because of Mr. Coffey's breath.

As the meeting progressed, Mr. Coffey seemed to sober up. He disposed of his stock during the course of the proceedings. When the meeting broke up, he seemed quite himself. But he still had his breath, as Sheriff Wright noticed when he went over and introduced himself.

Mr. Coffey, who was almost twice Wright's age, beamed, "Lyall," he said, in a rich, ingratiating baritone, "I've heard a great deal about you. You are, young man, destined to go far."

Wright was flattered, and completely charmed. He was face to face with the most compelling and hypnotic personality he had ever encountered. Mr. Coffey placed a pudgy hand at his throat. "Tonsilitis," he explained. "I had a druggist give me something for it, and do you know, I believe it contained alcohol."

Wright had Coffey's relative engage the man in conversation, while he took a look at the stock that Mr. Coffey had turned in. The signatures of Mrs. Coffey on the stock somehow looked stereotyped. Wright had in his pocket one of the letters that the Rockford relatives had received, signed by the widow, and he superimposed the signature on the letter over the signature on a share of stock. Holding the letter and the stock up to the light, he could see that the signatures didn't vary one iota. Then Mr. Wright compared the signatures on the various shares of stock and found that they, too, were precisely the same, showing none of the variations of genuine signatures of the same person. The answer was simple. The signatures had been made by a rubber stamp.

The Boy Sheriff was no dope. He knew a crime when he saw one, and he saw one now—a murder. Coffey had married Hattie Hales for her money, got it, murdered her, disposed of her body somewhere, and then fixed up a likely story to account for her disappearance.

It was all plain enough, and simple enough, Wright reflected, except for the vital problem of establishing the corpus delicti. He had no actual proof that the former Hattie Hales was dead, let alone that she had been murdered. Sheriff Wright told himself that if he knew anything about men, William N. Coffey—devastatingly charming, supremely cunning—stood in a fair way to get away with murder.

Now Wright let go with a jab at the suspect. He pointed out to him that the stock certificates and one of the letters, supposedly from Hattie, all bore the same rubber stamp signature. Was William N. Coffey caught off balance with that one? He was not.

He drew Wright into a corner, so that what he was about to say would not be overheard. "Lyall," he began, in a con man tone, "the truth of the matter is that the signature on the letters and on the stock *are* rubber-stamp signatures."

"You admit, then," said Wright, "that you are guilty of forgery?"

"Certainly not," said Mr. Coffey. "Hattie left me the third week of our marriage. I had to think of her dear old mother. Had I written immediately to her mother and her other relatives in Rockford and broken the news that Hattie had run off with Mr. St. Claire, the shock would have been too great for them. Hattie's mother would have died. She has a bad heart, you know."

"So?"

"So I had a rubber stamp made up, and began writing letters to the Rockford folks—fine, righteous people, bless them—so that this Mr. St. Claire's relationship with Hattie would be broken to them gradually. Then I wrote a letter myself. The whole idea of the rubber stamp was to save Hattie's mother from what might have been a fatal shock." Mr. Coffey fingered the knot of his white,

ministerial necktie and studied Sheriff Wright. "Praise the Lord," he added.

Wright admitted later that he had to fight an impulse to like Mr. Coffey, even though his intelligence told him that the man was a three-alarm scoundrel. "Why did you use a rubber stamp on the stock certificates?" the boy sheriff wanted to know.

Mr. Coffey had an answer for that one, too. He didn't intend to keep the money he was to receive for the certificates, he said. "I'm going to give it to Mother."

"Your wife's mother?"

"Yes." Mr. Coffey was, among other things, something of a Thespian. Tears came to his eyes again. "She reminds me so much of my own dear mother," he said.

Sheriff Wright told Mr. Coffey that he was sorry, but that he would have to lock him up on a technical charge of forgery.

Mr. Coffey's house of cards quickly tumbled about his head—apparently. A more intensive probe into the man's past disclosed that he had served time in Iowa, several years previously, for larceny in the form of holding out considerably more than his commissions from funds he raised. Moreover, Hattie Hales had never been his legal wife: Mr. Coffey had for many years been married and maintaining a family in Madison, Wisconsin —a wife and family who were still there to confound him.

Other peace-enforcement officials, including Sheriff Frank J. Kennedy of Dubuque County, Iowa, District Attorney Robert Clark of Juneau County, and the gendarmes of Mr. Coffey's home town of Madison, entered the picture. It developed that Mr. Coffey and Mrs. Hales had stayed at an automobile trailer camp in Dubuque during three days in October —the last trace available of Mrs. Hales over the entire itinerary Mr. Coffey had covered from the time of his departure from Rockford until the time of his arrest. Sheriff Kennedy's men carefully went over Dubuque and its environs. They came up with nothing.

But the Madison gendarmes came up with something. They found in Mr. Coffey's modest Madison residence a couple of bundles that he had dropped off there around Christmas time, when he had put in a short and sweet appearance for the holidays. The bundles contained clothes and jewelry belonging to Hattie Hales.

The evidence was building up. But it was by no means complete, and Mr. Coffey wasn't talking. They had him on forgery and bigamy, but not on murder. He just sat in his cell, reading his Bible and singing psalms, and refusing to admit anything. He was still Mr. Coffey to the sheriff and the sheriff continued to be Lyall to him.

More of Mr. Coffey's past began to come under the official magnifying glass. Mr. Coffey had, some eight years previously, become enamored of a pretty choir singer whose voice had blended well with his own in a small Wisconsin church of a Sunday morning. He had married the girl and gone off somewhere with her. She, like Hattie Hales, had vanished. Her parents had last heard from her from Boston. She had written them saying that she had been with child, but not Mr. Coffey's child—which was hardly the type of thing that a girl would put in writing. That had been the last that anybody had heard of her. Mr. Coffey's great heart had, of course, been broken when he returned to Wisconsin with the tale that his wife had left him, but time had healed his wound.

Sheriff Kennedy, Sheriff Wright, District Attorney Clark and just about everybody else associated with the case were taking a crack at Mr. Coffey. "Gentle-men," he said one day to the group of them, in that forgiving way of his, "why don't you begin proceedings against me for forgery and bigamy if you must proceed against me? Don't you realize you'll never convict me of murder?"

Lyall Wright was in an ugly spot. Not only was he failing to gain state-wide prominence by breaking William N. Coffey, but Coffey was making a monkey out of him. This kind of thing would be no help to his career.

Then Wright came up with an idea which, to this day, remains quite individual in crime history. He began talking one morning to a deputy sheriff in a tone of voice that was designed to appear confidential, but which he knew would carry to Coffey's cell. "We'll have to try the Berlin system on him," Wright said to the deputy. "I've just got a cable from the police of Berlin, Germany, and they've told me about their newest system in establishing whether a man's guilty of murder or not."

"The Berlin system?" asked the carefully-rehearsed deputy. "What's that, Lyall?"

"The damnedest thing you ever heard of," said Wright. "All I have to do is put Coffey on the scales at six in the morning and six at night and take careful note of his weight. When a man's guilty of murder he loses from half a pound to a pound a day. The Berlin police tell me it never misses."

"It sure sounds worth a try," said the deputy.

"It sure does," said Wright.

At six that evening Wright, explaining to Coffey, who he knew had heard everything, that weighing him twice a day was part of the jail routine, began the business on the scales. Coffey noted his weight, which was 190 pounds on the dot, smiled to himself and went back to his cell. In the morning at six, Wright got him up and weighed him again. Coffey blinked. He weighed only 189. He seemed to have lost a pound during the night. He had no way of knowing that Wright had adjusted the scales during the night.

At the third weighing in, at six the second night, Coffey scaled only 188½, despite the fact that he had eaten three big meals that day. He began to look alarmed.

Wright kept up the trickery and Coffey continued to lose weight. Then, one morning, when Coffey should have weighed 184, according to the way Wright had set the scales, he weighed, instead, 186. At first, Wright couldn't understand it. But he understood it when he frisked Coffey. The prisoner had secreted in his clothing his Bible, which weighed two pounds.

The Boy Sheriff knew he had Coffey now. "You can't beat the Berlin system," he said to the prisoner. "You'd better tell me all you know."

Coffey hung on for a couple of days more. He tried every dodge he could think of to beat Wright's "Berlin system," including soaking his underclothes and socks in water, and concealing heavy articles in his mouth at weighing-in time. But the big prisoner began to suffer from lack of sleep, as fear really took hold of

him, and one night he sent for Wright. "Lyall," he said, "call a stenographer; I'm ready to tell you everything."

Coffey's story was that he had killed his wife by accident during a quarrel—a quarrel that had begun when she accused him of running around with another woman.

The body, carefully cut into many pieces, was discovered in a series of graves near an automobile camp at Bratton's Woods, Wisconsin. There was little question in the minds of the investigators that Coffey had deliberately slain his wife; he had obtained her money, and that was all he had married her for.

Bitter feeling developed between Sheriff Wright of Juneau County and Sheriff Kennedy of Dubuque. Kennedy was of the opinion that the murder had been committed in his county—and the finding in Dubuque of a blood-stained baseball bat, which Coffey admitted having used in the crime, appeared to substantiate Kennedy's theory. But Coffey maintained that the death had taken place in Wisconsin—possibly because Wisconsin's punishment for murder was life imprisonment, while Iowa had the death penalty. Sheriff Wright, eager to wrap up the case, decided that the murder had been committed in Wisconsin. Coffey was sent away for life.

The Lady in the Bath Tub

There's an old saying that the cops can make a hundred mistakes, the murderer only one. Here's proof, unfortunately for Nancy Titterton.

If there was one thing that Police Commissioner Lewis J. Valentine of New York City could have done without on April 10, 1936, it was a bath tub murder. April 10 was Good Friday. The Commissioner, a man of heroic conviviality, had been on the wagon for Lent. He still had a day to go. A bath tub reminded him of water—something he had grown to loathe.

A bath tub murder was precisely what was deposited in Valentine's lap late in the afternoon. What was worse, it was the kind of murder that would generate intense heat on the police department until it was cleaned up. It had all the elements that enchanted the newspapers, especially the tabloids—a lady victim, sex, glamorous locale, sex, mystery, and sex. If the case wasn't cracked fairly promptly, Fiorella LaGuardia, the Mayor, who became physically ill at the mere thought of newspaper criticism, would be on the phone every half hour screaming, "Lew, for *cry*-sake get the goddam lead out and bring somebody *in, will* you, Lew!"

What had happened was that a couple of upholsterers had gone to the apartment of a Mr. and Mrs. Lewis Titterton, at 22 Beekman Place, about half past four in the afternoon, to deliver a love seat that they had repaired, found the door of the apartment ajar, walked in and discovered Mrs. Titterton dead in the bath tub. The lady, almost nude, had been garrotted by a pink pajama top before being placed in the tub, which was partly filled with water.

The upholsterers—a man named Theodore Kruger, and his assistant, a fellow named John Fiorenza—began a prowl of the premises. Fiorenza, a pocket-billiard addict from Brooklyn, summoned his employer into the bedroom. He pointed to a rumpled blue candlewick counterpane, and a large insinuating stain thereon, and remarked, "Prolly a sex feen."

Detectives agreed with Fiorenza. Robbery had not been the motive; nothing in the apartment had been tossed except Mrs. Titterton.

The victim's husband, dug out of Rockefeller Center, where he worked for the National Broadcasting Company, turned out to be a spare, blond Englishman in his middle thirties. He spoke and behaved like a man who had been educated at both Cambridge and Harvard, which he had. This made him a suspicious character to a couple of manhunters who had been weaned in Hell's Kitchen.

"When'd you see your wife last?"

"At breakfast."

"What time was that?"

"Hawlf past eight."

"It's a quadder after five now. Where you been all day? You come home to lunch? You talk to your wife on the phone at all?"

"Which question do you wish me to awnswer? You've awsked three, old boy."

"Oh, a *wise* guy."

Titterton, a connoisseur of dry humor, had telephoned his wife from his office at about nine-thirty that morning and relayed to her a piece of amusement he

333

had come upon in the morning post. He had been in and out of his office at the wireless concern all day. A couple of times, once during mid-morning, he had been absent long enough to have returned to his apartment, less than fifteen minutes by cab. He had been absent more than an hour around lunch time. He had lunched alone at a sandwich counter in the NBC Building.

"Who seen you there?"

The detective who posed that query obviously had not spent much time in the NBC Building. Nobody ever saw anybody in the NBC Building. People in the corridors and in the lifts there were usually too intent on their own business to notice other people. It was the NBC Building that contributed to the disintegration of the marriage of Sinclair Lewis and Dorothy Thompson. Once asked whatever had happened to his wife, Lewis said, "She disappeared into the NBC Building two years ago and I haven't heard from her since."

Big-city detectives, especially the New York variety, out on a front-page murder case, are seldom enthusiastic subscribers to the theory that a man is innocent until proven guilty. When a man could conceivably have committed a crime, even though he is not the type and would have had no apparent motive, he is, to the average detective, guilty until proved innocent. Titterton divined this attitude on the part of the detective team from Hell's Kitchen. "A chap," he said, "would hardly rape his own wife, you know."

The state of the body indicated Mrs. Titterton had been done up between ten-thirty and eleven-thirty that morning. A woman friend had telephoned her at ten-thirty and spoken to her about a social engagement. Another woman friend had phoned at eleven-thirty and received no answer. A delivery boy from a neighborhood dry-cleaning establishment had called at the apartment at eleven-thirty, with a dress for Mrs. Titterton, rung the bell and received no answer. He had noticed that the entrance door was ajar, as it still was when the upholsterers called almost five hours later. While the dry-cleaning boy had been at the door he heard the phone ringing inside, concluded nobody was home when nobody answered it, and went away with the dress.

Although the Tittertons lived on a very tony thoroughfare—the building they lived in was a run-of-the-mill five-story brownstone without a doorman or an elevator. The Titterton apartment was a seventy-five-dollar-a-month four-room layout on the fourth floor. Anybody with the legs to climb the stairs could go up and ring the bell. Mrs. Titterton, a devotee of crime and horror stories, had learned in such literature the value of caution. She never opened the door to anyone without first calling through and finding out who was there.

The locking mechanism of the door had not been tampered with. Apparently Mrs. Titterton had let her murderer in and he had, upon leaving after killing the lady, thoughtlessly left the door ajar, unmindful of burglars. It appeared, then, that Mrs. Titterton had known the man who murdered her.

Mrs. Titterton, a thirty-three-year-old native of Ohio, was hardly the classic rape victim. She was the intellectual, rather than the casting couch, type. She was a tiny woman, with an average figure. She was dark, even-featured and sparkling in conversation. But, at a party, she was definitely not the kind of woman that a wolf would back into a corner. The bed on which the crime had quite obviously been perpetrated was disassembled and the component parts removed to the police laboratory with the care that would have been accorded to so many crates of eggs. Mrs. Titterton's wrists bore marks of binding by stout cord. A piece of quarter-inch five-ply cord was found in the bath tub under the body. It matched in thickness the marks on the victim's wrists. It was thirteen inches long. Apparently it had been part of a larger piece that the murderer had removed before leaving.

The cord looked as if it had come from a Venetian blind. There were Venetian blinds in the Titterton apartment but the cords on them were intact. The murderer, then, had brought the cord with him. This meant that he had come with rape in mind, which in turn indicated premeditation rather than a crime of impulse.

The cord angle suggested to some of the dicks that the murderer had been a social acquaintance of Mrs. Titterton's rather than a tradesman or a delivery man. The reasoning here was that run-of-the-mill people seldom lived in homes with Venetian blinds whereas those likely to know the Tittertons socially probably did.

While the boys in the laboratory were sweating over the bed, sixty-some dicks were infiltrating themselves into the front-parlor and below-stairs life of the murder neighborhood, and Commissioner Valentine was assuring himself that high noon of Easter Saturday—the hour when Lent officially ended—*would* come, despite its slowness of approach.

The town's two morning tabloids, whose readers had been on a long and monotonous diet of unimaginative homicides among the working classes, prepared to dish up the feast inherent in an upper-class sex murder. Not content with the basic ingredients, the tabloids, and then the more conservative papers, began to douse on the seasoning of exaggeration. Mrs. Titterton, by virtue of some old soft-focus pictures and prose by reporters unburdened by the demands of accuracy, now became a ravishing beauty. Her husband, who at the time was in the $5,000-a-year brackets in the semi-important post of authority on literary rights for NBC, became, in at least one tabloid, a big network executive making five hundred dollars a week.

Mrs. Titterton, who had dabbled in long-hair literary efforts, and who had a bureau drawer half filled with rejected manuscripts, became a highly successful author. The basis for this stature derived principally from the fact that she had recently sold a short story to the highbrow magazine *Story*, whose co-editor, Whit Burnett, a man who never completely understood why writers had to eat, had mailed her a check for twenty-five dollars. The Titterton apartment, which gave off on a bright orange fire escape, and which was furnished chiefly by things picked up in side-street secondhand shops, became the lush dream of an interior decorator.

The Tittertons, represented as being close friends of top-drawer figures in the literary, publishing, and radio fields, actually circulated on a semi-Bohemian intellectual level where promise, rather than accomplishment, predominated. Their friends included minor executives in publishing and radio circles, radio and magazine writers, and artists, who, whatever they have accomplished since, weren't worried about income taxes then.

Among the Titterton acquaintances was a fellow who wrote soap operas for the radio. He was a genius at involving the characters of his creation in dilemmas that caused cry water to drop on

numberless washboards. On the morning
after the murder, this man woke up to
find himself in a situation more dramatic,
and certainly far less hopeful of solution,
than any he had ever contrived in his
five-times-weekly assaults on feminine
tear ducts.

The fellow woke up in the back room
of a watering hole in the heart of the
lost-weekend district on Third Avenue.
He had been there all night. Since he
was a steady patron, he had been accorded lodging privileges when the joint
locked up at four A.M. It was now half-
past ten and the beer spigots were being
polished up for the late breakfast trade.

The soap-opera writer won the fight to
get the hair of the dog that bit him past
his nose and, a few minutes later, when
it decided to stay down, he took a chance
on bleeding to death by opening his eyes
all the way. When he did, he saw Mrs.
Titterton's picture on the front page of
the *Daily News*. He shut his eyes quick,
then opened them again. Mrs. Titterton's picture was still there. She had been
murdered about twenty-four hours previously.

Mrs. Titterton was a friend of his. He
had always had a secret yen for her. He
had started to raise a fog on the Thursday night and, sometime early on Good
Friday morning—he judged now that it
had been around ten o'clock—he had
found himself in the vicinity of Beekman Place and had decided to go up and
call on Mrs. Titterton. He had been in
the apartment many times before—always
at night when the lady's husband was
there—and he knew his way around the
building. He had figured that he would
find Mrs. Titterton alone, and, with the
unrealistic conceit of the drunk, that she
would be receptive to what he had in
mind.

As he sat reading the story of the mur-

der—the murder that had been committed by some friend of Mrs. Titterton's—the writer attempted to penetrate
the Scotch mist that lay between the
present and the morning before. He
could not remember a thing after making the decision to go up and see Mrs.
Titterton. He knew from past experience
that, when out on a red-paint job, he
had sometimes travelled considerable
distances, carried on conversations with
people, propositioned women, fought
with men, and wrote out checks, and
then, next morning, had been unable to
recollect a single minute of it. Now he
wondered if he had made his way to the
Titterton apartment, committed the
crime, and then wandered away undetected.

He learned that he hadn't shown up
in the saloon until early afternoon the
day previously. He inquired at other
spots on his Third Avenue beat. He
couldn't establish where he had been at
the hour of the murder. He couldn't
begin to guess where he had been—unless
in the Titterton apartment.

He made his way to East Forty-second
Street and bought the early editions of
the Saturday afternoon papers. One paper had gotten hold of the fact that nail
marks from the heel of a shoe—no doubt
the shoe of the murderer—had been
found on the inside of the footboard of
the bed.

The writer went into a shoe store and
bought himself a pair of new shoes—with
rubber heels. He took his old shoes with
him. He threw them into the East River.
He had never felt so much like a drink
in his life. He was too scared to take one.
He walked over to one of the parks in
Tudor City. There he sat down to try to
think things out, to see if he could somehow get through the fog and establish

his innocence of the thing he feared he had done.

It was noon. Commissioner Valentine was having an early lunch in an Irish restaurant on Center Street across from headquarters. He downed a rye, neat, then called to the waiter. "Another one quick," he said. "A bird can't fly on one wing, you know."

A janitor is always one of the first things the dicks try on for size in a case like the Titterton one. The janitor in the murder building—Dudley Mings— was a good-natured, slow-moving big man who was somewhat hard of hearing when tenants called to him to do something, except around Christmas time. It was the habit of the residents of 22 Beekman Place, whether they lived on the first floor or the fifth, to go to their doors and yell for Dudley at the top of their lungs when they wanted a chore performed.

During the one-hour time block in which the murder had been committed, Mrs. Titterton, whose voice was distinctive, had called out, "Dudley! Dudley!" Tenants who had heard had assumed that she had discovered a leaky faucet or something. The dicks wondered whether she had been yelling to Dudley to do something or to stop doing something.

A contributing editor of *The Reader's Digest*—a man named W. A. DeWitt— had, during the murder hour, been struggling with a problem of condensation in his Beekman Place study, which overlooked the roof of the murder building. The magazine man had been gazing out of a window, perhaps trying to think of one word that would take the place of six, when he noticed a big man in blue denims walking suspiciously, whatever that form of ambulation might be like, over the roof of the Number 22.

The man in the blue denims turned out to be Mings, the janitor. His expla-nation for his presence on the roof was that he had gone up there to repair a trap door. The trap door had, indeed, been recently repaired, but *how* recently the janitor couldn't prove. The dicks who had Mings on the suspect list figured that he had gone to the roof, made his way to the roof of an adjoining building and then gone down a fire escape by way of returning to his own quarters. To have returned to his quarters by way of the stairs in his own building would have, the way the dicks figured it, entailed the risk on Mings' part of being seen by tenants who had heard Mrs. Titterton calling, "Dudley! Dudley!"

Commissioner Valentine, feeling better than he had in six weeks, returned to his desk at headquarters after lunch on the Saturday afternoon to find there a breakdown of what the laboratory boys had found out about the bed.

The presence of male semen, a protein substance, on a piece of material or clothing, could not be positively established in a laboratory test. Certain tests, however, could establish its absence. An analysis of the spot on the counterpane failed to establish that it was not semen. In view of the circumstances, it was assumed that it was—and it was on this very point that the case was eventually to be broken.

A piece of horsehair—a single piece— showed up in the debris sucked from the counterpane by a small police vacuum sweeper. The piece of hair was gray and black. It was a quick, simple matter to check it against horsehair used for padding in the clothing of every suspect who was being screened. The hair did not match that taken from the clothing of Titterton, the husband; Mings, the janitor; or several delivery men and boys who either admittedly had been, or could have been, in the Titterton apartment building Good Friday morning.

The nail marks on the footboard of the bed, obviously made by the heel of the rapist's shoe, weren't distinctive enough to be matched up against the nails in the shoe heel of a suspect. They offered a lead of sorts, however. The killer wore leather heels on his shoes, not rubber ones. Nails sometimes stick out of leather heels; never out of rubber heels. Titterton wore rubber heels; Mings leather heels with nails protruding from them.

A smudge of paint had shown up on the counterpane. It was bright orange— the color of the fire escape at 22 Beekman Place.

The fire escape gave off from the Titterton bathroom. It had been painted only a week or so before the murder. Several painters and other workmen had been engaged in maintenance work not only at Number 22 but on adjoining buildings.

Since it was known that Nancy sometimes walked around the apartment in a semi-state of attire there were several Peeping Toms among the artisans. One man even carried field glasses as part of his equipment. One of the painters admitted to Deputy Chief Inspector Francis J. Kear, in charge of all dicks in the department, "We're not gettin' rich. So what the hell, we might as well have a little fun."

Since the fire escape on the building at Number 22 ran past not only the Titterton bathroom but the bathrooms of apartments above and below the Tittertons, there had been a brisk demand by the painters to be assigned to it. "I bet we painted that damned thing three times," a painter told Inspector Kear. "It wasn't worth it, either. Why, I seen better lookin' dames in the Bronx."

Whatever else the men on the fire escape may have seen or may have missed, none of them would admit having laid eyes on Mrs. Titterton, with or without her clothes on. Dicks were assigned to look into every man.

Late on the Saturday afternoon, the soap-opera writer who didn't know whether or not he had murdered Mrs. Titterton, decided to go home. He found a dick waiting for him. A dick had been assigned to question every man whose name was down in the Titterton address book.

"Where were you yesterday morning between half past ten and half past eleven?"

"In a saloon."

"Where abouts?"

"On Third Avenue."

"Okay. We'll go over there."

"No, I was visiting a friend."

"Okay, we'll go see the friend."

"To tell the truth, I don't remember *where* I was."

"I know. You been on a bender. You got new shoes on—with rubber heels. The other shoes in your clothes closet have leather heels. Come on."

The dicks who were ringing doorbells on Beekman Place began to hear about a tall thin man with a sandy moustache. A character thus described had appeared at half a dozen apartment doors in the Titterton and an adjoining building the night before and the morning of the murder. He had inquired for a Miss Claxton, a Miss Poindexter, a Miss Haverstraw and several other ladies. He had appeared at one apartment on the third floor of the murder house shortly after ten o'clock the morning of the crime.

Half a dozen dicks were doing nothing except examining the trip sheets of the city's thousands of taxi drivers for the morning of Good Friday. The trip sheets recorded the starting points and destinations of passengers and the approximate times they were carried. More than a hundred cabs had left the vicinity of the murder scene around the time of the crime. One driver recalled having picked up a tall thin man with a sandy moustache half a block from the Titterton house shortly after eleven o'clock the previous morning. He had dropped the man at an apartment house on East Seventieth Street.

"What was you doin' on Beekman Place askin' for a Miss Claxton and a Miss Poindexter and a lot of other names?"

"Not so loud, please. My wife's in the next room."

"Well, get your hat and tell her you won't be back for a little while."

On Monday morning—seventy-two hours after the murder—Commissioner Valentine feared the worst, and it happened. LaGuardia, the Little Flower, having spent Easter Sunday resting and reading the papers, was on the wire bright and early. "What you got on that murder, Lew? You think maybe that janitor's in it?"

"We're inclined to eliminate him, Mr. Mayor."

"Then how about that fellow you picked up Saturday night—the fellow who was inquiring for all those girls?"

"He's out. Seems he met a girl at a party and didn't get her name or exact address straight. All he knew was she lived at number twenty something Beekman Place. He decided to hunt for a needle in a haystack and didn't find it."

"Anything new on the painters, on the husband?"

"Not a thing, Mr. Mayor. We found out how that paint got on the counterpane. It was put on the fire escape to air."

"Well, what about that radio writer? For cry-sake Lew, haven't you got anything!"

"He's our best bet. We've taken pictures of him and we're passing them around Beekman Place. If anybody saw him around twenty-two Friday morning, we'll wrap it up."

The piece of horsehair found on the murder bed didn't match up with any in the padding of the writer's suits. The piece of cord that had bound Mrs. Titterton's wrists couldn't be tied to him, either. There wasn't a single clear fingerprint in the Titterton apartment that didn't belong to the dead woman, her husband or a maid who came in occasionally. There were some partial prints, probably those of the murderer, on the bed, on the bath tub and on Mrs. Titterton's garter belt, where they had been brought up by the then-new silver-nitrate process. The prints were so smudged, due to the fact that whoever had made them had been in motion, that they were completely useless. The police sent samples of the cord and the horsehair to cord and horsehair manufacturers and hoped for the best.

Nobody on Beekman Place had seen the radio writer Good Friday morning. That didn't mean anything one way or the other. The man himself now admitted to the police that he could very well have committed the murder without recalling it. "I wish," he said, "you'd get it cleared up, even if clearing it up means pinning it on me. Anything would be better than the torture of this suspense."

In a way, the fellow was getting a dose of his own medicine. He himself had inflicted upon countless housewives the torture of not knowing, until the following day, same time, same station, whether the heroine would give the next dance to the honest bricklayer, the handsome tin-smith or the lecherous drummer.

By Tuesday, the department was leaning heavily on the piece of horsehair and the thirteen-inch length of quarter-inch five-ply cord. They got word from a cord-age company in Pennsylvania. They got word from the horsehair people. A turn-key walked to a cell in a police station, unlocked the door, and said to the radio writer, "You can go. You didn't do it."

The cord, which the cops had thought was a product used in Venetian blinds, was really made for use in the upholstery business. It was utilized in binding the padding of stuffed furniture. The horse-hair, too, was of a type used to stuff fur-niture.

Commissioner Valentine felt a head-ache coming on. Two upholsterers had discovered the body. It had never oc-curred to the department to include the two men in the suspect list. If one of them were guilty of a crime which had had the department in a wheel for five days, the Little Flower would have a hemorrhage.

Kruger, the boss upholsterer, had a clean record. Fiorenza, his assistant, didn't. As a boy, he had played cops and robbers—with real cops. He had done time. At the moment, he was on proba-tion. His specialty was hot cars. That didn't rule out a sex crime. Fiorenza looked like a hot greaseball.

Fiorenza hadn't come to work until about noon on Good Friday. He had called up earlier to tell Kruger, who knew of his criminal past, that he would be late since he was reporting to his pro-bation officer. Kruger hadn't known, but the dicks knew, that probation offices were closed on Good Friday.

The dicks had their man, but they knew that a mouthpiece with an eye to loopholes and dramatics stood a good chance of beating a rap that hung on a piece of horsehair and a piece of cord. They had to have a confession.

The dicks tailed Fiorenza for five days. Then, when they were sure that he felt he was in the clear, they nailed him. He was a shrewd cookie. "Nobody can prove nothin' on me." He started to scream for a lawyer. A lawyer could wait.

The dicks told Fiorenza they had an ace in the hole—an ace that Fiorenza himself was holding. They reminded him of the spot on the counterpane—the spot that he himself had called his em-ployer's attention to. Then they took a sample of his semen. Next day they told him that a laboratory comparison analy-sis showed that the spot on the counter-pane had been made by him. The dicks were, of course, bluffing, but they might as well have hit the Brooklyn boy with a brick outhouse. "Okay. Okay. I done it."

What Fiorenza had done had been clever enough. In fact, the boldness of the execution of the crime had com-pletely fooled the cops. He had first seen Mrs. Titterton, none too fully clothed, when he had called for some work some months previously. For some reason or other—probably, the dome doctors claimed, because she was so cultured and he was such a mugg—Mrs. Titterton be-came the ideal woman to possess in the mind of Fiorenza. For months he thought of nothing else except Mrs. Titterton.

The night before the murder he fig-ured it all out. He conceived an excuse for absence from work the following morning. He went to the Titterton apartment and had no trouble getting in because Mrs. Titterton knew him. He said his boss had sent him around to ask something about the love seat that was to be delivered that afternoon. When he learned that Mrs. Titterton was alone with him, he bound her wrists with some cord he had brought for the purpose, raped her, then strangled her. Fiorenza said he put his victim in the bath tub to make the death look like a suicide. He forgot to remove from Mrs. Titterton's throat the pajama top he had strangled her with. He overlooked the piece of cord when he cut the binding from her wrists. He had no way of knowing that he had, by way of driving an extra nail in his own coffin, left on the counterpane a piece of horsehair that had clung to his clothing at least from the previous day.

The Titterton case was something less than a classic example of brilliant police work. It was, rather, a classic example of the axiom in station houses that the cops can make a hundred mistakes but the criminal can make only one.

The Snatch That Made the G-Men

*We are sometimes prone to take the work of J. Edgar Hoover and his
G-Men for granted. But there was a time when the F. B. I. locked
horns with the underworld—when the underworld threatened
to take over the country—and came out ahead. Here is the
case—one that outstrips fiction at every bend in the
investigative road—that made the country sit up
and take notice.*

In the summer of 1933, J. Edgar
Hoover's G-Men, then only cutting their
investigative teeth, pulled off a job that
connoisseurs of crime detection regard
as unsurpassed even to this day. The
crime itself wasn't extraordinary per se;
it wasn't, in fact, even a murder. It was
a kidnapping, a snatch—one of a wave
of big-league jobs that broke out like an
epidemic back in the thirties. It was how
it was solved that made it one for the
book. And it was what its solution represented—the twilight of the public enemy
—that made it a milestone in the history
of law-enforcement. By the same token,
this particular case spotlighted the
G-Men as they had never been spotlighted before and brought about public
realization that Hoover's boys were not
boys but men.

The snatch that made the G-Men came
in the midst of the gangster era—the era
of John Dillinger, Baby Face Nelson,
Pretty Boy Floyd, Machine Gun Kelly,
Creepy Karpis, Ma Barker and her sons
Clyde and Marvin, and Clyde's cigar-
smoking moll, Bonnie Parker; Al Capone,
the Lindbergh kidnapping, the Kansas
City Union Station massacre, the battle
of Little Bohemia Lodge, and that contribution to Chicago's civic improvement wherein one gang, masquerading
as cops carrying machine guns, went into

a garage and mowed down another gang
on St. Valentine's Day.

The Lindbergh Law—the statute that
was to give G-Men authority to chase the
hoodlums across state lines—was just a
gleam in J. Edgar Hoover's eye. The
gangsters were calling practically all the
shots. The real-life counterparts of such
movie baddies as James Cagney, Hum-
phrey Bogart and Edward G. Robinson
were putting the snatch on affluent citizens, heisting jugs and otherwise scaring
the hell out of people, then jumping into
jallopies with souped-up motors, crossing
state lines into areas of asylum, and lying
doggo until things cooled off.

Even when, after the Lindbergh kidnapping, the G-Men were authorized to
cross state lines and carry guns, the gangsters weren't particularly impressed. Nor
was the public or many of the country's
police departments. Hoover himself was
a mild-looking lawyer of thirty-eight,
hardly a fellow to throw the fear of Hell
into anybody by his mere appearance;
and his clean-cut, clear-eyed young law-
trained G-Men, some of them just a little
on the righteous side, hardly looked like
the crew to pull the rug from under the
gangsters. "A bunch of Boy Scouts," wise-
cracked Jimmy Walker, New York's
clothes-conscious Mayor. "Publicity
hounds," said a politically-appointed

police chief, who got sore when the G-Men suddenly appeared in town one night, lit up a building with spotlights, then went in and made an important pinch a stone's throw from police headquarters.

Small wonder, then, that a couple of hoods, who, even though they couldn't write very well, could read, and thus knew about Hoover's threat to crush the public enemies, went right ahead with their plans to snatch Charles Urschel, a multi-millionaire Oklahoma oil man, on the night of July 22, 1933, and hold him for a ransom of two hundred thousand dollars—a fifth of a million, tax free. The pair got the caper rolling about eleven o'clock on a steaming Saturday night when they appeared on the sun porch of Urschel's mansion, a movie-type showplace in Oklahoma City. There were four persons on the sun porch—Urschel and his wife, and Walter B. Jarrett, another multi-millionaire oil man, and his wife. The quartet had, before the appearance of the two hoods, been enjoying a nightcap after an evening of high-stakes bridge.

"Which one of you is Urschel?" asked one of the hoods—a six-footer with broad shoulders and a snap-brim hat yanked well down over his forehead. He was carrying a sub-machine gun. Nobody answered. "Hell," said the second hood, "a smaller man holding a pistol, "let's take *both* uv thum."

Urschel and Jarrett were hustled out, shoved into a car and driven away. Mrs. Urschel put through a call to the F.B.I. in Washington and got J. Edgar Hoover on the phone. Hoover told her to keep mum and stand by.

An hour or so later, Jarrett turned up. He had been dumped out of the car at a dark spot a dozen miles out of town after the hoods had discovered which captive was Urschel. He had not gotten the license number of the car but said it had been a Chevrolet sedan.

G-Men soon arrived and stationed themselves in the Urschel mansion as well as in the Oklahoma City telephone exchange, alerted for the next move of the kidnappers. Nothing happened for four days. Then, on the Wednesday, a small boy was walking along a street in Tulsa, a hundred odd miles northeast of the snatch scene, when a faceless sort of stranger stopped him, handed him a small package and a dollar and told him to deliver the package to a prominent local oil millionaire named Catlett. Catlett was a close friend of Urschel's.

The package contained four letters— two typewritten by the kidnappers and two handwritten by Urschel. What the letters boiled down to was that another oil-rich friend of the abducted man—a tall, weather-beaten ex-Texas Ranger named Kirkpatrick—was to make up a package of two hundred grand in old, unmarked twenty-dollar bills, put a blind money-ready ad in the real-estate columns of the Daily *Oklahoman* and stand by for instructions.

Kirkpatrick telephoned the Urschel home and talked to a G-Man. "Go ahead with the ad," he was told. "We'll get the money from Mrs. Urschel and deliver it to you." What the G-Men wanted to do, of course, was to record the serial numbers of the bills.

The day after the ad appeared, Kirkpatrick received a typewritten letter postmarked Joplin, Missouri. It instructed him to pack the ransom in a bag of light color, so that it would be visible at night, and then, on Saturday night—just a week after the snatch—board the Katy Sooner Flyer, which left Oklahoma City at tenten for an overnight run eastward to Kansas City. Kirkpatrick was to sit on the rear platform of the observation car of the train and keep his eyes peeled for a bonfire on the right side of the tracks in the direction the train was moving. When he saw the bonfire he was to alert himself for the appearance of a second bonfire farther on. When he saw this second fire he was to toss the bag of ransom to the tracks.

If Kirkpatrick didn't see the bonfires that would mean that the kidnappers had changed their plans. If so, he was to proceed to Kansas City, register at the Muehlebach Hotel and stand by for further communication.

So the ex-Texas Ranger was sitting on the rear platform of the observation car of the Katy Sooner Flyer, with the ransom in a light-colored bag, when the train pulled out on the Saturday night. The G-Men were making no attempt to catch up with the snatchers at this stage of the game for fear of jeopardizing the life of the hostage. They would move—and move fast—at the proper time.

Not long out of Oklahoma City the Katy Sooner Flyer made an unscheduled stop to put on two extra cars to accommodate week-end travellers. The extra cars were coupled to the end of the train so that the observation car become the third car from the end rather than the end car. That bitched things up and Kirkpatrick never did see any fires.

When, on the Sunday morning, Kirkpatrick registered at the Muehlebach Hotel, there was a telegram for him from Tulsa. The wire said the kidnappers understood how the two extra cars attached to the Katy Sooner Flyer had prevented Kirkpatrick from following instructions, but that everything would be all right if he would wait in his hotel room for a phone call.

That night Kirkpatrick got a phone call instructing him to walk to the La-Salle Hotel, several blocks distant, and to take the bag of money with him. Kirkpatrick had covered part of the distance when he heard a voice behind him saying, "I'll take that bag, Mr. Kirkpatrick." Kirkpatrick turned around but didn't get a good look at the speaker's face. Kirkpatrick asked the man what assurance he had that Urschel would be returned safely. "Never mind about that," said the man. "He'll be okay." Kirkpatrick decided to chance it.

Late on the Monday night—nine nights after he had been snatched—Charles Urschel returned home after having been driven around blindfolded since early that morning, then shoved out of the car on the outskirts of the city. The oil man —a compact, middle-aged gent with moxie to spare—looked very tired. The G-Men asked him if he wanted to sleep before he gave them a day-to-day account of what had happened to him and answering a couple of thousand questions. "Hell, no," said Urschel. "Let's get after the bastards as fast as we can."

On the Saturday night he was abducted, Urschel had gotten only fair-to-middling descriptions of his abductors before Jarrett was released. Both had been in their thirties. One had been big and broad-shouldered, the other of medium size. After Jarrett was dumped out of the car the two snatchers manacled Urschel hand and foot, blindfolded him, stuck cotton in his ears and told him to lie on the floor in the rear. Both of the snatchers rode in front.

"What was the last thing you saw that you could recognize before you were blindfolded?" a G-Man asked Urschel.

"The lights at the power plant at Harrah." Harrah was to the east of Oklahoma City.

Now, lying there in the back seat, deprived of his sense of sight, Urschel knew he would have to rely largely on his other senses to determine where he was being taken. One of his first impressions was that the car was to some extent back-tracking.

"How did you know *that*?"

"I don't know. I guess I just *felt* it."

"How fast would you say the car was going?"

"Oh, at moderate speed. Say thirty miles an hour, maybe."

"Did you get jounced much, lying there in the back seat, as if you were going over bumpy roads instead of smooth ones?"

"*I'll* say I got jounced. Those fellows certainly knew how to pick out the bad roads."

By way of loosening the cotton that had been stuck in his ears, Urschel began to work his jaws. After a while he had loosened the cotton sufficiently to hear fairly well.

About an hour, so nearly as Urschel could judge, from the time the car had left the point near Harrah, he smelled oil and heard the sound of pumps. Oil wells. Then, about half an hour later, he smelled oil and heard pumps again. More oil wells.

"You're pretty sure about the time— say an hour before you heard the first pump, then half an hour later when you heard the second one?"

"Pretty sure."

"And those were oil pumps you heard and that was oil you smelled?"

Urschel reminded the G-Men that he had been an oil man all his life.

Sometime around four o'clock in the morning, as Urschel figured time, the car stopped. One of his captors stayed with him while the other one walked away. In about fifteen minutes, the man who had walked away returned. Now Urschel could hear the sound of metal striking metal and the odor of gasoline was quite distinct. The man had gone off for some gasoline, returned with it in a metal container and was filling the tank of the car.

Urschel knew when daybreak came because some light filtered through the covering over his eyes and he could hear the crowing of roosters. It was not long after daybreak that the car swerved sharply into what was obviously a very bumpy dirt road. It travelled at a crawl for about three minutes, then Urschel heard one of the snatchers getting out and opening a gate. Now the car moved forward a short distance and stopped. Judging from a creaking sound, the gate was closed.

"How could you be sure the car was only crawling?"

"I could hear the driver shifting into second gear."

About three minutes after going through the first gate the car went through another gate.

"So the car went through two gates after turning in off the road?"

"Yes."

About a minute after passing through the second gate, the car entered a structure of some sort. How, his questioners wanted to know, did Urschel know that? Urschel knew by the diminution of light coming through his bandages and the sound that a motor makes when inside a building.

Now Urschel was transferred from one car to another. When the second car started out, Urschel, who knew quite a lot about engines, judged, from the sound of the motor, that he was in a Cadillac. There was a bed of sorts in the rear of this second car and Urschel was told to lie down on it and was then completely covered over by a blanket.

At about eight o'clock in the morning,

so nearly as Urschel could determine, the men in the front seat told him they were going to pull into a gas station and that if he peeped they would let him have it. At the gas station one of the kidnappers passed the time of day with a woman who was attending to the pumps. Urschel heard the woman complaining about the weather. The region, she said, had lacked rain and the crops were burning up. But she was hopeful. A big storm, she said, was brewing.

"What did that woman's voice sound like? Was it low or high or screechy or what?"

"It was high and kind of cracked."

"Would you say she was a young woman or an old woman?"

"Now that you speak of it, I would say she was elderly."

The woman checked the oil in the car, put some water in the radiator, and filled up the gas tank. The whole bill came to a dollar seventy-five. "Here's a five spot, Mother," said one of the snatchers. "Keep the change." The woman was thanking the man for his generosity when the car started up with a jerk.

A couple of hours later, or about ten o'clock, one of the snatchers said to the other, "Jesus, will you look at that sky over there." Thunder began to roll, and Urschel, even under the blanket, could hear the wind whistling around the car. Then a terrific rain storm broke. Presently the car, still travelling on secondary dirt roads, began to slither in mud.

The car drove slowly through the storm for about an hour. One of the kidnappers said he was hungry. "To hell with that," answered the other one, "we gotta get there while the gettin's good." Sometime in the afternoon, probably around three o'clock, the car entered a garage or barn. One of the abductors left and returned in a little while with some sandwiches and coffee. They undid Urschel's handcuffs so that he could eat the sandwiches and drink the coffee. Then they bound his hands behind his back again.

Some hours later, Urschel was uncuffed, hand and foot, and, with a captor on each side of him, gripping an arm, led out of the enclosure. He walked a few steps, passed through a gate, walked some more, then entered a house.

The G-Men stopped him at this point to fill themselves in on what would obviously be vital details. Had he been turned to the right or the left when taken out of the barn or garage? To the left. How many steps had he taken before coming to the gate? About six. Once through the gate, how many steps had he taken before reaching the house? About fifteen or sixteen. What had he been walking on all this time—dirt, gravel, boards? He had walked on dirt from the enclosure to the gate, then on boards. When he reached the house, had he gone up any steps before going through a door? Yes. How many steps? Three. Wooden steps, or stone steps, or concrete? Wooden. Because they gave under his weight? Yes.

"All right, Mr. Urschel, you're in the house now. What happened then?"

Urschel had the impression that he was led from the first room into a second room. There his two captors told him to feel his way around and make himself comfortable. "Can't I take this bandage off my eyes?" Urschel asked. "You think we're *nuts*?" said one of the captors. There were two iron beds in the room and a wash stand. "Where's the toilet?" asked Urschel. There was, he was told, an outhouse in its usual place.

Urschel was chained to the bed, hand and foot, and soon pretended to be asleep by simulating heavy breathing. His two captors were still in the room.

The walls were thin. He could hear voices in an adjoining room (probably the room he had passed through upon entering the house)—the voices of more than one man, and the voice of at least one woman.

One of the snatchers brought Urschel a big meal of ham and eggs and bread and coffee. The ham tasted wonderful; Urschel figured it was home-cured. "How did you know that?" "It just tasted different than ham you buy in stores."

"The weather's been very hot this past couple of weeks," said a G-Man. "Were the windows open in the room you were in? Yes. "Did you hear the sounds of any farm animals—cows or chickens?" Yes. Urschel had heard cows, chickens and guinea hens. "How do you know you heard guinea hens?" Guinea hens, Urschel said, made a peculiar sound which, once heard, would always be recognized. "And you know a guinea hen when you hear one." "Positively."

"You say this ham you got was home-cured. Didn't you hear any pigs?" No. "Did you hear machinery of any kind?" No. "He was," said a G-Man to another one who was making notes, "probably on a small farm. But we can't be sure. That was on a Sunday."

Later that same day—the Sunday—Urschel was taken to a second house, about a fifteen-minute drive over bumpy dirt roads from the first place. This was where he was to remain for a week. Here the two kidnappers left for a while.

Urschel, still blindfolded, now found himself in the custody of two new men —one of whom, judging from the timbre of his voice, was young, the other, from the same observation, elderly.

"You're sure one of those men was elderly? What makes you think that besides his voice?"

"He didn't seem to move very fast.

And every once in a while he would get short of breath."

The sounds from without that Urschel heard were similar to those he had heard at the first place, with one notable substitution. He had heard guinea hens at the first place but he heard none here. He had heard no pigs at the first place but he heard pigs here. This was probably where the home-cured ham had come from that Urschel had been served at the first farm.

Urschel's elderly captor was a not-unfriendly old cuss and talkative to boot. He liked to spout about politics, agricultural problems, and the weather.

"Was he a Democrat or a Republican?"

"A Democrat."

Dwelling on the weather one day the old man remarked that the farmers must have been hit hard by the drought up in Oklahoma. *Up* in Oklahoma. He stopped short after making the remark and Urschel had the impression that the old man could have bitten his tongue off for having made it.

Urschel decided that the old man was a native of the Southwest, probably a Texan, natively intelligent but formally uneducated.

"How do you figure he was a Texan?"

"I just happen to recognize a Texas accent when I hear it."

"You say he was natively intelligent but not formally educated. How did you decide that?"

"I could just *tell*. He had a good mind and pretty well thought-out opinions but his grammar was bad."

One day Urschel asked the old man for a drink of water. The old man shouted to somebody in another room to bring some. Then Urschel heard, not far from the house, a creaking sound. When the water was brought in he noticed that it was in a battered tin cup.

"How did that water taste? Did it taste like regular tap water?" No. The water had had a pronounced mineral taste. The creaking sound, the battered tin cup, the mineral taste—it all added up to a well near the house.

As the days passed and the two kidnappers began to work out details of their plot, they would occasionally come to the room and question Urschel as to who his friends were and who could dig up a fifth of a million on short notice, and still keep his lips buttoned up. That was when Urschel decided that his friend Catlett, the Tulsa oilman, could help him.

The kidnappers told Urschel they were going to remove the blindfold so that he could write a couple of letters—the letters that were eventually given to the boy on the street in Tulsa for delivery to Catlett. They added they would stand behind him while he wrote and they dictated and warned him not to try to turn around and get a look at them or they would drill him. So Urschel didn't try. But, through the corner of his eye, he did get a look at part of the room he was in—enough to recognize it again.

All during his incarceration in the second house, Urschel occasionally heard the voice of a woman in another room. His impression was that the woman was middle-aged or elderly. "Would you recognize her voice again if you heard it?"

"I sure as hell would."

From the very first, Urschel had heard the sounds of airplanes passing overhead—one in the morning, the other in the afternoon. When, the third day of his captivity, it became obvious to him that the airplane sounds fell into a pattern, that the ships were maintaining a schedule, he made it a point to inquire of the old man what time it was. He didn't make his inquiries immediately after hearing the sounds of the planes, but allowed a few minutes to elapse, so as not to arouse suspicion.

By the end of six days Urschel satisfied himself that the morning plane passed overhead about nine-forty-five and the afternoon one about five-forty-five. *About* those times, that is. He couldn't be certain right on the button, but he was fairly certain. On occasion he had asked the old man what time it was, right when the plane was passing overhead, and the old man had always answered nine-forty-five or five-forty-five. Other times Urschel had sat with his back to the old man and began to count his pulse beat when a plane was passing overhead. Knowing how many times his heart beat in a minute he was able to measure off a minute, or two or five before asking the old man what time it was. It always wound up about the same—nine-forty-five in the morning and five-forty-five in the afternoon, give or take a minute.

On the eighth day of Urschel's captivity—a Sunday—the rain came down in torrents all morning. Urschel didn't hear the sound of a plane that morning. He wondered if the storm had drowned out the sound of the plane, or whether the plane had not gone over because of the weather, or whether no flight was scheduled on Sundays.

On the Monday forenoon—the ninth day after he had been snatched—Urschel was told the ransom had been paid and that he was going to be released. He was stowed in the back of a car, under a blanket, and driven around all day. This time the kidnappers had brought an extra supply of gasoline along with them so that no stops were made. Urschel had the feeling that the car was frequently backtracking for miles at a stretch. Late that night he was dumped out on the outskirts of Oklahoma City and by the time he had removed the bandages from his eyes the car had disappeared.

The G-Men pondered that slip-of-the-tongue the elderly captor had made—his reference to Oklahoma as "up there." This posed the possibility that Urschel's place of imprisonment had been in Texas. Such a theory was further buttressed by the fact that the abductors' car had, up to the time Urschel was bound and taped, travelled in an easterly direction from Oklahoma City, whereas Texas lay to the west and south. It would have been normal criminal psychology for the kidnappers to have first travelled in a direction practically opposite to the spot they were really headed for, then, after blindfolding their victim, double back on their tracks.

G-Men, using watches and speedometers as instruments of detection, got into automobiles at the point where Urschel had been taped and bound, and hit dirt roads in the general direction of Texas. They began to draw blanks. Then one pair of G-Men came to an oil field about an hour from Harrah, and to another one half an hour later—just as Urschel had done. Both of the fields were to the southwest of Oklahoma City, in the direction of Texas.

Other agents, poring over meteorological records, were trying to find out the locale of the two severe storms that Urschel had experienced during his captivity—the first one around ten o'clock the morning after his abduction, the second one the day before he had been released. They discovered that the vicinity of Ardmore, Oklahoma, had been lashed by a storm around ten o'clock the morning after the kidnapping—and Ardmore, too, was in the direction of Texas.

Now the G-Men went on the prowl for the woman—the elderly woman—who had sold gas to the abductors two hours before the Ardmore storm and had been told to keep the change from a five-spot. So they backtracked two hours from where the storm had struck, in the direction of the oil fields that had previously interested them, screening the countryside for an elderly woman who manned a gas pump on Sundays.

They drew blank after blank but then they found their woman. She vividly recalled the man who had given her the five-dollar bill and told her to forget the change. The benefactor had been a big man, broad of shoulder, hard and handsome of countenance. Man in his thirties. "Would you know him again if you saw him?" "Know him," said the old woman. "Why, I'd *kiss* him."

Backtracking still farther, Hoover's sleuths came to a deserted farm reached over a road containing two gates—the very road, they suspected, the snatchers had traversed to reach the spot where they changed from the Chevvy to the Caddy. There were tire marks on this road—apparently the marks of two cars, one large, one small. The G-Men took impressions of the tire marks.

Now they backtracked some more, on the prowl for the person who had supplied a can of gasoline to one of the kidnappers around four o'clock on the Sunday morning, some five hours after the snatch. They figured that this person, whoever he was, had been asleep at that hour. The deduction was, therefore, that he probably had his place of business and his home in one spot, otherwise how would the kidnapper have known that the man could supply him with gas?

Such a man was found. He said the man who had awakened him in the middle of the night for a can of gas had been a big fellow, in his middle thirties, with powerful shoulders. And he would recognize the man again? He thought so.

Now Hoover's bright boys got a record of that second storm they were hunting for—the one the morning before Urschel was driven from his unofficial prison to be released. Or at least they thought so. There had been a terrific storm over Wise County, Texas, that Sunday morning. Texas was continuing to add up. The kidnap car had headed toward Texas, the old confederate of the kidnappers had talked like a Texan, and there had been a terrific storm in the area where Urschel might well have been held.

Now Hoover's men devoted themselves to airline schedules. Was there any spot in Wise County where planes regularly passed over around nine-forty-five in the morning and around five-forty-five in the afternoon? The flight schedules of the American Airways Fort Worth-Amarillo run began to look most interesting. In fact, downright exciting. Each morning, Sundays included, an American Pilgrim plane left Fort Worth at nine-fifteen and was passing over Wise County at nine-forty-five. In the afternoon, on the way back from Amarillo to Fort Worth, the same plane passed over Wise County at five-forty-five and was due in at six-fifteen. The American Airways logs disclosed that on the Sunday morning when Urschel had heard the terrific storm, but no plane overhead, American had cancelled its regular Fort Worth-Amarillo flight because of weather. Bingo.

Now the G-Men took to the air. They got into those Amarillo-Fort Worth ships and, at nine-forty-five in the morning and at five-forty-five in the afternoon, day after day, peered down through powerful field glasses on the terrain below. What they were looking for were two farms, about a fifteen-minute automobile drive, over bumpy roads, from each other —one farm with a board walk leading from a barn or garage to a house entered by a stoop containing three steps, and with farm animals, including guinea hens; the second place with a well in back of the house and pigs but not guinea hens among the farm stock.

The sleuthing from the sky, good as it was, was somewhat easier than it might have been because of the groundwork that had gone before it. The G-Men soon spotted two farms that fitted right into the pattern of suspicion. They were little more than a mile apart, or about a quarter of an hour's drive from one another over bumpy roads—the roads, the G-Men figured, that Urschel had traversed while being taken from his first to his second place of incarceration. One of the farms had a board walk leading from an outbuilding to the back door—a walk about the length of the one Urschel had traversed when taken out of the car to go into the house where he spent his first Sunday night. The second farm had a well behind the house, as had Urschel's second place of imprisonment.

Now the G-Men came down out of the sky and got to work on the ground. Two of them, travelling in a rattletrap with Texas plates, invaded the area of suspicion in the guise of travelling drummers. They didn't call immediately at the two farms they had under the glasses. First they wanted to find out something about who lived on those farms. Regional farmers on whom the phony drummers called divulged that the farm where Urschel was suspected of first being held was operated by a man named Armon Shannon, and that the second place was operated by Armon Shannon's old man—R. G. (The Boss) Shannon. The old gent was known as The Boss because he had, in his earlier years, been a political big shot. The elderly captor of Urschel had liked to spout about politics. So far, so good.

When the spurious drummers called at Armon Shannon's place they noticed that Armon, who looked like a country jake, complete with shaved neck, kept cows, chickens and guinea hens. At the farm of Boss Shannon, a garrulous old character with a Texas drawl down to his knees, they observed that there were no guinea hens but that there were pigs. Boss Shannon cured his own hams—and Urschel had unquestionably partaken of some Shannon ham during his incarceration.

There were two cars—a Cadillac and a Chevrolet—in a garage on Boss Shannon's place. Hoover's sleuths sneaked in one night and made impressions of the tires on the cars. The impressions matched with those they had picked up in the road leading to the barn where the kidnappers had changed cars.

The G-Men kept the farm of Boss Shannon under glasses for a couple of days. That hunch that all good detectives have when the chips are down told them that somebody was lying doggo in the Boss' house. And so, in the middle of one night—a night three weeks after Urschel had been snatched from his sun porch—half a dozen G-Men let themselves into the Shannon house, inching around silently, carrying machine guns, just like in the movies.

In a bedroom on the second floor a sleeping figure lay in the moonlight. It wasn't Boss Shannon and it wasn't his wife—for they had meantime been clapped over the mouths and taken in another room just as Armon was being taken at his place. So the G-Men grabbed *this* character before he could wake up. He turned out to be a forty-five-minute egg by the name of Harvey Bailey—a citizen with a record down to his insteps. Less than three months previously, he had crashed out of the Kansas State

pen, where he had been doing half a century for heisting a jug, and gone right into business again by joining up with the mob who, trying to spring a pal being taken to the big cage, went to the Union Station Plaza in Kansas City and murdered three cops and a G-Man and, by mistake, their prison-bound pal, too.

Bailey was as talkative as Charlie McCarthy without Bergen. He wasn't carrying much cash, for a public enemy—little more than a grand. But most of it was Urschel ransom lettuce. He hadn't, however, been one of the two men who had appeared on the Urschel sun porch. And those were the pair of G-Men really wanted.

The G-Men had picked up a new machine gun in Bailey's room. It took them only a couple of days to trace it to its place of purchase—a store in Fort Worth. There it had been sold shortly before the snatch to a thirtyish dame with a pretty but hard face and flaming red hair.

The description of the red-headed doll made sense. While one group of Hoover's boys had been tracing the tommy rod, another group had been running down the family lines that extended from the home of Boss Shannon and his wife. Thus they learned that Boss Shannon's wife, who had been married before, had a daughter named Kathryn—a lady with red hair. Kathryn, the G-Men learned, was married to a big-time bad boy named Kelly—Machine Gun Kelly. And Machine Gun Kelly was known to be palsy-walsy with another cop-hating gentleman named Albert Bates.

Both Kelly and Bates had, for a long time, been stars in the Rogues Gallery. Urschel immediately identified their official portraiture as that of the two hoods who had plucked him off his porch. Kelly, who had big broad shoulders, was also identified as the fellow who had bought a can of gas from the man in the middle of the night, and as the generous gent who had given the old lady at the gas pump the five spot and told her to keep the change. But where were Kelly and Bates—and Machine Gun's red-headed wife?

Urschel was brought back to the homes of the Shannons. He immediately identified the surroundings as those of his period of captivity. He was most positive in his identification of the room in Boss Shannon's house where, when he had written the letters for the kidnappers, the bandages had been temporarily removed from his eyes. Boss Shannon and his wife, and their son Armon, were told to talk in front of Urschel. Urschel couldn't have been more positive in his identification of their voices.

Now it was all over but the shooting— or almost. The G-Men sunk pipelines into the underworld and stool pigeons— or informants, as they are called in official circles—began working for Uncle Sam. That was how Albert Bates was picked off a street in Denver before he could reach into an arsenal he was carrying. Machine Gun Kelly and his wife, however, had really faded. So Uncle Sam decided to go to bat in Texas against Old Man Shannon and his wife, their son Armon, Bates and Bailey. But before the trial got under way, Bailey, the old crasher-outer, did it again. With guns, hacksaws, keys and other tools of his trade smuggled into him through a crooked jailor, he locked several honest jailors up in cells, took another honest one along with him as a hostage and said good-bye. But the G-Men surprised him, with his arms down, that very night and slapped him back in the can.

Armon Shannon, the fellow with the rube's haircut and shaved neck, was the only lucky one at the trial. He got ten years' probation. His pop and mom and Bailey and Bates got life.

Late in September—two months after the Urschel snatch—the Hoover underworld pipelines paid off. Machine Gun Kelly and his red-haired wife were taken in their sleep—a favorite dodge of the G-Men to avoid blood-letting—in a private home in Memphis, Tennessee. When they were being tried, Machine Gun drew the index finger of his right hand slowly across his throat—for the benefit of the Federal Prosecutor. The Prosecutor happened to be a gutsy Irishman named Joe Keenan, the same Keenan who later went to Japan to prosecute World War Two criminals. Keenan ran his right index finger across *his* throat and went right on with the case. So Machine Gun and his wife got life, too.

The G-Men didn't make out so good about the two hundred grand. Less than half of it was recovered, seventy thousand being found hidden in a dry well in the home of an acquaintance of the snatchers. But Urschel, who was paying the freight, didn't mind about that. He figured the loss was a small price to pay for coming out of the business in one piece.

By way of wrapping it up good, the G-Men got the goods on everybody who had handled any of the ransom money, or who had helped to give asylum to the hoods in flight. When the score was finally tallied up, twenty-one bad guys and dolls had been jolted for a total of six life sentences, and fifty-eight years, two months and two days in durance vile. What was more important, the G-Men had thrown the fear of Hell into the public enemies and, while they were still to meet up with such characters as Dillinger, Pretty Boy Floyd and Creepy Karpis, the sun was beginning to set. The Urschel case was the twilight of the gangster.

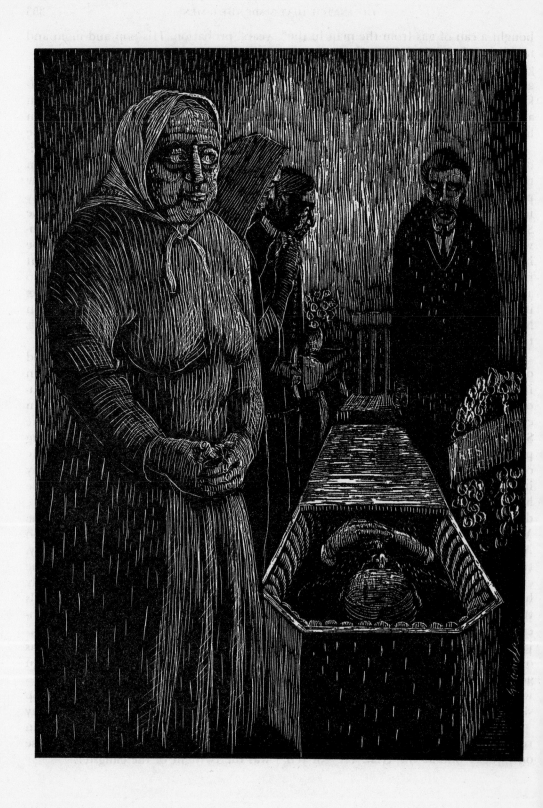

Chicago's Constant Widow

*Mrs. Tillie Mitkiewitz-Ruskowski-Kupczyk-Klimek, the Prophet of
Chicago's Little Poland, could foretell the approach of
death—with or without a crystal ball.*

Tillie Gburek, who first appeared more than half a century ago in that section of the Chicago slums known as Little Poland, was hardly the type of girl to attract a man. She was short, broad, muscular and red-faced. Feminine finery left her absolutely cold and, to bottom things off, she had piano legs that were usually encased in brown cotton stockings. At the age of twenty, in the year of 1885, Tillie developed a penchant for mannish sweaters that buttoned down the front, thereby smothering whatever natural resources she may have possessed. Our heroine, however, was a superb cook—one of the best, in all of Little Poland—and it was that attribute that was one day to bring the drab and forlorn Tillie Gburek into, of all places, the public eye.

Tillie, the offspring of Polish immigrants, worked from dawn to dusk in a North Side sweatshop owned and operated by a flesh-and-blood Simon Legree. As she approached her twenty-first birthday, the cosmic urge overpowered her to the extent that she paid a visit to one of the many marriage brokers who then flourished in Little Poland. After laying fifty dollars on the barrelhead, Tillie came up with a husband—a young gentleman by the name of John Mitkiewitz—who was more interested in eating than in other biological processes.

For a solid quarter of a century, Tillie lived in a Little Poland tenement with John Mitkiewitz. During the greater part of that time she continued to work in the sweatshop because her husband, a woefully inefficient jack-of-all-trades, was something less than a good provider. Mitkiewitz missed considerable time from his varied labors because he was usually engaged either in entering into or emerging from serious hangovers.

Tillie moused through the years, meek and uncomplaining. By 1911, when she was forty-six, she seemed to be totally immersed in the mists of obscurity. The only thing that saved her from being a complete nonentity was a certain amount of neighborhood renown that attached itself to her because of her ability as a cook. Beef stews were Tillie's specialty, and she clung to her recipe with jealous secrecy, no doubt realizing that the recipe in question was her sole claim to individuality.

Suddenly a great change came over Tillie. Almost overnight a certain intentness of purpose shone from her watery blue eyes, and, instead of facing each day with fear and docility, she seemed to attack it with outright belligerence. On one memorable occasion she became a heroine to her fellow peons in the sweatshop when she interrupted the whip-cracking activities of the proprietor, a frail little man, by planting her right fist on his teeth and his nose and knocking him cold.

Tillie was so pleasantly surprised at her own strength that she went straight home and, finding her husband in one of his periodic stupors, gave him a shellacking that the neighborhood talked about for weeks. Thus, for the first time in her totally uninteresting life, Tillie found herself being pointed out with admiration as she walked the streets of Little Poland. Her ego, which had long suffered from malnutrition, was being fed at last, and, for the first time, Tillie experienced the sweet taste of power.

Next Tillie cast about for a means to enhance her prestige. She decided to plow the fertile soil of superstition in Little Poland. Most of the inhabitants of the district were unenlightened immigrants who still embraced strange and fearful customs and beliefs that dated back to the Middle Ages. They looked with a mixture of awe and reverence, for example, on the wrinkled old crones who claimed to possess the gift of prophecy. Tillie decided, therefore, to become a prophet.

One sultry evening in the summer of 1911, when Tillie was sitting on a fire escape with a woman neighbor, she pointed to a yellow mongrel dog in a foul alley below. "That dog," said Tillie, "will be dead within a week."

"How do you know?" asked the neighbor.

"The powers tell me so."

And, sure enough, the yellow mongrel was found stiff and cold on the seventh day. Tillie had begun a fabulous career as a seeress.

For three years the squat seeress predicted canine deaths with stunning accuracy. As a result Little Poland came to respect and fear her. The corner butcher no longer incorporated his right hand in the gross weight of beef that Tillie bought for stews because she hinted to him that evil might befall him if he overcharged her. Men, women and children went out of their way to be nice to Tillie, convinced that she had the power to put a curse on them. About the only person who knew Tillie and who wasn't impressed by her claims of prophecy was her husband. That, as it was to turn out, was Mitkiewitz's misfortune.

"I don't think that John is long for this world," Tillie said as she sat on the fire escape with a neighbor one night in the summer of 1914. "The powers tell me that I'll be a widow within three weeks."

One morning, three weeks later on the button, Tillie charged into the corner butcher's to buy some beef for a stew and announced, almost parenthetically, that her husband had passed away during the night. The butcher and two customers inquired as to the cause of death. "He just got numb all over," said Tillie. "Where is a good place to get a coffin—cheap?"

The seeress was singularly dry-eyed as John Mitkiewitz was lowered into a grave in All Saints Cemetery. After the funeral Tillie invited some friends to her flat and everybody got good and high. Along toward the end of the party the merry widow let it be known that despite the fact that her late husband had been a quarrelsome lush she thought matrimony was a fine institution. So fine, in truth, that she contemplated another marriage.

The earth was still soft, as the saying goes, on John Mitkiewitz's grave when Tillie visited a marriage broker. She had received, she disclosed, one thousand dollars from an insurance company following the death of Mitkiewitz, and this monetary consideration, coupled with Tillie's culinary artistry, was sufficient, in the eyes of the fee-hungry broker, to counterbalance the woman's lack of physical magnetism when it came to arranging a match. Thus, within six weeks of her first husband's death, Tillie became a bride again. The lucky man was one John Ruskowski, who had recently accepted a position as a section hand with the Pennsylvania Railroad and who, as fortune would have it, carried a paid-up insurance policy for two thousand dollars.

Ruskowski, who sported luxurious blond handlebar mustachios, was a great man with a knife and fork, and Tillie saw to it that he never went hungry. He particularly liked his bride's beef stew. "I don't know what she puts in them stews," he told a fellow pick-swinger one day, "but I never tasted anything like them."

One night, during the third month of his marriage to Tillie, Handlebar John was sitting at the table, belching happily after five ample helpings of beef stew. "You had somethin' different in the stew tonight," John said to Tillie. "What was it?"

"A new spice," said Tillie. "Was it bitter?"

"A little bit," said John, "but I liked it."

The following afternoon Tillie, who had by this time taken up the hobby of drinking, had some women friends in to kill a jug of new wine. As the guests were departing, Tillie told them that she was about to make another prophecy.

"Who is this time, Tillie?" asked one of the women, trembling.

"Don't say anything about it to him because it would worry him—but it's my husband."

Two weeks later, Tillie was in the butcher shop buying meat for another stew and, just before departing, informed the butcher that she had become a widow again during the night. "It was the same thing as happened to my first husband," said Tillie. "He just got numb and died."

And so John Ruskowski, mustachios and all, was laid to premature rest in All Saints Cemetery only a few graves away from Tillie's first husband. As on the occasion of the previous burial, the widow displayed an admirable stoicism in her hour of grief. Once again there was a party in Tillie's flat after the funeral, and once again Tillie, oiled to the ears, reaffirmed her faith in matrimony and expressed her intention of taking unto herself a third husband.

A man by the name of Joseph Guszkowski, a towering big gent with a flat face and a flat head, had put in a bid for a wife with the very marriage broker whom Tillie consulted about a third husband. Guszkowski, a railroad laborer, was known to his intimates as Blunt Joe because he was so honest that it hurt. If he didn't like a person's face, he said so. As it was to turn out, Blunt Joe didn't like Tillie's face when the marriage broker brought the two of them together— and he didn't bother wrapping up his highly articulate impressions of the woman as he slowly appraised her from her thick ankles to her red face and back to her ankles again.

"What I had in mind," said Blunt Joe to the broker in Tillie's presence, "was somebody young and pretty." Blunt Joe thereupon went into detailed physical specifications. Although Tillie looked almost as much like a misshapen man as a woman, her pride was strictly feminine and it was stung to the quick by Blunt Joe's remarks. Tillie, as it was subsequently to develop, was overcome by the fury of a woman scorned.

Tillie played it smart. She cloaked her real feelings and put on such a show of good grace that Blunt Joe felt ashamed of himself and agreed to move into Tillie's flat on a trial basis. His compromise with his preconceived notions as to what a bride should be was somewhat alleviated by the fact that Tillie was such an excellent cook and that she had a bank account, by virtue of insurance on two husbands, that was far from hay back in 1914.

Evidence developed on a later and sadder day seems to indicate that Blunt Joe underwent a change of opinion about Tillie after he had been domiciling with her for a month. Tillie's stews, it seems got him—and you can take that two ways.

Tillie never forgot Blunt Joe's derogatory remarks about her on the occasion of their first meeting. It is, of course, entirely conceivable that she may have thought less of the remarks in time and might even have married Blunt Joe. When she discovered, however, that the man carried no insurance whatever and, moreover, that he was reluctant to take any out, something apparently died within her.

The seasoning in Tillie's stews began to grow bitter and, within two months of her second husband's death, Blunt Joe took to his bed. "He's numb all over, poor man," Tillie divulged to an impressed neighbor. "The powers tell me he has less than two weeks of this life." And so Blunt Joe was laid to rest in All Saints Cemetery—not very far from the mortal remains of Tillie's first spouse and Handlebar John.

Thirteen months after she had buried her first husband, Tillie became a bride for the third time. The happy man was named Frank Kupczyk, better known to intimates in the sweatshop where he worked as Kuppy.

Kuppy was an easy-going little Pole who, for reasons best known to himself, was utterly sincere in his belief that Tillie was the most attractive woman he had ever laid eyes on. This astigmatic view was to operate in his favor, as shall be seen, for it was a new experience for Tillie to be married to a man who liked her for herself alone rather than for her

cooking. It might be said, in fact, that Tillie Mitkiewitz - Ruskowski - Kupczyk was, at fifty, in love for the first time in her life.

On the day of Tillie's wedding to Kuppy, the newlyweds threw a brawl in Tillie's flat. There were hams, chickens and rib roasts and almost every kind of beverage except non-alcoholic ones. The tenement rocked from the vibrations of Polish dances and the cop on the beat stopped in out of sheer curiosity. The civil servant became so caught up with the spirit of things that he gave his cap, badge and billy to a pretty feminine guest and didn't go near his call box for two days.

Midnight came, and the only merrymaker who wasn't either staggering or lying somewhere in a stupor was pretty twenty-five-year-old Rose Chudzinski, a distant relative of the bride, who lived in a near-by tenement. Rose, as a matter of fact, had participated only slightly in the festivities. She had drunk but little and had for the most part remained off by herself, apparently brooding about something. Several times Tillie and various of the guests had tried to imbue her with their gaiety, but Rose would have none of it. And now, at midnight, she began to rivet a burning gaze on the three-time bride.

Tillie was in the act of downing a mug of beer when she noticed Rose staring at her. "What in the hell," shouted Tillie, "is wrong with you?"

The remark had a somewhat sobering effect on the guests who were still conscious, but not nearly so sobering as Rose's answer. "I have been wondering," said the girl, who had become quite Americanized, "how long your new husband is going to live."

Tillie drained the mug of beer and strode belligerently forward until she was face to face with the girl. "What do you mean?"

"I mean I think it's very funny," said Rose, "that both of your husbands died so soon after you married them. And it's funny about Blunt Joe, too."

Tillie's thin lips twitched into a sneer. "It's not my fault that they died," she said. "I fed them well enough."

Rose bit her lower lip and left. Several of Tillie's admirers, who had been temporarily sobered by the untoward incident, waited in embarrassed silence for some sort of an explanation from the bride. If Tillie was unnerved, she quickly recovered herself. "Poor child," she explained. "We must be sorry for her rather than angry. She's going to die, you see."

"*Rose* is going to *die!* But she's so healthy and young."

The seeress shook her head sideways. "There's nothing I can do about it," she said. "The powers have willed it that way."

Tillie enjoyed such status as a prophet that the auditors who heard her wedding-night forecast never made any connection between the coming death of Rose Chudzinski and the fact that the girl had made some very pointed remarks to Tillie. These same witnesses were, in fact, greatly impressed by Tillie's magnanimous nature when it became known that Tillie was making frequent visits to the home of Rose in an effort, as Tillie explained, to patch things up before the girl died. When Rose Chudzinski—the fourth person close to Tillie to come to a sudden end—died within six weeks of Tillie's third wedding night, the seeress, rather than drawing any suspicion to herself, took on added stature as a prophet. For she had foretold, ten days previously, the exact day of Rose's death.

In retrospect it seems incredible that Tillie could have been so closely associated with four sudden deaths within such a short space of time without drawing official suspicion to herself. The orbit in which she moved, however, offers considerable of the explanation. To speak against a prophet in the valley of ignorance and fear that was Little Poland in those days, let alone suspect one of ulterior motives, was considered tantamount to signing one's own death warrant by way of courting a prophet's curse. Rose Chudzinski had cast reflection on Tillie, and Rose's fresh grave was a frightening reminder of terrible things in store for anyone entertaining ideas similar to Rose's.

Then, too, Tillie had seen to it that four different doctors and four different undertakers had been summoned following the four deaths. Two different insurance companies had paid policies on Tillie's dead husbands. There was, therefore, no outsider in possession of sufficient facts upon which to draw a suspicious inference. Add to all that the fact that the Chicago Police Department in those days was hardly on a par with Scotland Yard and it will be seen that there was clear sailing ahead for Tillie.

Following the death of Rose Chudzinski, Tillie went into a period of quiescence. She kissed the sweatshop goodby and was apparently quite content to make beef stews for her third husband, Kuppy, and bask in the warmth of his inexplicable adoration for her. But, against a possible emergency, Tillie retained her status as a prophet by continuing to call the death shots on dozens of neighborhood dogs and cats.

Early in the year of 1920—when she was fifty-five, and in the fifth year of her marriage to Kuppy — certain circumstances arose that caused Tillie to rejoice in the fact that she had maintained her status as a seeress. She somehow got into arguments with the parents of three small children, and the children died, one by one, just as Tillie prophesied they would.

Shortly after the death of the third child, Tillie turned her attention to Kuppy, whose ardor had somehow cooled along the way. Moreover, Tillie, in a fire-escape chat with a woman neighbor, disclosed that Kuppy had developed a roving eye. By a strange coincidence the powers told Tillie that Kuppy was not long for this world simultaneously with her discovery that his amorous interests lay elsewhere.

Tillie went into a neighborhood notions store and bought some black cloth. "It's for a funeral," she explained.

"Whose?" asked the clerk.

"My husband's," said Tillie.

"When did he die?"

"Ten days from now."

Tillie's next stop was at an undertaker's, where she bought the cheapest coffin in the place and had it delivered to the basement of the tenement where she lived one day while Kuppy was at work.

Kuppy, who was a staunch believer in his wife's prophetic powers, came upon her one night making a black hat. "That looks like a widow's hat," he said.

"It is," said Tillie. "The powers tell me of a death eight days from now and I'll have to go to the funeral."

Six days later Kuppy took to his bed, with pains in his legs and stomach. On the seventh day he was in very bad shape and on the eighth day Tillie went down to the basement, drew the janitor aside and said, "It's all right to bring the coffin up now."

Tillie threw quite a wake the night Kuppy was laid out. With a mug of beer in her hand, she stood with a woman neighbor, gazing down at Kuppy's mortal remains. "It's too bad," she said, "that I have such bad luck with husbands. I hope my next one lasts longer."

"Your *next* one, Tillie?"

Tillie drained the beer mug. "Yes," she said. "A man named Anton Klimek. He works in a brewery."

It was in the summer of 1921, shortly after she collected insurance on Kuppy, that Tillie married Klimek—a mild, wide-eyed little man in his fifties whose distinguishing characteristic was a rich brown walrus mustache. Tillie left the old flat where three husbands and a prospective groom had had such bad luck, and moved to another thoroughfare in Little Poland.

Tillie and Anton Klimek were quite happy for the first few months of their marriage until two large dogs, which Klimek had owned for several years, caused something of a rift in the marital lute. Tillie complained to a neighbor one day that Klimek spent most of his evenings petting the dogs instead of her. But Mrs. Mitkiewitz-Ruskowski-Kupczyk-Klimek had a happy solution to her problem: the dogs, she said, were doomed by the powers to die within an hour of each other. Klimek was not let in on the prophecy, and the first he knew about it was one night in October, when, returning from his day's work in the brewery, he stumbled over the bodies of both of the dogs as he let himself into his flat.

Anton went around to tell his brother, John, who ran a blacksmith shop, about his misfortune. The brother stared curiously at Anton as the man spoke. When Anton had finished telling about the dogs, John said, "That's too bad, but I'm not so worried about the dogs as I am about you."

"Why," asked Anton, "what's the matter with me?"

"Your face is all puffed up and it's purple. You ought to take a look at it."

Next day Anton called on his brother John again. "I feel awful," he said. "I have pains in my legs and something has gone wrong with my hearing."

"About that wife of yours," said John. "How many times did you say she has been married before?"

"Three."

"And what happened to her husbands?"

"They all died."

"I think you're going to die too, Anton, if you don't get to hell away from that woman. You look worse today than you did yesterday."

Anton Klimek went home and began to question his wife about his predecessors. "Everybody has to die sometime," said Tillie.

"But did they take sick all of a sudden?"

"Stew's on," said Tillie, completely ignoring the question. Anton wasn't hungry, and anyway the stew tasted bitter, just like the ones he had been eating for several days now. "You've got to have some nourishment," said Tillie. "I'll make you some soup." The soup, too, was bitter, but Tillie forced Klimek to take it.

It was Anton Klimek's brother who finally connected with the Chicago Police Department. The gendarmes barged into Tillie's flat on October 27, 1921—and not a minute too soon. Anton Klimek, freshly insured, was in bed, at death's door. It would have taken just one more stew to have done him in—and Tillie had the stew on.

Klimek eventually came around—the only man or beast, as far as is known, to have escaped with his life after Tillie brought out the Indian sign. That bitter flavor that Klimek and all the others had noticed had been arsenic. The authorities had to dig up only one body, Kuppy's, to prove that Tillie was a female Bluebeard.

Students of the criminal mind say that the former Tillie Gburek was propelled by more than one motive. After almost half a century as a nonentity, she became an egomaniac; the role of prophet nourished her ego and her lust for power over others, and murder secured her status as a seeress. The companion criminal driving force to Tillie's ego was of a monetary nature—good old insurance on arsenic victims. And, in the case of Blunt Joe, Tillie's distaff pride had been hurt.

Tillie had a field day at her trial for murder. More than anything else, the trial was her hour in the glare of the spotlight. She struck corny poses on the witness stand, sneered and snarled at the prosecutor, and even made another prophecy. She said that the powers told her that she would escape the gallows. And she did; she got off with life, later to be turned down by prison authorities in numerous requests to be allowed to cook for fellow inmates.

At the trial it was brought out that Tillie was below par mentally. Pondering on the eight murders that she had gotten away with, a cynical Chicago reporter was prompted to inquire, "I wonder what the hell would have happened if she had been *smart?*"

Long Island's Messy Murder

Billy Burns, the great detective, was a dog lover who knew that canines barked at strangers. What puzzled him, for a time, when he set out to probe this murder, were a couple of dogs that hadn't barked.

Of a windy morning in late March, in the year of 1919, William J. Burns, the country's number-one private eye, stepped off a train at Long Beach, Long Island, to address himself to a puzzling problem in murder. Burns, he of the brisk walk, the natty attire, the sandy hair and the snapping blue eyes, brushed past several news hawks who had been awaiting his arrival and hustled over to an ugly stucco house less than six blocks from the railroad station. It was in that house, more than three weeks previously —at about half past nine on the night of Thursday, February 27—that Mrs. Robert Keene Wilkins, a woman of sixty, had been fatally done in.

The District Attorney of Nassau County, an able and conscientious public servant named Charles A. Weeks, was waiting for Burns at the murder scene. The District Attorney's patience with the local gendarmes had finally disintegrated; they had not only failed to draw a lead on a single suspect, but had begun to display all the enthusiasm of men bent on kicking the case around until it got lost. And so the D.A. had telephoned to the William J. Burns Detective Agency in New York and, after settling a question that arose before he ever went out on a case—the question of how much he was to be paid for his services—Burns walked into the murder scene to brief himself on the known facts and take over.

For several weeks prior to the murder of Mrs. Wilkins, the wife of a sixty-seven-year-old New York physician, Long Beach, a summer resort of less than three hundred winter residents, had been visited by a pair of nocturnal second-story men. Although the cops had been unable to catch up with the prowlers, several Long Beachers had caught fleeting glimpses of them. While descriptions of the pair varied, all observers agreed on two points: the men had been above average in height and had worn gray caps.

As crime goes, the after-dark visitations of a pair of second-storymen in a small and sleepy summer resort in the dead of winter was pedestrian stuff. It wasn't until Mrs. Robert Keene Wilkins was murdered and William J. Burns was called in that the crime wave in Long Beach was raised to the classic level. For the Wilkins case turned out to be a real doozer—one that detectives still talk about when they get together to shoot the breeze.

Doctor and Mrs. Wilkins had two homes—the one in Long Beach and another in New York City, on West Sixty-fifth Street near Central Park. The New York property was a three-story theatrical boarding house, which Mrs. Wilkins operated and where she and her husband maintained two rooms for themselves. The Doctor, who specialized in the treatment of tape worm, maintained an office on the ground floor. Sometimes, when the winter weather was bad, the old couple remained overnight in the New York house. But, the month of February,

1919 being unseasonably mild, the Wilkinses had kept the Long Beach house open and commuted to New York each weekday, catching an eight o'clock train in the morning and returning on one that arrived in Long Beach at 9:06 at night.

On the night that she was to be murdered, Mrs. Wilkins stepped off the 9:06 with the Doctor, who was, despite the fact that he was approaching seventy, spry, big, bewhiskered of face, ruddy of cheeks and twinkling of eyes. The gentleman physician, who was something of an amateur chef, was carrying a package containing a Spanish mackerel, which he had purchased on the way home. He informed a neighbor, a man named Mayer, a New York furrier, who had ridden out on the train in the seat directly behind the Wilkinses, that he was going to cook the mackerel for himself and his wife upon reaching home.

But, as it turned out, the Doctor never got around to cooking that fish and, before the night was out, his wife was as dead as the mackerel. Half an hour after Wilkins and his wife had stepped off the 9:06, the Doctor stumbled into the home of Mayer, the neighbor, his head and face worked up, his clothes torn, and blood spattered all over him.

The Wilkinses, it seemed, had come home and surprised the two housebreakers who had been appearing in Long Beach for weeks now—the tall fellows wearing the gray caps. In an ensuing struggle, the Doctor had been banged over the head and rendered temporarily unconscious and his wife had been fatally battered with a ball-point machinist's hammer. The hammer, which apparently had been a tool of the burglars' trade, had been left behind at the murder scene, seemingly when the killers had panicked,

and was in the possession of District Attorney Weeks.

There it was, then: a murder apparently as simple and commonplace as it was brutal. The problem: merely to find the two tall burglars wearing gray caps. Or so it seemed.

Burns began to prowl through the Wilkins house, not looking for anything in particular but his five senses sharpened for anything of possible value. Two things quickly impressed him. The house was a monument to bad housekeeping, dusty and unkempt. And it smelled like a zoo.

Why, Burns asked the D.A., did the house smell that way. Weeks explained that Mrs. Wilkins had been fond of birds and animals but that her affection had not extended to properly caring for them. She had owned two collie dogs, Duke and Duchess by name, a monkey, a parrot and several canaries, all of which had been removed to the home of women friends.

It was when Burns got to the second floor that he noticed an interesting thing. The Doctor and his wife had occupied separate bedrooms. Her bedroom looked like a cyclone had hit it while his was immaculate. The Doctor and his wife, Burns decided, had been a curiously assorted pair.

Photographs of the couple—that of the Doctor in his wife's bedroom, that of her in his bedroom—seemed to corroborate the little sleuth's deduction about the Wilkinses. The Doctor's mutton-chop whiskers were carefully trimmed, his hair neatly in place, and his tie meticulously knotted. Mrs. Wilkins, on the other hand, looked like a regular old frump, even in the portrait. Her mouth was open, showing buck teeth, the collar of her dress was mussed, and her gray hair looked as if it had been arranged with an egg beater.

On the way to the District Attorney's office to examine the physical evidence, Burns kept wondering why a man of the Doctor's apparent fastidiousness had married, and stuck with, an obviously slovenly woman like the murder victim. He began to wonder, in fact, if this seeming contradiction in personalities would have any bearing on the solution of the murder.

The only potentially valuable piece of evidence in the District Attorney's office, from Burns' point of view, was the machinist's hammer that had been used as a murder weapon. The handle of the hammer was wrapped in a piece of newspaper and the newspaper was fastened to the handle by a piece of white twine.

Removing the paper, Burns saw that the handle of the tool had been bound by ordinary picture wire, apparently to strengthen a fracture in the wood. The hammer was old and seemingly bore no marks that would quickly lead to its origin so Burns laid it aside for the time being. Other things were, as Burns saw the picture, more urgent.

Ever since the murder of his wife, Doctor Wilkins had been staying in the rooming house in New York. Burns decided to go in and have a talk with the old boy. Wilkins appeared to be devastated over the loss of his wife. While Wilkins moaned to Burns over the tragedy that had befallen him, the detective observed that the Doctor was wearing a fresh pink rose in his lapel and that the physician smelled strongly of lilac water. The flower and the smell of lilac seemed somehow incongruous under the circumstances.

Now that he had met the Doctor face to face, Burns was increasingly struck by the fact that a man like Wilkins had been married to a woman such as the one who was slain. He began to suspect that the reason was money.

When Doctor Wilkins was unable to add to the rather sketchy facts about the murder, Burns returned to Long Beach and began to poke around among the people who had known the Doctor and his wife. When he approached the home of the woman who was keeping Duke and Duchess, the Wilkins collies, the dogs began to bark loudly. The barking of the dogs was something that the average detective wouldn't have paid any attention to. But Burns did. He dropped the incident into his mental don't-forget file.

The woman who was keeping the two dogs told Burns that Doctor Wilkins and his wife had been married thirteen years previously—in 1906. The marriage was the third for each of them. Mrs. Wilkins, whose maiden name had been Julia Kraus, was from an old German family and, at the time of her marriage to the Doctor, was heiress to about one hundred thousand dollars from a cheese fortune. The fact that Mrs. Wilkins was an heiress cleared up quite a lot for Burns. The fastidious Doctor had decided to put up with the unattractive appearance and slovenly habits of his third wife after getting a whiff of that cheese money.

Although Julia Wilkins had been an heiress, she had always remained a penny pincher. She had been too niggardly with money to hire a maid, or even a cleaning woman, in the Long Beach house; nor had she ever hired any help in the New York rooming establishment, preferring to cut corners by personally making the beds and rearranging the dust.

The Doctor, on the other hand, liked

to spend money. He patronized expensive tailors, scorned anything less than the best in food and liquor, and liked to take a flier in the market when he had the money. The picture of the basic incompatibility between Wilkins and his wife was coming into sharper focus for Burns.

Next move for Burns: A visit to the New York lawyer who handled fiscal affairs for the slain women—a timid, mousey little man. The lawyer had not yet filed Mrs. Wilkins' will for probate. "Why?" asked Burns. "I'm almost afraid to," answered the lawyer. "Why?" "Well, I don't want any trouble with Doctor Wilkins."

And why would the mouthpiece be expecting trouble from the Doctor? Mrs. Wilkins had left all her money to charity, nothing to the Doctor. She had made the charitable bequests after divorcing her second husband and, on the advice of counsel, had never gotten around to changing the will.

"Why was that?" Burns wanted to know.

"I advised her not to change her will but to give the Doctor the impression that she *had* changed it."

"But *why?*"

Well, for more than one reason. Mrs. Wilkins had been in frail health when she married Wilkins. Seemed that the cheese heiress had been coming apart at the seams and had been just the kind of a woman that the actuarial-risk boys in the insurance companies would have wanted no part of. Doctor Wilkins had prescribed various medicines for his third wife but she never took the stuff. Didn't believe in medicine. Curiously enough, she started to pick up the year after her marriage to the Doctor.

"How do you account for that?" asked Burns.

"I don't know," answered the lawyer, "except that Doctor Wilkins is a most fascinating man. Why, he could charm a bird out of a tree. His charm must have had a therapeutic effect on his wife. But I'll always think he hoped she would die so he could inherit her money."

Since Doctor Wilkins was now beginning to get a little brown around the edges, Burns wondered if the old boy had ever been in trouble as a Doctor. Thus he found that Wilkins had a black mark against him in the records of the New York Medical Society. He had gotten the black mark because he had been in some bottled-water trouble with the Board of Health.

Just prior to marrying the heiress to the cheese money thirteen years before, Wilkins, although having a license to practice medicine, had not exactly been practicing. He had, rather, been in a sort of business, operating out of a hole in the wall off Broadway. He had been peddling a mud-colored bottle product called Doctor Wilkins' Wonder Remedy.

The Doctor's Wonder Remedy, which retailed at a dollar a bottle, was, according to the label, guaranteed to cure tape worm or money back. One day a woman patient who had consumed several bottles of the stuff without results, demanded her money back. The Doctor made the mistake of ordering her out of his office and she wound up at the Board of Health.

An investigator for the Board of Health, palming himself off as a host to a tapeworm, bought a bottle of the Wilkins Wonder Remedy. Analysis disclosed that it was nothing but Hudson River water, alive with assorted bacteria. "Maybe that water didn't kill a tapeworm," a Board of Health investigator told Burns, "but we wouldn't be a bit surprised if it killed some of the people who drank it. Why, that stuff was practically poison."

Why, Burns wanted to know, had Wilkins used Hudson River water instead of a colored product of some kind. The contaminated stuff, it seemed, looked and tasted as medicinal as all hell.

It was now time, Burns decided, to take a good hard look into the past of the old boy with the twinkling eyes and the mutton-chop whiskers. So Burns went back a third of a century and, using people who had known the Doctor as stepping stones, brought himself up to date on the Wilkins saga.

Walter Keene Wilkins was a California boy who wasn't born with a silver spoon in his mouth but should have been. By the time he reached voting age he had highly accented appetites for expensive clothes and jewelry, good food, strong liquor and weak women but was short at the pockets. He went up and down the Golden State selling carpet sweepers, his eyes always peeled for a likely opening. It wasn't until he was thirty-five that he found what he wanted —a young lady named Grace Mansfield.

Miss Mansfield, the daughter of well-heeled people in the Napa Valley, was swept off her feet by the carpet-sweeper salesman. Young Wilkins was a strapping big hunk of beef cake, handsome of countenance, rich of voice, courtly of manner—altogether a fascinating fellow. He not only talked Grace into marrying him but conned her old man into forking over the dough for the newlyweds to move to New York so that he could study medicine.

It was while Wilkins was serving his internship at Bellevue Hospital that the marital bark hit the rocks. The handsome big intern had a habit of pinching and propositioning the nurses and the girls in white began to squeal to his wife.

When enough of them squealed, Mrs. Wilkins went back to California and got a divorce. So there was Doc, when he completed his internship, alone in the big city and finding the competition in medical circles something fierce.

The Doctor, who was developing a penchant for show girls, eventually hung his shingle out in front of a theatrical boarding house on West Thirty-eighth Street—a casual establishment run by a devastatingly homely widow named Suzanne Kirkland. The widow was well heeled and when Doc found that out, he laid siege to the lady's heart and married her.

After the honeymoon the Doctor practically gave up what practice he had to devote himself to the management of his wife's rooming house. He promptly threw out all the male guests and installed show girls in their places. Wilkins, now forty, was a very busy man, anticipating the slightest whim of the guests. An ex-roomer of the place told Burns that Wilkins prescribed sleeping pills for his wife, convincing her that she suffered from a nervous condition, and sometimes roamed the halls practically all night, making certain the guests were not in need of anything.

One night the Doctor and Mrs. Wilkins were standing at the head of a steep flight of stairs, when, somehow or other, Mrs. Wilkins lost her balance and toppled down the stairs. She got off with minor bruises but the Doctor was greatly disturbed about the whole thing. He went around telling the roomers that the fall had made his wife a nervous wreck and that he would have to take drastic measures to cure her.

The Doctor's remedy was cold baths— baths with big chunks of ice in the water. Mrs. Wilkins complained that she felt dreadful after such baths but the Doctor insisted that she take two a day—one in the morning and one at night. One morning Mrs. Wilkins died among the chunks of ice.

Examining the death certificate of the second Mrs. Wilkins, Burns saw that the lady's demise had been ascribed to apoplexy. The certificate had been signed by a physician other than Wilkins. Burns hunted up the second Doctor and asked him if he remembered anything unusual about the death. "As a matter of fact, I do," said the sawbones. "The body had already been embalmed before Doctor Wilkins summoned me, so that I couldn't make a thorough examination of it. I thought that was a little unusual but since Wilkins was a doctor I didn't question it at the time. He told me his wife had died of apoplexy and I had no reason to doubt him."

"Did you know that he had his wife take two baths a day in chunks of ice?"

"Never heard of anything like that."

The Doctor, Burns learned, inherited his second wife's roominghouse. What with chasing the tenants, lavish spending and general neglect it took Wilkins just ten years to run the roominghouse into the ground. And so, as he reached his fiftieth year, Doctor Walter Keene Wilkins was both out at the pockets and out of practice. It was then that he went into the bottled-water dodge and after the Board of Health drew a bead on him, he began to hunt around for another wife.

The same mail man had been delivering mail on Sixty-fifth Street to the house owned by the third Mrs. Wilkins for about fifteen years. Burns found the letter carrier to be a fund of background information about the Doctor and the third Mrs. Wilkins. It seemed that the Doctor, after learning that the lady with the buck teeth was heiress to the cheese fortune, had rented one of her rooms

and began to pour on the old oil. But the cheese heiress wasn't interested. Doc, though, smelling that cheese money, refused to be discouraged.

There was a wheezy old organ in the rooming house and Wilkins learned that the proprietress of the establishment, while being fond of organ music, couldn't play herself. So Doc went out and took enough organ lessons so that he was soon able to sit down at the thing and play a few old German tunes. That did it. Wilkins and his landlady got married and Doc went into practice on the ground floor as a tapeworm specialist. He was still up to his old tricks. He tossed out all the male guests and installed ladies, mostly chorines, in their places.

Things rocked along pretty evenly, at least on the surface, with the third marriage of the Doctor and the former Julia Kraus. The Doctor, ignoring the encroachment of age, was still doing a little darting around the halls of the rooming house, but if his wife ever questioned him about his nonprofessional activities he apparently gave her a satisfactory one for nobody ever heard the couple quarreling.

In going out to Long Beach of an evening, Doctor and Mrs. Wilkins took the Broadway subway at Sixty-sixth Street to Pennsylvania Station. During the walk to the subway they crossed Broadway at Sixty-fifth Street and thus became acquainted with a traffic cop on post there —a cop bearing a name that tickles the fancy of certain hateful critics of the New York Police Department. The cop's name was Crooks.

Often times the Doctor and his wife would stop beside a little wooden platform that Officer Crooks stood on while he directed traffic and chat with the cop while the stream of commerce roared past them. There were times when Mrs.

Wilkins remained in the rooming house all night and Doc went out to Long Beach alone, principally to air the two collies, feed the monkey and put water in the cages of the parrot and the canaries. On such occasions Doc would stop to chat with Officer Crooks longer than usual.

One evening, about a year before the murder of Julia Wilkins, Crooks told Burns, Doc was standing there, out in the middle of Broadway, chatting with the cop over the roar of traffic. Officer Crooks happened to be in a reminiscent mood that evening and he told Wilkins about a murder case that the New York Police Department had once handled. Seemed that a husband, wishing to get rid of his wife so that he could inherit her money, bashed her head in with a hammer, then mussed himself up and called the police, claiming he and his wife had been set upon by robbers. "But there never had been no robbers in the neighborhood," Crooks had told Wilkins, "and the police got suspicious. Anyway, there was other things about the case I don't remember that made the police suspicious of the husband and he got electrocuted."

Old Doc Wilkins used to stop at Officer Crooks' post and stand there in the midst of that roaring Broadway traffic and have Crooks repeat the story of that murder over and over again. It was practically like a kid asking his parent to repeat a fairy tale that he particularly liked. Officer Crooks told Burns that Old Doc just hadn't been able to get enough of that story.

Why, Burns wondered, would Doctor Wilkins have been so fascinated by Officer Crooks' recital of a murder story? Was it possible that Old Doc, the fastidious, carefully-brushed, neatly-pressed, perfumed, skirt-happy old gentleman had finally become so fed up on his third wife's slovenly habits, and so weary of waiting for her to kick off and leave him that cheese fortune, that he had seen in Officer Crooks' recital of a plan for murder the answer to his two-fold problem?

Considering the Wilkins background, especially the circumstances surrounding the demise of his second wife, Burns began to believe so. The appearance of those two robbers in Long Beach would have been grist for Old Doc's murder mill. Who would have doubted his story about the two tall men in the gray caps when all of Long Beach had been talking of little else for weeks? Who indeed —except William J. Burns?

Now, definitely suspicious of Wilkins, Burns' mind went back to those two collies that had barked so loudly at his approach to the home of the woman who was keeping them. Certainly two dogs that barked at the approach of Burns would have barked if two intruders—the men in the gray caps—had gone near the Wilkins home the night of the murder.

A man who lived right next door to Wilkins had been bothered for two years by the barking of the dogs. He told Burns, "Christ, we haven't had so much peace since the murder and those two damned dogs were taken away." The dogs barked at everybody who approached the Wilkins house.

"You could hear them barking even when all the windows in the Wilkins house were closed?"

"Oh sure."

"And they barked even when Doctor and Mrs. Wilkins came home at night?"

"Now that's a funny thing. They never let out a sound when the Doctor or his wife came home. They seemed to know their footsteps."

The neighbor had been in his home from shortly after six o'clock the night of the murder right up until the time of the crime. He clearly recalled that the dogs had not barked that night. By now more than a month had passed since the murder and Burns wanted to know how the neighbor could recall that the dogs had not barked. "Because," answered the man, "I said to my wife the next day when we read in the papers about the robbers it was a funny thing we hadn't heard the dogs barking." That was good enough for Burns. The neighbor had not heard the dogs bark because the two tall men wearing the gray caps had been nowhere near the Wilkins home that night.

Now Burns got around to the murder hammer again—the hammer with the handle wrapped in newspaper. A small puzzle within the larger one was now cleared up—the puzzle as to why the hammer handle had been wrapped in paper. The paper had been wrapped around the handle because fingerprints wouldn't come up on newsprint. But why would such a precaution have been taken unless the murderer had known *beforehand* that the hammer was to be used as a lethal weapon?

Thinking that there might be a trademark on the handle of the hammer beneath the wire, Burns began to unwind the wire. As he did so he came upon a tiny piece of green feather. The feather had apparently been floating through the air and come to rest on the hammer handle just as it was being bound and had been unnoticed by the person who had bound it.

Burns wrapped the piece of feather in a piece of tissue paper, went into New York, bought a magnifying glass, and went into a pet shop. "I want you to take a look at this feather through this glass," he said to the proprietor of the pet shop, "and tell me what kind of a bird you think it's from."

"Looks like it comes from a bird in the parrot family," said the proprietor.

"That's what I hoped you'd say," said Burns.

Burns now devoted his attention to something else that had previously seemed unimportant—a smudge of bright green paint on the hammer handle. Burns learned from neighbors that Old Doc had, one unseasonably warm weekend a couple of months before, painted a fence behind his house a bright green —exactly the same shade of green as the smudge on the hammer handle. While painting the fence, Wilkins had also done a little repair work—driving in a nail here and there. It was obvious to Burns that Old Doc had used the ballpoint hammer in the repair work and that the handle had thus taken on the bright green smudge.

The wire around the hammer handle and the string that had held the newspaper in place weren't too hot as clues. But they weren't exactly cold, either. The wire was of the same kind used to hang pictures in the Wilkins Long Beach home. The string was the same kind as that used in a Long Beach butcher shop where the Wilkinses dealt.

The newspaper looked hotter than the string or the wire. The murderer had torn it around the edges so that it could not be identified at sight. But it wasn't a New York paper. Burns determined that simply by comparing the type with that of the big New York dailies.

Setting out on a canvass of newspaper plants in the vicinity of Long Beach, Burns learned that the newsprint had come from a daily sheet called The Lynbrook *Era*. Moreover, the print around the murder hammer was from an issue of The *Era* published the morning of the day of the murder.

Burns went into Manhattan, to the house on Sixty-fifth Street, and fell to talking with Wilkins about this, that and the other thing. He asked the Doctor, apparently quite casually, what newspapers he read. The Doctor said he read nothing but The New York *Times*. "Ever read any Long Island papers, Doctor?" "I wouldn't be seen with them," answered Wilkins with some vehemence. "They're nothing but rubbish."

"The Lynbrook *Era* doesn't seem to be so bad," said Burns.

"I disagree with you, sir," said Old Doc. "That's one of the worst of the whole lot."

"How do you know that if you don't read it?"

"I saw a few issues a year or so ago," answered Wilkins. "That was enough."

Wilkins had not subscribed to The *Era*, but he could have bought it at a news stand—either in Long Beach, at the railroad station, before he left for New York the morning of the murder, or at Pennsylvania Station in New York, on his way back to Long Beach to commit the murder. The man who sold papers at the Long Beach station couldn't recall whether or not Wilkins had bought anything from him a morning more than a month previously. And of course nobody at the news stands in such a busy place as Penn Station could recall such a thing.

Now Burns began to think of Mayer, the furrier who had ridden in on the train, in the seat directly behind the Wilkinses, the night of the murder. Did Mayer, Burns wanted to know, by chance recall whether Wilkins had been reading a newspaper on the train that night. "No," said Mayer. "As I recall it, Doc and his wife had just made the train that night because they had stopped some-

where to buy a mackerel. I had two newspapers and I gave him one of mine when I was through with it."

"Remember what paper that was?"

"Sure," said Mayer. "It was The *Era*— The Lynbrook *Era*. I get it every morning but sometimes I don't have time to read it until I come back at night."

Burns turned his attention toward establishing Wilkins as the owner of the murder hammer. He couldn't locate the store where the hammer had been purchased. But he came up with something almost as good. He got hold of a workman who had, while making repairs in the Wilkins Long Beach home more than a year previously, borrowed, from Old Doc's tool chest, a ball-point hammer with a handle bound by wire.

Now Burns went to District Attorney Weeks with a pretty package of circumstantial evidence—pointing the finger of guilt at the fastidious old wolf who had found himself tied down to a rich and slovenly old sack in discouragingly good health—the parrot feather, the wire, the string, the piece of The Lynbrook *Era*; the repairman's story about the bound-up hammer, the bright green paint smudge on the hammer handle and its relation to the Wilkins fence; Old Doc's fascination by Officer Crooks' tale of the man who had bludgeoned his wife; and the barking dogs that had not barked.

The District Attorney liked the feel of Burns' package. Old Doc was pinched for the murder, clapped in durance vile, and indicted by the grand jury. While Wilkins was awaiting trial the Eden Musee at Coney Island put on a grim tableau for the peasants—a reconstruction of the murder.

Wilkins, still smelling money there in the can, started suit against the Eden people for invasion of privacy. But he never lived to prosecute the suit. He hanged himself in jail.

It seems that Old Doc's lawyer imparted to him a piece of news that decided Wilkins that there was nothing to live for, let alone fight for.

The mouthpiece told his client that his third wife had failed to provide for him in her will. So there was poor fastidious Wilkins, after living with the sloppy old bag for thirteen years and then having to murder her to get her money, winding up with nothing to show for all his toil and trouble.

Gaston Bullock Means:
Con Cum Laude

Introducing Gaston Bullock Means of the North Carolina Meanses—by all odds the most versatile criminal of the twentieth century. Gaston, who began where other criminals left off, capped a career of infamy by swindling Evalyn Walsh McLean out of $104,000 on his false promise to restore to her the kidnaped Lindbergh baby.

When, in the first decade of the present century, William J. Burns, a red-haired, freckled-faced little man in his early forties, resigned as star operative of the United States Secret Service to form the William J. Burns International Detective Agency, he looked upon himself, with all the impartiality at his command, as the greatest detective alive. Over a period of years, Billy Burns had, in tangling with counterfeiters, cranks with designs on the lives of two Presidents, and other assorted criminals, displayed an investigative acumen that gave him considerable justification for this opinion of himself. So in 1910, when his agency was rolling and he began telling people that he had hired an operative who was, next to himself, the greatest natural detective he had ever known, a certain curiosity began to surround the object of his enthusiasm.

The operative to whom Burns referred was a thirty-year-old moon-faced ex-school superintendent, cotton broker and part-time lawyer from Cabarrus County, North Carolina, named Gaston Bullock Means. Although somewhat old to be entering a new profession, Gaston Means had three of the principal attributes of the successful private gumshoe of the era —natural guile, little or no conscience,

and a right hand totally ignorant of the behavior of the left one.

Gaston Means became practically invaluable around the New York headquarters of the Burns Agency, on lower Broadway, not only because of his unique and never-failing knack for uncovering blots on the escutcheons of families under investigation by the agency, but for ability to cope with the agency's founder. Burns had a habit of ascending into monumental rages, particularly at any mention of the word Pinkerton, the name of a rival agency. Means was the one person who could bring him down again. "Here, here, Chief," Means would say, in a soothing, resonant voice, coated with an accent from the mint-julep belt, "you are far too important a man to let a thing like that upset you." Burns would search Means with an icy blue glare, and then say, "I guess you're right, Gaston."

Burns and Means were, on the surface, an ill-assorted pair—the one, Burns, small, natty and explosive; the other huge of frame, baggy of attire, slow-moving. It was an attraction of opposites; the two men complemented each other. What they had in common was an incandescent desire to get ahead in life; and as each did, in his own way, their paths crossed many times throughout the years. When Burns died in the 1930's, the New York *Times* shared his own estimate of himself, referring to him as probably the greatest detective this country had ever produced. When Gaston Means died, also in the 1930's, in a federal jail, ranking criminologists pegged him as the most cunning, the most intelligent and the most versatile criminal of the twentieth century. His swindling of Evalyn Walsh McLean, Washington's Cinderella woman, of one hundred and four thousand dollars in connection with the Lindbergh kidnaping case, was merely an anticlimax to the criminal career of Gaston Means.

Burns, who had taken to asking, "Gaston, what the hell would I ever do without you?", was shocked out of a week's sleep when, one day in the fall of 1915, after he had been a Burns dick five years, Means eased himself into the founder's office and tendered his resignation. "Is it money?" asked Burns. The question was natural. Burns himself was noted for his one-way pockets, and if an agency operative ever got rich, it was in experience. "It's not exactly money, Chief," said Means. "I'm getting out of the detective business."

"Where are you going, Gaston?"

"I'm going to manage the affairs of Maude King."

"No!"

"Yes."

Maude Robinson King, an ex-ribbon counter clerk with one million dollars, was a darling of the Sunday-supplement editors. She was, at thirty-eight, an international screwball whose intelligence was in inverse ratio to her beauty, and she was gorgeous. She was always on the verge of announcing her engagement to some horse jockey, prize fighter, or bell captain, until a restraining hand was clapped over her pretty mouth; she had

great fun planting stink bombs in the Houses of Parliament in London and dropping empty champagne bottles off the Eiffel Tower. She had, in 1901, at the age of twenty-four, negotiated passage from the ranks of Chicago's department-store workers to a mansion on the Gold Coast by marrying James C. King, a flinty-eyed lumber tycoon who still had the first toothpick from his first forest. King was exactly fifty years older than his bride, and, while there was one school of thought that discounted the difference in ages, pointing out that when Mrs. King was one hundred and ten years old her husband would be only one hundred and sixty, cynical observers were certain that the old boy had married an aphrodisiac and that she had married a bank book.

King wore out, in one way and another, in four years. And although the wood man left most of his fortune—four million dollars—for the founding of the James C. King Home for Old Men, his widow still had one million dollars and a whole world to spend it in. Her principal regrets were that she could wear only one fur coat and ride in only one automobile at a time. She drew fortune hunters like an open window draws a draft. Her mother, Mrs. Anna Robinson, a loud-mouthed old character who gave the impression of having consumed great quantities of carbohydrates in her time, established herself as a layer of insulation between her daughter and the dough-happy chasers, but as mama got along in years the task became too arduous. She decided that what Maude needed was somebody to manage both her and her affairs. Although old Mrs. Robinson and Gaston Means had never met, they had a mutual friend who suggested Means as ideal for the job of taking over Maude King's affairs. Means was hired at one hundred dollars a week, more than twice his Burns salary.

Means moved into a corner room of a ten-room layout that Mrs. King and her mother occupied in the Edgewater Beach Hotel in Chicago. He disappeared behind a mountain of canceled checks, paid and unpaid bills, lists of securities, bank statements and other papers relating to Maude King's fiscal life. He left the door of his room open; Mrs. King and her mother could hear him making loud ticking sounds with his tongue as he struggled to bring order out of chaos. Occasionally he would emerge with a pencil clenched crosswise between his teeth and a sheaf of papers in each hand, to question either Mrs. King or Mrs. Robinson about some item or other. The ladies would later hear him on the telephone, arguing with somebody about the price they had been charged for something.

Although given to loose-fitting single-breasted suits usually stuffed with miscellany, and unshined blucher shoes, Means was a man of great personal magnetism and solid family background. The Meanses were, in Cabarrus County, North Carolina, the rough equivalent of the Cabots and the Lodges in Massachusetts. Gaston's grandfather had once been governor of the state; an uncle, George Means, had been a U. S. Treasury Department investigator and chief of police of Concord; and Gaston's father, Colonel W. G. Means, was a prominent Concord attorney, landowner and onetime mayor of the town. Upon graduating from the University of North Carolina, Gaston had studied law in his father's office, helped in the preparation of briefs, and investigated the dark recesses of important cases. For a time he had taken up the educational life, becoming superintendent of schools in Albemarle, North Carolina, with thirty-two teachers under him. Then, prior to meeting William J. Burns at a Washington social gathering, he had been a cotton broker in Concord and Washington.

Maude King had a childlike taste for adventure. She found life with Means very exciting. Something thrilling and dramatic was always happening. At the theater, Means would point out people in the audience whom, he said, he had investigated as a Burns detective, and tell simply fascinating stories about them. Mysterious telephone calls would come into the King apartment at the Edgewater Beach Hotel. Means would take the calls, listen intently to what the person on the other end of the wire had to say, look around at either Mrs. King or Mrs. Robinson, roll his eyes and say, "If you come within a block of this hotel, you'd have *me* to deal with!" Then he would hang up, wipe his brow, and make light of the whole thing. If one of the ladies questioned him about the call, he would smile and say, "Now let *me* worry about it; after all, that's what I'm being paid for." Means had a dimple in each cheek, his forehead was high and his brown hair was thinning. The total effect, which was cherubic, was made even more so by the polka-dot bow ties which Means favored; all in all, his face radiated warmth and inspired confidence. His brain, of course, was something else again.

One night Means was strolling with Mrs. King and her mother near the hotel. A young man with a gun appeared dramatically from the shadows. "Your money or your life!" he rasped, in the tradition of the era. Means, who stood over six feet and weighed about two hundred pounds, could manipulate his bulk with surprising dexterity. He made a couple of lightning moves, pinioned the stick-up man to the pavement and took his gun away from him. Mrs. Robinson started to scream for the cops. "S-s-s-h-h," said Means. Maude King's protector took the hold-up man by the coat collar and propelled him out of earshot. He came back alone. "I let him go," he said. "The poor fellow's wife's in the hospital and he needs money for an operation. He's never done anything like this before," Means sighed. "I gave him ten dollars."

Gaston Means became the indispensable man of the Edgewater Beach Hotel. Mrs. King and Mrs. Robinson depended upon him so much that they even took him along, to avail themselves of the benefit of his advice, when they bought clothing. He ordered all meals that were sent up to the apartment in the hotel; he made elaborate personal investigations of the room-service waiters who served the meals. When he dined out with the ladies, he bustled into the kitchen for a personal inspection before ordering. "We have to watch out for poison, you know." He went over all bills and he was now making out all checks for Mrs. King to sign. He decided eventually to relieve Mrs. King of the chore of signing checks; he had her give him power of attorney over two of her checking accounts.

Means was spending a great deal of time in the ticker rooms of Chicago brokerage houses. He sat up nights, preparing lengthy statements for Mrs. King purporting to disclose profits from his market manipulations on her behalf. Mrs. King, who thought bulls and bears were animals and that red ink was prettier than black, would take a quick look at the profits, impulsively throw her arms around Means, kiss him on the cheek and say, "Mr. Means, you're *won*derful!"

There was in the Edgewater Beach Hotel an assistant manager named Phillips—a man of brittle mien—who had always regarded Gaston Means as the type of patron he would ask to pay in advance, baggage or no baggage. Phillips had noticed Means in a ticker room in the hotel wearing a worried expression. Knowing that Means handled Mrs. King's financial affairs, Phillips was curious. He snagged Mrs. King into a conversation one day in July of 1917. "How are you doing in the stock market these days?" Phillips asked. "Oh," said Mrs. King, "Mr. Means makes all kinds of money for me in the market." She told Phillips about the financial statements. "Such statements are all very well," said Phillips, "but have you ever seen the actual stocks?" Come to think of it, Mrs. King had not. "Ask him to let you see the stocks," said Phillips.

Means' next statement showed losses of about five thousand dollars and profits of about twenty-eight thousand dollars. "Or a net profit," he explained to Mrs. King, "of twenty-two thousand, eight hundred and fifty-three dollars and eighty-six cents." He folded the statement and placed it in his pocket. "Where," asked Mrs. King, "are the stocks?"

Means gave the lady a double take. "What did you say?"

"Where are the stocks—the stocks themselves?"

"Who have you been talking to?" asked Means. "Who told you to ask that question?"

"Mr. Phillips, the assistant manager."

The Means countenance darkened. He milked the story of her talk with Phillips from Mrs. King, then went downstairs and rocked the hotel. When he returned, he said to Mrs. King, "I never want you to speak to Phillips again. Do you understand that?"

"Yes, Mr. Means." Mrs. King, with her

little one-track mind, wasn't in the least suspicious, but she wanted to see those stocks. "They're in the safety deposit vault at the bank," said Means.

"What bank?"

"The Northern Trust Company."

"Well, let's go down there in the morning, Mr. Means; I want to see the actual stocks."

"Come to think of it," said Means, "they're not in the Northern Trust at all. I shipped them to the Colonel for safekeeping in his vault."

"The Colonel? You mean your father?"

Means nodded. Mrs. King still insisted upon seeing the stocks. Means indulged her. Very well, she could see the stocks, but she would have to go to North Carolina to see them. It was August. It was hot in North Carolina in August. "I don't mind the heat," said Mrs. King. "In fact, I like heat—and anyway, I want to see the stocks."

Maude King and Gaston Means arrived in Concord late in August. They were guests at the home of Gaston's father, Colonel Means. The Colonel's home was quite a place—a huge Colonial mansion where the white folks lounged around in white linens, fanning themselves, and the colored servants mixed and served mint juleps all the livelong day. The Colonel, a white-haired, goateed old tale spinner, told Maude King a story about Gaston, later widely repeated, that explained much about Means. "When Gaston here was only eight," the Colonel said, "he used to pick up information for me. I bought him a pony and he used to ride all around the countryside, keeping his eyes and ears open, mostly while buying candy in country stores. He would come home and tell me who he saw and what

he heard people saying and who was where and doing what.

"Well, sir, I'd make careful notes of everything Gaston picked up. You'd be surprised how those notes came in handy later. A witness for the other side would get on the stand and he'd say he was in a certain place on a certain date. I'd look up my notes. I'd find Gaston'd seen him someplace else that day and I'd get other people to prove it. Yes, Ma'am, Gaston was a lot of help to me—him and his little pony."

Maude King never did get to see the stocks. Means took her hunting instead. Late one afternoon he organized a little expedition to go after rabbits in a wooded region known as Blackwelder's Spring, on the edge of Concord. Mrs. King had never hunted before. "Oh," said Means, "it's fun." Afton Means, an older brother of Gaston, a Captain Bingham, a local dog fancier, Means and Mrs. King made up the party. When the hunters went into the woods, Means said to his brother and to Captain Bingham, "You two go on ahead; I want to take Mrs. King to the spring. She's thirsty."

"I'm not thirsty, Mr. Means," said Mrs. King.

"Oh, you are, too," said Means. "Anyway, it's no trouble." Means and Mrs. King went off by themselves. In a little while, Afton Means and Captain Bingham heard a loud report. Means came running out of the woods. "My God!" he was shouting. "Mrs. King has shot herself!" Tears were streaming down his cheeks. He dropped to the ground; his big body shook with sobs as he buried his face in his hands. "Poor Mrs. King," he said. "Oh, *poor* Mrs. King."

A coroner's jury of apple knockers exposed their tonsils as Gaston Means of the North Carolina Meanses explained how Maude King had met death. "I had this twenty-five-caliber blue-steel Colt automatic," he said, fighting back the tears, "and I put it in the crotch of a tree while I went to the spring to get a drink. Mrs. King insisted she wasn't thirsty, so I left her standing by the tree where the gun was while I went to the spring to quench my thirst." It had been fairly dark in the woods. Means had reached the spring, leaned down, and struck a match to see if there were any insects on the surface of the water before drinking. He heard Mrs. King giggling. He looked back and there, some two hundred feet distant, he saw that the lady had taken his automatic from the tree crotch and was twirling it. "Mrs. King, poor soul, was very light-headed," Means explained. "I shouted to her to put the gun back. Then I leaned down to get my drink and I heard this report." A bullet had gone into Mrs. King's head, behind her left ear. The jurors decided that she had either committed suicide or met death by accident when she dropped the Colt, causing it to explode.

Old Mrs. Robinson, who had come east with her daughter and who was staying at the Oak Grove Hotel in Asheville, began arrangements to send the body back to Chicago. "I'm going to put Maude in a vault," she told Means, "until I decide where she'll be happiest."

"Oh," said Means, "didn't I tell you?"

"Didn't you tell me *what?*"

"It was practically your daughter's last wish—she wanted to be cremated."

"There ain't going to be no cremation," said old Mrs. Robinson, "and that's final."

The remains of Maude King had hardly been placed in a vault in Graceland Cemetery in Chicago than that threat to all evil-doers, the author of the anonymous letter, put in an appearance. Somebody from Concord dropped a note to the Chicago cops saying that if they would go to the trouble of taking Maude King out of the vault and examining the bullet hole behind her ear, they'd sure as hell find proof she had been murdered.

The bullet hole behind Mrs. King's ear seemed to rule out even the most remote possibility of suicide or accident. The bullet had gone in straight, not on an angle. In order to have shot herself, Maude King would not only have had to be a contortionist, but left-handed, and she had been neither. Had death been due to the accident of a dropped gun exploding, the bullet would certainly have entered her head at an angle. Even to the Chicago cops, who were not exactly unacquainted with miscarriages of justice, it was fantastic that anybody could have got away with so obvious a murder.

The State Solicitor of North Carolina, a man named Hayden Clement who was fast on the uptake, was not an admirer of the Means clan. When he received the intelligence from Chicago he decided to take a look at the minutes of the coroner's hearing that had resulted in the suicide-or-accident verdict. Clement was struck by what he thought was a serious inconsistency in Means' story. Means had said he had struck a match to see if there were any insects on the surface of the spring he was about to drink from. If it was so dark that he couldn't see the water in front of his face, how could he have seen Mrs. King, two hundred feet away, twirling a gun?

Clement went to Chicago. He began to thread his way through the labyrinth of Maude King's fiscal life. Everywhere he turned he found cleaned-out bank accounts and safety-deposit boxes. Gaston Means had had power-of-attorney to dip into some of the accounts and the boxes;

others, in the Northern Trust Company in Chicago and in the Netherlands Bank in New York, Means had entered after submitting written orders from Maude King—orders which, under examination, proved to be forgeries. Mrs. King had, some years before, established a trust fund for her mother at the Merchants Loan and Trust Company in New York. The bank had paid the old lady one hundred dollars a week until a few months previously when, she now told investigators, Means had begun to pay her in cash.

At the bank, Clement and some men from the New York D.A.'s office found a forged order revoking the trust fund. Means, who was at his father's place in North Carolina, grieving over Maude King's death, had, it now developed, a secret apartment on Park Avenue in New York. The D.A.'s men gave it a toss and found evidence that Means had, over a period of eighteen months, lost one hundred and twenty-three thousand dollars in the stock market. This was within twenty-five thousand dollars of the shortages discovered in Maude King's accounts. Some old blotters were found in the Means apartment. When they were held up to a mirror the signatures of Maude King and Mrs. Robinson appeared—evidence that Means had forged the names, since neither Mrs. King nor her mother had ever been in the apartment.

It seemed abundantly clear that Gaston Means had murdered Maude King when he faced possible exposure for having gypped her out of one hundred and fifty thousand dollars. Means went on trial for the murder of Maude King in November, 1917. Business in Concord was practically at a standstill; the spirit of carnival gripped the populace. The judge was a close friend of the Means

clan. Means' lawyer threw a lot of weight around in the community. State Solicitor Clement, with a sharp nose for odors, asked for a change of venue—to some place, any place, where Justice might get a reasonably fair shake. The judge almost busted his gavel in denying the motion.

Eight farmers, four of them members of the Ku Klux Klan, were drawn on the jury. The state produced expert witnesses to prove that it would have been muscularly impossible for Maude King to have shot herself, and that it would have been equally impossible for her to have died accidentally. The story of Means' assault against the fortune of his employer was reduced to the simplest possible terms, so as to be understandable to the agriculturists in the box.

Gaston Means took the stand in his own defense. He launched into the story of his life. He gradually abandoned the theme of Mrs. King's death and took up that of white supremacy. The state solicitor grew hoarse shouting objections to irrelevancies. Means talked like a Southern senator during a filibuster. After covering the subject of white supremacy, he returned briefly to Mrs. King. His face was suffused with piety. He raised his eyes toward the ceiling. "If there is a God in Heaven," he asked, "why did He take this wonderful woman away in the bloom of her lovely life?" State Solicitor Clement had practically the only dry eyes in the courtroom.

On top of that, William J. Burns—the great Burns of Secret Service fame—testified as a character witness for Means. Burns seemed to take the position that the state solicitor, rather than Gaston Means, was on trial. Burns corroborated what the jury knew all along—that Gaston Means was the salt of the earth, the victim of some deep-dyed big-city conspiracy. The boys in the box were out all night. A couple of men thought Means might be partly guilty of something or other and maybe ought to be punished, say by a five-dollar fine and ten days in jail or something. These radicals were severely overruled by the other ten. In the morning Gaston Means walked out of court a free man. Maude King, it seemed, had, after all, committed suicide.

Means was free, but he was broke. He now entered a long period of litigation. Maude King had always been humiliated to think that her husband had left her only one million dollars while bequeathing four times as much to the James King Home for Old Men. She had frequently mentioned to Means how nice it would be if King's will could sometime be set aside, the old men turned out of their home into the cold, and the four million dollars directed to her. Means, agreeing, had got Mrs. King to sign an agreement with him whereby she would give him one-quarter of the proceeds if he somehow succceeded in getting King's will set aside. He had been so busy with one thing and another that he hadn't had time to take up the matter of the will. Now, however, he addressed himself to the problem of getting King's will set aside and making himself one million dollars. He went into seclusion in the ancestral home at Concord, emerging only to go to a local stationery store to purchase such items as rubber stamps, parchment paper, gold seals, and sealing wax. He came up with a handsome-looking document—the long-lost second, final and official will of James C. King. He went up to New York with it, to the law offices of Charles Evans Hughes, defeated the previous year by Woodrow Wilson for the Presidency of the United States. He got the bum's rush from Hughes.

Undiscouraged and undismayed, Means consulted another law firm. Then another and another. Everybody seemed to be looking around for a twenty-foot pole, not wishing to handle Means with a ten-foot one. He finally found a Philadelphia lawyer in Chicago. The barrister agreed that the second will was genuine. It was filed for probate. Means went out and bought a new automobile and several suits on credit. He sat down and wrote a letter to the trustees of the James C. King Home for Old Men, advising them that, for the good of everybody concerned, they had better begin placing their indigent charges elsewhere. Means met with disappointment. The second will was thrown out of court and, moreover, branded a preposterous forgery.

Means retired to the family homestead to lick his wounds and marshal his thoughts. He was sincerely dedicated to the proposition that only suckers did an honest days work. He went into court again. This time he was suing to protect what he actually termed his good reputation. He sued a group of law enforcement officials, bankers and lawyers who had been concerned with the gathering of evidence against him showing his motive for murdering Maude King. He asked a total of one million dollars in damages. Again he found his cases thrown out of court.

Next Means devoted himself to finding lawyers to sue the judge who had thrown the will out, and the judges who had dismissed his damage suits. He even consulted shysters on the possibility of suing other lawyers who had refused to handle his actions. He waded between Concord, New York and Chicago in an ever-flowing stream of legal red tape, technicalities and shenanigans. All of it came to nothing.

Gaston Means, as he reached his fortieth birthday in 1920, was a deeply frustrated man. The compensation for the frustration took the form of over-long sessions at the groaning board and the polished mahogany. He developed a paunch, in the classic J. P. Morgan tradition, and the capillaries in his nose gave way under inner pressure generated by mint juleps and straight Kentucky bourbon.

Gaston Means was faced with the depressing necessity of making a living. He was married to a woman who thought he was simply wonderful, and who believed everything he told her—the former Julie Patterson of Chicago. They had a son, and Means had the average fatherly pride in the boy. He could have gone back with the Burns Agency as a private dick, but the thought of the low pay there, after the dough he had either handled or tried to get, acted practically as an emetic. Means latched on as an investigator for a Chicago lawyer named Roy D. Keehn. Late in 1920, while he was still looking around for something big, Means found it right in the office of Lawyer Keehn. There was a large cash sum—fifty-seven thousand dollars, to be exact—due Mr. Keehn from a New York settlement. Means mentioned that he would like to take a run down to the old homestead in Concord. "While I'm in the East, I can pick up that money for you," he said to Keehn.

Means picked up the money. Then he went to Concord. There he entered the offices of the Southeastern Express Company and sent a registered package to Keehn. When Keehn got the package and opened it, expecting to find the fifty-seven thousand dollars, he found instead a newly-cut block of wood—North Carolina pine, no less. Another beautiful friendship came to an end; Keehn entered suit against Means for the money.

You can't, as the saying goes, get blood out of a turnip. The case never came to trial. Now Means sued the express company for the money. He claimed an express clerk had removed the money he had sent to Keehn and substituted the block of wood. A jury decided that if anybody substituted anything for anything, Gaston Means had exchanged a block of wood for fifty-seven thousand dollars. Whatever had happened, Gaston Means was in the chips. He addressed himself to a cask of Kentucky bourbon at the ancestral home in Concord. He followed with interest the Presidential election campaign of 1920 between Warren G. Harding and James M. Cox, a couple of Ohio newspaper publishers.

When the great American public, in its infinite wisdom, elected Warren G. Harding to the Presidency in November, 1920, Gaston Bullock Means emerged from a horrible bourbon hangover to read a telegram from William J. Burns in New York. The wire asked Means to come at once to discuss a matter of import. Burns was a man who never forgot a favor if he had done the favor. Certainly he had done Means a good turn by being a character witness at his murder trial; Means was cute enough to know that Burns now wanted a favor himself.

What Burns wanted was Means' assistance in getting him appointed Chief of the Division of Investigation, United States Department of Justice, later to be known as the F.B.I. The publicity value to Burns' detective agency, with its founder in such a job, would be incalculable. Means didn't quite see how he could help. Burns had it all figured out. Harry Daugherty, a midde-aged lawyer of Washington Courthouse, Ohio, who had been instrumental in wangling Harding's nomination at the Republican national convention, was a close personal friend of Burns. Daugherty, who was slated to become Harding's Attorney General, wanted to appoint Burns to the Division of Investigation job, but Harding wasn't too keen on the appointment. He had somebody else in mind. What Burns wanted Means to do was to travel throughout the country, during the four months that would elapse before Harding would be inaugurated, and get influential politicians to write letters to Daugherty insisting that Burns would be a great man to head the Division of Investigation. "Then Harry can show the letters to the President," Burns explained to Means, "and maybe make him change his mind." "What are the chances of my getting a job under you at the Department of Justice?" Means wanted to know. Burns gave him a quick stare. Means just sat there blinking. "Why fine, Gaston, just fine. You help me get in and I'll take care of you."

Burns paid Means' expenses as he roamed the country. Some politicians were pleased to write the kind of letter Means wanted them to write; others weren't. Means had learned that there is a skeleton in everybody's closet; it is just a question of how big the skeleton is. He uncovered the skeletons in the closets of recalcitrant politicos, whereupon they became only too glad to write to Daugherty endorsing Burns.

When, in March of 1921, Harding took the oath as the twenty-ninth President of the United States, an assorted crew of the most unsavory characters ever to congregate outside of a jail yard packed their bags in cities, towns and villages the length and breadth of the land, but mostly in Ohio, and entrained for Washington. The Ohio Gang was fixing to take over the country. This was the crowd of political blackguards who were to peddle practically everything but the Washington Monument to the highest bidder. Privileges, opportunities and physical assets were placed on the block. Oil lands, judgeships, whisky from bonded warehouses in an era of prohibition, power sites on Indian reservations, stock-market tips, government timber lands, in fact anything and everything that could be price-tagged was to go up for sale. Most of the boys, such as Harry Daugherty, the Attorney General, were to leave under a cloud, and some of them, like Albert B. Fall, Secretary of the Interior, were to go to prison as common crooks, but it was to be great while it lasted. The curtain was up on the era of wonderful nonsense, little black bags, and pay-offs under two-watt bulbs.

William J. Burns got in as Chief of the Division of Investigation largely because of the letters Means had inspired for him. It was Burns who set up the original national fingerprint identification system, the forerunner of the present FBI identification system. The present head of the F.B.I., J. Edgar Hoover, was, in fact, in the department when Burns took over, having thoroughly familiarized himself with the mechanics of the place as a young clerk while the First World War was being fought.

One of Burns' first moves was to send for Gaston Means. "You're in, Gaston," he said. "I want you to be one of my chief investigators." The salary broke down to eighty-nine dollars a week. "But there are little extras," Burns went on. "Like expenses. It'll all help. You'll like the work. It should be exciting." Burns cleared his throat. "And by the way," he said, "you'll not only take orders from me, but from Jesse Smith."

Jesse Smith turned out to be a fluttery, pink-cheeked man of fifty-five with a great deal of suet around the waistline.

He had once been in the dry-goods business in Ohio, but had been brought to Washington by Attorney General Daugherty as his Man Friday. Smith held no official position, but he had an office on the seventh floor of the Department of Justice Building, right next to Burns' office. "Where," Smith asked Burns, "are you living?"

"At the Bellevue Hotel with my wife and son."

"You are moving," said Smith. Means was too old a hand to ask questions. He went back to the Bellevue Hotel with Smith, threw a few things into a couple of suitcases and told his wife and boy to follow him. They followed him to an opulently-furnished three-story white brick house in the 900 block of Sixteenth Street, northwest, a little more than a block from the Department of Justice Building. The place, Means soon learned, rented for one thousand dollars a month, a fortune in those days. "Goodness, Gaston," Mrs. Means whispered, "you'll never be able to keep this place up on your salary." "Quiet," said Means.

Jesse Smith gave Means one thousand dollars in cash. "Buy a photostat machine," he said. Then Smith turned the keys over to Means. "I'll see you later," he said, and went off.

The house had a full English basement. It was the basement that appealed to Means; it was to be Means' private domain in the dramatic months to come. The basement had three rooms. The front room, facing on Sixteenth Street, contained a mahogany rolltop desk, a couch, bathroom, fireplace, and had three windows that looked out on a lawn facing the street. Means promptly had these windows double-barred. Then he personally constructed a mail box that ran the length of the middle window. The second basement room Means fixed

up as a dining room, and the third as a bar. There were two stationary wash tubs in the third room that later proved useful for icing champagne.

It didn't take Means long to find out where the bodies were buried around town. He caught on quick that there was an important body buried right in the White House. The scuttlebutt was that the President of the United States had an illegitimate child. That explained much; it explained why Harding, who wasn't basically any more crooked than the average politician, wasn't lifting a hand against the palace guard as they busily polished the capitol dome so as to enhance its appeal to prospective purchasers when it came time to put it on the market.

Means was given routine assignments to handle under Burns. Jesse Smith used to drop into his office occasionally, and also visit the house on Sixteenth Street to use the photostat machine. The rent was presumably being paid every month, by Smith, or somebody, because Means never saw a rent bill. He knew the house somehow figured in the plans of the Ohio Gang, but he couldn't figure out just how. The answer would come later.

It would be unfair to Gaston Bullock Means to suggest that he was the only scoundrel operating as an early day F.B.I. man. No less an authority than J. Edgar Hoover said that the department was honeycombed with grafters. "Those of us who were honest," Hoover said, "kept quiet about where we worked. We didn't want people to think we were crooks."

One of the honest agents was a young man of Greek ancestry named John Maragon, who achieved renown of a sort in the Washington Five-Percenter probe of the Truman era. Maragon's qualifications for the job were unique. He happened to arrive in Washington with a politician whose baggage included a suitcase filled with bootleg liquor. The bag began to leak, right in Union Station, and a prohibition agent pounced on it. The snooper demanded to know who owned the bag. John Maragon, to save the politician embarrassment, claimed ownership of the leaking suitcase and took the rap. By way of showing his appreciation to Maragon, the politician had him appointed to the Division of Investigation of the Department of Justice.

Straws began to appear in the wind in the fall of 1921, after the Ohio Gang had had six months to orient itself. Jesse Smith would call Means on the phone and say, "Gaston, I'm coming over with a man. I'd like to talk privately in your basement. When I get there would you like to take a walk for about an hour?" Smith would appear with various characters. Some of them carried little black bags, others didn't. The first man that Means recognized was a furtive-looking little man with a great walrus moustache —Albert B. Fall, Secretary of the Interior.

William J. Burns sent for Means. "Gaston," he said, "Mrs. Harding has asked me to send her my most trusted man to work on a confidential assignment of some kind." Burns lit a cigar. "Now don't ask me what the assignment is about; I haven't the slightest idea. But you're my best man. You better get right over to the White House and see Mrs. Harding. I'll phone and say you're on your way."

Here was a commentary of some kind on the type of early-day F.B.I. men operating in Washington—a proved scoundrel, a man who had been up on a murder rap four years before, easing his bulk into the White House to work on a confidential mission for the Frst Lady of the land. Mrs. Harding, a prim, nervous little woman, who had had one disastrous marriage before marrying Harding, received Means in a sitting room on the second floor. She didn't mince words. She told Gaston Means a story which, with its sequels, later circulated throughout subterranean Washington. Her husband was being forced to submit to certain things because the men around him knew that he had at one time been indiscreet with a young lady from Ohio named Nan Britton. "There is even a report that Miss Britton has a child and that the President is the father of it. That of course is preposterous. But I want you to find out all you can for me about Miss Britton. Find out, by all means, if there are any incriminating letters or diaries or anything like that that could be used against the President."

"And if I find such evidence, Madam, what do you wish me to do?"

"Bring it to me. I want nothing to interfere with the President. I want him to be in a position to get rid of these men around him who are forcing him to do things against his will."

Mrs. Harding didn't know where Nan Britton was. To Means that was no problem; he was adept at smelling out people. He went back to Burns and told him that his assignment for Mrs. Harding would take him out of town for a few weeks. "What is the assignment, Gaston?" asked Burns.

Means explained it. "No!" said Burns. "On my word of honor, Chief." "Well, I'll be damned," said Burns. "Keep me in touch with things, Gaston."

Means checked into Marion, Ohio, Harding's home town, as a traveling salesman for a linoleum company. He was loaded down with samples. He posed as a great admirer of the President, which didn't make him any enemies in town.

The President owned and published the Marion Daily *Star*. Means got linoleum orders from two employes there. He learned from his customers that Nan Britton, the daughter of a doctor who lived near Marion, had frequently contributed poetry to the *Star* while Harding was in the United States Senate. While not in Washington making laws, Harding had spent a good deal of his time at the paper. The poetry of Nan Britton—love stuff and pretty sophisticated for the Middle West—had interested him. He had sent for the girl to have a talk with her; she turned out to be blonde, shapely, pretty, and some thirty years his junior. The senator had always been a man who loved to look; there was a general suspicion around the paper that he had done more than look at the fair young verse writer.

Means got a tip that Nan Britton was living with relatives in Chicago. He ran the girl down to a swank apartment house on Chicago's North Side. Means was of that school of Hawkshaws who would rather spend six months figuring out how to do a thing neatly than do it in an hour and make a mess of it. He rented a room across the street from the apartment building, bought himself a pair of seven-power field glasses and began to study the faces of the building employes as they reported for work and left at nights. He became interested in a fellow who looked worried, who looked as if he could use some money. The fellow was an elevator operator. Means moved into the lift jockey's home neighborhood. The fellow liked a beer at night in a neighborhood speakeasy. Means began to patronize the speak. He quickly roped the subject. "How'd you like to make a hundred dollars," he asked. The elevator operator had a girl in trouble; a hundred seemed like a fortune. "How?"

Means smiled. "Just let me into that apartment where Nan Britton lives."

One night, when Nan Britton was at the movies, Means went through the young lady's effects. He found a stack of post cards bearing the initials W.G.H. He found a box of cheap costume jewelry. He found a large candy box containing four small diaries. A fast shuffle of the diaries revealed a pass-by-pass account of Warren Harding's affair with Nan Britton, including details of the birth, care and feeding of a baby daughter.

Means returned to Washington early in February. The snow was flying on the afternoon that he was ushered into a White House sitting room. He found Mrs. Harding seated before a grate fire; she was white with excitement. "What did you find, Mr. Means?" She glanced expectantly at a large briefcase Means was carrying. "Not very much, Madam," he said, "but enough to let us know we are on the right track." Means showed Mrs. Harding the post cards; they had been mailed to the Britton girl from various points that Harding had hit during his campaign a year and a half previously. The quality of the observations on the cards wasn't very original; they were on the wish-you-were-here level. The Harding postals were to give the nation a belly laugh when, subsequently, they were dwelt upon at length in a volume of Nan Britton's authorship called *The President's Daughter*. One card asked "Have you learned to sing the campaign song?" The Republican campaign song had been *Harding, You're the Man for Us*, and, from the way things eventually turned out, the author of both words and music probably felt like chopping his hands off for ever having composed it—fellow by the name of Al Jolson.

The walls had ears that February day when Means visited Mrs. Harding. A couple of White House maids, who knew from what they had seen and heard around the place that things were not as they might be between the President and the First Lady, glued their ears to the door of the sitting room. They caught snatches of what Means said, since his voice was resonant and carried well. By nightfall practically everything that transpired in the sitting room was carried by spent runners into the DuPont Circle gossip stockades.

Means showed Mrs. Harding some jewelry—cheap costume stuff that had set the donor back not more than a couple of hundred dollars. The postals and the jewelry didn't prove anything damaging against Harding as far as the Britton girl was concerned. Mrs. Harding inquired of Means if he hadn't found "letters or a diary or anything." Means assured Mrs. Harding that he had not; he suggested, however, that such evidence might well have fallen into other hands.

President Harding, according to the story that went the rounds in Washington, walked in on Means and Mrs. Harding. As a result, he ordered Means canned from his Department of Justice job. Things had got somewhat out of hand; Means found himself in a ticklish spot. Actually, he was in the employ of the Ohio Gang, and here he had found himself working against the very boys who were buttering his bread. Nobody had figured on Mrs. Harding entering the picture. So far all Means had got was a lousy eighty-nine dollars a week; now he wouldn't even get that. He had come to like the house that rented for one thousand a month. He decided to go into business for himself, and to hell with the Ohio Gang.

Means holed up in his English basement with a case of bourbon, some cheese and crackers, and his photostat machine. He gave a good imitation of a beaver for two nights and a day, stopping only for naps on his couch. What happened after that seems to have been pretty incredible. It became common scuttlebutt around Washington that Gaston Means phoned the President of the United States, informing Harding he had in his possession something of vital import to him, and thus got Harding to visit the house on Sixteenth Street. There, according to the story, Means showed Harding two of the four Britton diaries. Harding is supposed to have shown interest in throwing the diaries into a roaring fire, whereupon Means informed him that he had made photostats of the important pages. Harding thereupon asked Means what his price for the diaries was. Means' price was to be appointed a special agent for the enforcement of prohibition—with a roving assignment. A job like that was worth a fortune. Grafting prohibition agents were naming their own figures not to interfere with big bootleggers.

In the light of subsequent events, the story seems believable. Harding's Secret Service guards later admitted that they had taken the President to the house on Sixteenth Street. A Means butler remembered a visit by the President. Means, in his book, *The Strange Death of President Harding,* which on a later day was to become a best-selling confession tome, made no secret of the fact that he had had the President of the United States right where he wanted him.

The night after Harding's visit, Mrs. Harding, according to a story she later divulged to certain intimates, called at the Means home in response to a phone call. Means showed her the two diaries he had held out on the President. Mrs. Harding examined the diaries for fifteen minutes before she spoke a word. "Where did you get these, Mr. Means?" she asked.

"I'm afraid I can't disclose the source, Madam," said Means. "Sufficient to say that they were right here in Washington all the time."

"Here in Washington!"

Means nodded. "Yes. Apparently somebody got to Miss Britton's quarters in Chicago before I got there. Whoever it was represented a person who is now very close to the President." Means folded his hands behind his back and rocked back and forth in his feet. "It explains a lot, doesn't it, Madam?"

"It certainly does." Mrs. Harding took the diaries and put them in a large handbag she carried. "Mr. Means, how can I ever thank you?" Means rolled his eyes and cleared his throat. Many people, over a period of years, were to learn that when Gaston Bullock Means cleared his throat it cost somebody money. "There is a little question of expenditures," he said. "It was necessary for me to do something most unethical to lay hands on those diaries."

"You mean you had to *pay* for them?" Means nodded. "How much, Mr. Means?"

"Fifty thousand dollars."

"Fifty thousand dollars! Why, that's a *fortune,* Mr. Means." Mrs. Harding hadn't been born that morning, or even the day before. "Mr. Means, you are not a wealthy man. Where did you get that much money—and why did you pay it out without first consulting me?"

Means appeared startled that his actions were being questioned. "I had to make up my mind on the spot, Madam,"

he said, with an obvious effort to retain his patience. "My wife's father, Dad Patterson, arranged a loan for me." He cleared his throat again. "I knew of course that you would consider the money secondary to the protection that possession of these diaries will afford the President from now on."

"Yes. Yes, of course. I'll raise the money. I am not a wealthy woman, but I'll raise it somehow." Means said there was no hurry. This was March 3, 1922; the end of the month would do.

Two days later, William J. Burns phoned Means. "I've had an inquiry about you, Gaston, from Roy Haynes. I'm sending him a very nice letter; I'll send you a carbon so you'll know just what I've said."

"Thank you very much, Chief. That's nice of you."

Roy Haynes was the Prohibition Commissioner of the United States. He had called Burns and told him that he understood that Gaston B. Means would make a good special investigator and wanted to know a little about him. "Just for the files," said Haynes. Haynes also got in touch with the Attorney General's office, which had just fired Means, and inquired there about the man. The whole procedure was typical of the phony gestures that were carried on in the upper echelons of the Harding Administration. Haynes didn't have to ask Burns, or the Attorney General's office, for information about Means; he had himself read in the newspapers of the man's trial for murder and about other things, including the block of wood that Means had substituted for fifty-seven thousand dollars. Yet two men—William J. Burns and one Guy D. Goff, an assistant to the Attorney General—sat down and, with perfectly straight faces, dictated the following letters:

Department of Justice,
Division of Investigation,
Washington, D. C.
March 10th, 1922.

Hon. Roy A. Haynes,
Prohibition Commissioner,
Treasury Department,
Washington, D. C.
My dear Mr. Haynes:

I received a request from your office the other day asking me to let you know something about Gaston B. Means. I immediately called up your office when I returned to Washington, but was told you were in conference. I then told your secretary to tell you that Gaston B. Means was absolutely all right; honest, intelligent, straightforward, and would make a first class man for you.

Of course, I do not want to relinquish the services of Mr. Means and if there is any specific case you have in mind that requires the aid of a resourceful, courageous, intelligent man, Mr. Means is the one you want.

Mr. Means has been suspended in our service by the Attorney General through a complaint of some kind which the Attorney General has not explained to me, but I know it cannot be anything serious, and only a question of giving Mr. Means an opportunity of being heard.

As you know, no man can do his duty without making enemies, and Mr. Means has made some very powerful enemies by the courageous manner in which he has gone after crooks who have robbed the Government, and therefore, I expect to have Mr. Means reinstated. In the meantime, I will be very glad indeed to have him go with your organization.

Very truly yours,
William J. Burns,
Director.

March 10th, 1922.

Maj. R. A. Haynes,
Federal Prohibition Comm.,
Treasury Dep't,
Washington, D. C.
My Dear Major Haynes:

I take great pleasure in indorsing and commending to your kindly consideration Mr. Gaston B. Means, who has been connected with the Division of Investigation here under Mr. William J. Burns. Mr. Means will be of great assistance to you in the work in which you are engaged if you can find a place for him. My advice to you is to find a place for him because you can rely upon what he does. He is able, experienced, industrious and he is not afraid. He will carry the message to Garcia, and what is better yet, he will come back with the answer.

Very cordially yours,
Guy D. Goff,
Ass't to the Attorney General
Acting Att'y General in the absence of Mr. H. M. Daugherty

Means got the job. As prohibition agent his salary again broke down to eighty-nine dollars a week. This was not only peanuts, it was peanut money. Means was fond of peanuts. He used to shell them and eat them by the hour. It was sometimes possible to tell how long Means had been in a given spot by the size of the mound of shells he left behind him. Immediately upon being notified that he had the job, Means phoned the White House. He got the President on the phone. "If you wish to send a Secret Service man over to my home, I will give him that material you are interested in, Mr. President."

"I'll send a man at once," said the President. "Remember, I want not only the books, but the photostats as well."

"To be sure, Mr. President," said Means. Means had two extra sets of photostats of the vital diary pages—one set in a safety deposit box in the Riggs National Bank in Washington, and another set in a secret well in the garden behind his home. He had followed the same procedure with the diaries he had sold to Mrs. Harding.

The well in the garden of the house on Sixteenth Street was to become a legendary part of the Washington of the Ohio Gang. Means had sunk an eighteen-foot length of pipe into the ground in his garden. The pipe was ten inches in diameter. Inside the pipe was a specially-made cylindrical tin box; this box, which rested at the bottom of the secret well when not being used, could be pulled to the surface by means of a chain. The pipe itself was covered by a movable flower bed. The flower bed, on a circular steel foundation, was padlocked in place, so that nobody could move it except Means, even if it were discovered. The whole well business was melodramatic in the best tradition of the times.

Means, as a prohibition agent, was given a desk in the Treasury Building. From his desk, he could see the White House. He was in no great hurry to get rolling as a roving investigator. There was business to be done in Washington first. For one thing, one of the occupants of the White House was indebted to him; Mrs. Harding had not yet dug up the fifty thousand she had promised him. Secondly, Means wanted to get first-hand confidential knowledge of the prohibition-enforcement situation throughout the country right at the source—at prohibition-enforcement headquarters. He began working at his desk nights; by studying the movements of the handful of patriots who also toiled at night, growing old in the service of their government, Means was able to move from office to office undetected, make wax impressions of desk and file locks, then get into the desks and files and leisurely peruse the contents.

Mrs. Harding had trouble raising the fifty thousand; Means let her settle with him for thirty-five thousand at the beginning of June, 1922. Then, late that month, he maneuvered an introduction to Mabel Walker Willebrandt, the glamour girl of the Harding Administration. Mrs. Willebrandt, one of the few highly-placed honest officials in Washington in 1922, was a Special Assistant Attorney General in charge of top-level bootleg prosecutions. Means informed her that, by virtue of his underworld connections, he could go to New York and other cities and uncover the biggest bootleggers in the country. Thus it was that Gaston Bullock Means, his dimpled face shining with anticipation, stepped off a Washington train in New York's Pennsylvania Station one steaming morning in mid-summer of 1922 carrying in his pocket the following letter:

Department of Justice.
Washington, D. C.
June 28, 1922.

Mr. Ralph Day,
Federal Prohibition Director
New York City, N. Y.
Dear Mr. Day:
This will be handed to you by Mr. Gaston B. Means, a special investigator who is conducting a special and confidential investigation of great importance to the enforcement of prohibition and my department.

I earnestly request that you accord him every possible cooperation and assistance for which this department will be greatly indebted.

Very truly yours,
Mabel Walker Willebrandt,
Assistant Attorney General

Means registered at the Vanderbilt Hotel on lower Park Avenue. He got on the telephone and started calling all the big-time bootleggers in New York—the men who operated fleets of boats that brought booze up from Cuba or Nassau, or that, more rarely, went to sea to meet a ship that had come from Europe with a cargo. "My name is Means," he would say to a bootlegger. "Gaston B. Means, formerly of the Department of Justice, now with the Treasury Department. I'd like to make an appointment to meet you somewhere." Means knew, from sneaking looks at the confidential files at prohibition headquarters in Washington, who the big boys were, the rough extent of their operations and take, to whom they had probably paid protection money in the past, and about how much.

Means oozed good will as he ambled across the Vanderbilt lobby to pump the hand of a dark, over-dressed little character he was meeting for the first time— Manny Kessler, the first of the big-shot bootleggers to run afoul of the man who had come up from Washington on a confidential mission. He looked Kessler right in the eyes, smiled warmly so that his dimples showed, and began to look around for a quiet corner where they could talk. It was a hot day. Means sat down with Kessler on a big sofa under a potted palm and wiped his brow. "The way the boys have it figured," he said, smiling quickly, "you're in for thirty-five thousand."

"Lord," said Kessler, "that's a lot of dough."

Means blinked innocently. "It *is* quite an amount, isn't it," he said. "But headquarters knows your approximate gross, and they have things figured out on a sort of percentage basis." Means glanced around as if to make sure there were no eavesdroppers in the potted palms. "One

trouble is," he went on, "there are so many fingers in the pie. Why, do you know that some of the jack gets all the way up to Andy?" In fact, Andrew W. Mellon, the Pittsburgh aluminum magnate who was Harding's Secretary of the Treasury, was one of the few men in the Washington of that day who were *not* interested in getting money by graft. But Means was never one to let his style be cramped by truth.

When Manny Kessler expressed surprise that the Secretary of the Treasury should have his hand out, Means shook his head from side to side, made a ticking sound, and said, "Manny, you'd think the man had enough money already. I simply can't understand it."

"What about the ten thousand I paid to that fellow at the McAlpin Hotel six weeks ago?" asked Kessler.

"Oh, *that*. That doesn't count," said Means. "We're starting a new system."

Gaston Means rated as an actor of superior talent and broad repertoire. David Belasco, the greatest theatrical producer of them all, and an outstanding actor in his own right, studied Gaston Means when Means was testifying before a Congressional Committee probing the Ohio Gang. "What I could have done with that man had I got him earlier!" Belasco told friends. "He has the perfect instinct for delivering a line." The Means countenance had a pliability that could express any degree of any emotion convincingly. He could cry at will; turning on tears, if the situation called for it, as easily as he could turn on a water faucet. He never looked so utterly innocent as when he was dripping with guilt.

Being an actor, Means liked things to be theatrical, and slightly unreal. He often went to elaborate lengths to create an atmosphere. This was not only because he liked to savor the full drama of a given situation; he had found that a dramatic atmosphere often took a man's mind off the fact that he was being hoodwinked. Means created an atmosphere especially for the bootleggers during his stay in New York. Kessler and the others could have gone to a room Means had on the eighth floor of the Vanderbilt and given him the cash in an envelope. Such simplicity was not for Means; the mere transfer of cash was too cold and might produce a subsequent reaction of resentment.

Means took over the room adjoining the one he occupied. He placed in this room a large goldfish bowl on top of a table. The table was placed in such a position that Means, from his own room, could look through the keyhole of a door between the two rooms and see the bowl. The idea was that the bootleggers were to go into the room containing the goldfish bowl and drop their graft into the bowl. Nobody was to be in the room when they left the money. They were just to go in, deposit it in the bowl, and leave.

The business of paying money to a goldfish bowl, rather than to a human being, was supposed to have its advantages. There had never been an instance on record, Means pointed out to Kessler, of a goldfish bowl turning government's evidence and testifying against somebody for attempting to bribe it; the same could not be said of law-enforcement officers, including a submicroscopic quantity of prohibition agents whose passion for honesty appeared to many people as an eccentricity bordering on the lunatic.

Means soberly instructed the bootleggers to time their visits to the room with the goldfish bowl so that they would drop their graft into the bowl on the split second of a given minute. Kessler, for example, was to deposit his dough at eight-five exactly on a Thursday night. Means lent Kessler an expensive platinum watch, as thin as a tea wafer. "This watch has Naval Observatory time," Means told Kessler, "and is synchronized with mine. Consult it to see that you drop the money in the bowl at exactly eight-five. Then drop the watch in after the money." Means never explained why it was necessary that the money be dropped in the bowl at a precise minute; he requested his victim not to inquire as to the reason. Actually, there was no reason at all for the split-second timing, but it was dramatic and mysterious. The bootleggers, by making their payoffs on the dot, went away with a vague sense of achievement in having surmounted some invisible obstacle.

Means had still another touch—one based on the philosophy that misery loves company and designed to make the boys feel a little less pain in parting with important currency. When Kessler arrived to put his thirty-five grand in the goldfish bowl, he was pleased to note that somebody had been there before him, doing the same thing. Means had filled the bowl with a stack of money— the cash that Mrs. Harding had paid him for the diaries—then placed on top of the money a thin platinum watch, just like the one with which Kessler weighted down his contribution.

Means faded across the Hudson River to Newark, New Jersey. There at the Robert Treat Hotel, a stream of leaders in the beverage business made trips to the goldfish bowl. Then Means went to Boston. Again the goldfish bowl paid off. He returned to Washington in August, some six weeks after he had left with the promise to Assistant Attorney General Mabel Walker Willebrandt that he would turn up some of the country's biggest bootleggers.

When Means walked into Mrs. Willebrandt's office, the lady was struck by the fact that he had lost considerable weight; he was down to around one hundred and seventy pounds, which was light for him, and he was leaning heavily on a cane. He looked haunted.

What he had done was go on a starvation diet for this very meeting. He dropped into a chair, rolled his eyes and began to play the role of a man who had undergone a dreadful experience. He informed Mrs. Willebrandt that he had been held a prisoner on a boat in Long Island Sound for almost a month. "I wasn't as cautious as I might have been," he explained. "I was so eager to get the goods on this gang—Manny Kessler and those fellows—that I wasn't looking around to see who was observing me. I was picked up right on Park Avenue, in front of the Vanderbilt Hotel, and chloroformed and shanghaied on this underworld boat in the middle of the night."

"Why," said Mrs. Willebrandt, "I must report this to Mr. Burns at once!" Means held up a restraining hand and smiled weakly. "No," he said, "don't breathe a word about it, please. Let me get my strength back and go after these blackguards single-handed. It is a question of honor with me—Southern honor." Mrs. Willebrandt, who thought no evil and saw none, was deeply moved.

Means bought a farm down along the Eastern shore of Maryland. He took his wife and boy there while he recuperated from his ordeal with the gangsters. He was visited one afternoon by Jesse Smith. Means had seen or heard little from Smith since his discharge from the Department of Justice. Smith was a weather vane; he always pointed in the direction of the wind. "Nice place you have here,

Gaston," he said to Means. "I looked up the records; I see you paid cash for it." Smith got right down to business. He said he had heard the story around town that Means had been held prisoner on a gangster boat. "I don't believe a word of it, Gaston," he said. "On the other hand, you seem to have done pretty well up in New York."

"What makes you say that?"

"Well, we sent a fellow up there to make a little proposition to a certain gentleman whose initials are M.K. and the man said he already paid *you* thirty-five thousand. What's all this about a goldfish bowl and synchronized watches?"

"What of it?" said Means. "It's a free country; I've got my wife and family to think of."

Smith began to uncover his hand. The boys, as Smith always spoke of the Ohio Gang, had been considering the case of Gaston Means. The Gang now realized that Means had been placed in a difficult position by being called upon by Mrs. Harding to investigate the President, and to get evidence for Mrs. Harding that would have made the President a free man. "Why," said Smith, "a thing like that could have cut us all off at the pockets." The Gang had learned through its access to the records of the movements of the White House Secret Service detail that two operatives had accompanied the President to Means' home on a date subsequent to the one on which Means had been discharged from the Department of Justice. That meant to the Gang that Means must have had something very vital on the President. "We figure it was one of those Nan Britton diaries," said Smith. "Like the two you sold Mrs. Harding. We figure that's why the President issued orders that you were to be appointed to the prohibition department."

Means knew better than to try to deny

what Smith was saying. He wanted to know just one thing—how the Gang had found out he had sold Mrs. Harding two diaries. It turned out that apparently Evalyn Walsh McLean, a close friend of both Mrs. Harding and the President, had been told about the diaries in confidence by Mrs. Harding and had then blabbed.

The point of Smith's visit was to take Gaston Means back into the Ohio fold; a man as adept as Means at murder, swindling, blackmail and shakedown was too valuable to lose. Means returned from his Maryland farm to the house on Sixteenth Street after the Labor Day holiday in 1922. Thereafter things began to hum.

There were three focal points of activity of the Ohio Gang. One was the basement of the Means home. The second was a residence that was to become known as the Little Green House on K Street. The Means basement was to be the unofficial business headquarters of the Gang; the Little Green House the playtime headquarters. The Little Green House was maintained strictly for revelry —revelry of the unsophisticated kind enjoyed by men with rough hands and red necks. The tone of the joint, although it was frequented by cabinet officers, bureau heads, ranking members of the federal judiciary, and, on some occasions, by the Chief Executive himself, was that of a stag smoker. Earl Carroll, producer of The Vanities and other Broadway girl shows, was entrusted with the job of shipping cargoes of blonde bums to Washington on weekends. Pornographic motion pictures, some of them featuring a couple of dolls who later put on clothes, changed their names and became famous in Hollywood, were shown nightly. Catering firms all over the East always had trucks somewhere on the road, headed for the Little Green House with Vermont turkeys, Virginia hams, Russian caviar. Champagne came in from France, whisky was sprung from bonded warehouses, and lager was always on tap.

The third focal point of the Ohio Gang was Friendship, the home of Evalyn Walsh McLean. Little Evalyn, as some people called her, was just taking over the social reins in the capital. Mrs. McLean was noted for bad English and misuse and mispronunciation of words, but she had several million dollars in her own right, from a copper fortune amassed in Colorado by her father, and she had married another fortune in Edward Beale McLean, a rich man's son who published the Washington *Post* by day and chased women by night. Friendship was a sort of early-day Stork Club; if you weren't seen there, you didn't count. Gaston Means, smiling and observant, was in frequent attendance.

Evalyn McLean derived most of her social drag from friendship with the Hardings. Her husband, who also published the Cincinnati *Enquirer*, had supported Harding for the Presidency; Mrs. McLean and Mrs. Harding patronized the same fortune teller—a lady subsequently to become widely known in Washington as Madame X. Mrs. Harding had sworn by Madame X since the days when her husband was a senator. It developed that four senators' wives, among them Mrs. Harding, had made a practice of going to Madame X in a body twice a month. Madame X, a three-alarm fraud, had one day gazed inscrutably at first one and then another of the senators' wives, and murmured, "One of your husbands will some day be President." When Senator Harding became President Madame X was made.

Through her friendship with Mrs. Harding, and also with the President,

Mrs. McLean was hep to a lot of scuttle-butt. Since Washington social promi-nence has always depended in large meas-ure on access to scuttlebutt, this placed Little Evalyn in an enviable position. In addition to her White House sources, she had a private detective force of her own. This detective force was roughly divided into three divisions. One division put on smoked glasses, the better to be able to keep an eye on Mrs. McLean's collection of jewelry; another division kept an eye on her husband, and the third division circulated around town picking up scan-dal. Mrs. McLean began to play a cute game called You Tell Me Something and I'll Tell You Something. To impart something to Little Evalyn in confidence was tantamount to putting it on the As-sociated Press wire.

Gaston Means now became investi-gator-in-chief for the Ohio Gang. If a Federal judgeship was vacant and some-body applied for it, it was up to Means to make a personal investigation of the applicant's qualifications, which meant how much he could afford to pay for the job. Means acted as the contact man be-tween the Gang and big stock-market operations in New York, Chicago and San Francisco who cleaned up by ad-vance information of Washington moves and pronouncements and kicked back part of the loot. Attorney General Daugh-erty, Albert B. Fall and others of the palace guard, who were playing market sure things under assumed names, took a herring into the ticker rooms of the brokerage firm of Ungerleider and Com-pany in the Willard Hotel and painted it bright red. At Ungerleider's the palace guard played openly and on a small scale; they chose stocks that they knew would make only small advances, if any. Some-times the Gangsters even chose stocks that they knew were due to dive. The Ungerleider dealings created a surface impression of integrity in high places. Means still retained his eighty-nine dol-lars-a-week job as a special prohibition agent. Occasionally, just to keep the franchise, he would actually turn in a bootlegger—usually one who either balked at paying graft or who wasn't in a position to. Means, who was in a posi-tion to know, estimated, in his book, *The Strange Death of President Harding,* that he personally collected a total of seven million dollars from bootleggers during the fiscal year beginning July 1, 1922.

Between trips to various parts of the country to investigate applicants for Fed-eral jobs, Means shuttled between Wash-ington and various points on the Atlan-tic seaboard, putting the bite on big bootleggers. He always brought the loot back in a suitcase and deposited it in the well under the movable flower bed in his back yard. He retained about 10 per cent for himself and turned the rest over to Jesse Smith.

Curiously enough, Gaston Means, for all the money that passed through his hands, was usually broke. He loved lux-ury and lived in rajah style. He had three custom-built cars, each at five thousand dollars a copy, a large staff of servants, and a yacht. Caught up in the spirit of the times, he had strayed from the connu-bial couch; he maintained women in ex-pensive apartments in New York, Boston and Los Angeles. He didn't see them very often but the girls had to eat and dress well and pay the rent so that it all added up. Means also acquired a taste for horse-racing and roulette. Like many an-other smart, big-time crook, he was just another sucker at the track and the wheel.

By the spring of 1923, after the Gang had been in for two years, such influen-tial papers as The Chicago *Tribune,* The Philadelphia *Record* and The Los Angeles *Times* began to put the blast on some of the shenanigans in Washington. The lid was still on, but it wasn't on tight enough to seal in all the odors.

In what should have been the merry month of May, 1923, Jesse Smith began to emerge as the weak link in the crooked chain. He sat one night in the basement of the house on Sixteenth Street, mopping his brow and puffing. "What's eating you, Jesse?" asked Means. "Oh, Gaston," said Smith, "something terrible is going to happen one of these days. A Congressional Committee will begin a probe into all of us and when it does, we'll all go to the penitentiary. That'll be the end of the music and the girls and the champagne."

Means smiled until his dimples showed. "Jesse," he said, "you worry too much."

"Maybe I do," said Smith, "but I'd like to get this thing off my mind. Do you know what I feel like doing, Gaston?"

"No, what?"

"Spilling everything I know. Maybe I could stay out of prison that way."

Means wasn't the only person to hear Smith talk that way; half of Washington knew he was thinking of blowing his top. Jesse Smith, the blubbery, big ex-dry-goods man, was probably in a position to reveal more about the Ohio Gang than any other man alive. That made him a strategic figure in more ways than one; he was a threat to the lives of a baker's dozen of scoundrels, and, by the same token, they were a threat to him.

In the middle of May, Attorney General Harry Daugherty and Jesse Smith took a trip to their home town in Ohio. They returned to Washington together on Monday, May 28, so that Daugherty could be in the capital on Memorial Day

to participate in some eulogies to the restless dead in Arlington Cemetery. Jesse Smith seemed more relaxed than he had been in some weeks when he got back; he was his old jovial self.

Daugherty and Smith, who was divorced, shared an apartment on the fourth floor of the Wardman Park Hotel. Daugherty said he wasn't feeling too hot; he thought that instead of going with Smith to the hotel apartment he would stay at the White House. "Warren and I will keep each other company," was the way Daugherty explained it. "Warren's not feeling so good either." That night, Smith visited the home of Gaston Means. The Means butler let him in shortly after eight o'clock, and let him out about an hour later. The butler heard Means saying to Smith, "I'm glad to see you in better shape after your trip, Jesse. I *told* you there wasn't anything to worry about."

Jesse Smith went straight from the house on Sixteenth Street to the Wardman Park Hotel. There he stopped at the cigar stand and bought three sixty-cent cigars. He settled himself in an easy chair in the lobby, lit a cigar, and, to hotel attaches who observed him, gave every appearance of a man at peace with the world. Fashionably gowned women, some of them young enough still to have fine figures, paraded before the observant eyes of Jesse Smith while the soft strains of chamber music floated in from another room. The Washington night was soft, and up in New York the stock market would remain steady over the holiday. Everything, as Jesse Smith remarked to a friend who stopped long enough to inquire how he was, was just fine and dandy. Smith remained in the lobby until around midnight, when he bought an early edition of the next day's

Post from a bellboy. Then he went up-stairs, too.

In the middle of the night, a door slammed in the house on Sixteenth Street —the front door. The slamming awakened the Means butler. He went to a front window on the second floor and looked out. There was a street light near the Means home. The butler saw the hulking figure of his employer passing under the light and walking off into the darkness. Means had many odd habits, but strolling in the middle of the night was not one of them. About six o'clock the following morning, a milkman making deliveries on Sixteenth Street North-west saw a big man getting out of a taxi-cab in the 700 block and walking in the direction of the Means home. He didn't know Gaston Means, but later, when he saw full-length pictures of him in the newspapers in connection with a Con-gressional investigation, he said that the man he had seen getting out of the taxi-cab was Means.

At six-thirty in the morning—half an hour after the milkman had seen Means getting out of the cab—the phone rang in the sixth-floor apartment of Elmer Dwyer, the manager of the Wardman Park Hotel. "This is Mr. Burns," said the voice on the phone. "William J. Burns. Will you please come to Mr. Daugherty's apartment immediately. Something terrible has happened." Dwyer threw a dressing gown over his pajamas and stepped into a pair of slip-pers and hastened from his apartment down two flights of fire stairs to the fourth floor. He was wondering, as he approached the Attorney General's suite, just what had happened, and who it had happened to. He was about to press the buzzer of a door that opened into a small foyer when the door was swiftly opened. William J. Burns, also attired in dressing gown, motioned the manager inside and locked the door. Jesse Smith, dressed in purple silk pajamas, lay on the floor of the living room. "Suicide," said Burns. A bullet had entered Smith's right tem-ple, passed completely through his head, come out the left temple and lodged in a door jamb. A gun lay on the floor near the body.

Dwyer looked around the room. Burns, who occupied the apartment directly below that of Daugherty, explained to Dwyer that he had heard the shot and come right up.

"I'd better call Dr. Schoenfeld," Dwyer said to Burns. Dr. Herbert H. Schoenfeld was the Wardman Park house doctor.

"No," said Burns. "That can wait. Anyway, Jesse's dead. Stay here while I make a call." In the presence of Dwyer and Martin, Burns put through a call to the White House. It was now about a quarter to seven in the morning. Burns got the President on the wire. "This is Burns of the Bureau of Investigation, Mr. President. I'm deeply sorry to bother you at such an hour, but there is dread-ful news and I wanted you to be the first to hear it."

Dwyer could hear Harding's voice cut-ting in to ask what the news was. "Jesse Smith has just committed suicide."

"That's terrible, Mr. Burns," said the President. "Simply terrible. Don't let the news out until I tell Mr. Daugherty. He hasn't been feeling well and I want to break the news gently to him. Thank you for calling me. Is there anything else?

"No, nothing else, Mr. President."

In a little while, Lieutenant Com-mander Joel T. Boone, the White House physician, arrived. He pronounced Jesse Smith dead. Burns now permitted Dwyer to summon the hotel physician. Dr.

Schoenfield said later that the atmosphere in the suite seemed to discourage a thorough examination of the body. The trend seemed to be to get Jesse Smith out of the hotel, embalmed and back to Ohio for burial with all possible haste.

The death of Jesse Smith turned out to be something that jobholders in Washington didn't discuss, even with one another, if they knew which side their bread was buttered on. Jesse, the ex-dry-goods man who had been transplanted to never-never land, was shoved safely six feet under in Washington Courthouse, Ohio, and the world moved on. There was, it turned out, one fact about Jesse Smith that had a tendency to make suicide by gun incongruous, if not impossible, and that was Smith's mortal dread of firearms of any kind. His ex-wife, Roxie Stinson, who lived in Washington and with whom he had remained on friendly terms, had been out window-shopping with him in downtown Washington only a few weeks before his death. "I stopped to look into a window," Roxie told Evalyn Walsh McLean, "and Jesse started to turn green. I hadn't realized what kind of window I was looking in. It was the window of a sporting goods store and there were some guns on display. Once Jesse fainted—passed out cold—at the mere sight of a gun. I don't know why he was so afraid of guns; I just know he was."

Was it likely that a man who had felt about guns as Smith had felt about them would have chosen a gun with which to take his own life, assuming that he had been so disposed to begin with? Was it likely that a man who had come back from Ohio as relaxed as Smith had been, and who had obviously been at such peace with both the world and himself less than seven hours before his body was found—was it likely that this man had been in the frame of mind to take his life with a gun or by any other means?

The questions were discussed in low tones over tea cups, whisky glasses and pewter mugs of fine Canadian ale. There were other questions, too. What had happened to Jesse Smith's private papers? No personal papers of Jesse Smith ever turned up after his death—not even such non-incriminating correspondence as several unpaid bills which he was known to have possessed the afternoon before his end. Smith was known always to have carried on his person a little green notebook in which he had marked down such trivial personal expenditures as postage stamps—a hangover from his dry-goods days. Even this notebook, which was perhaps as innocent as anything in Washington, had disappeared.

Gaston Means rode around town, in his five-thousand-dollar custom-built cars, looking for all the world like the cat that had swallowed the canary. Evalyn Walsh McLean, who had an affinity for intrigue, assigned two of her private dicks to make her up a dossier on the passing of Jesse Smith. Mrs. McLean soon satisfied herself that Gaston Means had murdered Jesse Smith by way of dispensing with the weak link in the graft chain. Just who Means had acted for, aside from himself, Mrs. McLean's private dummies couldn't guess; any number of important men were sleeping again nights, now that Jesse Smith had gone back to Ohio in a box. One of Mrs. McLean's detectives dug up a handsome bellboy in the Wardman Park who, after spending most of the night in the room of a lady guest on a floor below that of the Attorney General's suite, had been sneaking down a flight of fire stairs when he had passed a big man who had smiled at him. The bellboy recalled that the big man had had dimples when he smiled.

Mrs. McLean began telling friends she had proof that Gaston Means had murdered Jesse Smith. It wasn't long before Means heard about this. Always the jealous guardian of his reputation, Means paid Mrs. McLean a visit. He asked her why she was telling people he had murdered Jesse Smith. "Because it's true," said Mrs. McLean. The Means countenance darkened. "Some day," he said, melodramatically, "you'll pay dearly for this!" And years later, when she was least expecting it, she did.

Three months after Jesse Smith's death, in August, President Harding died suddenly in San Francisco while on his way to an Alaskan vacation. One official, after issuing the usual irreparable-loss stuff, said to another member of the Ohio Gang, "Why in hell did he have to go and *die? Now* what will we do for a living?" The question was far from academic. When the life spark passed out of the worry-and-rum-racked body of Warren Harding, the source of power of the Ohio Gang went with it. An eccentrically honest character whom nobody outside of Massachusetts and Vermont had ever heard of—a Vice President named Calvin Coolidge—was sworn into the Presidency in a Vermont farmhouse in the dead of the night by his father, old John Coolidge, a Justice of the Peace who removed some cut plug from his right cheek for the occasion.

One by one, the Ohio Gang disappeared from the capital, some of them already under clouds, some of them not to be under clouds until later. A few, such as Secretary of the Interior Fall, were to go to prison. Attorney General Daugherty was twice to achieve hung juries when tried for crookedness. The man who could have hung him—Jesse Smith—was in his grave. William J. Burns, Gaston Means' great friend, returned to his own agency, a bigger man than ever after having devoted himself to the service of his country.

In the upheaval, Gaston Means was dropped from his job in the prohibition department. This was a serious blow to him; he needed official status of some kind to give him leverage in prying graft from bootleggers. He was broke and forty-three; he wandered around Washington, in the mid-summer heat, wearing an alpaca jacket. He resembled a captain without a ship. He moved out of the house on Sixteenth Street and settled with his wife and son in the Gordon Hotel, a small, inexpensive hostelry.

Means locked himself up with a case of bourbon and pondered the future. He was to say later that he thought of numerous business firms around the country that had been mixed up with the Ohio Gang; it would probably have been possible for him to have made a pretty good connection with some such firm. But the thought of honest work repelled Means. Judges, in dishing out sentences to confidence-type criminals like Means, completely miss the point when they mouth the old bromide about what a successful person the criminal would have been had he devoted his energies to honest enterprise. Superior confidence men like Yellow Kid Weil, The Deacon Buckminster, Dapper Don Collins and Wilson Mizner, all of whom had a great deal in common with Means, wanted no part of the legitimate life. To the golfer the ultimate thrill is a hole in one; he gets sent by blasting out of a trap onto the green. The fisherman gets a charge out of a strike, the football player a bang out of a ninety-yard run. To the confidence man life holds no thrill like that of taking a sucker. The matching of wits, the suspense as the plot gets rolling, the high inner excitement, the sense of accomplishment, the feeling of superiority, that accompany the take—these things are to be found only outside the law; the legitimate life offers nothing quite like them.

Means was slowly working his way through the bourbon when he had a hot flash. If status was all he lacked to take bootleggers, what was stopping him from *creating* status? What indeed? Andrew Mellon was still the Secretary of the Treasury and prohibition enforcement was Treasury business. Secretary Mellon wasn't to find out about it until later, but he now had a new, confidential agent named Means.

Gaston Means began to introduce into his work, late in 1923, what the theatrical profession calls props. His principal prop was a fake telephone. This instrument was connected to a set of batteries concealed in the desk it sat on. A buzzer under the desk rang the phone when pressed by a foot. Means set the phone up in a room of his quarters in the Gordon Hotel. He explained to his wife, who still believed everything he said, that he was going to play jokes on some people with the phone. In a way, Gaston Means never uttered truer words.

Means went up to New York and got in touch with a bootlegger named Charles W. Johnson. Johnson was anxious to lay hands on some bonded liquor from a government warehouse, which was priceless stuff. "I can fix you up," said Means. "How?" said Johnson. "You're no longer with the Treasury Department." Means just smiled. He produced a note on engraved personal stationery bearing the name of Andrew W. Mellon that was as spurious as it was impressive. The note, in handwriting that Means had simulated as Mellon's, said:

G. M.—I will approve limited number of releases if sufficient contributions are made to anti-Ford fund.

A.W.M.

"What does Mellon mean?" asked Johnson. Means had a way of looking at people that made them feel stupid. "Surely you've heard that Henry Ford wants to be President. Well, Secretary Mellon is raising a fund to keep Ford out of the White House. He's willing to release a limited quantity of bonded whisky to contributors to the fund." Means cleared his throat. "It's not exactly crooked," he said, "but it's not exactly legal, either."

Johnson wanted to know how much stuff he could get, where it would be sprung from, and how much it was going to cost him. Means said they'd have to go to Washington to get such details. Thus Johnson was taken into the room with the fake phone. Means deposited himself in a swivel chair at his desk, picked up the phone and called the number of the Treasury Department. A less artful man than Means would have got right through to the Secretary of the Treasury. But Mellon was too busy to talk to Means right then; the Secretary would call back within an hour.

It was more than an hour before the phone rang. It was Mellon. In guarded language, Means said he had a campaign contributor lined up and asked the questions Johnson had asked him. Then he merely nodded or said, "uh-huh," as he got the answers; he was scribbling things on a pad as Mellon talked. When the conversation was over, Means turned around on his swivel chair, put the fingertips of his right hand against the fingertips of his left hand, smiled, and said, "Well, it's all fixed."

Mellon was going to okay the release

of one hundred thousand dollars worth of rye from the Sam Thompson Distillery in Pennsylvania if John was willing to contribute twenty thousand dollars to keep Henry Ford out of the White House. It was a deal; the trouble was Johnson had only fifteen thousand dollars cash with him. "Just make out a check for the balance," said Means. "To Mellon?" asked Johnson. "No, to cash." Johnson made out the check. Means went up to New York, opened a bank account under the name of Williams, deposited the check and got the dough.

Weeks passed. Johnson phoned Means from New York at all hours of the night and day. Means improvised as he went along; he never planned very far ahead, but wrote the scenario to fit developing circumstances. He kept stalling Johnson. Then Johnson came to Washington. "I gave Mellon the money," said Means. "I can't help it if he hasn't gone through with his end of the bargain."

Means had meanwhile lured other bootleggers to the room in the Gordon Hotel, there to let them listen in fascination as he talked over his fake phone, then take them for amounts ranging from five thousand dollars to twenty-five thousand dollars. As time passed, Means convinced the other bootleggers that Mellon, while accepting their contributions, had been afraid to go through with the liquor-springing deals. "Too much pressure on him," Means would say. The bootleggers shrugged and charged the contributions off to profit and loss. They couldn't have done much anyway; to "expose" Mellon, they would have had to admit conspiracies on their part. Johnson, the original sucker, was different. "You get that dough up or I'm going right to Mellon!" he told Means. Means couldn't get the dough up for the simple reason that he didn't have it.

He had bought a forty-thousand-dollar home in Chevy Chase, a fashionable Washington suburb, and shot the rest in the market and at the wheels. Johnson lodged a squawk and Means was indicted.

While this indictment was hanging over him, Means was summoned as a witness before a Congressional committee that was investigating the Department of Justice under the Burns regime. Looking unruffled and very important as he arrived in the hearing room carrying several briefcases bulging with documents, Means got off a crack that was widely relished in Washington. When asked what his occupation was, he smiled until his dimples showed and replied brightly, "Answering indictments."

Means went on trial for the Johnson whisky deal. Secretary Mellon was the principal witness against him. Johnson produced the check that Means had cashed under the name of Williams. The Williams signature was pronounced by handwriting experts to be that of Means. Means maintained that the Secretary of the Treasury, acting for mysterious unnamed interests, was framing him out of circulation. He was found guilty. He entered Atlanta Penitentiary in 1924 at the age of forty-four.

In 1927, when Means was in the third year of his four-year stretch, Nan Britton, President Harding's ex-flame, came out with her sensational book, *The President's Daughter,* a fairly well documented volume that pretty well established that Harding had been the father of a daughter born to her near Asbury Park, New Jersey. Means got hold of a copy of *The President's Daughter;* he saw at once that there was big dough to be made in expose-type literature and Means was no man to let big dough lie.

Immediately thereafter, Gaston Means got religion. He was either praying or reading the Bible whenever the Reverend Fred Ladlow, a prison chaplain, saw him. The Reverend Ladlow was both moved and impressed. The angle was that the minister was a close friend of Mrs. May Dixon Thacker, a prominent writer, and the sister of the Reverend Thomas Dixon, whose novel *The Clansman* was used as the basis of D. W. Griffith's motion picture *The Birth of a Nation.* Mrs. Thacker often visited the Atlanta can in the course of welfare work. The chaplain introduced Means to her.

Means suggested that Mrs. Thacker collaborate with him on a book exposing the Ohio Gang. Mrs. Thacker thought such a book would be in the nature of a public service. Immediately upon being sprung in 1928, Means and Mrs. Thacker got busy on their collaboration. She was just what he needed; the book, to be called *The Strange Death of President Harding,* would bear the names of both Means and Mrs. Thacker. He was banking on her reputation to overcome his.

During the collaboration, Means got out his prop phone again. He turned out to be a hound for accuracy. To check such trivial details as the precise hour when someone had arrived at his house on Sixteenth Street years before, he would get on the prop phone and call various important personages in Washington and elsewhere. His meticulousness made a deep impression on Mrs. Thacker; his fussing over the details of small, true things completely blinded her to the large untruths in the book. Means backed up everything he said, with counterfeit letters and artificially-aged documents.

The book, while it did reflect the intrigue and the sinister glamour of the Washington of the Harding administration, was packed with fiction masquerading as fact. It implied, among other things, that Mrs. Harding had poisoned her husband. Cynical and well-informed readers thought that such an act wouldn't have been a bad idea, but they knew it wasn't true.

The Strange Death of President Harding became an overnight best-seller; it went through printing after printing. Means was rolling in the first legitimate money of his life—if money derived from a basic fraud could be called legitimate. He went around to bookstores, beaming and signing autographed copies for charmed and fascinated readers. He was having a great time. Suddenly, he realized that he had become respectable. The thought of an honest life appalled him.

Means took to the newspapers. He saw that a society lady in Tarrytown, New York—Mrs. Finley Shepherd, formerly Helen Gould of *the* Goulds—had organized a committee to combat Communism. Gaston Means thereupon became the first man in the United States to put anti-Communism on a paying basis. He went to Montreal and wrote a long letter to Mrs. Shepherd, warning her that she and everybody in her family would get theirs for her attitude. He signed the letter Agents of Moscow.

Then Means dropped down to New York again and wangled an introduction to Mrs. Shepherd. He began to talk about one thing and another and then said that he had heard, through his vast connections, that the Communists were involved in a plot against her life. "Why, you are absolutely right, Mr. Means," said Mrs. Shepherd. "I received a threatening letter only two weeks ago." Means asked to see the letter. He studied it, made that ticking sound with his tongue, shook his head, and rolled his eyes. "This is terrible," he said. "I hope it's not too late to do something about it." Mrs.

Shepherd hired Means at one hundred and fifty dollars a week, plus expenses, to track down the letter writers. He asked her if he could take with him the letter she had received. "It'll help me find out who wrote it," he explained. So he walked away, on a new investigation, carrying as his first clue the letter of his own authorship.

Means sent more letters from Montreal, then rushed back to Tarrytown to get them and investigate them. All the while he was running up fantastic expense bills. When Mrs. Shepherd began to develop writer's cramp from signing checks, Means announced that he had located the letter writers. Apparently he had; as if by magic, the letters from Montreal stopped coming.

Means put the anti-Communism racket on a nation-wide assembly-belt basis. He took people all over the country for two years. His killings didn't compare with those of his precan days, but he was averaging around one thousand dollars a week. The trouble was he was spending twelve hundred. It was, then, with a profound sense of relief that he heard, in March of 1932, that the Lindbergh baby had been kidnaped. Here was a big-scale operation, high-echelon stuff; a smart operator, himself for example, should be able to make it pay off handsomely.

Means went to none other than Evalyn Walsh McLean. He had vowed that she would pay dearly for telling Washington that he had murdered Jesse Smith. Now was his chance. Means sold Mrs. McLean on the story that because of his underworld connections, he could get in touch with the kidnapers. He got in touch with them. They wanted $100,000; he would need $4,000 for expenses.

Some of the details of Means' dealings with Mrs. McLean, while he took her and her entourage around the country, pretending to be on the verge of finding the Lindbergh child, reveal that the man was really at the height of his powers. When, at the outset, he asked Mrs. McLean for $104,000, he was off on the right foot. The amateur would have asked for an even amount—fifty or a hundred thousand. That added four grand was the Means touch. Mrs. McLean might have been suspicious of Means had he asked for the even hundred thousand, or for fifty thousand, but when a man used to the money Means was used to asked for an extra four thousand, it seemed plain that he was getting no part of the basic hundred.

Means juggled well; he kept the balls in the air for several weeks. Then Mrs. McLean's lawyers got hep to what was up and stepped in. They demanded that Means return the hundred grand; he could keep the four thousand. A couple of days later he phoned the lawyers. "Will you please be courteous enough to send me a receipt for that hundred thousand dollars?" The lawyers said they hadn't seen the dough. That was odd; Means had given it to a man who had approached him on the street and said he represented the lawyers. So it was into the federal can with Gaston—Leavenworth for fifteen years.

In 1938, Means had a heart attack in prison. G-men—men from the very Department of Justice where once Means had operated—were anxious to clear up many secrets about the criminal of the century. What had he to say about the death of Maude King? What about the death of Jesse Smith? Most important, where was Mrs. McLean's cash? Means simply hadn't had time even to get started on it. Where had he buried it? Gaston Means smiled until his dimples showed, said nothing, and died.

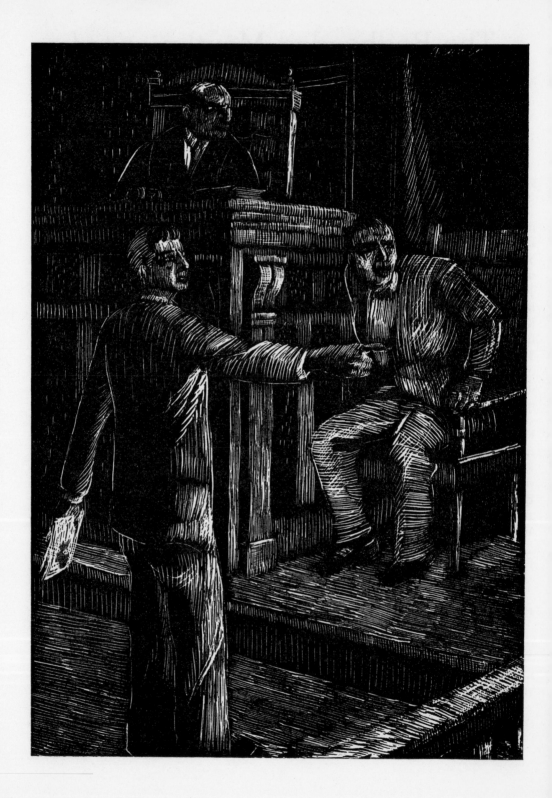

The Redheaded Mouthpiece of Broadway

Introducing William J. Fallon, the Great Mouthpiece, who, drunk or sober, could charm the birds out of the trees and not-guilty verdicts out of impressionable juries.

One fine day back in the Twenties, a meek-looking little man walked into the law offices of Fallon & McGee at Times Square, New York City, desperately in need of legal advice. Consulting William Joseph Fallon, then the greatest criminal lawyer in the country, he divulged that he was a teller in one of the city's largest banks, that he had gambled and lost $10,000 of the bank's money in the stock market, and that the bank examiners, due any day, would be certain to find him out.

"I'm afraid I'll be sent to prison, Mr. Fallon," said the meek little man. "I've read a lot about you in the papers and I was wondering if there was anything you could do to keep me out of prison. I've got a wife and family and the disgrace to them would be something awful."

"You say you stole $10,000," said Fallon.

"That's right, Mr. Fallon."

"How much more can you get?" asked Fallon.

The prospective client didn't exactly understand the question.

"I say," repeated Fallon, "how much more can you get? How much more can you lay hands on?"

"You mean how much more can I *steal?*"

"If you want to put it that way, yes."

"Oh, I could get practically any amount, I guess. But I don't understand why you should ask me that."

"Could you get $50,000 and be back here with it before the examiners get there?"

"Oh, sure. I could get practically any amount, I guess. But I don't want to take any more. God, Mr. Fallon, I'm in enough trouble already."

"You just do as I say," said Fallon. "Be here as quick as you can with the $50,000 and I'll guarantee to keep you out of jail. Otherwise you're sure to go."

The little man didn't understand it. If he was in deep trouble because he had stolen $10,000, why wouldn't he be in deeper trouble if he ran his take up to $60,000? Fallon grew impatient. His client could follow his advice—or else.

Next day the little man appeared with the $50,000. Fallon counted the money, then told his client to register at a certain hotel under an assumed name and lie low until he heard from him. Then Fallon telephoned to the president of the bank. He was short and sweet. "You're $60,000 short in your accounts," he informed the banker. "I represent the teller who took the money. I think I can recover $40,000 of it for you if you agree not to prosecute."

The banker was outraged at the proposition. But when he thought it over and weighed both sides of the problem, he decided that it wasn't worth $40,000 to send the teller to prison and get his bank a heap of bad publicity to boot. So a few days later he phoned Fallon and agreed to the deal. By this time Fallon had begun to feel a little sorry for the thief. The man had been working for the bank since he left grammar school and was still getting coolie wages. "You'll not only agree not to prosecute," Fallon told the banker, "but you'll give my client a fine recommendation so that he can get another job somewhere."

The banker, having no other course, agreed to that, too. So Fallon returned the $40,000, pocketed the remaining $10,000 and got rid of it within a week by hitting the hot spots and buying a couple of automobiles for lady friends.

That's a story that's been going the rounds these many years about William J. Fallon, the great mouthpiece. It is in all probability true, for it would have been typical of Fallon. He was the trickiest, cleverest, shadiest big-time criminal lawyer New York has ever known, and the big burg has had a few. Fallon, in fact, rates with the celebrated courtroom strategists in all American criminal history—right up there with Clarence Darrow of Chicago and Earl Rogers of Los Angeles.

Fallon, a stalwart redhead who dripped with magnetism, could charm a bird out of a tree, let alone a lady into a hotel room. He wanted no truck with dry legal cases; the colorful criminal stuff was his meat. He defended gunmen, gangsters, prohibition racketeers, income-tax evaders, such underworld big shots as Arnold Rothstein, and such glamor pusses as Peggy Hopkins Joyce, who once got in trouble with the customs people for forgetting to declare a bagful of diamonds that she had brought in from Europe.

Legends spring up about lawyers and if the lawyers are smart they capitalize on the legends. The legend that fastened it-self to Bill Fallon was that the worst that could happen to a client of his was a hung jury—eleven for conviction and one for acquittal. Then the case would be retried and retried and finally kicked around until it got lost.

The story along the Broadway grapevine was that Fallon, acting through underworld intermediaries, bought off the twelfth juror in a tough case. He sometimes denied this. "Most jurors are dumb," he once told Fanny Brice, when he was hiding her husband, Nicky Arnstein, from the law. "All I have to do is to pick out the dumbest of the dozen, concentrate everything on him, and my client is sure of a hung jury."

By concentrating everything, Fallon meant more than the evidence. Sometimes the prosecution had evidence so damaging to Fallon's client that Fallon was obliged to divert attention from it. On such occasions, *he* became the defendant, rather than the man who was on trial. He deliberately did things that brought the wrath of the prosecutor and the judge down upon him, then turned that wrath to his advantage.

Once, for example, he was cross-examining a detective who was the state's star witness against a crook client. The questioning began in normal enough fashion, with Fallon speaking in a moderate tone of voice and standing a respectful distance from the witness. As the cross-examination progressed, Fallon's voice grew louder and he inched closer to the witness until he was practically in the man's lap and shouting at the top of his voice.

The district attorney, speaking in a normal tone, told the judge he objected to Fallon's tone of voice. Fallon kept right on shouting at the witness. Now the judge banged his gavel so hard he almost broke it and instructed Fallon to stop talking. Fallon, not taking his eyes from the witness, kept right on shouting. Now the judge began to shout at Fallon. Finally Fallon turned to His Honor, cupped a hand to his ear, and inquired if the judge was talking to him.

"*Yes,* I'm talking to you!" shouted the judge. "What did Your Honor say?" asked Fallon.

"I said I'm talking to you," roared the judge, "and instructing you not to stand so close to the witness and shout at him." Fallon cupped his hand to his ear again and stood there looking puzzled. "What did Your Honor say?" Now the judge began to roar even louder. Fallon looked startled, then hung his head. He couldn't, he said, help it if he had recently suffered an injury that had impaired his hearing. "You mean you are deaf?" asked the judge. Fallon couldn't hear the man. The judge roared a repetition of his question. "Yes, Your Honor," said Fallon, looking at the jury out of the corner of his eye. "I fear that I may never be able to hear normally again."

For the balance of the trial, poor Fallon had to shout at the state's witnesses and practically sit in their laps while the prosecutor and the judge had to interrupt him frequently. "Your Honor," said the prosecutor, "I think counsel is only pretending he is deaf." Fallon asked the judge what the man had said. The judge shouted the information. Fallon looked sad again. "Would that I were but pretending," he said.

The jury was obviously touched by Fallon's plight. Fallon didn't put the defendant on the stand because he, not the crook, had become the defendant. And of course the crook was acquitted.

Outside the courtroom after the verdict was in, Fallon tapped the prosecutor on the shoulder. "Pardon me, sir," he whispered, "but if I'm not mistaken I heard you drop a pin back there."

No less an authority than David Belasco, the great theatrical producer, who was a close friend of Fallon's thought that Fallon had missed his true destiny when he took up law instead of acting. In Belasco's considered opinion, Fallon would have made a great tragedian. There was something tragic about his square, Hibernian face, something wistful in his China-blue eyes, and he was born to the dramatic gesture. His voice had a rich, throbbing timbre not unlike that of his friend John Barrymore but he didn't always have to use it to produce an effect. He could cock his head and convey more anger or surprise than a pedestrian prosecutor could with a thousand words and when, in the midst of a fiery exchange with a reluctant witness, he would abruptly stop talking, hunch his shoulders and hang his head, he was as tragic as Hamlet.

Fallon was at his dramatic best in the summer of 1924 when, after being tried in federal court for jury bribing, he summed up his own case. His ancient enemy, William Randolph Hearst, had instigated the charge and the evidence against Fallon seemed so completely and utterly damning that Fallon's lawyer could do little to rebut it. There was only one thing to do, and that was for Bill Fallon to plead his own case by summing up to the jury.

Thus it was that on a steaming morning Fallon got up to begin his address to the jurors—the address that he hoped would save his legal life. Dressed in a finely cut blue-serge suit and wearing a burgundy necktie, he was, more than ever, Hamlet in a tragic hour. He talked in low tones, with sweet reasonableness, and he talked not so much about the evidence that the prosecution had presented, but about life in general and about his own life in particular. He had only gotten into his summation, if it could be called that, when there was a break for lunch.

"That was a dumb thing to do Bill," his counsel told him as the jurors went out to lunch, "breaking up your summation like that. The whole effect of the thing will be lost while they're out eating."

"On the contrary," said Fallon. "I've planted the seed. It will grow while they're out stuffing themselves at government expense."

And so in the afternoon the jurors came back, well fed and looking very interested in what Fallon had to say. He took up where he had left off, pacing up and down, addressing his remarks first to this juror, then to that one. He was, that steaming day in July of 1924, not a lawyer addressing a jury but, rather, an actor performing before an audience.

Once in a while he would supply a little comedy to relieve the tension—some anecdote about his early life as a lawyer, how unresourceful he had been on certain occasions. As the sun sank lower in the white-hot sky, Fallon became more and more the underdog. He spoke of his mother—his dear sainted mother—and he whipped a snow-white handkerchief from his breast pocket and dabbed at his eyes. He spoke of his days at Fordham Law School, when he had had dreams of becoming a great lawyer—for his dear old mother's sake. He told the jurors how, in his early days as a prosecutor in Westchester County, New York, he had once, in his zeal to do his job, sent an innocent man to prison—without knowing it, of course—and how, ever after that he had been dedicated to seeing that there would never be another

miscarriage of justice if he could do anything about it.

But of course he had made mistakes in his life, Fallon told the jurors. To err, he pointed out, was human; to forgive, divine. The judge interrupted him at this point. He instructed an attendant to show a woman out of the courtroom. It was all right to cry, but this woman was practically wailing.

And so it came to pass that late in the afternoon William Joseph Fallon came to the end of his summation. He ceased his walking and stood in the center of the jury box. He tilted his head slightly upward and he outstretched his arms in supplication. "Gentlemen of the jury," he said, in a voice lowered almost to a whisper, "all that is dear to me, all that life means to me, I now place in your hands." His arms dropped to his sides and he lowered his head until his chin rested on his chest. Thus he stood, completely motionless, for fully thirty seconds.

And so the jury filed out to decide upon the fate of William Joseph Fallon. There was no doubt in the minds of anybody, even Fallon's friends, that he had been guilty of purchasing a juror. The big question along the Broadway grapevine was: Had Fallon succeeded, once more, in making the jury forget the evidence and, by his own dramatic charm, sold it a bill of goods? The verdict this time was the most important one of Bill Fallon's life. For if the verdict was guilty, the great mouthpiece would not only be finished; he would go to prison.

The whole town was pulling for Fallon because the man was indeed a beloved rogue. Headwaiters and bellhops loved him because he threw money around like confetti. Practically every rooter for the New York Giants followed the Fallon bribery trial in the papers as if it were a World Series because Fallon was one of the town's top Giant rooters and a close friend of John J. McGraw, the Giant manager. Politicians, society figures and mobsters were offering Jack Doyle, Broadway's betting commissioner, 6 to 5 that Fallon would get at least a hung jury—and not one he hung himself.

Although Fallon was married, and had been for twelve years, he didn't work at it. He had a wife who was part human, part angel. Whenever, after flying long and high, he came home to roost, she never so much as asked him where he had been or what he had been doing, probably because she knew the answers in advance and because she simply loved the big fellow.

Fallon's partner, Eugene McGee, was several years older than he, and had frequently lectured at Fordham Law School when Fallon was a student there. The firm of Fallon and McGee was known as the Broadway and Forty-second Street Bar Association. McGee did the research on a case and handed it over to Fallon. Then Fallon would dramatize the research in the courtroom.

The Broadway and Forty-second Street Bar Association operated on strictly a cash basis, except when the client was a pretty woman. Then Fallon would refuse to accept any money. "Gosh, Bill," McGee complained one day when Fallon refused to take a fee from a chorus girl who had come in to be defended for assaulting a woman who had caught her with her husband, "we've got to eat." "How can you think of food, Gene," countered Fallon, "when you look at anything as beautiful as that?"

Both Fallon and McGee were late sleepers, not usually getting into the office until late morning or early afternoon unless there was a big trial going on. Although they took in elaborate sums, they had a crummy office and just one secretary. The secretary would accept retainers from prospective clients who called when neither of the partners was in. Many mornings the secretary would collect one or more retainers, often totalling $2,000 or $3,000 and put the money in a tin box. Whichever of the partners arrived for work first rifled the box. Sometimes Fallon got the money and sometimes McGee got it.

Although Fallon and McGee were, for all practical purposes robbing each other, they never had so much as a loud word about these trips to the till. It was all part of the game. Anyway, the larcenies were about evenly divided between the two men. A friend once asked Fallon if he thought McGee was getting the better of him by this unique method of dividing the spoils.

"Not at all," said Fallon. "In fact, we're both better off because of it. It saves bookkeeping."

Apparently, neither Fallon nor McGee ever made the slightest effort to beat one another to the morning's bag unless they just happened to arrive in the vicinity of Broadway and Forty-second Street about the same time. Then, spotting one another, they would, instead of greeting each other as partners, begin a race to the office. Since each man tossed it away at night, he was usually flat in the morning. The last one in would usually have to borrow $50 or $100 from the other— until the next day. The next day never arrived.

McGraw, the manager of the Giants, who was one of Fallon's drinking companions, once asked him why he didn't dispense with McGee and go it alone. "John," said Fallon, "every comedian would be dead without a straight man. I'm a comedian and Gene's a straight man."

Although Bill Fallon had the generosity of a drunken sailor in most things, such as buying gems and automobiles for his lady friends and handing out big tips, there was a stingy side to his nature. He shined his own shoes, cut his own hair and, when escorting a handsomely attired lady to her diggings after an evening on the town, always rode in the subway or street cars, never in a taxi.

Belasco, the sage of the make-believe world, once asked him about these apparently stingy traits. Fallon, never at a loss for an explanation, explained that he thought it was degrading for a man to be a bootblack and that he didn't want to contribute to the degradation of anybody. He offered Belasco the same explanation for cutting his own hair, although the general opinion was that Fallon had such a handsome shock of the stuff that he didn't want to take a chance on any barber cutting it improperly. So far as his refusal to use taxis went, he insisted that he considered them dangerous. "Just look at all the accidents taxis get into," he would say. "You never hear of street cars and subway trains getting into trouble like that. Anyhow, subways are faster and you see such interesting people in them."

In his later years, in the days before he went on trial for jury bribing, Fallon became a real drunk, an authentic lush. His devotion to liquor, however, never seemed to take the edge off his sharp mind, and it never road-blocked his way to a courtroom when the chips were down. Fallon did, however, frequently appear in the august portals of justice with whisky on his breath. After a night on the town he would often have only enough time to shave, take a bath and change his clothes before grabbing a quick breakfast and hustling off to court. In his later years, Fallon's breakfast more

often than not consisted of a couple of raw eggs dropped in half a tumblerful of rye. That would carry him through to the noon recess when he would repeat the nourishment—often without the eggs.

One morning, down in the old Criminal Courts Building on Centre Street, near Police Headquarters, Fallon appeared before a straight-laced judge to argue for a reduction of bail for a client. Fallon was in particularly good form that morning and his words had wings. But the judge didn't seem so intent on what Fallon was saying as on sniffing the air around him. Finally His Honor leaned forward, fixed Fallon with a severe stare, and inquired, "Is it possible that counsel has been drinking?"

Fallon blinked, smiled warmly, stepped back a few feet, and bowed from the waist. "If," he said, "Your Honor's sense of justice is as keen as Your Honor's sense of smell, I shall have no fear that my client's bail will be reduced."

The judge was completely enchanted. As he smiled, he seemed to be fighting back the desire to laugh out loud. He sat back and told Fallon to proceed with his argument. The bail was reduced.

William Joseph Fallon was that *rara avis*—a native New Yorker. He was born in the home of his parents—Joseph and Mary Fallon, natives of Ireland—in a handsome four-story red brick house in the 200 block of West Forty-seventh Street. Fallon senior, though under thirty when Willie was born, ran a highly successful market. He had already been blessed with two daughters, not entirely to his satisfaction, since he preferred boys. Willie Fallon's mother was a gentle, retiring woman, but the old man was a belligerent character. "What the hell use is a girl in a corner street fight?" he used to inquire of neighbors. "Why, she can't *defend* herself." So the drinks were on Old Man Fallon on January 23, 1886, when Willie, the first of two sons, checked in.

When, a couple of years after Willie's birth, the second son came along, making a family of six, not counting a couple of servants, Old Man Fallon decided to get out of Manhattan, out somewhere in the country where the air was fresh and there was room to move around. So the Fallons sold the red-brick house on West Forty-seventh Street and moved to Mamaroneck, on Long Island Sound, up in Westchester County. There the elder Fallon opened another market and the kids went to school.

Although there was always whisky around the house, it never occurred to Willie Fallon, as it does to so many boys, that he would drink the stuff when he grew up. If anything, he had the makings of an abstainer by the time he was 10 years old. The smell of whisky practically nauseated him.

As Willie Fallon reached his teens, he began to worship his mother—something that he did to the end of his days. To him, there was no woman on earth like his mother, which was probably one reason why he was to make such a poor husband. Willie, as his mother and father always called him, was, despite his practically unnatural love for his mother, a boy's boy—handy with his fists and good at sports. Girls never interested him. He was, in fact, shy in their presence—something of a Ripley considering what a wow he later became with them.

Fallon's mother wanted him to become a priest so he began to study at Fordham University in New York City. But by the time he had completed his regular college course, the ham in him cropped out. He thought of going on the stage and becoming a great star but he knew that such a course would break the heart of his mother. The next best thing, then, was the law. Stalwart, handsome, and with a lightning mind and a golden voice, he could picture himself strutting before juries, spellbinding them in the cause of justice. Fallon's parents, his mother in particular, had always stressed the terrible wages of sin. God was on the side of the just—and it was with that in mind that Fallon began the study of law at Fordham.

Eugene McGee, a big, rough-hewn young Irishman who was already practicing law in Manhattan, frequently did special teaching at Fordham. McGee was quick to recognize in Fallon a future whiz at the bar. Came graduation day and McGee approached Fallon. "Bill," he said, "why don't you come in with me as a junior partner? We would be a great success together."

Fallon wasn't interested. For one thing, he didn't want to go to New York. His mother had begun to picture him as practicing, preferably as a prosecutor, up in Westchester County. So Fallon opened up a little office in White Plains, the county seat. He was twenty-three at the time. He didn't find private practice as exciting as he had hoped it would be. For one thing, there weren't many exciting cases—mostly dry legal stuff.

Still worshipping his mother, Fallon never bothered with girls. Until, that is, he was twenty-six. Then he met a girl named Agnes Rafter—an Irish colleen who reminded him of his mother. Agnes' father ran a chain of grocery stores. She and Fallon were married at the Church of the Holy Trinity in New York City in June of 1912.

Agnes thought it would be fine if her young and handsome husband ran for the state legislature. Dreamer that she was, she pointed out that if he got into politics he might someday become governor. So he went around making speeches and his charm got him elected.

Up in Albany, Fallon was distressed to find himself among a bunch of political hacks and windbags who were pumping for a lot of legislation that was, to him anyway, as dull as the law books. So he sat out most of his term back in White Plains. But by now the Fallon charm had attracted quite a bit of local attention. The fellow was not only brilliant and handsome but witty and winning. The district attorney of Westchester County, a fine public servant named Frederick E. Weeks, decided that Fallon was just the boy he needed on his staff—the boy to handle the tough ones with juries. So Fallon was appointed Assistant District Attorney in 1914, when he was twenty-eight.

Prosecuting, with its opportunity for courtroom dramatics, suited Fallon just fine. All the tough cases—the ones the D.A. stood a fair chance of losing—were turned over to him. Young Fallon had an unerring instinct for finding the flaw in the story of a witness for the defense. And if there wasn't a flaw to be found, Fallon would create one. He seemed to take the position that the end justified the means. If he could, by trickery, trip up an obviously honest witness for the defense, he used trickery. Once, for example, he was cross-examining a man who was testifying to the good character of a fellow charged with breaking into a home. At one stage of the testimony of the character witness the man said that during the night of the robbery he had left his home to go out and buy a quart of milk.

"How long would you say you were out of your house going for that quart of milk?" asked Fallon.

"Maybe twenty minutes."

"How far from your house was the store where you bought that milk?"

"Three doors away."

"Yet it took you twenty minutes to buy that quart of milk?"

The witness nodded.

"Was the store crowded so that you didn't get waited on for about twenty minutes?"

No, the store had been empty.

"Well, then, why did it take you twenty minutes?"

"I didn't go right to the store. I took a walk."

"Oh! So you didn't really go out to buy the milk at all. What you really went out for was a walk. May I ask where you went during that walk—and what the *real reason* was behind that walk?"

The witness began to squirm a little bit. He couldn't quite explain why he had taken such a roundabout course to buy a quart of milk. Fallon kept pressing the man for an explanation. The witness couldn't supply an explanation, for there was none to give. He had just taken a walk, that was all. But every time he was hesitant about answering why he had taken the walk, for fear of walking into a trap, Fallon would turn to the jury and raise his eyebrows. It is axiomatic that a sharp lawyer can make an innocent witness appear to drip with guilt. And that was exactly what Fallon did to the man who had gone out for a quart of milk but, once on the street, decided to take a little walk before returning home.

When he summed up to the jury, Fallon ignored practically everything except the walk of the milk purchaser. The jury decided that the milk purchaser had been hiding something—something he had done during that walk—and that if he was the kind of a character witness the defense produced the defendant must be guilty. So guilty it was.

In preparing a case against a defendant, Fallon had an unerring instinct for digging up something in the man's past which, sprung in the courtroom, usually threw a third strike at the defendant. Once he was trying a middle-aged man for stealing from his employer. The defendant had a good lawyer—a lawyer who put the defendant on the stand and established the fact that the man had led an honorable life from the cradle to the time he was accused of stealing. Everybody in the courtroom, including Fallon, knew that the defendant was making an excellent impression on the jury—an impression that cast serious doubt on the charge against him.

Now Fallon, taking over, asked the defendant if it weren't true that he had graduated from high school twenty-three years before.

"Yes, sir."

"And you had trouble in making a passing grade in history during your senior year in that high school. Isn't that correct?"

"Yes, sir." The defendant, who had been calm up to now, began to look a little uneasy.

"And you were accused of cheating in your final examination in history. Isn't that true?"

"No, not exactly."

"What do you mean not exactly?"

"Well, sir, several students in the senior class did a little copying from each other in history. But . . ."

"And you were one of those accused. Isn't that correct?"

"Well, you see . . ."

"Were you accused of cheating or weren't you!"

"I was. But . . ."

"Oh, so you *were* accused of cheating. That's all."

The man was sent up.

Fallon and Gene McGee used to go together to baseball games at the Polo Grounds. It was McGee who was a friend of John J. McGraw, the Giant manager, and it was McGee who introduced Fallon to the Little Napoleon. As Fallon and McGee would sit in a box between home plate and first base, near the Giants' dugout, McGee would ask Fallon why he didn't quit Westchester County and come down to the big town and go into partnership with him. The pair, McGee pointed out, would make an unbeatable team. Fallon wasn't interested. His life, he said, was dedicated to meting out justice to evildoers. "It's how my mother wants it," he said to McGee more than once.

One day in 1915, after Fallon had been prosecuting for more than a year, he was trying a youth charged with a run-of-the-mill robbery. The defendant was a clean-cut, innocent-looking kid and the case against him was far from open and shut. There was some question in the district attorney's office, in fact, that the kid in the toils was guilty of the robbery. That, and the fact that the defendant had a clean record, was why the case was far from open and shut. But when Fallon laid hands on it, he proceeded to button it up. What he actually did, from all available accounts, was to blow up a fine circumstantial case against the youth and knock down everything in the defendant's favor introduced by a third-rate lawyer who was no match for him. So the kid went to prison. While the youth was in the big house his mother died of a stroke brought on, the doctor said, by emotional turmoil over her son's plight.

And then, a year later, another robber —an old pro—was caught in Westchester County. He began to sing, hoping to lessen his sentence. He included in his song a verse about the robbery that the kid had been sent up for a year before. The old pro had pulled that job, too.

Fallon, thinking the singing man was off key about the robbery he had sent the kid up for, questioned the singer in great detail. "How do I know you're not lying about that robbery?" Fallon asked the prisoner. "I can tell you the details about the house you say the kid broke into," said the old fellow. "All right," said Fallon, "go ahead and tell me." The old one described the interior of the house in great detail. Fallon was still not satisfied. "Well, will *this* satisfy you?" asked the prisoner. "I knocked over a piece of bric-a-brac and broke it when I pulled that job. I didn't see nothing about that in the papers."

Fallon now realized the criminal was speaking the truth. A piece of bric-a-brac *had* been broken during the robbery but never been mentioned in the press or during the trial of the boy in prison.

Fallon left his office early that afternoon. He walked into a saloon near the railroad station in White Plains—a saloon on the ground floor of a little broken-down hotel run by a couple of midgets who had once been performers in the Ringling Brothers-Barnum & Bailey Circus. The midgets were a husband-and-wife team and the husband, who stood about 40 inches high, and who went under the name of Admiral Dot, was the bartender. He had a special platform built behind the bar so that he could reach the beer spigots and the liquor bottles.

"Well, Bill," the Admiral said to Fallon that afternoon, "what'll it be—the usual?" "No," said Fallon, "give me a drink of whisky." The Admiral blinked. He had long served Fallon ginger ale and thought the fellow was kidding. But as he studied Fallon's face, he saw differently, and reached for a bottle.

Fallon later said that the first drink was hard to get down. But once he got it down he began to feel that creeping joy that inhabits thirsty wayfarers once they reach the oasis. The second drink was easy—and the third one was easier yet. Admiral Dot, who was a handy man with a bottle himself, and therefore something of a connoisseur of drinkers of heroic stature, began to look upon Bill Fallon in a new and admiring light. "Bill," said the Admiral, "I must say you're off to a pretty good start for a fellow who's never touched the stuff."

Then Fallon told Admiral Dot that he had sent an innocent man to prison and that he had killed the prisoner's mother. "You're kiddin', Bill," said the Admiral. Fallon convinced the Admiral, and everybody else to whom the Admiral relayed the story, that he wasn't kidding. He chucked his job as assistant D.A. He was going to New York to practice law—criminal law—and give the Blind Goddess one of the worst beatings she was ever to get. Before he left, he saw that the innocent kid was pardoned.

The firm of Fallon & McGee began to operate out of a desk-and-hat rack office in the Singer Building on lower Broadway. The word had soon seeped down from Westchester County, to the ears of the sharpies, that Bill Fallon was a smart mouthpiece who was out to beat the law. There was plenty of business for a fellow like that.

One of Fallon & McGee's first clients was a handsome big fellow in his middle thirties by the name of Robert Arthur Tourbillon, better known as Dapper Don Collins. Dapper Don had a vast repertoire of dodges for extracting money from people, his specialties being blackmail, card sharping on transatlantic liners, and confidence work.

It was Fallon who first asked Dapper Don how he had ever come to get into a career of taking the suckers. The answer was really quite simple. As a youth of eighteen in his native Georgia, young Tourbillon, seeking adventure, had latched onto a job as a trick bicycle rider with a broken-down one-ring circus. Tourbillon, his manly frame set off in tights and spangles, rode a bicycle in a groove around the top of a roofless cage filled with lions. The lions appeared to be particularly nasty as they growled and leaped upward, trying to get at the handsome young cyclist. The peasants, who had paid their money to witness the death-defying spectacle, stood around the cage, awe-stricken and gawking, impressed by the belief that if the daring Tourbillon should make a slip and fall into the cage he would be torn to pieces.

Tourbillon laughed to himself as he rode around the rim of the cage and occasionally glanced at the yokels. While the lions looked particularly vicious actually they were completely harmless. They were all practically coming apart at the seams with age, and their teeth had been drawn and their claws clipped. It was while studying the spectators as he rode around the rim of the cage that the fellow who was later to become Dapper Don, con man de luxe, embraced the unshakable conviction that at least 25 percent of the population were boobs ripe for the kill. And so he went on from there, cutting a high, wide and hilarious swath through Larceny Lane.

The trouble for which Dapper Don Collins engaged the services of Fallon & McGee was quite pedestrian, really. Dapper Don had taken a well-known Bronx delicatessen dealer for about $20,000 in a crooked card game. Fallon, who instinctively liked the dapper one, asked Don if he had any of the money left—to put down as a retainer fee. "No, I haven't," said Collins. "But I expect to go over to New Jersey this coming week end and I ought to have plenty Monday morning."

The situation was a ticklish one for Collins, even though the delicatessen dealer didn't have evidence for criminal prosecution. The mark swung a lot of weight with the Democratic political machine in the Bronx and he had told Collins to get up the money he had taken from him or he would apply political pressure to Dapper Don and see that he was run out of town.

"Have $20,000 here Monday if you can, Don," said Fallon. "I'll be thinking of what to do over the week end."

Fallon telephoned to a private detective and asked the dick to give him a quick rundown on the private life of the delicatessen dealer. On the Monday morning, when Dapper Don appeared with the $20,000, Fallon counted it and put it in his pocket. "I'll just take this as my fee, Don," said Fallon. That was all right with Don, an easy-come-easy-go character, but he wanted to know what went with the delicatessen dealer.

It seemed that Fallon had run into a stroke of great fortune. The private dick he had put on the case had smelled out Bronx gossip to the effect that the big pastrami man, who had a wife and four children, also had a few mistresses around the Bronx, one of whom had given birth to a little bundle of illegitimate joy. Don beamed. "You mean . . . ?" Fallon smiled and nodded. "The kid's a two-year-old boy and he looks exactly like that delicatessen man."

"But how sure are you, Bill?"

"I'll know tomorrow." The delicatessen man was coming into Fallon's office to talk about the Collins matter.

When, next day, the complainant appeared, he was the picture of upright belligerence. "I suppose," he told Fallon, "that you have sent for me so that you can settle up that crooked card game I was in."

"Well," said Fallon, "yes and no."

"Yes and no. What the hell do you mean!"

"How many children do you have?"

"Two boys and two girls."

"I mean *illegitimate* children. How many little bastards do you have besides that two-year-old boy on East 116th Street?"

The man said he didn't know what Fallon meant. But Fallon knew he had him. Fallon reached into a folder (as he later explained the dodge to drinking companions) and, holding the folder below the level of his desk top, out of range of the delicatessen man's vision, began to look at sheets of blank paper, one at a time. He would look at a sheet of blank paper, purse his lips, then make a ticking sound with his tongue and look up at the man sitting across the desk from him. Then he would shuffle the papers, look at another blank piece, and do the same thing. By the time he had pulled that a few times the delicatessen man was sweating. "My wife and family, Mr. Fallon!" he said. "You've got to think of *them*."

Fallon told him he didn't have to worry about a thing. "Just forget about going to your political friends about Mr. Collins," he told the man, "and everything will be all right." Fallon put the blank papers back in the folder and put the folder in the safe. "Just what have you *got* in that folder, Mr. Fallon?" asked the man. "Never mind," said Fallon. "It'll never go any farther so long as you keep your big mouth shut." That wrapped it up.

It was through Dapper Don Collins that Fallon met Arnold Rothstein, the big-time gambler who was later knocked off in the Park Central Hotel for welching on a big bet. Fallon, Collins and Rothstein used to hang around the Astor Hotel and Times Square and, just for fun, play a little game with both the yokels and native New Yorkers, who are supposed to be very smart. They would bet with strangers that they could guess what make of automobiles would pass the hotel in preponderant numbers—five Fords before two Buicks, and so on, in a given period of time. They always won simply by "stacking" some automobiles around the corner and, after the bets were down, giving the signal to the drivers of the cars to infiltrate them into the Times Square traffic.

Another game that Fallon, Collins and Rothstein played was to approach a stranger and say that they would give him odds that a friend of theirs—a fellow with a remarkable X-ray mind—could identify a given playing card simply by being called on the phone and asked what the card was. The feat sounded impossible but, after the bet was down, it always worked. The sucker would pick a card out of Rothstein's deck—the five of clubs, say—call a number, ask for a certain party, and ask him what card he was holding in his hand. The man with the X-ray mind would think a few seconds, then say, "Why, the five of clubs, of course."

The secret, since widely used, simply revolved around a code. Rothstein and the man on the other end of the phone had a file of fifty-two names, each representing one of the fifty-two cards in the deck. Thus if the sucker called the number and asked for Mr. Brown, the name Brown would indicate that he had picked the ace of spades, say. If he asked for Mr. Smith, that would indicate he had picked the two of spades. And so on. It was foolproof and, when they were short of lunch money, Fallon and McGee would pull the dodge, Fallon hanging around The Astor and McGee sitting in his office, with the code at his elbow and waiting for the phone to ring.

Fallon was hired to defend a little confidence man named Petey the Kid, who had sold Grant's Tomb to a sucker. The law had Petey the Kid bang to rights, as the saying went—identification of Petey by the sucker, witnesses to the swindle, and everything. The case was a real toughie, but Fallon took it because Petey the Kid was in a position to plunk down around $10,000.

The district attorney was Ferdinand Pecora, later a state supreme court justice. Pecora, who felt his stomach muscles tightening every time he so much as heard Fallon's name, assigned one of his best assistants to prosecute Petey.

By way of revealing to the jury what a bad character the Kid was, Pecora's assistant reached into the records of Petey's past. Every time the prosecutor would bring out the pertinent data on something Petey had been mixed up in, Fallon would yowl an objection. He was overruled every time. "But what has this got to do with the issue at hand, Your Honor?" Fallon would ask the judge. "The evidence is admissable," the court would reply. Fallon would fold his arms and stare at the judge.

When it came time for Fallon to put his client on the stand, he knew that his only out was to play the case for laughs. "Petey," he asked, "are you acquainted with King George of England?" The prosecutor howled an objection. "The question is as pertinent as those asked by the State of New York," Fallon maintained. "Objection sustained," said the Court.

"Petey," Fallon next asked, "were you—" and now he consulted some notes

—"were you, on the night of February 12th last, a guest of President Wilson in the White House?" The prosecutor screamed and the judge almost broke his gavel and the jury began to laugh. Fallon insisted that the prosecutor had asked witnesses questions far less relevant. "Petey," Fallon next inquired, "have you ever climbed the large pyramid—the pyramid of Cheops?" Petey said he hadn't. "One of the two smaller ones, then?" No.

"Petey," said Fallon, consulting more notes, "an elderly couple were murdered in Pennsylvania, near Lancaster, several days before you were taken into custody. Do you deny that you murdered them?" Petey denied that he was a murderer. The jury was still laughing. "Petey," asked Fallon, "did you ever throw a baby out of a second-story window?" Petey hadn't. "Did you ever kick your mother downstairs?" Petey hadn't.

The jurors were practically laughed out when it came time for Fallon to sum up. "Take a look at this little man, gentlemen," he advised the jurors. "He has never thrown a baby out of a second-story window and he has never kicked his mother downstairs. And he has never climbed any of the pyramids." The jurors apparently spent their remaining laughter in the jury room because they brought in a split verdict.

Before Petey the Kid went on trial the second time, Fallon thought up a way of hanging another jury. His tack this time would be to concentrate on one juror, to the exclusion of other members of the panel. To do that he would have to find some common bond with the man.

A great one for improvising as he went along, Fallon had no idea of how he was going to establish a common bond with any of the jurors until, when questioning prospective members of the panel, he noticed that one man had difficulty walking. Obviously the man had rheumatism. Fallon accepted him without a question but with a comment: "May I say that I like your face?"

Next day Fallon appeared with a pained expression on his face. He didn't seem as spry as usual; in fact, he had difficulty moving around. The judge asked him if anything was wrong. "Nothing," said Fallon bravely. "Nothing at all, Your Honor, thank you."

"But there *is* something wrong with you, Mr. Fallon. You seem to be in pain."

"I'm afraid Your Honor has caught counsel in a falsehood," said Fallon. "I am indeed in great pain."

"What from, Mr. Fallon?"

"Rheumatism, Your Honor."

Eleven of the jurors voted to convict Petey the Kid but the rheumatic juror hung the panel. Thereafter the case of Petey the Kid was kicked around until it got lost.

Fallon was defending a big-time thief down in the Criminal Courts Building one day when the prosecutor appeared with a spanking new briefcase. The briefcase was filled with enough stuff to send Fallon's client up for a couple of hundred years. During the noon recess the prosecutor took the briefcase out to lunch with him. While at lunch, he got a telephone call. He got up from the table to go to the phone, taking the briefcase with him. There was a woman's voice on the other end of the wire. She inquired of the prosecutor if he were aware of the fact that his wife was unfaithful to him. The prosecutor was aware of no such thing but the inquiry startled him. It startled him so much that he forgot all about his briefcase, lying on the floor beside him. When the conversation was over, the briefcase was gone.

When the afternoon court session began, Fallon appeared, immersed in papers and bathed in innocence. The prosecutor didn't show up. Fallon demanded to know where the man was. The judge explained that the session would have to be adjourned because the prosecutor had lost his briefcase. Fallon seemed shocked. But he quickly recovered from his shock. He demanded that the trial proceed. The judge overruled him. Finally the proceedings were adjourned until next morning while the prosecutor combed lower Manhattan for his briefcase.

Next morning the prosecutor still didn't have his briefcase. He had to admit that all his evidence had vanished. Fallon demanded that the trial proceed. It did. Fallon's client was, naturally, acquitted.

Bill Fallon was a whiz at taking a case that most other lawyers would have considered hopeless and, by a combination of artifices, pulling it out of the fire—always providing, of course, that the fee was right. Flossie Brooks, a shapely miss known on both sides of the law as a blackmailer de luxe, walked into the office of Fallon and McGee one day and announced that she was up to her pretty blue eyes in trouble.

"What have you done, Flossie?" asked Fallon, who knew the girl by reputation. Flossie had shaken down an Armenian rug merchant for a couple of thousand dollars and got caught at it.

"How did you get caught?" asked Fallon, looking at Flossie's legs. Flossie had learned that the Armenian, who was married and who lived in Manhattan, had done considerable nocturnal romping in Atlantic City while at the shore resort displaying rugs at a stand on the Boardwalk. In possession of this dreadful information, Flossie telephoned to the rug merchant's home. His wife answered the phone. "Let me speak to your husband," said Flossie. "Who is this?" asked the wife. "Never mind who it is," said Flossie. "Just let me speak to him."

Flossie got right to the point with the rug merchant. She thought maybe it would be worth a couple of thousand to the man if his wife didn't find out about what had happened at Atlantic City. "Sure," said the Armenian. "I'll be glad to attend to that matter. Where will I meet you?" A rendezvous was arranged for a spot in Central Park the following night.

The rug man began to think things over. He had heard somewhere that trying to buy off a blackmailer was like trying to get hold of a will-o-the-wisp. Then, too, his wife seemed curious about the call from the lady after business hours. He decided that confessing everything to his wife would entail less trouble in the long run than holding still for blackmail. So he confessed everything, took his beating, called the cops and appeared in Central Park next night with a couple of thousand in marked bills and two dicks hiding in the bushes.

"So when I took the money," Flossie told Fallon, "they pinched me."

When Flossie Brooks disclosed that she was in a position to plunk down a handsome fee in advance, Fallon began to see the vague outlines of an acquittal. When the trial began, Fallon, keeping Flossie's legs in mind, told her to make sure she kept them crossed while he examined the jurors. As he questioned each prospective juror as to his political affiliations, his religion, and other subjects having nothing whatever to do with the subject at hand, he didn't listen to any of the replies but studied the quizee to see how much attention he was paying to Flossie's legs. If the prospective juror seemed to be paying more attention to Flossie's

legs than to Fallon, Fallon accepted him. His theory was that a man interested in a pretty pair of legs would, other things being equal, hardly be constrained to cast a vote to put them out of circulation.

The principal witnesses against Flossie were the Armenian rug merchant, his wife, and the two detectives who had grabbed Flossie after the rug man had given her the two grand in Central Park. "You admit," asked Fallon when he began cross-examination of the rug merchant, "that the basis of this whole case against Miss Brooks arises from the fact that you were unfaithful to your wife on numerous occasions in Atlantic City?" "Yes," said the witness. "In other words," said Fallon, "you deceived your wife while you were in Atlantic City. Is that correct?" "Yes." Or, to put it another way, you lied to your wife about what you did at nights in Atlantic City." "Yes."

Fallon stepped closer to the rug man, who was squirming now, folded his arms across his chest, and looked at the witness with contempt. "My dear man," he said, "since you are a confessed liar, how do you expect these twelve fine gentlemen in the jury box here to believe you *now*?" Fallon, his arms still folded across his chest, turned to the jury and raised his eyebrows. "That is all," he said, still looking at the jury.

Then Fallon began to cross-examine the rug merchant's wife. He asked her if she were quite comfortable. Yes, she was. "Can I get you a drink of water or anything, Madam?" he inquired. No, she wasn't thirsty. "I think this courtroom is a little too warm," he said. "Shall I have a window opened for you?" No. The temperature was just right.

"Now, then, Madam," said Fallon, who seemed to put a low connotation on the word *madam*, "you have testified that you are positive that Miss Brooks here is the lady who telephoned to your husband the night of May 3rd last?" Yes, Madam was positive. "How many times have you heard Miss Brooks speaking?" Madam had heard Miss Brooks twice—the night she telephoned and after Miss Brooks was arrested.

"And you were certain, Madam, just from hearing the lady on the phone that night, that she was the same person that these two sterling detectives arrested in Central Park." The witness was positive. "In other words, Madam, if a stranger called your home on the telephone you could, just by hearing them speak two sentences, positively identify them later?" The witness gave an affirmative answer, but she didn't seem too sure of herself.

"Have you received any telephone calls lately from people you didn't know who asked to speak to your husband?" Madam had received several such calls. "When did you receive the last such call?"

"Last night."

"What time?"

"Why, about half past nine."

"And you would recognize the caller's voice if you heard it again?" The lady would. Fallon asked a man in the second row of spectators to stand up and come forward. He gave him a newspaper clipping to read. After the man had read for a minute or so, Fallon stopped him and asked the rug merchant's wife if she had ever heard the man before. "No," said the lady. "I've never heard the gentleman until just now."

Now Fallon put the man on the stand. He testified that he had, in the presence of witnesses, called the rug merchant's home the previous night.

"What time?"

"Half past nine."

"Who answered?"

"A lady."

"Thank you, sir," said Fallon, who now turned to the jury, folded his arms, and raised his eyebrows. "That will be all," he said to the witness.

Fallon didn't have anything on the two detectives who had pinched his client but by the time he got through asking them questions that had nothing to do with the case some of the jurors were probably convinced that the kindest act either of the dicks had ever performed was to hold a lantern while his old mother went to a dark cellar to chop wood.

Everybody figured that Fallon was afraid to put his client on the stand. That was where Fallon fooled them. Flossie Brooks had a bad record and Fallon, taking the wind out of the prosecution's sails, brought out all the sordid details. Now he asked Flossie if she had a father and mother. Flossie did. "Do you support them?" Flossie had to. "Why?" "Well, my father has tuberculosis," said Flossie. "Oh," said Fallon. "I'm *so* sorry. And your mother?" Mother had a fatal heart ailment. Fallon looked as if he was about to break down and cry.

"Were you," Fallon now asked Flossie, "ever approached by any member of the New York Police Department and asked to pay tribute in lieu of being framed?" Flossie had been so approached. By whom? Why, by two detectives. "Do you see them in this courtroom?" Flossie pointed out the two prosecution witnesses. Fallon turned to the jury, folded his arms again and raised his eyebrows.

When the prosecutor began to cross-examine Flossie, Fallon kept shouting objections to practically every question. Finally the judge asked him to explain the basis of his objections. Fallon was glad the judge had raised the point. "Because, Your Honor," he said, "the prosecutor has political ambitions. He is not so much concerned about accepting the testimony of shaky and lying witnesses as he is to forward his political career."

The prosecutor began to scream. When the screaming stopped, Fallon asked the judge if he could make just one more statement. "I myself once had political ambitions," he said, "and, in my zeal, I sent an innocent man to prison. I have vowed to the memory of my dear mother that I shall do all in my power to see that no innocent man—or lady—ever goes to prison." Now Fallon turned on the actual tears. As he wiped them away, he apologized, in choking voice, to the judge and the twelve good men and true. It took the jury almost twenty minutes to bring in an acquittal for Flossie Brooks.

As time passed, Fallon became the darling of the newspaper boys. He was a man who was always good for some copy. There were always a couple of bottles of rye in the shabby little office of Fallon & McGee—one for Fallon and one for the scribes. By now Fallon was a fairly steady drinker—not a drunk by any means, but surely a man who could stand up to the rail with practically anybody. As a result he would often wake up in the morning with quite a head but, so far, he had never taken a hair of the dog that bit him before breakfast. It wasn't until later that he was to live on rye and raw eggs

Fallon bought a house in the West Eighties—a four-story brownstone affair— and seemed devoted to his wife. He claimed that he always wanted children, particularly a son, but it was becoming increasingly apparent that his wish was not to be granted.

Now Fallon's mother died. When she died, something died inside him. He disappeared for a week—off on his first long bender.

The Broadway wise guys, such as Ar-nold Rothstein, the gambler, wondered how long it would be until Bill Fallon broke his marriage vows. The girls, particularly the type who hung around the Astor Hotel in Times Square, were, as Noel Coward might say, simply mad about the boy. Once in a while, he would go out on a party without his wife, but he always got home by midnight. His sole purpose in life seemed to be to hoodwink the law—by fair means if possible, by unfair means if need be.

Because so much of the business of Fallon & McGee—con men, con women, card sharps, and early-day racket boys— originated in the vicinity of Times Square, the firm, at Fallon's suggestion, left their downtown office and took one in Times Square. After a day in court, or in his office consulting with clients, Fallon would go into the Astor Hotel for dinner alone, then go out to see a show. He found that he got along fine with theatrical people. Some of them, such as David Belasco, used to attend his trials just to see him perform. He would return the compliment by going backstage after a performance and complimenting the actors.

Thus it was that Bill Fallon came to become an intimate friend of Fannie Brice. Fannie, a little East Side girl, had the emotional depth and the capacity for sympathy indigenous to the Jewish race. Though short on looks, with a large nose and a large mouth, when Fannie kneeled down on the stage of the New Amsterdam Theatre as a star of the Ziegfeld Follies and, bathed in a purple spotlight, sang a torch song, even the Broadway gamblers in the audience began to cry. Fallon, with his Irish capacity for sentiment, thought Fannie Brice was one of history's ten greatest women.

There was only one thing Fallon didn't like about Fannie and that was her husband—Nicky Arnstein. Arnstein, who was some fifteen years older than Fannie, was a fastidious gentleman, a highly sharpened product of a bitterly competitive society. He was a real hustler, mixed up in just about everything. One of the best capsule descriptions of Arnstein was set down by Gene Fowler in *The Great Mouthpiece,* the definitive biography of William J. Fallon. "He," says Fowler of Arnstein, "played a severe game of cards on transatlantic liners."

The Broadway wise guys—the Runyon-esque characters who are supposed to know everything — could never understand why Fannie Brice, a very good girl, ever fell for a man like Arnstein. Fallon wondered, too. "Well, Bill, I'll tell you," Fannie said to Fallon one night, "I just love the man. I guess I'll love him till the day I die."

Fallon knew that Arnstein, in spite of his protestations to Fannie that he was engaged in various legitimate enterprises, would come a cropper sooner or later. When, then, one day in February, 1920, some brokerage-house messengers were stuck up in the Wall Street district and relieved of $5 million in negotiable securities, Fallon's underworld pipelines advised him that Brother Arnstein had probably masterminded the little plot.

Fallon dropped into the Arnstein apartment on Central Park West. Arnstein was just having breakfast. Fannie, who had worked in the Follies the night before, was still in bed. "Nicky," said Fallon, "a little bird tells me you know about that job down on Wall Street." Arnstein went on with his breakfast. "You don't have to tell me anything, Nicky," said Fallon. "But when they catch up with you, let me know. I'll handle the case for Fannie's sake." Arnstein went on with his breakfast and Fallon left.

A couple of days later Fannie Brice telephoned to Fallon. "Nicky's gone, Bill," she said. "I'm afraid he's in some kind of trouble." Nicky was in big trouble. Some rat had peeped to the law and put the finger on Arnstein as the master-mind behind the big robbery. The New York District Attorney, hearing that Fallon and Fannie Brice were close friends, and deducing that Fallon would be the lawyer in Arnstein's case, sent a couple of flatfeet to question Fallon as to where Arnstein was. "How should I know?" said Fallon. "But maybe if the district attorney agrees to a low bail for Arnstein I can find out where he is."

The D. A. wasn't in a mood to talk bail. Arnstein was a slippery customer and he wanted to put him practically in irons once he laid hands on him. So the D. A., figuring that Arnstein might be in touch with Fallon by long-distance phone, put taps on Fallon's office phone. Fallon was a little too cute for that. The dicks listening at the other end of the taps never heard Arnstein's voice. But Fallon, ever the joker, made certain that the eavesdropping of the dicks would be exciting. He had different friends phone him from public booths and say, "I just got a call from Nicky. He's leaving where he is and going where you told him to." The D. A.'s men, then the New York police, were run ragged trying to catch sight of the men who were calling Fallon with the exciting intelligence. But they never reached a phone booth in time to catch the callers.

Months passed. Arnstein was still lying doggo. Fallon kept in touch with the D. A. Finally the D. A. agreed to release Arnstein on bail of $100,000 if Fallon produced him. "All right," said Fallon, "I'll bring Nicky in if you give me your word he won't be arrested on the way. This has to be a surrender, not a pinch.

Nicky's a very sensitive fellow." It was a deal.

Fallon's partner, McGee, had been in touch with Arnstein all along—by long-distance phone and by letters Arnstein sent to intermediaries. Fallon met Arnstein one night at an inn in Mamaroneck. "I've arranged bail for you, Nicky," he said. "Who's putting it up?" asked Arnstein. "Arnold Rothstein." "Why, Rothstein hates me." "Yes, but he admires Fannie."

Fallon and Arnstein motored down from Mamaroneck to Manhattan next day in a new car Fallon had bought. The plot was to pick up Fannie Brice before Arnstein went down to Centre Street, surrendered to the D. A., and got out on bail. While on the way to pick up Fannie, Fallon and Nicky swung into Fifth Avenue and what did they do but run smack into the annual police parade. Arnstein was all for getting to hell off the avenue but Fallon thought it was a great joke. So there they were—the most wanted man in New York, and his mouthpiece—riding on Fifth Avenue with the cops.

Down on Centre Street, Arnstein went into the D. A.'s office alone to go through the formality of surrendering and getting out on bail. Fallon and Fannie left the car to go out and take a short walk. When they got back the car had been stolen. Fallon ducked into a phone booth and made a few calls. In a little while a hairy gangster called Monk Eastman returned the car. "*Crise,* Bill," he said to Fallon, "how'd I know it was *your'n.*"

Although Arnstein was quickly released on bail, there ensued a succession of developments that served as a springboard to make William J. Fallon a national figure. Arnstein was ordered to appear before a United States commissioner and answer some questions relat-

ing to his financial standing. Fallon knew that if Arnstein answered the questions truthfully he would hang himself and that if he lied he could be indicted for perjury.

Fallon, who could soak up information like a sponge when he had to, sat up all night reading the federal statutes that might be of help to him in getting his client out of the jam. He thus became intrigued by the possibilities inherent in the constitutional amendment that holds that a man may refuse to testify on the grounds that his own testimony may degrade and incriminate him.

So, when Arnstein appeared before the United States commissioner to answer questions, he began to answer, then suddenly clammed up on the grounds that he might degrade and incriminate himself. Nicky's fear of degrading himself seemed somewhat academic but he was on solid ground in fearing to incriminate himself. The commissioner blinked when he heard Arnstein parroting the words that Fallon had obviously put in his mouth, then looked at Fallon. There stood Fallon, with his arms folded across his chest. "I suppose," the commissioner said to Fallon, "that your client is acting on your instructions." "He certainly is," said Fallon.

The commissioner, not exactly a pushover, had heard the refusal-to-answer-on-constitutional-grounds dodge before and so had other judges. But up until now the men on the bench had brushed the dodge by simply saying, in effect, "You'll answer or go to jail," and the defendants had usually answered. But this time it was to be different. Nicky refused to answer and the commissioner ordered him to jail.

Fallon dived into the statutes again. While Arnstein sweated it out in durance vile Fallon whipped up an application for habeas corpus. But no judge would sign the application. "Don't worry about a thing," Fallon told Arnstein. "I'm going to take this whole matter direct to the United States Supreme Court."

By a series of intricate legal maneuvers, Fallon quickly got his habeas corpus proceedings on the calendar of the highest court in the land. And so Mr. Fallon went to Washington.

As a rule, attorneys suffer from stage fright when making a maiden appearance before the austere justices. But not Fallon. He strutted like a peacock when he made his appearance before the Nine Old Men as he argued that his client should be legally sprung.

Most lawyers appearing before the august tribunal wore formal morning attire. Fallon wore his usual blue serge suit and burgandy necktie. Veteran reporters, witnessing his appearance, thought they detected an unusual stiffness in some members of the bench.

Fallon was obviously steeped in the statutes relating to habeas corpus, thoroughly grounded, however recently. As he spoke, his tone was just the right combination of confidence and respect. He hadn't been at his argument long when the colder justices seemed to start thawing out. Although Fallon was talking about dry legal technicalities he might as well have been telling a smoking-car story for the interest he created.

Once in a while, a justice would interrupt him to ask him a question. During one such interrogation, Fallon forgot himself and folded his arms across his chest—something that was and is unthinkable in the Supreme Court chambers. But he quickly remembered where he was and dropped his arms to his sides. When it was all over he bowed like somebody in a palace in Versailles in the

eighteenth century, and left the chambers. Outside, he inquired of a lawyer acquaintance, "Where can I get a drink?"

The Supreme Court quickly handed down its decision—in favor of Fallon. Legally sprung, all Arnstein had to worry about now was going to jail again—on the bond robbery charge.

It was while in Washington that Fallon met the great love of his life. He went alone to Keith's Theatre one night to see a vaudeville show. One of the acts featured a young dancer named Gertrude Vanderbilt — no relation to *the* Vanderbilts since she had red, rather than blue, blood. Miss Vanderbilt, a divorcee, was in her twenties, some ten years younger than Fallon.

Fallon became so entranced with the girl that he went around to the stage door afterward and sent in his card. Gertrude Vanderbilt had heard all about Fallon, both in New York and in Washington.

"I've fallen in love with you," Fallon said to Miss Vanderbilt as he talked to her in her dressing room. Gertrude thought he must be kidding. "No," said Fallon, "I'm serious. I've never been so serious. You're what I've been looking for all my life." Gertrude leaned forward and smelled Fallon's breath. "I thought so," she said. "You've been drinking."

By this time, Fallon was used to having his way with women. He began to pout. "You are," said Gertrude Vanderbilt, showing him to the door of the dressing room, "the most conceited man I've ever met in my whole life. I'd be much obliged if I never laid eyes on you again."

Fallon went back to New York talking to himself. Back in the big town, he began to strut. He also began to play the field. But he told Gene McGee that he couldn't get the Vanderbilt girl out of his mind. He said he would have liked to marry her but that naturally his religion forbade divorce. McGee, who knew of Fallon's almost unnatural attachment for his dead mother, asked him if the dancer in any way resembled his mother. "That's the odd part of it," said Fallon. "Not the slightest."

The bond robbery case involving Arnstein took an unexpected turn. The federal authorities decided that they had a better chance of going to bat against Arnstein in Washington than in New York. It turned out that Arnstein had been seen in the nation's capital in company with several men known to have disposed of some of the stolen bonds through a fence there. He had been registered at a hotel under an assumed name and a porter on a New York-Washington train had served him in a drawing room the night before he had registered at the hotel. The case against Arnstein was, in fact, circumstantial, but dangerous to the man, principally because of his unsavory reputation.

At Arnstein's trial, Fallon pulled out the usual stops—confusing the government's witnesses and making them contradict themselves and causing them to create unfavorable impressions on the jurors. Fallon gave the colored porter quite a rough ride on the witness stand. He felt on pretty sure ground there for some of the jurors, he knew, had southern, anti-Negro sentiments. Result: a hung jury.

Fallon was still carrying the torch for Gertie Vanderbilt. Arnstein, an unreasonable character, blamed Fallon's interest in the dancer for the jury disagreeing rather than acquitting him. He started to call Gertie foul names. Fallon told him to take back what he said. Arnstein wouldn't do it. "All right," said Fallon, "you can get another lawyer to handle your next trial."

Arnstein ate crow. He pleaded with Fallon to keep the case. Fallon gave him a withering look and left for New York. He disappeared. Fannie Brice tried to find him and make him reconsider her husband's case. Fallon paid no attention.

One night Fallon went to a performance of the Ziegfeld Follies. He sat down front watching Fannie singing her greatest song, one that was written especially for her to express her feelings about Arnstein—*My Man*. Fallon was moved—but not moved enough to go to bat for Arnstein. Arnstein had said something nasty about the girl Fallon loved and, despite the fact that he had not, as yet, reached first base with Gertrude Vanderbilt, he was completely off his head about the girl.

Eugene McGee handled Arnstein's second trial in Washington. Arnstein was convicted of complicity in the bond robbery and given a jolt in the federal penitentiary.

Arnstein's conviction sent Fallon's stock up. The Broadway wise guys—the characters that Damon Runyon, then a young reporter, was already studying—were more than ever convinced that Bill Fallon was unbeatable.

Eventually, Fallon and Gertie Vanderbilt came to terms. He bought her a handsome house on the upper West Side. If the man was in love with her she was, by now, completely in love with him. The Fallon-Vanderbilt love affair became, in fact, the eighth wonder of the world to Broadway, which didn't know what the other seven wonders were. The pair were always seen around town when Gertie was playing in or near New York. When she was on the road, Fallon was on the road, too, leaving McGee to take care of the firm's business. Mrs. Fallon of course knew about Miss Vanderbilt but she always hoped the affair would run its course.

Fallon was a great believer in the benefits of delaying a trial. There were several reasons for such a belief. Witnesses died, or their memories grew dim or blacked out all together. Evidence deteriorated or, more happily, vanished. The winds of public sentiment shifted.

Fallon had one case dumped in his lap which he immediately set about delaying because public sentiment was so unfavorable to his client. The client was a taxi driver named Schmidt. He owned his own cab and, after driving fares around town, picked up women on his own time. One night, in the back seat of his cab, he injured a woman internally and she bled to death.

Schmidt was held without bail on a charge of murder. The papers wanted Schmidt's scalp and Schmidt screamed for Fallon.

Fallon, learning that Schmidt was well heeled, took the case. He pulled every trick out of the bag to put as much time as possible between the girl's death and the beginning of Schmidt's trial. He would have to appear in another court somewhere on a prior matter. He would have to be out of town on legal business.

Then, to, Fallon would fake illness. Some broken-down doctor would appear in court for him, on the eve of Schmidt's trial, and convince the judge that counsel was practically at death's door. Once Fallon appeared himself to ask for a postponement because of illness. McGee and another man held him up as he appeared before the bar and, in a loud whisper, requested the delay. Court attendants, though used to Fallon's trickery, were afraid the man was in such bad shape that he might not leave the courtroom alive.

A whole year passed. During that time the fires of public resentment against Schmidt lessened in intensity. But Schmidt signed three separate confessions to the murder. The confessions didn't worry Fallon. He would find a way to get around them.

For several days before the trial began, Fallon boned up on medical books. Thus he went into court knowing practically as much about the physical pecularities of the female body as the average doctor —more, in fact, than some medicos.

The state, which had its innings first, produced enough doctors to staff a small hospital to prove the death was murder. By way of conditioning the jury to the line he was to take, Fallon, in cross-examining the state's doctors, continually referred to the girl's death as "this accident." The prosecutor, growing tired of that, began to bellow objections. This was no accident; it was murder. The more the prosecutor objected, the more Fallon referred to "this accident."

When the state's case was in, Fallon pulled his first big surprise. He summoned as a defense witness Dr. Otto H. Schultz, a medical examiner who had helped prepare the case *against* Schmidt. The prosecution objected to the move on a technicality. The prosecution lost.

Fallon played cat-and-mouse with Dr. Schultz. Finally he got Dr. Schultz to admit that the death of the woman could have been accidental.

Next Fallon called on the woman's husband—from whom she had been separated at the time of her death. He inquired of the husband if it were true that his wife had frequently suffered internal hemorrhages. Yes, it was true. "Then you don't believe what the police say," said Fallon, "that your wife died because of any guilty act on the part of the defendant?" No, the husband did not believe such a thing.

Next morning, when court opened, something new had been added—the taxi cab in which the death had occurred. The taxi cab was as essential to the case as a fifth wheel is to a wagon. But it produced a very dramatic effect.

Now Fallon summoned Schmidt to the stand in his own defense. "Now I want you to tell the truth—the whole truth, Mr. Schmidt," said Fallon. "I want you to hold nothing back from these gentlemen of the jury. You are married?" Yes, Schmidt was married. "Then you were unfaithful to your wife in consorting with other women?" Yes, Schmidt had been unfaithful. "Did you love your wife?" Yes, Schmidt had loved his wife. "Did you love any of the other women you consorted with?" No—except one.

"Which one, Mr. Schmidt?" Schmidt had loved the lady he was accused of killing. "You didn't love any of the other women, but you loved the woman you are accused of killing?" "Yes, Mr. Fallon." "Did you kill your wife, Mr. Schmidt?" "No." "Why?" "Well, I love her." "Did you kill the lady who had this *accident*, Mr. Schmidt?" "Why, no. She just bled to death."

Fallon turned to look at the taxi cab. "This is the cab where the accident occurred?" That was the cab. Fallon opened the front door of the cab. "You were here in this front seat with the lady, Mr. Schmidt?" No, Schmidt had been in the back seat. Fallon opened the rear door and peered in. "In *here?*" Yes, in there.

"Who suggested that the two of you go into the back seat?" "I object," yelled the prosecutor. The objection was overruled. Fallon smiled sadly. "I am certain, Mr. Prosecutor," he said, more in sorrow than anger, "that my client is not going

to give the answer you feared he would give." Now to Schmidt: "As I was asking, before we were interrupted, who suggested that you and the lady leave the front seat of your cab and go into the back seat?" "I did," said Schmidt. "You are a very honest man, Mr. Schmidt. And now, may I ask, did the lady object in any way, either by word or action, to your suggestion that the two of you go into the back seat?" "No, she didn't." "Are you sure of that—dead sure she didn't object?" "Yes. Matter of fact, she said she wanted to go to the back seat." Fallon turned to look at the jury and slightly raised his eyebrows.

"Mr. Schmidt, I notice that your right arm seems to pain you. Is something wrong with it?"

"Yes, sir. It was twisted."

"Twisted? By whom?"

"By the people who got the confessions from me."

"Mr. Schmidt, you have made three confessions. Which one resulted in your twisted arm?"

"My arms were twisted *twice.*"

Fallon appeared shocked. "Twice! Then you were constantly mistreated by the police so you would sign those three confessions?"

"All the time."

"In other words, the confessions were forced out of you."

"Yes, sir."

The D. A. was up screaming an objection. "Objection sustained," said the judge. "Why, Your Honor?" asked Fallon. "My client has marks all over his body." "Objection sustained." Fallon told Schmidt to pull up his pants legs. Schmidt's legs were cut and otherwise marked up. The D. A. yelled that the marks had been there at the time of Schmidt's arrest. He objected and the objection was sustained. "What has happened to justice?" Fallon muttered so that only the jurors could hear him.

Fallon had completely knocked the wind out of the state's sails before the prosecutor got to Schmidt. He had revealed the worst about Schmidt, then capitalized on it. Schmidt was acquitted.

Fallon was a great one for keeping an ear to the ground, the better to tune in on anything that he could twist to his financial advantage. He was talking to his friends, Jack Doyle, the Broadway betting commissioner, and John J. McGraw, manager of the Giants, a couple of nights before the 1919 World Series between the Chicago White Sox and the Cincinnati Reds was about to begin at Redland Field in Cincinnati.

"There's somethin' goddamed funny goin' on out there," McGraw said to Fallon. "Jack here'll tell you why." Doyle had become suspicious of all the money that had suddenly appeared in support of the Reds, who were very much the underdog in the series. The betting had originally started out 5-2 in favor of the White Sox, a superb baseball machine, and then, as the opener in the series drew near, Cincinnati partisans were offering even money that their club would take the autumn classic.

"Sounds like something has been fixed," said Fallon.

"You can bet your ass somethin's been fixed," growled McGraw.

The first game at Redland Field seemed to bear out McGraw's and Doyle's suspicions. Eddie Cicotte, the star pitcher of the White Sox, whose most puzzling delivery was the shine ball, didn't have his stuff; the Reds hit him almost at will. The White Sox sluggers—Shoeless Joe Jackson and a couple of others—didn't seem to be giving it the old college try. Sports writers noted that Jackson in particular seemed to be off

balance at the plate. So the White Sox dropped the opener.

The series of 1919 went to the first club that took five games, not four. The Reds took the classic five games to three. The Sox looked like the champs they were in the three games they won. They looked incredibly bad in the five games they lost. It didn't add up.

Fallon saw McGraw when McGraw returned to New York from the series. "If any damned thing was ever fixed," McGraw said to Fallon, "that series out there was."

"Who'd you see that looked suspicious, John?" asked Fallon.

"Well, I saw Abe Attell hanging around the Stinton Hotel in Cincinnati lookin' like the cat that ate the bird."

Abe Attell rang a bell with Fallon. Attell, the onetime flyweight boxing champion of the world, had quit the ring with a quarter of a million dollars but got rid of it fast. It had behooved him to turn a buck practically any way he could. So he had taken to turning quite a few bucks on sure-thing gambling.

The rumor that the World Series had been fixed—that Eddie Cicotte, Shoeless Joe Jackson and several other White Sox players had taken a dive—gained momentum all winter long. It was still very much alive when the baseball season opened in April of 1920. All this while, Fallon was trying to figure a way of putting the big swindle on a paying basis.

Still keeping his ear very close to the ground, Fallon was eventually able to reconstruct just about what had happened. Some weeks before the series had opened, some gamblers had approached Arnold Rothstein, the big-time Broadway gambler, with a fine proposition. The White Sox looked like a shoo-in for the American League pennant and the

Reds ditto for the National League flag. Although the White Sox were the greatest club in baseball, they were torn by internal strife. Many of the star players, including Eddie Cicotte, the star pitcher, were dissatisfied with the coolie wages they were getting. They were so dissatisfied, in fact, that they were sore. "So you see, A. R.," one gambler said to Rothstein, "the boys would listen to a proposition." The proposition that the gamblers had was that Rothstein put up $100,000 as an advance payoff for certain key White Sox players to throw the series, then everybody could get down on Cincinnati to take the series, at very attractive odds, and mop up.

Rothstein asked who had thought up the bright idea. "Abe Attell," said one of the boys. "I don't think I'll put up the money," said Rothstein. Rothstein was smart enough there. He knew that if Attell was behind the plot that he would somehow scrape up the hundred grand, or part of it, someplace else. So why should *he* put up the money?

Rothstein's listening posts advised him that Attell and some of his pals had scraped up enough for the fix. So Rothstein, without actually underwriting the fix, plunged heavily at highly favorable odds.

Learning all this, Fallon now had his angle. He called on Rothstein. "Arnold," he said, "you're in trouble." How? "It's that World Series business." Rothstein said he had had nothing to do with it. "I know," said Fallon. "I know. But that's not what Charley Comiskey thinks." Charles Comiskey, known as the Old Roman, was the tough-minded, tough-talking owner of the White Sox. "Why," Rothstein asked Fallon, plainly scared, "what's Comiskey saying about me?"

"Don't worry about a thing," said Fallon. "But phone me if he starts getting tough."

Old Roman Comiskey came to New York when the White Sox came in to play their first 1920 series with the Yankees. Fallon phoned him at his hotel. "You don't know me," Fallon said to Comiskey, "and who I am doesn't matter. I just love the game of baseball and I thought you'd like to know something about that World Series last fall."

"Keep talking," said the Old Roman.

"You might call to see Arnold Rothstein. He's the man who fixed it."

Next day Fallon got a phone call from Rothstein. Rothstein was frantic. "Get up here right away," he told Fallon. "That man from Chicago is waiting outside my office."

Fallon burst in on Rothstein and Comiskey. "Who are you?" he demanded of the man he had telephoned the day before. Comiskey identified himself. "Well, I'll have to ask you to get out of here." Comiskey said he hadn't a mind to leave. Fallon picked up a telephone. He called the precinct station house. "This is William J. Fallon speaking," he said. "I'm with Mr. Arnold Rothstein. I wish you would send an officer around here immediately to arrest a man for trespassing."

"Wait a minute!" shouted Comiskey, who probably figured he was in enough trouble. "I'll go." Fallon called off the cops and the Old Roman left with his toga tattered.

But the Old Roman was not through. He put private detectives on the trail. As a result several gamblers, associates of Attell in the fix, were picked up in Chicago. They sang. Attell, six White Sox players, and three other gamblers were indicted for conspiracy—then a serious charge in Chicago.

Fallon dropped in to see Rothstein.

"Arnold," he said, "I'm afraid they'll indict you next. You better go out there and appear before the grand jury."

"Are you *crazy?*" said Rothstein.

"On the contrary, you'll be crazy if you don't go out there and demand that the grand jury hear you. Some of those other rats are trying to frame you." Of course nothing of the kind was happening, but after Comiskey's visit, Rothstein thought the roof was caving in. "What'll I *say* to the grand jury?" asked Rothstein. "Just tell them the whole truth. Say you were approached by men you didn't know and that you decided not to go into the thing because if it was going to be fixed you could clean up without incriminating yourself."

"*Say,*" said Rothstein, "I see what you mean."

"The truth, Arnold," said Fallon, "is always the best policy." And now, Fallon added, he was a little short. Could Rothstein advance him a little matter of $10,000 or so? Rothstein was glad to oblige.

Rothstein made quite a hit in Chicago with the jurors. The man's honesty appealed to the jurors. So he returned to New York with a clean bill of health.

Now Fallon decided he could pick up some extra money from Abe Attell. He contacted Attell and cautioned the little man that he was in desperate need of good counsel. Attell agreed. "Fine," said Fallon, "I think I can square that matter out in Chicago for about $15,000."

Attell handed over the money and Fallon left town for a few days. During his absence, Attell was arrested by the New York authorities at the request of the Chicago authorities, to be held pending extradition to face the conspiracy indictment. Fallon, who had apparently been very busy while out of town, now returned and pulled one out of the hat.

He went before a judge and, demanding that Attell be released, claimed that the Abe Attell who was arrested was not the same Abe Attell who had been indicted in Chicago.

"On what grounds do you base such an assertion?" asked the judge.

"Either there are two Abe Attells, Your Honor," said Fallon, "or somebody in Chicago *posed* as my client."

"What proof have you to back up your assertion?" asked the judge.

Fallon said he could produce a Chicago man who had gone before the grand jury in Chicago and contributed to the indictment of Abe Attell simply by identifying a picture of the man he said he had worked with to fix the series.

So Abe Attell was brought before the judge and Fallon produced the man who had testified before the Chicago grand jury. "No," said the Chicagoan, "that ain't the man I worked with on the series. That ain't him at all." So Abe Attell was never extradicted to Chicago and the case against him collapsed of its own weight. The other conspirators got off, too, but the guilty players were banned for life from organized baseball and Judge K. M. Landis became baseball's first commissioner.

Precisely what went on between the time Fallon approached Abe Attell to become his counsel and the day Attell was pointed out by the Chicagoan as *not* the Abe Attell who had fixed the series has never come to light. But we can *guess,* can't we?

Fallon was perhaps the first of several smart New York lawyers who have pulled what some legal strategists call the smell trick in a courtroom. He was defending a fierce-looking big Russian who was accused of arson. The defendant had a record that was somewhat against him. He had been convicted twice previously of setting fire to furniture stores he had operated and attempting to collect insurance on the fires. And now here he was with his liberty on the line for his third try at the jackpot.

The whole case, by the time Fallon got through twisting it around, revolved around some rags that a fireman had come across in the burning building. A fireman got on the stand and testified that the rags had been soaking wet and that when he had smelled them he had smelled kerosene. Fallon just sat there, eyeing the fireman as the man testified.

When it came Fallon's time to cross-examine the witness, he approached the fireman in what seemed to some veteran courtroom attachés as a deceptively friendly manner. "You are, I suppose," Fallon began, "an expert on smells."

"Well," answered the fireman, "I kind of have to be. You got to look out for suspicious smells when you go out on a fire so's to make sure it ain't incendiary."

"I see," said Fallon. "And so when you went out to fight this particular blaze you were looking for suspicious smells. Is that correct?"

"Well, kind of."

"You knew, of course, that the defendant in this action had been convicted of arson twice before?"

"Yes, I knew that."

"You were aware of that fact when the bell rang in the firehouse and you found out where the fire was."

"No. Not when the bell rang, but when I got to the fire."

"At any rate, you were *suspicious* that this particular fire might have been of incendiary origin when you got to it to put it out?"

"Yes, sir."

"That being the case, you naturally looked around for some evidence to corroborate your suspicions."

"Naturally. Yes, sir."

"And so you picked up these rags which you say were soaked in this highly inflammable fluid."

"Yes, sir."

"You smelled the rags and decided they were soaked with kerosene?"

"Right."

"I notice those rags were not produced in evidence. Why is that, may I ask?"

"Well, I dropped them to go on fighting the fire and by the time I got back to where I found them they had been burned up."

"But you're sure you're not *lying* about those rags. You really found such rags when you first reached the blaze."

Of course the fireman was not lying.

"All right," said Fallon, "I'll take your word for it that you are telling the truth. You *look* like a truthful man. But now I want to ask you something else. Are you sure that that was kerosene—and not *water*—that you smelled on those rags?"

The fireman seemed puzzled that Fallon should ask him such a question. Fallon repeated the question. Certainly the fireman was sure. He certainly knew the difference between water and kerosene when he smelled the two. "You're *absolutely* sure about that?" said Fallon. The fireman was absolutely sure.

"Then," said Fallon, "you would not object to *proving* to these fine gentlemen here"—Fallon pointed to the jurors—"that you can tell the difference between water and kerosene when you smell them." No, the fireman would not object; he was, in fact, slightly amused. "Do not take this matter lightly," said Fallon. "A man's liberty depends on whether you can tell the difference when you smell kerosene and water."

Fallon went back to counsel table and produced five bottles, each filled with liquid. The bottles were numbered 1, 2,

3, 4 and 5. He took the cork out of bottle No. 1 and handed the bottle to the witness. "Smell that," he said, "and tell me what's in it." The fireman took a smell. "Kerosene," he said. "Take a *good* smell," said Fallon. "I want you to be certain that you do not make a mistake." The fireman took a deep smell. "Kerosene," he repeated.

Now Fallon handed the witness bottle No. 2 and had him repeat the test. "Kerosene," said the fireman. The witness said that bottles 3, 4 and 5 also contained kerosene. When Fallon took bottle No. 5 from the fireman he put it to his lips and took a drink of it. Now he held the bottle to the nose of each juror. "Gentlemen," he said to the jurors, "the contents of this bottle do not taste like kerosene to me. And I am very sure they do not smell like kerosene to you." He paused to savor the drama of the situation. "And now I'll tell you why the contents of this bottle do not taste or smell like kerosene. This bottle—this bottle that the gentleman on the witness stand would have you believe contains kerosene—doesn't contain kerosene at all. It contains water. When you get into the jury room I wish you would all help yourselves to a taste of its contents. If what you taste in the slightest resembles kerosene I think it is your duty to convict my client. If what you taste is water, then it is your duty to acquit my client."

Of course the client was acquitted. What Fallon had done, simply, was to fill the fireman's smelling apparatus with kerosene fumes by having the man inhale deeply of the first four bottles. Then, when he whiffed the water, the kerosene fumes from the previous four bottles were still in his nostrils and he thought the water was kerosene.

The early twenties in New York was the golden age for the Bucket Boys. They were the fellows who operated bucket shops, or crooked brokerage houses. There was no Securities and Exchange Commission to regulate brokerage houses in the twenties and the way the boobs were taken by the sharpers was really something awful.

All a crooked outfit needed to make a quick quarter of a million or so was an office somewhere and a few telephones. A squad of sharpers would sit at the telephones, systematically go through the telephone directory and, in golden tones, call people all day long. They would pose as customer's men from a respectable brokerage and take orders for listed stocks at the market price. The gimmick was that they didn't buy the ordered stock, but just took the customer's money and held it in the hope that the stock would go down. Then they'd have a profit of the price difference instead of a lousy brokerage fee. If the stock went up, they'd talk the client into reinvesting in some other stock until that went down —for a while a very profitable enterprise.

Finally, however, the federal people began to bring down a few of the bucketeers and that's where Fallon got into the act. He added to his repertoire the defense of about half the city's crooked brokers.

There were two ways to get a bucketeer off the federal hook: confusing the jury so that the least it would bring in would be a disagreement, or purchasing a juror. In the light of subsequent events, it would seem that Fallon purchased quite a few jurors. Newspaper reporters, not to say federal judges and prosecutors, began to take notice of the imposing number of eleven-to-one verdicts Fallon got when representing a bucketeer. The New York *American* made one reference to him as Eleven-to-One Fallon.

When, however, there was something

less than an open-and-shut case against a bucketeer, Fallon tried for an acquittal. He had quite a bag of tricks in trying for acquittals. In one typical case, which rotated around a sucker identifying a bucketeer on the witness stand, Fallon simply had his client completely alter his appearance. He put the man on a severe diet and reduced him from 200 pounds to 140. He changed the color of the defendant's hair from brown to black, mixed with gray. He had the man shave off a naturally imposing moustache and wear needless glasses so thick that they looked like magnifying glasses. To top off everything, he sent the defendant to a dramatic coach and vested him with a southern accent.

After the sucker had testified for the government, Fallon cross-examined him at length about the appearance of the villain who had bilked him out of his life's savings. The sucker described the villain as a moustached brown-haired man weighing about 200 pounds who talked like a typical New Yorker. "And did he wear eyeglasses?" asked Fallon. "No." "You're *sure* about that?" Positively.

When Fallon put the defendant on the stand, the man got up from the counsel table and began to walk toward the witness chair. He walked into the counsel table and fell over it. "Why," said Fallon, "you're so nervous you forgot to put on your glasses. There's nothing to be nervous about. The complainant in this case certainly wasn't talking about *you*."

So the villain put on the thick-lensed glasses and took the stand, and made a categorical denial of the charge against him in moss-and-honeysuckle tones. Then Fallon asked the sucker to stand up. "Is this the man you say took your money?" he asked the sucker, pointing to the defendant. "No," said the sucker.

Acquittal.

In the case of another bucketeer, Fallon brought his defendant into court on a stretcher with a doctor and nurse in attendance. The federal prosecutor protested that the defendant was faking. Fallon had half a dozen doctors testify on the stand that the crook had a few months to live—if he was lucky. The government prosecutor demanded that *his* doctors examine the defendant. The Fallon doctors, men who were hardly burdened by adherence to the Hippocratic oath, had dosed the man with drugs that had made his heart beat almost twice as fast as normal, and coached the crook in how to simulate symptoms of half a dozen fatal ailments. The government doctors had to admit that the defendant was at death's door. It took the jury almost ten minutes to acquit the man.

Fallon's eleven-to-one verdicts in the cases of bucketeers eventually aroused the suspicion of William Randolph Hearst's New York *American*. So the Hearst paper assigned a flock of reporters to shadow the jurors who had thrown the verdicts into disagreement. The boys dug up a man named Rendig who seemed to be unexplainably flush with money. Rendig had cast the sole dissenting vote when a jury wanted to convict two partners in a bucket shop who were represented by Fallon in federal court. The *American* reporters turned their dope over to the United States Attorney and Rendig confessed that Fallon had paid him $5,000 to hang the jury.

Thus it was that William J. Fallon went on trial in the summer of 1924 at the age of thirty-six. The trial was looked upon by a sweating populace as something of a circus. Gene McGee, Fallon's partner, was the counsel of record in the case but when things got under way, Fallon personally took over. He had been hitting the bottle hard for some weeks before the trial but Gertie Vanderbilt got him to lay off at least until the trial was over.

Fallon, dressed in a new blue suit and wearing a new burgundy necktie, was his old self in the courtroom—the actor responding to the stimulus of an appreciative audience. He cocked his head, folded his arms across his chest, and bowed from the waist as the judge spoke to him.

The crux of the whole case was, of course, the testimony of Rendig, the purchased juror. The money that had been paid to Rendig had reached him by way of two checks, which in turn had gone through half a dozen persons before Rendig endorsed them. Fallon made a great deal of that. Rendig's receipt of the checks had been part of a plot—a plot by William Randolph Hearst to ruin him. And why had Hearst tried to plot his ruin?

Fallon pulled another spectacular one out of the hat. He took the stand in his own defense. He began to question himself.

Hearst had tried to ruin him, Fallon said, because he had gone to Mexico and there dug up birth certificates of twins that Hearst had fathered through a certain motion-picture actress. The jurors sat there with their mouths open, inhaling the scandal.

The government's prosecutor screamed objections until he practically wore himself out. The Mexico business, true or false, had nothing to do with the jury purchasing yet Fallon made it, rather than the issue at bar, the big thing. He made so much of it, in fact, that the jurors were thinking more about Hearst and the movie actress than about Fallon. One of Hearst's editors, shaken at the testimony, telephoned Hearst at the Hearst ranch in California and told him

what Fallon had said. "Well," said Hearst, "you won't have to think twice about what your lead headline will be tomorrow."

Then, of a steaming midsummer morning, William J. Fallon got up to address the jury—to plead for his professional life. That was the day he made his great, tear-jerking summation on his own behalf—one of the most dramatic summations in American courtroom history. It wasn't altogether *what* Fallon said in his summation; much of the power was in *how* he said it—the tone of voice, the facial expressions, the dramatic gestures. Spectators who were in that courtroom that torrid day more than a third of a century ago never, to their dying day, will forget the performance of the great mouthpiece pleading for his professional existence. And then, at the end of his summation, when Fallon stood there, with his head bowed and his arms at his side, a strange stillness enveloped the entire courtroom.

That night, after the prosecution had summed up to the jury and the judge had charged it, the jurors brought in their verdict. *Not guilty.* Fallon, sitting there waiting for the verdict, jumped to his feet, rushed over to the jury box, and shook the hand of each juror. Then, on his way out of the jury room, he walked over to Nat Ferber, one of the *American* reporters who had helped build up the jury-bribing case against him. "Nat," Fallon whispered, "so help me God, *I'll never bribe another juror.*"

Fallon went to the Polo Grounds next day to watch the game between the Giants and the Reds. He sat in a box near the Giants' dugout and was practically mobbed. He was the town's hero because New York has always had an affinity for Broadway-type characters who are a little sharper than the law.

But now a curious thing happened. The firm of Fallon & McGee, which had expected to do a big business when and if Fallon was acquitted, found itself getting the old go-by. The anticipated rush of clients just failed to materialize. Clients were afraid to ask Fallon to defend them. They were afraid that Hearst would still be gunning for him. That being so, he wouldn't dare pull any tricks. And Fallon without tricks would be like a juggler without Indian clubs.

Fallon, strapped for money, sold the house he and his wife lived in for a fraction of its worth and the couple moved to a small apartment in the Oxford Hotel. He began to hit the bottle so steadily that he was drunk more often than he was sober. He went around town, babbling that David Belasco was going to make a big stage star of him. But by now Belasco, too, was laying off him. Gertrude Vanderbilt gave him money now and then and then went to Europe to fill theatrical engagements.

Some of Fallon's legal enemies—men he had beaten in the courtrooms—sold the Bar Association on the idea that it would be a good move to disbar Fallon. But Fallon, like a phoenix rising from its own ashes, became his old self again—just long enough to argue successfully before the Bar Association that he should not be disbarred.

Once in a while, Fallon would latch on to a case in which he defended a bootlegger. But by now he was so shot with booze that he began to flub the cases and a couple of his bootlegger clients went to Atlanta. He was through but he didn't realize it. The old vanity was still there. He had done it once; he could do it again.

His friend McGraw threw one in his lap—the case of a Giant player accused of participating in a fixed game. Fallon appeared before Baseball Commissioner Landis to argue the player's case. Landis handed down his decision: the banishment of the player from organized baseball.

One day in the summer of 1926—two years after he had gotten his acquittal in the juror-bribing case—Fallon was holed up in a midtown hotel room. There was a knock on the door. Fallon, thinking it was a bootlegger delivering another quart, opened the door. A jealous woman friend, not a bootlegger, was standing at the door. She, too, was carrying liquid in a bottle—acid. She threw it in Fallon's face.

Taken to a hospital, Fallon was seriously burned. Some of the acid had gotten into one eye. It was thought that Fallon would lose the sight of the eye. He had a few dollars in his pocket. He bribed an attendant to go out and bring him in a bottle of whisky. He got high right there in the hospital room.

Fallon got out of the hospital, not only with the sight of the eye saved, but with hardly a scar to show for the dose of acid. "It's the luck of the Irish," he told a reporter.

Fallon, who was occasionally stricken by remorse because of the shabby treatment he had given his wife over the years, vowed when he left the hospital that he would never cheat on her again. The woman believed him. They were together, in their apartment in the Oxford, when the New Year of 1927 came in. "*This* year will be different," Fallon said to his wife. "I've been through the worst. And after all, I'm only thirty-nine."

But Fallon's past had more than caught up with him. His shady legal work through the years, his failure to live up to the hopes that his mother had had for

him, his failure as a husband, his failure
even as a lover—all those elements had
combined to drive him to drink. And,
once he became an alcoholic, he couldn't
pull himself together sufficiently to make
up for his past mistakes, even had he sincerely wanted to.

And so, one day in late April of 1927,
William Joseph Fallon, the man who just
missed genuine greatness, died of a gas-
tric hemorrhage and a heart attack in his

rooms in the Oxford Hotel. Hardly any
of the fair-weather friends attended the
funeral—which was par for the Broadway
course. The man who had tossed thousands around like confetti didn't leave
even enough to buy a coffin. It didn't
come out until later that the handsome
coffin that Fallon went away in, dressed
in blue serge and wearing a burgundy
necktie, was purchased by that rugged
Irish friend named John J. McGraw.

Philadelphia's Murdering Faith Healer

Introducing Doctor Bolber, the faith healer who made the Quaker City lose faith in faith healers—the behind-the-scenes account of the hilarious and murderous goings-on of an arsenic specialist who wrote criminal history.

Doctor Morris Bolber, who functioned as a faith healer in the Italian district of South Philadelphia back in the Thirties, could never quite bring himself to subscribe to the theory that murder will out. This attitude of the doctor, who wasn't a physician at all but who just called himself one, sprang in part from unique conditions right in his own bailiwick. Bolber, a man whose ear was never very far from the ground, was aware of three specific instances wherein ladies, for a variety of reasons, had poisoned their spouses with nobody—or *practically* nobody—being the wiser.

The Philadelphia Police Department, without realizing it, or in fact caring much, was lending an assist to this shocking state of affairs. The Department in the Thirties was honeycombed by grafters from City Hall down to the flatfeet on the beat with the result that many honest cops were usually so preoccupied by worry over getting the rug pulled from under them that they didn't notice what was going on among the citizens. Thus a murderer who was sly enough not to throw his victim out with the garbage or appear in the New Year's Day Mummers Parade with somebody's head stuck to a broomstick stood in a fair way to go unmolested indefinitely. And, for a man who was *really* clever, the field of pre-meditated homicide offered opportunity practically beyond limit.

What set Doctor Bolber to brooding over all this was the fact that he wasn't doing so well at the bank. The pickings in the faith-healing field had, since the Great Depression of 1929, been slim. The faith healer's patients had either lost faith in him or couldn't afford to be healed.

The doctor, with a wife and a houseful of offspring to support, had gone into a side line—selling bottles of stale ginger ale spiked with saltpeter to women whose husbands had strayed from the connubial couch. The saltpeter had slowed down the husbands but it hadn't slowed down a parade of creditors to the doctor's domicile and office in a faded-red brick house on the corner of Ninth Street and Moyamensing Avenue, in the heart of the Quaker City's Italian district.

One morning in February, 1932, Bolber was in a state of acute depression as he sat in a gloomy front room that he used for professional purposes, against a background of scuffed leather volumes on fortune telling and faith healing while a howling wind rattled the windowpanes. The faith healer looked somewhat incongruous in such a setting, for he was an affluent-looking little man of forty-two, neatly barbered, alert of eye and sharply turned out. As he sat there in his office, railing at the fates, somebody pulled the bell at the front door and Bolber rushed to a window to see whether it was friend or foe—patient or creditor.

The caller was a new patient—a moderately attractive woman of about thirty, the wife of a man named Anthony Giacobbe, who ran a dry-goods store. She had come to get a bottle of that stuff she had been hearing about—the stuff that slowed men down.

Mrs. Giacobbe told Bolber that her husband was spending so much time and money on drink and other women that he was letting his business go to pot. "We're even having a hard time keeping up his insurance," said Mrs. Giacobbe.

"Insurance?" said Bolber, all ears. "How much insurance does your husband carry?"

"Ten thousand dollars' worth."

Doctor Bolber was visited by an inspiration. He gave Mrs. Giacobbe a bottle of stale ginger ale spiked not with saltpeter but with an aphrodisiac strong enough to transform a broken-down wreck into a howling wolf. "Come back in a couple of weeks," said the doctor, "and let me know if this has any effect on your husband."

As soon as Mrs. Giacobbe left, Bolber, according to an admission he was one day to make to the cops, hustled around the corner to a hole-in-the-wall tailor shop run by a friend of his named Paul Petrillo. This Petrillo, a chubby man in his thirties, with heavily greased black hair and the smell of Sen Sen on his breath, had for some time been collaborating in a unique arrangement with the faith healer. Petrillo made free suits for Doctor Bolber in return for the names of women married to men who were neglecting their home work. Petrillo was one day to be revealed in a courtroom as a

gent with phenomenal amorous powers.

This particular day, when the fraudulent faith healer slipped the wolfish tailor the name of Mrs. Giacobbe, something new had been added. Petrillo was not only to seduce the lady; he was to pretend to fall in love with her and propose marriage. "But what about the husband?" Petrillo asked. "Never mind about him," said Bolber. "Just get the wife nuts about you and I'll take care of the husband."

"How?"

"Kill him."

"But why knock the guy off, Doc?" asked Petrillo. "What's the angle?"

"Insurance. He's got ten thousand dollars' worth of insurance. We can get half of it from the wife. That'll give us twenty-five hundred apiece."

Petrillo was all for it. In 1932 twenty-five hundred dollars was a bundle. "How you goin' to knock the guy off, Doc?"

"Poison," said Bolber. "I got a poison that'll fool any doctor."

"What's the name of it?"

The substance Bolber had in mind was conium, a lethal herb known to the layman as hemlock—the stuff that was in the mickey that did in Socrates, the Greek philosopher, in 500 B.C. The attractive feature of conium, which was easily disguised in food and drink, was that when it was administered to a patient suffering from any one of a wide variety of diseases it caused the ailment to worsen materially.

Next morning Petrillo sprayed himself with perfume and, posing as a book salesman, called on Mrs. Giacobbe after her philandering husband had left for his place of business.

In a couple of weeks, Mrs. Giacobbe called on the faith healer again. The stuff that he had given her to slow down her husband had had no effect. "But I don't care," said Mrs. Giacobbe. "I've met somebody else."

"And you're in love with him?"

"Yes."

Bolber sat in his office half the night writing a dramatic act, complete with instructions for gestures, by which Petrillo was to propose marriage to Mrs. Giacobbe. Next day, after Giacobbe, the marked man, was away at business, Petrillo called on the wife. On bended knee, he professed his undying love for the lady. "Let's get married and run away somewheres," he said, beating his chest.

"But what about my husband?" asked Mrs. Giacobbe.

"Something could happen to him."

Mrs. Giacobbe had never thought of such a happy eventuality. "What could happen?" she asked.

"We could take all his clothes off when he comes home drunk some night and he could get pneumonia from layin' there naked with the cold wind blowin' right on him."

A few nights later Bolber was sitting in his office listening to Petrillo relating developments. "Giacobbe didn't go to work today," the tailor was telling the faith healer. "Me and his wife stripped him when he come home drunk last night. He woke up with an awful cold this morning." Mrs. Giacobbe had gotten her husband thoroughly starched again that night. "So we stripped him again a little while ago," Petrillo went on. "The weatherman says it's gonna be down to ten above tonight. When Giacobbe wakes up tomorrow morning he ought to be practically blue."

Next night Petrillo reported to Bolber that Giacobbe had contracted pneumonia. The family doctor had been called and had prescribed two kinds of liquid medicine. "Good," said the faith healer.

"Tell Mrs. Giacobbe to come around with that medicine."

The patient quickly began to come apart at the seams. The bona fide doctor wasn't surprised. "Your husband was a heavy drinker," he explained to Mrs. Giacobbe. "Heavy drinkers often fail to survive pneumonia."

After the funeral, Bolber sent for the widow. There would be a fee, he explained, for his doctoring up that medicine—a fee of half that insurance money. Mrs. Giacobbe, not too bright and happy to be rid of her faithless spouse so that she could marry the ardent tailor, willingly forked over the five grand—in cash.

It wasn't long before Mrs. Giacobbe appeared in Bolber's office greatly distraught. Petrillo had banked his romantic fires. The doctor made a ticking sound and shook his head sadly. The male animal was an unpredictable beast. There was nothing, he feared, he could do to help the lady.

One night, after office hours, the faith healer suggested to Petrillo that they get busy on another husband. Where, Petrillo asked, would they find a man carrying enough insurance to make the enterprise worthwhile?

"We'll insure somebody ourselves," said Bolber.

The doctor went to his card file. "Now here's a woman named Lorenzo whose husband is a roofer. We could insure the husband for say ten thousand dollars, with double indemnity in case of an accident, and then get him pushed off a roof."

How, Petrillo inquired, would they get Lorenzo insured without his knowing it? And who would push him off the roof?

Bolber ignored the questions. "You got a cousin," he said to Petrillo. "The one that was pinched a couple of years ago for counterfeiting."

"Oh, you mean Little Herman. Herman Petrillo."

"That's the fellow. He used to be an amateur actor, didn't he?"

"Yeah, before the Secret Service pinched him for that bum money. He used to act in church plays."

"What's he doing now?"

"He's a spaghetti salesman."

"Get him here," said the faith healer.

Herman Petrillo, the ex-counterfeiter, was a foxy-looking toy man given to loud checked suits and overcoats with belts in the back. Doctor Bolber decided that Little Herman would blend perfectly into his scheme.

Bolber explained to Little Herman that he was to pose as Lorenzo, the roofer, in taking out an insurance policy. Then, after the policy was issued, Herman would contrive, by some method Bolber would think up, to shove the real Lorenzo off a roof. Little Herman, a real stinker, was simply mad about the plot.

Paul Petrillo, carefully coached by Bolber, assumed the role of a canvasser and called at Lorenzo's home one day when Lorenzo was up on a roof in a distant part of the city. A few weeks after laying the groundwork, Paul asked Mrs. Lorenzo if she would marry him. The lady said she would be glad to except that she was already married. "But supposin' something should happen to your husband," said Petrillo. "Like what?" asked the seduced wife. "Like him fallin' off a roof." Mrs. Lorenzo, who caught on quickly, liked the idea.

Now Doctor Bolber instructed Little Herman to telephone to the Philadelphia offices of the Prudential Insurance Company, palm himself off as Lorenzo, and ask that a salesman come to the Lorenzo home—next day at noon, when the real Lorenzo would be up on a roof somewhere.

When the salesman called, there was Mrs. Lorenzo, the faithless wife, and Little Herman, the stand-in husband, looking for all the world like what they weren't, applying for a ten thousand dollar policy with double indemnity for accidental death and with cash in hand to pay for the first quarterly premium.

A Prudential doctor called the following day, found Herman to be a sound actuarial risk, and in due time the policies arrived in the mail and Mrs. Lorenzo intercepted them.

Doctor Bolber began to follow the real Lorenzo around, the better to spot some plausible way of striking up an acquaintanceship with the man. He fell into converse with the roofer in a bar one night. Thus he discovered that Lorenzo was mad for French post cards.

Doctor Bolber acquired a supply of the French art and gave the stuff to Little Herman. Late one afternoon Little Herman buttonholed Lorenzo when the marked man came down off a roof and sold him some cards. "Get a hold of me any time you got more of this stuff," Lorenzo told Herman.

Doctor Bolber, too cagey to be hasty, allowed a few months to elapse before giving Little Herman the nod to take care of Lorenzo. Next day Little Herman appeared on a roof that Lorenzo was repairing. He had a new batch of French post cards for the roofer.

"Gee," said Lorenzo, "these are pippins. How much." The question was to remain unanswered. Little Herman, looking around to make sure nobody was observing him, gave the actuarial risk a shove and in a twinkling Lorenzo was plunging eight stories to the street.

Six months passed before Doctor Bolber summoned Little Herman again.

"You ever go fishin'?" Bolber asked. No, Little Herman didn't know anything about fishing. Bolber told him to bone up on the sport and to buy himself some tackle. "We've found a man by the name of Fierenza who's got five thousand dollars in double indemnity already," the faith healer said. "He fishes every Saturday afternoon in the Schuylkill River. Your cousin is going to make love to his wife."

One fine Saturday afternoon, when Fierenza was about to go out in a rented rowboat, who just happened along but Little Herman. Actor that he was, Little Herman, carrying bait and tackle and wearing hip boots and a battered hat bright with artificial flies, looked more like an Izaak Walton devotee than a real fisherman.

"You goin' out in that there boat alone?" Little Herman asked Fierenza. "Yeah," said Fierenza. "How about me and you sharin' the boat and we'll split the expense," suggested Little Herman. The diminutive fiend patted his hip pocket. "I got a bottle with me, too."

Out on the water, in a cove where nobody could see them, Little Herman asked Fierenza if he could swim. "No," said Fierenza.

"Not a stroke?"

"Nope."

"Hey," said Little Herman, pointing to something behind Fierenza. "What's that?"

"What's what?"

"There. *Behind* you."

Fierenza turned and there was a shove, a cry and a splash. Little Herman, who could swim, dove off the other side of the boat. Then, good and wet, he climbed back in the boat again and rowed ashore. There he acted the role of heart-broken friend. "It's all my fault," he said. "I should of saved him."

With three victims—Giacobbe, the dry-goods merchant; Lorenzo, the roofer and Fierenza, the fisherman—disposed of within a year and a half, for an over-all take of twenty-five thousand dollars, Doctor Bolber saw nothing ahead but a golden future. "There's no telling," he said to the Petrillo cousins while the three sat around the faith healer's office over a jug of Chianti one night in the summer of 1933, "where a thing like this could end. Why, we could establish branches all over the country—like Household Finance."

Doctor Bolber, having his ear to the ground, had gotten a rumble about a most remarkable woman in North Philadelphia—a woman named Carino Favato who was known in her own bailiwick as the Witch. The Witch, who was a widow, was in the same profession as Doctor Bolber—faith healing, saltpeter and general mumbo jumbo. She got rid of husbands for wives—not for insurance money but just to get rid of them. This impressed Bolber as a wanton waste of golden opportunity and that was why, on one hot summer night, he journeyed across town to have converse with Mrs. Favato.

One look at the Witch convinced Doctor Bolber why she had taken on that appellation. The woman, in her early forties, was strictly out of a bad dream —short, squat, with a hooked nose and a face that reminded Bolber of a batch of fresh dough with two currants for eyes.

The Witch, it developed, had heard of Bolber and so, since the two immediately understood each other, they dispensed with the preliminaries and began to talk shop. What, Bolber inquired, did the Witch use to poison errant husbands?

"Best stuff, arsenic," said the Witch. "What you usin'?"

"Conium."

"What that?"

"It's from the carrot family. It's also known as hemlock. It's what they used to poison Socrates with."

"Who?"

"Socrates."

"Philadelphia man?"

Doctor Bolber asked the Witch if she was married. "Had five husbands," said the Witch. "Poisoned three."

"And did you collect insurance on the ones you poisoned?"

The Witch nodded.

Now Bolber explained how simple it was to collect insurance on the husbands of other women. The Witch was fascinated and craved details. Bolber supplied them. "Jesus," said the Witch. "Look all the money I could made if I think of that."

Bolber patted the Witch's hand. "Never mind," he assured her. "We'll make up for lost time."

The Witch went to *her* card file. A hapless janitor named Dominic Petrino emerged from the file as a sound prospect. Petrino's wife had been buying saltpeter from the Witch for some time without appreciable results.

The faith healer explained to the Witch that Paul Petrillo, the wolfish tailor, would romance the janitor's wife and condition her for the plot. Then Little Herman would pose as the janitor for the benefit of the insurance people and when the real janitor was bumped off the Witch would be cut in on the take. "Good," said the Witch. "While you doin' that I be lookin' for more husbands."

After Paul Petrillo had set things up in the Petrino home, Little Herman, the actor, hovered in the wings, ready to go on stage and essay one of his finest roles. One day when the real janitor was at work, Little Herman, dressed like a jani-tor, and smelling like one, sat around the Petrino flat with the faithless wife when a salesman for the Prudential Life Insurance Company called.

Herman said he would like to take out a ten thousand dollar policy with double indemnity. The salesman inquired how a janitor could keep up the payments on such a big policy.

Doctor Bolber, the sly one, had prepared well in advance for that very question. He had fixed up a couple of fake books that made it appear that the janitor had twelve thousand dollars in savings. "Me and my wife here turn over houses," Little Herman explained, meaning that the couple dabbled in real estate. That made everything all right.

It was two days later, when a doctor for the Prudential called to give the stand-in applicant a physical examination that Little Herman had a few bad moments. This same sawbones had examined Little Herman more than a year before, when Little Herman had posed as Lorenzo, the doomed roofer.

"Haven't I seen you someplace before?" asked the doctor. "Never seen you in my life, Doc," said Little Herman. "But I could swear that I've examined you for insurance before." "You couldn't of, Doc. I ain't never taken out insurance before." The doctor ascribed the whole thing to a case of mistaken identity, examined Little Herman, found him a sound actuarial risk, and the policy was issued.

A few months passed. Then Doctor Bolber gave the nod for the end of the real janitor. Petrino worked in a tenement house. The faith healer handed Little Herman a monkey wrench, instructed him to pose as an inspector for the gas company, sneak up behind Petrino when the janitor was at the top of a flight of steep stairs, and crown him with the wrench. "It'll look," Bolber explained, "like that janitor just fell down the stairs and fractured his skull."

One night, a couple of weeks later, Doctor Bolber again crossed the city to pay another visit to the Witch. He handed her five hundred dollars for her cut of the Petrino take. "Who else you got for us?" he asked.

The Witch had a fishmonger named Luigi Primavera. It was the same evil story all over again, with Paul Petrillo romancing the wife and Little Herman Petrillo standing in for the doomed man —but with a new twist. Doctor Bolber, warming up to his work decided to take a more personal hand in matters. "I'm going to kill this man Primavera personally," he informed the Petrillo cousins. "How, Doc?" asked Little Herman. "I'm going to run over him with an automobile," said the faith healer.

So one rainy day, while Primavera was hawking fish on a lonely street in South Philadelphia, Doctor Bolber, at the wheel of a car with a souped-up motor and fake license plates, waited until the victim left his wagon to knock on some doors. Then the doctor stepped on the gas, ran up on a sidewalk and sent poor Primavera and his fish flying.

Late that night, the doctor sat in his office reading the early editions of the morning papers. The papers carried the story of the hit-and-runner who had killed the fishmonger. Some people living on the street where the fatality had occurred had told the cops that the driver of the car, whose description fitted that of Bolber, had apparently been deliberate in running Primavera down.

The faith healer sat in his office most of that night, drinking and thinking. Just as daylight was peeping through the blinds in his office he reached a momentous decision. Henceforth he would eschew accidental deaths in favor of natural ones. True, a natural death paid only half the insurance money that a double-indemnity one did, but it was less likely to excite suspicion.

Next Doctor Bolber was visited by an inspiration that was to prove a bright milestone in the history of premeditated homicide. He decided that a canvas bag, filled with about twenty pounds of sand, would, if brought down on a man's head, render the victim temporarily unconscious. Repeated additional blows would induce a cerebral hemorrhage and a sand bag would leave no outward traces of having been applied.

Doctor Bolber's sand-bag technique proved just as successful as he predicted it would be. For three solid years, from 1934 to 1937, Paul and Little Herman, working stealthily under the faith healer's supervision, traveled throughout the Quaker City, respectively romancing wives and sandbagging sleeping husbands. The Witch proved to be a most valuable scout for the satanic doctor.

By January of 1937, some five years after Mrs. Anthony Giacobbe had first appeared in Doctor Bolber's crummy office asking for some saltpeter for her errant spouse, the faith healer had given the nod for an officially estimated fifty killings. By now Bolber's faded red-brick home at the corner of Ninth Street and Moyamensing Avenue had taken on a new look by an expensive mid-town decorating outfit. The Petrillo boys were doing splendidly at the bank and chasing around town in expensive automobiles. The Witch, who was a baseball fan, devoted to the fortunes of the Athletics, was to be seen regularly in a field box at Shibe Park, eating hot dogs by the half dozen, spilling mustard on expensive satin dresses, and invoking the wrath of the nether regions on the players of visiting clubs. Everybody was fat and rich. But were they happy? You just bet they were.

So far as the Philadelphia Police Department went, Doctor Bolber might very well still have been sitting there in his office in South Philly today, giving the lethal nod to the Petrillo boys. Only one cop in the entire department—a smart and honest dick by the name of Sam Ricardo—got a whiff of what was going on. Ricardo, like Doctor Bolber, was a fellow who kept an ear to the ground. Thus, in the early months of 1937, he heard the first faint rumbles of a murder-for-insurance ring at work. Ricardo didn't hear any names, just that there were, and had been for some time, some not-so-brotherly goings on in the City of Brotherly Love.

Detective Ricardo went to his superiors and asked to be assigned to investigate the rumors he had heard. His superiors looked at Ricardo as if the man were not quite bright. So Ricardo was assigned to some pedestrian investigations while Doctor Bolber continued on his satanic way.

It was in a jail house, of all places, where something developed that was, in the final analysis, to trip up Doctor Bolber. There was a fellow named Harrison, not a bad jake, who was doing a stretch in a workhouse for a minor offense. Harrison put his time in durance vile to good advantage by inventing a cheap cleaning fluid. So when he was about to get out of the can in the spring of 1937 he asked a fellow con if the con knew of anybody on the outside who might be able to finance the cleaning fluid so that Harrison could get it on the market. "Yeah," said the fellow con. "Look up a guy by the name of Herman Petrillo. He's got all kinds of dough."

Little Herman only half listened as Harrison expounded the prospects for his cleaning fluid. "I ain't inarrested in nothin' like that," said Little Herman. "But tell you what. You go out and dig up a guy we can get insurance on and knock off and I'll cut you in on it."

Harrison, playing it straight, asked for more details. Little Herman supplied the details. Harrison, still playing it straight, said he'd think it over. Harrison yelled to the law. Detective Sam Ricardo, the only man on the cops who had even gotten wind that something was going on, began to follow Little Herman around. But Little Herman didn't seem to contact anybody. So he was pinched on suspicion of murder.

Among those who saw Little Herman's picture in the papers was the Prudential insurance doctor who, after having examined Little Herman as Lorenzo the roofer, had thought the fellow looked somehow familiar when he later turned up as Petrino the janitor. So the wise doctor went to the cops.

The cops put the wives of the roofer and the janitor on the griddle. Thus they found out about Paul Petrillo, the wolf. The Petrillo boys, knowing the law had them bang to rights, began to sing. Doctor Bolber, the faith healer, and the Witch emerged from the vocalizing.

The Witch was nabbed and she began to sing, too. But when the cops went around to the brick house on the corner of Moyamensing Avenue and Ninth Street, Doctor Bolber had vanished. It was months before the law caught up with the doctor. Guess where he was. He was in Brooklyn, running a delicatessen store. *That's* where *he* was.

Bolber, too, decided to sing. Everybody was singing his own tune, to save the flesh around his vocal chords. A whole raft of faithless wives were dragnetted as a result of the confessions of the master plotter and his associates. Some of the wives went to prison, others got off for testifying for the state against Bolber, the Petrillo cousins and the Witch. The Witch was lucky; she got off with life in prison. Doctor Bolber got life, to die in durance vile, and the Petrillos were executed—some half a hundred murders too late.

Brooklyn's Two Million $ Torch

Sam Scarlow, Brooklyn's $2,000,000 Torch, was a man who didn't believe in doing things by halves. When Sam launched his career as a professional fire bug, he made a scientific study of his profession and, continuing far beyond where other fire bugs had left off, sure lit up the City of Churches.

At a few minutes before ten o'clock, on a marrow-chilling night in October 1932, a chunky, owl-eyed little man parked his beat-up blue Essex across the street from a one-story women's clothing store on Brooklyn's Flatbush Avenue. He peered out through his thick-lensed horn-rim glasses, noting to his satisfaction that the building was in darkness and the street was deserted. Then he removed a small black bag from the car, silently let himself into the blacked-out store with a passkey, and got down to business.

Working with swift professional confidence, the little man opened up his bag, which contained about one hundred strips of celluloid, each about two inches wide and a foot long. He carefully spread the celluloid on the floor in rows, fanning out from a central point, each row reaching to a bundle of highly inflammable dresses. At the hub of the rows of celluloid he placed a candle, which was just three inches high and which, he knew from long experience, would burn exactly one inch per hour. Then he lit the candle, scrutinized his handiwork with a professional eye, and left the store with all the nonchalance of a man leaving business for the day. Which, indeed, he was.

His name was Samuel Scarlow, but he was to become better known to every fire insurance company in the land as Sam

the Torch. A careful study of his career is equivalent to a textbook course in arson, and his activities so stimulated the insurance boys that, when Sam finally went out of business, they cut rates in Brooklyn by as much as twenty per cent.

Like any artist, Sam, now leading an upright life, looks back on his work with a good deal of affection. "It was the softest money a man ever made," he says today. "The hours were short and the work was easy. And the tax rates," he adds, with a sigh for days which will not come again, "were not the murder that they are today."

The morning after the Flatbush Avenue job, Sam arose around noon, in his room at the Lafayette Hotel, and turned on a local newscast. The announcer imparted the information that a fire of undetermined origin had broken out early that morning in a clothing store on Flatbush Avenue, and had reduced the establishment to ruins. Sam smiled with professional satisfaction, put on a snappy doublebreasted suit, ate breakfast, bestowed a fond kiss upon the doll with whom he was then in residence and drove to a building on Court Street in downtown Brooklyn.

There Scarlow dropped into the office of Samuel J. Wurzberg, a free-lance insurance adjustor who was hired, on a percentage basis, to estimate fire losses for insurance companies. Wurzberg, a pale, moon-faced little man with a double chin, rimless glasses and dark hair which he parted in the middle, was a monument of civic and political prestige. Every summer he spearheaded a municipal drive for funds to get the kids out of the hot city and into the country. And his political power seeped into every section of the borough. If a new cop made the mistake of giving a traffic ticket to one of Wurberg's friends, he could expect a sharp reprimand from his superiors.

Scarlow sat down and smiled amiably at the civic leader. "You been to the burn-out yet?"

"Just got back."

"How do you figure the damage?"

"Thirty thousand."

Sam the Torch rubbed his hands together. "Then that's three grand I got coming."

Wurzberg was breaking open a bottle when a seedy looking little man with cold poached eyes and liver lips entered the room. His name was Abe Goldner, and he was an insurance salesman. He had a jaunty walk, like that of W. C. Fields, and was an amateur story teller who usually killed himself with his own jokes. Goldner had sold the insurance to the clothier who, business being rotten, had wanted his place burned down. Along with the Torch and Wurzberg, he came in for a 10 per cent cut of the loot, the clothier getting the rest.

Working as an incendiary trio, the salesman, the Torch and the adjustor were driving the insurance companies nuts. Over a period of twelve months, the Torch had averaged an incendiary job every five nights for an estimated total loss exceeding $1,000,000. Which gave each of the trio a cool hundred grand for their year's labor.

The only trouble with the Torch was

that, like many practitioners of illicit trades, he fancied himself a good picker at the track and in the stock market. As a result, his firebug earnings slipped through his fingers almost as fast as the money came in, and he was usually broke and eager to get on with the next job—a circumstance that kept things lively in the borough of Brooklyn.

At the same time that Scarlow, Wurzberg and Goldner were having their little meeting, two men were engaged in serious conference on the other side of the East River. They were in the office of the National Board of Fire Underwriters, which represented the big fire insurance companies, and their discussion stemmed directly from the activities of Sam the Torch. One was Tom Brophy, the rugged fire marshal of Greater New York, and the other was A. Bruce Bielaski, the cagey, quiet-mannered chief of the National Board's arson squad.

Brophy, who had just returned from the Flatbush Avenue fire, was red-faced with anger. "That clothing store job was arson surer than hell!" he shouted at Bielaski. "The place was burned to the ground before the boys could even start pumping. I wish to hell I could prove it."

Both Brophy and Bielaski had long suspected that there was a professional firebug to end all professional firebugs at work in Brooklyn. Statistics don't lie and Brophy and Bielaski knew that, for a year now, there had been a thumping 20 per cent increase in the number of Brooklyn fires of undetermined origin. As a result, fire-insurance rates had gone up, and honest policy-holders were screaming to high heaven.

What the Brooklyn boys knew and what Brophy and Bielaski were painfully aware of was that arson is the hardest crime in the books to prove. In committing arson, the criminal usually burns up the very evidence needed to convict him.

Business in Brooklyn was generally rotten, the country being smack in the middle of the great depression, and salesman Goldner, as he prowled through the city of churches, baby carriages and rubber plants, had little trouble locating merchants who were glad to go along with his plan.

Goldner, Sam Scarlow says, could almost smell a commercial enterprise that was in the red. "He would," Sam says, "bust in on the proprietor of a place and ask the man how business was. Then he would look around and say: 'I see you ain't doin' so good.' Then Goldner would tell the man he ought to sell his business to the insurance company."

A common goal established, Goldner would get right down to details, fixing up his new customer with about three times as much insurance as his property warranted and then doctoring the man's books to make it all look right. If the businessman was completely broke, Abe would volunteer to pay the premiums himself. Once everything was set, Goldner would explain the set-up to Wurzberg. If it looked all right to him, they would call in Sam the Torch.

Sam Scarlow was born in Russia, in 1888, but, by the time he was around twenty, he and his family had emigrated to New York's teeming East Side. His first major business venture, which he had embarked upon within a few short years, was operating a fleet of taxicabs. But Sam, who apparently came into this world with larceny in his heart, was never content to do anything legitimately. His cabs were usually to be found lurking around the trans-Atlantic docks, waiting for trusting immigrants who could, after asking to be driven to

Brooklyn, be hauled there by way of Southern Connecticut and soaked accordingly.

Being a man to whom the grass always looked greener on the other side of the street, Sam eventually drifted out of the taxi dodge and into the fur business. At first he operated out of a hole-in-the-wall on the Lower East Side but, palming off dyed-squirrel for mink, he soon made a bundle. By the time he was thirty, he had enough money to open up a big wholesale fur outfit on lower Fifth Avenue, and was soon grossing about a million dollars a year.

Along about this time Sam gave up wearing off-the-rack suits and began patronizing the fashionable custom tailors. He also took to losing large bundles at the race track, buying heavily in the stock market, and panting around after the dolls. Sam was living high and riding for a fall. It came in 1929.

When Wall Street laid an egg, Sam was divested of everything but a business stuffed with inventory that nobody could afford to buy. He was then forty-one years old, married, and the father of four children. Drastic measures were called for.

He was sitting around his establishment one day, looking gloomily at all that unwanted fur, when a friend dropped by. "You should," the friend observed, leaping straight to the heart of the problem, "have a fire."

Sam blinked, thought a minute and then looked up. "It's a good idea," he said, "but I don't know nothin' about fires. I might just ruin the stuff and mess up everything."

"Don't do it yourself," the friend said. "I know a *macher*."

Macher is a Hebrew word meaning "He who lights a fire," and the *macher* did just that, burning Sam's business to the ground. It was a smooth, professional job, and the insurance money was paid without question. As Sam was paying off the *macher*, he suddenly realized that here was a business with many advantages. The only inventory you would need would be a small bag filled with the stuff to start the blaze. You collect your money quickly, and there would be no more worrying about the fickle winds of commerce. In fact, Sam realized, the worse business conditions were for everybody else, the better they would be for him. "I decided right then and there," Sam says, "that as soon as I had learned the ropes, I would become a firebug."

There were, Sam found out by going to the public library and delving into statistics, about 30,000 fires a year in the five boroughs of New York City, 95 per cent of them from such natural causes as overloaded electric circuits, rats nibbling on matches, workmen leaving oily rags on a job, and lightning. Only 5 per cent were of incendiary origin; that is, started intentionally. That 95 per cent area, Sam figured, would give him plenty of room in which to move around.

Premeditated fires were set for profit or, by pyromaniacs, for kicks. Pyromaniacs (of whom there were then about five hundred on the loose in Greater New York), who set off about one fourth of the incendiary blazes, do so because they are frustrated firemen or because they are so mixed up sexually that the only way they can get a reproductive charge is to stand in the street, usually at night, and watch a building burning to the ground. One notorious pyromaniac who was widely publicized had, it seemed, fallen in love with a West Side warehouse and, like a wolf with a dish, simply couldn't look at the building until he burned it down. "I was intrigued by this stuff about pyromaniacs," Sam

says, "and determined to use it to advantage."

Sam spent weeks in that library, fighting his way through the language barrier, boning up on arson, arsonists and how they had been caught. Some had been detected because they had used inflammable liquids, such as gasoline, that left a suspicious odor behind. Others had done themselves in by cutting holes in ceilings to create drafts and then, for some reason or other, the ceilings had not burned and the holes were still there, gaping at the suspicious firemen.

The *macher* who had burned down Sam's place had used oil-soaked rags for the job. Sam, who was then living on the ground floor of a two-family brick house in the Bensonhurst section of Brooklyn, went down to his cellar and conducted several experiments with oil-soaked rags. He didn't like the ash that the rags left. Putting his thinking cap on, Sam's mind went back to the clothing business. He remembered that he had once accidentally flicked a cigar ash on the celluloid button on a coat and that the button had immediately flared up into nothing.

Working in his cellar like a dedicated scientist, Sam practically fell in love with celluloid. The material not only flared up more quickly than anything else but the odor it gave off when burning lingered only a minute or so. The biggest feature of all, though, from Sam's point of view, was that the stuff, unlike oily rags, left practically no residue.

As his experiments progressed, Sam was able to judge, almost to the minute, the length of time it would take a candle to burn down to the celluloid. He was the originator of this timing, which has since been widely copied.

In his research, Sam says, he discovered certain basic truths. The lunatic-type of firebug usually sets off a blaze during or around a full moon. Certain businesses tend to have fires at certain times of the year. The fur business, for instance, had a high incidence of fires in the spring, when the weather got warm and the furriers were stuck with heavy inventories. Most hat and cap businesses that went up in flames did so in the spring and the summer when people were prone to go bare-headed. Cloak-and-suitors took the insurance way out when, with a sudden change of fashions, they were caught with heavy stocks of out-of-date apparel.

Sam decided to make it a policy never to burn a business that was in the seasonal doldrums. But if he had to, he would do it during a full moon when the finger of guilt would point toward a pyromaniac.

Sam had, since taking up residence in Brooklyn, infiltrated himself into the borough and come to casually know Wurzberg, the civic and political leader. Being a shrewd judge of character, Sam had always figured Wurzberg as being something less than the knight in shining armor that he pretended to be. So Scarlow, preliminary to starting his career as a firebug, dropped in on Wurzberg.

After some preliminary jockeying around, Sam got to the point. "The two of us," he said, "could make a hell of a lot of money with your connections and my knowledge."

Wurzberg just sat there, his eyes pleasantly narrowed, and said: "Go on, I'm listening."

"I can," said Scarlow, who was sufficiently acquainted with the law to know that he was perfectly safe in thinking out loud so long as there was no third party in the room, "set a fire so that nobody will ever know it's incendiary."

"How?" asked Wurzberg.

"When I told him about my experiments," Sam says, "Wurzberg clasped his hands behind his head, leaned back in his swivel chair and grew very thoughtful. 'You know something?' he said. 'We could make a million dollars on a thing like this.'"

Wurzberg could, he told Sam, okay a claim for insurance after Sam burned a building down but the problem would be to get policyholders who would go along with the plot. The solution to the problem would be to locate business men who were in the red and his friend Abe Goldner would be just the boy to do that.

The plot, Sam says, got off to a flying start. Within a week, Goldner had lined up ten small businesses carrying an aggregate of about a quarter of a million dollars in insurance. Within sixty days Sam had torched them all, Wurzberg had put through the claims, and the three conspirators, each getting 10 per cent of the loot, were splitting up a total of $75,000.

As time passed, Sam, instead of growing careless, grew more meticulous about every phase of his work. The candle and the celluloid merely capped long and painstaking preparation. Sam turned down as many jobs as he accepted. He would never set a fire during the day, when it would be immediately noticed, nor would he accept an assignment that wasn't in a neighborhood where the fire would get a good start before people woke up and turned in an alarm. He wanted no part of cops, watchmen, sprinkler systems or automatic alarms. Of course, if there was sufficient incentive, he could find ways of coping with such obstacles.

One time Sam was assigned to torch a small clothing factory. In company with the owner, he examined the project with the dedication of the true scientist. The factory, a three-story building of faded red brick, contained a sprinkler system that automatically went into operation when the temperature reached a certain level. There was a watchman on the premises. And it was the dead of winter.

"You got three problems here that got to be solved," Sam told the owner. "You got to take care of that sprinkler system; you got to get in a fight with that watchman and fire him, and you got to wait for warm weather."

"I don't get you," said the puzzled owner. "I thought you was going to burn this place down."

"I am," said Sam. "But you got practically no air circulation to cause a good draft, and the only way to get it is throw open all the windows."

"Well, let's throw them open."

"In the dead of winter? Why, them fire people'd get suspicious right away."

"Well, okay," said the owner, "but why do I have to get into a fight with the watchman? Why can't I just fire him?"

"Well," said Sam, looking at the owner as if he were a half-wit, "how would it look if you just told the man you didn't need him no more? I'll tell you how it would look: it would look suspicious. You got to pick a fight with him."

And so, four months later, in June, the owner of the factory picked a fight with the watchman and canned him. A couple of weeks later, he and Sam short-circuited the fire-alarm system — something that could have happened naturally—and, the windows being open for the warm weather, there was a nice draft blowing through the building. Now all Sam had to do was sneak in with his candle and his strips of celluloid, move the stock into the line of draft, light the candle, and slip away.

One day, about a year and a half after the rash of Brooklyn fires had first broken out. Bielaski was sitting in his office, studying a map of the borough that was dotted by red pins indicating the locations of the questionable blazes. His eyes came to rest on a certain block in the Sheepshead section of Brooklyn where, in the space of six months, eight little business establishments had mysteriously burned to the ground—every one of them insured.

Bielaski decided to infiltrate a plant into the area. The man he chose, who operated under the name of Stanley Patchkowski, was a stubby, bald Hungarian linguist who had had long experience as an under-cover man. Patchkowski's most valuable characteristic was a guilty, hang-dog look which unfailingly conveyed the impression that he either had compounded or was just about to compound a felony.

Patchkowski moved into a rooming house in the suspicious block and, with that guilty look of his, had little trouble getting on friendly terms with the residents. Posing as a man who owned a business somewhere in Manhattan, he began buying his evening meals at a corner delicatessen and muttering constantly about business conditions.

One night, a couple of weeks after he had moved in, Patchkowski got into conversation with the proprietor of the delicatessen.

"How's everything?" asked the proprietor as he wiped off the counter.

"Rotten," said Patchkowski.

"What's the matter?"

"Business. I'd burn it if I knew how to go about it."

The sleuth let things drop there. A few nights later, the delicatessen man said to him: "You *really* want a fire?"

"You bet I do. Why do you ask?"

"I can fix you up," said the man behind the counter. "I know a man who knows the best *macher* in the business."

Patchkowski said he'd like to meet the friend who knew the best *macher* in the business. So, a couple of nights later, when Patchkowski walked into the delicatessen, he saw a seedy-looking little man sitting at a marble table in the corner. An introduction was effected and Patchkowski found himself talking to Abe Goldner.

Goldner and Patchkowski sat at the marble table, munching pastrami sandwiches and talking business. Patchkowski said he owned a woolen goods factory on East Seventeenth Street, across the river in Manhattan, and wanted it burned down.

"How much you carryin' on it?" asked Goldner.

"Twenty thousand."

"Let's look it over."

Next day the two men were standing on East Seventeenth Street, looking over a three-story dirty brick dress manufacturing building that was humming with activity. A friend of Bielaski's owned the building, which was why it was chosen.

Goldner said he'd have a *macher* look it over. Patchkowski asked who the *macher* was. "Nobody ever sees him," Goldner said. "He don't like to be known."

While Patchkowski stalled on one pretext or another, Bielaski stuck a couple of tails on Goldner. The first thing the tails turned up was a visit of Goldner to the office of Sam Wurzberg. Bielaski now turned up the fact that Wurzberg was adjusting a hell of a lot of claims.

The faint outlines of the picture were coming into focus. Goldner was insuring the doomed properties. Wurzberg, a Jekyll-Hyde type, was winking at the incendiary work, which made the insur-

ance swindles possible. But who, Bielaski wondered, was the firebug?

Bielaski got a couple of his agents, posing as real-estate men, to rent a suite of offices right down the hall from Wurzberg's offices. The idea was to keep an eye on everybody who dropped in on Wurzberg. This was done by means of a transom periscope through which the two insurance dicks, sitting there in their spurious office, could keep a constant eye on Wurzberg's front door.

As the days wore on, and the detectives began to get a good look at Wurzberg's various callers, one man showed up in the periscope with great frequency —an owl-eyed little man wearing thick-lensed glasses who, as he walked through the hallway, seemed to leave a conspiratorial wake behind him.

Now that his undercover agent had put the finger on Sam Scarlow, Bielaski and Brophy decided to put tails on the man. Bielaski supplied two veteran insurance investigators, who holed into a room across the street from Scarlow's house in Brooklyn. But, they quickly learned, tailing Scarlow was next to impossible. Sam the Torch consistently went through red lights and the wrong way on one-way streets, and they knew that if they attempted to follow his illegal moves he would notice them.

One night, after they had been on the job several weeks, Bielaski's men were trailing the Torch through some downtown Brooklyn traffic when Sam suddenly cut loose, went through a red light, turned the wrong way into a one-way street and left his pursuers cursing to themselves. Three hours later, about one o'clock in the morning, fire broke out in a warehouse in the Red Hook section and burned with such speed and ferocity that the building was practically a shell by the time the firemen got there.

There was a full moon that night, but
Bielaski was under no illusions that the
Red Hook job was the work of a pyromaniac. To begin with, it had been done
too skillfully. And Sam had pulled that
dodge and given his tail the slip. "That's
no full-mooner job," Bielaski told his
men. "He's just trying to use the moon
as a cover. Stay with him."

It was along about this time that Sam's
wife died. Sam, a very religious man,
went into mourning and didn't come out
of the house for three weeks. During
those three weeks there wasn't a fire of
suspicious origin in all Brooklyn.

Emerging from his period of mourning, Sam left his four kids in the care of
a housekeeper and checked into the
Lafayette Hotel. He was in residence
only a few hours when a couple of
Bielaski's men, hanging around the
lobby, saw that Sam was joined by an
attractive redhead. It was obvious that
the two were having a ball because Sam
didn't come out of his room, except for a
few short walks around the block, for
several days.

One morning Scarlow popped out of
the elevator and was passing one of the
dicks when he gave Bielaski's man a double take, scudded to a stop, and stood
there glaring at the sleuth. "All right,
gumshoe!" yelled Sam. "I'll give you all
the evidence you want."

"I don't know what you're talking
about," said the dick.

"The hell you don't! You're sitting
here to keep an eye on me." Sam put his
hands on his hips. "Well, let me tell you
something: Come up to Room Five
Twenty-three and I'll give you all the
evidence you want."

"What kind of evidence do you
mean?"

"Divorce evidence. The lady up in

that room'll be glad to give her husband
evidence for a divorce."

Next day Brophy and Bielaski were
discussing the incident in the hotel
lobby. "If we ever had the slightest
chance of tailing that monkey," Brophy
was saying, "it's out the window now."

"I have an idea," said Bielaski. "The
only reason I haven't suggested it up to
now is that it'll take so many men to do
the job—and I'm not sure it'll pay off.
But it's our only move now."

"What is it?"

"Well, we're both agreed that Scarlow
is using celluloid to start these fires. Why
don't I assign about twenty men to cover
all the places in Brooklyn that sell celluloid in wholesale quantities?"

"Why wholesale?"

"With Scarlow's background as a fur
merchant it'd be second nature for him
to buy things wholesale."

Brophy nodded.

"Now," Bielaski went on, "if we find
out that he's buying a batch of celluloid
somewhere, we'll know he's ready to start
a new fire. Then we'll listen in on the
telephone in his hotel room."

It wasn't until the ninth day after the
celluloid watch was begun that one of
Bielaski's sleuths ran into a piece of luck.
He was covering a wholesale store when
Sam Scarlow scurried in, bought twenty-
five dollars' worth of celluloid strips,
each two inches wide and a foot long,
and scurried out.

Shortly after returning to the Lafayette, Sam sent his red-headed friend
out, probably on a pretext of some sort,
so that she wouldn't know what he was
up to. Bielaski's dick at the phone tap
heard Sam calling a number in Brooklyn.
"Tonight's the night," he said. "I'll meet
you at your apartment and bring the
stuff." A check of the phone number dis-

closed that it was the apartment of a man in the fur business.

That night, Brophy and several cops, this time not having to face the insurmountable problem of tailing Sam, were secreted in the shadows around the furrier's apartment house. Along toward ten o'clock that blue Essex pulled into the street. The thoroughfare was deserted but Sam the Torch, ever on guard to make sure he wasn't being followed, drove around the block three times before he parked the car and got out, carrying his little black bag.

The Torch was standing in the lobby, pressing the door bell of the man he was going to do the job for, when Brophy barged in. The fire marshal let go with a haymaker and knocked Sam flat. A search quickly revealed the tools of Sam's nefarious trade.

While the cops emerged from the shadows and took Scarlow into custody—after more than 150 fires and over $2,000,000 up in smoke—Brophy went in and began to give the Torch's client a hard time. The client quickly came apart at the seams and admitted that Scarlow had been hired to set a fire for him.

Later that night, when Wurzberg and Goldner were seized, they, like Scarlow, clammed up. The three yelled for mouth-pieces and were sprung on bail. But Bielaski was ahead of them. For months now he had been probing the reputations and backgrounds of the insured business men whose burned establishments had aroused his suspicion. He rounded them up and they broke out in a rash of confessions.

One day, a week after Scarlow had been pinched, Bielaski visited him in the Lafayette Hotel, where he was still holed up with the red-head. "You could," said Bielaski, "get about a hundred and fifty years in prison for all the confessions I

have in my office. I thought may be you'd like to help us and probably get off with a lesser sentence."

"I'm not going to confess anything," said Scarlow.

"Maybe," said Bielaski, "you'd like to know that Wurzberg has been gypping you."

Scarlow glared at Bielaski. "What do you mean?"

"We have, said Bielaski, "been studying the bank accounts of you and Goldner and Wurzberg and the way we figure it is that in the beginning Wurzberg paid you 10 per cent of the insurance on every job you did. But lately he's been paying you less."

Sam the Torch leaned forward, his mouth open, his eyes wide.

"Take that job you did on Fulton Street seven weeks ago," Bielaski went on. "Your bank balance shows you were paid 10 per cent of eighteen thousand dollars in insurance. Actually, Sam, that place was insured for thirty-three thousand."

Months passed and, as he rode around town with Bielaski, putting the finger on co-conspirators whose places he had burned down, Sam underwent a metamorphosis. Gradually, he changed from criminal to man-hunter. In fact, he became so dedicated to his work of cleaning up the ring that he offered to sock anybody who didn't cooperate with Bielaski. Sam, despite all his ill-gotten gains, was flat broke—the horses and the market. But he was proving so valuable at cleaning up the whole arson plot that Bielaski put him on the payroll of the National Board of Fire Underwriters at twenty-five dollars a week.

At the trials of Wurzberg and Goldner, Sam went on the witness stand and told a jury how his erstwhile partners had collaborated with him in burning up a couple of million dollars worth of property. Sam also got several of his one-time clients to testify to the same thing. Sam's two ex-partners drew 12½ to 25 years in the big cage. Some of the ring's customers got off with light or suspended sentences or, because they cooperated with the State, no sentences at all.

Sam, who had been unofficially promised leniency because of his cooperation, had expected a light sentence and had, in fact, even toyed around with the hope of getting a suspended one. Instead, there was some kind of a slip-up and he found himself facing a bookthrowing judge who gave him worse than Wurzberg and Goldner had got 20 to 40 years. Sam just stood there, blinking at the judge behind those thick-lensed glasses. "It don't," he muttered, "pay to be honest."

Bielaski, who had grown to have a sneaking admiration for the little man, told Sam that he would pull every legal string he could think of to get that sentence lightened.

It wasn't until 1946, when Sam was in the twelfth year of his jolt, that Bielaski found a string with something on the other end. Sam's two eldest sons had distinguished themselves in the Second World War. Their uniforms dripping with medals, they appeared before Governor Thomas E. Dewey to plead for their father's release. Bielaski dispatched a letter to Dewey respectfully recommending clemency. So Sam, at the age of fifty-eight, was sprung on parole.

Sam was a sad sight when he came out of prison, his face drawn and pale, the thick lenses of his glasses thicker than ever. Aside from his four children, he had only two friends in all the world—Bielaski and the red-head he had been living with in the Brooklyn hotel. During the entire time Sam had been in prison, she had taken care of his two smaller children. The trouble was she was still married and her husband wouldn't give her a divorce.

The parole board wouldn't sit still for their living together without benefit of clergy, and Sam, who by this time had gotten used to taking his troubles to Bielaski, came to him with this one. Bielaski nosed around and discovered that there was nothing to prevent the red-head from getting herself a Mexican divorce. She did, and, at long last, married Sam.

Until a few years ago Sam Scarlow made his living by running a laundromat, having made a successful switch from cleaning out insurance companies to cleaning shirts. Then he suffered a coronary thrombosis.

Today, Sam, viewing his career with a certain amount of pride, feels that he made a significant contribution to law and order by helping the cops nail down the arson ring. He even considers his torching activities to have been of benefit to mankind. "For instance," he says, "you can't deny that I did a favor for the insurance companies by teaching them more about arson than they could have learned in a hundred years."

Coster-Musica: Man Who Doped the Drug Houses

Here, in all truth, was a living, breathing Jekyll-Hyde—a respected business tycoon and banker by day, masquerading under an assumed name, and a criminal and blackmail victim by night, known to the denizens of the underworld under his real monicker. Meet Mr. Coster-Musica!

It was a few minutes after ten o'clock one morning of 1933. In Fairfield, Connecticut, an owl-faced paunchy little man, his brisk step belying his fifty-six years, breezed past his secretary into his sumptuous office as president of McKesson & Robbins.

"Oh, Mr. Coster," the secretary called, trailing after him. "Mr. Robert Vernard wants to see you. He says it's very urgent."

"All right. Tell him to come right in." The man's manner was impatient.

While he waited for his assistant treasurer to arrive, he drummed his fingers on his desk and looked possessively around the walls. He had not done badly —not badly at all. Little Phil Musica, the one-time slum kid, was now head of one of the country's most respected drug manufacturing companies. There was hardly a medicine chest in the land that didn't contain at least one McKesson & Robbins label.

He leaned back in his upholstered swivel chair and tapped his fingers together. He'd done a good job, too. The firm had been slipping when he bought it, and he'd brought it right back up to the top. Of course, there were those who might say he and his brothers were robbing the company blind, but that was all in how you looked at it. He smiled contentedly.

Things were going so well, in fact, that he did not dream the world would soon be ranking him among the cleverest crooks of the twentieth century. For Philip Musica, as Frank Donald Coster, had both revitalized a great company and stolen so much of its assets that the total amount never could be figured out. With a criminal past, he had the ruling bankers eating out of his hand. And as a result of his skulduggery, every auditing firm in the country had to alter its methods of checking accounts. After Phil Musica was through, *nobody* took *anyone's* word for *anything*.

The door opened, and the man called Robert Vernard—born Robert Musica— walked in. He was thirty-seven years old and he looked as though he had been worrying all his life. Behind him came the purchasing agent, who had begun life as George Musica but later decided he'd better be known as George Vernard. A baldish man of forty-two who didn't act very happy either, he carefully closed the heavy door behind him.

"What's the matter?" demanded Phil Musica. "Have my brothers seen a ghost?"

"It's worse than that," Robert chittered. "Look at this," He handed Phil a letter.

Phil's piercing black eyes leaped to the signature. "Brandino," he gasped, his voice high and strained. "After all these years. . . ." He darted through the letter:

I saw your picture in the papers and see that you are now calling yourself Frank Donald Coster. It's been a long time now but I know you are Philip Musica. Maybe you could help an old friend who needs some money.

JOE BRANDINO

"Good God!" he muttered.

"It's blackmail," said George. "Are you going to pay?"

Phil shrugged despairingly. "We have no choice," he sighed.

"How much?"

"Give him five thousand dollars. Take it out of petty cash."

"But if we start a thing like this it'll never stop," the assistant treasurer protested.

"Do as I say!" Phil snapped. "There's only one other way—and we're not murderers."

"All right." Robert was not the man to argue a point. He knew he himself would never kill anyone, but one couldn't be sure about Phil.

"Take it to him at his address," Phil continued. He shuddered and passed a hand over his face. "Whatever happens, keep him away from here."

The intercom buzzed, and Robert, a nervous type, shot into the air. Phil held up a cautioning hand and flipped a switch.

"Mr. Coster," the secretary said in alarm, "there's a state trooper here and he wants to see you."

Phil stiffened momentarily, then relaxed with a slow smile. "Ask him to come in," he said.

He glanced at his brothers knowingly. "Nothing to worry about," he whispered. "He'll just be bringing us the news about

last night. Remember, we don't know a thing."

The door opened and the trooper stepped in. "Mr. Coster?" he asked, properly deferential before so great and powerful a man.

"Yes," Phil said easily.

"I'm afraid I have some bad news to report, sir."

"What about?" Phil demanded, leaning forward as though suddenly apprehensive.

"Another of your trucks was hijacked last night. Up near Old Lyme. Somebody held up the driver with a gun and bound and gagged him."

"Good Lord!" moaned Phil, staring at his brothers. "That must have been the shipment of morphine and cocaine."

"Can you tell me how much it was worth?" asked the trooper.

"Robert," said Phil, "you took out the insurance on that shipment. How much was it?"

"A little over ninety thousand dollars."

The trooper whistled. "It'll be worth even a good deal more than that on the illegal drug market."

"The money is secondary," said Coster. "What about the driver? Was he hurt?"

"No, just roughed up a bit."

When the trooper left, Phil sat back and grinned at his brothers. This little scheme was working out perfectly—just as the others had. He'd tip off one of his gangster friends when a valuable shipment of drugs would be passing a given point—and later get his cut when the shipment had been knocked off and disposed of.

George sourly picked up Brandino's letter—and the grin broke. For the rest of Phil Musica's life it was never really to return.

With his brothers instructed on how

to handle the blackmailer, the president of the third largest drug house in the world buzzed for his secretary and tackled the morning's mail. In the middle of that job he had a few minutes' conference with Julian Thompson, treasurer of Mc-Kesson & Robbins. Shortly before eleven o'clock he clapped on his hat, stepped out into a chauffeur-driven black limousine, and was driven to the Fairfield branch of the Bridgeport-City Trust Company. As a pillar of the community, he was a director of the bank. The other directors, awaiting his arrival, greeted him deferentially and got down to the business of the weekly meeting.

Philip Musica, alias Donald Coster, was at his con-man best when, playing the role of bank director, he cast his piercing eyes on security being put up for a loan.

"Who is this asking us for fifteen thousand dollars?" Phil demanded that day as he ran his tongue over his lips and swiveled his gaze to the other directors. "What kind of collateral is he offering? I don't see any."

"Mr. Coster," said one of the directors, "I know this man personally. He has a sound little business and is good for the money. He's unable to put up the kind of collateral we normally require—but I'll vouch for him personally."

"All right," said Phil, staring at the speaker intently. "But I want to go on record as saying that I don't like this kind of borrowing. I don't like it at all."

The meeting over, Phil rushed to the Barnum Hotel in nearby Bridgeport, where the Rotary Club was to hold its weekly luncheon. Philip Musica, the man with the criminal record, was to speak that day on "Honesty and Integrity."

When the time came Phil arose to an ovation. He stood quiet for fully half a minute, blinking soberly at his audience like an owl.

"Mr. Toastmaster, honored guests and Rotarians," he began, his voice mellow and confident. "It is an honor and a privilege for me to address you today on simple honesty . . ."

Philip Musica was feeling pretty sure of himself—pretty smug and unafraid. He almost forgot Joe Brandino.

What manner of man was this character who called himself Coster? What hidden springs made him go? How had he succeeded in becoming a flesh-and-blood Jekyll-Hyde, obliterating a criminal record, assuming a new background and identity, and rising to a position of great influence in legitimate business?

The story of Philip Mariana Fausto Musica, alias Frank Donald Coster, is one of the most singular in the annals of crime. Phil Musica, dedicating his life to separating honest people from their money, took up where other con men left off. Phil thought big and operated in millions when his brothers under the skin-game settled for thousands.

He was born in Naples, Italy, in May, 1877, the eldest of what was to be a family of seven children. The parents, Antonio and Assunta Musica, emigrated to the United States shortly after Phil's birth. Antonio, a barber, had heard that in this country the streets were paved with gold because men shaved every day. On the lower East Side of New York City he didn't find much gold.

Phil and the rest of the kids didn't have much of a raising, lower Manhattan being the home ground of aspiring young crooks who eventually moved onward and upward to the electric chair. As soon as he got his bearings, Phil proved he wasn't going to be part of the ordinary run of punks. In a region where being neatly dressed was practically an invitation to mayhem, Phil was a neat dresser. And he got away with it despite the fact that he was a smallish kid who couldn't swap knife slashes with his playmates. Instead, he got himself out of jams by charm and wit. Dark-eyed and alert, he was always buzzing around the neighborhood straightening things out for others, and he was such a whiz at school that he did the homework for all his knuckle-headed pals.

By the time Phil was sixteen he had developed a fierce hatred of poverty and a decided taste for the finer things of life. He was considered the dandy of the slums. His shoes were always highly polished and his clothes neatly pressed, and he wore a flower in his buttonhole. (The flower was a phony that lit up when he pressed a concealed bulb.) He had an open, impudent face and a way of blinking his eyes and clearing his throat before speaking.

He quit school now (later he was to palm himself off as the recipient of a doctor-of-philosophy degree from the German University of Heidelberg), and went to work for his old man, who had finally given up clipping hair and opened a hole-in-the-wall Italian grocery. Although the store was in the old man's name, Phil, the smart one, was soon running things.

By the time he reached his twenty-first birthday Phil Musica had really got going. He swaggered through the streets in loud suits and headlight stickpins, and proclaimed to everyone his conviction that the way to get ahead was by perseverance and an early start. A man had to be honest, too. Phil was so prominently honest you couldn't believe it. Unfortunately, most people did. No one could deny that he was a success—the little grocery had now become A. Musica & Son,

an importing firm specializing in Italian foods, and business was booming. In fact, there was so much money around that Phil convinced the family the lower East Side was no longer good enough. So mama and papa and all the children moved into an architectural monstrosity in the fashionable Bay Ridge section of Brooklyn.

As time passed, A. Musica & Son began to gobble up much more than their share of business, and there were cries of anguish as one competitor after another bit the dust. "I don't know how they're doing it," was the complaint, freely translated, of one fallen cheese-and-salami man. "They're selling their stuff cheaper than it costs to import it."

It wasn't until 1909 that anyone found out just how they did it. That year the City of New York was undergoing one of its periodic reform waves. Investigators, tipped off by desperate competitors, drew a bead on Dandy Phil and decided to find out how Musica & Son were able to sell cheese for less than the import price and still make a handsome profit.

One day a hard-faced man wearing the gold badge of a deputy United States marshal walked into Musica & Son and asked for Phil.

"You're speaking to him," said Phil.

"You're under arrest," said the deputy.

Phil stayed cool. "What for?"

"Bribing customs inspectors."

"I don't know what you're talking about," said Phil. This was a slight exaggeration.

What the man was talking about was that Philip Musica had been indicted by a federal grand jury for bribing customs inspectors to let cheese consigned to Musica & Son slip in without duty. That was how the firm had been able to undersell its competitors. Phil was all set to deny everything until Musica senior was indicted, too, and then he gave in. Rather than see the old man risk the clink, he beat his breast and yelled that it was all his fault. And as a matter of fact, it was. Papa got off, and Phil drew a year in the pen.

Coming out, Phil, now thirty-three, took up socially where he had left off. He hit the hot spots and basked under the bright lights around Times Square. In this atmosphere the legitimate cheese business now seemed a little too dull, so Phil began to look around for something more exciting. One day he read a news item stating that switches of human hair, known as "rats" and used to build up ladies' pompadours, were in great demand and that suitable hair, in 12-to-20-inch lengths, was selling for eighty dollars a pound. Since much of the hair came from Italy and since the elder Musica, having been a tonsorial artist, knew more than the average man about hair, Phil knew where his future lay.

Thus, within a few months after his release from prison, Phil and his father were in the business of importing hair. As his first move Phil sent his old lady and two of his brothers to Naples as purchasing agents. Soon the hair, in properly long lengths, began to arrive in New York, and the United States Hair Company was in business. For the next few years the profits were good. There was enough for Phil and his family if he'd only been content to remain in its Brooklyn bosom. He wasn't. He was still running from poverty, and after awhile he took an apartment for himself in the Knickerbocker Hotel, at Broadway and Forty-second Street, began to wear spats and custom-tailored suits, and became a regular fixture at such tony and expensive restaurants as Rector's and Delmonico's. Somewhere he had to get the

money to pay for these delusions of grandeur.

Once Phil put his devious mind to work on the problem, the solution seemed simple enough. What had worked once, he figured, ought to work again. He promptly wrote a detailed letter of instructions to his mother in Naples, telling her to forget about buying long hair and concentrate instead on hair sweepings from Italian barber shops. These sweepings were, of course, slightly less than worthless, since they were unwelcome even on the heads where they originated. Presently the docks in New York were loaded with crates filled with sweepings for the United States Hair Company.

There must have been more than one screw loose in Phil's head at this time, for what he tried simply didn't make sense if he had any idea of getting away with it indefinitely. He began to bribe customs inspectors—the ploy that had sent him to the pen before. The inspectors gave Phil reports on crates of genuine long hair when in fact the crates contained nothing but valueless hair sweepings. Phil took these reports to banks and borrowed money on them, as would often be done in the ordinary course of business.

One day, though, several of Phil's crates fell afoul an honest customs man who happened to shove one of them out of the way after unsuspectingly glancing at a crooked report on it.

"Wait a minute," he said to a fellow inspector. "Does this crate feel heavy enough to be filled with hair switches?"

The second man tilted the crate and dropped it back. "Hard to say," he muttered. "It does seem light."

And so the crate was opened and the two customs men looked first at the sweepings, then at each other.

There was hell to pay when the news

got out, and Uncle Sam bustled a couple of men along to put the nippers on Phil. But the hair specialist—and all the other Musicas—had got a tip and flown the coop.

The banks that Phil had swindled were all protected by the William J. Burns International Detective Agency, and a Burns gumshoe was assigned forthwith to track Phil down. Going through Phil's desk, the detective found a book on extradition laws. It was evident that the section which stated this country had no extradition treaty with Honduras had been well thumbed, and the eye reached for a phone. The fugitive Musicas were picked up in New Orleans as they were about to board a banana boat.

One thing must be said for Phil: he loved his family. He'd taken the rap for papa before, and that had seemed very noble—although, of course, he'd got the old man in the mess. Now, after a heart-to-heart talk with himself, he pleaded guilty to grand larceny, shouldering all the blame for the hairy swindle so that the charges against his family, suspected of having been co-conspirators, could be dropped. He was remanded to The Tombs to await sentence.

It was in this famous jail that Phil, feeling life beginning at forty, really proved his mettle. He became a stool-pigeon. Conning fellow prisoners into confessing to him, he turned their stories over to the cops. This show of public spirit made such a hit with the district attorney, an ambitious man, that a deal was made and Phil was given a suspended sentence.

And what field of endeavor did Philip Musica enter when he was released? He became an investigator on the staff of the district attorney. Going under the name of William Johnston, he developed into a busy little beaver smelling out vice

for the D. A. and, in his role of stool-pigeon, cuddling up to new prisoners and getting confessions from them.

Phil's double identity—salaried stool-pigeon and ex-con still reporting to his parole officer—caused occasional confusion and frequent double-takes around the prosecutor's office. A new assistant D. A. might notice Phil, docile and self-effacing, waiting to see his parole officer, and a few minutes later spot the same little man, in his role of investigator Johnston, bristling with authority.

One day Phil received a visit from a mild-mannered man by the name of Edward Walter Hubbard, a partner in a small Wall Street brokerage outfit.

"Mr. Johnston," Hubbard said, "there's some dirty work going on in my office and I want to hire you to find out about it."

"What kind of dirty work?"

"I think my partner is plotting against me."

Phil took a retainer and got to work. He soon found out there wasn't anything to the story. Hubbard was simply an over-sensitive man given to imaginary problems, and if someone absent-mindedly gave him a blank stare he was apt to interpret it as a plot on his life. Phil, naturally, decided to make the most of the situation.

"I'm afraid," he reported to Hubbard, "that there's more to this than you've suspected."

One night the broker invited Phil out to his home in Brooklyn, where Phil met Hubbard's wife. Carol Hubbard was a beautiful brunette still young enough to tell the truth about her age. Up to now, Phil had been so busy that he had never taken any woman seriously. But as he sat in Brooklyn that night with the Hubbards watching Carol sparkle, he succumbed to the age-old sinking feeling known as the common crush.

Phil made it a point thereafter to discuss the progress of his investigation in Hubbard's home, while Carol was present. Darting glances at Carol as he spilled tall tales to her husband, he could see that he was making progress with the lady. But Eddie was very obviously in the way.

Phil gave the problem some serious study and shortly came up with an answer. He began to send poison-pen letters to Hubbard, advising the man that his life was in danger and he'd better get out of town.

"Who do you suppose is sending these letters?" Hubbard asked querulously when the third one arrived.

"Probably that partner of yours," said Phil, running his tongue over his lips and blinking.

"But what can I do?"

"Nothing," Phil pointed out smoothly. "You'd have to prove he's sending those letters and that's pretty hard."

He lifted the letters from Hubbard's hand. "Let me try, though," he said. "I'll take them to a handwriting expert."

As time passed, the letters continued to arrive and Phil journeyed regularly to Brooklyn to collect them for his handwriting expert—a nameless individual who seemed to get nowhere. In the course of this business Phil saw more and more of Carol as her husband slowly but surely began to come apart at the seams. And when he figured the time was right he made his next move.

"I have a suggestion," he said one night to the old man. "This thing has been getting you down. Why don't you take a trip somewhere for your health— say, Arizona. The change might do you a lot of good."

Hubbard jumped on the idea as though he'd just been shown a way out of the madhouse. "Carol," he said, "how soon can we leave?"

"Carol," Phil declared, his black eyes restless, "better stay here. She ought to keep an eye on the investigation."

When Hubbard had left for the West, Phil lost no time taking the broker's wife out to dinner. One remark leading to another, Phil, finally, over the coffee, batted his eyes and murmured dramatically, "Carol, I have fallen in love."

Legally, however, it wasn't as simple as that. It was to be several years before Phil could change Carol's name. And by that time he'd switched his own again.

Phil was forty-four when he decided to quit the D. A.'s office and get back in business for himself. Sufficient time had elapsed, he figured, for everybody—well, practically everybody—to have forgotten about the cheese and hair scandals.

During his sojourn in The Tombs, Phil had met a Sicilian gangster named Brandino—an individual of spectacular depravity up to his eyeballs in all sorts of rackets. Now he looked the man up.

"The two of us," Phil said, "ought to go in business together."

"What you got in mind?" asked Brandino, a hairy, apelike man with long arms and a rolling walk.

"Well," said Phil, "they tell me there's a lot of money in flowers—second-hand flowers." And he explained his idea.

So Phil and Brandino went into the flower business in Brooklyn. Their source of supply was somewhat unusual —they hung around cemeteries, keeping an eye peeled for funerals. Loitering in the shrubbery and peering over tombstones, they'd keep watch on a graveside funeral service until the mourners left. Then they stole the wreaths and sold them to ghoulish florists, who resold them to newly bereaved families. Sometimes the same wreaths went the route two or three times. It looked like a good thing—until the cemetery guards drew a bead on Phil and Brandino and began driving them away.

The two then tried selling flavoring extracts, but this started working into too honest a business and one day they got into a fight about money. Phil dissolved the partnership then and there, before it had really got off the ground.

A vindictive character, Phil decided that Brandino should be punished for having opposed him—a mistake that he was one day deeply to regret. Knowing all about the gangster's past, he sat down and wrote a series of poison-pen letters to the D. A. As a result, Brandino found his tail in a sling.

"I know who done this to me," he growled to the cops. "And I'll get him for it if it takes a hundred years."

Shortly after the bust-up Phil dropped into the Knickerbocker bar to swap drinks with a Broadway acquaintance. They were to be the most important drinks he ever had.

"What's the next idea?" asked the pal, after Phil had spilled the news.

"I don't know yet," said Phil.

"Friend of mine tells me there's a lot of money in hair tonics and stuff like that. He was broke a year ago and now he's making more than he can spend."

A tip like that, with such a pleasant jingle of silver, Phil couldn't pass by. So in 1923 he popped up in Mount Vernon, a Westchester County suburb of New York, and rented a broken-down two-story brick factory. His landlord knew him as Coster—Frank Donald Coster. And because he was through with the identities of William Johnston, stool-pigeon and wife-stealer, and Philip Musica, crook and ex-con, Phil decided to change his appearance, too. He raised

a mustache and began to wear horn-rimmed glasses. He bought a pair of elevator shoes, adding two inches to his height, and switched to high-calorie foods to add to his weight. Previously he had favored single-breasted suits of loud design; now, as a business executive, he laid in a wardrobe of subdued double-breasted numbers. The transformation was striking. Most people who had seen the convicted criminal of a few years back wouldn't have made the connection with the business executive in Mount Vernon. Most—but unfortunately for Phil, not all.

In his desire to put as many layers of insulation as possible between his true identity and his new one, Phil incorporated the outfit as Girard & Company, listing himself as president and as vice president and holder of practically all of the stock, a totally fictitious character on whom he bestowed the monicker P. Horace Girard.

Phil next advertised for a chemist and got a smallish man with watery blue eyes who gave his name as Doctor Emil Fanto and said he was a native of Vienna. However that may have been, he made it clear he knew his stuff. Getting right down to work, he was soon busy producing such a fine line of toilet waters that Phil, doubling in brass as head salesman, had little difficulty peddling them to several New York department stores. Soon Girard & Company had a payroll of ten persons compounding drugs and making up cosmetics.

Then came the day that Phil was sitting in his office adding up a column of figures when Doctor Fanto eased himself in.

"Do you have a minute, sir?" he asked humbly.

"Just about," said Phil.

"It's about Mr. Girard, our vice president."

Phil shot a sharp glance up at his chemist. "What about Mr. Girard?" he demanded.

"Nothing," said Fanto, "only I've been here several months now and I've never even seen him."

"He's not here very much," said Phil, blinking as he relaxed a bit.

"But I would like to meet him."

"Why?"

Fanto spread his hands.

"In the other places I've worked, here and in the old country, I've always been introduced to all the officers of the company."

"Well," Phil said easily, "I'll see that you meet him next time he comes to town."

"Oh." The chemist nodded wisely. "He's not in town, then?"

"No," said Phil. "He travels a lot."

When Fanto left the office Phil looked after him speculatively. The man was curious—too curious.

Not long after Phil got rolling in Mount Vernon, he brought in three brothers—Robert, 5 feet 3 of jittery nerves, George, docile and rather shy, and Arthur, tall, dolorous, and thirsty. Robert was useful because he was always so scared things would go wrong that he could generally pick out the weak points of a scheme. George simply did everything he was told. Arthur was smart—and besides that, he looked so honest.

Naturally, none of them could hang onto the name of Musica, so Phil introduced them as Robert Vernard and George Vernard, while Arthur (who really hated his name) became George Dietrich. At first their main function was to keep their eyes open—especially for anyone who gave a sign of knowing that F. Donald Coster wasn't all he seemed.

Phil stuck pretty much to his knitting that first year and did all right. After meeting all expenses he cleared about twenty-five thousand dollars for himself. He was batching it now in a modest furnished home on a residential street, going into New York nights to chase dolls and Carol Hubbard. Fond of the opera, he brought Carol to hear practically every big star of the time. The dolls he took elsewhere.

But although things were rocking along nicely with a comfortable and legitimate profit, Phil couldn't bring himself to feel that an honest buck had the kick of a crooked one. So his screw came loose again the day he had a visitor—a grim-faced man who stepped out of a long black limousine.

The visitor got right down to cases. "My name," he growled, "is Schultz, Dutch Schultz. Ever hear of me?"

Phil nodded blandly. Dutch Schultz was one of the important bootleggers of the era. A gangster in the classic tradition, he usually gave a police department that wouldn't play ball twenty-four hours to get out of town.

"I'll lay the cards on the table," Schultz said. "In your business you're usin' a lot of good alcohol. Right?"

"Right," said Phil.

"How much alcohol you allowed a month?"

"5,250 gallons."

"What you payin' for it?"

"A dollar and a half a gallon."

"I'll pay you five."

"Cash?"

"Cash."

It was a deal, and Dutch made it plain that if Phil could get more alcohol, he'd buy it.

A couple of days later, Phil went down to the Treasury Building in Washington to see about getting his alcohol allowance increased. Waiting for the official concerned, he was dressed to kill—dark gray double-breasted suit with fedora and spats to match, a flower in his buttonhole, and his little mustache neatly trimmed. He tapped his fingers on a black briefcase and felt very confident. But then, when he was ushered into the inner office, he staggered back on his heels. He had recognized at once the man behind the desk —a former customs inspector who'd been working on the very docks where Phil had made his arrangements for evading Uncle Sam's cut.

The official glanced briefly at Phil, then did a double take.

"Haven't I seen you before?" he asked.

"Not that I know of," said Phil, looking the man straight in the eye.

There was a slight pause while the official riffled through Phil's papers on the desk before him. "Coster, Coster, Coster," he repeated. "Is that your real name?"

"What do you mean?" demanded Phil with the proper degree of indignation. "Of course it is."

The Treasury man cocked his head and narrowed his eyes. "I've seen you someplace," he said, "without those glasses and that mustache. I don't believe your name's Coster at all."

Phil was just working up a good sputter of rage when the official snapped his fingers. "I've got it!" he exclaimed. "You're Philip Musica, and you were mixed up in that customs bribery in New York several years ago."

Phil's sputter died. "All right," he sighed, "what if I am Musica?"

"How do you expect me to recommend an increase in your alcohol allowance if you're an ex-convict?"

There was something in the way the government man spoke that prompted Phil to take heart. "Look here," he said,

leaning closer and talking low, "there's an awful lot of money involved here. Plenty to go around."

The Treasury man got up to close the door. "Are you offering me a bribe?" he asked bluntly.

"Well, now look. It isn't—"

"I'm not complaining. Where are you staying?"

"At the Willard."

"I'll meet you there at eight o'clock. What's your room number?"

That night the official rapped lightly on Phil's door promptly at eight.

"Call me Joe," he said, accepting a drink. "And now, let's get down to cases. I know very well what you want all this alcohol for. Everybody's doing it—treating the stuff to make it palatable, then selling it to bootleggers."

"Keep talking," said Phil, leaning forward eagerly."

"Well," said Joe, "you won't get it on the application you've made. The department will never okay a big alcohol increase just because you say you're going to expand. You've got to show you're going into another line—branching out."

"What do you recommend?"

"Spirits of camphor. Buy a lot of solid camphor and tell us you've got to have alky to make spirits of camphor. We'll release the stuff for a thing like that. Then all you've got to do is put down on your books that you used the alky for this purpose, and you can sell the alky and throw the damned camphor away."

"What's your cut?"

"The price down here is standard—10 per cent."

Back at his office in Mount Vernon, Phil made his plans. He decided to set up a dummy branch company, ostensibly to manufacture spirits of camphor, and put Arthur in charge of it as president. This fictitious subsidiary was to be known as W. W. Smith & Company—a name Phil picked out of thin air. As a hole-in-the-wall address, complete with dummy books on non-existent business, it would function as a transfer point for turning over the alcohol to Dutch Schultz.

And with the setting up of W. W. Smith & Company, on Hanson Place in Brooklyn, things boomed for Phil Musica. Dutch paid cash for all the alcohol Phil wanted to sell, and just to get into the spirit of things, the legitimate business of Girard & Company—thanks to new toilet-goods products thought up by Doctor Fanto—soared. Phil began to act like a juggler with several balls in the air. The money was rolling in, but it can't be said that he wasn't working for it.

Phil began to dream of expanding what was now the parent operation. He ordered Girard's books audited by the renowned firm of Price, Waterhouse & Company. To do the job there appeared at the Mount Vernon plant one morning a little man with a wispy mustache and a blue serge suit, a senior accountant who had fooled a lot of people into thinking he could be fooled.

Phil hovered in the background as the man started to work. He had no qualms about the books of Girard & Company because all the entries there were on the level. It was when the accountant began to delve into the fake books of W. W. Smith & Company that he had a few bad moments. The accountant would pore over an entry, purse his lips, look up at Phil, and ask, "Just what does this mean?" Actually, it turned out, the accountant wasn't questioning a thing—he was only making sure he understood all the entries.

At the end of three days the accountant stacked his papers, put them in a briefcase, and reached for his hat.

"Well, Mr. Coster," he said, "I must say that you have kept everything in apple-pie order."

"No problems, then?" asked Phil.

"No problems at all."

Phil had got more out of the audit, however, than just the green light for his books. He had stumbled upon an invaluable piece of information that was one day to shape the course of the great McKesson & Robbins swindle—and make Price, Waterhouse wish to high heaven they had never heard of Frank Donald Coster. What Phil had figured out was this: an accountant making an audit never bothered to check whether the inventories noted in the books actually existed. Today auditing firms always check inventories—Phil taught them they'd better.

Phil was in a Mount Vernon bank a few days later having a little chat with the president about business conditions in general.

"I'd like to expand," Phil said. "Really branch out. But I don't know just how to go about it."

The banker, who had seen Phil's progress reflected in the monthly statements of Girard & Smith, grew thoughtful.

"Tell you what I'm going to suggest," he said. "I'll give you the name of a man to get in touch with. He's with one of the big investment houses in Wall Street. His name's Thompson—Julian Thompson. Fine chap. He'll probably come up and look your plant over."

A few days later, after a couple of pleasant telephone conversations, Thompson appeared at Phil's office, shook hands and sat down. Julian Thompson was a delicately featured man, tall and spare, in his late forties, who looked levelly at people through pince-nez glasses. Though Phil didn't learn it then, Thompson was also leading a sort of double life—but of quite a different type from the Musica variety.

By day he was a financial man; by night, a playwright. A few years before he had written the Broadway success, *The Warrior's Husband,* which introduced Katharine Hepburn to Manhattan first-nighters. He was a fine judge of food and potables and liked his Martinis so dry you could blow the dust off them.

Thompson prided himself on being a sharp judge of character—a talent that had stood him in good stead in both business and playwriting. Now, as he sat looking at the impostor who called himself F. Donald Coster, he took an instant liking to the man. "He exuded integrity," Thompson was to say on a later and sadder day. "After five minutes with him, I would have trusted him with my checking account."

There were reasons other than Phil's personality that sold Thompson. Two fraudulent diplomas, neatly framed, hung on the wall behind Phil's desk—one attesting to Phil's graduation from Heidelberg, the other to his license to practice medicine in New York City.

Phil was going good that day. He chattered away about the merits of his products as he showed the finance man the Price, Waterhouse accounting sheets. Thompson was as impressed by the report as the auditing accountant had been with Phil's books.

Now Phil brought out the fake books of the phony W. W. Smith & Company, and Thompson, never thinking to question any of the entries, looked them over, made some notes, and said, "Mr. Coster, I am impressed."

Thompson went back to New York and conferred with his superiors. After mature considerations, it was decided that Phil's company wasn't of sufficient stature yet to be listed on a stock exchange, but that it certainly merited friendly consideration by the loan committee of any bank.

"Will you put that in writing?" Phil asked, and Thompson did.

Beginning to move fast now, Phil bought an abandoned factory in Fairfield, Connecticut. Then, bearing Thompson's letter, he walked into the local office of The Bridgeport-City Trust Company and inquired about the possibility of a loan for the expansion of his business.

"We're always glad to help anybody bringing industry to our area," Phil was told by an officer.

"In that case," said Phil, "I'd like to meet your loan committee."

He was all set for one of his best conman performances when he appeared before the committee, composed of the bank's directors. Those dark eyes of his, behind rimless glasses, bulged with integrity as he pulled out a batch of spurious documents showing the progress Girard & Company and its subsidiary, W. W. Smith, had made.

Phil was operating on his new theory that the bankers would never dream anybody would have the nerve to flash papers that could be checked by a few phone calls and found to be spurious. This theory, in fact, was to become an article of faith with him.

One of the directors asked Phil a technical question about spirits of camphor, the product that W. W. Smith & Company was supposedly so successfully manufacturing.

"I'm glad you asked that, sir," said Phil, whereupon, having boned up in advance, he went into a sound dissertation on spirits of camphor.

"And just how do you propose to expand?" asked another director.

Phil reached for a sheaf of carefully worked-out figures showing the production he proposed to attain and how the expansion would pay for itself over a comparatively brief period of time.

"What amount of money would you require, Mr. Coster?" asked one of the bank directors.

"I think," said Phil, "a hundred thousand dollars should be sufficient."

If Phil didn't bat an eye, neither did any of the directors. By now they were passing around Phil's phony papers, which purported to show not only his track record but, on the basis of his companies' financial condition, his future performance.

"I think I can say," one of the directors finally opined, "that we shall probably look with favor on this request within the next week or two."

"Thank you, gentlemen," said Phil. "Thank you very much."

Phil got the hundred thousand, all right, and pretty soon the Fairfield plant was booming as Phil transferred all his activities there from Mount Vernon.

When Girard & Company got under way in its new location, Phil received a government okay for even more alcohol. The result was that the plant hummed both day and night, with most of the new alky going to Dutch Schultz and other bootleggers during the after-hours shift.

With the big move, George and Robert were given offices adjoining Phil's. The master crook himself settled into a large room with heavy red carpeting on the floor, drapes to match, and a massive mahogany desk. All three offices opened on a common reception room, which was presided over by a secretary. Phil's door was always closed, but Robert and George kept their offices open so they could see what was going on. In a way they functioned as a sort of flying wedge to protect Phil against any unwelcome intruder.

A few months after Phil had got going in Fairfield a police officer dropped in on him.

"You got a lot of trucks goin' out of here nights," the cop said. "What's in them?"

"Oh, products of various sorts." Phil was used to inquisitive cops.

"We think them trucks is cartin' alcohol," the man in blue said bluntly.

Phil didn't miss a breath. "Why would you think a thing like that?" he asked calmly.

"Because of the Dutchman."

"The Dutchman?"

"We been tappin' your phone, Mister Coster, and we hear Schultz talkin' to you all the time."

Phil buffed his fingernails before talking. He had never run into this problem in Mount Vernon. And it would be a waste of time to argue. He came out straight.

"How much do you fellows want?"

"It's goin' to cost plenty, but we'll guarantee you one thing."

"What's that?"

"First-class protection."

"Tell your superior to arrange the details," Phil sighed.

With this arrangement and the connection in Washington, Girard & Company continued to expand. Inside a year it had about fifty employes, including Doctor Fanto, the little chemist, who had by now become an indispensable man to Phil.

There came the day when the good doctor, whom the Musicas personally thought of as that little pest, walked into Phil's office.

"Mr. Coster," he said, "for a long time now I have been trying to get on friendly terms with you."

That approach made Phil see red. "Fanto," he snapped, "just what the hell is it you want?"

"I want to help you, Mr. Coster." The chemist was as smooth in his way as some of the preparations he bottled.

"How?"

"I know you are in the bootleg business."

"What!" Phil was really rocked back on his heels.

"I know what's going on here and in Brooklyn," Fanto pursued. "You're selling alcohol to bootleggers instead of making spirits of camphor."

Phil swallowed sourly. If the man knew that, he could be dangerous. "Keep talking," he said.

"I have discovered a way of taking the flavoring out of many of our alcoholic products at practically no cost. Now, what I was thinking was that if you raised my salary—gave me a sort of a commission, you might say—I could reveal my secret. Then we'd both be the financial gainers."

Phil got up and began to laugh. "Fanto," he said, clapping the man on the back, "you know, I was always a little afraid of you. Here I've been trying to keep secrets from you all along and you've been way ahead of me." He grabbed the little chemist's hand. "Shake," he crowed. "It's a deal."

Partly because of Fanto's genius in making shampoo fit for human consumption, Phil paid off his bank loan in half a year—which was six months ahead of time. Thereafter when he walked into The Bridgeport-City Trust Company Phil was looked on as wearing a halo.

In the spring of 1926, when Phil had been in Connecticut for about a year, he heard that the old and highly respected Brooklyn drug manufacturing company of McKesson & Robbins was on the market. The McKesson & Robbins name was to drugs what Tiffany was to gems. The trouble was that younger and more ag-gressive companies had stolen some of the old firm's thunder.

Phil got a brainstorm and went into conference with his brothers. "It's just what we need," he argued, "an old reliable name. Why, with that label we can get enough alcohol to make all of us millionaires!"

So Phil addressed another loan meeting at The Bridgeport-City Trust Company.

"Gentlemen," he said, standing at the head of the table, his head cocked, his eyes flashing with earnestness, "we are here confronted by a rare opportunity. I can buy McKesson & Robbins—surely you've all heard of McKesson & Robbins —for slightly less than a million and a half." He tossed the figure off as if it were small potatoes.

Soon the air was white with flurries of statistics. It was the same old story. Phil completely won over the bank directors. The following week the bank, in collaboration with a Connecticut brokerage house, arranged to float a stock issue. Phil got the biggest chunk of the stock, but there were many other investors, too, in on what they thought was a good thing, and there had to be a board of directors for the firm. Thus Phil merged Girard & Company with McKesson & Robbins and moved the old, respected outfit and its more than one hundred employes to his Fairfield plant.

Phil and his brothers had no sooner warmed their seats as officials of the new drug combine than a reporter and a photographer for The Bridgeport *Post* popped into the plant and made their way toward the president's office. They were just entering the reception room when George popped out. His features darkened as he heard the two explain to the secretary who they were.

Abruptly he turned to the girl. "Tell these men that the president is busy."

"Who are you?" asked the reporter.

"An official of this company," said George, who had just been appointed purchasing agent.

"Are you authorized to speak for Mr. Coster?"

"I am."

The photographer made an impolite sound. "Look, toots," he said to the secretary, "you tell Coster that I want a picture of him for our files."

Under George's glare the secretary timidly asked the visitors to wait while she consulted the great man. She was back in less than a minute.

"I'm sorry," she said, "but Mr. Coster says he is too busy to grant an interview or pose for a picture at this time."

The newsmen left, muttering under their breaths. They were only the first of what was to be a long line of disappointed journalists.

That same morning Phil's secretary got on the inter-com and summoned all the old McKesson & Robbins executives to an immediate conference in the president's office. Within minutes about a dozen men were standing before the mahogany desk while Phil, sitting behind it, looked at them as if they were duck-billed oddities from another world. His brothers stood back of him, one on each side.

"Gentlemen," Phil began, "may I present Mr. Robert Vernard—here on my right—who is the new assistant treasurer of this organization? Mr. Vernard will handle many important details on my behalf. And here on my left is Mr. George Vernard, his brother, who is our new purchasing agent and who will, like Robert, take many details off my shoulders.

"I might say," Phil went on, "that these two gentlemen have been associated with me in the past and when you are dealing with them you may consider yourselves as dealing with me." Phil stopped, ran his tongue over his lips, and blinked his eyes as his head swiveled to take in everybody present. Then he added, "Is that clear, gentlemen?"

"Yes," spoke up one man, "but may I ask how we are to deal with you, sir?"

"I'm glad you asked," said Phil, his face blank. "You are to deal with me by not dealing with me."

"I'm afraid I don't quite understand."

"I mean," said Phil, "that I intend to be too occupied with plans for expansion to be bothered with administrative details. All such details are to be handled by the Vernards." Phil's features darkened as he again looked over the group. "Talk counts for nothing, gentlemen," he said. "It's action that counts. And now, if you'll excuse me . . ."

The executives filed out, feeling they had got a pretty cold shoulder for a start. "But he looks like a smart guy," said one official. "Maybe this'll work out okay after all."

For a short time after taking over McKesson & Robbins, Phil commuted between his home in Mount Vernon and the plant in Fairfield by a chauffeur-driven limousine. But taking a liking to the lush Fairfield County countryside, he asked a local real-estate dealer to look around for a piece of property befitting his new station in life.

All this time Phil had kept an eye on Carol Hubbard. Maneuvering things from behind the scenes, he had seen to it that she divorced her husband. And now that he was a big drug man and needed a wife as part of his front, he told Carol he was going to jump off the Woolworth Building if she didn't marry him. And so they were married.

Very soon the real-estate man dug up a suitable place for them to set up housekeeping—a twenty-room Spanish-type mansion of yellow stucco and red tile, set back behind high walls and graced with expensive shrubbery and dogwoods where whip-poor-wills sang. Carol called in a New York decorator and furnished the place with about ninety thousand dollars worth of period stuff. Then, in January 1928, on a day when it was cold enough to freeze a pawn shop sign, the great Phil Musica, whose right hand had spent fifty-one years trying to figure out what the hell his left was up to, moved in, with his wife.

It is the custom in Fairfield County to stick to New England social protocol, which demands that old residents call on a newcomer to pay their respects. What happened to one middle-aged couple, who lived only a stone's throw away, was typical of what awaited every caller. It was a Sunday afternoon, and the Costers had moved in the previous Friday. The neighborly couple walked up to the front door of the mansion and rang the bell. The butler answered.

"We are neighbors of Mr. and Mrs. Coster," they said. "We've come to pay our respects."

"Mr. and Mrs. Coster are not in," said the butler flatly.

The door was half open as he spoke, and the callers saw a smallish gentleman with an owl-like face coming down a flight of stairs. They heard him demand: "Who's that?" The butler, obviously embarrassed, retreated into the house and reappeared in half a minute. "As I said," he repeated, "Mr. and Mrs. Coster are not at home."

It would be an exaggeration to say that Phil and Carol, after a few such incidents, were well liked in the neighborhood. And it didn't help their reputation any when Phil began raising chows, a

harmless-sounding breed of dogs that will cheerfully disassemble a man. He kept them in runs back of the house, where they erupted in blood-curdling warning whenever they heard the slightest unusual sound.

Although he wanted nothing to do with his neighbors, who could become too nosey for comfort, Phil did all right socially in a formal way. One of his banker friends got him into the nobby Black Rock Yacht Club of Bridgeport, and another put him up for the equally posh Brooklawn Country Club in Fairfield. But Phil, who stuck pretty close to his office during business hours, was always too busy to make the most of the memberships. He confined himself to an occasional meal at either place, usually with Carol.

If his fellow club members thought Phil rather stand-offish and his neighbors thought him awful, the tradesmen around Fairfield considered him one of God's chosen people. His bills for meats and groceries were enormous and he never questioned them, however padded they were. On those rare occasions when Phil bumped into a delivery boy at the estate, he'd even stop to inquire how things were going. He could afford to be nice to the kids because they didn't threaten his house of cards.

One day a youngster of about sixteen was leaving the place as Phil arrived home in his limousine.

"Hello there, son," said Phil. "How's the world treating you?"

"Pretty good, Mr. Coster."

"You say that with reservations."

"Well," the lad admitted, "to tell you the truth, sir, I'm having my troubles."

"Tell me about them."

The boy wanted to go through college but didn't have the funds. "I don't want to be like my old man," he finished, "working himself to death in his old age."

"You're really serious about wanting to make something of yourself?"

"Yes, sir."

"Fine," said Phil. "I'll look into things and you'll hear from me."

The kid didn't understand what the kind man was driving at. But Phil followed through. He had his brother Robert investigate the boy's story and reputation. Both held up. Then Phil sent for him.

"I've been asking some questions about you," he started out. "I must say I find you deserving."

"Thank you, Mr. Coster," said the boy, still wondering what this was all about.

"Now here's what I'm going to do," Phil said. "I'm setting up a scholarship fund for you. Maybe someday you'll turn out to be a doctor or lawyer or a big corporation executive like me. Then if you feel like it—you can pay me back."

The kid began to cry. Coster put his arm around him. "What's the use of living," he asked, his voice lumpy with sympathy, "if we can't help one another?"

A couple of years passed while Phil was putting the spark of life back into the old McKesson & Robbins outfit. Although he didn't know the first thing about the wholesale drug business, he had a genius for picking men who did. He raided other companies for brilliant chemists, having the money to pay them superior salaries, and he hired crackerjack salesmen to canvass the drug trade.

When a scientific question relating to drugs arose at a meeting, Phil would rub his hands over his mustache, gaze off into space, and say, "I'll have to devote some thought to this." Then later Fanto filled him in on enough technical stuff to enable him to carry on a limited discussion

at the next meeting. Before he ran out of dope Phil always singled out a chemist and confided, "I've decided you're just the man to handle this. Regard it as your baby."

Phil never feared being tripped up. He was such an autocratic little squirt that nobody dared to pursue a question once Phil had put an end to the discussion.

Late in 1928 McKesson & Robbins began to attract the attention of Phil's old financial friend, Julian Thompson. He got in touch with Phil, and Phil said he had something he wanted to talk over. So they made a date.

"What I have in mind," said Phil, aggressively imaginative, "is to take over several of the small drug companies and make my firm a giant."

Thompson's ears went up. "I believe I can help you do just that," he said happily.

All this time Phil had been working nights with Robert and George and Arthur on fake books for W. W. Smith & Company, showing large profits in the camphor game. The cagey-eyed accountants of Price, Waterhouse were continuing to audit the books, but it never occurred to any of them to question an entry relating to inventory. Thus, when Coster showed Thompson the books, the finance man was soundly impressed once more. This time he set the Wall Street machinery in motion for McKesson & Robbins to start taking over some of the competition.

By the spring of 1929 Phil had gobbled up about fifty of the smaller companies, and McKesson & Robbins had become the third largest drug outfit in the world. Julian Thompson was now installed as treasurer of the company in the greatly expanded building in Fairfield.

Meanwhile Phil had kept up his profitable little sideline of siphoning off alcohol for Dutch Schultz and other bootleggers, while buying protection from Fairfield cops and federal prohibition agents for the privilege of doing so. In the space of a couple of years he collected about a million dollars for this under-the-counter enterprise. You'd think he'd run far enough from poverty by this time. But not Phil. He started gambling on the stock market with his bootleg money.

This was 1929, remember, and there came a day in October when Phil almost wished he was back selling cheese. In the market crash he lost everything he had except his home. At the age of fifty-two he had to start all over. There was, of course, one thing in his favor: he had a good job.

But if he'd lost his money, he had gained, by this time, considerable confidence that his past was dead. He'd changed his appearance successfully, and he was showing some signs of the advancing years. It had been a long time since his picture had been taken for the rogues' gallery, and although that picture was still there—in a place where Phil couldn't very well lay hands on it—there was little likelihood that anybody would have reason to dig it up. Yet Phil continued to refuse his picture to the newspapers. "He's too modest a man," one of his brothers explained, "to have his picture taken at all."

Although he seemed to be comparatively secure from exposure, Phil nonetheless was determined to leave no loopholes. He sent his brother Arthur to South America. There Arthur bribed a newspaper reporter to cable a story back to the states saying that Philip Musica, the man who had been involved in the

cheese and hair scandals in New York some years before, had died of typhoid fever.

With that, everything seemed to be clear sailing for Phil, and the years went by uneventfully, with the money pouring in. Looking for a drain to take care of some of it, he bought a yacht—a 134-foot job with a twenty-man crew that had once belonged to Marconi, the wireless wizard—and he named it the *Carolita,* for his wife. Even with that, however, he could never relax completely. On his weekend cruises around Long Island Sound he never used the yacht's telephone to call anyone but his brothers, and the eavesdropping stewards never heard him say much more to them than: "Is everything all right?"

Then one day in 1933 Phil's wife presented him with a problem that, as any husband knows, could only be solved her way.

"Donald," she said, "I want a picture of you for my vanity table."

"Why?" demanded Phil, instantly suspicious of anything that might be used as a clue to his real identity.

"I just do," said Mrs. Coster. "Every wife wants a picture of her husband."

"All right," said Phil reluctantly. "If you insist. But there's only to be that one picture—none for your relatives or the newspapers or anybody else."

So Phil had a formal portrait taken— a bust-length shot showing him looking straight into the camera, mouth firm, eyes exuding integrity—a man you could trust.

The picture hadn't been on Carol's vanity very long when a Bridgeport reporter, tired of getting the brush-off from Phil, decided to take things into his own hands. He simply bribed one of the servants to lend him the photo while Carol was out shopping. Taking it to his office, he had it copied and returned it before anyone was the wiser.

A couple of mornings later Phil picked up his copy of The New York *Times* and, over breakfast coffee, was thumbing through the financial section when he spied his picture. He blinked his eyes—this time in genuine shock—and stared across the table at his wife.

"Carol!" he barked. "How in hell did my picture get in here?"

Carol looked at the page as Phil held it up and shrugged. "How should I know?"

"There's only one in existence," Phil declared grimly. "It has to be a copy of the one in your bedroom."

Carol still couldn't explain it. Any explanation, though, was almost beside the point—which was that a picture of Phil Musica was now in general circulation. Anything might happen.

And it did. Shortly after that, in the spring, the letter arrived from Phil's old prison pal and double-crossee, Joe Brandino. Knowing Brandino, Phil must have been aware, even then, that his goose was cooked. Brandino had sworn to get even—and the time had come.

Phil took some hope, however, in that the letter Brandino wrote was not unduly threatening. If he could be bought off for five thousand dollars, the price would be cheap. Yet Phil knew that the price could not possibly be that cheap. It wasn't.

Sometime later, there appeared one morning in Phil's outer office a tall, hawk-nosed man.

"I want to see Mr. Coster," he said to the secretary.

"Do you have an appointment?"

"No."

"Mr. Coster never sees anyone without an appointment."

"He'll see me," hawk-nose growled.

Just then little Robert, hearing trouble through his ever-open door, popped out. "What do you want with Mr. Coster?" he asked.

"That's between him and me," the visitor snarled. "Now where's his office and get out of my way!"

The man's bellow was so loud that Phil put his head out. His gaze locked with that of the visitor. "Come in," he said softly, a catch in his voice. "Come in."

When Phil closed his door, Robert pulled out his watch. "It's almost lunch time," he said to the secretary. "You can go now." And thus the somewhat bewildered girl missed overhearing a most interesting conversation in Phil's office.

"Well, Phil," hawk-nose began, "it's been a long time and you've come quite a way."

Phil was cornered, but like many another rat he wasn't going to give up without a fight. "My name is Coster—F. Donald Coster," he shrilled indignantly. "And what do you mean—a long time? I've never seen you before in my life."

The visitor gargled a laugh. "You play it well. You play it real close." His face suddenly snapped to an ugly glare. "But don't play it too close, Musica. Don't try again the double-cross you gave your old friend Brandino the last time we did business. This time you do things my way—or *I'll* go to the cops."

He laughed again. "That would be real novel, wouldn't it—me going to the cops about you, Phil Musica. You cheese-swindling, hair-peddling, grave-robbing double-crosser!"

"Not so loud!" Phil dashed to the door and peeked out. Seeing only Robert, he closed it again and darted back. "What do you want? I'm a busy man—come to the point."

"The point is ten grand. And I want

it right now." Brandino shouted the words.

"For God's sake, keep your voice down!" Phil whispered hoarsely. "I'll give you the money. You'll have the money. Only keep quiet."

Hurriedly he scratched out a personal check payable to cash and carried it out to Robert. "Take this to the bank," Phil said, "and bring back the money immediately."

When Robert returned, Brandino took the wad with a leer. "I'll be seeing you, Phil," he said happily.

The blackmailer had latched onto a good thing. It would have been even better if he hadn't started to spill the news around in his drunken moments. From then on the word traveled fast among Phil's old associates.

Only three weeks had passed since Brandino's visit when a thin, smallish, inconspicuous man appeared at the desk of Phil's secretary.

"I'd like to see Mr. Coster," he said meekly. "I don't have an appointment, but we're old friends and I'm sure it'll be all right."

The secretary was puzzled, for the caller was the type of man her boss wouldn't normally have flicked ashes on. But then, she reflected, he'd had some odd visitors before, and she decided she'd better check.

"By all means," said Phil nervously to her question. "Show him in."

Ten minutes later Phil called the secretary in while the visitor sat puffing at a cigar. "Cash this at the bank," Phil said, handing her a check for two thousand five hundred dollars, "and bring the money back to me."

After she had returned with the roll and the meek little man had left, she said to Phil, "I hope I didn't do wrong letting him in."

"On the contrary," said Phil glumly. Then he expanded with a phony brightness. "On the contrary. That was the husband of one of my former employes. He needed help. Life isn't worth much, is it, if we can't lend a helping hand now and then."

"Then it's all right if I disturb you when people call without appointments?"

Phil was thoughtful for a moment. "Yes," he said slowly, "show anybody in."

Two months later an insolvent-looking blonde appeared in the outer office. She, too, demanded to see Mr. Coster without an appointment. By now, Phil had developed ears that could hear through walls and the visitor was hardly into her spiel when Phil opened the door and beckoned her inside. Again he sent the secretary to the bank for two thousand five hundred dollars. When the blonde left, Phil called the secretary in for dictation. "Charity," he mused half aloud, "where will it ever end?"

It was a good question.

About a month afterwards Phil was in his inner sanctum dictating one afternoon when the door opened a crack and Robert motioned. Phil flushed and broke into a cold sweat.

"We'll finish some other time," he said to his secretary. "You may go for the day."

As she returned to the outer office Robert passed her with Brandino—back again.

Phil's old friends—not to say his enemies—had discovered a pigeon.

And by the first months of 1934 Philip Musica stood in a fair way to becoming one of the plumpest pigeons in the history of extortion. The word had spread throughout New York's Little Italy that the big drug man and the fellow with the criminal record were one and the same and that Phil was up to his assets in hush money. The result was that hardly a week passed without Phil's receiving a letter from somebody who had known him when, or getting a visit from a bindlestiff in need of ready scratch.

Yet the McKesson & Robbins legitimate business was booming. Phil was in great demand at luncheon clubs throughout New England as a speaker, and his picture was now constantly being printed in the papers. He received an invitation, which he accepted, to become a director of the Bridgeport-City Trust Company. But with all this success his blackmail problem was increasing, because the more prominent he became legitimately the bigger prey he was regarded by the bloodsuckers.

Phil had just put through a couple of big deals one afternoon when his secretary popped in and said there was a visitor to see him.

"What's his name?" asked Phil.

"Simon. Benjamin Simon."

Phil ran his hand over his chin. "I don't seem to know any Benjamin Simon. What's he look like?"

"He's rather short. About forty-five or so."

"Does he say what he wants?"

"No. But he says you'll know him when you see him."

The words were like magic, and Benjamin Simon, a stooped little man, trotted into the office. He stood silent a moment looking at the president of McKesson & Robbins, then he said, "Remember me?"

"I can't say that I do," answered Coster, his features darkening. He tried never to remember anybody, but it was a vain hope.

"From the district attorney's office—twenty years ago."

Phil remembered. Simon had been a process server in the D.A.'s office when Phil had been jugged for the wig wagging.

"What do you want?" he asked calmly.

"A job."

"What kind of a job?"

"Oh, I'm not particular. But I figure I can be useful to a man in your position."

Coster swiveled about and stared through the window down into the street. "Perhaps you could," he said, feeling quietly desperate. "Perhaps you could."

So Benjamin Simon was put on the payroll as a confidential assistant to the president at one hundred dollars a week —good pay in those days. Simon knew the score on Phil's hush-money pay-offs, and he pointed out that his value lay in his experience in dealing with blackmailers. Knowing the ins and outs of the law, he would be able to bargain with them, fighting them with their own weapon—fear.

But his first attempt was a flop. A couple of weeks after Simon had been put on the payroll, Phil was standing in his office looking down into the street when he saw a man getting out of a taxicab. Brandino.

Phil buzzed for his secretary. "Get Mr. Simon in here right away," he said in considerable agitation.

When Simon entered, he waved Phil's words back into his mouth. "Brandino?" he asked. "I just saw him outside."

"He's been here before. Can you deal with him?"

"I'll try."

Simon took Brandino out for a walk. After a while he left him in a lunch wagon and returned to Phil's office.

"He wants ten thousand dollars," he told Phil. "Says if he doesn't get it he'll spill everything to the papers."

"For heaven's sake give it to him!" said Phil, reaching for his checkbook.

Phil was now far from keeping his head above water. The killing of Prohibition in 1933 had cut off the major source of his income, while at the same time his blackmail costs had soared. He was already paying out in hush money several times his fifty thousand-dollar salary from McKesson & Robbins. It was imperative that he augment his income.

Up till then Phil had kept his hands off the McKesson & Robbins treasury. Arranging for the hi-jacking of its trucks had been simply a profitable little sideline that bit only into the insurance companies. But the books had been kept straight. Whatever crooked business had been done was under the name of W. W. Smith & Company. Now he cooked up the idea of tapping the big firm's till and using the money to gamble in the market, thereby making enough to keep his ball from being shot out of the air. To make it as difficult as possible to check his shenanigans, he decided to establish a crude-drug department. Withdrawing real McKesson & Robbins money, he'd put it on the books as having purchased crude drug stocks that actually would never exist.

Basically, the idea was simple enough. In actual practice, though, it would require a bit of legerdemain—which was just Phil's strong point.

The first move he made was to address the drug firm's board of directors. "Gentlemen," he said, "we are going to branch out. My researches have disclosed that there is a fortune to be made in trading in crude drugs."

"Why do you think so, Mr. Coster?" asked one of the directors.

"War," said Phil, dramatically.

"Do you really think there will be a war?"

"I certainly do," said Phil. "And if a world war comes, you know how scarce drugs will be. We could make a fortune."

With that bait the board voted to give Phil a free hand at establishing a depot for crude drugs.

The swindle would be carried out, Phil decided, in the name of the subsidiary, W. W. Smith & Company. That would make things much harder for any nosy investigator to trace. And to add another barrier the depot would be set up in Canada. To get the works running, Phil and his brother Arthur, who was president of W. W. Smith, made a trip to Montreal. There they hired a couple of beginning young stenographers and rented an office, five broken-down warehouses and a vacant lot. The stenographers, who were obviously not to know what it was all about, were to have it pretty soft. As the plan worked out, all they ever did was to receive the large envelopes mailed by Arthur in Brooklyn, break them open, and remail the smaller envelopes they contained. These were all addressed to W. W. Smith & Company in Brooklyn. They held forged letters and bills reflecting huge purchases of crude drugs that W. W. Smith had made from fictitious Canadian companies. To accountants they would constitute evidence that the drugs were actually stored in those Canadian warehouses. The bills for the drugs would eventually be sent by W. W. Smith to McKesson & Robbins, and the drug company would pay the non-existent firm for the non-existent purchases. Arthur would cash the checks and slip the cash to Phil.

There was quite a bit of spurious correspondence to be done to make it look as though a big business was going on, so Arthur bought eight typewriters, each with a different type face. His job now was to sit all day long in the Brooklyn hole-in-the-wall pecking away at orders and receipts, which he mailed to Canada to be postmarked and mailed back. Then he forwarded these papers to Phil in Fairfield, and Phil presented them at board meetings.

"Gentlemen," Phil would say to the board, shuffling a batch of the phony correspondence, "I am pleased to report a net gain of 22 per cent on that purchase of gum opium we made last month."

The directors would chitter in glee. "Fine, fine," they'd echo.

Then Phil would add, "And I've plowed the profit right back into the business."

That took care of any demands for dividends in hard cash.

The months passed, during which Phil and his brothers were running around in circles trying to keep up with the necessary correspondence and book-keeping. Phil used to wake up in the middle of the night adding columns of figures on the wall.

The money poured out from McKesson & Robbins without difficulty, but the plan to make a killing in the market wasn't working out so well. The trouble was that Phil was as unsuccessful at speculating in stocks — recklessly plunging huge sums—as he was successful at hoodwinking his associates.

On a summer evening of 1936 Julian Thompson, the honest treasurer, was a guest at Phil's home for dinner. After dessert, Phil and Thompson retired to the library. There the treasurer, swirling his brandy in a fist-sized snifter, glanced meaningfully at Phil.

"I've been thinking," he said, "that we might make the stockholders happy if we cashed in on some of those crude-drug operations."

Phil downed his brandy and poured another before answering. "I don't know,

Julian," he said. "We're making such a handsome profit on that operation that I hate to touch it."

"But you've been plowing all the profits back into it, Donald," Thompson persisted. "One of the stockholders said to me just the other day that he'd like to see at least 10 per cent of those profits reflected in a dividend check."

Phil's face darkened.

"Who said that?" he asked sharply.

"It doesn't matter. Just one of the stockholders."

No one did anything more about those wonderful if evasive profits then. But after sitting on the idea through the winter, the drug company's board of directors decided, in the spring of 1937, that the time had come. To pay off some bank loans they voted to sell about four million dollars' worth of inventory. A million of this amount, they directed, was to be realized by the sale of the crude-drug stocks.

A few months passed and the directors met again, while Phil was home nursing a cold. To their surprise, they found that, instead of having sold a million dollars' worth of crude drugs, he had added another half million.

"Who authorized him not only to ignore our recommendation but to run counter to it?" one of the directors asked Thompson indignantly.

"I'm sure I don't know," the treasurer said, obviously puzzled. "But I'll make it my business to find out."

Next morning Thompson walked into Phil's office.

"Donald," he said, "the directors are a little angry at you."

Phil raised his brows. "Angry at me?"

"Yes. They're wondering why you bought more crude drugs when you were instructed to sell."

His eyes suddenly wintry, Phil got up

and walked around his desk. "Tell the directors," he said, his voice high and strained, "that I am running this business and I'll stand on my record."

That night, Thompson couldn't sleep. Tossing and turning, he got up several times to smoke. A little after seven o'clock, as he was dressing, his strange uneasiness suddenly crystallized. Nobody, he recalled, except Coster and Dietrich and the Vernards knew anything about that crude-drug operation. Among the four of them they had been handling every detail of the Canadian business—okaying purchases and payments and keeping a close watch over the records, which indicated that there was roughly four million dollars' worth of crude drugs stored in Canada. Now that he thought of it, Thompson realized he had never really examined the books of the Canadian operation.

Secretly looking over the entries that day, Thompson could detect nothing wrong with them. They were apparently in fine order. For more than two years now, the drug firm's subsidiary, W. W. Smith & Company, had been purchasing huge supplies of crude drugs, and these had appreciated in value and been sold at a profit. According to the books, the profits had gone right back into the business in the form of more purchases, which were stored in six different warehouses in Montreal.

Everything seemed all right, and for the next few days Thompson did nothing more. But he kept wondering about those Canadian stocks and how to check on them. Acting on a bright idea, he sneaked another look at the records and made a startling discovery. Although millions of dollars' worth of drugs were apparently stored in Canada, there wasn't a nickel's worth of insurance on the stuff.

Now thoroughly suspicious, Thompson got off a letter to a company in England which, according to the records, had sold eighty-five thousand dollars' worth of crude drugs to W. W. Smith & Company and asked for details. In due course back came a reply: the English firm had never heard of W. W. Smith & Company.

All this time Thompson had realized that suspicions alone were not enough on which to make a move that might create a scandal and jeopardize the position of the company. Now he seemed to have something definite to go on, but he needed more. So, one weekend, he slipped quietly up to Montreal and took a look around. According to the volume of its transactions on McKesson & Robbins records, W. W. Smith & Company should have had a good-sized office here. Instead its address was simply a small room. The six warehouses where the crude drugs were supposed to be stored weren't warehouses at all, but empty broken-down mercantile buildings and, in one instance, a vacant lot. Thompson stood in front of that vacant lot, on the windy Sunday afternoon, looking at it with narrowed eyes, his lips tight and his heart pounding.

Monday, back in Connecticut, Thompson was about to barge into Phil's office without knocking when Robert saw him.

"Don't go in there!" Robert yelled, so intently that Thompson stopped in his tracks.

"Why not?"

"The president is on long-distance. Something very important. He can't be disturbed."

Thompson glared at Robert and turned the knob regardless. But the door was locked. In a moment, however, it opened and out popped Phil, hat on and briefcase clutched under his arm.

"I want to see you," said Thompson.

"Not now," said Phil. "I'm on my way home to bed."

"What's wrong with you?" asked Thompson.

"A splitting headache." Phil ran his hand over his brow and looked pained.

"What I have in mind can't wait."

Phil turned an icy stare on Thompson. "It'll *have* to wait!"

He was walking away when Thompson said, "I've been in Montreal over the weekend."

Phil stopped, wheeled around and stared at Thompson. "You've been *where!*"

"Montreal."

"What for?"

"Looking into things."

"I'll phone you," said Phil. "I'll phone you from home in a little while."

In less than an hour he was on the wire. "Julian," he said, sounding quite pleasant, "I feel much better. What do you say we take a cruise this afternoon on my yacht—out on the Sound? It'll be cold, but we can talk."

"Good idea," said Thompson. He didn't care particularly where he cornered Phil, as long as he could pin him down.

Late in the day the two were on the boat heading out into Long Island Sound. They sat alone at the stern, the chill winds of late November whipping by them, and Phil seemed his old self—defiant and unbruised.

"Tell me, Julian," he said, "what's disturbing you?"

"Canada."

"What about Canada?"

"That address of W. W. Smith & Company. It's only a hole in the wall."

Phil looked straight at his guest, his thoughts scurrying like mice inside his skull.

"Of course it is," he said. "That's all

that's necessary. All that goes on there is clerical work."

"But," said Thompson, returning Phil's fishy stare. "I've been looking into those warehouses where all the drugs are supposed to be stored."

"And?"

"They're nothing but vacant buildings. In fact, one address is that of a vacant lot."

"What you say can't be so."

"It *is* so."

"There must be some mistake—somebody's foolish error in writing things down."

Phil got up and, walking to the rail, hunched over it and gazed down into the water. He muttered something under his breath, and Thompson moved up beside him.

"You're insulting me with your doubts," Phil said.

"I can't help it." The treasurer's tone was cold. "This must be gone into."

Darkness was falling now as Phil turned to Thompson, his eyes swiveling up from the churning waters. At his look Thompson shuddered. He felt that he was suddenly dealing with a fiend. Phil's hands worked, as if to grasp the treasurer, and he leaned toward him.

Then a crewman came to ask instructions.

Thompson made damned sure that he kept within sight of the crew until he got back to shore. He returned at once to New York, got on the telephone, and summoned a meeting of the board of directors at the Sherry-Netherland Hotel for the next morning. There he laid all the facts on the table.

Within a day a couple of Dun & Bradstreet investigators were on their way up to Canada. They confirmed Thompson's story that the four million dollars in crude drugs existed only in Coster's imagination.

When the report was in, the stockholders forced McKesson & Robbins into receivership and all hell broke loose. Still Phil stuck to his desk, issuing orders while the furies swirled about his head. He was bluffing to the last ditch because no one of the powers-that-be yet suspected he was anything other than F. Donald Coster. His unveiling, however, was inevitable. The newspapers ran the story that the great drug company was in serious financial trouble, and Phil's photo appeared on all the front pages.

At a few minutes after eight the evening the story broke, a mild-mannered man by the name of Henry Unterweiser, a veteran investigator for the New York State Attorney General, left his apartment to buy an early edition of next day's *Daily News*. On the way back he glanced at the front page picture of F. Donald Coster. Studying the face for a few minutes, he wondered why it looked vaguely familiar, then shrugged and continued on home.

Later that night the investigator read the story and kept coming back to the picture of Coster.

"I'd bet my life that I've seen this man before," he said to his wife.

"Where do you think it could have been?"

Dawn broke for Unterweiser. "In our rogues'-gallery! That *must* be the place."

Next day Unterweiser neglected his official duties to concentrate on the collection of crooks' mug shots. It was late in the afternoon when, having thumbed through thousands of cards, his hand suddenly stopped. His eyes widened as he pulled out a picture of Philip Musica.

"By God," muttered Unterweiser, "I *knew* I was right."

The investigator took the story to his boss and ended with a suggestion. "Let's send the fingerprints up to Connecticut," he said. "Then we'll get positive proof that Coster is Phil Musica—and a crook." He shook his head. "What a killing that guy must have made!"

In Fairfield, where Phil was still being treated with great respect, the police faced him in his home with the identification. Phil denied it vehemently. While he was busy shrilling protests, a dick slipped into his bathroom and swiped a glass with fingerprints on it. At police headquarters a loops-and-whorls man went to work on it with brush and powder. Half an hour later, having compared prints, the expert looked up.

"No doubt about it," he said. "Philip Musica, ex-con, and F. Donald Coster, the industrialist, are one and the same."

The end came with the morning. It was December 6, 1937, and Phil got up a little after ten o'clock. He dressed with his usual care and appeared for breakfast in a gray double-breasted suit with spats to match. Carol sat quietly at the table with him.

"Bourbon!" he snapped at the butler. "And be quick about it."

He poured a good four fingers into a glass, downed it in a gulp, and poured another drink. "I'm not hungry," he said to his wife, and tossed off the second shot.

The phone rang, and Phil leaped across the room to get it. It was George, the amiable brother.

"They're picking me up," he said. "I just got away long enough to sneak in this call. In a little while they'll be coming for you."

"What about Robert and Arthur?" Phil barked.

"I don't know about Arthur. They've already got Robert." George hesitated a moment. "Phil!" he burst out. "I couldn't help it—I've told them who we all are!"

"Thanks," said Phil abruptly. He slammed the receiver down, and Carol could hear his snarl. "Thank you very much, my dear little brother."

"What was it?" she asked.

Phil glanced at her, and then, averting his eyes, told her. He ran his hand over his head, and his tongue kept moistening his lips. Slowly he made his way upstairs.

Carol followed, keeping her distance, and saw him stop in his bedroom to read a motto hanging on the wall: When you get into a tight place and everything goes against you, till it seems as if you could not hold on a minute longer, never give up, for that is just the time the tide will turn.

He was still staring at it when he heard a car pull into the driveway. Going to a window, he saw two officials get out and come up to the front door.

Then Philip Mariana Fausto Musica, sixty years old, who had made quite a couple of names for himself, went into the bathroom, locked the door, put a gun to his head, and blew his brains out.

After Phil's exposure, the stock in McKesson & Robbins took such a nose dive it practically went through the floor of the Stock Exchange. Yet in time, with honest men running the company, it again not only recovered its position but regained the respect its name had earlier possessed.

A few days after the suicide, when everybody was wondering what Phil had done with the four million bucks, a couple of the cops who had been taking Phil's pay-offs during the alcohol-running period went to Phil's house. Pacing the grounds and discussing the big question, they came to the dog runs in back. One of them stopped short to stare.

"All right," he said, "put yourself in Musica's place. You got a lot of dough and you want it safe in a place nobody would think of looking for it."

The other had swung about to follow his partner's gaze. "You mean it's under the concrete in those runs?"

"Could be. He'd of known if anybody went near it then because of the howl those dogs would have let out."

They eyed each other.

"Be a job to rip them up."

The first officer shook his head. "It's not the job, it's the dogs," he said.

"A little poison will take care of them."

They nodded in agreement and moved on.

But government investigators had suspected the same things as the cops. They moved in immediately and dug up the runs. Not a cent was found—there or anywhere else.

Phil Musica, the boy with contempt for suckers, had proved the biggest sucker of them all in the end. Most of the money he'd stolen had gone to his blackmailers.

His brothers, who broke down to spill the whole story, received prison jolts for collaborating in the swindle.

The Scrambled Sleepers

Arsenic and a pair of mixed-up bed partners made for a parlay which paid off in high voltage at the big cage. Just who was in residence with whom was sometimes not too simple to divine, but the Appelgate-Creighton caper ended on a simple note—they both sat in the same chair.

Everett Appelgate, a thin, seamy little man of forty, with shifty champagne-colored eyes, oversized lips and a strained, chalky countenance, was a man of unswerving fidelity to carnal pursuits, a gentleman who knew his way around a woman. He had, for all his surface unattractiveness, a certain wayward charm. His trouble, as it was to turn out, was that he lived too late in the world's history. He should have lived back around the fifth century, in the era of Saint Ursula, the virgin martyr of Cologne, where he could have had access to Ursula's thousands of maiden companions. But that, alas, was not to be.

After women, Appelgate, a veteran of the First World War, gave priority to American Legion affairs. He was, in 1934, Commander of the Legion's Second Division in Nassau County, which comprised ten posts, and he held a full-time administrative job in the Nassau County Veterans' Bureau. He was married to a torpid woman in her mid-thirties who, though only about five feet tall, weighed exactly an eighth of a ton and was shaped like a Boston bean pot. The couple had an eleven-year-old daughter, Agnes. The Commander, busy as he was elsewhere, spent just enough time with his wife to hold the franchise.

Appelgate's adjutant in the Legion was an easygoing man of his own age—John Creighton, a salesman. Creighton's wife Frances, a buxom, darkly vivacious lady

of Spanish antecedents, worked as a clerk in the County Engineer's office. For some unexplained reason, Mrs. Creighton had escaped Appelgate's notice until one night at an American Legion social affair. After dancing with the lady, Appelgate, who sometimes did things in a complicated manner, called his adjutant aside and said, "Jack, why don't your family and my family take a house together and cut expenses?"

That was how the Creightons and the Appelgates came to move into a small stucco bungalow on Bryant Place in Baldwin in the summer of 1934. The Creightons had two children—Ruth, aged sixteen, and John, Jr., eleven—which meant that there were a total of seven occupants in a house designed for four at the most. Partially as a result of this overcrowding, and partially as a result of Commander Appelgate's glandular demands, the little white bungalow was to be the scene of some absurd and unique activity, none of which was to come to any good end, and little of which was, at first blush, believable. But, as Pirandello observed in *Six Characters in Search of an Author*, life is full of infinite absurdities, which, since they are true, do not need to seem plausible.

There were two bedrooms in the Baldwin bungalow. Mr. and Mrs. Appelgate took one, and Mr. and Mrs. Creighton the other. The Creighton girl and the Appelgate girl slept in a half-finished

491

attic, and the Creighton boy slept on a cot on an enclosed porch. In order to go from the Appelgate bedroom to the attic it was necessary to pass through the Creightons' bedroom. The little bungalow became, then, a place of organized confusion.

Commander Appelgate, always an active man after dark, frequently passed through the Creighton bedroom on his way to the attic to see, as he explained it, if the girls were comfortable for the night. This sometimes proved embarrassing to Mrs. Creighton, not to say her husband, for the Commander invariably chose as the time for his march through the bedroom those moments when Mrs. Creighton was hardly in a state of attire to receive visitors. On one or two occasions Creighton was on the point of speaking to Appelgate about the intrusions but he thought better about it when he realized that Appelgate had promised to back him for a prominent Legion post at the next election. Ah, politics!

One day in September, when the children were in school, Creighton out at work, and Mrs. Appelgate visiting friends in Mineola, Appelgate and Mrs. Creighton found themselves alone in the house for the first time. Mrs. Creighton was in bed with a cold and Appelgate had, at the last minute, suddenly decided that the affairs of the veterans in Nassau county were in such shape that he could be spared for a day to take care of his adjutant's wife.

Silence had no sooner settled over the house than Appelgate went into Mrs. Creighton's bedroom and sat on the edge of the bed. He was the possessor of an elaborate collection of pornographic photographs and, as he rummaged through his pockets, he found that he just happened to have some pictures on him. He

showed them to Mrs. Creighton. Mrs. Creighton, although a woman with a low boiling point, had not, up to now at least, been unfaithful to her husband. She glanced at the photos, frowned, handed them back to Appelgate, and inquired what, precisely, he had in the back of his mind.

When Appelgate informed the lady, in so many words, that he was in the mating mood, she threatened to tell her husband. And now Mrs. Creighton discovered that Appelgate had a face uniquely equipped to accommodate a Bobby Clark type of leer. "While you're telling Jack about me," Appelgate said, "I'll be telling your two kids about that poison trial in Newark in 1923."

Mrs. Creighton made a show of pretending that she didn't know what Appelgate was talking about. "You know damned well what I'm talking about, Frances," he said. "You and Jack were tried for feeding arsenic to your brother —Raymond Avery, I believe his name was—to collect his insurance. You never thought I'd find out about that, did you?"

"We were acquitted," snapped Mrs. Creighton. "That's all behind us."

"It would still be a shock to your kids, especially Ruth, to know that their father and mother were accused of murder."

Such are the foundations upon which liaisons are laid.

Now that she had discovered him, however unwillingly, Frances Creighton couldn't get enough of Appelgate. She began to spend more and more time at home, under the pretext that she was ill, and then contrive to get everybody out of the house—everybody, that is, except Appelgate, whose mating season seemed to run from January to January.

A whole year passed. Mrs. Creighton's

husband seems to have been a very un-suspicious man, while Mrs. Appelgate was usually too preoccupied preparing some new starchy dish for herself to no-tice what was going on.

And then Appelgate began to weary of Mrs. Creighton. For one thing, he was a man who didn't like to be tied down. Then, too, he heard the wild clear call to a frolic in distant meadows.

There was, for example, Appelgate pleasantly discovered, in the summer of 1935, Frances Creighton's own daughter, Ruth. In the year since he had known Ruth, she had changed from a child to a structurally arresting young lady.

Appelgate took Ruth out in his sex-mobile while he called at the homes of veterans on relief. During the ride, he asked her if she liked reading. She did. It just happened that Appelgate had a book with him—the kind of book that is sent through the mails in a plain wrap-per.

Ruth glanced through the book while the Commander went into the home of a destitute veteran. When he came out and asked her how she liked the book, Ruth, her mother's daughter, said, "Oh, Uncle Ev, it's *thrilling!*"

Uncle Ev followed through with some of his postals. And then, one night in July, he maneuvered Ruth into, of all places, a motion-picture projection booth at an American Legion social af-fair—adding, after a fashion, new weight to the argument that motion pictures contribute to delinquency.

Appelgate's waning enthusiasm for Mrs. Creighton did not go unnoticed by the lady. The Commander avoided being alone with his adjutant's wife, and the only opportunity she had to glare at him was at the breakfast or dinner table. The relations between the two became so strained that Jack Creighton laughingly inquired one Sunday, "Say, have you two had a fight or something?"

The summer heat descended on the little bungalow in Baldwin, producing a sort of tropical effect on the inhabit-ants. Appelgate wandered around the house in a state of semi-undress, like an English remittance man on the beach of a South Seas island. He paraded through the Creighton bedchamber so frequently that the Creightons took his passages for granted. Sometimes he was up in the attic all night, sleeping, as he put it, with the kids.

Eventually the sleeping arrangements became very scrambled. Somehow or other Ruth Creighton often passed through her parents' room, going in the opposite direction to the route usually taken by Uncle Ev. The heat, it seems, had made her restless, too. Just how she found relief from the heat by sleeping in a big bed with Uncle Ev and Aunt Ada, as she insisted on doing, was a ques-tion that her parents (at least her father) never thought to answer. As for Ada Ap-pelgate, she made no connection between Ruth's nocturnal visits to the bedroom of her and her husband and her hus-band's insistence that she take sleeping pills each night to insure better rest.

Early one night in August Mrs. Creighton surprised her daughter and Appelgate in the garage behind the house where, theoretically, Appelgate had taken Ruth to show her how to put water in an automobile battery.

"I *thought* this was going on!" said the mother. "I could tell from the way you two looked at each other at supper to-night."

"Mother," said Ruth, "don't be old-fashioned!"

"Get into the house," said the mother

to the daughter, "and I'll speak to you later!"

Alone with Appelgate, Mrs. Creighton said, "Well, what have you got to say for yourself?"

"What do you intend to do, Fran?" asked Appelgate.

"I haven't made up my mind yet," said the woman. That was understandable. Mrs. Creighton couldn't decide what her dominating emotion was—whether it was hatred of Appelgate for seducing her daughter, hatred of Appelgate for spurning her, or jealousy of Ruth for taking a man away from her. And, on top of everything, she was in no position to go to her husband with the whole story.

Next day Mrs. Creighton confronted Appelgate. "Ruth tells me," she said, "that she thinks she's pregnant."

"She couldn't have been for long."

"That's not the point," said the girl's mother. "One of these days she's sure to have a baby, and an illegitimate baby would be a terrible thing." Mrs. Creighton, like many women of low instincts, had a passion for respectability. The thought of murdering somebody presented no moral problem, but the idea of possibly having a neighbor point her out as the mother of a girl who had given birth to an illegitimate child was simply horrifying.

"I suppose an illegitimate kid wouldn't be so good at that," said Appelgate.

"Appy," said Mrs. Creighton, "I'm a mother and I've got to think of my daughter. Have you ever thought of marrying Ruth?"

"To tell the truth," said Appelgate, "I haven't. I never thought of it because I'm married already."

"Do you love Ruth enough to marry her?"

"Fran, I'm nuts about the kid."

"Answer my question: do you love Ruth enough to marry her?"

"Sure, but I'm married to Ada."

"We'll get rid of Ada."

"Get *rid* of her? What do you mean—a divorce? She'd never give me one."

"Divorce nothing. I'll put something in her food."

Appelgate, for the first time, saw Frances Creighton in a new light. He saw no longer a darkly handsome woman. He saw instead a woman who dripped with unadulterated evil.

"Then you and Jack *did* poison your brother for his insurance!" he said.

"Jack didn't have anything to do with it," Mrs. Creighton said. "I did it alone. It was easy."

But Appelgate didn't want to poison his wife. "Either we poison Ada," said Mrs. Creighton, "or I'll get Jack to move us so far away you'll never see Ruth again." Appelgate had to decide whether to lose his latest conquest or become a murderer. He chose to become a murderer.

From one viewpoint, Everett Appelgate and Frances Creighton chose a propitious time to poison Ada Appelgate. The Appelgate family doctor had just decided to treat the woman for obesity. She was now nearing two hundred seventy pounds, and was more asleep than awake as she pushed herself around the bungalow, between her bed and the kitchen. Aside from putting the woman on a near-starvation diet, the physician prescribed certain medicines, one of which was bitter. The bitter medicine, the plotters were quick to realize, would be an ideal medium for the introduction of arsenic, the type of poison that had been decided upon because of Mrs. Creighton's previous experience with it.

From another viewpoint, the plotters couldn't have chosen a less propitious time to begin operations. Mrs. Creighton had run afoul of a neighbor who didn't like her face and who vaguely associated it with a scandal of some sort. The neighbor, a devotee of the tabloid New York *Daily News,* journeyed in to Manhattan and did a little research in the public file room of the paper. She thus came upon accounts of the Creighton poison trial in Newark in 1923 and returned to Baldwin with pursed lips and photostats of some of The *News* stories about the trial.

During the first week in September—on the very day, it was to turn out, that Appelgate and Mrs. Creighton went to a cut-rate drugstore right in Baldwin and purchased twenty-three cents' worth of a rodent-killer called Rough On Rats—the neighbor called on Ada Appelgate and showed her the photostats. That night, after dinner, Ada Appelgate called her husband into the bedroom.

"Ev," she said, "I've got something awful to tell you. Fran and Jack were tried for murder in New Jersey twelve years ago."

Appelgate was shocked, but not for the reason his wife thought.

"We'll have to put them out," said Mrs. Appelgate.

"Not so fast," said her husband. "Give me time to think this over. You say they were tried for murder. Were they convicted?"

"Well, not exactly. They were found not guilty."

"Oh," said Appelgate, "that's different. They only let people off who are innocent. You should know that."

"All I know," said Ada Appelgate, "is that where there's smoke there's fire."

"Now you just keep your mouth shut about this. I'll figure it out and handle it myself."

Later that night, Appelgate broke the bad news to Mrs. Creighton. "Who told her about the trial?" Mrs. Creighton wanted to know.

Appelgate mentioned the neighbor's name.

Mrs. Creighton called on the woman. She wanted to explain things, she said. She explained that her brother had committed suicide by taking arsenic over a period of time. "He didn't want to make it appear to be a suicide," said Mrs. Creighton, "because he wanted us to get the insurance on his life and the insurance companies wouldn't have paid on a suicide."

Mrs. Creighton's auditor, through years of devotion to the columns of The *News,* had become a connoisseur of violent ends. "Why," she asked, "did your brother commit suicide, Mrs. Creighton?"

"He was underdeveloped sexually," she said, speaking the truth. "He knew he could never marry the girl he was in love with."

The *News* reader, conditioned to the importance of sex in life's little race, was appalled at Mrs. Creighton's revelation.

Mrs. Creighton learned that the neighbor was a very devout woman, especially on Sundays, and she closed her visit with a little prayer for a long and happy friendship for the two. "And now," she said, "I wonder if you would go to Ada, like the good Christian woman I've found you to be and set her right about me."

The neighbor refused. This wounded Mrs. Creighton's sensibilities. "I feel," she told Appelgate, speaking of the neighbor, "like baking her a cake."

Despite the fact that Ada Appelgate now knew that Frances Creighton had once been accused of an arsenic murder, the two plotters plunged into their work with the clinical detachment of scientists. It was decided that Mrs. Creighton would mix the doses of poison and that Appelgate would administer them.

Mrs. Appelgate was a superstitious woman. She dreaded the number 13. This, as it was to turn out, was a well-founded dread. It was on the 13th of September, while Mrs. Creighton hovered in the background, that Appelgate fed his wife the first dose of arsenic in a wineglassful of medicine.

The girl Ruth, meantime, received pleasantly unexpected lunar news. She informed Appelgate that she wasn't going to have a baby, after all. Appelgate passed the news on to Mrs. Creighton, and suggested that it would now not be necessary to murder his wife. Mrs. Creighton decided, however, to go right ahead with the plot, no doubt to be on the safe side.

Two days later, on the 15th, Mrs. Appelgate took to her bed. She felt generally miserable, and the soles of her feet felt, as she described them, funny. "You've been on your feet too much," said her husband. "Here, take this. It's your medicine."

The next day, Mrs. Appelgate was seized with one of the classic symptoms of arsenic poisoning—violent vomiting. The doctor who had been treating Mrs. Appelgate for obesity dropped in. "Just as I thought," he said after diagnosing the patient's new symptoms. "The gall bladder." He ordered Mrs. Appelgate removed to a hospital.

"I wish there was a way of mixing a solution, melting somebody in it, and flushing them down the toilet," Mrs. Creighton said to Appelgate after they took Mrs. Appelgate away. "I'd put that doctor in the solution."

Mrs. Appelgate's condition straightened out by itself in the hospital and in a few days she was home again, but con-

fined to bed. The poisoners took up where they had been obliged to leave off. Mrs. Appelgate was in a very weakened condition. The doctor ordered eggnogs and beef broth at frequent intervals. Mrs. Creighton volunteered to stay home from work and personally prepare nourishment for her friend. Mrs. Appelgate was too weak to protest the preparation of the broth and eggnogs by the woman she had come to dislike. Thus, Mrs. Creighton poisoned by day, and Appelgate by night. On the 27th of September, fourteen days after the plotters had begun operations, Ada Appelgate died in her sleep.

By way of celebrating the success of their joint effort, which now left the way clear for the marriage of Ruth and Appelgate, Appelgate and Mrs. Creighton resumed their former illicit relationship. "I feel a little mean about this," Mrs. Creighton is known to have said—"cheating on my own daughter and all."

Appelgate finally got around to phoning the doctor. "You better come at once, Doc," he said. "My wife has taken a turn for the worse."

The doctor looked over his late patient. "Just as I thought," he said. "Coronary arterial occlusion." Then he signed a death certificate.

The *Daily News* reader, seeing the crepe on the Creighton-Appelgate door, called to offer condolences and acquire details. Mrs. Creighton somehow got the impression that the neighbor was suspicious about the death. She dropped everything and went into the kitchen and baked a cake. That afternoon she went over to the neighbor's house with a big piece of the cake. If Mrs. Creighton had done a foolish thing in baking the cake, the neighbor did a foolish thing, too. She ate the piece of cake. That night she became violently ill. Her husband, little realizing how right he was, remarked that her illness must have been due to something she had eaten.

The woman had a talk with the driver of a bakery wagon the next morning. She asked him if it would be possible for somebody to put poison in a cake in such a way that it couldn't be tasted when eaten. "I guess so," said the driver. "I read about somethin' like that someplace once."

"Wait," said the woman. "I want to show you something." She showed the driver the photostats. The driver looked across the street at the bungalow with the crepe on the door. "Jeez," he said, "who'd a believed it? Mrs. Creighton buys rolls from me."

While Ada Appelgate lay in the widest coffin that her husband could procure, the neighbor called at the bungalow and, in private conversation with Mrs. Creighton, accused her of trying to poison her. Mrs. Creighton's reaction was hardly what the neighbor expected. "You and your husband own that house you live in, don't you?" Mrs. Creighton asked.

"Yes. But what has that got to do with what we're talking about?"

"Just this," said Mrs. Creighton. "Poisoning is a very hard thing to prove. The prosecutor found that out in Newark twelve years ago. So go ahead and prove I tried to poison you. Go ahead— and after you don't prove it, I'll sue you for false arrest and take that house away from you."

The neighbor decided to bide her time. The matter, however, was out of her hands. The bakery-wagon driver told a friend about Mrs. Creighton's past, the friend told a detective in the office of Inspector Harold R. King, Chief of Nassau County Detectives.

Inspector King briefed himself on the Newark poison trial and then sent for Everett Appelgate, whom he knew by sight and reputation. He asked Appelgate if he knew that Mrs. Creighton had once been tried for murder by poison. "Sure," said Appelgate. "But that was a bum rap. I've never known a finer woman."

"Mrs. Creighton never had any fights with your wife?"

"They were like sisters."

"Then you're not suspicious about your wife's death in the slightest?"

Now Commander Appelgate made a reply that was a classic of double meaning. "I'd as soon suspect myself," he said, "as Frances Creighton."

Appelgate returned to the bungalow. "You know Inspector King, don't you?" he asked Mrs. Creighton.

"I've seen him around the courthouse."

"Well, he's just had me over for questioning."

"What!"

Appelgate nodded. "He was asking me about you."

"Asking you *what* about me!"

"Now don't get excited, Fran. Everything's all right. He found out about the Newark trial, and he was just checking up on Ada's death, that's all."

"Who told him about the Newark trial!"

Appelgate shrugged. "Search me."

"What did you tell him about me?"

"I said I'd never known a finer woman."

Mrs. Creighton studied Appelgate. "You act," she said, "as if you weren't in this at all."

That night, Inspector King summoned Appelgate to his office again. "I might as well be frank with you," he said. "Things look very suspicious about the death of your wife. The doctor tells me she vomited violently and that the soles of her feet were tender but that those conditions cleared up in the hospital—only to come back again when she was taken home. It sounds just like arsenic to me. Here!" King shoved a paper at Appelgate. It was a form giving the authorities permission to perform an autopsy. "Sign that," King said.

Appelgate signed the paper and returned to the bungalow. He called Mrs. Creighton into the kitchen, and John Creighton wondered what all the secrecy and whispering was about. "Things look bad for you, Fran," Appelgate told the woman.

"Bad for *me*? What do you mean?"

"Inspector King suspects arsenic."

Mrs. Creighton rushed to the kitchen closet, grabbed the box of Rough On Rats, hustled out into the yard, and tossed it over a fence, into a garbage pile. A detective, having been assigned to watch the house, was right there to retrieve the box of poison.

Inspector King and other officials called at the bungalow later that night. They separated Mrs. Creighton and Appelgate and questioned them. They couldn't budge Appelgate. He was sitting comparatively pretty; it was the woman who had a record as a suspected poisoner, not him. Mrs. Creighton, too, was holding her own. She would admit nothing.

Then one of the detectives asked Appelgate if he had ever had relations with Mrs. Creighton? "Her?" Appelgate said. "Too old!"

The detective was a regular tattletale. He ran right to Mrs. Creighton and repeated the remark. Whatever else Frances Creighton was, she was a woman. "Too old, am I?" she said. "Well, he didn't think I was too old before he spied my daughter!"

The woman scorned may have been cutting off her nose to spite her face, but she fixed Commander Appelgate then and there. She confessed the whole horrible business, every detail of it. When chemists found arsenic in Ada Appelgate's body, it was anticlimactic. Ruth, the girl, corroborated certain features of her mother's story on the witness stand at the trial of Mrs. Creighton and Appelgate, dwelling, among other testimony that gladdened the hearts of the tabloid editors, on the details of her seduction by and subsequent affair with the Legion Commander. The girl's testimony sounded more like something from the hillbilly realm of the Ozarks than from metropolitan New York.

Before Frances Creighton and Everett Appelgate went to the electric chair in Sing Sing, Frances Creighton had one source of satisfaction: the lover who had scorned her would never be her son-in-law.

The Captain's Lethal Paradise

*The Captain was a charmer . . . and the lady was lonely. So they got
married and the bride paid and paid—and then she disappeared.
There was no question that the Captain was the responsible
party—but how to nail him to the mast was the problem.*

It is the little things that often change
the course of a person's life. In the case
of Miss Agnes Tufverson, an austere
American career woman on a holiday in
Europe in the summer of 1933, the little
thing was the heel of her right shoe. It
gave way as she was going up the gangplank of a Channel steamer at Tilbury
Dock in London and she lurched forward. She might have fallen on her plain,
honest and intelligent face had it not
been for a quick, strong arm from the
rear. When Miss Tufverson turned to
thank the proprietor of the arm, she
found herself gazing into the dark and
oily countenance of Captain Ivan Poderjay, age thirty-five, late of the Jugoslavian
Army. The lady's goose, as it was to turn
out, went into the oven then and there,
later to be done to a turn, all on account
of a heel.

The English Channel has done as much
as any body of water in the world to pro-
mote the sale of remedies for seasickness;
it was at its promotional best the day
Miss Tufverson and Captain Poderjay
made the crossing to Dunkirk, France.
Miss Tufverson was traveling, as the saying goes, by rail, when, to her great embarrassment, whom should she notice
standing alongside of her but Captain
Poderjay. "Here," he said, "take a sip of
this." He offered her a flask of brandy.

By the time the steamer reached
France, Agnes Tufverson, who had im-
bibed freely of equal drafts of brandy

and Poderjay, felt a new and alien sensation stirring inside her. She knew, as the
Captain bowed low and gave her hand
the continental business, that the feeling was l-o-v-e.

Agnes Tufverson returned to New
York in September, there to reassume her
duties as a member of the legal staff of
the Electric Bond and Share Company.
She was a changed woman. Her age was
generally suspected to be what today
might be called a Jack Benny 38, and,
prior to her holiday, she had acted every
hour of it; now, however, she had the
gaiety and lightheartedness of twenty-
one.

The lady's co-workers, having at least
average intelligence, suspected a man.
Miss Tufverson was very reticent about
his identity. Well she might have been;
she had seen Captain Poderjay for only
a few hours during the Channel crossing
four months before and had not heard
from him since. She took a trip to Detroit, to visit her father and four sisters,
who were solid Swedish stock, and told
them her wonderful secret.

"But Agnes," said one of the sisters,
"you know nothing whatever about this
Captain Poderjay, and the chances are
you'll never hear from him again."

"Oh, I just *know* I'll see him again,"
said Miss Tufverson.

The lady was right. She was sitting
alone, reading, in her tastefully furnished
three-room apartment in a doggy build-

501

ing on East Twenty-second Street, one night late in November, when the phone rang. It was Dream Boat. He just happened to be in New York for a few days on business. Could he drop up? *Could* he.

When, in a little while, the door buzzer sounded and Miss Tufverson answered, the Captain was all but obscured behind the largest box of flowers she had ever seen. When he unburdened his gift, he stood resplendent in white tie, evening cape, topper and stick.

"Goodness gracious, Captain Poderjay," said Miss Tufverson, who had been born in Grand Rapids, "what is the *occasion?*" The question surprised the Captain. The flowers? He was, after all, calling on a lady. The evening clothes? It was, after all, after six P.M.

Miss Tufverson played some classical music on the phonograph. Then she served some spirits. Between times she told the Captain, at his urging, her life story. She had been a government clerk in Washington, had worked her way through law school at nights, and now was regarded as one of the topmost women lawyers in New York. "And," asked Poderjay, who had the habit of referring to himself in the third person, "would you be so kind as to inform the Captain how it is that such a vibrant woman as you never married?"

For ten days and ten nights, Agnes Tufverson lived in never-never land.

At dinner, the theater and dancing, he was intriguingly noncommittal. "The Captain," he would say, "thinks you look particularly charming tonight, my dear," or, "The Captain feels as if he were dancing on a cloud when he dances with you." Then, one night, after a round of the correct spots, they wound up at her apartment and he took her hand. "Agnes," he murmured, "you have stolen Ivan's

heart." Seventy-two hours later—on December 4—Captain Ivan Poderjay and Agnes Tufverson were married at the Little Church Around the Corner.

"Where," asked the bride, "do we go from here, Ivan?"

"Back to your place," he said. The Captain was expecting a cable from an English law firm that owed him some royalties on a lock he had invented.

"I didn't know you were an inventor, Ivan," said Mrs. Poderjay in a taxi on the way back to her apartment. The lady had not, as a matter of fact, asked a single direct question of the man since he had first anesthetized her.

The cable from London, which the Captain had requested be sent to his wife's address, had not arrived. "This," said Poderjay, "places the Captain in a ridiculous position."

"How is that, Ivan dear?"

"Oh, it isn't anything really, except that the monthly remittance from my properties on the continent—a matter of thirty thousand dollars in American money—will not arrive until around Christmas. I was depending on the royalties from my lock to tide me over."

The bride made so bold as to ask her husband how much the royalties amounted to.

"A silly sum to be worried about," said the Captain. "Twelve thousand dollars."

The bride, whose salary was in excess of ten thousand dollars a year, consulted a bankbook that she kept in a desk in the living room. As it happened, she had twelve thousand dollars, almost to the penny, in the bank. She offered to let her husband have the money until his delayed royalties came through. Poderjay fell into a fit of bitter laughter.

"To think," he said, "of a Poderjay accepting money from a *woman*."

"But I am your *wife,* Ivan, and it's only a *loan.*"

Poderjay moved into his wife's apartment while waiting for the cable from London. When, after a couple of days, it still hadn't shown up, he suggested to her that she might as well start going to the office again. "No use neglecting your work, my dear," he said. "The cable might not be here for a couple of weeks. You know how slow the English are." So, while the bride checked in at the Electric Bond and Share against the day when a honeymoon would materialize, Captain Poderjay spent his days lolling around the apartment, drinking gin.

His capacity for gin was impressive. He usually ordered it over the house phone that connected with one of the uniformed attendants in the lobby of the apartment building, tipping the attendant a dollar each time a quart was delivered. He averaged three quarts between the time his wife left for work at nine in the morning and when she returned around five-thirty in the afternoon.

The former Miss Tufverson had a maid—an attractive girl named Emily—who came in each morning to straighten up. Emily, a good girl, soon learned that being alone in the apartment with Poderjay was both an occupational and moral hazard. "That oily Captain's no good," she told another maid in the building. "I would tell his wife on him only she's such a nice woman I wouldn't want to start trouble."

When the bride returned from work the afternoon of December 19, fifteen days after her marriage, the groom had good news for her. His money had arrived during the day. They were sailing for Europe at midnight the following night—the 20th—on the *S.S. Hamburg* of the Hamburg-American Line. Poderjay handed his wife a check on a London bank in repayment of her loan. "I must call my sisters in Detroit," said Mrs. Poderjay, "and say good-by."

The Captain got on the phone during the conversation and spoke to a Miss Sally Tufverson. "All of you," he said to Miss Tufverson, "are to come to Europe to be the Captain's guests."

"But Captain," said Miss Tufverson jokingly, "what would we use for money?"

"Money?" The Captain laughed. "Poof! The Captain will arrange all transportation and expenses." He handed the phone back to his bride. "I see what you mean," said Sally Tufverson to her sister. "He's *charming.*"

Right after the phone call, the curtain went up on one of the most baffling sleight-of-hand performances in the history of the Missing Persons Bureau of the New York Police Department. Poderjay went to the house phone and called Dan O'Neill, the porter, and asked him to bring up from the basement three trunks —two belonging to his wife and one belonging to him. Next morning, the porter called on the house phone and asked Mrs. Poderjay if she cared to have him arrange for a truck to take the three trunks to the Hamburg-American pier, about fifteen minutes distant. The wife asked her husband what his wishes were. "Ivan," he informed her, "has attended to that."

When Emily, the maid, came in, Mrs. Poderjay, who had not yet decided what to do about her apartment, asked that Emily come in the following morning to straighten up as usual. When Emily left, Poderjay followed her out into the hall.

"Mrs. Poderjay has changed her mind about you coming in tomorrow to straighten up," he said. "You are to come the day *after* tomorrow." Emily thought that was strange, but, since she was a maid, not a detective, she accepted the instructions without giving them a second thought.

All day long, Poderjay dashed in and out of the apartment house on last-minute errands relating to the *Hamburg's* midnight sailing. Late in the afternoon, a truck called for the three trunks. At eight that night—four hours before the *Hamburg* was to sail—Captain and Mrs. Poderjay appeared in the lobby of the apartment building. There were hurried good-bys to the elevator men and lobby attendants.

At twenty minutes past midnight—twenty minutes after the *Hamburg* had weighed anchor—Captain Poderjay walked into the lobby of the apartment house.

"Why, Captain," said one of the attendants, "I thought you were supposed to sail at midnight."

The Captain, who seemed to be preoccupied, mumbled something about a last-minute business development having detained him. His wife, he divulged, had sailed ahead of him and he would join her abroad later. He peeled a ten-spot from a wad and sent the doorman around the corner for a quart of juniper juice.

Next afternoon—the afternoon of December 21—Poderjay went out on foot around five o'clock. He returned about eight o'clock and told O'Neill, the porter, that a trunk was coming for him and to see that he was notified the moment it arrived. The trunk—a big shiny black one that looked brand-new—arrived about eight-thirty by truck. O'Neill called Poderjay on the house phone and asked him if he should bring the trunk up. "Don't touch it," said Poderjay. "The Captain will attend to it." Poderjay went downstairs and shepherded the trunk up the freight elevator to the apartment. In a

little while he called down for a quart of gin—his fourth since morning.

In the morning—the morning of December 22, the second morning after the *Hamburg* had sailed—Emily, the maid, let herself in to the apartment to straighten up. She was startled to see the Captain. He gave her the same explanation for his presence as he had given to the lobby attendant the second night previously. Poderjay was busy straightening up; he was particularly occupied destroying papers of various kinds. A big black trunk—the trunk that had been delivered the night before—stood in the middle of the bedroom, shut tight.

Poderjay handed Emily a pile of papers that he had just taken from his wife's desk. "Here," he said, "take these out and put them in the incinerator." The incinerator was in the hallway just outside the apartment. Emily glanced at the papers.

"But, Captain," she said, "these belong to my mistress. Look, her name is on them. I can't burn these, sir."

The Poderjay features clouded. "Do as the Captain commands you!" The maid, buckling under Balkan force, went out and put the papers in the incinerator. Later in the morning Emily told another maid, "That Captain that married Miss Tufverson is up in her apartment drinking and burning everything up." By noon the remark had gained currency among the employes of the building; somehow it generated a feeling of uneasiness.

Shortly after nightfall, a wagon that needed a coat of paint, drawn by a horse that needed a good feed, arrived at the service entrance of the building. The driver, a nondescript character, told O'Neill, the porter, that he was calling for a trunk belonging to Captain Poderjay. O'Neill notified the Captain on the house phone.

"Shall I come up and get it?" O'Neill asked Poderjay.

"No," said Poderjay. "Send the driver up."

The Captain, whose breath this night was practically a fire hazard, stuck close to the trunk. He went down the freight elevator with the truckman and the trunk. He gave the truckman a democratic hand in hoisting the trunk on the wagon. Then he hopped up on the driver's seat with the truckman and was off. Poderjay's presence on the seat of a decrepit wagon was incongruous enough; what made it all the more incongruous was the fact that he was formally starched out, complete to opera cape, topper and stick.

So much for the night of December 22. Ten days later, on the first day of January, 1934, Sally Tufverson, in Detroit, received a cable signed by her sister. The cable was from London. In it, Mrs. Poderjay stated that she could not stand the cold English climate and was leaving for France and India. The remark about the English climate struck Sally Tufverson as singular; Agnes, being of Swedish extraction, had greatly enjoyed cold weather, the colder the better.

Five months passed. The woman in whom romance had bloomed late had vanished into the deep silences. So had Lover Boy. In May, Sally Tufverson journeyed to New York and called at the Missing Persons Bureau of the Police Department.

The first thing the cops did was give the apartment a toss. There wasn't much to toss. The bride had left no papers behind. The place was *too* clean; everybody leaves *some* kind of papers behind. The building help was screened and the

bulls got hold of the story of Emily the maid and the burned papers.

The dicks wanted to know of Sally Tufverson if Captain Poderjay had borrowed any money from her sister. That was one item that the bride had not mentioned to her folks. Banks were combed; Agnes Tufverson's savings account was located. The woman had withdrawn twelve thousand dollars in cash the day after her marriage. On December 20—the last day she had been seen in New York—she had deposited a check on a London bank in the amount of twelve thousand dollars and signed by Ivan Poderjay. The check had proved highly resilient, but the bank had been unable to get in touch with Mrs. Poderjay to impart the dreary tidings.

That wasn't all the dicks found out. The missing woman had disposed of thirty thousand dollars in securities the day she had last been seen. The investigators saw in this transaction the outline of another loan to Poderjay. Agnes Tufverson had written to her family that the Captain's monthly remittances from his European properties totalled thirty thousand dollars. Since the December remittance would have arrived in New York around Christmas, or some days after the sailing of the *Hamburg,* was it not possible that the Captain had permitted his wife to lend him the thirty thousand until the remittance, which would pass on the high seas, caught up with him?

The records of the Hamburg-American Line disclosed no reservations or cancellations under either the name of Poderjay or Tufverson for the night of December 20. What, the dicks now asked themselves, had happened during the four hours between the time Poderjay had left with his wife and the time he had come back to the apartment house without her? Where was the former Agnes Tufverson during those hours, and what had happened to her?

The White Star liner *Olympic,* outbound for England, had sailed at midnight December 22—the night Poderjay had been seen driving off formally attired on the truck bearing the new black trunk. The *Olympic's* passenger list disclosed that Ivan Poderjay had been aboard. He had occupied Stateroom 86 on C Deck—alone. The cops wanted to know more about that stateroom. It was an outside room. It contained one porthole opening directly on the sea. A diagram of the ship showed that the porthole was two feet in diameter—plenty big enough to stuff an average-size body through, and Agnes Tufverson had been average size.

Poderjay had been allowed sixty feet of trunk space aboard the *Olympic* free of charge on his ticket. Records of the ship showed he had been charged for thirty cubic feet in excess of the free allotment, making ninety cubic feet in all. There was no breakdown as to how many trunks had been included in the ninety cubic feet, but a pretty good guess was that there had been four—the black one that had been delivered to Poderjay the night before he had gone away, and the three trunks, one belonging to him and two to his wife, that had been carted off in a truck the day the *Hamburg* sailed. Since the *Hamburg* had sailed forty-eight hours before the *Olympic,* that meant that Poderjay had checked the three trunks somewhere and later picked them up and had them sent to the *Olympic.*

The cops were very much interested in the origin and travels of the black trunk that Poderjay had taken with him when last seen. They screened trunk stores in the neighborhood and found a place on Third Avenue, within a few minutes' walk of the apartment house, where the Jugoslav had bought the trunk. Although five months had elapsed since the purchase, the proprietor of the place remembered Poderjay because of the Captain's habit of gulping gin from a bottle while he looked over the stock. Poderjay had bought the trunk at five-thirty in the afternoon. The hour was fixed because the trunk store closed at five-thirty and Poderjay had selected his trunk just at closing time. He had taken the trunk with him, strapped to the back of a taxi.

The trunk had not arrived at the apartment house, however, until eighty-thirty —three hours after it had been purchased —and then not by taxi but by truck. This fact was established for the cops because O'Neill, the porter at the apartment house, was a very methodical man. He kept detailed records of practically everything relating to his job. Where had Poderjay gone with the trunk for three hours, and why had he changed from a taxi to a truck?

The dicks figured a lot would be answered to their satisfaction if they could locate the drivers of two taxis and three trucks. There had been, in addition to the cab that had hauled the trunk, the taxi in which Poderjay and his wife had left for the Hamburg-American Line pier. There had been the truck that called for the three trunks the day of the *Hamburg* sailing, the truck that had delivered the black trunk three hours after Poderjay had purchased it, and the wagon that had hauled the trunk, and Poderjay, away the next night. The dicks didn't make out so well. They couldn't locate either of the taxi drivers. They located only one of the three truckmen—the driver of the wagon, who couldn't tell them any more than what they already suspected; he had taken Poderjay and the trunk to the White Star pier where the outgoing *Olympic* was berthed.

The *Olympic* itself was in Southampton when the dicks became interested in it. The New York cops cabled Scotland Yard. Long-winded cables began to arrive from England, collect, every few hours. Two stewards on the *Olympic* remembered Poderjay, after all those months, because of three peculiarities the man had displayed during the crossing. He had always referred to himself in the third person. He had never once left his stateroom. His capacity for gin had been heroic.

Since the stewards remembered the man, they remembered something of his surroundings. He had had just one trunk in his stateroom during the crossing—a shiny black trunk that looked new. During the first day of the voyage, Poderjay had asked one of the stewards to move the trunk from one part of the stateroom to another part. The trunk had been quite heavy. Near the end of the voyage, the same steward had removed the trunk from the stateroom; it had then been noticeably lighter.

The Yard dug out the original of the can't-stand-the-climate cable that had been sent from London to Sally Tufverson in Detroit on New Year's Day. The former Agnes Tufverson had not sent the message; Poderjay had. The handwriting on the cable original and on *Olympic* bar chits signed by the Jugoslav was identical.

Poderjay himself had vanished, probably in the direction of the Continent, after disembarking from the *Olympic*.

The way the cops doped it was that Poderjay, after laying hands on forty-two thousand dollars of his bride's money, had knocked her off, probably on the night he left in the cab with her, presumably bound for the Hamburg-American pier. A clever fellow like Poderjay could very well have rented a room somewhere, and, detouring his wife there under a subterfuge of some sort while on the way to the pier, murdered her and left her body there until the next night. Then, after purchasing the black trunk, he could have had it delivered to the point where he had secreted the body, put the body in it, then had the trunk taken to the apartment house until it was time for his own departure.

The Yard caught up with Poderjay in Vienna in June, six months after his American bride had vanished. He was living in a nobby flat in the fashionable Hintzerstrasse with a woman who turned out to be his legal wife of some years. Two trunks identified as the property of Agnes Tufverson, plus such personal effects of the woman as her clothing, brief case and books, were found in the Hintzerstrasse flat. Poderjay had a long record for swindling women.

The New York dicks now assured themselves as they pondered the cable intelligence from abroad that they had the Tufverson mystery all wrapped up— well, *practically* wrapped up.

When, in January 1935—thirteen months after Agnes Tufverson's disappearance—Dream Boat returned to New York on a wave of extradition, a delegation of dicks showed up at the pier with greetings. The Captain, dashing as hell in a polo coat with upturned collar a la Hollywood, cast the first shadow of coming events when, sauntering down the gangplank wearing bracelets, he asked two sleuths to turn their heads the other way while he posed for photographers.

"The Captain," he explained to his captors, "wishes to look nice for the ladies —and he does not wish other faces to spoil the picture." The dicks might have taken a crack in their stride; what threw them off their stride was what the crack implied. It implied that Captain Ivan Poderjay did not bruise easily. A character who did not bruise easily, in combination with the complete and utter absence of the most vital piece of evidence in the whole case—the body of the missing woman—was a combination just too dreadful to contemplate.

At headquarters, the cops worked in relays on Poderjay, right around the clock. The net result, at the end of the first twenty-four hours, was as if Poderjay had been working in relays on the cops. The suspect was like a daisy; the cops looked like weeds that had been sprayed with an insecticide, then trampled on.

"Why, you bastard," said one dick, "you know you threw that woman's body out of the porthole! Why don't you admit it?"

"Why," asked Poderjay, "don't you prove it?"

"All right. If you didn't murder that woman, where is she?"

The Captain shrugged. "Canada, perhaps."

"Canada. Now he says she's in Canada."

"The Captain did not say Canada," Poderjay corrected. "He said Canada *perhaps*."

It was at this point that the Captain decided to oblige the cops—to an extent. If they *must* know what happened to Agnes Tufverson, he could, perhaps, give them some leads to work on. Anything to be of help. No hard feelings.

"Miss Tufverson," began Poderjay, "fell hopelessly in love with the Captain. That had happened to the Captain many times, women falling in love with him, so he tried to be understanding and sympathetic." The dicks were looking first at Poderjay, then at each other, as the man talked. Miss Tufverson, Poderjay con-

tinued, had threatened to commit suicide if he didn't marry her. "And so the Captain married the poor woman to rehabilitate her." They quarreled that night on their way to the Hamburg-American pier. "Women of that age are unreasonable." She walked off the pier, leaving her trunks behind, saying she was going to Canada to forget the Captain. He returned to the apartment. "The Captain was in no hurry. He thought the poor woman would come back to the apartment." When, after forty-eight hours, she didn't return, Poderjay left for Europe. "The trunks and the other belongings that you gentlemen found in the Captain's possession in Vienna and which you seem to make so much about—those the Captain took for safekeeping." Poderjay paused to look around at his auditors. "The Captain," he added with a very straight and earnest face, "has no interest in those belongings. The owner may have them when she returns."

At the end of forty-eight hours, the cops stopped talking to Poderjay and began talking to themselves. The Chinese are supposed to be the toughest people to crack. The rumor began to spread around the Building, as they call headquarters, that, compared to Poderjay, a Chinese is a magpie. It just wasn't believable; the cards had been stacked against Ivan the Uncrackable when he stepped off the boat, yet here he was, winning the game. The answer lay in the joker—the absence of a corpse.

As time passed, the situation, as they say in diplomatic dispatches, worsened. There were, unfortunately, new mysteries to be solved. The cops simply couldn't afford to make a life work of the Tufverson case. Then came the Ripley.

Poderjay, believe it or not, was charged with bigamy. After many months of investigation and weeks of having Poderjay on the carpet, that was absolutely the best the law could do.

The Captain, looking for all the world like the cat that snapped up the bird, was led out of a courtroom with nothing more bothering him than two and a half to five years in Sing Sing.

"Don't let anybody tell you," said a detective to a reporter, when they took the bigamist away, "that a man can't get away with murder."

When he got out, Captain Ivan Poderjay, late of the Jugoslavian Army, was deported to his native land. There, at last reports, he dwells behind the Iron Curtain. Which beats, at that, an electric curtain.